Financial
Advisor's
Desk Reference

Financial
Advisor's
Desk Reference

Jonathan D. Pond

New York Institute of Finance
New York   London   Toronto   Sydney   Tokyo   Singapore

Library of Congress Cataloging-in-Publication Data

Pond, Jonathan D.
  Financial advisor's desk reference / Jonathan D. Pond.
    p.   cm.
  Includes index.

  ISBN 0-13-319278-4
  1. Investments—Handbooks, manuals, etc. I. Title.
HG4527.P66   1992
332.6—dc20   91-47148
                                                              CIP

This publication is designed to provide accurate and authoritative information in regard to the subject matter covered. It is sold with the
understanding that the publisher is not engaged in rendering legal,
accounting, or other professional service. If legal advice or other expert assistance is required, the services of a competent professional
person should be sought.

ISBN 0-13-319278-4

© 1992 by NYIF Corp
Simon & Schuster
A Paramount Communications Company

Printed in the United States of America
10 9 8 7 6 5 4 3 2 1

CONTENTS

INTRODUCTION

Financial services professionals need timely and readily accessible reference information—more so, perhaps, than any other profession. The dynamic and highly interrelated nature of financial services requires that generalists, for example, financial planners and specialists, have convenient access to information on all areas of financial services. For example, financial services specialists such as stockbrokers sell insurance products, insurance agents sell investment products, and both sell products that require an understanding of taxation, retirement planning, and estate planning. *Financial Advisor's Desk Reference* will help financial service professionals do a better job in an increasingly complex environment.

Financial Advisor's Desk Reference entries address a plethora of matters of importance to financial services professionals. It contains:

- *Highlights* of recent innovations and trends
- *Summaries* of performance
- *Descriptions* of relevant legal and tax matters
- *Lists* of information sources
- *Illustrations* of historical trends
- *Analyses* of statistical and economic data
- *Explanations* of complex technical concepts
- *Tables* that are commonly used in financial analysis
- *Glossary* that explains industry products and jargon

A brief explanation accompanies each entry to show how the information can be used. A summary at the beginning of each chapter describes important events and conditions relating to the particular topic and will offer a forecast of expected future conditions and trends.

The demand for financial services and the demands on the financial services professional will both increase during the 1990s for several reasons.

Post-World War II baby boomers will be entering their peak earning years. An increasing rate of savings as well as inheritances will also fuel the need for financial products and services. Concern over achieving financial security, fueled by the recession of the early 1990s will cause people to seek the assistance of financial professionals. Many financial institutions are redoubling their efforts to educate both their professional staff and clients to meet these demands.

The competent financial services professional recognizes that in order to provide appropriate counsel to clients, he or she must develop an understanding of a wide range of areas. These areas are becoming an understanding of a wide range of areas. They are also becoming increasingly complex as a result of changes in and interpretations of the tax laws, the introduction of new products, a changing economy, and the constant evolution of new strategies. *Financial Advisor's Desk Reference* will assist the financial services professional in providing timely, well-informed services to his or her clients. It will also provide a convenient means of answering the many questions that arise in day-to-day professional practice.

ACKNOWLEDGMENTS

The assistance of several very capable people who helped prepare this reference is gratefully acknowledged. They include Lisa Schkolnick, Marla Brill, Donald Carleton, Viveca Gardiner, Ivan Kreilkamp, and Natalie Liu. Sheck Cho at the New York Institute of Finance skillfully guided this volume through the editorial process. Thanks also to Jacqueline Roulette at NYIF who oversaw the production process. Finally, I appreciate the guidance of the many financial services professionals who made helpful suggestions regarding the content of this volume.

Chapter 1_____

CAPITAL ACCUMULATION

The accumulation and preservation of wealth are the central purposes of financial planing. The task of the investment professional is to find the optimal balance of equity, fixed-income, cash-equivalent, and perhaps real estate investments that provide growth and, at the same time, preserve principal.

The importance of proper diversification in achieving these goals on a long-term basis is immeasurable. Consider that between August and October 1987, the stock market lost almost 28 percent of its value. While the market subsequently regained all of that drop, those who were fully invested in stocks during that period would have lost much of their hard-earned financial assets if, for some reason, they were forced to sell all their holdings shortly after the downturn.

Determining the optimal investment allocation for a particular individual requires thorough, ongoing analysis based on investment needs, age, marital status, income, life-style, objectives, and personal preferences. Generally, younger investors can afford to take on greater investment risk in exchange for greater opportunity because their earning potential is greater than that of an older or middle-aged person. However, a retiree should generally opt for a less aggressive investment approach because his or her earning potential is much lower now than it was during his or her working years.

These rules of thumb, of course, must be tempered by each individual's situation. For example, a retiree who has substantial income from a pension and Social Security can afford to take a greater degree of investment risk than can someone who depends largely on personal savings for income. A young, high-earning individual who feels uncomfortable with investment risk may be better suited for a relatively conservative portfolio, even though it offers less potential for growth than a more aggressive one.

Another factor that must be taken into account in the asset allocation process is the relative attractiveness of various types of investments. This does not mean that investors must shift their asset mix frequently to achieve financial success. However, the investment professional should periodically review an individual's portfolio to help ensure than an existing asset mix is appropriate in light of prevailing market conditions.

Because the markets will not rise as much in the 1990s as they did in the 1980s, investors will have to spend more time evaluating their portfolios and analyzing investment alternatives if they are going to outpace inflation on an after-tax basis. To help accomplish this, diversification into international securities will become increasingly commonplace even for the average investor, although these investment opportunities should generally be sought through worldwide diversification rather than by concentrating on a single country or region.

Several trends that will affect many clients will influence the role the financial services professional plays in the capital accumulation process. Many clients will accumulate large investment portfolios as a result of a variety of factors, including an aging population, an increased rate of savings, and more concern about achieving financial security. Inheritances that will total several trillion dollars are predicted for the 1990s. There is also a trend toward requiring employees to take more responsibility for setting aside and managing their own retirement-oriented resources. All these trends will challenge the financial services professional who will need to keep abreast of the ever-changing investment environment throughout the 1990s to serve his or her clients better.

1.1   INVENTORY OF INVESTMENT ALTERNATIVES

Table 1.1 describes the various commonly used investment alternatives, including their advantages and disadvantages. It is divided into three sections representing the three investment categories of stock investments, interest-earning (including cash-equivalent) investments, and real estate investments. Each of these categories is discussed in more detail in Chapters 2 through 6. Even though they may not be involved in all categories of investment, financial services professionals need to be familiar with the wide range of investment alternatives, particularly the role that each might play in meeting client investment objectives.

Table 1.1   Commonly Used Investment Alternatives

Investment	Description	Advantages	Possible Disadvantages
Stock Investments			
Common stock	Security that represents ownership in a company	Potential for high rate of return through capital gains; may pay dividends	Risk of market decline; not protected by government; value fluctuates daily
Convertible preferred stock	Preferred stock that may be exchanged by owner for common stock	Combines usually attractive dividend payout with potential of capital appreciation of common stock	Lower yield than bonds; sells at a premium to conversion value of the common stock
Futures contracts	Contracts covering the sale of financial instruments or commodities for future delivery; includes agricultural products, metals, Treasury bills, foreign currencies, and stock index futures (i.e., Standard & Poor's 500)	High potential return through use of leverage	Highly speculative and volatile; favorite of investment "scamsters"
Options	The right to buy (call) or sell (put) at a given price (strike price) for a given period of time	Inexpensive way to speculate; possible high return for small investment; covered option writers can add income with low risk	Option buyers usually lose entire investment
Preferred stock	Stock sold with a fixed dividend; if company is liquidated, it has priority over common stock	Fixed rate of return; safer than common stock dividends	Dividend is usually never increased; stock price appreciation potential may be limited

Stock Investments (continued)			
Stock mutual fund	Investment trust in which your money is pooled with those of other investors and invested in stocks by professional managers	Professional management; diversification reduces risk; can switch from one fund to another within a family of funds; wide selection; low costs; low investment minimums	Not federally insured; subject to fluctuations in the stock market
Unit investment trust (stocks)	Fixed portfolio of securities deposited with a trustee; offered to public in units	Diversification; professional selection; usually can redeem units	Portfolio is not managed actively; subject to price fluctuation
Warrant	Gives holder right to purchase a given stock at stipulated price over a fixed period of time	If underlying shares rise in value, so will warrant; can exercise warrant at any time	If warrant expires, value of investment is lost
Interest-Earning Investments			
Bond mutual fund	Investment trust in which your dollars are pooled with those of others and invested by professional managers in various bond issues	Professional management; diversification reduces risk; can switch from one fund to another within a family of funds; wide selection; low costs; low investment minimums	Not federally insured; subject to fluctuations in interest rates
Certificate of deposit (CD)	Receipt for money left in bank for set period of time at an agreed-upon interest rate; at end of period, bank pays deposit plus interest	Insured up to certain limits by federal government; competitive interest rates	Penalty for early withdrawal; interest rates may rise while your money is locked in

Interest-Earning Investments (continued)			
Convertible bonds	Bond that may be exchanged by owner for common stock of same company	Combines safety of bonds with potential for capital appreciation of common stock	Lower yield than similar quality nonconvertibles; sell at premiums t the conversion value of common stock
Corporate bond	Debt obligation of corporation	Receive fixed return over specified time; assured return; low risk with highly rated bond issues	May be called prior to maturity, particularly if interest rate declines
Money market deposit account	A type of money market fund at a bank or savings and loan association; has limited checking privileges	No federal regulation of rates: banks set their own rates; insured by federal government up to certain limits; no withdrawal penalties	Minimum balance required; limited check writing rates often lower than money market mutual funds
Money market mutual fund	An investment company which buys short-term money market instruments	High short-term interest rates; no withdrawal penalties; handled by professional money managers; check-writing privileges	Usually not insured; no capital growth potential
Mortgage-backed securities	Securities representing a shared ownership in pools or mortgages; backed by federal, state, or local governments; include Ginnie Maes, Fannie Maes, Freddie Macs, etc.	Backed by government or government agencies; high yields; liquidity; receive regular monthly income	Prices decline if interest rates increase; payments dwindle as mortgages are paid off
Municipal bond	Debt obligation of state, city, town, or their agencies	Interest earned is tax-free at federal level and in state and city where issued	Subject to price fluctuations; after-tax return may be lower than other bonds

Interest-Earning Investments (continued)			
NOW account	Negotiable order of withdrawal; interest-bearing checking account	Funds in account earn interest; unlimited checking; federally insured up to certain limits	Interest rates are low; must maintain minimum balance
Savings account	Account in which money deposited earns interest	Federally insured up to certain limits; guaranteed yield; can be used as collateral	Low interest rates
Treasury bills	Short-term U.S. Treasury securities; maturities: 13, 16, and 52 weeks	Backed by U.S. government; interest earned is exempt from state and local taxes	Rates often lower than other short-term investments
Treasury bonds	Long-term U.S. Treasury securities; maturities: 10 years or more	Backed by U.S. government; interest earned is exempt from state and local taxes	Value declines if interest rates rise
Treasury notes	Medium-term securities of U.S. Treasury; maturities: not less than 1 year and not more than 10 years	Backed by U.S. government; interest earned is exempt from state and local taxes	Value declines if interest rates rise
Unit investment trust (bonds)	Fixed portfolio of securities deposited with a trustee; offered to public in units; categories include municipal bonds, corporate bonds, public utility common stocks, etc.	Diversification; professional selection; usually can redeem units; available in small dollar amounts	Portfolio is not managed; most have 25-30 year maturities

Interest-Earning Investments (continued)			
U.S. savings bonds	Debt obligation of U.S. Treasury	Backed by U.S. government; if held 5 years, return is 85% of the average yield on 5-year Treasury securities with a 6% minimum guaranteed; exempt from state and local income taxes; may defer federal tax; registered, so it can be replaced if lost or stolen	Generally lower rate of interest than available elsewhere
Zero-coupon bonds	Debt instrument; sold at discount from face value with no (zero) annual interest paid out; capital appreciation realized upon maturity	Low initial expenditure leads to balloon payment upon maturity; you know exact amount you will receive	Yields lower than for regular bonds; must pay taxes annually as though you received interest unless invested in tax-deferred account
Real Estate Investments			
Income-producing real estate	Do-it-yourself real estate investing involving the purchase and management of properties ranging from apartments to commercial and industrial buildings	Total control over acquisition, management, and sale of the property; opportunity for significant tax-favored wealth accumulation	Expensive to get into; risk of loss through vacancies or declining prices; management of property can be a hassle
Real estate investment trust (REIT)	REITs invest in or finance real estate projects including offices, shopping centers, apartments, hotels, and so on; REITs are sold as stock and trade on the stock exchanges	Provides participation in real estate with small amount of money	Subject to fluctuations of real estate and the stock market

Real Estate Investments (continued)			
Real estate limited partnerships	A real estate ownership arrangement involving one or more general partners and limited partners; liability is generally limited to the extent of actual investment; can invest in all kinds of real estate	Provides participation in real estate with small investment; limited partners are relieved of chore of managing the property	Potential for profits is limited versus buying property yourself; many deals have soured over past years
Undeveloped property	Do-it-yourself investment in raw land that, it is hoped, will eventually be developed	Well-situated property can appreciate a great deal; minimal management responsibility	Good raw land is very expensive and difficult to finance long term; lack of income requires ability to commit money over a long period of time.

1.2   ALLOCATING INVESTMENTS ACCORDING TO INVESTOR NEEDS

Allocating investments, on the one hand, is an overused and abused approach that entails a frequent reallocation of investments in response to short-term market indicators, and, on the other hand, it is a very important concept for long-term investment success. The following section describes a long-term approach to asset allocation.

Most people tend to invest in extremes. Some invest too conservatively, restricting their investments to low-risk interest-earning securities like certificates of deposit (CD)s and money market funds. Other investors speculate too much by investing their hard-earned money on high-risk stocks or some other supposed high-return investment. Successful long-term investors and their advisors, however, usually take a middle-of-the-road approach to investing by allocating their money among stocks, interest-earning securities, and, perhaps, real estate investments. If they speculate on high-risk investments, they risk only a small portion of their portfolio, perhaps 5 percent.

In order to invest successfully over the long term, investors should periodically review how their assets are allocated based upon current market values. This is a particularly challenging task since the so-called asset allocation decision hinges on so many diverse and rapidly changing factors, including stock market conditions, interest rates, economic prospects, and tax regulations, not to mention the client's own financial status, objectives, and preferences. Unfortunately, all too often insufficient attention is directed toward asset allocation. It is easier to focus on individual investments such as a stock mutual fund, municipal bond, or real estate limited partnership rather than to step back and look at present and future investments in their totality.

1.2.1 The Four Steps of Investment Allocation

Many people simply make an investment when they have the money available to do so. However, before making a specific investment, the investor and his or her financial advisor should review how it will fit into his or her total portfolio. The investment allocation process involves up to four steps, culminating in actually selecting specific investments.

Step 1. First, the investor should determine the appropriate percentage of total funds available for investment in each of the three major investment categories, that is, stock investments, interest-earning investments, and real estate investments. The investor may not be interested in making or may not be able to afford to make real estate investments, in which case the allocation decision is between stock investments and interest-earning investments. The following tips may assist in making this important decision.

- Younger or middle-aged investors should generally have a considerable portion of their investments in stock and, if they are so inclined, income-producing real estate because over the long term, these investments have performed very well, particularly in comparison with interest-earning investments. However, a portion of the portfolio should remain conservatively invested. A typical portfolio allocation may be 40 percent stocks, 30 percent real estate, and 30 percent interest-earning for investors who opt for real estate investments. For those who do not, 60 percent stocks and 40 percent interest-earning is widely considered to be a desirable allocation—or 50 percent and 50 percent, which is not a bad allocation, either, and is a lot easier to remember.

- Preretirees within ten years of retirement, as well as retirees themselves, should have a somewhat more conservative asset allocation. This tactic minimizes the possible adverse effects of being caught in a protracted downturn in the stock or real estate markets for older investors who don't have as long a time period to make up for it. An appropriate allocation depends on many factors, of course, but a typical preretiree or retiree who will need to rely on his or her personal investments to help pay living expenses might consider an appropriate portfolio balance to consist of 40 percent stocks and 60 percent interest earning investments or, if the preretiree or retiree has real estate investments; 30 percent stocks, 20 percent real estate, and 50 percent interest-earning investments. Note that even retirees need stocks in their personal portfolios because stocks have generally been consistent in providing an inflation-beating return which retirees, most of whom have long life expectancies, still need.

Step 2. The second step involves evaluating the general types of investments within each of the two or three investment categories that are suitable, for example, "direct" ownership of stocks, interest-earning investments and real estate and/or "indirect" ownership via mutual funds or limited partnerships. Most often, the appropriate course is one of diversifying across investment vehicles. For example, with respect to stock investments, the investor may be best served by having some of his or her portfolio invested in specific company shares and some in mutual fund shares.

- If a client's portfolio is relatively small, he or she should probably be encouraged to restrict investments to mutual funds. As the client's portfolio increases, he or she can start making direct investments like individual stock issues and corporate or municipal bonds.

- Deciding how much to place in indirect versus direct investments also requires much judgment. If the investor wants to keep things simple, the following formula could be a perfectly good way to split up investments in order to maintain a 50 percent/50 percent split between total stocks and total interest-earning securities:

	25% in directly owned common stocks
	<u>25%</u> in stock mutual funds
Subtotal:	50% in stock investments
	25% in directly owned interest-earning investments
	<u>25%</u> in interest-earning mutual funds
Subtotal:	50% in interest-earning investments
Grand total:	100%

Step 3. The third step in the investment allocation process further breaks down the general categories of investment into specific industry, market or fund categories. Appropriate directly owned interest-earning investments might consist of short-term investments (money market accounts, certificates of deposit), municipal bonds, corporate bonds, and Treasury bonds. Assuming, as is usually the case, that the investor should also invest in interest-earning mutual funds, he or she might consider, for example, intermediate-term municipal bond funds, long-term corporate bond funds, and convertible bond funds.

- Many inexperienced investors are unfamiliar with a number of investment products that may be worthwhile additions to their portfolios. Financial services professionals should strive to familiarize their clients with the many excellent investment securities that are available.

- Just as it is unwise to place too large a portion of one's funds in one category of investment, interest-earning securities, for example, the investor should also never place too much money in a single type of investment. A few years ago, many people put too much money into junk bond mutual funds. They suffered when the market for these securities collapsed. The investor should thus be sure to spread his or her investments among several categories of interest-earning securities and stocks.

Step 4. The final step consists of selecting specific investments within each of the industry or fund categories that were identified in step 3—a particular bond or stock issue or mutual fund, for example.

1.2.2 Developing a "Permanent Portfolio Structure"

Table 1.2 depicts the investment allocation process, including typical types of investments that might be included in each investment category. Investors can use it to decide how to allocate their investments. They should view their asset allocation plans as a "permanent portfolio structure," which they will refrain from altering significantly even in the face of market uncertainty. Successful investors establish reasonable investment allocation parameters—and stick to them.

Table 1.2   Investment Allocation

Form of Ownership	*Investment Category*		
	Equity	*Fixed Income*	*Real Estate*
Direct	Common stocks	Bonds, Treasury securities, etc.	Directly owned real estate
Mutual fund / Partnership	Stock mutual funds	Fixed-income mutual funds	Limited partnerships

1.3   DEALING WITH MARKET VOLATILITY AND INVESTMENT UNCERTAINTY

Beginning in the latter half of the 1980s, the markets for both stock and interest-earning investments became increasingly volatile and uncertain—enough to frighten experienced and novice investors alike. The 1990s have started out in the same manner, so investors and their advisors should probably resign themselves to the fact that volatile stock and interest-rate markets are becoming the norm. Successful investors will continue to maintain a steady, consistent course, as they should under any market conditions. Nevertheless, there are several important matters that investors need to remember when learning to cope with market volatility and investment uncertainty.

Most investors have been adversely affected from time to time by large, often sudden declines in stock prices and/or by rapidly rising or declining interest rates. Many investors are prone to act rashly as a result of unexpected and/or major market fluctuations. Some bail out of most or all of their stock and bond investments, retreating to the safety and flexibility of short-term investments such as money market funds. Yet the yield on short-term investments barely keeps pace with inflation after taxes have been paid on the interest. There are 10 important principles that investors and financial services professionals alike should keep in mind, particularly in the face of market uncertainty.

1. *Maintain a balanced portfolio.*
   Investment portfolios should consist not only of common stock investments, but also of fixed-income investments and, perhaps, real estate. Otherwise, the investor will always risk having a substantial portion of his or her assets eroded by unfavorable market conditions.

2. *Diversify.*
   Many investors overcommit their portfolios to the stock of one or a very few companies and/or a single mutual fund. This lack of diversification is often the result of an individual's participation in his or her employer's stock option and/or stock purchase plans. Although such participation is usually advisable, there is always a danger that the price of the particular shares will collapse. Most investors who are exposed in this way can't afford this level of risk and should therefore liquidate some of their single-issue portfolios.

3. *Buy quality.*
   Shares of quality, dividend-paying companies and higher-rated debt issues are favored during volatile markets. These companies have more staying power if, in fact, economic conditions continue to deteriorate.

4. *"Ladder" the maturities of interest-earning investments.*
   Investors should pick interest-earning investments with varying maturities so that if interest rates rise or fall, they won't be stuck with a large portion of their interest-bearing investments maturing at the same time. Investors who purchase bonds of varying maturities will be at least somewhat insulated from the effects of fluctuating interest rates.

5. *Opt for mutual funds that have superior long-term track records.*
   Stock mutual funds have typically performed abysmally during bear markets. Similarly, investors are often surprised to discover that the value of most bond mutual funds declines when interest rates rise. Nevertheless, some funds, usually those that have been around for a long time and have produced strong long-term performance records (in comparison with similar funds), are consistently better at handling

adverse market conditions than are others. Conversely, today's high flier is often tomorrow's crash victim.

6. *Use stop-loss orders on stocks.*
A stop-loss order will protect stocks somewhat against a sharply and rapidly declining market. They are not foolproof, however. For example, in a volatile market, the investor who relies on stop-loss orders may at some point find himself or herself sold out of a stock that subsequently rebounds in price.

7. *When in doubt, seek safe havens.*
In times of total confusion and fear, investors should park at least some of their money in safe short-term investments such as money market funds, Treasury bills, and short-term certificates of deposit. While these investment vehicles may not provide a particularly attractive rate of return, at least they can protect one's assets until market conditions stabilize.

8. *Doing nothing is often the best response to crisis.*
Most investors who react to suddenly adverse market conditions almost always do the wrong thing. They are selling when they should be holding, if not buying. In general, investors should not "sell into weakness." Wait until things settle down.

9. *Avoid investing with borrowed money.*
The investors who were really hurt by the 1987, 1989, and 1990 market downturns were generally those who had invested on margin. The only way for them to cover their margin calls was to sell their holdings at an inopportune time. Margin investing can be an effective means of leveraging a stock portfolio, but fully margined investors expose themselves to considerable risk.

10. *Take a long-term investment perspective.*
The 500-point single-day drop in the Dow on October 19, 1987 was a heartstopper for nearly everyone even remotely involved in equity investing. For many, including some Wall Street insiders, it looked as though the world was coming to an end. Yet the total decline during the October 1987 market erased only one year's gain on the Dow. Flat (if not down) 12-month stock markets are not that uncommon, as was the case in 1990. By investing for the long term, investors and investment advisors can save themselves a great deal of anguish over shorter-term market vacillations.

1.4 CUMULATIVE GROWTH OF STOCKS AND TREASURY SECURITIES DURING THE 1980S

Figure 1.1 shows the cumulative growth of a dollar invested in common stocks, small-company stocks, long-term government bonds, and Treasury bills from the

FIGURE 1.1 CUMULATIVE GROWTH OF U.S. STOCKS, BONDS, TREASURY
BILLS AND INFLATION, 1980–1990

Exhibit 1   The Decade: (Year-End 1979 = 1.00)
                   Wealth Indices of
                   Investments in U.S. Stocks,
                   Bonds, Bills, and Inflation

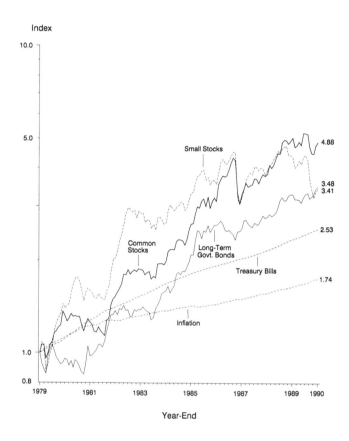

Source: Ibbotson Associates, *Stocks, Bonds, Bills and Inflation, 1991 Yearbook,* (Chicago: Ibbotson
Associates,1991).

end of 1979 to the end of 1989. The cumulative increase in the consumer price index is also presented. Despite considerable volatility, common stocks, as measured by the S&P 500 stock index, outperformed the other depicted categories over the decade.

1.5 AVERAGE ANNUAL RETURNS OF STOCKS, CORPORATE BONDS, AND TREASURY SECURITIES FOR THE DECADES SINCE 1920

Table 1.3 lists the compound annual returns of stocks, bonds, and Treasury securities for the last six decades and for the period 1926 to 1929. Inflation figures over comparable periods are also presented. Note that over most of the decades surveyed, stocks provided superior returns to those of fixed-income securities and Treasury bills.

Table 1.3   Compound Annual Rates of Return for Decades, 1920s–1980s

	1920s[1]	1930s	1940s	1950s	1960s	1970s	1980s
S&P 500	19.2%	0.0%	9.2%	19.4%	7.8%	5.9%	17.5%
Small-company stocks	–4.5	1.4	20.7	16.9	15.5	11.5	15.8
Long-term corporate	5.2	6.9	2.7	1.0	1.7	6.2	13.0
Long-term government	4.4	4.9	3.2	–0.1	1.4	5.5	12.6
Intermediate government	4.2	4.6	1.8	1.3	3.5	7.0	11.9
Treasury bills	3.7	0.6	0.4	1.9	3.9	6.3	8.9
Inflation	–1.1	–2.0	5.4	2.2	2.5	7.4	5.1

[1]Based on the periods 1926–1929.

Source: Ibbotson Associates, *Stocks, Bonds, Bills and Inflation, 1991 Yearbook*, (Chicago: Ibbotson Associates,1991).

1.6 CUMULATIVE GROWTH OF STOCKS AND TREASURY SECURITIES 1925–1990

Figure 1.2 shows the cumulative growth of a dollar invested in common stocks, small company stocks, long-term government bonds, and Treasury bills from the end of 1925 to the end of 1990. The cumulative increase in the consumer price index is also presented.

FIGURE 1.2 CUMULATIVE GROWTH OF U.S. STOCKS, BONDS, TREASURY BILLS, AND INFLATION, 1926–1990

Exhibit 9   Wealth Indices of   1925 - 1990
                 Investments in the
                 U.S. Capital Markets   (Year-End 1925 = 1.00)

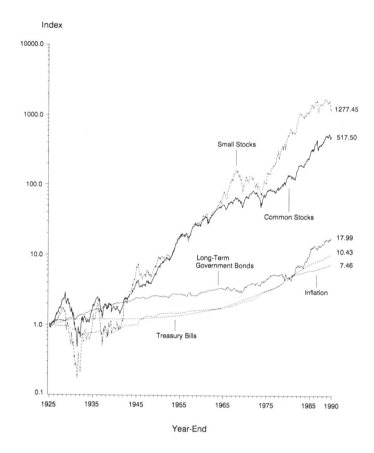

Source: Ibbotson Associates, *Stocks, Bonds, Bills and Inflation, 1991 Yearbook*, (Chicago: Ibbotson Associates,1991).

1.7 BOND AND STOCK YIELDS

Table 1.4 shows the annual average yields of various categories of fixed-income securities and common and preferred stocks from 1970.

Table 1.4 Bond and Stock Yields, 1970–1990

TYPE	1970	1980	1982	1983	1984	1985	1986	1987	1988	1989	1990
U.S. Treasury, constant maturities: [1][2]											
3-year	7.29	11.55	12.92	10.45	11.89	9.64	7.06	7.68	8.26	8.55	8.26
5-year	7.38	11.48	13.01	10.80	12.24	10.13	7.31	7.94	8.48	8.50	8.37
10-year	7.35	11.46	13.00	11.11	12.44	10.62	7.68	8.39	8.85	8.49	8.55
U.S. Govt., long-term bonds [2][3]	6.58	10.81	12.23	10.84	11.99	10.75	8.14	8.64	8.98	8.58	8.74
State and local govt. bonds, Aaa [4]	6.12	7.86	10.86	8.80	9.61	8.60	6.95	7.12	7.36	7.00	(NA)
State and local govt. bonds, Baa [4]	6.75	9.02	12.46	10.17	10.38	9.58	7.75	8.17	7.84	7.40	(NA)
High-graded municipal bonds (Standard & Poor's) [5]	6.51	8.51	11.57	9.47	10.15	9.18	7.38	7.73	7.74	7.24	7.25
Municipal (Bond Buyer, 20 bonds)	6.35	8.59	11.66	9.51	10.10	9.11	7.32	7.63	7.68	7.23	7.27
Corporate Aaa seasoned [4]	8.04	11.94	13.79	12.04	12.71	11.37	9.02	9.38	9.71	9.26	9.32
Corporate Baa seasoned [4]	9.11	13.67	16.11	13.55	14.19	12.72	10.39	10.58	10.83	10.18	10.36
Corporate, by years to maturity: [6]											
AA Industrial, 10 years	(NA)	12.05	13.98	11.06	12.91	11.11	8.35	8.91	9.40	9.26	(NA)
AAA Utilities, 30 years	8.72	12.57	14.95	12.21	13.46	11.79	9.15	9.40	9.75	9.39	(NA)
A Utilities, 30 years	9.17	13.68	15.84	12.82	13.87	12.20	9.63	9.89	10.19	9.89	(NA)
Corporate (Moody's) [4]	8.51	12.75	14.94	12.78	[7]13.49	12.05	9.71	9.91	10.18	9.66	9.77
Industrials (49 bonds) [8]	8.26	12.35	14.54	12.25	13.21	11.80	9.96	9.83	9.91	9.66	9.77
Railroads (13 bonds) [9]	8.77	11.48	13.68	12.08	13.07	11.94	9.85	9.63	10.03	(NA)	(NA)
Public utilities (51 bonds) [10]	8.68	13.15	15.33	13.31	[7]14.03	12.29	9.46	9.98	10.45	9.66	9.76
Stocks (Standard & Poor's): [5]											
Preferred (10 stocks) [11]	7.22	10.60	12.53	11.02	11.59	10.49	8.76	8.37	9.23	9.04	8.96
Common: Composite (500 stocks)	3.83	5.26	5.81	4.40	4.64	4.25	3.48	3.08	3.64	3.45	3.61
Industrials (400 stocks)	3.62	4.95	5.48	4.04	4.05	3.76	3.09	2.62	3.14	3.01	3.16

NA Not available. [1] Yields on the more actively traded issues adjusted to constant maturities by the U.S. Treasury. [2] Yields are based on closing bid prices quoted by at least five dealers. [3] Averages (to maturity or call) for all outstanding bonds neither due nor callable in less than 10 years, including several very low yielding "flower" bonds. [4] Source: Moody's Investors Service, New York, NY. [5] Source: Standard & Poor's Corp., New York, NY, *Standard & Poor's Outlook*, weekly. [6] Based on first trading day of each month, deferred call, new issue estimate. Source: Salomon Brothers, Inc., New York, NY, *An Analytical Record of Yields and Yield Spreads*. [7] The Aaa public utility average was suspended on Jan. 17, 1984 because of a lack of appropriate issues. The average corporate does not include Aaa utilities from Jan. 17 to Oct. 12. The Aaa utility average was reinstated on Oct. 12. Thirty public utility bonds were used during the period Jan. 17-Oct. 12, 1984. [8] Covers 40 bonds for period 1970-1983, 38 bonds for 1984-1986, and 37 bonds for 1987 and 1988. [9] Covers 23 bonds for period 1970-1981, 15 bonds for 1982, and 17 bonds for 1983. Beginning 1989 there was not an acceptable number of issues to continue a yield average. [10] Covers 40 bonds for period 1970-1988. [11] Yields based on 10 stocks, 4 yields. Issues converted to a price equivalent to $100 par and a 7 percent annual dividend before averaging.
Source: Except as noted, Board of Governors of the Federal Reserve System, *Federal Reserve Bulletin*, monthly.

1.8 ASSETS AND LIABILITIES OF HOUSEHOLDS

Table 1.5 shows trends in the composition of household assets and liabilities from 1970, including the percentage distribution. Pension fund reserves increased significantly as a percentage of total household assets over the periods surveyed while "other corporate equities" decreased.

1.9 COMPOSITION OF SAVINGS

Table 1.6 shows the changes in the composition of savings from 1970. Total individuals' saving is equal to the increase in financial assets plus the net investment in tangible assets minus the net increase in debt.

Table 1.5 Assets and Liabilities of Households, 1970–1989

TYPE OF INSTRUMENT	TOTAL (bil. dol.)							PERCENT DISTRIBUTION		
	1970	1980	1985	1986	1987	1988	1989	1970	1980	1989
Total financial assets	**2,488**	**6,541**	**9,905**	**10,830**	**11,390**	**12,324**	**13,770**	**100.0**	**100.0**	**100.0**
Deposit and market instrument [1]	791	2,124	3,594	3,851	4,153	4,561	5,012	31.8	32.5	36.4
Checkable deposits and currency	118	260	379	467	487	491	499	4.7	4.0	3.6
Small time and savings deposits	411	1,141	1,830	1,946	2,005	2,138	2,228	16.5	17.4	16.2
Money market fund shares	-	65	215	248	269	287	372	-	1.0	2.7
Large time deposits	15	112	120	95	114	151	185	0.6	1.7	1.3
Credit market instruments	247	546	1,052	1,096	1,277	1,495	1,728	9.9	8.3	12.5
U.S. Government securities	101	266	581	626	716	799	933	4.1	4.1	6.8
Treasury issues	85	221	483	499	522	580	607	3.4	3.4	4.4
Savings bonds	52	73	80	93	101	110	118	2.1	1.1	0.9
Other Treasury	33	148	404	406	421	471	490	1.3	2.3	3.6
Agency issues	16	45	98	126	194	218	326	0.6	0.7	2.4
Tax-exempt obligations	47	78	219	196	238	282	299	1.9	1.2	2.2
Corporate and foreign bonds	34	53	38	78	102	94	148	1.4	0.8	1.1
Mortgages	52	107	128	114	115	177	191	2.1	1.6	1.4
Open-market paper	14	41	86	84	106	144	157	0.5	0.6	1.1
Mutual fund shares	45	52	203	357	406	416	463	1.8	0.8	3.4
Other corporate equities	683	1,111	1,685	1,849	1,719	1,809	2,140	27.4	17.0	15.5
Life insurance reserves	131	216	257	274	300	326	354	5.3	3.3	2.6
Pension fund reserves [2]	241	916	1,802	2,058	2,248	2,559	2,942	9.7	14.0	21.4
Equity in noncorporate business	567	2,033	2,197	2,231	2,339	2,396	2,565	22.8	31.1	18.6
Security credit	4	16	35	44	38	45	53	0.2	0.2	0.4
Miscellaneous assets	26	72	133	165	187	213	241	1.1	1.1	1.8
Total liabilities	**493**	**1,489**	**2,401**	**2,707**	**2,970**	**3,265**	**3,561**	**100.0**	**100.0**	**100.0**
Credit market instruments	472	1,430	2,296	2,592	2,865	3,152	3,442	95.8	96.1	96.7
Mortgages	309	974	1,484	1,713	1,956	2,189	2,411	62.7	65.4	67.7
Installment consumer credit	106	302	527	582	618	671	728	21.4	20.3	20.4
Other consumer credit	29	53	75	78	75	72	63	5.8	3.6	1.8
Tax-exempt debt	-	17	81	79	78	79	81	-	1.1	2.3
Bank loans, not elsewhere classified	8	30	44	50	45	42	60	1.6	2.0	1.7
Other loans	21	55	84	89	92	98	100	4.2	3.7	2.8
Security credit	10	29	57	66	50	54	54	2.1	1.9	1.5
Trade credit	5	17	34	36	40	44	49	1.1	1.2	1.4
Unpaid life insurance premiums [3]	5	13	15	14	15	16	16	1.0	0.9	0.4

- Represents zero. [1] Excludes corporate equities. [2] See also table 597. [3] Includes deferred premiums.

Source: Board of Governors of the Federal Reserve System, *Annual Statistical Digest.*

1.10 TAXATION OF INVESTMENTS

This section describes the general income tax rules pertaining to investments.

1.10.1 Interest Income

1.10.1.1 Taxable Interest. All interest received or accrued is fully taxable, with the exception of interest on tax-exempt state or municipal bonds and on employee stock ownership plans (ESOP) loans. For a cash-basis taxpayer, interest becomes taxable as received.

Interest on corporate obligations becomes taxable when it is received by or credited to a cash-basis taxpayer; the same rule applies to interest on certificates of deposit, time obligations, and similar kinds of deposit arrangements on which interest is credited periodically and can be withdrawn without penalty (even though the principal cannot be withdrawn without penalty prior to maturity). However, interest on certificates of deposit of a maturity of up to one year that is not credited or made available to the holder without penalty before maturity is not counted as part of the holder's income until the certificate is redeemed or matures.

When a bond is sold between interest dates and the amount of interest earned up to the date of sale is added to the selling price, the buyer reports as income only that part of the full interest payment in excess of what he had paid the seller. The seller must include in her interest income the portion

Table 1.6 Composition of Savings, 1970–1989

COMPOSITION OF SAVINGS	1970	1975	1980	1984	1985	1986	1987	1988	1989
Increase in financial assets	**80.7**	**176.4**	**321.3**	**563.7**	**568.0**	**561.2**	**512.1**	**549.5**	**595.1**
Checkable deposits and currency	8.7	6.0	8.9	23.0	32.6	94.8	22.8	8.5	12.1
Time and savings deposits	43.5	77.6	124.9	229.6	133.0	106.5	97.8	159.6	134.4
Money market fund shares	-	1.3	24.5	44.0	12.1	33.0	21.4	18.1	84.9
Securities.	0.5	9.3	9.0	72.8	137.7	51.1	144.7	75.1	114.1
U.S. savings bonds.	0.3	4.0	-7.3	3.0	5.3	13.6	7.8	8.5	8.2
Other U.S. Treasury securities	-10.6	14.2	30.3	64.2	53.3	3.8	18.8	48.2	19.3
U.S. Government agency securities	4.6	-5.6	9.4	32.4	24.2	4.8	71.4	72.8	114.7
Tax-exempt obligations	-0.1	5.0	1.1	26.2	38.1	-24.5	42.6	30.7	16.8
Corporate and foreign bonds	9.2	9.6	-18.2	-4.1	4.2	39.3	24.1	-4.1	24.3
Open-market paper	-2.2	-11.7	3.7	4.4	47.0	-2.2	4.8	34.8	8.0
Mutual fund shares.	2.0	-0.4	1.1	24.0	68.5	141.4	73.1	-1.7	28.3
Other corporate equities	-2.8	-5.8	-11.0	-77.3	-102.8	-125.0	-97.9	-114.0	-105.4
Private life insurance reserves	5.2	7.9	9.7	5.0	10.4	17.2	25.7	24.9	27.6
Private insured pension reserves	2.9	8.7	22.3	46.7	63.4	82.5	70.6	88.8	86.8
Private noninsured pension reserves.	7.2	40.2	51.2	42.1	39.5	24.4	25.0	11.7	-23.3
Government insurance and pension reserves.	8.9	15.1	35.3	63.9	72.3	78.7	73.9	84.9	84.8
Miscellaneous financial assets.	3.9	10.1	35.4	36.6	67.0	72.9	30.2	78.0	73.8
Gross investment in tangible assets.	**150.5**	**236.4**	**403.4**	**608.0**	**640.5**	**699.5**	**727.6**	**773.5**	**805.7**
Owner-occupied homes	28.1	51.9	113.6	155.4	161.4	181.7	204.0	224.3	243.5
Other fixed assets [1]	36.4	45.1	79.6	100.9	105.9	108.5	100.2	89.6	78.2
Consumer durables	85.7	135.4	219.3	335.6	372.2	406.0	421.1	455.2	473.3
Inventories [1].	0.4	4.0	-9.1	16.1	5.0	3.4	2.4	4.4	10.7
Capital consumption allowances	**102.9**	**173.0**	**311.1**	**399.3**	**424.8**	**456.3**	**490.5**	**517.0**	**549.5**
Owner-occupied homes	13.5	24.4	47.0	60.0	64.4	67.1	70.0	73.0	76.0
Other fixed assets [1]	23.7	41.6	76.8	102.6	105.9	108.7	115.2	120.4	132.9
Consumer durables	65.8	107.0	187.4	236.7	254.6	280.6	305.4	323.7	340.7
Net investment in tangible assets	**47.6**	**63.4**	**92.3**	**208.7**	**215.7**	**243.2**	**237.1**	**256.5**	**256.1**
Owner-occupied homes	14.6	27.5	66.6	95.4	97.1	114.6	134.0	151.3	167.5
Other fixed assets [1]	12.7	3.5	2.9	-1.6	-4.0	-0.2	-15.0	-30.7	-54.6
Consumer durables	19.9	28.4	31.9	98.8	117.6	125.4	115.7	131.6	132.6
Inventories [1].	0.4	4.0	-9.1	16.1	5.0	3.4	2.4	4.4	10.7
Net increase in liabilities [2]	**38.7**	**80.7**	**209.3**	**381.0**	**437.5**	**395.2**	**372.0**	**390.6**	**360.2**
Mortgage debt on nonfarm homes	13.5	38.8	96.4	136.7	157.0	216.8	234.0	230.9	217.2
Other mortgage debt [1]	16.4	16.8	57.4	87.4	103.1	71.2	75.0	61.4	51.0
Consumer credit	4.6	8.0	2.6	81.6	82.5	58.0	32.9	51.1	39.1
Security credit.	-1.8	0.7	7.2	-2.4	19.4	8.2	-15.3	3.1	0.8
Other liabilities [1]	3.7	14.7	38.9	77.3	75.6	41.2	45.5	43.0	48.8
Individuals' saving	**89.6**	**159.1**	**204.4**	**391.4**	**346.1**	**409.2**	**377.2**	**415.4**	**491.0**
Less: Government insurance and pension reserve	8.9	15.1	35.3	63.9	72.3	78.7	73.9	84.9	84.8
Net investment in consumer durables	19.9	28.4	31.9	98.8	117.6	125.4	115.7	131.6	132.6
Capital gains dividends from mutual funds .	0.9	0.2	1.8	6.0	4.9	17.5	22.4	6.3	15.0
Net saving by farm corporations	(Z)	0.5	0.5	0.7	0.9	0.6	0.9	1.4	1.8
Equals: Personal saving, flow of funds basis [3].	**59.9**	**114.8**	**134.9**	**221.9**	**150.5**	**187.0**	**164.3**	**191.3**	**256.8**

- Represents or rounds to zero. Z Less than $50 million. [1] Includes corporate farms. [2] Includes items not shown separately. [3] Personal saving on national income account basis measures personal saving as income less taxes and consumption; flow-of-funds basis measures the same concept from acquisition of assets less borrowing.

Source: Board of Governors of the Federal Reserve System, *Flow of Funds Accounts*, quarterly.

of the selling price representing interest accrued to the date of sale. This interest adjustment is a purchase of accrued interest and has no effect on the cost of the bond.

Holders of certain bonds or other obligations issued at a discount may be required to include in income a portion of the discount as "imputed interest" in each year the obligation is held, even though no interest corresponding to the amount is paid or accrued during the period. Certain other notes, debt instruments, or loans bearing interest at less than the applicable federal rate may also result in "imputed interest" income to the lender.

1.10.1.2 Municipal Bonds. The Tax Reform Act of 1986 altered rules governing tax exemption for interest of bonds issued after August 15, 1986. Interest on obligations of a state or local government is usually excludable from gross income, but bond interest is not tax free when it is derived from

- Nonexempt private activity bonds

- State or local bonds that have not been issued in registered form
- Arbitrage bonds

Private activity bonds qualifying for tax exemption include

- Exempt-facility bonds
- Qualified mortgage bonds
- Qualified veterans' mortgage bonds
- Qualified small-issue bonds
- Qualified student loan bonds
- Qualified redevelopment bonds
- Qualified Internal Reserve Code Section 501(c)(3) bonds meeting applicable restrictions

1.10.1.3 U.S. Savings Bonds. A taxpayer on the cash basis need not be taxed on the increase in value of a U.S. savings bond until the value is realized upon surrender of the bonds. However, a cash-basis taxpayer may elect to treat the yearly increase in value as income.

A taxpayer on the accrual basis must include the increase in value of a U.S. savings bond (issued at a discount and payable at par on maturity) each year in an amount equal to the increase in redemption value.

An exception to the rules discussed exists for an individual who, in a year in which she redeems a qualified U.S. savings bond, pays qualified higher education expenses. In such a case, the individual may exclude from income amounts received upon such redemption. To qualify, the bond must be issued after 1989 to an individual who has reached age 24 before the date of issuance. Tuition and fees required for a taxpayer, or a taxpayer's spouse or dependents, for enrollment and attendance at an eligible educational institution, count as eligible higher education expense.

However, if the total proceeds of U.S. savings bonds redeemed by a taxpayer during a tax year exceed the qualified higher education expenses paid by the taxpayer, limits to the amount that may be excluded apply. Limits also apply if the modified gross income of the taxpayer exceeds $40,000 (or $60,000 in a joint return).

Before the limits defined are applied, the amount of qualified higher education expenses must be reduced by the sum of the amounts received under a qualified, tax-exempt scholarship.

1.10.2 Dividends

1.10.2.1 Cash Dividends For income tax purposes, "dividend" means any distribution of money or property made by a corporation to its shareholders out of earnings and profits. Dividends are fully included in gross income.

A dividend is taxable when the check is actually received, even though it may be dated and mailed in an earlier year—time of payment, rather than declaration, governs taxability. An accrual-basis stockholder's dividend does not need to be included in income until it is made subject to the stockholder's demand.

If a dividend is both cash and noncash property, the total value of the dividend is the amount of cash plus the fair market value of the property at the date of distribution. This amount is reduced (but not below zero) by the amount of liability to which property is subject.

1.10.2.2 Stock Dividends and Stock Rights As a general rule, a stockholder need not include in gross income the value of a stock received as a stock dividend, although there are several exceptions. Cash that is paid in lieu of fractional shares is taxable however, even though fractional shares themselves would not be.

1.10.3 Capital Gains and Losses

1.10.3.1 Capital Assets A capital gain or loss is a gain or loss from the sale or exchange of a capital asset. "Capital asset" means property, but does not include the following:

- An inventoriable asset
- Property held primarily for sale to customers in the ordinary course of the taxpayer's trade or business
- A note or account receivable acquired in the ordinary course of trade or business for services rendered or from the sale of stock in trade or property held for sale in the ordinary course of business
- Depreciable business property
- Real property used in the taxpayer's trade or business
- A copyright; a literary, musical, or artistic composition; a letter or memorandum; or similar property (but not a patent or invention) held by the taxpayer who created it, or by one whose basis in the property is determined by reference to the basis of one who created it.

A taxpayer's household furnishings, personal residence and automobile are "capital assets" to which the capital gains provisions apply. Although gain on the sale of this kind of property is treated as capital gain, no loss is recognized for income tax purposes unless the property was held for the production of income. For example, if an individual sells a residence that had been partially used as rental property, he or she would have to make a proper allocation of the cost of the building, the selling price, depreciation (applicable to the rental portion only), and the selling expenses between the personal and rental portions of the building as if there were two separate transactions. Gain on either portion would be recognized for income tax purposes, but loss would be recognized only on the rental portion. Stock and securities are generally considered to be held for production of income so that loss on their sale is a capital loss.

1.10.3.2 Computing Capital Gains and Losses Gains or losses from the sale or exchange of a capital asset must be characterized as either short term or long term, depending on how long the asset was held by the taxpayer. If a taxpayer has both short-term and long-term transactions during the year, each type is reported separately, and gains and losses from each type are netted separately. After this netting process has been achieved, the net long-term capital gain or loss for the year is combined with the net short-term capital gain or loss for the year to arrive at an overall (net) capital gain or loss for the year. If capital gains exceed capital losses, the overall gain is included with the taxpayer's other income and is taxed at the regular tax rates. If capital losses exceed capital gains, the overall losses are subject to deduction limitations.

All capital gains of individuals, estates, and trusts are taxed as ordinary income at the regular rates of 15 percent, 28 percent, or 31 percent.

In determining the extent of deductibility of capital losses in the tax year, all short-term and long-term gains and losses are grouped, and the total losses are deductible only to the extent of the aggregate gains, plus, in the case of taxpayers other than corporations, ordinary income of up to $3,000. Both short-term and long-term capital losses may be used to offset up to $3,000 of ordinary income: An individual with $20,000 of ordinary income, a short-term capital loss of $800 and a long-term loss of $200 would be able to make a capital loss deduction of $1,000.

Individuals may carry over a net capital loss for an unlimited time until the loss is exhausted. A capital loss that is carried over to a later tax year retains its long-term or short-term character for the year to which it is carried. In determining the character and amount of the capital loss that can be carried over, short-term capital gain is increased by the lesser of

1. The ordinary income offset ($3,000 or the amount of the net loss)
2. Taxable income increased by that offset and the deduction for personal exemptions

A short-term capital loss carry-over first offsets short-term gain in the carryover year. If a net short-term capital loss results, such loss offsets net long-term capital gain, and thus up to $3,000 of ordinary income.

A long-term capital loss first reduces long-term capital gain in the carryover year, then net short-term capital gain, and finally up to $3,000 of ordinary income.

Chapter 2 _____

CASH EQUIVALENTS

Not long ago, the only place for investors to earn interest on funds they wanted to keep relatively liquid was a low-yielding passbook savings account. Today, there is a broad range of more appealing choices for cash equivalent investments, that is, short-term, interest-earning investments. For example,

- Money market mutual funds invest in short-term debt such as commercial paper, Treasury bills, and certificates of deposit. Shares are generally redeemable at any time, either through the mail or by telephone.

    There are a variety of different types of money market mutual funds, including tax-exempt funds that invest solely in short-term municipal debt and U.S. government money market funds, that invest in Treasury bills and/or government-guaranteed, mortgage-backed securities.

- Money market deposit accounts, offered by banks and other savings institutions, have liquidity features similar to money market mutual funds, although they may require higher investment minimums and have more stringent restrictions on withdrawals. Their rates tend to be lower than money market mutual funds.

- Certificates of deposit, also offered by banks, can offer competitive yields. Maturities range from 90 days to 10 years, although investors who may need access to their money should limit themselves to maturities of 6 months or less. There is usually an early withdrawal penalty if a certificate of deposit is accessed before its stated maturity.

- Treasury bills, along with U.S. savings bonds, are the only debt instruments guaranteed directly by the full faith and credit of the U.S. government. For investors seeking liquidity, maturities of under 1 year, which require a minimum of $10,000 are most appropriate.

Investors may use these cash equivalents for a variety of purposes. Often, they serve as a "parking place" for money awaiting more attractive investment opportunities. During times of high short-term interest rates, cash equivalents can be attractive investments themselves. In addition, liquid savings accounts may be used to house emergency funds to help meet living expenses should regular sources of income be suddenly reduced or suspended or if unexpected expenses arise.

Since there may be substantial differences in yield among cash-equivalent investments, it is advisable to check prevailing rates regularly on both fully taxable and federal and/or state tax-exempt investments to achieve the highest possible after-tax returns. However, investors and financial professionals should keep in mind that cash-equivalent investments will, at best, barely beat inflation on an after-tax basis.

2.1 CASH EQUIVALENT INVESTMENT SUMMARY

Investors should keep at least a portion of their portfolios in highly liquid, cash equivalents such as Treasury bills, money market funds, or other interest-bearing investments that are readily convertible into cash with little or no risk of loss of principal. These funds can be used as an emergency cash reserve, as well as a convenient "parking place" for money awaiting investment in equities, fixed-income securities, real estate, or other, more attractive investment opportunities. This section describes the most commonly used cash equivalent investments.

2.1.1 Certificates of Deposit

A certificate of deposit (CD) is a receipt for funds deposited in a financial institution at a specified interest rate for a specified period of time. Some institutions offer low minimum deposits; time of maturity ranges from 3 months to 10 years. There are three different kinds of CDs. *Fixed-rate negotiable CDs* require a minimum investment of $100,000; maturities usually fall between 14 and 180 days. On maturity, both principal and interest are paid. *Variable-rate CDs* also typically require a minimum deposit of $100,000, but are much more responsive to fluctuating interest rates. Interest payments occur monthly, quarterly, or semiannually, and on each payment date the rate is readjusted to prevailing rates. Then there are a variety of *Small savings CDs* designed for investors with smaller amounts of money to invest, with varying interest rates, maturities, and minimum deposits.

Accounts of depository institutions offering CDs may be insured by a private insurance company, a state insurance fund, or a federal agency. Federal agency-insured institutions are far safer than are other kinds, and a prudent investor will limit investment to these. Federal deposit insurance programs make a deposit a riskless investment up to a certain amount. This limit is currently $100,000 of a depositor's principal and interest (for all kinds of deposits—savings and checking accounts, NOW accounts, money market deposit accounts, and CDs) although Congress is considering limitations on federal deposit insurance. An investor depositing large amounts in a CD or other kind of deposit should keep this limit in mind. For example, a 5-year, 7 percent CD with a principal deposit of $90,000 will earn about $13,041 interest after the second year, pushing the balance over $100,000 and leaving several thousand dollars uninsured.

Several brokerage firms sell so-called brokered CDs. In essence, they offer a CD shopping service which may result in the investor obtaining a better CD rate than he or she could at a local financial institution.

2.1.2 Money Market Funds

When, in the mid-1970s, money market rates climbed far above the rates offered by banks and thrifts, a new kind of mutual fund was invented to capitalize on the money market's high return and liquidity. Money market funds are designed to appeal to the small investor, for whom direct investment in money market securities is awkward. Transaction costs are very small, and since money market funds are able to buy a broad range of securities, credit risk is negligible. The three types of money market funds are general-purpose funds, which invest in a wide range of good-quality money market instruments and which have an average maturity of 30 to 40 days; U.S. government short-term funds, which invest solely in U.S. Treasury securities and U.S. government agency issues and have an average maturity of 40 days; and tax-exempt money market funds, which invest in short-term municipal securities and are exempt from federal income taxes but which have a lower yield than the other two types.

2.1.3 Money Market Deposit Accounts

Institutions are free to pay any interest rate they like on money market deposit accounts, as with CDs. Money market deposit accounts (MMDAs), however, unlike CDs, have no maturity rate, and as their interest rate varies, a set yield is not guaranteed. Disadvantages to MMDAs, compared to money market funds, include a generally higher minimum balance, limited check-writing privileges, and the inconvenience of going to the bank to transfer or withdraw funds. Unlike money market funds, however, money market accounts offered by federal insured depository institutions are insured up to $100,000.

2.1.4 Treasury Bills

Treasury bills, one of the several securities issued by the U.S. government to the investing public, offer investors no risk, very high liquidity, exemption from state and local taxation, and a wide range of maturities. Treasury bills or T-bills are negotiable, noninterest-bearing securities with an original maturity of 1 year or less. Currently, bills are offered in minimum denominations of $10,000 and increments of $5,000 thereafter. An investor in a bill earns a return by receiving more for the bill at its maturity than he or she paid for it at issue—bills are always issued at a discount face value, the amount being determined in bill auctions held by the Fed.

At the time of bill auctions, an investor may submit a bid, either competitive or noncompetitive. A nonexpert, individual investor will generally put in a noncompetitive bid, permitting him or her to buy bills at the average accepted bid. An institutional investor buying large quantities of bills makes a competitive bid of a yield—expressed in percentage points—that he or she is willing to pay. Once all bids are received, the Fed allocates the supply of bills among those bidders who have offered to pay the highest prices (i.e., to accept the lowest yields). Successful bidders will, therefore, pay different prices for their bills, and an investor who manages to be near to the stop-out yield—the highest yield the Fed will accept—will get the most favorable return. Obviously, an investor must study the market very carefully before submitting a bid.

In terms of salability on the secondary market, a bill's yield is unlikely to be constant over time. It will fluctuate due to changes in the general level of interest rates, as rates falling after the bill is issued will make the bill more desirable and will make it command a higher price and lower yield. Conversely, if rates rise after a bill is issued, it will become less attractive to buyers—since its discount is less than that on current bills—and its yield will be forced up. Even if interest rates remained constant, a bill's yield would vary according to the yield curve, which dictates that the shorter a bill's current maturity, the lower its yield. This reliable rule of thumb is not invariably true, for when interest rates are expected to fall, yields will be lower on bills with a long time to maturity than on bills with a short maturity.

The price paid for a bill will generally be higher the closer it is to maturity, the steeper the yield curve, and the lower the current level of short-term interest rates.

2.1.5 Savings Accounts

Passbook savings accounts are the most convenient and liquid of investments, but they also pay the lowest interest (usually around 5 percent). Savings accounts are insured by the Federal Deposit Insurance Corporation (FDIC) up to $100,000 and can be used as collateral against a bank loan. Negotiable order of withdrawal (NOW) accounts and Super NOW accounts are hybrids of checking and savings accounts that require a minimum deposit and pay higher interest rates.

2.1.6 Municipal Notes

State and local governments issue municipal notes, which bear interest and are issued with maturities ranging from a month to a year. These securities are secured by the issuer's pledge of credit, a pledge that does not absolutely remove debt risk, as it is possible that a municipality might default on its securities. Municipal notes' primary attraction is that interest income on them is exempt from federal taxation, and often from state taxes as well. The muni market, thus, attracts only highly taxed investors for whom the tax exemption provides substantial after-tax return.

2.2   IMPORTANT CONSIDERATIONS IN MAKING CASH EQUIVALENT INVESTMENTS

Many investors become accustomed to always making the same kind of short-term investment. By devoting some time to evaluating the various types of short-term investments, investors and their advisors will be able to make the most of the money that is invested in these securities.

2.2.1   Finding the Highest Rates

Rates on short-term (cash equivalent) investments vary, sometimes considerably. Local and financial newspapers usually provide extensive coverage of rates offered on certificates of deposit, money market accounts, and Treasury bills. Interest rates on certificates of deposit vary not only from one local bank to another, but also from one region to another. CDs are often advertised nationwide and can be purchased by mail. Investors should ascertain whether the bank or savings institution is federally insured before committing money.

Investors can benefit from the intense competition for their money. Local banks may engage in price wars to attract money. Many mutual fund companies are temporarily waiving all or part of the fees charged to money market investors in order to attract deposits. The effort to stay abreast of conditions in the short-term investment markets will often be handsomely rewarded.

For investors in the higher income tax brackets, it may be appropriate to compare the after-tax yields on taxable short-term investments, such as CDs and ordinary money market accounts, with yields on tax-exempt money market accounts. Since T-bills are also exempt from state and local taxes, they are particularly attractive for investors who live in high-tax areas. The after-tax return is the amount of total interest that would be received on any short-term investment minus any taxes that would be due. The yields on tax-exempt money market funds are frequently higher than the after-tax yields on taxable instruments, although conditions do change periodically. After-tax rates of return should be compared frequently.

2.2.2   Selecting Convenient Features

Short-term investments vary in the number of convenient features they offer. In general, money market mutual funds are the most convenient and flexible, but individual investors will find many of the following conveniences more important:

Telephone switching between funds

Check-writing privileges

Immediate confirmations and regular statements

Expedited redemptions

Low investment minimums

Timely resolution of problems

Weighing the financial returns against the availability of such features as those just listed will complete the picture of exactly what a specific short-term investment can do for an investor.

2.3 SHORT-TERM MONEY MARKET RATES OF INTEREST

Table 2.1 shows historical interest rate relationships among various types of money market securities. Since rates can vary widely among these instruments, financial professionals as well as individual investors should compare them carefully before making a purchase.

Finance Paper vs. Treasury Bills

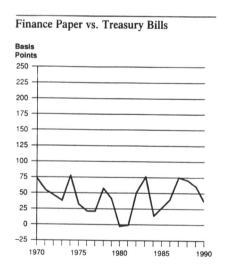

Commercial Paper vs. Treasury Bills

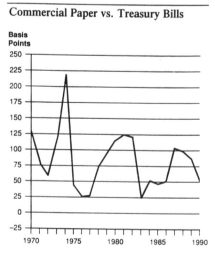

Bankers Acceptances vs. Treasury Bills

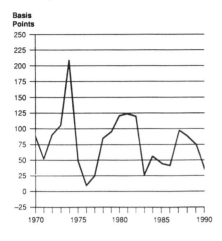

Certificates of Deposit vs. Treasury Bills

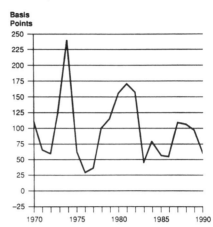

Finance Paper and Commercial Paper Compared with Treasury Bills

Certificates of Deposit and Bankers Acceptances Compared with Treasury Bills

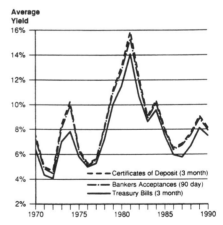

(Courtesy of the Federal Reserve)

2.4 RELATIVE YIELDS OF CASH EQUIVALENTS

Table 2.2 is a comparison of interest rates on cash equivalent securities and home mortgages. Note the significant interest rate fluctuation that occurred during this period, particularly in the last decade.

Table 2.2 Cash-Equivalent Rates and Mortgage Rates, 1970–1990

TYPE	1970	1980	1981	1982	1983	1984	1985	1986	1987	1988	1989	1990
Federal funds, effective rate [1]	7.18	13.36	16.38	12.26	9.09	10.23	8.10	6.80	6.66	7.57	9.21	8.10
Commercial paper, 3-month [1][2]	(NA)	12.66	15.33	11.89	8.88	10.10	7.95	6.49	6.81	7.66	8.99	8.06
Prime rate charged by banks	7.91	15.27	18.87	14.86	10.79	12.04	9.93	8.33	8.21	9.32	10.87	10.01
Eurodollar deposits, 3-month	8.52	14.00	16.79	13.12	9.57	10.75	8.27	6.70	7.07	7.85	9.16	8.16
Finance paper, 3-month [2][3]	7.18	11.49	14.08	11.23	8.70	9.73	7.77	6.38	6.54	7.38	8.72	7.87
Bankers acceptances, 90-day [2][4]	7.31	12.72	15.32	11.89	8.90	10.14	7.92	6.39	6.74	7.56	8.87	7.93
Large negotiable CDs, 3-month, secondary market	7.56	13.07	15.91	12.27	9.07	10.37	8.05	6.52	6.86	7.73	9.09	8.15
Federal Reserve discount rate [5]	5½ -6	10-13	12-14	8½ -12	8½	8-9	7½ -8	5½ -7½	5½ -6	6-6½	6½ -7	6½ -7
Taxable money market funds [6]	(NA)	12.68	16.82	12.23	8.58	10.04	7.71	6.26	6.12	7.11	8.87	7.82
Certificates of deposit (CDs): [7]												
6-month	(NA)	(NA)	(NA)	(NA)	(NA)	9.99	7.83	6.51	6.47	7.18	8.34	(NA)
1-year	(NA)	(NA)	(NA)	(NA)	(NA)	10.37	8.29	6.75	6.77	7.47	8.41	(NA)
2 1/2-year	(NA)	(NA)	(NA)	(NA)	10.06	10.82	9.00	7.13	7.16	7.77	8.33	(NA)
5-year	(NA)	(NA)	(NA)	(NA)	(NA)	11.25	9.66	7.60	7.66	8.11	8.30	(NA)
U.S. Government securities: [8]												
3-month Treasury bill	6.39	11.43	14.03	10.61	8.61	9.52	7.48	5.98	5.77	6.67	8.11	7.50
6-month Treasury bill	6.51	11.37	13.80	11.07	8.73	9.76	7.65	6.03	6.03	6.91	8.03	7.46
1-year Treasury bill	6.48	10.89	13.14	11.07	8.80	9.92	7.81	6.08	6.32	7.13	7.92	7.35
Prime 1-year municipals [9]	4.35	6.25	7.92	7.88	5.29	6.05	5.12	4.33	4.44	5.15	6.11	(NA)
Home mortgages:												
HUD series: [10]												
FHA insured, secondary market [11]	9.03	13.44	16.31	15.31	13.11	13.82	12.24	9.91	10.16	10.49	10.24	10.17
Conventional, new-home [12][13]	8.52	13.95	16.52	15.79	13.43	13.80	12.28	10.07	10.17	10.30	10.21	10.08
Conventional, existing-home [12]	8.56	13.95	16.55	15.82	13.45	13.81	12.29	10.09	10.17	10.31	10.22	(NA)
Conventional, 15 yr. fixed [7]	(NA)	(NA)	(NA)	(NA)	(NA)	(NA)	(NA)	10.05	10.04	10.14	10.05	(NA)

NA Not available. [1] Based on daily offering rates of dealers. [2] Yields are quoted on a bank-discount basis, rather than an investment yield basis (which assumes a higher figure). [3] Placed directly; averages of daily offering rates quoted by finance companies. [4] Based on the most representative daily offering rates of dealers. Beginning Aug. 15, 1974, closing rates were used, and from Jan. 1, 1981, rates of top-rated banks only. [5] Federal Reserve Bank of New York, low and high. The discount rates for 1980 and 1981 do not include the surcharge applied to frequent borrowings by large institutions. The surcharge reached 3 percent in 1980 and 4 percent in 1981. Surcharge was eliminated in Nov. 1981. [6] 12 month yield for period ending December 31. Source: The Donoghue Organization, Inc., Holliston, MA, *IBC/Donoghue's Money Fund Report*, weekly (copyright). [7] Annual averages. Source: Advertising News Service, Inc.; North Palm Beach, FL, *Bank Rate Monitor*, weekly (copyright). [8] Averages based on daily closing bid yields in secondary market, bank discount basis. [9] Averages based on quotations for one day each month. Source: Salomon Brothers, Inc., New York, NY, *An Analytical Record of Yields and Yield Spreads*. [10] HUD = Housing and Urban Development. [11] Averages based on quotations for 1 day each month as compiled by FHA. [12] Primary market. [13] Average contract rates on new commitments.

Source of tables 835-837: Except as noted, Board of Governors of the Federal Reserve System, *Federal Reserve Bulletin*, monthly, and *Annual Statistical Digest.*

2.5 SELECTED TIME DEPOSITS AND OTHER ACCOUNTS AT INSURED COMMERCIAL BANKS

Table 2.3 shows trends in amounts outstanding and average rates paid for time deposits and retail repurchase agreements, and amounts outstanding for IRA and Keogh plan deposits. Although average rates paid on money market accounts increased in 1987, 1988, and the first quarter of 1989, amounts outstanding declined, at least partially as a result of the increasing popularity of money market mutual funds. IRA and Keogh plan deposits at insured commercial banks increased steadily over the periods surveyed.

Table 2.3 Selected Time Deposit and Other Accounts at Insured Commercial Banks—Deposit and Rates, 1985–1990

[As of **December**. Estimates based on data collected from a sample of about 500 banks]

TYPE OF DEPOSIT	AMOUNT OUTSTANDING (bil. dol.)						AVERAGE RATE PAID (percent)					
	1985	1986	1987	1988	1989	1990	1985	1986	1987	1988	1989	1990
NOW accounts [1]	44.5	164.2	174.8	190.5	196.8	209.2	5.99	5.00	4.95	4.96	5.02	4.93
Money market deposit accounts [2]	330.1	380.0	353.8	346.4	350.3	376.3	6.71	5.19	5.43	5.87	6.40	(NA)
Interest-bearing time deposits: [3]												
7-31 day	5.3	6.1	7.1	6.4	} 45.4	} 50.2	} 6.85	5.45	6.02	6.77	} 7.64	} 6.94
32-91 day	21.0	21.6	23.3	24.8			} 7.16	5.62	6.26	7.20		
92-182 day	147.8	131.5	132.4	136.3	152.8	167.6	7.50	5.70	6.75	7.84	7.83	7.19
183 day-1 year	66.1	72.2	96.8	128.0	177.4	220.8	7.77	5.93	7.14	8.19	7.86	7.33
1-2 year	81.2	83.8	89.6	107.2	125.0	150.0	8.24	6.22	7.46	8.30	7.88	7.43
2 year or more	115.4	120.7	121.3	133.0	129.2	138.1	8.73	6.61	7.86	8.39	7.86	7.52
All IRA and Keogh Plan deposits	59.4	73.1	83.2	94.0	109.2	131.2	(NA)	(NA)	(NA)	(NA)	(NA)	(NA)
Retail repurchase agreements [4]	1.3	1.1	0.8	1.6	(NA)	(NA)	6.77	5.37	5.46	6.77	(NA)	(NA)

NA Not available.   [1] Negotiable order of withdrawal accounts containing an agreement between depositor and depository such that some or all funds deposited are eligible to earn more than 5.25 percent. As of January 1, 1986 interest rate ceilings were removed from all NOW accounts. Beginning with the December 1986 data the NOW accounts category includes all NOW accounts, including those accounts which were subject to a 5.25 percent regulatory interest rate restriction prior to January 1, 1986. Estimates for NOW accounts beginning in December 1986 are based on reports of deposits.   [2] Deposits with no minimum balance requirement and no required minimum maturity but institutions must reserve the right to require at least seven days' notice prior to withdrawal, no restrictions on depositor eligibility, or limitations on the amount of interest that may be paid; such accounts may allow up to six transfers per month, no more than three of which may be draft and may permit unlimited withdrawals by mail, messenger, or in person. Estimates based on reports of deposits.   [3] All interest-bearing time deposits and open account time deposits with balances of less than $100,000, including those held in IRAs and Keogh Plan deposits.   [4] Retail repurchase agreements are in denominations of less than $100,000 with maturities of less than 90 days that arise from the transfer of direct obligations of, or obligations fully-guaranteed as to principal and interest by, the U.S. Government or an agency thereof.

Source: Board of Governors of the Federal Reserve System, *Money Stock, Liquid Assets, and Debt Measures, Federal Reserve Statistical Release H.6,* weekly.

Chapter 3

EQUITY INVESTMENTS

Stock investments have long played a major role in investing, although in recent years interest-earning investments and real estate investments have become worthy contenders for the investor's dollar. Individual investors will reenter or enter the stock markets, either through individual stock purchases or through stock mutual funds, in greater numbers during the 1990s as they bear witness to the superior total return performance of stocks versus other investment alternatives. Although there will be more participation in the stock market, individuals still remain skeptical of a market increasingly dominated by institutions and frequently buffeted by market uncertainty. Also, program trading and leveraged buy-outs reinforce the individual investor's opinion that he or she is at an unfair disadvantage in the market.

The financial services professional is often called upon to recommend appropriate investments, evaluate a specific investment, and/or evaluate an entire portfolio. The complexity of these tasks is substantial, yet they are an integral part of the financial services business. It is essential that the financial services professional develop an awareness of what products are available and of how various products may be appropriate in meeting an individual's unique capital accumulation needs.

As the market reaches all-time highs, investors will become more uncertain about the short-term prospects for stocks. Concerns over the economy will continue unabated due in part to the slow recovery from the recession. Conflicting forecasts by leading market observers will exacerbate the uncertainty, but equities will continue to offer long-term investment opportunities, particularly when compared with other categories of investment.

Tax initiatives will most likely be beneficial to equity investors. Lower capital gains rates (possibly tied to length of holding period) and/or indexation of capital gains are receiving bilateral support on Capitol Hill.

More attention will be paid to international stock markets, particularly with the demise of communism and the focus on the removal of European trade barriers culminating in 1992.

Stocks and stock mutual funds (see Chapter 5) will provide investors with above-average long-term investment return opportunities, in spite of the twin deficits, economic uncertainty, and other problems that have always provided the timid with sufficient reason to avoid stocks. Other equity markets, for example, options, futures, and collectibles, will continue to be successfully exploited only by specialists. In fact, the increasingly knowledgeable and affluent individual investor of the 1990s will become more conservative in his or her equity investing.

3.1 SUMMARY OF STOCK AND OTHER EQUITY INVESTMENTS

Table 3.1 summarizes the characteristics of the various kinds of stock investments, derivative securities such as options, and other "ownership" (equity) investments. All these investments confer on the owner the right to profit from any appreciation in value of the investment or to suffer the effect of any decline in value.

As the table indicates, the categories vary considerably with respect to risk as well as other characteristics. Many are very risky and, therefore, are usually appropriate only for investors with the resources and/or expertise to manage the risk effectively.

3.2 STOCK INVESTMENT STRATEGIES

The following well-respected strategies are among the most commonly used for investing in stock. This is not a compendium of esoteric or high-risk investment techniques. Instead, this section summarizes basic strategies for achieving long-term stock investment success.

1. *Never buy stocks indiscriminately.* Many investors buy stocks haphazardly simply because they have money to spend. Investments should be made only when you have a good reason to buy a particular stock. If possible, the investor should keep some cash available to take advantage of new opportunities as they arise.

2. *Select a promising industry.* At any given time, most industries in the economy are either on the upswing or the downswing with respect to earnings potential. When choosing a stock to buy, the investor should start by selecting a promising industry. He or she should have a good reason for selecting an industry and a company within it whose future looks promising.

3. *Diversify.* Investors should try to own stocks in several different industries. Overdiversification on a small amount of money is unwise, however, because the investor may have difficulty keeping track of

Table 3.1 Characteristics of Stock Investments, Derivative Securities, and Other Equity Investments

Instrument	Role in Portfolio	Liquidity	Price Volatility	Leverage Available	Investing Strategies Available	Tax Comments	General Comments
Common stock	Inflation hedge	High	Varies	Buying on margin	Stop-loss orders and/or dollar-cost averaging		Reinvestment plans available for many companies
Preferred stock	Stable income	High	Lower	Buying on margin	Dividend reinvestment		Features are important considerations
Mutual funds	Inflation hedge and/or instant diversificaton	High	Medium[1]	No	Dividend reinvestment and/or dollar-cost averaging		"Families" allow flexibility
Options	Portfolio insurance and/or speculative instrument	High	Higher	Margin available under limited conditions	Can provide downside price protection	Tax liability depends on exercise date	Covered option writing can add income to investment portfolio
Commodity futures	Speculative instrument	High	High	Buying on margin	Selling short	Trading not allowed on IRAs, Keogh plans	Speculative
Stock-index futures	Speculative instrument and/or portfolio insurance	High	High	Buying on margin	Hedge against downside risk of overall portfolio	Considered capital asset by IRS	Speculative

Table 3.1 (continued)

New issues	Growth or speculative instrument	Medium[2]	Higher	No margin on primary issue	Possibility for speculative gains		No commissions in primary market
Foreign equities	Global diversification and/or inflation hedge	Medium[3]	Varies[4]			Some countries impose local taxes	American depositary receipts remove custodial and trading inconveniences
Warrants	Speculative and/or portfolio hedge	High	Higher	Yes[5]	Warrant hedging	Considered capital asset by IRS	
Precious metals	Inflation hedge	High[6]	Higher	No		Considered capital asset by IRS	Investor should trade only with established dealer
Collectibles	Growth and/or value stability	Low	Varies	No	Significant appreciation probably only with high-priced items		Significant upkeep expenses usually required

[1]Specialty or sector funds could have a less stable value than fully diversified stock mutual funds.

[2]Liquidity of a new issue in the secondary market depends on the number of shares offered, the underwriters' active marketing, and whether the issue is listed. These factors are not usually considerations for market-established instruments.

[3]Low turnover on smaller foreign exchanges—other than British, Canadian, and Japanese stock markets—could result in liquidity limitations.

[4]The combination of currency exchange and price fluctuations generally makes the value of foreign equities less stable than that of their U.S. counterparts.

[5]Transactions with overseas brokerage firms could result in time lags between order and execution, or order and delivery, in sales of securities.

[6]Platinum is much less liquid than gold or silver.

individual stock holdings. Mutual funds should be considered by investors of any size portfolio as a convenient way to achieve broad diversification.

4. *Buy low and sell high.* Investors should condition themselves to buy stocks when business is down and sell them when business is up. Stocks can gain when prices are low, and major selling opportunities come when stocks are hot and prices are high.

5. *Stay abreast of market trends.* It is always important to look at general trends in the market. A stock that has already risen in value might be a good candidate for continued gains if the market is still rising. Conversely, a stock that does not respond to a general market rise might be a poor investment.

6. *Use stop-loss orders to protect against loss.* Potential losses can be limited by using stop-loss orders, which "fence in" gains by restricting the effects of a market downturn on an investor's stocks. Stop-loss orders can also be used to force investors to sell. For example, if an investor buys a stock at $12 per share and it rises to $18 per share, he or she might put a stop-loss order in at $15 per share by a volatile stock price, but this is often preferable to a larger loss due to plummeting stock prices.

7. *Maintain long holding periods.* The buy-and-hold strategy of investing usually works for high quality stocks because the general market gains ground over time, and thus the value of most holdings increases. Only more experienced investors who can devote considerable time to managing their portfolios are consistently successful with a trading strategy. Studies have shown that over most holding periods of 10 years or longer, investors have enjoyed returns well in excess of inflation; shorter holding periods generally produce much lower returns.

8. *Use dividend reinvestment programs.* Dividend reinvestment programs (DRPs) are a useful way for investors to begin a stock accumulation program. Investors purchase modest amounts of stock in companies that they intend to hold onto and then have all their dividends reinvested to purchase additional shares regularly. Investors may also want to augment their holdings by making additional optional purchases through the DRP.

9. *Buy good performers.* Investors should try to buy value. Companies with strong balance sheets and solid earnings growth are consistently better long-run performers.

10. *Look for regular small stock dividends.* Investors may want to consider buying stock in companies that habitually pay regular small stock dividends. A small stock dividend (20 percent or less) often does not result in a lower stock price consistent with the dilution of ownership. This strategy therefore allows investors to increase the value of their holdings with no current tax effect.

11. *Buy low price/earnings, high-dividend stocks.* Many successful long-term

investors use the investment strategy of purchasing common stocks of companies with low P/E ratios and high dividend yields. A "7 and 7" strategy, for example, involves buying stock in companies with a P/E ratio of less than 7 and a dividend yield of greater than 7. The logic behind this is that the stock price is depressed (a low P/E ratio), and hence, the stock is being purchased when no one else wants it, which in itself is often a good strategy. So long as the company is fundamentally sound, the dividend yield of such stocks is relatively attractive, and the investor is betting that when the P/E ratio returns to normal (perhaps 12), the company will eventually increase its dividend to maintain an attractive yield.

12. *Know the risks of short selling.* Short selling is a very risky approach to playing bear markets; most investors are usually wrong in predicting them. In fact, the odd-lot short-sale index has been one of the most consistent contrary indicators of future market performance. In other words, an increase in odd-lot short-selling activity almost certainly means a bull market. For most bearish investors, buying put options is preferable to short selling.

13. *Write covered call options.* Writing call options on stocks in the portfolio provides additional income from the premiums received. A conservative covered call writing program can be implemented with minimal risk to the investor.

3.3   STOCK RATING INDEXES

This section explains the stock rating symbols used by Standard & Poor's and Value Line. These ratings can provide a quick appraisal of the relative ranking of a particular stock, but, of course, this represents only one piece of relevant information in the security analysis process. Relative quality of bonds or other debt, that is, degrees of protection for principal and interest, cannot be applied to common stocks, and therefore these rankings should not be confused with bond quality ratings, which appear in Section 4.12.

3.3.1 Standard & Poor's Ratings

Growth and stability of earnings and dividends are deemed key elements in establishing Standard & Poor's earnings and dividend rankings for common stocks, which are designed to capsulize the nature of this record in a single symbol (see Table 3.2). These rankings are based upon a computerized scoring system that considers pershare earnings and dividend records from the most recent 10 years. Basic scores computed for earnings and dividends are adjusted for growth, stability within the long-term trend, and cyclicality. A Standard & Poor's common stock ranking is not a forecast of future market price performance, but is basically an appraisal of past performance and relative current standing. The S&P preferred stock rating is an assessment of the capacity and willingness of an issuer to pay preferred stock dividends and any applicable sinking fund obligations.

Table 3.2 Standard & Poor's Stock Rating Symbols

Common Stocks			*Preferred Stocks*		
A+	=	Highest	AAA	=	Prime
A	=	High	AA	=	High grade
A–	=	Good	A	=	Sound
B+	=	Medium	BBB	=	Medium grade
B	=	Speculative	BB	=	Lower grade
B –	=	Highly speculative	B	=	Speculative
C	=	Marginal	C	=	Nonpaying
D	=	In reorganization	NR	=	No rating
NR	=	No ranking			

3.3.2 Value Line Rankings

The Value Line Investment Survey ranks each of the 1700 stocks that it monitors (see Section 3.5) according to timeliness and safety (see Table 3.3). These ranks are updated every week. The timeliness rank indicates the probable relative price performance of a stock within the next 12 months and is based upon such measures as current earnings and stock price in relation to the past 10 years' experience, earnings momentum, and the past deviation between actual and estimated quarterly earnings. The safety rank is a measure of risk avoidance. It is based mainly on the company's relative financial strength and the stock's price stability. The safety rank changes infrequently.

Table 3.3 Value Line Stock Rating System

Common Stock: Timeliness Rank

Rank 1 (highest) Expect this stock to be one of the best price performers during the next 12 months.

Rank 2 (above average) Expect better than average price performance.

Rank 3 (average) Expect price performance in line with market.

Rank 4 (below average) Expect below-average price performance.

Rank 5 (lowest) Expect poorest price performance relative to that of other stocks.

Common Stock: Safety Rank

Rank 1 (highest) This is probably one of the safest, most stable, and least risky stocks.

Rank 2 (above average) This stock is probably safer and less risky than most stocks.

Rank 3 (average) This stock is probably an average safety and risk stock.

Rank 4 (below average) This stock is probably riskier and less safe than most stocks.

Rank 5 (lowest) This stock is probably one of the riskiest, least safe stocks.

3-4 NEW YORK AND AMERICAN STOCK EXCHANGE COMPANIES

This section lists the companies traded on the New York (NYSE) and American (AMEX) stock exchanges together with their trading symbols. It can be used to determine quickly if a particular stock is traded on either of these exchanges. Most New York and American stock exchange companies are followed by security analysts; therefore, research information on these companies is probably available from one or more sources.

The list contains NYSE and AMEX stocks as of April 1991. Note that the composition of these exchanges is subject to frequent modification through original new listings, technical new listings resulting from changes in corporate structure or mode of operation in companies previously listed, and removals. Also note that if a company has more than two issues of a single class of stock, Table 3.4 indicates "various" rather than describing each issue separately.

Table 3.4 New York and American Stock Exchange Listed Companies

Exchanges: American (A) and New York (N)

Stock	Symbol	Exchange	Stock	Symbol	Exchange
AAR Corp.	AIR	N	Action Industries	ACX	A
Abbott Laboratories	ABT	N	Acton Corp.	ATN	A
Abiomed, Inc.	ABD	A	Acton Corp. Pfd	ATN Pr	A
Abitibi-Price	ABY	N	Acuson Corp.	ACN	N
ACM Government Income Fund	ACG	N	Adams Express	ADX	N
			Adams Res & Energy	AE	A
ACM Government Opportunity Fund	AOF	N	Adobe Resources	ADB	N
			Adobe Resources Pfd	various	N
ACM Government Securities	GSF	N	Advanced Medical Technology	AMA	A
ACM Government Spectrum Fund	SI	N	Advanced Micro Development	AMD	N
ACM Managed Income Fund	AMF	N	Advanced Micro Development Pfd	AMD Pr	N
Acme-Cleveland	AMT	N	Advest Group	ADV	N
Acme Electric	ACE	N	Aetna Life/Casualty	AET	N
Acme United	ACU	A			

Stock	Symbol	Exchange

Stock	Symbol	Exchange
Affiliated Publications		
Class 'A'	AFP	N
Ahmanson (H.F.) & Co.	AHM	N
Aileen, Inc.	AEE	N
AIM Strategic Income Fund	AST	A
Air Express International	AEX	A
Air Products and		
Chemicals	APD	N
Airborne Freight	ABF	N
AIRCOA Hotel Partners L.P.	AHT	A
Airgas, Inc.	ARG	N
Airlease Ltd L.P.	FLY	N
Alamco, Inc.	AXOO	A
Alaska Air Group	ALK	N
Alba-Waldensian	AWS	A
Albany Int'l Class 'A'	AIN	N
Alberto-Culver Class		
'A' (1/10 vtg)	ACV A	N
Alberto-Culver Class 'B'	ACV	N
Albertson's, Inc.	ABS	N
Alcan Aluminum Ltd	AL	N
Alco Standard	ASN	N
Alexander & Alex Sv	AAL	N
Alexander's, Inc.	ALX	N
Alfin, Inc.	AFN	A
A. L. Labs Class 'A'	BMD	N
Allegheny Corp.	Y	N
Allegheny Int'l	AG	N
Allegheny Int'l Pfd	various	N
Allegheny Ludlum	ALS	N
Allegheny Power Systems	AYP	N
Allen Group	ALN	N
Allen Group Pfd	ALNPr A	N
Allergan, Inc.	AGN	N
Alliance Capital		
Management L.P.	AC	N
Alliance Global Enviro Fd	AEF	N
Alliant Techsystems	ATK	N
Allied Irish Banks	AIB	N
Allied Products	ADP	N
Allied-Signal, Inc.	ALD	N
Allstar Inns L.P.	SAI	A
Allstate Muni Income		
Trust	ALM	N
Allstate Muni Income II	ALT	N
Allstate Muni Income III	ALT	N
Allstate Muni Income		
Opportunity	AMO	N
Allstate Muni Income		
Opportunity II	AOT	N

Stock	Symbol	Exchange
Allstate Muni Income		
Opportunity III	AIO	N
Allstate Muni Premium		
Fund	ALI	N
ALLTEL Corp.	AT	N
ALLTEL Corp. Pfd	AT Pr	N
Alpha Industries	AHA	A
Alpine Group	AGI	A
Aluminum Company of		
America	AA	N
Aluminum Company of		
America Pfd	AA PR	A
ALZA Corp. Class 'A'	AZA	A
ALZA Corp. Class 'A'		
Units (Wrrt, Purch 1		
Class 'A' at $30)	AZA.U	A
AM International	AM	N
AM International Wrrt	AML WS	A
AM International Pfd	AM Pr	N
Amax Gold, Inc.	AU	N
Amax, Inc.	AMX	N
Amax, Inc. Pfd	AMXPrB	N
Ambase Corp.	ABC	N
AMC Entertainment	AEN	A
Amcast Industrial	AIZ	N
Amdahl Corp.	AMH	A
Amdura Corp.	ADU	N
Amdura Corp. Pfd	ADU PrD	N
Amerada Hess	AHC	N
Amer 1st Prep Fund 2 L.P.	PF	A
Amer Adj Rate Tri 1995	ADJ	N
Amer Adj Rate Tri 1996	BDJ	N
American Bank, Conn	BKC	A
American Barrick Res	ABX	N
Amer Biltrite	ABL	A
American Brands	AMB	N
American Brands Pfd	various	N
Amer Building		
Maintenance	ABM	N
American Business		
Products	ABP	N
American Capital	ACC	A
American Capital Bond		
Fund	ACB	N
American Capital Cv Sec	ACS	N
American Capital		
Income Trust	ACD	N
American Cyanamid	ACY	N
American Electric Power	AEP	N
American Exploration	AX	A

Stock	Symbol	Exchange
American Exploration Wrrt	AX WS	A
American Express	AXP	N
American Express, Americus	various	A
American Family	AFL	N
American Fructose Class 'A'	AFC.A	A
American Fructose Class 'B' (10 votes)	AFC.B	A
American General	AGC	N
American Government Income Fund	AGF	N
American Government Income Portfolio	AAF	N
American Government Term Trust	AGT	N
American Health Prop	AHE	N
American Healthcare Management Class 'A'	QAHI	A
American Heritage Life	AHL	N
American Home Products	AHP	N
American Home Products Pfd	AHP Pr	N
American Home Products, Americus	various	A
American International Group	AIG	N
American Israeli Paper Ord	AIP	A
American List	AMZ	A
American Maize-Products Class 'A'	AZE.A	A
American Maize-Products Class 'B' vtg	AZE.B	A
American Medical Holdings	A	A
American Oil & Gas	AOG	A
American Petrofina Class 'A'	API.A	A
American Precision Industries	APR	A
American President Companies	APS	N
American R.E. Partners	ACP	N
American Realty Trust SBI	ARB	N
American Reliance Group	ARI	A
American Restaurant Partners Class 'A'	RMC	A
American Savings Bank	ASB	N
American Savings Bank Pfd	ASB Pr A	N

Stock	Symbol	Exchange
American Science & Engr	ASE	A
American Science & Engr Wrrt	AS WS	A
American Shared Hospital Sv	AMS	A
American Ship Building	ABG	N
American Southwest Mtge Inv	ASR	A
American Stores	ASC	N
American Technical Ceramics	AMK	A
American Telephone & Telegraph	T	N
AT&T Series, Americus Ser 2 (Unit)	various	A
American Waste Services Class 'A'	AW	N
American Water Works	AWK	N
American Water Works Pfd	various	N
Americana Hotels/Realty	AHR	N
AmeriHealth, Inc.	AHH	A
Ameriscribe Corp.	ACR	N
Ameritech	AIT	N
Ameron, Inc.	AMN	N
Ames Dept Stores	ADD	N
Ametek, Inc.	AME	N
AMEV Securities	AMV	N
AmocoCorp	AN	N
Amoco (Americus)	A	A
AMP, Inc.	AMP	N
Ampal-Amer Israel Class 'A'	AIS.A	A
Ampco-Pittsburgh	AP	N
AMR Corporation	AMR	N
AMRE, Inc.	AMM	N
AMREP Corp.	AXR	N
AmSouth Bancorp	ASO	N
Amwest Insurance Group	AMW	A
Anacomp, Inc.	AAC	N
Anadarko Petroleum	APC	N
Analog Devices	ADI	N
Andal Corp.	ADL	A
Andrea Radio	AND	A
Angeles Corp.	ANG	A
Angelese Mtge Investment Trust	ANM	A
Angelese Ptc Mtge Class 'A' SBI	APT	A

Stock	Symbol	Exchange		Symbol	Exchange
Angelica Corp.	AGL	N	Atalanta/Sosnoff	ATL	N
Angell Real Estate	ACR	N	Atari Corp.	ATC	A
			A.T.&E. Corp.	ATW	A
Anheuser-Busch			Athlone Industries	ATH	N
Companies	BUD	N	ATI Medical	ATI	A
Anthem Electronics	ATM	N			
Anthony Industries	ANT	N	Atlanta Gas Light	ATG	N
AOI Coal	AOI	A	Atlantic Energy	ATE	N
Aon Corp.	AOC	N	Atlantic Richfield	ARC	N
			Atlantic Richfield Pfd	various	N
Apache Corp.	APA	N	Arco, Americus Unit	various	A
Apex Muni Fund	APX	N			
Applied Magnetics	APM	N	Atlantis Group	AGH	A
ARC International	ATV	A	Atlas Con Mining/		
Archer-Daniels-Midland	ADM	N	Development	ACM.B	A
			Atlas Corp.	AZ	N
ARCO Chemical	RCM	N	Atlas Corp. Wrrt	AZ WS	A
Arctic Alaska Fisheries	ICE	A	ATMOS Energy Corp.	ATO	N
Arizona Land Income					
Class 'A'	AZL	A	Audio/Video Affiliates	AVA	N
Arizona Public Service Adj			Audiovox Class 'A'	VOX	A
Rt Q Pfd	ARPPrQ	N	Augat, Inc.	AUG	N
Ark Restaurants	RK	A	Austria [Republic] SIGNs	SPJ	N
			Austria Fnd	OST	N
Arkla Exploration	ARK	N			
Arkla, Inc.	ALG	N	Automatic Data Processing	AUD	N
Arkla, Inc. Pfd	ALG Pr A	N	Avalon Corp.	AVL	N
Armatron International	ART	A	AVEMCO Corp.	AVE	N
Armco, Inc.	AS	N	Avery Dennison Corp.	AVY	N
			Avnet, Inc.	AVT	N
Armco, Inc. Pfd	various	N			
Armco, Inc. Class 'B' Pfd	various	N	Avon Products	AVP	N
Armstrong World			Aydin Corp.	AYD	N
Industries	ACK	N	B&H Maritime Carriers	BHM	A
Arrow Automotive			B&H Ocean Carriers	BHO	A
Industries	AI	A	Badger Meter	BMI	A
Arrow Electronics	ARW	N			
			Bairnco Corp.	BZ	N
Arrow Electronics Pfd	ARW Pr	N	Baker, Fentress & Co.	BKF	N
Artra Group	ATA	N	Baker Hughes, Inc.	BHI	N
Arvin Industries	ARV	N	Baker (Michael)	BKR	A
Arvin Industries Pfd	ARV Pr	N	Baldor Electric	BEZ	N
ARX, Inc.	ARX	N			
			Baldwin Technology		
ASA Ltd.	ASA	N	Class 'A'	BLD	A
ASARCO, Inc.	AR	N	Balfour, Maclaine	BML	A
Ashland Coal	ACI	N	Ball Corp.	BLL	N
Ashland Oil	ASH	N	Bally Mfg	BLY	N
Asia Pacific Fund	APB	N	Baltimore Bancorp	BBB	N
Asset Investors Corp.	AIC	N	Baltimore Gas & Electric	BGE	N
Astrex, Inc.	ASI	N	Bamberger Polymers	BPI	N
Astrotech International	AIX	A	Banc One Corp.	ONE	N
Astrotech International			BancFlorida Fin'l	BFL	N
Wrrt	AIX WS	A	Banco Bilbao Vizcaya ADS	BBV	N
Astrotech International			Banco Central SA ADS	BCM	N
Pfd	AIX Pr	A	Banco Santander ADS	STC	N

Stock	Symbol	Exchange
Bancroft Convertible Fund	BCV	A
BancTEXAS Group	BTX	N
Bandag, Inc.	BDG	N
Banister Cont'l Ltd	BAN	A
Bank of Boston	BKB	N
Bank of New York	BK	N
Bank of San Francisco	BOF	A
BankAmerica Corp.	BAC	N
BankAtlantic Fin'l	BFC	A
Bankers Trust NY	BT	N
Banner Indus Class 'A'	BAR	N
Barclays pic ADS	BCS	N
Bard (C. R.)	BCR	N
Barnes Group	B	N
Barnett Banks, Inc.	BBI	N
Barnwell Industries	BRN	A
Baroid Corp.	BRC	N
Barr Laboratories	BRL	A
Barrister Information Systems	BIS	A
Barry (R. G.)	RGB	A
B.A.T. Indus Ord ADR	BTI	A
Battle Mtn Gold	BMG	N
Bausch & Lomb	BOX	N
Baxter International	BAX	N
Bay Financial	BAY	N
Bay Meadows Oper'g (Unit)	CJ	A
Bay State Gas	BGC	N
Bayou Steel Class 'A'	BYX	A
BCE, Inc.	BCE	N
Bear Stearns Companies Pfd	BSC Pr A	N
Beard Oil Co.	BOC	A
Bearings, Inc.	BER	N
Beazer PLC ADR	BZR	N
Beckman Instruments	BEC	N
Becton, Dickinson	BOX	N
Belden & Blake Energy	BBE	A
Belding Heminway	BHY	N
Bell Atlantic Corp.	BEL	N
Bell Industries	BI	N
BellSouth Corp.	BLS	N
Belo (A. H.) Class 'A'	BLC	N
Belvedere Corp.	BLV	A
Bemis Co.	BMS	N
Beneficial Corp.	BNL	N
Beneficial Corp. Pfd	various	N
Benetton Group ADS	BNG	N

Stock	Symbol	Exchange
Benguet Corp. Class 'B'	BE	N
Bergen Brunswig	BBC.A	A
Bergstrom Capital	BEM	A
Berkshire Hathaway	BRK	N
Berlitz Int'l.	BTZ	N
Berry Petroleum Class 'A'	BRY	N
Best Buy Co.	BBY	N
Bet Public Ltd ADS	BEP	N
Bethlehem Corp.	BET	A
Bethlehem Steel	BS	N
Bethlehem Steel Pfd	various	N
Beverly Enterprises	BEV	N
BIC Corp.	BIC	A
Binks Mfg	BIN	A
Bio-Rad Labs Class 'A'	BIO.A	A
Bio-Rad Labs Cv Class 'B'	BIO.B	A
Biocraft Labs	BCL	N
Biomagnetic Technology	BMT	A
Biopharmaceutics	BPH	A
Birmingham Steel	BIR	N
Biscayne Hldg	BHA	A
Black & Decker Corp.	BDK	N
Black Hills Corp.	BKH	N
Blackstone Advantage Term	BAT	N
Blackstone Income Trust	BKT	N
Blackstone Strategic Term	BGT	N
Blackstone Target Term	BTT	N
Blair Corp.	BL	A
Blessings Corp.	BCO	A
Block (H & R)	HRB	N
Blockbuster Entertainment	BV	N
Blount, Inc., Cv Class 'B'	BLT.B	A
Blount, Inc., Class 'A'	BLT.A	A
Blue Chip Value Fund	BLU	N
BMC Industries	BMC	N
Boeing Co.	BA	N
Boise Cascade	BCC	N
Bolar Pharmaceutical	BLR	A
Bolt Beranek/Newman	BBN	N
Bond International Gold Ord	BIG	N
Bond International Gold Ord Wrrt	BIG WS	N
Borden, Inc.	BN	N
Borden Chem/Plastics	BCP	N
Borden Chem/Plastics Cm Ptc Common Units	BCU	N
Boston Celtics L.P.	BOS	N

Stock	Symbol	Exchange		Symbol	Exchange
Boston Edison	BSE	N	Burlington Resources	BR	N
Bow Valley Industries	BVI	A	Burnham Pacific Properties	BPP	A
			Bush Industries Class 'A'	BSH	A
Bowater, Inc.	BOW	N	Businessland, Inc.	BLI	N
Bowl America Class 'A'	BWL.A	A	Cabletron Systems	CS	N
Bowmar Instruments	BOM	A			
Bowne & Co.	BNE	A	Cablevision Sys Class 'A'	CVC	A
BP Prudhoe Bay Royalty	BPT	N	Cabot Corp.	CBT	N
			Caesars World	CAW	N
Brascan Ltd Cv Class 'A'			Cagle's, Inc.	CGL.A	A
Ord	BRS.A	A	Cal Fed Income Partners	CFI	N
Brazil Fund	BZF	N			
BRE Properties Class 'A'	BRE	N	California Energy	CE	A
Briggs & Stratton	BGG	N	Calif REIT SBI	CT	N
Bristol-Myers Squibb	BMY	N	Callahan Mining	CMN	N
			CalMat Co.	CZM	N
Bristol-Myers Pfd	BMY Pr	N	Calprop Corp.	CPP	A
Bristol-Myers, Americus					
Unit	various	A	Calton, Inc.	CN	N
British Airways ADS	BAB	N	Cambrex Corp.	CBM	A
British Gas ADS	BRG	N	Campbell Resources	CCH	N
British Petrol ADS	BP	N	Campbell Soup	CPB	N
			Canadian Marconi	CMW	A
British Petrol ADS					
WRRT/Purch	BP WS	N	Canadian Occidental Petrol	CXY	A
British Steel ADS	BST	N	Canadian Pacific Ord	CP	N
British Telecommunications			Canal Capital Corp.	COW	N
ADR	BTY	N	Canal Capital Corp. Pfd	COW Pr	N
Broad, Inc.	BRO	N	Canandaigua Wine		
Broad, Inc., Pfd	BRO Pr A	N	Class 'B'	CDG.B	A
Broken Hill Prop ADR	BHP	N	Canandaigua Wine		
Brooklyn Union Gas	BU	N	Class 'A'	CDG.A	A
Brown-Forman Class 'B'	BF.B	A	Capital Cities/ABC	CCB	N
Brown-Forman Class 'A'			Capital Holding	CPH	N
vtg	BF.A	A	Capital Housing/Mtge	CAP	A
Brown-Forman (other)	various	A	Capstead Mortgage	CMO	N
Brown Group	GB	N	Capstead Mortgage Pfd	CMO Pr	N
Brown & Sharpe Mfg			Careercom Corp.	PTA	N
Class 'A'	BNS	N	Carlisle Companies	CSL	N
Browning-Ferris Ind	BFI	N	Carmel Container Systems	KML	A
BRT Realty Trust SBI	BRT	N	Carnival Cruise Class 'A'	CCL	N
Brunswick Corp.	BC	N			
			Carolco Pictures	CRC	N
Brush Wellman	BW	N	Carolina Freight Corp.	CAO	N
BSD Bancorp	BSD	A	Carolina Power & Light	CPL	N
BSN Corp.	BSN	A	Carpenter Technology	CRS	N
BSN Corp. Wrrnt	WS	A	Carriage Industries	CGF	N
Buckeye Partners L.P.	BPL	N			
			Carter Hawley Hale	CHH	N
Buffton Corp.	BFX	A	Carter-Wallace	CAR	N
Bunker Hill Income			Cascade Natural Gas	CGC	N
Securities	BHL	N	Cash American		
Burger King Investors	BKP	N	Investments	PWN	A
Burlington Coat Factory	BCF	N	Caspen Oil, Inc.	CNO	A
Burlington Northern	BNI	N	Caspen Oil, Inc., Pfd	CNO Pr	A

Stock	Symbol	Exchange		Symbol	Exchange
Castle (A. M.)	CAS	A	Cheshire Financial	CFX	A
Castle & Cooke	CKE	N	Chevron Corp.	CHV	N
Castle Convert Fund	CVF	A	Chevron (other)	various	A
Catalina Lighting	LTG	A	Chicago Milwaukee	CHG	N
			Chicago Milwaukee Pfd	CHG Pr	N
Cattelus Development	CDX	N			
Caterpillar, Inc.	CAT	N	Chicago Rivet & Mach	CVR	A
Cavalier Homes	CXV	A	Chieftain International	CID	A
CBI Indus	CBH	N	Chile Fund, Inc.	CH	N
CBS, Inc.	CBS	N	Chiles Offshore Corp.	CHC	A
			Chili's, Inc.	EAT	N
CBS, Inc., Pfd	CBS Pr	N			
CCX, Inc.	CCX	N	Chiquita Brands Int'l	CQB	N
Cedar Fair L.P.	FUN	N	Chock Full O' Nuts	CHF	N
Centel Corp.	CNT	N	Chris-Craft Industries	CCN	N
Centennial Group (New)	CEQ	A	Chris-Craft Pfd	various	N
			Christiana Companies	CST	A
Centerior Energy	CX	N			
Centex Corp.	CTX	N	Chrysler Corporation	C	N
Central Fund, Cda Class 'A'	CEF	A	Chubb Corporation	CB	N
Central Hudson Gas &			Church & Dwight	CHD	N
Electric	CNH	N	Chyron Corporation	CHY	N
Central La Elec	CNL	N	CIGNA Corporation	CI	N
Central Maine Power	CTP	N	CIGNA High Income Shares	HIS	N
Central Nwspprs Class 'A'	ECP	N	CII Financial	CII	A
Central Securities	CET	A	CILCORP, Inc.	CER	N
Central & So. West	CSR	N	CIM High Yield Securities	CIM	A
Central Vt Public Service	CV	N	Cincinnati Bell	CSN	N
Centura Banks	CBC	N	Cincinnati Gas & Electric	CIN	N
Century Communications			Cincinnati Milacron	CMZ	N
Class 'A'	CTY	A	Cineplex Odeon	CPX	N
Century Telep Enterprises	CTL	N	Circle K	CKP	N
Cenvill Development			Circuit City Stores	CC	N
Class 'A'	CVL	A			
CF Income Ptnrs L.P.	CFI	N	Circus Circus Enterp	CIR	N
			Citadel Holding	CDL	A
Chambers Development	CDV.B	A	Citicorp	CCI	N
Chambers Development			Citizens 1st Bancorp	CFB	N
Class 'A'	CDV.A	A	Citizens 1st Bancorp		
Champion Enterprises	AHB	A	Pfd	CFB Pr A	A
Champion International	CHA	N			
Chaparral Steel Company	CSM	N	Citizens & Sthn Corp.	CTZ	N
			Citytrust Bancorp	CYT	N
Chart House Enterpr.	CHT	N	Claire's Stores	CLE	N
Charter Company	CHR	N	Clark Equipment	CKL	N
Charter Power Systems	CHP	A	Clayton Homes	CMH	N
Chase Manhattan	CMB	N			
Chaus (Bernard) Inc.	CHS	N	Clear Channel Commun	CCU	A
			Clemente Global G	CLM	N
Chemed Corp.	CHE	N	Cleveland-Cliffs	CLF	N
Chemical Banking Corp.	CHL	N	Clorox Co.	CLX	N
Chemical Banking Corp.			Club Med, Inc.	CMI	N
Class 'B'	CHL.B	N			
Chemical Waste			CMI Corp.	CMX	A
Management	CHW	N	CML Group	CML	N
Chesapeake Corp.	CSK	N	CMS Energy	CMS	N

Stock	Symbol	Exchange
CMS Enhancements	CME	N
CNA Financial	CNA	N
CNA Income Shares	CNN	N
Coachmen Industries	COA	N
Coast Distribution Systems	CRV	A
Cost Savings Fin'l	CSA	N
Coastal Corp.	CGP	N
Coastal Corp. Pfd	various	N
Coca-Cola Co.	KO	N
Coca-Cola, Americus Unit	KKU	A
Coca-Cola Enterprises	CCE	N
Coeur d'Alene Mines	CDE	A
Cognitronics Corp.	CGN	A
Cohu, Inc.	COH	A
Coles Myer Ltd ADR	CM	N
Colgate-Palmolive	CL	N
Collins Food Int'l	CF	N
Collins Industries	GO	A
Colonial High Income Muni	CXE	N
Colonial Interm High Income	CIF	N
Colonial Investment Grade Muni	CXH	N
Colonial Muni Income Trust	CMU	N
Color Systems Technology	CLR	A
Columbia Gas System	CG	N
Columbia Labs	COB	A
Columbia R.E. Investments	CIV	A
Com Systems	CTM	A
Comdisco, Inc.	CDO	N
Cominco Ltd	CLT	A
Commercial Intertech	TEC	N
Commercial Metals	CMC	N
Commodore International	CBU	N
Commonwealth Edison	CWE	N
Commonwealth Edison Cv Wrrt	various	N
Commonwealth Edison Pfd	various	N
Commwlth Energy Systems	CES	N
Commtron Corp. Class 'A'	CMR	A
Communication Satellite	CQ	N
Community National Bancorp	CNB	A
Community National Bancorp Wrrt	WS	A

Stock	Symbol	Exchange
Community Psychiatric Centers	CMY	N
COMPAQ Computer	CPQ	N
Comprehensive Care	CMP	N
Comptek Research, Inc.	CTK	A
CompuDyne Corp.	CDC	A
Computer Association International	CA	N
Computer Factory	CFA	N
Computer Sciences	CSC	N
Computer Task Grouop	TSK	N
Computrac, Inc.	LLB	A
Comstock Partners Strategy	CPF	N
ConAgra, Inc.	CAG	N
Concord Fabrics Class 'A'	CIS	A
Concord Fabrics Cv Class 'B' (10 votes)	CIS.B	A
Connecticut Energy	CNE	N
Connecticut Natural Gas	CTG	N
Conner Peripherals	CNR	N
Conseco, Inc.	CNC	N
Consolidated Edison	ED	N
Consolidated Edison Pfd	various	N
Consolidated Freightways	CNF	N
Consolidated Natural Gas	CNG	N
Consolidated Rail	CRR	N
Consolidated Stores	CNS	N
Constar International	CTR	N
Conston Corp. Class 'A'	KCS	A
Contel Corp.	CTC	N
Continental Airlines Hldg	QCTA	A
Continental Bank	CBK	N
Continental Corp.	CIC	N
Continental Homes Hldg	CON	A
Continental Information Systems	CNY	N
Continental Materials	CUO	A
Continuum Co.	CNU	A
Control Data	CDA	N
Conversion Industries	CVD	A
Convertible Holdings	CNV	N
ConVest Energy Corp.	CEP	A
Cooper Cos	COO	N
Cooper Indus	CBE	N
Cooper Indus Pfd	Pr	N
Cooper Tire & Rubber	CTB	N
Copley Properties	COP	A
Corcap, Inc.	CCP	A
Core Indus	CRI	N

Stock	Symbol	Exchange		Symbol	Exchange
Corning, Inc.	GLW	N	Danaher Corp.	DHR	N
Corona Corp. Class 'A'	ICR.A	A	Daniel Indus	DAN	N
Counsellors Tandem	CTF	N	Data-Design Labs	DDL	N
Countrywide Credit Ind	CCR	N	Data General	DGN	N
Countrywide Credit Ind Pfd	Pr	N	Datametric Corp.	DC	A
Countrywide Mtge Inv	CWM	N	Datapoint Corp.	DPT	N
Cortaulds, pic ADR	COU	A	Dataram Corp.	DTM	A
CPC Int'l	CPC	N	Davis Water & Waster	DWW	N
CPI Corp.	CPY	N	Daxor Corp.	DXR	A
Craig Corp.	CRA	N	Dayton Hudson	DH	N
Crane Co.	CR	N	De Rose Indus	DRI	A
Crawford & Co. Class 'B'	CRD.B	N	Dean Foods	DF	N
Crawford & Co. Class 'A'	CRD.A	N	Dean Witter Gvt Income SBI	GVT	N
Cray Research	CYR	N	Decorator Indus	DII	A
CRI Insured Mtg Assn	CMM	N	Deere & Co.	DE	N
Crompton & Knowles	CNK	N	Del Electronics Corp.	DEL	A
Cross (A. T.) Class 'A'	ATX.A	A	Del Laboratories	DLI	A
Crossland Savings F.S.B.	CRL	N	Del-Val Fin'l	DVL	N
Crossland Savings Pfd	various	N	Delmarva Power & Light	DEW	N
Crowley, Milner & Co.	COM	A	Delmed, Inc.	DMD	A
Crown Centl Pet Class 'A'	CNP.A	A	Delta Air Lines	DAL	N
Crown Centl Pet Class 'B'	CNP.B	A	Delta Woodside Indus	DLW	N
Crown Cork & Seal	CCK	N	Deltona Corp.	DLT	N
Crown Crafts	CRW	A	Deluxe Corp.	DLX	N
CRS Sirrine, Inc.	CRX	N	Designatronics, Inc.	DSG	N
Cruise America	RVR	A	Designcraft Indus	DJI	A
Crystal Brands	CBR	N	DeSoto, Inc.	DSO	N
Crystal Oil Corp.	COR	A	Detroit Edison	DTE	N
CSS Industries	CSS	A	Detroit Edison Pfd	various	N
CSX Corp.	CSX	N	Devon Energy	DVN	A
CSX Corp. Pfd	CSX Pr A	N	Dexter Corp.	DEX	N
CTS Corp.	CTS	N	DI Industries	DRL	A
Cubic Corp.	CUB	A	Diagnostek, Inc.	DXK	N
Culbro Corp.	CUC	N	Diagnostic Products	DP	N
Cummins Engine	CUM	N	Diagnostic/Retr'l Cv		
Cummins Engine Pfd	CUM Pr	N	Class 'A'	DRS.A	A
Current, Inc., Shares	CUR	N	Diagnostic/Retr'l Cv		
Curtice-Burns Foods Class 'A'	CBI	A	Class 'B'	DRS.B	A
Curtiss-Wright	CW	N	Dial REIT	DR	N
Customedix Corp.	CUS	A	Diamond Shamrock Offsh	DSP	N
CXR Corp.	CXR	A	Diamond Shamrock R&M	DRM	N
CyCare Systems	CYS	N	Diana Corp.	DNA	N
Cyclops Industries	CYC	N	Diasonics, Inc.	DIA	A
Cypress Fund	WJR	A	Dickenson Mines Ltd		
Cypress Semiconductor	CY	N	Class 'B'	DML.B	A
Cyprus Minerals	CYM	N	Dickenson Mines Ltd		
Cyprus Minerals Pfd	CYM Pr	N	Class 'A'	DML.A	A
Dallas Semiconductor	DS	N	Diebold, Inc.	DBD	N
Dana Corp.	DCN	N	Digital Commun Assoc	DCA	N

Stock	Symbol	Exchange		Symbol	Exchange
Digital Equipment	DEC	N	EAC Indus	EZC	A
Dillard Dept Str Class 'A'	DDS	N	Eagle Financial	EAG	A
Dime Svgs Bank N.Y.	DME	N	Eagle-Picher Indus	EPI	N
Diodes, Inc.	DIO	A	Eastern Co.	EML	A
Discount Corp.	DCY	N	Eastern Enterprises	EFU	N
Disney (Walt) Co.	DIS	N	Eastern Util Assoc.	EUA	N
Diversified Indus	DMC	N	EastGroup Properties SBI	EGP	A
Divi Hotels N.V.	DVH	A	Eastman Kodak	EK	N
Dixon Ticonderoga	DXT	A	East Kodak, Americus		
Dixons Group ADR	DXN	N	Unit, Score, Prime	various	A
Dominion Resources	D	N	Eaton Corp.	ETN	N
Domtar, Inc.	DTC	N	ECC International	ECC	N
Donaldson Co.	DCI	N	Echlin, Inc.	ECH	N
			Echo Bay Mines Ltd	ECO	A
Donnelley (R. R.) & Sons	DNY	N			
Donnelly Corp. Class 'A'	DON	A	Ecolab, Inc.	ECL	N
Dover Corp.	DOV	N	Ecology/Environment		
Dow Chemical	DOW	N	Class 'A'	EEI	A
Dow, Americus Unit,			Edison Bros Stores	EBS	N
Score, Prime	various	A	Edisto Resources	EDS	A
			Edisto Resources Pfd	Pr	A
Dow Jones & Co.	DJ	N			
Downey S & L Assn	DSL	N	EDO Corp.	EDO	N
DPL, Inc.	DPL	N	Edwards (A. G.), Inc.	AGE	N
DQE, Inc.	DQE	N	EG&G, Inc.	EGG	N
Dravo Corp.	DRV	N	Ehrlich Bober Fin'l	EB	A
			1838 Bond-Deb Trad'g	BDF	N
DRCA Med Corp.	DRC	A			
Dresser Indus	DI	N	Ekco Group	EKO	N
Dreyfus Cal Muni Income	DCM	A	Elcor Corp.	ELK	N
Dreyfus Corp.	DRY	N	Eldorado Bancorp	ELB	A
Dreyfus Muni Income	DMF	A	Electronic Assoc	EA	N
			ElectroSound Group	ESG	A
Dreyfus N.Y. Muni					
Income	DNM	A	Eljer Industries	ELJ	N
Dreyfus Strategic Gvt	DSI	N	Ellsworth Cv Growth/		
Dreyfus Strategic Muni			Income	ECF	A
Bondfund	DSM	N	Elscint Ltd	ELT	N
Dreyfus Strategic Muni	LEO	N	Elsinore Corp.	ELS	A
Driver-Harris	DRH	N	EMC Corp.	EMC	N
Ducommun, Inc.	DCO	A	Emerald Homes L.P.	EHP	N
Duff/Phelps Util Income	DNP	N	Emerson Electric	EMR	N
Duke Power	DUK	N	Emerson Radio	EME	N
Duke Realty Inv	DRE	N	Empire of Carolina	EMP	A
Dun & Bradstreet	DNB	N	Empire Dist Elec	EDE	N
Duplex Products	DPX	A	Empresa Nac'l Elec ADS	ELE	N
du Pont (E.I.) de Nemours	DD	N	Endevco, Inc.	EI	A
Du Pont, Americus Unit,			Energen Corp.	EGN	N
Score, Prime	various	A	Energy Service	ESV	A
DWG Corp.	DWG	A	Energy Service Pfd	ESV Pr	A
Dycom Indust	DY	N			
			Engelhard Corp.	EC	N
Dynamics Corp. Amer	DYA	N	Engex, Inc.	EGX	A
E-Systems	ESY	N	Ennis Business Forms	EBF	N

Stock	Symbol	Exchange		Symbol	Exchange
Enron Corp.	ENE	N	Fansteel, Inc.	FNL	N
Enron Corp. Pfd	ENE Pr J	N	Far West Financial	FWF	N
ENSERCH Corp.	ENS	N	Farah, Inc.	FRA	N
Enserch Explor Ptnrs	EP	N	Fay's, Inc.	FAY	N
Entergy Corp.	ETR	N	Fedders Corp.	FJQ	N
Enterra Corp.	EN	N	Federal Express	FDX	N
Entertainment Mktg	EM	A	Fed'l Home Ln Mtg Sr		
			Ptc Pfd	FRE Pr	N
Entertainment Publishing	ENT	A			
Environmental Systems	ESC	N	Federal-Mogul	FMO	N
Environmental Systems			Federal Nat'l Mtge	FNM	N
Pfd	ESC Pr A	N	Federal Paper Board	FBO	N
Environmental Techtonics	ETC	A	Federal Paper Board Pfd	various	N
Enviropact	ENV	A	Federal Rlty Inv Tr SBI	FRT	N
Enzo Biochem	ENZ	A	Federal Signal	FSS	N
EQK Green Acres L.P.	EGA	N	Ferro Corp.	FOE	N
EQK Realty Inv I SBI	EKR	N	FFP Partners L.P.	FFP	A
Equifax, Inc.	EFX	N	Fiat ADR	various	N
Equimark Corp.	EQK	N	Fibreboard Corp.	FBD	A
Equimark Corp. Pfd	EQK Pr	N	Fidelity Nat'l Fin'l	FNF	A
Equitable R.E. Shop'g	EQM	N	Fieldcrest Cannon	FLD	N
Equitable Resources	EQT	N	Filtertek, Inc., (Unit)	FTK	N
Equitec Fin'l Group	EFG	N	Finevest Foods	FVF	N
Equity Income Fund	ATF	A	Fingerhut Cos	FHT	N
Escagenetics Corp.	ESN	A	Fireman's Fund	FFC	N
ESI Industries Class 'A'	ESI	A	First of America Bank	FOA	N
Espey Mfg & Electr	ESP	A	First Australia Fund	IAF	A
Esquire Radio & Elec	EE	A	First Australia Prime	FAX	A
Essex Financial Partners			First Bank System	FBS	N
L.P. (Unit)	ESX	A			
			First Bank System Pfd	FBS	N
Essette Business Sys	ESB	N	First Boston Income	FBF	N
Esterline Corp.	ESL	N	First Boston Strategic	FBI	N
Ethyl Corp.	EY	N	First Brands Corp.	FBR	N
Etz Lavud Ltd Ord	ETZ	A	First Capital Hldgs	FCH	N
Europe Fnd	EF	N			
			First Capital Hldgs Pfd	FCH	N
Everest/Jennings Int'l			First Central Fin'l	FCC	A
Class 'B'	EJ.B	A	First Chicago	FNB	N
Everest/Jennings Int'l			First Chicago Pfd	various	N
Class 'A'	EJ.A	A	First City Banc Tex	FBT	N
Excel Industries	EXC	A			
Excelsior, Inc., Shares	EIS	N	First City Banc Tex Pfd	FBT Pr B	N
Exxon Corp.	XON	N	First Empire State	FES	A
			First Federal Bancorp	FFS	A
Fab Indus	FIT	A	First Fidelity Bancorp	FFB	N
Fabri-Centers Amer	FCA	N	First Fidelity Bancorp		
FAI Insurances Ltd ADS	FAI	N	Pfd	various	N
Fairchild Indus	FEN	N			
Fairchild Indus Pfd	FEN Pr A	N	First Financial Fund	FF	N
			First Iberian Fund	IBF	A
Fairfield Cmnties	FCI	N	First Interstate Bancorp	I	N
Falcon Cable Sys L.P.	FAL	A	First Interstate Bancorp		
Family Dollar Stores	FDO	N	Class 'A'	IA	N

Stock	Symbol	Exchange		Symbol	Exchange
First Interstate Bancorp Pfd	various	N	Franklin Multi-Income Trust	FMI	N
First Mississippi	FRM	N	Franklin Principal Maturity	FPT	N
First Nat'l Corp. (Cal)	FN	A	Franklin Resources	BEN	N
First Union Corp.	FTU	N	Franklin Universal Tr	FT	N
First Union R.E. Eq SBI	FUR	N	Fredericks of Hollywood	FHO	A
First Virginia Banks	FVB	N	Freeport-McMoRan	FTX	N
First Wachovia	FW	N	Freeport-McMoRan Pfd	FTX Pr	N
Firstar Corp.	FSR	N	Freeport McMoRan Copper		
FirstFed Financial	FED	N	Class 'A'	FCS	N
Fischer & Porter	FP	A	Freeport-McMoRan O/G		
Fitchburgh Gas & Elec	FGE	A	Realty	FMR	N
			Freep't-McMoRan Resources	FRP	N
Flanigan's Enterprises	BDL	A	Frequency Electrs	FEI	A
Fleet/Norstar Fin'l	FNG	N			
Fleetwood Enterpr	FLE	N	Friedman Indus	FRD	A
Fleming Cos	FLM	N	Fries Entertainment	FE	A
Flexible Bond Trust	FLX	A	Frisch's Restaurants	FRS	A
			Frontier Insurance Gr	FTR	N
Flightsafety Int'l	FSI	N	Frozen Food Express	JIT	A
Floating Point Sys	FLP	N			
Florida East Coast Indus	FLA	N	Fruit of the Loom Class 'A'	FTL	A
Florida Progress	FPC	N	Fund America Cos	FFC	N
Florida Public Utilities	FPU	A	Fuqua Indus	FQA	N
			Fur Vault, Inc.	FRV	A
Florida Rock Indus	FRK	A	Furr's/Bishop's L.P.	CAF	N
Flowers Indus	FLO	N			
Fluke (John) Mtg	FKM	A	Future Germany Fund	FGF	N
Fluor Corp.	FLR	N	Gabelli Equity Trust	GAB	N
FMC Corp.	FMC	N	Gainsco, Inc.	GNA	A
			Galactic Resources	GLC	A
FMC Gold	FGL	N	Galaxy Cablevision L.P.	GTV	A
Foodarama Supermkts	FSM	A			
Foote, Cone & Belding	FCB	N	Gallagher (Arthur J.)	AJG	N
Foothill Group Class 'A'	FGI	N	Galoob (Lewis) Toys	GAL	N
Ford Motor	F	N	Galoob (Lewis) Toys Pfd	GAL Pr	N
			Galveston Houston	GHX	N
Ford, Americus Unit, Score, Prime	various	A	Gamma Biologicals	GBL	N
Ford Motor of Canada	FC	A	Gannett Co.	GCI	N
Forest City Enterp			Gap, Inc.	GPS	N
Class 'A'	FCE.A	A	Garan, Inc.	GAN	A
Forest City Enterp Cv			GATX Corp.	GMT	N
Class 'B'	FCE.B	A	GATX Corp. Pfd	GMT Pr	N
Forest Labs	FRX	A			
			Gaylord Container Class 'A'	GCR	A
Fort Dearborn IncSec	FTC	N	GEICO Corp.	GEC	N
Forum Retirem't Ptnrs	FRL	A	Geiman Sciences	GSC	A
Foster Wheeler	FWC	N	Gemco Nat'l	GNL	A
Foundation Health	FH	A	Gemini II	GMI	N
Foundation Powerboat Ind	FPI	A			
			GenCorp	GY	N
FPA Corp.	FPO	A	Genentech, Inc.	GNE	N
FPL Group	FPL	N	Gen'l Amer Investors	GAM	N
France Fund	FRN	N	General Automation	GA	A
Franklin Hldg Corp.	FKL	A	General Cinema	GCN	N

Stock	Symbol	Exchange
General Cinema Ser A	GCN PrA	N
Gen'l DataComm Ind	GDC	N
General Dynamics	GD	N
General Electric	GE	N
G.E., Americus Unit, Score, Prime	various	A
General Employ Enterpr	JOB	A
General Host	GH	N
General Housewares	GHW	N
General Microwave	GMW	A
General Mills	GIS	N
General Motors	GM	N
General Motors Cl E, Cl H	various	N
General Motors, Americus Unit, Score, Prime	various	A
General Public Util	GPU	N
General Re Corp.	GRN	N
General Signal	GSX	N
Genesco, Inc.	GCO	N
Geneva Steel Class 'A'	GNV	N
Genisco Technology	GES	A
Genovese Drug Str Class 'A'	GDX.A	A
GenRad, Inc.	GEN	N
Genuine Parts	GPC	N
GEO Int'l	GX	N
Georgia Gulf Corp.	GGC	N
Georgia-Pacific	GP	N
Gerber Products	GEB	N
Gerber Scientific	GRB	N
Germany Fund	GER	N
Getty Petroleum	GTY	N
Giant Food Class 'A'	GFS.A	A
Giant Group	GPO	N
Giant Yellowknife Mn	GYK	A
Gibson (C. R.)	GIB	A
Gillette Co.	GS	N
Gitano Group	GIT	N
Glatfelter (P. H.)	GLT	A
Glaxo Hldg Plc ADR	GLX	N
Gleason Corp.	GLE	N
Glenfed, Inc.	GLN	N
Glenmore Distill Class 'B'	GDS.B	A
Global Gvt Plus Fund	GOV	N
Global Income Plus Fund	GLI	N
Global Marine	GLM	N
Global Marine Wrrt	GLM WS	N
Global Nat'l Res	GNR	A
Global Ocean Carriers	GLO	A
Global Yield Fund	PGY	N
Go-Video	VCR	A
Go Video Wrrnt	Vcr Ws	A
Golden Nugget	GNG	N
Golden Valley Microwave	GVF	N
Golden West Fin'l	GDW	N
Goldfield Corp.	GV	A
Goldome	GDM	N
Goodrich (B. F.)	GR	N
Goodrich (B. F.) Pfd	various	N
Goodyear Tire & Rub	GT	N
Gorman-Rupp	GRC	A
Gottschalks, Inc.	GOT	N
Gould Investors L.P.	GLP	A
GR Foods	GRX	A
Grace (W. R.)	GRA	N
Graco, Inc.	GGG	N
Graham Corp.	GHM	A
Graham-Field Health	GFI	A
Grainger (W. W.)	GWW	N
Granada BioSciences	GBI	A
Granada Foods	GNF	A
Granges, Inc.	GXL	A
GRC International'l	GRH	N
Great American Bank, FSB	GTA	N
Great Atl & Pac Tea	GAP	N
Great Lakes Chemical	GLK	N
Gr North'n Iron Ore	GNI	N
Greater Wash Investors	GWA	A
Green Mountain Power	GMP	N
Green Tree Accept	GNT	N
Greenman Bros	GMN	A
Greiner Engineering	GII	A
Greyhound Dial Corp.	G	N
G.R.I. Corp.	GRR	A
Grow Group	GRO	N
Growth Stock Outlook Tr	GSO	N
Grubb & Ellis	GBE	N
Grumman Corp.	GQ	N
Grumman Corp. Pfd	GQ Pr	N
GTE Corp.	GTE	N
GTE Corp. Pfd	various	A
GTE, Americus Unit, Score, Prime	various	A
GTI Corp.	GTI	A
Guardian Bancorp	GB	A
Guardsman Products	GPI	N
Guilford Mills	GFD	N

Stock	Symbol	Exchange		Symbol	Exchange
Gulf Canada Resources	GOU	A	Health-Rehab Ppty	HRP	N
Gulf Resources/Chem	GRE	N	Healthcare Int'l Class 'A'	HII	A
			HEALTHSOUTH Rehab	HRC	N
Gulf Resources/Chem			HealthVest SBI	HBT	A
Pfd	GRE PrB	N	Hecla Mining	HL	N
Gulf States Util	GSU	N			
Gundle Environmental Sys	GUN	A	HEICO Corp.	HEI	A
GW Utilities Ltd	GWT	A	Heilig-Meyers	HMY	N
H&Q Healthcare Inv	HQH	N	Hein-Werner	HNW	A
			Heinz (H. J.)	HNZ	N
Hadson Corp.	HAD	N	Heinz (H. J.) Pfd	HNZ Pr	N
HAL, Inc.	HA	A			
Halifax Engineering, Inc.	HX	A	Helene Curtis Ind	HC	N
Hall (Frank B.)	FBH	N	Helm Resources	H	A
Hall (Frank B.) Pfd	FBH Pr B	N	Helmerich & Payne	HP	N
			Helvetia Fund	SWZ	N
Halliburton Co.	HAL	N	Henley International	HEN	A
Hallwood Group	HWG	N			
Halsey Drug	HDG	A	Hercules, Inc.	HPC	N
Halsey Drug Wrrt	HDG WS	A	Heritage Entertainment	HNIS	A
Hampton Indus	HAI	A	Heritage Media Class 'A'	HTG	A
			Hershey Foods	HSY	N
Hampton Utilities Tr	HU	A	Hewlett-Packard	HWP	N
Hancock Fabrics	HKF	N			
Handleman Co.	HDL	N	Hewlett-Packard, Americus		
Handy & Harman	HNH	N	Unit, Score, Prime	various	A
Hanna (M. A.) Co.	MAH	N	Hexcel Corp.	HXL	N
			High Income Advantage	YLD	N
Hannaford Bros	HRD	N	High Income Advantage II	YLT	N
Hanson pic ADR	HAN	N	High Income Advantage III	YLH	N
Hanson Wrrt	HAN WS	N			
Harcourt, Brace/Jov	HBJ	N	High Yield Income Fund	HYI	N
Harcourt, Brace/Jov Pfd	HBJ Pr	N	High Yield Plus Fund	HYP	N
			Hillenbrand Indus	HB	N
Harken Energy	HEC	N	Hillhaven Corp.	HIL	A
Harland (John H.)	JH	N	Hills Dept. Stores	HDS	N
Harley-Davidson	HDI	N			
Harman International	HAR	N	Hilton Hotels	HLT	N
Harnischfeger Indus	HPH	N	Hipotronics, Inc.	HIP	A
			Hi-Shear Indus	HSI	N
Harris Corp.	HRS	N	Hitachi Ltd ADR	HIT	N
Harsco Corp.	HSC	N	HMG/Courtland Prop	HMG	A
Hartford Steam Boiler Ins	HSB	N			
Hartmarx Corp.	HMX	N	Holco Mtge Accept I	HOL.A	A
Harvey Group	HRA	A	Holiday Corp.	HIA	A
			Holly Corp.	HOC	A
Hasbro, Inc.	HAS	A	Hollnam, Inc.	HCN	A
Hastings Mfg	HMF	A	Home Depot	HD	N
Hatteras Income Sec	HAT	N			
Hawaiian Elec Indus	HE	N	Home Shopping Network	HSN	A
Health Care Prop Inv	HCP	N	HomeFed Corp.	HFD	N
			Homestake Mining	HM	N
Health Care REIT	HCN	A	Homestead Fin'l Class 'A'	HFL	N
Health-Chem	HCH	A	Homestead Fin'l Cv Class		
Health Concepts IV	HCF	A	'B' (10 votes)	HFL B	N
Health Equity Prop	EQP	N			
Health-Mor	HMI	A	Honda Motor ADR	HMC	A
			Honeywell, Inc.	HON	N

Stock	Symbol	Exchange		Symbol	Exchange
Hong Kong Telecom ADR	HKT	N	IMCERA Group	IMA	N
Hooper Holmes	HH	A	Imo Industries	IMD	N
Hopper Soliday	HS	N			
			Imperial Chem Ind ADR	ICI	N
Horizon Healthcare	HHC	N	Imperial Corp. Amer	ICA	N
Hormel (Geo A)	HRL	A	Imperial Holly Corp.	IHK	A
Horn & Hardart	HOR	A	Imperial Oil Cv Class 'A'	IMO.A	A
Horsham Corp.	HSM	N	INA Investment Sec	IIS	N
Hotel Inv Tr SBI Unit	HOT	N			
			Inco, Ltd.	N	N
Hotel Inv Tr SBI Unit			Income Opportunity Rlty	IOT	A
Wrrt	HOTWS.BN		Incstar Corp.	ISR	A
Houghton Mifflin	HTN	N	India Growth Fund	IGF	N
House of Fabrics	HF	N	Indiana Energy	IEI	N
Household Int'l	HI	N			
Household Int'l Pfd	HI Pr D	N	Ingersoll-Rand	IR	N
			Indonesia Fnd	IF	N
Houston Indus	HOU	N	Inefficient Market Fnd	IMF	A
Houston Oil Roy UBI	RTH	N	Information Display Tech	IDT	A
Houston Oil Trust UBI	HO	A	Inland Steel Indus	IAD	N
Hovnanian Enterpr	HOV	A			
Howell Corp.	HWL	N	Inspiration Resources	IRC	N
			Insteel Industries	III	A
Howell Indus	HOW	A	Instron Corp	ISN	A
Howtek, Inc.	HTK	A	Instrument Systems	ISY	A
HRE Properties	HRE	N	Instrument Systems Pfd	ISY Pr I	A
Hubbell, Inc., Class 'B'	HUB.B	A			
Hubbell, Inc., Class 'A'	HUB.A	A	Integra-A Hotel/Restaurant	ITG	N
			Intellicall, Inc.	ICL	N
HUBCO, Inc.	HCO	A	Intelligent Sys Master Unit	INP	A
Hudson Foods Class 'A'	HFI	A	Intelogic Trace	IT	N
Hudson General	HGC	A	Intercapital, Inc., Sec	ICB	N
Huffy Corp.	HUF	N			
Hughes Supply	HUG	N	INTERCO, Inc.	ISS	N
			Interlake Corp.	IK	N
Humana, Inc.	HUM	N	Intermark, Inc.	IMI	A
Hunt Mfg	HUN	N	Intermark, Inc. Pfd	IMI Pr	A
Huntingdon Int'l ADR	HTC	N	Int'l Aluminum	IAL	N
Huntway Ptnrs L.P.	HWY	N			
Hydraulic Co.	THC	N	Int'l Bus. Machines	IBM	N
			IBM, Americus Unit,		
Hyperion Total Return			Score, Prime	various	A
Fund	HTR	N	Int'l Flavors/Fragr	IFF	N
IBP, Inc.	IBP	N	Int'l Multifoods	IMC	N
I.C.H. Corp.	ICH	A	Int'l Paper	IP	N
I.C.H. Corp. Pfd	ICH Pr A	A			
ICM Property Investors	ICM	N	Int'l Pwr Machines	PWR	A
			Int'l Recovery	INT	A
ICN Biomedicals	BIM	A	Int'l Rectifier	IRF	N
ICN Pharmaceuticals	ICN	N	Int'l Technology	ITX	N
Idaho Power	IDA	N	International Telecharge	ITI	A
IDEX Corp.	IEX	N			
IE Industries	IEL	N	Int'l Thoroughbred	ITB	A
			Int'l Thoroughbred Pfd	ITB Pr A	A
IGI, Inc.	IG	A	Interpublic Grp Cos	IPG	N
Illinois Tool Works	ITW	N	Inter-Regional Fin. Gr.	IFG	N
IMC Fertilizer Group	IFL	N	Interstate Gen'l L.P.	IGC	A

Stock	Symbol	Exchange		Symbol	Exchange
Interstate/Johnson Lane	IS	N	Kansas Pwr & Light	KAN	N
Interstate Power	IPW	N	Kappa Networks	KPA	A
InterTan, Inc.	ITN	N			
Ionics, Inc.	ION	A	Katy Indus	KT	N
Iowa-Ill Gas & Elec	IWG	N	Kaufman & Broad Home	KBH	N
			Kaufman (H. W.) Fin'l Grp	HWK	A
IP Timberlands Class 'A'	IPT	N	Keithley Instruments	KEI	A
IPALCO Enterprises	IPL	N	Kelley Oil & Gas Ptnrs	KLY	A
Irish Investment Fund	IRL	N			
Iroquois Brands Ltd	IBL	A	Kellogg Co.	K	N
IRT Corp.	IX	A	Kellwood Co.	KWD	N
			Kemper Corp.	KEM	N
IRT Property	IRT	N	Kemper High Income	KHI	N
Italy Fund	ITA	N	Kemper Interm Gvt Tr	KGT	N
ITEL Corp.	ITL	N			
ITEL Corp. Pfd	ITL Pr C	N	Kemper Multi-Mkt Income	KMM	N
ITT Corp.	ITT	N	Kemper Muni Income	KTF	N
			Kemper Strategic Muni Tr	KSM	N
ITT Corp. Pfd	various	N	Kennametal, Inc.	KMT	N
IVAX Corp.	IVX	A	Kent Electronics	KEC	A
Iverson Technology	IVT	A			
Jackpot Enterprises	J	N	Kentucky Utilities	KU	N
Jaclyn, Inc.	JLN	A	Kenwin Shops	KWN	A
			Kerkhoff Industries	KIX	A
Jacobs Engr Group	JEC	A	Kerr Glass Mfg	KGM	N
Jakarta Growth Fund	JGF	N	Kerr Glass Mfg Pfd	KGM PrDN	
James Madison Class 'A'	JML	A			
James River Corp.	JR	N	Kerr-McGee	KMG	N
James River Corp. Pfd	various	N	Ketchum & Co.	KCH	A
			Ketema, Inc.	KTM	A
Jamesway Corp.	JMY	N	KeyCorp.	KEY	N
Jan Bell Marketing	JBM	A	Keystone Consol Ind	KES	N
Jefferson-Pilot	JP	N			
Jetronic Indus	JET	A	Keystone Int'l	KII	N
Jewelmasters Class 'A'	JEM	A	Killearn Properties	KPI	A
			Kinark Corp.	KIN	A
JHM Mte Sec Pfd L.P.	JHM	N	King World Prod'ns	KWP	N
John Hancock, Inc., Sec	JHS	N	Kirby Corp.	KEX	A
John Hancock Inv Tr	JHI	N			
Johnson Controls	JCI	N	Kit Mfg	KIT	A
Johnson & Johnson	JNJ	N	Kleer-Vu Indus	KVU	A
			Kleinwort Benson Aus	KBA	N
J&J, Americus Unit, Score,			KLM Royal Dutch Air	KLM	N
Prime	various	A	K mart	KM	N
Johnson Products	JPC	A			
Johnston Indus	JII	N	KN Energy	KNE	N
Jones Intercable Inv	JTV	A	Knight-Ridder, Inc.	KRI	N
Jones Plumbing Sys	JPS	A	Knogo Corp.	KNO	N
			Koger Equity	KE	A
Jostens, Inc.	JOS	N	Koger Properties	KOG	N
Joule, Inc.	JOL	A			
JWP, Inc.	JWP	N	Kollmorgen Corp.	KOL	N
Kaneb Services	KAB	N	Korea Fund	KF	N
Kaneb Services Pfd	KAB Pr A	N	Kroger Co.	KR	N
			Kubota Ltd ADR	KUB	N
Kansas City Pwr & Lt	KLT	N	Kuhlman Corp.	KUH	N
Kansas City So. Ind	KSU	N			
Kansas Gas & Elec	KGE	N	K-V Pharmaceutical	KV	A

Stock	Symbol	Exchange		Symbol	Exchange
Kyocera Corp. ADR	KYO	N	Lincoln Nat'l Cv Sec	LNV	N
Kysor Ind'l	KZ	N	Lincoln Nat. Dir. PFd	LND	N
L & N Housing	LHC	N	Lincoln National Income Fd	LND	N
L.A. Gear, Inc.	LA	N	Linpro Specified Prop SBI	LPO	A
			Lionel Corp.	LIO	A
La Quinta Mtr Inns	LQM	N			
La Quinta Motor L.P.	LQP	N	Littlefield, Adams	LFA	A
La-Z Boy Chair	LZB	N	Litton Indus	LIT	N
LaBarge, Inc.	LB	A	Live Entertainment	LVE	N
LAC Minerals	LAC	N	LL&E Royalty Tr UBI	LRT	N
			Lockheed Corp.	LK	N
Laclede Gas	LG	N			
Lafarge Corp.	LAF	N	Loctite Corp.	LOC	N
Laidlaw, Inc., Class 'B'	LDWB	N	Loews Corp.	LTR	N
Laidlaw, Inc., Class 'A'	LDWA	N	Logicon Inc.	LGN	N
Lamson & Sessions	LMS	N	Lomas Financial Corp.	LK	N
			Lomas Mortgage	LMC	N
Lancer Corp.	LAN	A			
Landmark Bancshrs	LBC	N	Lomas/Neft Mtg Inv SBI	LOM	N
Landmark Land	LMS	A	Lone Star Indus	LCE	N
Landmark Savings Assn	LSA	A	Long Island Lighting	LIL	N
Lands' End	LE	N	Long Island Lighting Pfd	various	N
			Longs Drug Stores	LDG	N
Landsing Pacific Fund	LPF	A			
Larizza Industries	LII	A	Longview Fibre	LFB	N
Laser Indus Ltd Ord	LAS	A	Loral Corp.	LOR	N
Latin America Inv. Fnd	LAM	N	Lori Corp.	LRC	A
Laurentian Capital	LQ	A	Louisiana Land/Exp	LLX	N
			Louisiana Pacific	LPX	N
Lawrence Ins Group	LWR	A			
Lawson Mardon Gr Class 'A'	LMG	A	Lowe's Cos	LOW	N
Lawter Int'l	LAW	N	LSB Indus	LSB	A
Lazare Kaplan Int'l	LKI	A	LSB Indus Pfd	LSB Pr C	A
LeaRonal, Inc.	LRI	N	LTV Corp.	QLTV	N
			LTV Corp. Pfd	various	N
Lee Enterprises	LEE	N			
Lee Pharmaceuticals	LPH	A	Lubrizol Corp.	LZ	N
Legg Mason, Inc.	LM	N	Luby's Cafeterias	LUB	N
Leggett & Platt	LEG	N	Lukens, Inc.	LUC	N
Leiner P. Nutrit'l Prod	PLI	A	Lumex, Inc.	LUM	A
			Luria (L.) & Son	LUR	A
Leisure & Technology	LVX	N			
Leisure & Technology Pfd	LVX Pr	N	Luxottica Group ADS	LUX	N
Lennar Corp.	LEN	N	LVI Group	LVI	N
Leslie Fay Cos	LES	N	LVI Group Pfd	LVI Pr	N
Leucadia National	LUK	N	Lydall, Inc.	LDL	A
			Lynch Corp.	LGL	A
Liberty All-Star Eqty	USA	N			
Liberty Corp.	LC	N	Lyondell Petrochem	LYO	N
Lifetime Corp.	LFT	N	M/A-Com, Inc.	MAI	N
Lillian Vernon	LVC	A	Magma Copper Class 'B'	MCU	A
Lilly (Eli)	LLY	N	Magma Copper Class 'B'		
			Wrrt	MCU WS	A
Lilly (Eli) Wrrts	LLY WS	N	MagneTek, Inc.	MAG	N
Lilly Ctgnt Pymt Units	HYU	A			
Limited, Inc.	LTD	N	Maine Public Service	MAP	A
Lincoln Nat'l Corp.	LNC	N	Major Group	MJR	N
Lincoln Nat'l Corp. Pfd	LNC Pr	N	Malartic Hygrade Gold	MHG	A

Stock	Symbol	Exchange		Symbol	Exchange
Malaysia Fund	MF	N	M.D.C. Holdgs	MDC	N
Manhattan Nat'l Corp.	MLC	N	MDU Resources Group	MDU	N
			Mead Corp.	MEA	N
Manor Care	MNR	N	Measurex Corp.	MX	N
Mfrs Hanover	MHC	N	MedChem Products	MCH	A
Manville Corp.	MVL	N			
Manville Corp. Wrrt	MVL WS	N	Media General Class 'A'	MEG.A	A
MAPCO, Inc.	MDA	N	Medical Properties	MPP	A
			Medicore, Inc.	MDK	A
Marcade Group	MAR	N	MEDIQ, Inc.	MED	A
Marion Merrel Dow	MKC	N	MEDIQ, Inc Pfd	MED Pr	A
Maritrans Ptnrs L.P.	TUG	N			
Mark IV Industries	IV	N	Meditrust SBI	MT	N
Marlton Technologies	MTY	A	Medtronic, Inc.	MDT	N
			Medusa Corp.	MSA	N
Marriott Corp.	MHS	N	MEI Diversified	MEI	N
Mars Graphic Services	WMD	A	Mellon Bank Corp.	MEL	N
Marsh & McLennan	MMC	N			
Marshall Indus	MI	N	Mellon Bank Corp. Pfd	various	N
Martech USA	MUS	N	Melville Corp.	MES	N
			MEM Co.	MEM	A
Martin Lawrence Ltd			Mercantile Stores	MST	N
Editions	MLE	N	Merchants Group	MGP	A
Martin Marietta	ML	N			
Masco Corp.	MAS	N	Merck & Co.	MRK	N
MassMutual Corp. Inv	MCI	N	Merck, Americus Unit,		
MassMutual Part'n Inv	MPV	N	Score, Prime	various	A
			Mercury Air Group	MAX	A
MATEC Corp.	MXC	A	Mercury Finance	MFN	N
Material Sciences	MSC	A	Meredith Corp.	MDP	N
Matlack Systems	MLK	A			
Matsushita El Ind ADR	MC	N	Merrill Lynch	MER	N
Mattel, Inc.	MAT	N	Merrimac Industries	MRM	A
			Mesa Limited Ptnrshp	MLP	N
Matthews & Wright Gr	MW	A	Mesa Offshore Tr UBI	MOS	N
Mauna Loa Macadamia			Mesa Royalty Tr UBI	MTR	N
Class 'A'	NUT	N			
Maxus Energy	MXS	N	Mesabi Tr Ctfs SBI	MSB	N
Maxus Energy Pfd	MXS Pr	N	Mestek, Inc.	MCC	N
MAXXAM, Inc.	MXM	A	Met-Pro Corp.	MPR	A
			Metro Mobile Cts Class 'A'	MMZ.A	A
May Dept Stores	MA	N	Metro Mobile Cts Class 'B'	MMZ.B	A
Maytag Corp.	MYG	N			
MBIA, Inc.	MBI	N	Metrobank N.A.	MBN	A
McClatchy Newspapers	MNI	N	Metropol Ed 3.90% Cm		
McDermott Int'l	MDR	N	Pfd	MTT.C	N
			Metropolitan Fin'l	MFC	N
McDermott Int'l Pfd	various	N	Metropolitan Realty	MET	A
McDonald & Co. Invest	MDD	N	Mexico Fund	MXF	N
McDonald's Corp.	MCD	N			
McDonnell Douglas	MD	N	MFS Charter Income Tr	MCR	N
McGraw-Hill	MHP	N	MFS Gvt Mkts Income Tr	MGF	N
			MFS Income & Opt Tr	MFO	N
McKesson Corp.	MCK	N	MFS Interm Income SBI	MIN	N
McKesson Corp. Pfd	MCK Pr	N	MFS Multimkt Income	MMT	N
McRae Indus Cv Class 'B'	MRI.A	A			
MC Shipping	MCX	A	MFS Multimkt Total		
MCN Corp.	MCN	N	Return	MFT	N

Stock	Symbol	Exchange		Symbol	Exchange
MFS Municipal, Inc., Tr	MFM	N	Mtge & Rlty Trust	MRT	N
MFS Special Value Trust	MFV	N	Mtge & Rlty Trust Wrrt	MRT WS	A
MGI Properties	MGI	N			
MGM Grand	MGG	N	Morton International	MII	N
			Motorola, Inc.	MOT	N
MGM/UA Commun'ns	MGM	N	Mott's Holdings	MSM	A
MHI Group	MH	N	Mountain Med. Eq	MTN	N
Michael Anthony Jewelers	MAJ	A	MSA Rlty	SSS	A
Michaels Stores	MKE	A			
Mich Consol Gas $2.05			MSR Exploration	MSR	A
Cm Pfd	MCN Pr	N	Muni High Income Fd	MHF	N
			MuniEnhanced Fund	MEN	N
Mickelberry Corp.	MBC	N	MuniInsured Fund	MIF	A
Micron Products	PMR	A	MuniVest Fund	MVF	A
Micron Tech	MU	N			
Mid-America Bancorp	MAB	A	Munsingwear, Inc.	MUN	N
Mid-Maine Savings Bank	MMS	A	Murphy Oil	MUR	N
			Mutual Omaha Int Sh	MUO	N
Middleby Corp.	MBY	A	Myers (L. E.) Gr	MYR	N
Midland Co.	MLA	A	Myers Indus	MYE	A
Midway Airlines	MDW	N			
Midwest Resources	MWR	N	Mylan Labs	MYL	N
Millipore Corp.	MIL	N	Nabors Industries	NBR	A
			Nabors Industries Wrrt	NBR WS	A
Minnesota Min'g/Mfg	MMM	N	NACCO Indus, Inc., Class 'A'	NC	N
Minnesota Pwr & Lt	MPL	N	Nalco Chemical	NLC	N
MIP Properties, Inc.	MIP	A			
Mission West Prop	MSW	A	Nantucket Indus	NAN	A
Mitchell Energy/Dev	MND	A	Nashua Corp.	NSH	N
			Nat'l Australia Bk ADR	NAB	N
Mitel Corp.	MLT	N	National City Corp.	NCC	N
Mitsubishi Bank Ltd ADS	MBK	N	Nat'l Conven'ce Strs	NCS	N
MNC Financial	MNC	N			
Mobil Corp.	MOB	N	Nat'l Conven'ce Strs Pfd	NCS PrE	N
Mobil, Americus Unit,			National Education	NEC	N
Score, Prime	various	A	National Enterprises	NEI	N
			National Fuel Gas	NFG	N
Molecular Biosystems	MB	N	National Gas & Oil	NLG	N
Monarch Capital	MON	N			
Monarch Mach Tool	MMO	N	National HealthCorp. L.P.	NHC	A
Monsanto Co.	MTC	N	National Heritage	NHR	N
Montana Power	MTP	N	Nat'l Intergroup	NII	N
			Nat'l Intergroup Pfd	NII Pr	N
Montedison S p A ADS	MNT	N	Nat'l Medical Entpr	NME	N
Montgomery St, Inc., Sec	MTC	N			
Moog, Inc., Class 'B'	MOG.B	A	Nat'l Patent Devel	NPD	A
Moog, Inc., Class 'A'	MOG.A	A	Nat'l Presto Indus	NPK	N
Moore Corp. Ltd	MCL	N	Nat'l Realty L.P.	NLP	A
			Nat'l Semiconductor	NSM	N
Moore Medical Corp.	MMD	A	Nat'l Semiconductor Pfd	NSM Pr	N
Morgan's Foods	MR	A			
Morgan (J. P.)	JPM	N	Nat'l Semiconductor		
Morgan Grenfell Smallcap	MGC	N	Wrrt	NSM WS	N
Morgan Keegan, Inc.	MOR	N	Nat'l Service Indus	NSI	N
			National-Standard	NSD	N
Morgan Products Ltd	MGN	N	Natl Westminster ADS	NW	N
Morgan Stanley Group	MS	N	Nationwide Health Prop	NHP	N
Morrison Knudsen	MRN	N			

Stock	Symbol	Exchange		Symbol	Exchange
Navistar Int'l	NAV	N	Norsk Hydro A.S. ADS	NHY	N
Navistar Int'l Wrrt	various	N	Nortankers, Inc.	VLC	A
Navistar Int'l Pfd	various	N	Nortek, Inc.	NTK	N
NBB Bancorp	NBB	N			
NBD Bancorp	NBD	N	North America Vaccine	NVX	A
			North Canadian Oils	NCD	A
NBI, Inc.	NBI	N	No Europ'n Oil Rty Tr	NET	N
NCH Corp.	NCH	N	North Fork Bancorp	NFB	N
NCNB Corp.	NCB	N	Northbay Financial	NBF	A
NCR Corp.	NCR	N			
NECO Enterprises	NPT	A	Northeast Federal	NSB	N
			Northeast Federal Pfd	NSB PrA	N
Neiman-Marcus Group	NMG	N	Northeast Utilities	NU	N
NERCO, Inc.	NER	N	North'n States Pwr	NSP	N
Network Equip Tech	NWK	N	North'n Telecom Ltd	NT	N
Nevada Power	NVP	N			
New Amer Hi Income Fd	HYB	N	Northgate Explorat'n	NGX	N
			Northrop Corp.	NOC	N
New American Shoe	NSO	N	North West Gold Class 'A'	NWG	A
New England El Sys	NES	N	Northwestern Pub. Svc.	NPS	N
New Germany Fund	GF	N	Norwest Corp.	NOB	N
New Jersey Resources	NJR	N			
New Line Cinema	NLN	A	Nova Corp. of Alberta	NVA	N
			Novo-Nordisk A/S ADR	NVO	N
New Mexico/Ariz Land	NZ	A	NS Group	NSS	A
New Plan Rlty Tr SBI	NPR	N	Nucor Corp.	NUE	N
New York State E&G	NGE	N	Nu Horizons Electronics	NUH	N
N.Y. Tax Exempt Income	XTX	A			
New York Times Class 'A'	NYT.A	A	Nu Horizons Electronics		
			Wrrt	NUH WS	A
Newcor, Inc.	NEW	A	NUI Corp.	NUI	N
Newell Co.	NWL	N	Numac Oil & Gas	NMC	A
Newhall Land/Farming	NHL	N	Nuveen Cal Inv Qual Muni	NQC	N
Newmark & Lewis	NLI	A	Nuveen Calif Muni Income	NCM	N
Newmont Gold	NGC	N			
			Nuveen Cal Muni Mkt Oppt	NCO	N
Newmont Mining	NEM	N	Nuveen Muni Value Fd	NUV	N
News Corp. Ltd ADS	NWS	N	Nuveen N.J. Inv Qual Muni	NQJ	N
Niagara Mohawk Pwr	NMK	N	Nuveen N.Y. Inv Qual Muni	NQN	N
Niagara Share	NGS	N	Nuveen N.Y. Muni Income	NNM	A
Micholas-Applegate Gr	GEF	N			
			Nuveen N.Y. Muni Mkt		
Nichols Institute	LAB	A	Oppt	NNO	N
Nicolet Instrument	NIC	N	Nuveen N.Y. Muni Val Fd	NNY	N
NICOR, Inc.	GAS	N	Nuveen N.Y. Perform Plus		
NICOR, Inc., Pfd	GAS Pr	N	Muni	NNP	N
NIPSCO Industries	NI	N	Nuveen Pa Inv Qual Muni	NQP	N
			Nuveen Perform Plus Muni	NPP	N
NL Indus	NL	N			
Noble Affiliates	NBL	N	Nuveen Prem Income Muni	NPI	N
Norcen Energy Res	NCN	A	NVR L.P.	NVR	N
Norcen Energy Res			NWNL Cos	NWN	N
Subordinate Class 'A' vtg			NYNEX Corp.	NYN	N
(1 vote)	NCN.A	A	Oak Indus	OAK	N
Nord Resources	NRD	N			
			Oakwood Homes	OH	N
Norex America	NXA	A	O'Brien Energy Sys Class 'A'	OBS	A
Norfolk Southern	NSC	N	Occidental Petrol'm	OXY	N

Stock	Symbol	Exchange		Symbol	Exchange
Ocean Drill & Expl	ODR	N	Pacific Gas & Elec	PCG	N
Odetics, Inc Class 'B'	O.B	A	Pacific Scientific	PSX	N
Odetics, Inc., Class 'A'	O.A	A	Pacific Telesis Group	PAC	N
OEA, Inc.	OEA	A	Pacific Western Bancshrs	PWB	A
Ogden Corp.	OG	N	PacifiCorp.	PPW	N
Ogden Corp. Pfd	OG Pr	N	Page America Group	PGG	A
Ogden Projects	OPI	N	PaineWebber Group	PWJ	N
Ohio Art	OAR	A	PaineWebber Group Pfd	PWJ Pr	N
Ohio Edison	OEC	N	Pall Corp.	PLL	A
OHM Corp.	OHM	N	Pan Am Corp.	PN	N
Oklahoma Gas & Elec	OGE	N	Pan Am Corp. Wrrt	PN WS	N
Old Republic Int'l	ORI	N	Panhandle East'n	PEL	N
Olin Corp.	OLN	N	Pansophic Systems	PNS	N
Olsten Corp.	OLS	A	Par Pharmaceutical	PRX	N
OMI Corp.	OMM	A	PAR Technology	PTC	N
Omnicare, Inc.	OCR	N	Paramount Commun'ns	PCI	N
Omnicom Group	OMC	N	Park Electrochemical	PKE	N
On-Line Software Int'l	OSI	N	Parker Drilling	PKD	N
One Liberty Properties	OLP	A	Parker-Hannifin	PH	N
One Liberty Properties Cv Pfd	OLP Pr	A	Parker/Parsley Petrol	PDP	A
Oneida, Ltd.	OCQ	N	Pathe Communications	PCC	N
Oneita Industries	ONA	A	Patrick Petroleum	PPC	N
ONEOK, Inc.	OKE	N	Patriot Premium Divd Fd	PDF	N
O'okiep Copper ADR	OKP	A	Patriot Premium Divd Fd II	PDT	N
Oppenheimer Cap L.P.	OCG	N	Patten Corp.	PAT	N
Oppenheimer Multi-Gvt Tr	OGT	N	Paxar Corp.	PXR	A
Oppenheimer Multi-Sector	OMS	N	Pay-Fone Systems	PYF	A
Orange-Co.	OJ	N	PEC Israel Economic	IEC	A
Orange/Rockland Util	ORU	N	Peerless Tube PLS	PLS	A
Oregon Steel Mills	OS	A	Pegasus Gold	PGU	A
Organogenesis, Inc.	ORG	A	Penn Central	PC	N
Orient Express Hotels	OEH	N	Penn Engr & Mfg	PNN	A
Oriole Homes Cv Class 'A'	OHC.A	A	Penn Traffic	PNF	A
Oriole Homes Class 'B'	OHC.B	A	Penney (J. C.)	JCP	N
Orion Capital	OC	N	Penna Power & Light	PPL	N
Orion Capital Pfd	various	N	Penna R.E. Inv Tr SBI	PEI	A
Orion Pictures	OPC	N	Pennzoil Co.	PZL	N
Ormand Indus	OMD	A	Penobscot Shoe	PSO	A
Oryx Energy Co.	ORX	N	Penril Corp.	PNL	A
O'Sullivan Corp.	OSL	A	Peoples Energy	PGL	N
Outboard Marine	OM	N	Pep Boys-Man, Mo, Ja	PBY	N
Overseas Shiphldg	OSG	N	PepsiCo, Inc.	PEP	N
Owens-Corning	OCF	N	Perini Corp.	PCR	A
Owens & Minor	OMI	N	Perini Corp. Pfd	PCR Pr	A
Oxford Energy	OEN	A	Perini Invest't Prop	PNV	A
Oxford Indus	OXM	N	Perkin-Elmer	PKN	N
Pacific Am'n, Inc., Shrs	PAI	N	Perkins Family Rest	PFR	N
Pacific Enterprises	PET	N	Permian Basin Rty Tr	PBT	N
			Perry Drug Stores	PDS	N

Stock	Symbol	Exchange		Symbol	Exchange
Peters (J. M.)	JMP	A	Premier Industrial	PRE	N
Petrie Stores	PST	N	Presidential Rlty Class 'B'	PDL.B	A
Petroleum & Resources	PEO	N	Presidential Rlty Class 'A'	PDL.A	A
Petroleum & Resources			Presidio Oil Class 'B,'	various	A
Pfd	PEO Pr A	N	Presidio Oil Class 'A'	various	A
Petroleum Heat & Pwr					
Class 'B'	PHP	A	Price Communications	PR	A
			Primark Corp.	PMK	N
Pfizer, Inc.	PFE	N	Prime Fin'l Ptnrs Class 'A'	PFP	A
Phelps Dodge	PD	N	Prime Motor Inns	PDQ	N
PHH Corp.	PHH	N	Prime Motor Inns L.P.	PMP	N
Philadelphia Elec	PE	N			
Phila Suburban	PSC	N	Primerica Corp.	PA	N
			Princeton Dignostic Labs	various	A
Philip Morris Cos	MO	N	Prism Entertainment	PRZ	A
Philip Morris, Americus			Proctor & Gamble	PG	N
Unit, Score, Prime	various	A	Proctor & Gamble, Americus		
Philippine Long D Tel	PHI	A	Unit, Score, Prime	various	A
Philips NV	PHG	N			
Phillips Petroleum	P	N	Professional Care	PCE	A
			Progressive Corp., Ohio	PGR	N
Phillips-Van Heusen	PVH	N	Proler Int'l	PS	N
PHL Corp.	PHX	N	Pro-Med Capital	PMC	A
PHM Corp.	PHM	N	Property Cap Tr	PCT	A
Pico Products	PPI	A			
Piedmont Nat'l Gas	PNY	N	Property Tr Amer SBI	PTR	N
			Prospect Street Hi Income	PHY	N
Pier One Imports	PIR	N	Providence Energy	PVY	A
Pilgrim Reg'l Bk Shr	PBS	N	Prudential Interm Income	PIF	N
Pilgrim's Pride	CHX	N	Prudential Realty SBI	PRT	N
Pinnacle West Capital	PNW	N			
Pioneer Electron ADR	PIO	N	PS Group, Inc.	PSG	N
			PSI Resources	PIN	N
Pioneer Financial Svcs	PFS	N	Public Sv Colorado	PSR	N
Pioneer Financial Svcs			Public Sv New Hamp	PNH	N
Pfd	PFS Pr	N	Public Sv New Mexico	PNM	N
Pitney Bowes	PBI	N			
Pitney Bowes Pfd	PBI Pr	N	Public Svc Enterpr	PEG	N
Pitt-DesMoines, Inc.	PDM	A	Publicker Indus	PUL	N
			Puerto Rican Cement	PRN	N
Pitts & W Va RR SBI	PW	A	Puget Sound P&L	PSD	N
Pittston Co.	PCO	N	Putnam Diversif'd Prem	PDN	N
Pittway Corp.	PRY	A			
Potlatch Corp.	PCH	N	Putnam Dividend Income	PDI	N
Potomac Electric Pwr	various	N	Putnam Hi Income Cv/Bd		
			Fd	PCF	N
Potomac Electric Pwr Pfd	Pr	N	Putnam Hi Yield Muni	PYM	N
PPG Indus	PPG	N	Putnam Interm Gvt Income	PGT	N
Prairie Oil Royalties	POY	A	Putnam Inv. Grade Muni Tr	PGM	N
Pratt Hotel Corp.	PHC	A			
Pratt & Lambert	PM	A	Putnam Managed Muni		
			Income	PMM	N
Pre-Paid Legal Svcs	PPD	A	Putnam Master Income Tr	PPT	N
Precision Aerotech	PAR	A	Putnam Master Interm		
Preferred Health Care	PY	A	Income	PIM	N
Preferred Income Fund	PFD	N	Putnam Premier Income Tr	PPT	N
Premark Int'l	PMI	N	Qantel Corp.	BQC	N

Stock	Symbol	Exchange		Symbol	Exchange
QMS, Inc.	AQM	N	Rhone Poulenc, Americus		
Quaker Oats	OAT	N	Unit	RPU	N
Quaker State Corp.	KSF	N	Rhone-Poulenc Rorer	RPR	N
Quanex Corp.	NX	N			
Quantum Chemical	CUE	N	Richton Int'l	RHT	A
			Riedel Environm'l Tech	RIE	A
Quebecor Class 'A'	PQB	A	Rio Algom Ltd	ROM	A
Quest for Value Dual Fd	KFV	N	Riser Foods Class 'A'	RSR	A
Questar Corp.	STR	N	Rite Aid	RAD	N
Quick & Reilly Group	BQR	N			
RAC Income Fund	RMF	N	River Oaks Indus	ROI	N
			Riverbend Int'l	RIV	A
RAC Mtge Invest't	RMR	N	RJR Nabisco Holdings	RN	N
Racal Telecom ADR	RTG	N	RJR Nabisco Holdings		
Ragan (Brad)	BRD	A	Wrrnt	RN WS	N
Ralston Purina	RAL	N	RJR Nabisco Holdings		
Ranger Oil Ltd	RGO	N	Pfd	RN Pr	N
Raven Indus	RAV	A	RLI Corp.	RLI	N
Raychem Corp.	RYC	N	RMI Titanium	RTI	N
Raymond James Fin'l	RJF	N	RMS International	RMS	A
Rayonier Timberlands	LOG	N	Robert Half Int'l	RHI	N
Raytech Corp.	RAY	N	Robert-Mark Class 'A'	RMK.A	A
Raytheon Co.	RTN	N	Robert-Mark Wrrt	RMK WS	A
RB&W Corp.	RBW	A	Robertson-Ceco Corp.	Rhh	N
Re Capital Corp.	RCC	A	R.O.C. Taiwan Fund SBI	ROC	N
Reading & Bates	RB	N	Rochester Gas & El	RGS	N
Reading & Bates Pfd	Pr, Pr A	N	Rochester Telep	RTC	N
Real Est Inv Tr, Cal	RCT	N			
Real Est Sec Income Fd	RIF	A	Rockefeller Ctr Prop	RCP	N
Realty Refund SBI	RRF	N	Rockwell Int'l	ROK	N
Realty South Inv	RSI	A	Rockwell Int'l Pfd	various	N
Realty South Wrrt	WS	A	Rodman & Renshaw Cap	RR	N
			Rogers Corp.	ROG	N
Recognition Equip	REC	N			
Red Lion Inns L.P.	RED	A	Rohm & Haas	ROH	N
Redlaw Industries	RDL	A	Rohr Indus	RHR	N
Reebok Int'l	RBK	N	Rollins Environ Sv	REN	N
Reece Corp.	RCE	N	Rollins, Inc.	ROL	N
			Rollins Truck Leasing	RLC	N
Regal Beloit	RBC	A			
Regal Int'l	RGL	N	Rowan Cos.	RDC	N
Reich & Tang L.P.	RTP	N	Rowe Furniture	ROW	A
Reliance Group Hldgs	REL	N	Royal Dutch Petrol	RD	N
Repsol S.A. ADS	REP	N	Royal Palm Beach Col	RPB	A
			Royce Value Trust	RVT	N
Republic Gypsum	RGC	N			
Republic N.Y.	RNB	N	RPC Energy Systems	RES	N
Residential Mtge Inv	RMI	A	RPS Realty Trust	RPS	N
Resort Income Investors	RII	A	RTZ Corp. plc ADS	RTZ	N
Resource Recycling Tech	RRT	A	Rubbermaid, Inc.	RBD	N
			Ruddick Corp.	RDK	N
Rexene Corp.	RXN	N			
Reynolds Metals	RLM	N	Ruddick Corp. Cv Pfd	Pr	A
Reynolds & Reynolds Class			Russ Berrie & Co.	RUS	N
'A'	REY	N	Russ Togs	RTS	N

Stock	Symbol	Exchange
Russell Corp.	RML	N
Ryder System	R	N
Rykoff-Sexton, Inc.	RYK	N
Ryland Group	RYL	N
RYMAC Mtge Invest't	RM	A
Rymer Foods	RYR	N
Rymer Foods Wrrt	WS	A
Rymer Foods Cv Pfd	Pr	N
Saatchi/Saatchi ADS	SAA	N
Sabine Royalty Tr UBI	SBR	N
Safeguard Scientifics	SFE	N
Safety-Kleen	SK	N
Safeway, Inc.	SWY	N
Safeway, Inc., Wrrt	SWY WS	N
Sahara Casino Ptnrs	SAH	N
St. Joe Paper	SJP	N
St Joseph Lt & Pwr	SAJ	N
Salant Corp.	SLJ	N
Salem Corp.	SBS	A
Salomon Bros Fund	SBF	N
Salomon Phibro Oil Trust	SPO	A
Salomon, Inc.	SB	N
Samson Energy Co. L.P.	SAM	A
San Carlos Milling	SAN	A
San Diego Gas & El	SDO	N
San Diego Gas & El Pfd	Pr I	A
San Juan Basin Rty Tr	SJT	N
Sandy Corp.	SDY	A
Sanmark-Stardust	SMK	A
Santa Anita Rlty (Unit)	SAR	N
Sante Fe Energy Ptnrs	SFP	N
Santa Fe Pac Pipeline	SFL	N
Santa Fe Pacific	SFX	N
Sara Lee Corp.	SLE	N
Sara Lee Corp. Cv Pfd	Pr	N
Savin Corp.	SVB	N
Savin Corp. Cv Pfd A, B, D	Pr A,B,D	N
Saxon Oil Dv Ptnrs L.P.	SAX	A
Sbarro, Inc.	SBA	A
SCANA Corp.	SCG	N
Scandanavia Co.	SCF	N
SCECorp.	SCE	N
Sceptre Resources	SRL	A
Scheib (Earl)	ESH	A
Schering-Plough	SGP	N
Schlumberger Ltd	SLB	N
Schwab (Chas.) Corp.	SCH	N

Stock	Symbol	Exchange
Schwitzer, Inc.	SCZ	N
Science Management	SMG	A
Scientific-Atlanta	SFA	N
Scope Indus	SCP	A
SCOR U.S. Corp.	SUR	N
Scotsman Industries	SCT	N
Scott Paper	SPP	N
Scudder New Asia Fund	SAF	N
Scudder New Europe Fund	NEF	N
Scurry-Rainbow Oil	SRB	A
Sea Containers Ltd	SCR	N
Sea Containers Ltd Pfd	various	N
Seaboard Corp.	SEB	A
Seagram Co Ltd	VO	N
Seagull Energy	SGO	N
Sealed Air	SEE	N
Seaport Corp.	Seo	A
Seaport Corp. Cv Pfd	Pr A	A
Sears, Roebuck	S	N
Sears, Americus Unit, Score, Prime	various	A
Security Pacific	SPC	N
Seitel, Inc.	SEI	A
Selas Corp. of Amer	SLS	A
Seligman & Assoc	SLG	A
Semtech Corp.	SMH	A
Sequa Corp. Class 'A'	SQA.A	N
Sequa Corp. Class 'B'	SQA.Bs	N
Sequa Corp. Cv Pfd	Pr	N
Service Corp. Int'l	SRV	N
Service Merchandise	SME	N
ServiceMaster L.P.	SVM	N
Servotronics, Inc.	SVT	A
SFM Corp.	SFM	A
Shaw Indus	SHX	N
Shawmut Nat'l	SNC	N
Shelby Williams Ind	SY	N
Shell Transp/Trade ADR	SC	N
Shelter Components Corp.	SST	A
Sherwin-Williams	SHW	N
Sherwood Group	SHD	A
Shoney's, Inc.	SHN	N
Shopco Laurel Centre	LSC	A
Showboat, Inc.	SBO	N
Sierra Capital Realty IV	SZD	A
Sierra Capital Realty VI	SZF	A
Sierra Capital Realty VII	SZG	A
Sierra Capital Realty VIII	SZH	A
Sierra Health Services	SIE	A

Stock	Symbol	Exchange		Symbol	Exchange
Sierra Pacific Resources	SRP	N	SPI Pharmaceuticals	SPI	A
SIFCO Indus	SIF	A	Sprague Technologies	SPG	N
Signal Apparel Class 'A'	SIA	N	Springs Industries Class 'A'	SMI	N
Signal Apparel Cv Pfd vtg	Pr	N	SPS Technologies	ST	N
Signet Banking	SBK	N	SPX Corp.	SPW	N
Silicon Graphics	SGI	N	Square D	SQD	N
Singapore Fund	SGF	N	Stage II Apparel	SA	A
Sizeler Property Inv	SIZ	N	Standard Br Paint	SBP	N
SJW Corp.	SJW	A	Standard Commercial	STW	N
Skyline Corp.	Sky	N	Standard Fed'l Bank	SFB	N
SL Industries	SL	N	Standard Motor Prod	SMP	N
Smith (A. O.) Class 'A'	SMC.A	A	Standard-Pacific L.P.	SPF	N
Smith (A. O.) Class 'B'	SMC.B	B	Standard Products	SPD	N
Smith (A. O.) Cv Pfd	Pr C	A	Standex Int'l	SXI	N
Smith Corona Corp.	SCO	N	Stanhome, Inc.	STH	N
Smith Int'l	SII	N	Stanley Works	SWK	N
SmithKline Beecham			Starrett Housing	SHO	A
PLC ADS	SBH	N	Starrett (L. S.) Class 'A'	SCX	N
			State Mutual Sec Tr	SMS	N
SmithKline Beecham			Steego Corp.	STG	N
Unit Pfd	SBE	N	Stepan Co.	SCL	A
Smith's Food & Drug Class			Sterling Bancorp	STL	N
'B'	SFD	N			
Smucker (J. M.)	SJM	N	Sterling Capital	SPR	A
Snap-On Tools	SNA	N	Sterling Chemicals	STX	N
Snyder Oil Corp.	SNY	N	Sterling Electronics	SEC	A
			Sterling Software	SSW	A
Solitron Devices	SOD	N	Sterline Software Pfd	Pr	A
Sonat, Inc.	SNT	N			
Sony Corp. ADR	SNE	N	Stevens Graphics Class 'A'	SVG.A	A
Sotheby's Holdings Class 'A'	BID	A	Stevens Graphics Class 'B'	SVG.B	A
Source Capital	SOR	N	Stifel Financial	SF	N
			Stone Container	STO	N
South Jersey Indus	SJI	N	Stone & Webster	SW	N
Southdown, Inc.	SDW	N			
Southeast Banking	STB	N	Stoneridge Resources	SRE	N
Southern Co.	SO	N	Storage Equities	SEQ	N
South'n Indiana G&E	SIG	N	Storage Properties, Inc.	PSA	A
			Storage Technology	STK	N
Sthn New Eng Telecom	SNG	N	Stride Rite	SRR	N
Southern Union	SUG	N			
Southwest Airlines	LUV	N	Struthers Wells	SUW	A
Southwest Gas	SWX	N	Student Loan Mktg	SLM	N
Southwest Realty (Dep)	SWL	A	Suave Shoe	SWV	N
			Summit Tax Exempt Bond	SUA	A
Southwest Bell Corp.	SBC	N	Sun City Indus	SNI	A
Southwestern Energy	SWN	N			
Southwest'n Pub Sv	SPS	N	Sun Co.	SUN	N
Spain Fund	SNF	N	Sun Dstr L.P. Class 'A'	SDP	N
Spartech Corp.	SEH	A	Sun Dstr Class 'B'	SDP.B	N
			Sun Electric	SE	N
			Sun Energy Ptnrs	SLP	N
Sparton Corp.	SPA	N			
Speed-O-Print Bus Mach	SBM	A	Sundstrand Corp.	SNS	N
Spelling Entertainment	SP	A	Sunshine-Jr. Stores	SJS	A

Stock	Symbol	Exchange		Symbol	Exchange
Sunshine Mining	SSC	N	Templeton Emerg'g Mkts	EMF	A
SunTrust Banks	STI	N	Templeton Global Gvts	TGG	N
Super Food Services	SFS	A	Templeton Global Income	GIM	N
			Templeton Global Utilities	TGU	A
Super Valu Stores	SVU	N			
Superior Indus Int'l	SUP	A	TENERA, L.P. Ptnrs	TLP	A
Superior Surgical	SGC	A	Tenneco, Inc.	TGT	N
Superior Teletec	STT	A	Tenneco, Inc., Pfd	Pr B	N
Swift Energy	SFY	A	Tenney Engineering	TNY	A
			Teradyne, Inc.	TER	N
Swiss Helvetia Fund	SWZ	N			
Symbol Technologies	SBL	N	Tesoro Petroleum	TSO	N
Syms Corp.	SYM	N	Tesoro Petroleum Cv Pfd	Pr	N
Synalloy Corp.	SYO	A	Texaco, Inc.	TX	N
Syntex Corp.	SYN	N	Texas Indus	TXI	N
			Texas Instruments	TXN	N
Sysco Corp.	SYY	N			
System Indus	SYI	A	Texas Meridian Resources	TMR	A
Systems Center	SMX	N	Texas Pac Ld Tr	TPL	N
T/SF Communications	TCM	A	Texas Utilities	TXU	N
Tab Products	TBP	A	Texfi Indus	TXF	N
			Texscan Corp.	TSX	A
Tacoma Boatbldg	TBP	N			
Taiwan Fund	TWN	N	Textron, Inc.	TXT	N
Talley Indus	TAL	N	Textron, Inc., Pfd	various	N
Talley Indus Cv Pfd	Pr B	N	Thackeray Corp.	THK	N
Tambrands, Inc.	TMB	N	Thai Capital Fund	TTF	N
			Thermedics, Inc.	TMD	A
Tandem Computers	TDM	N			
Tandy Corp.	TAN	N	Thermo Cardiosystems	TCA	A
Tandycrafts, Inc.	TAC	N	Thermo Electron	TMO	N
Tasty Baking	TBC	A	Thermo Instrument Sys	THI	A
TCBY Enterprises	TBY	N	Thermo Process Sys	TPI	A
			Thermwood Corp.	TKC	N
TCF Financial	TCB	N			
TCS Enterprises	TCS	A	Thiokol Corp.	TKC	N
TCW Conv Sec Fund	CVT	N	Thomas & Betts	TNB	N
TDK Corp. ADS	TDK	N	Thomas Indus	TII	N
Team, Inc.	TMi	A	Thomson Advisory Group	TAG	N
			Thor Energy Res	THR	N
Tech/Ops Sevcon	TOC	A			
Technitrol, Inc.	TNL	A	Thor Industries	THO	N
Tech-Sym	TSY	N	Three D Depts Cv Class 'B'	TDD.B	A
TECO Energy	TE	N	Three D Depts Cv Class 'A'	TDD.A	A
Tejon Ranch	TRC	A	Tidewater, Inc.	TDW	N
			TIE/Communications	TIE	A
Tektronix, Inc.	TEK	N			
TeleCom Corp.	TEL	N	Tiffany & Co.	TIF	N
TeleConcepts Corp.	TCC	A	TII Indus	TI	A
Teledyne, Inc.	TDY	N	Timberland Co.	TBL	A
Teleflex, Inc.	TFX	A	Time Warner, Inc.	TWX	N
			Time-Warner, Inc. Pfd	various	N
Telefonica De Espana ADS	TEF	N			
Telephone & Date Sys	TDS	A	Times Mirror Class 'A'	TMC	N
Telesphere Conmun'ns	TSP	A	Timken Co.	TKR	N
Temco Nat'l Corp.	TEM	A	TIS Mtge Investment	TIS	N
Temco Nat'l Corp. Wrrt	WS	A	Titan Corp.	TTN	N
Temple-Inland	TIN	N	Titan Corp. Cv Pfd	Pr	N

Stock	Symbol	Exchange		Symbol	Exchange
TJX Companies (New)	JCX	N	TRW, Inc., Pfd	various	N
TNP Enterprises	TNP	N	TubosDeAceroMex ADR	TAM	A
Todd Shipyards	QTOD	N			
Tofutti Brands	TOF	A	Tucson Elec Power	TEP	N
Tokheim Corp.	TOK	N	Tultex Corp.	TTX	N
			Turkish Investment Fund	TKF	N
Toll Brothers	TOL	N	Turner Broadcast Class 'A'	TBS.A	A
Tolland Bnk	TBK	A	Turner Broadcast Class 'B'	TBS.B	A
Tonka Corp.	TKA	N			
Tootsie Roll Indus	TR	N	Turner Corp.	TUR	A
Torchmark Corp.	TMK	N	Twin Disc	TDI	N
			Two Pesos, Inc.	TWP	A
Toro Co.	TTC	N	Tyco Laboratories	TYC	N
Torotel, Inc.	TTL	A	Tyler Corp.	TYL	N
Tosco Corp.	TOS	A			
Total Petrol'm NA	TPN	A	UAL Corp.	UAL	N
Total Petrol'm NA Cv Pfd	Pr	A	UDC-Univ'l Dev L.P.	UDC	N
			UGI Corp.	UGI	N
Total Systems Svcs	TSS	N	UJB Financial	UJB	N
Town & Country Class 'A'	TNC	A	Ultimate Corp.	ULT	N
Toys R Us	TOY	N			
Trammell Crow R.E. Inv	TCR	N	UniCare Financial	UFN	A
Transamerica Corp.	TA	N	Unicorp American	UAC	A
			Unifirst Corp.	UNF	N
Transasmer'a, Inc., Shrs	TAI	N	Unilever N.V.	UN	N
Transatlantic Holdings	TRH	N	Unilever ADR	UL	N
TransCanada P.L.	TRP	N			
Transcapital Fin'l	TFC	N	Unimar Indonesian Ptc Units	UMR	A
Transcisco Class 'A'	TNI.A	A	Union Camp	UCC	N
			Union Carbide	UK	N
Transcisco Class 'B'	TNI.B	A	Union Corp.	UCO	N
Transco Energy	E	N	Union Electric	UEP	N
Transco Energy Cv Pfd	Pr A	N			
Transco Expl Ptnrs	EXP	N	Union Pacific	UNP	N
Transcon, Inc.	TCL	N	Union Pac, Americus Unit,		
			Score, Prime	various	A
			Union Planters	UPC	N
Transcontinental Rlty	TCI	N	Union Texas Pet Hldgs	UTH	N
Trans-Lux	TLX	A	Union Valley Corp.	UVC	A
TransTechnology	TT	N			
Tranzonic Cos	TNZ	A	UnionFed Fin'l	UFF	N
Tranzonic Cos Class 'B'	TNZ.B	A	Unisys Corp.	UIS	N
			Unisys Corp. Cv Pfd	Pr A	N
Travelers Corp.	TIC	N	Unit Corp.	UNT	N
TRC Cos	TRR	A	United Assets Mgmt	UAM	N
Tredegar Indus	TG	N			
Triangle Corp.	TRG	A	United Capital Corp.	ICU	A
Triangle Home Prod	THP	A	United Dominion Indus	UDI	N
			United Dominion Realty Tr	UDR	N
Tribune Co.	TRB	N	United Foods Cv Class 'B'	UFD.B	A
Tri-Continental	TY	N	United Foods Class 'A'	UFD.A	A
Tridex Corp.	TDX	A			
Trinity Indus	TRN	N	United Illuminating	UIL	N
TRINOVA Corp.	TNV	N	United Industrial	UIC	N
			United Inns	UI	N
Triton Energy	OIL	N	United Investors Mgm't	UTD	N
Triton Energy Cv Pfd	Pr	N	United Kingdom Fund	UKM	N
TRW, Inc.	TRW	N	United Medical	UM	A

Stock	Symbol	Exchange		Symbol	Exchange
United Merchants/Mfr	UMM	N	UtiliCorp United Pfd	various	N
United Park City Mns	UPK	N	Vader Group	VDR	A
U.S. Banknote	UBK	A	Valero Energy	VLO	N
U.S. Bioscience	UBS	A			
			Valero Energy Pfd	various	N
U.S. Cellular	USM	A	Valero Nat'l Gas Ptnr	VLP	N
U.S. Home	UH	N	Valhi, Inc.	VHI	N
U.S. Intec, Inc.	USI	A	Valley Forge	VF	A
U.S. Shoe	USR	N	Valley Indus	VI	N
U.S. Surgical	USS	N			
			Valley Resources	VR	A
U.S. West, Inc.	USW	N	Valspar Corp.	VAL	A
United Technologies	UTX	N	Van Dorn	VDC	N
United Telecom (Kan)	UT	N	Van Kampen Merritt Cal		
United Telecom (Kan)			Muni	VKC	A
Cv Pfd	various	N	Van Kampen Merritt Hi		
United Water Res	UWR	N	Income	VLT	N
Unitel Video	UNV	A	Van Kampen Merritt Interm	VIT	N
UNITIL Corp.	UTL	A	Van Kampen Merritt		
Unitrode Corp.	UTR	N	Inv Grade	VIG	N
Univar Corp.	UVX	N	Van Kampen Merritt Muni	VMT	N
Universal Corp.	UVV	N	Varco Int'l	VRC	N
			Varian Associates	VAR	N
Universal Foods	UFC	N			
Universal Health Realty	UHT	N	Varity Corp.	VAT	N
Universal Matchbox			Varity Corp. Cv Pfd	Pr A	N
Group	UMG	N	Verit Indus	VER	A
Universal Med Bldgs L.P.	UMB	N	Vermont Research	VRE	A
Universal Med Bldgs L.P.			Veronex Research	VX	A
Cv Pfd	Pr A	N			
			Versar, Inc.	VSR	A
Universal Voltronics	UVL	A	Vestaur Securities	VES	N
University Bank N.A.	UBN	A	Vestron, Inc.	VV	N
University Patents	UPT	A	V.F. Corp.	VFC	N
Uno Restaurant Corp.	UNO	A	Viacom, Inc.	VIA	N
Unocal Corp.	UCL	N			
			Viatech, Inc.	VTK	A
UNUM Corp.	UNM	N	Vicon Indus	VII	A
Upjohn Co.	UPJ	N	Vintage Petrol	VPI	N
URCARGO Inc.	KAR	N	Virco Mfd	VIR	A
URS Corp.	URS	N	Va'El & Pwr Pfd	VELPrH	N
USACafes L.P.	USF	N			
			Vishay Intertechn'gy	VSH	N
USAir Group	U	N	Vista Chemical	VC	N
USF&G Corp.	FG	N	Vista Resources	VS	N
USF&G Corp. Cv Pfd	PR A	N	VISX, Inc.	VSX	A
USF&G Pacholder Fd	PHF	A	Vivra, Inc.	V	N
USG Corp.	USG	N			
			VMS Hotel Inv't Fund	VHT	A
USLICO Corp.	USC	N	VMS Mortgage Inv Fund	VMG	A
USLIFE Corp.	USH	N	VMS Short Term, Inc.,		
USLIFE Income Fund	UIF	N	Tr SBI	VST	A
USP Real Est Inv Tr SBI	URT	A	Volunteer Capital	VCC	N
UST, Inc.	UST	N	Vons Cos	VON	N
USX Corp.	X	N	Voplex Corp.	VOT	A
UtiliCorp United	UCU	N	Vornado, Inc.	VNO	N

Stock	Symbol	Exchange
VTX Electronics	VTX	A
Vulcan Int'l Corp.	VUL	A
Vulcan Materials	VMC	N
Waban Inc.	WBN	N
Wackenhut Corp.	WAK	N
Wahlco Enviro Systems	WAL	N
Wainoco Oil	WOL	N
Walgreen Co.	WAG	N
Wallace Computer Svs	WCS	N
Wal-Mart Stores	WMT	N
Wang Labs Class 'B'	WAN.B	A
Wang Labs Cv Class 'C'	WAN.C	A
Warner Computer Sys	WCP	N
Warner-Lambert	WLA	N
Washington Gas Lt	WGL	N
Washington National	WNT	N
Washington National Cv Pfd	Pr	N
Washington Post Class 'B'	WPO.B	A
Washington REIT SBI	WRE	A
Washington Water Pwr	WWP	N
Waste Management	WMX	N
Watkins-Johnson	WJ	N
Watsco, Inc., Cv Class 'B'	WSO.B	A
Watsco, Inc., Cv Class 'A'	WSO.A	A
Waxman Indus	WAX	N
Wean, Inc.	WID	N
Weatherford Int'l	WII	A
Weatherford Int'l Pfd	Pr	A
Webb (Del) Corp.	WBB	N
Wedco Technology, Inc.	WED	A
Wedgestone Financial	WDG	N
Weingarten Rlty SBI	WRI	N
Weirton Steel	WS	N
Weis Markets	WMK	N
Weldotron Corp.	WLD	A
Wellco Enterprises	WLC	A
Wellman, Inc.	WLM	N
Wells American Corp.	WAC	N
Wells Fargo	WFC	N
Wells Fargo Mtg/Eqty	WFM	N
Wells-Gardner Electr	WGA	A
Wendy's Int'l	WEN	N
Wesco Financial	WSC	A
West Co.	WST	N
West Pt-Pepperell	WPM	N
WestAir Holding	WAH	A
Westamerica Bancorp	WAB	A
Westbridge Capital	WBC	A

Stock	Symbol	Exchange
Westcoast Energy	WE	N
Westcorp, Inc.	WES	A
Western Co. No Amer	WSN	N
Western Digital	WDC	A
Western Gas Resources	WGR	N
Western Inv't R.E. Tr SBI	WIR	A
Western Mining Hldg ADS	WMC	N
Western Union	WU	N
Western Union Pfd	various	N
Westinghouse Elec	WX	N
Westpac Banking ADS	WBK	N
Westvaco Corp.	W	N
Weyerhaeuser Co.	WY	N
Wheelabrator Tech	WTI	N
Wheelabrator Tech Wrrt	WS	N
Wheeling Pitt Steel	QWHX	N
Whirlpool Corp.	WHR	N
Whitehall Corp.	WHT	N
Whitman Co.	WH	N
Whittaker Corp.	WKR	N
Wichita River Oil	WRO	A
Wickes Cv Pfd	WIXPrA	A
Wickes Wrrt	WS	A
WICOR, Inc.	WIC	N
Wiener Enterprises	WPB	A
Wilfred Amer Educat'l	WAE	N
Willcox & Gibbs	WG	N
Williams Cos.	WMB	N
Williams Cos. Cv Pfd	Pr	N
Wilshire Oil Texas	WOC	N
Willis Corroon ADS	WCG	N
Windmere Corp.	WND	N
Winn-Dixie Stores	WIN	N
Winnebago Indus	WGO	N
Winston Resources	WRS	A
Winthrop Insured Mtge Inv II	WMI	A
Wisconsin Energy Corp.	WEC	N
Wisconsin Public Sv	WPS	N
Witco Corp.	WIT	N
WMS Industries	WMS	N
Wolf (Howard B.)	HBW	A
Wolverine World Wide	WWW	N
Woolworth (F. W.)	Z	N
Woolworth (F. W.) Cv Pfd	PrA	N
World Income Fund	WOI	A
WorldCorp, Inc.	WOA	N
Worldwide Value Fund	VLU	N
Worthen Banking Corp.	WOR	A

Stock	Symbol	Exchange		Symbol	Exchange
WPL Holdings	WPH	N	Zemex Corp.	ZMX	N
Wrigley (Wm.) Jr.	WWY	N	Zenith Electronics	ZE	N
			Zenith Income Fund	ZIF	N
Wyle Laboratories	WYL	N			
Wynn's Int'l	WN	N	Zenith Nat'l Insurance	ZNT	N
Xerox Corp.	XRX	N	Zero Corp.	ZRO	N
Xerox, Americus Unit,			Zurn Indus	ZRN	N
Score, Prime	various	A	Zweig Fund	ZF	N
XTRA Corp.	XTR	N	Zweig Total Return Fund	ZTR	N
XTRA Corp. Cv Pfd	Pr B	N			
Zapata Corp.	ZOS	N			

3.5 HOW TO INTERPRET A VALUE LINE REPORT

Figure 3.1 illustrates a typical Value Line report and provides explanations of the information offered there. The Value Line Investment Survey provides quarterly one-page reports on each of more than 1,700 stock issues. In evaluating a single stock, Value Line suggests first identifying stocks ranked 1 (highest) or 2 (above average) for timeliness (see section 3.3 for a further explanation of the rankings). Second, from the list of timely stocks, pick those that are in the industries also shown to be most timely. The weekly Value Line "Summary and Index" ranks industries in order of timeliness. The third step is to pick from the list of most timely stocks in the most timely industries those stocks that also conform to your safety constraints. Conservative investors should usually give preference to stocks ranked 1 or 2 for safety. Those seeking more volatile stocks might opt for lower rankings. Fourth, investors seeking dividend yield can find the estimated dividend yield of each stock in the weekly Value Line "Summary and Index."

Also see section 3.6 for a list of companies followed by the Value Line Investment Survey.

FIGURE 3.1 VALUE LINE REPORT AND DESCRIPTION

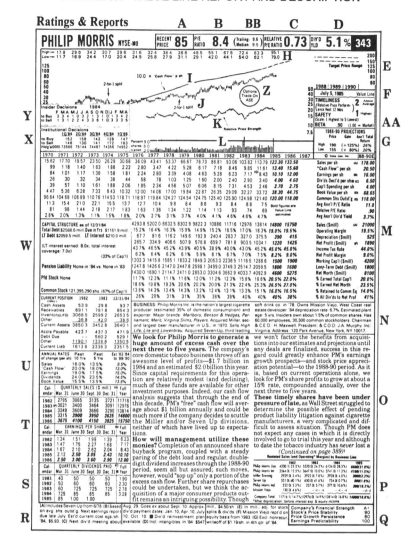

FIGURE 3.1 continued

SAMPLE VALUE LINE REPORT

A Recent price—nine days prior to delivery date.

AA Here is the core of Value Line's advice—the rank for Timeliness; the rank for Safety; Beta—the stock's sensitivity to fluctuations of the market as a whole.

B P/E ratio—the most recent price divided by the latest six months' earnings per share plus earnings estimated for the next six months.

BB P/E Median—a rounded average of four middle values of the range of average annual price-earnings ratios over the past 10 years.

C Relative P/E Ratio—the stock's current P/E divided by the median P/E for all stocks under Value Line review.

D Dividend Yield—cash dividends *estimated to be declared in the next 12 months* divided by the recent price.

E The 3-5 year target price range, estimated. The range is placed in proper position on the price chart, and is shown numerically in the "1988-90 Projections" box in the lower right-hand corner of the price chart.

F The date of delivery to the subscribers. The survey is mailed on a schedule that aims for delivery to every subscriber on Friday afternoon.

G Annual Total Return—the estimated future average annual growth plus current dividend yield—plus possible annualized change in the trend of the price-earnings ratio.

H The stock's highest and lowest price of the year.

I The Value Line—reported earnings plus depreciation ("cash flow") multiplied by a number selected to correlate the stock's 3- to 5-year projected target price with "cash flow" projected out to 1988-90.

J Monthly price ranges of the stock—plotted on a ratio (logarithmic) grid to show percentage changes in true proportion. For example, a ratio chart equalizes the move of a $10 stock that rises to $11 with a $100 stock that rises to $110. Both have advanced 10% and over the same space on a ratio grid.

K Relative price strength—describes the stock's past price performance relative to the Value Line Composite Average of 1700 stocks. The Timeliness Rank usually predicts the future direction of this line.

L The number of shares traded monthly as a percentage of the total outstanding.

M Statistical milestones that reveal significant long-term trends. The statistics are presented in two ways: 1) The upper series records results on a per-share basis; 2) the lower records results on a

company basis. On pages 30 to 33, you will find conclusions that might be drawn from an inspection of these milestones. Note that the statistics for the year 1985 are estimated, as are the figures for the average of the years 1988-90. The estimates would be revised, if necessary, should future evidence require. The weekly *Summary & Index* would promptly call attention to such revisions.

N A condensed summary of the business.

O A 400-word report on recent developments and prospects—issued once every three months on a preset schedule.

P Most large corporations engage in several lines of business. Hence sales and profit margins are shown by lines of business.

Q Value Line indexes of financial strength, price stability, price growth persistence, and earnings predictability.

R Footnotes explain a number of things, such as the way earnings are reported, whether "fully diluted," on a "primary" basis, or on an "average shares outstanding" basis.

S Quarterly dividends paid are actual payments. The total of dividends paid in four quarters may not equal the figure shown in the annual series on dividends declared. (Sometimes a dividend declared at the end of the year will be paid in the first quarter of the following year.)

T Quarterly earnings are shown on a per share basis (estimates in bold type). Quarterly sales on a gross basis.

U Annual rates of change (on a per share basis). Actual past, estimated future.

V Current position—current assets, current liabilities, and other components of working capital.

W The capital structure as of recent date showing the percentage of capital in long-term debt (33%), and in common stock (67%); the number of times that total interest charges were earned (7.0 in 1984).

X A record of the decisions taken by the biggest institutions (over $70 million in equity holdings)—including banks, insurance companies, mutual funds, investment advisers, internally managed endowments, and pension funds—to buy or sell during the past five quarters and how many shares were involved, and the total number of shares they hold.

Y The record of insider decisions—decisions by officers and directors to buy or sell as reported to the SEC a month or more after execution.

Z Options patch—indicates listed options are available on the stock, and on what exchange they are most actively traded.

Source: Value Line Inc., *How to Use the Value Line Investment Survey* (New York, 1985).

3.6 STOCKS FOLLOWED BY THE VALUE LINE INVESTMENT SURVEY

Table 3.5 can be used to identify stocks that are monitored by the Value Line Investment Survey.

All shares are traded on the New York Stock Exchange except where noted ASE (American Stock Exchange), PAC (Pacific), PHL (Philadelphia), MSE (Montreal), TSE (Toronto), or OTC (over the counter). The table represents stocks covered as of August 1991. Changes in coverage can and do occur regularly.

Table 3.5 Stocks Followed by the Value Line Investment Survey

Name of Stock	Ticker Symbol		Name of Stock	Ticker Symbol	
A & W Brands	(OTC)	SODA	Airgas, Inc.		ARG
AAR Corp.		AIR	Akzo N.V. (ADR)(g)	(OTC)	AKZOY
ACM Gov't Income Fund		ACG			
ADC Telecom.	(OTC)	ADCT	Alaska Air Group		ALK
ADT Ltd. (ADR)	(OTC)	ADTLY	Albany Int'l 'A'		AIN
			Alberta Natural Gas	(TSE)	ANG.TO
A.L. Laboratories		BMD	Alberto-Culver 'B'		ACV
AM Int'l		AM	Albertson's, Inc.		ABS
AMR Corp.		AMR			
ARCO Chemical		RCM	Alcan Aluminum		AL
ARX, Inc.			Alco Standard		ASN
			Alexander & Alexander		AAL
ASA Ltd.		ASA	Alexander & Baldwin	(OTC)	ALEX
AST Research	(OTC)	ASTA	Alexander's, Inc.		ALX
Abbott Labs.		ABT			
Abitibi-Price		AMY	Alico, Inc.	(OTC)	ALCO
Acme-Cleveland		AMT	Allegheny Corp.		Y
			Allegheny Ludlum		ALS
Acme Steel	(OTC)	ACME	Allegheny Power Sys.		AYP
Action Inds	(ASE)	ACX	Allen Group		ALN
Adams Express		ADX			
Adia Services	(OTC)	ADIA	Allergan, Inc.		AGN
Adobe Resources		ADB	Allied Products		ADP
			Allied-Signal		ALD
Adobe Sytems	(OTC)	ADBE	ALLTEL Corp.		AT
Advanced Micro Dev.		AMD	Allwaste, Inc.	(OTC)	ALWS
Advanced Telecom.	(OTC)	ATEL			
Advest Group		ADV	Aluminum Co. of Amer.		AA
ADVO-System	(OTC)	ADVO	ALZA Corp. 'A'	(ASE)	AZA
			Amax, Inc.		AMX
Aetna Life & Casualty		AET	Amcast Industrial		AIZ
Affiliated Publications		AFP	Amdahl Corp.	(ASE)	AMH
Agency Rent-A-Car	(OTC)	AGNC			
Ahmanson (H.F.)		AHM	Amerada Hess		AHC
Air & Water Techn.	(ASE)	AWT	Amer. Bankers Ins.	(OTC)	ABIG
			Amer. Barrick Res.		ABX
Air Express Int'l	(ASE)	AEX	Amer. Brands		AMB
Air Products & Chem.		APD	Amer. Building Maint.		ABM
Airborne Freight		ABF	Amer. Business Prod.		ABP

Name of Stock		Ticker Symbol	Name of Stock		Ticker Symbol
Amer. Capital Bond Fund		ACB	Armstrong World Inds.		ACK
Amer. Cyanamid		ACY	Arrow Electronics		ARW
Amer. Elec. Power		AEP	Artra Group		ATA
Amer. Express		AXP	Arvin Ind.		ARV
Amer. Family Corp.		AFL	Asarco, Inc.		AR
Amer. General Corp.		AGC	ASEA AB (ADR)	(OTC)	ASEAY
Amer. Greetings	(OTC)	AGREA	Ashland Coal		ACI
Amer. Home Products		AHP	Ashland Oil		ASH
Amer. Int'l Group		AIG	Ashton-Tate	(OTC)	TATE
Amer. Maize 'A'	(ASE)	AZEA	Athlone Ind.		ATH
Amer. Power Conv.	(OTC)	APCC	Atlanta Gas Light		ATG
Amer. President Cos.		APS	Atlantic Energy, Inc.		ATE
Amer. Ship Building		ABG	Atlantic Richfield		ARC
Amer. Software 'A'	(OTC)	AMSWA	Atlantic So'east Air	(OTC)	ASAI
Amer. Stores		ASC	Atlas Corp.		AZ
Amer. Tel. & Tel.		T	Augat, Inc.		AUG
Amer. Water Works		AWK	Austria Fund		OST
Ameritech Corp.		AIT	Autodesk, Inc.	(OTC)	ACAD
Ameritrust Corp.	(OTC)	AMTR	Automatic Data Proc.		AUD
Ameron, Inc.		AMN	Avantek, Inc.	(OTC)	AVAK
Ametek, Inc.		AME	Avery Dennison		AVY
Amgen	(OTC)	AMGN	Avnet, Inc.		AVT
Amoco Corp.		AN	Avon Products		AVP
AMP, Inc.		AMP	Aydin Corp.		AYD
Ampco-Pittsburgh		AP	Aztar Corp.	(OTC)	AZTR
AMREP Corp.		AXR	B.A.T. Ind. (ADR)(g)	(ASE)	BTI
AmSouth Bancorp		ASO	BB&T Financial	(OTC)	BBTF
Anacomp, Inc.		AAC	BCE Inc.	(TSE)	B.TO
Anadarko Petroleum		APC	BET PLC (ADR)(g)		BEP
Analog Devices		ADI	BP Canada	(TSE)	BPC.TO
Andrew Corp.	(OTC)	ANDW	BRE Properties		BRE
Angelica Corp.		AGL	Balmco Corp.		BZ
Anglo Amer. Cp S.A.	(OTC)	ANGLY	Baker Hughes		BHI
Anheuser-Busch		BUD	Baker (J)	(OTC)	JBAK
Anthem Electronics		ATM	Baldor Electric		BEZ
Aon Corp.		AOC	Baldwin Technology	(ASD)	BLD
Apache Corp.		APA	Ball Corp.		BLL
Apogee Enterprises	(OTC)	APOG	Bally Mfg		BLY
Apple Computer	(OTC)	AAPL	Balt. Gas & Elec.		BGE
Applied Biosystems	(OTC)	ABIO	Banc One Corp.		ONE
Applied Magnetics		APM	Bancorp Hawaii		BOH
Applied Materials	(OTC)	AMAT	BancTec, Inc.	(OTC)	BTEC
Applied Power 'A'	(OTC)	APWRA	Bandag, Inc.		BDG
Aquation Co.		WTR	Bank of Boston		BKB
Arbor Drugs	(OTC)	ARBR	Bank of Montreal	(TSE)	BMO.TO
Archer Daniels Midl'd		ADM	Bank of New York		BK
Arden Group 'A'	(OTC)	ADM	Bank of Nova Scotia	(TSE)	BNS.TO
Arkla, Inc.		ALG	BankAmerica Corp.		BAC
Armco, Inc.		AS			

Name of Stock		Ticker Symbol	Name of Stock		Ticker Symbol
Bankers Trust NY		BT	Bob Evans Farms	(OTC)	BOBE
Banta Corp.	(OTC)	BNTA	Boeing		BA
			Bohemia, Inc.	(OTC)	BOHM
Bard (C.R.)		BCR	Boise Cascade		BCC
Barnes Group		B			
Barnett Banks, Inc.		BBI	Bolar Pharmac.		
Barry (R.G.)	(ASE)	RGB	Bolt Beranek & Newman		BBN
Basic Amer. Medical	(OTC)	BAMI	Borden, Inc.		BN
			Boston Bancorp	(OTC)	SBOS
Bassett Furniture	(OTC)	BSET	Boston Edison		BSE
Battle Mtn Gold Co.		BMG			
Bausch & Lomb		BOL	Bow Valley Inds.	(ASE)	BVI
Baxter Int'l Inc.		BAX	Bowater, Inc.		BOW
BayBanks Inc.	(OTC)	BBNK	Bowne & Co.	(ASE)	BNE
			Brascan Ltd.	(ASE)	BRSA
Bay State Gas		BGC	Brazil Fund		BZF
Bear Stearns		BSC			
Bearings, Inc.		BER	Briggs & Stratton		BGG
Beazer PLC (ADR)		BZR	Bristol-Myers Squibb		BMY
Beckman Instruments		BEC	British Airways (ADR)(g)		BAB
			British Columbia Tel.	(TSE)	BCT.TO
Becton, Dickinson		BDX	British Gas PLC (ADR)(g)		BRG
Belding Heminway		BHY			
Bell Atlantic Corp.		BEL	British Petroleum PLC		BP
Bell Inds.		BI	British Steel (ADR)(g)		BST
BellSouth Corp.		BLS	British Telecom (ADR)(g)		BTY
			Broad, Inc.		BRO
Belo (A.H.) 'A' Corp.		BLC	Broken Hill (ADR)		BHP
Bemis Co.		BMS			
Beneficial Corp.		BNL	Brooklyn Union Gas		BU
Benguet Corp.		BE	Brown & Sharpe		BNS
Bergen Brunswig	(ASE)	BBC	Brown-Forman 'B'		BFB
			Brown Group		BG
Berldey (W.R.)	(OTC)	BKLY	Browning-Ferris Inds.		BFI
Berkshire Hathaway		BRK			
Best Buy Co.		BBY	Bruno's, Inc.	(OTC)	BRNO
Bethlehem Steel		BS	Brunswick Corp.		BC
Betz Labs.	(OTC)	BETZ	Brush Wellman		BW
			Buckeye Partners L.P.		BPL
Beverly Enterprises		BEV	Builders Transport	(OTC)	TRUK
BIC Corp.	(ASE)	BIC			
Big B, Inc.	(OTC)	BIGB	Burlington Coat		BCF
Bindley Western	(OTC)	BIND	Burlington Northern		BNI
Biogen, Inc.	(OTC)	BGEN	Burlington Resources		BR
			Burnup & Sims	(OTC)	BSIM
Biomet	(OTC)	BMET	Businessland		BLI
Bio-Rad Labs. 'A'	(ASE)	BIOA			
Bird Corp.	(OTC)	BIRD	Bulter Mfg.	(OTC)	BTLR
Birmingham Steel		BIR	C&S/Sovran Corp.		CVN
Black & Decker		BDK	CAE Inds.	(TSE)	CAE.TO
			CBI Inds.		CBH
Blair Corp.	(ASE)	BL	CBS Inc.		CBS
Block (H & R)		HRB			
Blockbuster Entertain.		BV	CDI Corp.		CDI
Blount, Inc., 'A'		BLTA	CIGNA Corp.		CI
Blyvoor Gold ADR	(OTC)	BLYVY	CIPSCO Inc.		CIP
			CML (Group)		CML
Boatmen's Bancshs.	(OTC)	BOAT	CMS Energy Corp.		CMS

Name of Stock		Ticker Symbol	Name of Stock		Ticker Symbol
CNA Fin'l		CNA	Centocor	(OTC)	CNTO
CPC Int'l		CPC	Cen. & South West		CSR
CPI Corp.		CPY			
CRSS Inc.		CRX	Cen. Hudson G. & E.		CNH
CSX Corp.		CSX	Cen. La. Elec		CNL
			Cen. Maine Power		CTP
C-TEC Corp.	(OTC)	CTEX	Cen. Vermont Pub. Serv.		CV
CTS Corp.		CTS	Century Tel. Enterprises		CTL
CUC Int'l		CU			
Cable & Wireless (ADR)(g)		CWP	Cetus Corp.	(OTC)	CTUS
Cabletron Sys.		CS	Chambers Dev. 'A'	(ASE)	CDVA
			Champion Int'l		CHA
Cablevision Sys 'A'	(ASE)	CVC	Charming Shoppes	(OTC)	CHRS
Cabot Corp.		CBT	Chase Manhattan		CMB
Cadbury Schweppes(g)	(OTC)	CADBY			
Caesars World		CAW	Chemed Corp.		CHE
Cal Fed Inc.		CAL	Chemical Banking Corp.		CHL
			Chemical Waste Mgmt.		CHW
Calgon Carbon		CCC	Chesapeake Corp.		CSK
California Energy	(ASE)	CE	Chevron Corp.		CHV
California Microwave	(OTC)	CMIC			
California Water	(OTC)	CWTR	Chieftain Int'l	(ASE)	CID
Callahan Mining		CMN	Child World		
			Chile Fund		CH
CalMat Co.		CZM	Chiquita Brands Int'l		CQB
Campbell Soup		CPB	Chock Full O' Nuts		CHF
Canadian Imperial Bk	(TSE)	CM.TO			
Canadian Marconi	(ASE)	CMW	Chris-Craft		CCN
Canadian Occidental	(TSE)	CXY.TO	Chrysler		C
			Chubb Corp.		CB
Canadian Pacific Ord		CP	Church & Dwight		CHD
Canon Inc. (ADR)(g)	(OTC)	CANNY	CILCORP, Inc.		CER
Capital Cities/ABC		CCB			
Capital Holding Corp.		CPH	Cincinnati Bell		CSN
Cardinal Distribution	(OTC)	CDIC	Cincinnati Financial	(OTC)	CINF
			Cincinnati Gas & Elec.		CIN
Carl Karcher Enterp.	(OTC)	CARL	Cincinnati Milacron		CMZ
Carlisle Cos.		CSL	Cineplex Odeon		CPX
Carlton (ADR)(g)	(OTC)	CCTVY			
Carnival Cruise 'A'		CCL	Cintas Corp.	(OTC)	CTAS
Carolina Freight		CAO	Circuit City Stores		CC
			Circus Circus Enterpr.		CIR
Carolina Power & Lt.		CPL	Citicorp		CCI
Carpenter Technology		CRS	Citizens Utilities 'B'	(OTC)	CITUB
Carter Hawley Hale		CHH			
Carter-Wallace		CAR	City National Corp.		CYN
Cascade Corp.	(OTC)	CASC	Claire's Stores		CLE
			CLARCOR Inc.	(OTC)	CLRK
Cascade Natural Gas		CGC	Clark Equipment		CKL
Casey's Gen'l Stores	(OTC)	CASY	Clayton Homes		CMH
Castle & Cooke		CKE			
Caterpillar, Inc.		CAT	Cleveland-Cliffs		CLF
Cedar Fair L.P.		FUN	Clorox Co.		CLX
			Clothestime	(OTC)	CTME
Centel Corp.		CNT	Club Med		CMI
Centerior Energy		CX	Coachmen Ind.		COA
Centex Corp.		CTX	Coastal Corp.		CGP

Name of Stock		Ticker Symbol	Name of Stock		Ticker Symbol
Coca-Cola		KO	Crane Co.		CR
Coca-Cola Enterprises		CCE	Crawford & Co. 'B'		CRDB
Coherent, Inc.	(OTC)	COHR	Cray Research		CYR
Colgate-Palmolive		CL	Crestar Financial	(OTC)	CRFC
			Crompton & Knowles		CNK
Collagen Corp.	(OTC)	CGEN			
Columbia Gas		CG	Cross & Trecker	(OTC)	CTCO
Comcast Corp.	(OTC)	CMCSA	Cross (A. T.) 'A'	(ASE)	ATXA
Comdisco, Inc.		CDO	Crown Cork		CCK
Comerica Inc.		CMA	Crystal Brands		CBR
			Cubic Corp.	(ASE)	CUB
Cominco Ltd	(TSE)	CLT.TO			
Commerce Bancshs.	(OTC)	CBSH	Culbro Corp.		CUC
Commerce Clearing 'A'	(OTC)	CCLRA	Culp Inc.	(OTC)	CULP
Commercial Intertech		TEC	Cummins Engine		CUM
Commercial Metals		CMC	Curtice-Burns Foods	(ASE)	CBI
			Curtiss-Wright		CW
Commodore Int'l		CBU			
Commonwealth Edison		CWE	Cyclops Inds.		CYC
Commonwealth Energy		CES	Cyprus Minerals		CYM
Communic. Satellite		CQ	DPL Inc.		DPL
Community Psych. Ctrs.		CMY	DQE		DQE
			DR European Equity	(MF)	DIEEX
Compaq Computer		CPQ			
Computer Associates		CA	DSC Communic.	(OTC)	DIGI
Computer Sciences		CSC	Dana Corp.		DCN
ConAgra, Inc.		CAG	Danaher Corp.		DHR
Conn. Energy		CNE	Daniel Indus		DAN
			Data General		DGN
Conn. Natural Gas		CTG			
Conner Peripherals		CNR	Datascope Corp.	(OTC)	DSCP
Conseco, Inc.		CNC	Dayton Hudson		DH
Consol. Edison		ED	De Beers Consol.	(OTC)	DBRSY
Consol. Freightways		CNF	Dean Foods		DF
			Deb Shops	(OTC)	DEBS
Consol. Natural Gas		CNG			
Consol. Papers	(OTC)	CPER	Deere & Co.		DE
Consol. Rail		CRR	DEKALB Energy Co.	(OTC)	ENRGB
Consol. Stores		CNS	DEKALB Genetics 'B'	(OTC)	SEEDB
CONSTAR Int'l.		CTR	Delchamps, Inc.	(OTC)	DLCH
			Dell Computer	(OTC)	DELL
Consumers Water	(OTC)	CONW			
Cont'l Airlines		QCTA	Delmarva Power & Lt.		DEW
Cont'l Bank Corp.		CBK	Delta Air Lines		DAL
Cont'l Corp.		CIC	Deluxe Corp.		DLX
Control Data		CDA	DeSoto, Inc.		DSO
			Detroit Edison		DTE
Cooper Cos		COO			
Cooper Indus		CBE	Dexter Corp.		DEX
Cooper Tire & Rubber		CTB	Diagnostic Products		DP
Coors (Adolph) 'B'	(OTC)	ACCOB	Dial Corp.		DL
Cordis Corp.	(OTC)	CORD	Diamond Shamrock		DRM
			Diasonics, Inc.		DIA
Core Indus		CRI			
CoreStates Fin'l	(OTC)	CSFN	Dibrell Brothers	(OTC)	DBRL
Corning, Inc.		GLW	Diebold, Inc.		DBD
Costco Wholesale	(OTC)	COST	Digital Equipment		DEC
Countrywide Credit		CCR			

Name of Stock		Ticker Symbol	Name of Stock		Ticker Symbol
Dillard Dept. Stores		DDS	1838 Bond-Debenture		BDF
Dime Svgs Bank N.Y.		DME	El Paso Elec. Co.	(OTC)	ELPA
Dionex Dorp.	(OTC)	DNEX	Elcor Corp.		ELK
Discount Corp. of N.Y.		DCY	Emerson Electric		EMR
Disney (Walt)		DIS	Empire Dist Elec		EDE
Diversified Inds.		DMC	Energen Corp.		EGN
Dixie Yarns	(OTC)	DXYN	Engelhard Corp.		EC
Dofasco	(TSE)	DFS.TO	Engraph, Inc.	(OTC)	ENGH
Dole Food		DOL	Ennis Business Forms		EBF
Dollar General Corp.	(OTC)	DOLR	Enron Corp.		ENE
Dominican Bankshs.	(OTC)	DMBK	ENSERCH Corp.		ENS
Dominion Resources		D	Entergy Corp.		ETR
Dominican Textile	(TSE)	DTX.TO	Enterra Corp.		EN
Domtar, Inc.		DTC	Equifax, Inc.		EFX
Donaldson Co.		DCI	Equimark Corp.		EQK
Donnelley (R. R.) & Sons		DNY	Equitable Resources		EQT
Dover Corp.		DOV	Ericsson (ADR)(g)	(OTC)	ERICY
Dow Chemical		DOW	Esterline Technologies		ESL
Dow Jones & Co.		DJ	Ethyl Corp.		EY
Dravo Corp.		DRV	Everex Systems	(OTC)	EVRX
Dress Barn	(OTC)	DBRN	Excel Inds.	(ASE)	EXC
Dresser Inds.		DI	Exxon Corp.		XON
Dreyer's Grand	(OTC)	DRYR	FHP Int'l	(OTC)	FHPC
Dreyfus Corp.		DRY	FMC Corp.		FMC
Driefontein (ADR)	(OTC)	DRFNY	FPL Group		FPL
Drug Emporium	(OTC)	DEMP	Fab Industries	(ASE)	FIT
Du Pont		DD	Fabri-Centers of Amer.		FCA
Duff & Phelps		DNP	Fairchild Corp. 'A'		FA
Duke Power		DUK	Family Dollar Stores		FDO
Dun & Bradstreet		DNB	Fansteel, Inc.		FNL
Duplex Products	(ASE)	DPX	Farah, Inc.		FRA
Duriron Co.	(OTC)	DURI	Fay's, Inc.		FAY
Durr-Fillauer	(OTC)	DUFM	Fedders Corp.		FJQ
Duty Free Int'l	(OTC)	DFII	Federal Express		FDX
Dynamics Cp. of Amer.		DYA	Federal Home Loan Mtg		FRE
Dynascan	(OTC)	DYNA	Federal-Mogul		FMO
Dynatech Corp.	(OTC)	DYTC	Federal Nat'l Mtg.		FNM
EG & G, Inc.		EGG	Federal Paper Board		FBO
E-Systems		ESY	Federal Rlty Inv Trust		FRT
Eastern Enterprises		EFU	Federal Signal		FSS
Eastern Util Assoc.		EUA	Ferro Corp.		FOE
Eastman Kodak		EK	Fieldcrest Cannon		FLD
Eaton Corp.		ETN	Fifth Third Bancorp	(OTC)	FITB
Echlin, Inc.		ECH	Figgie Int'l 'A'	(OTC)	FIGIA
Echo Bay Mines	(ASE)	ECO	Filtertek, Inc.		FTK
Ecolab, Inc.		ECL	First Alabama	(OTC)	FABC
Edison Bros Stores		EBS	First Australia Fund	(ASE)	IAF
EDO Corp.		EDO	First Bank System		FBS
Edwards (A.G.)		AGE	First Chicago		FNB

Name of Stock		Ticker Symbol	Name of Stock		Ticker Symbol
First Fidelity Bancorp		FFB	Gandalf Technologies	(OTC)	GANDF
First Financial Mgmt.		FFM	Gannett Co.		GCI
First Interstate Bancorp		I	Gap (The), Inc.		GPS
First Mississippi		FRM	Garan, Inc.	(ASE)	GAN
			Gaylord Container 'A'	(ASE)	GCR
First of Amer. Bank		FOA			
First Union Corp.		FTU	GEICO Corp.		GEC
First Union Real Est.		FUR	GenCorp		GY
First Va. Banks		FVB	Genentech, Inc.		GNE
First Wachovia Corp.		FW	Gen'l Amer Investors		GAM
			Gen'l Binding	(OTC)	GBND
Firstar Corp.		FSR			
Fischer & Porter	(ASE)	FP	Gen'l Cinema		GCN
Fiserv Inc.	(OTC)	FISV	Gen'l DataComm Ind		GDC
Fleet/Norstar Fin'l		FNG	Gen'l Dynamics		GD
Fleetwood Enterpr		FLE	Gen'l Electric		GE
			Gen'l Host		GH
Fleming Cos.		FLM			
Flexsteel Inds.	(OTC)	FLXS	Gen'l Housewares		GHW
FlightSafety		FSI	Gen'l Mills		GIS
Florida East Coast		FLA	Gen'l Motors		GM
Florida Progress		FPC	Gen'l Motors 'E'		GME
			Gen'l Motors 'H'		GMH
Florida Rock	(ASE)	FRK			
Flowers Inds.		FLO	Gen'l Public Utilities		GPU
Fluke (John) Mfg	(ASE)	FKM	Gen'l Re Corp.		GRN
Fluor Corp.		FLR	Gen'l Signal		GSX
Food Lion 'B'	(OTC)	FDLNB	Genesco, Inc.		GCO
			Genovese Drug 'A'		GDXA
Foote, Cone & Belding		FCB			
Ford Motor		F	GenRad		GEN
Forest Labs.	(ASE)	FRX	Genuine Parts		GPC
Forest Oil	(OTC)	FOIL	GEO Int'l		GX
Foster Wheeler		FWC	Georgia Gulf		GGC
			Georgia-Pacific		GP
Fourth Financial	(OTC)	FRTH			
Franklin Electric	(OTC)	FELE	Gerber Products		GEB
Franklin Resources		BEN	Gerber Scientific		GRB
Free State Consol.	(OTC)	FSCNY	Germany Fund		GER
Freeport-McMoRan		FTX	Getty Petroleum		GTY
			Giant Food 'A'	(ASE)	GFSA
Fremont Gen'l	(OTC)	FRMT			
Frisch's Restaurants	(ASE)	FRS	Giant Group		GPO
Frontier Ins. Group		FTR	Gibson Greetings	(OTC)	GIBG
Fruit of the Loom	(ASE)	FTL	Gilbert Assoc.	(OTC)	GILBA
Fuji Photo (ADR)(g)	(OTC)	FUJIY	Gillette		GS
			Gitano Group		GIT
Fuller (H.B.)	(OTC)	FULL			
Fund American Cos.			Glatfelter (P.H.)	(ASE)	GLT
Fuqua Inds.		FQA	Glaxo Holdings (ADR)(g)		GLX
Furon Co.	(OTC)	FCBN	Gleason Corp.		GLE
GATX Corp.		GMT	Glenfed, Inc.		GLN
			Global Marine		GLM
GRC Int'l		GRH			
GTE Corp.		GTE	Global Yield Fund		PGY
GWC Corp.	(OTC)	GWCC	Golden Enterprises	(OTC)	GLDC
Gabelli Equity		GAB	Golden Nugget		GNG
Galoob (Lewis) Toys		GAL			

Name of Stock		Ticker Symbol	Name of Stock		Ticker Symbol
Golden Valley		GVF	Hartford Steam Boiler		HSB
Golden West Fin'l		GDW	Hartmarx Corp.		HMX
			Hasbro, Inc.	(ASE)	HAS
Good Guys	(OTC)	GGUY	Haverty Furniture	(OTC)	HAVT
Goodrich (B.F.)		GR			
Goodyear Tire		GT	Hawaiian Elec.		HE
Gould Pumps	(OTC)	GULD	Healthdyne, Inc.	(OTC)	HDYN
Grace (W. R.)		GRA	Hechunger Co. 'A'	(OTC)	HECHA
			Hecla Mining		HL
Graco, Inc.		GGG	Heekin Can	(OTC)	HEKN
Grainger (W. W.)		GWW			
Grand Metropolitn (ADR)(g)		GRM	Hees Int'l Bancorp.	(TSE)	HILTO
Graphic Inds.	(OTC)	GRPH	Heilig-Meyers		HMY
Graphic Scanning	(OTC)	GSCC	Heinz (H. J.)		HNZ
			Helene Curtis		HC
G't Atlantic & Pacific		GAP	Helmerich & Payne		HP
G't Lakes Chemical		GLK			
G't Northern Iron		GNI	Henley Group		HEN
G't Wesstern Fin'l		GWF	Hercules, Inc.		HPC
Green Mountain Pwr.		GMP	Hershey Foods		HSY
			Hewlett-Packard		HWP
Green Tree		GNT	Hexcel Corp.		HXL
Greenman Brothers	(ASE)	GMN			
Grossman's, Inc.	(OTC)	GROS	Highland Superstores		
Groundwater Techn.	(OTC)	GWTI	Hillenbrand Indus		HB
Grow Group		GRO	Hilton Hotels		HLT
			Hi-Shear Inds.		HSI
Grubb & Ellis		GBE	Hitachi, Ltd (ADR)(g)		HIT
Grumman Corp.		GQ			
Guardsman Products		GPI	Holly Corp.	(ASE)	HOC
Guilford Mills		GFD	Home Depot		HD
Gulf Canada Res.		GOU	HomeFed Corp.		HFD
			Homestake Mining		HM
Gulf States Util		GSU	Honda Motor (ADR)(g)		HMC
H&Q Healthcare Inv		HQH			
HRE Properties		HRE	Honeywell, Inc.		HON
Hadson Corp.		HAD	Hong Kong Telecom (ADR)		HKT
Hall (Frank B.) & Co.		FBH	Hon Industries	(OTC)	HONI
			Hormel (Geo. A.)		HRL
Halliburton Co.		HAL	Horn & Hardart	(ASE)	HOR
Hallwood Group		HWG			
Hamilton Oil			Horsham Corp.		HSM
Hancock Fabrics		HKF	Houghton Mifflin		HTN
Hancock (John) Invs. Tr.		JHI	Household Int'l		HI
			House of Fabrics		HF
Handleman Co.		HDL	Houston Inds.		HOU
Handy & Harman		HNH			
Hanna (M. A.) Co.		MAH	Hovnanian Enterpr.	(ASE)	HOV
Hannaford Bros		HRD	Hubbell, Inc., 'B'	(ASE)	HUBB
Hanson PLC (ADR)(g)		HAN	Hudson's Bay Co.	(TSE)	HBC.TO
			Hudson Foods 'A'		HFI
Harcourt Brace Jov.		HBJ	Huffy Corp.		HUF
Harland (John H.)		JH			
Harley-Davidson		HDI	Hughes Supply		HUG
Harnischfeger Inds.		HPH	Humana, Inc.		HUM
Harris Corp.		HRS	Huntington Bancshs.	(OTC)	HBAN
			Hunt (J.B.)	(OTC)	JBHT
Harsco Corp.		HSC	Hunt Mfg		HUN

Name of Stock		Ticker Symbol	Name of Stock		Ticker Symbol
IBP, Inc.		IBP	Italy Fund		ITA
ICF Int'l	(OTC)	ICFIA	ITEL Corp.		ITL
IE Industries		IEL			
IES Industries		IES	JB's Restaurants	(OTC)	JBBB
IMC Fertilizer		IFL	JLG Industries	(OTC)	JLGI
			JSB Financial	(OTC)	JSBF
I.N.B. Financial	(OTC)	INBF	JWP Inc.		JWP
ITT Corp.		ITT	Jackpot Enterprises		J
Idaho Power		IDA			
IDEX Corp.		IEX	Jacobson Stores	(OTC)	JCBS
Illinois Power		IPC	James River		JR
			Jamesway Corp.		JMY
Illinois Tool Works		ITW	Jan Bell Marketing	(ASE)	JBM
Imasco Ltd.	(TSE)	IMS.TO	Jannock Ltd.	(TSE)	JN.TO
IMCERA Group		IMA			
Imo Industries		IMD	Japan OTC Equity Fund		JOF
Imperial Chem (ADR)(g)		ICI	Jefferson-Pilot Corp.		JP
			Johnson & Johnson		JNJ
Imperial Oil Ltd.		IMO	Johnson Controls		JCI
Inacomp Computer	(OTC)	INAC	Johnson Worldwide	(OTC)	JWAIA
Inco, Ltd.		N			
Indiana Energy		IEI	Joslyn Corp.	(OTC)	JOSL
Ingersoll-Rand		IR	Jostens, Inc.		JOS
			Justins Inds.	(OTC)	JSTN
Inland Steel		IAD	KLA Instruments	(OTC)	KLAC
Inspiration Resources		IRC	KLM Royal Dutch (g)		KLM
Instron Corp	(ASE)	ISN			
Integrated Device	(OTC)	IDTI	K mart Corp.		KM
Intel Corp.	(OTC)	INTC	KN Energy		KNE
			Kaman Corp.	(OTC)	KAMNA
Intelligent Electronics	(OTC)	INEL	Kaneb Services		KAB
Interface Inc. 'A'	(OTC)	IFSIA	Kansas City Power & Lt		KLT
Intergraph Corp.	(OTC)	INGR			
Interlake Corp.		IK	Kansas City South'n Ind.		KSU
Intermet Corp.	(OTC)	INMT	Kansas Gas & Elec		KGE
			Kansas Power & Light		KAN
Int'l Aluminum		IAL	Katy Inds.		KT
Int'l Business Mach.		IBM	Kaufman & Broad Home		KBH
Int'l Corona Corp. 'A'	(TSE)	ICRA.TO			
Int'l Dairy Queen 'A'	(OTC)	INDQA	Kaydon Corp.	(OTC)	KDON
Int'l Flavors & Frag.		IFF	Kellogg		K
			Kellwood Co.		KWD
Int'l Game Tech.		IGT	Kelly Services 'A'	(OTC)	KELYA
Int'l Multifoods		IMC	Kemper Corp.		KEM
Int'l Paper		IP			
Int'l Rectifier		IRF	Kemper High Income		KHI
Int'l Technology		ITX	Kennametal, Inc.		KMT
			Kentucky Utilities		KU
Interpublic Group		IPG	Kerr Glass Mfg		KGM
Inter-Regional Fin'l.		IFG	Kerr-McGee Corp.		KMG
Interstate Power		IPW			
InterTan, Inc.		ITN	KeyCorp.		KEY
Invacare Corp.	(OTC)	IVCR	Keystone Consol.		KES
			Keystone Int'l		KII
Iowa-Illinois G & E		IWG	Key Tronic	(OTC)	KTCC
Iowa Southern			Kimball Int'l 'B'	(OTC)	KBALB
IPALCO Enterprises		IPL	Kimberly-Clark		KMB

Name of Stock		Ticker Symbol	Name of Stock		Ticker Symbol
King World Productions		KWP	Lincoln Telecom.	(OTC)	LTEC
Kloof Gold Mng ADR	(OTC)	KLOFY	Litton Inds.		LIT
Knight-Ridder, Inc.		KRI	Liz Claiborne		LIZ
Knogo Corp.		KNO	Lockheed Corp.		LK
			Loctite Corp.		LOC
Koger Properties		KOG			
Kollmorgen Corp.		KOL	Loews Corp.		LTR
Korea Fund		KF	Logicon Inc.		LGN
Kroger Co.		KR	Lomas & Nettleton Mtg		LOM
Kuhlman Corp.		KUH	Lone Star Inds.		LCE
			Long Island Lighting		LIL
Kulicke & Soffa	(OTC)	KLIC			
Kyocera Corp. (ADR)(g)		KYO	Longs Drug Stores		LDG
Kysor Ind'l		KZ	Longview Fibre		LFB
L.A. Gear, Inc.		LA	Loral Corp.		LOR
L & N Housing		LHC	Lotus Development	(OTC)	LOTS
			Louisiana Land Expl.		LLX
LG&E Energy Corp.		LGE			
LTV Corp.		LTV	Louisiana-Pacific		LPX
Labatt (John) 'A'	(TSE)	LBT.TO	Lowe's Cos		LOW
Laclede Gas		LG	Lubrizol Corp.		LZ
Laclede Steel	(OTC)	LCLD	Luby's Cafeterias		LUB
			Lukens, Inc.		LUC
LAC Minerals		LAC			
LADD Furniture	(OTC)	LADF	Luria (L.) & Son	(ASE)	LUR
Lafarge Corp.		LAF	Lyondell Petrochemical		LYO
Laidlaw, Inc., 'B'		LDWB	M/A-Com, Inc.		MAI
Lamson & Sessions		LMS	MCI Communications	(OTC)	MCIC
			MCN Corp.		MCN
Lancaster Colony	(OTC)	LANC			
Lance, Inc.	(OTC)	LNCE	MDU Resources		MDU
Lands' End		LE	MEI Diversified		MEI
La Petite Academy	(OTC)	LPAI	MFS Multimarket Income		MMT
La Quinta Mtr. Inns		LQM	MGI Properties		MGI
			MNC Financial		MNC
Lawson Products	(OTC)	LAWS			
Lawter Int'l		LAW	M.S. Carriers	(OTC)	MSCA
La-Z Boy Chair		LZB	MTS Systems	(OTC)	MTSC
LeaRonal, Inc.		LRI	MacMillan Bloedel	(TSE)	MB.TO
Lee Enterprises		LEE	Magma Power	(OTC)	MGMA
			MagneTek, Inc.		MAG
Leggett & Platt		LEG			
Legg Mason, Inc.		LM	Malaysia Fund		MF
Lennar Corp.		LEN	Manitowoc Co.	(OTC)	MANT
Leslie Fay		LES	Manor Care		MNR
Leucadia National		LUK	Manufacturers Hanover		MHC
			Manufacturers Nat'l	(OTC)	MNTL
Liberty All-Star		USA			
Liberty Corp.		LC	Manville Corp.		MVL
Life Technologies	(OTC)	LTEK	MAPCO, Inc.		MDA
Lifetime Corp.		LFT	Marcus Corp.	(OTC)	MRCS
Lillian Vernon		LVC	Marion Merrell Dow		MKC
			Mark IV Inds.		IV
Lilly (Eli)		LLY			
Lilly Ind'l 'A'	(OTC)	LICIA	Marriott Corp.		MHS
Limited, Inc.		LTD	Marshall & Ilsley	(OTC)	MRIS
LIN Broadcasting	(OTC)	LINB	Marshall Industries		MI
Lincoln Nat'l Corp.		LNC			

Name of Stock		Ticker Symbol	Name of Stock		Ticker Symbol
Marsh & McLennan		MMC	Midwest Resources		MWR
Marsh Supermarkets 'B'	(OTC)	MARSB	Miller (Herman)	(OTC)	MLHR
			Millipore Corp.		MIL
Martin Marietta		ML	Minnesota Mining		MMM
Masco Corp.		MAS			
Masco Inds.	(OTC)	MASX	Minnesota Power & Lt		MPL
Material Sciences	(ASE)	MSC	Mirage Resorts		MIR
Matsushita Elec.(ADR)(g)		MC	Mitchell Energy & Dev	(ASE)	MND
			Mobil Corp.		MOB
Mattel, Inc.		MAT	Modine Mft.	(OTC)	MODI
Maxus Energy		MXS			
May Dept Stores		MA	Molecular Biosystems		MB
Maytag Corp.		MYG	Molex, Inc.	(OTC)	MOLX
McCaw Cellular 'A'	(OTC)	MCAWA	Molson Cos. Ltd 'A' (TSE)		MOLA.TO
			Monarch Mach Tool		MMO
McClatchy Newspapers		MNI	Monsanto.		MTC
McCormick & Co.	(OTC)	MCCRK			
McDermott Int'l		MDR	Montana Power		MTP
McDonald's Corp.		MCD	Montedison (ADR)(g)		MNT
McDonnell Douglas		MD	Montgomery St, Inc., Sec		MTC
			Moog, Inc., 'A'	(ASE)	MOGA
McGraw-Hill		MHP	Moore Corp.		MCL
McKesson Corp.		MCK			
Mead Corp.		MEA	Morgan Grenfell Smallcap		MGC
Measurex Corp.		MX	Morgan (J. P.) & Co.		JPM
Medco Containment	(OTC)	MCCS	Morgan Products		MGN
			Morgan Stanley		MS
Media General	(ASE)	MEGA	Morrison, Inc.	(OTC)	MORR
Medicine Shoppe Int'l	(OTC)	MSII			
MEDIQ, Inc.	(ASE)	MED	Morrison Knudsen		MRN
Medtronic, Inc.		MDT	Morton Int'l		MII
Medusa Corp.		MSA	Mosinee Paper	(OTC)	MOSI
			Motorola, Inc.		MOT
Mellon Bank Corp.		MEL	Multimedia, Inc.	(OTC)	MMEDC
Melville Corp.		MES			
Mentor Graphics	(OTC)	MENT	Murphy Oil Corp.		MUR
Mercantile Bancorp.	(OTC)	MTRC	Mut'l of Omaha Int Sh		MUO
Mercantile Stores		MST	Myers Inds.	(ASE)	MYE
			Mylan Labs		MYL
Merchants National	(OTC)	MCHN	NBD Bancorp		NBD
Merck & Co.		MRK			
Meredith Corp.		MDP	NCH Corp.		NCH
Meridian Bancorp.	(OTC)	MRDN	NCNB Corp.		NCB
Merrill Lynch & Co.		MER	NCR Corp.		NCR
			NEC Corp. (ADR)(g)	(OTC)	NIPNY
Merry-Go-Round		MGR	NIPSCO Inds.		NI
Mesa Ltd Part.		MLP			
Mexico Fund		MXF	NS Group		NSS
Meyer (Fred)	(OTC)	MEYR	NUI Corp.		NUI
Michael Foods	(OTC)	MIKL	NWNL Cos.		NWN
			NACCO Indus, 'A'		NC
Michigan Nat'l Corp.	(OTC)	MNCO	Nalco Chemical		NLC
Micron Technology		MU			
Micropolis Corp.	(OTC)	MLIS	Nash Finch Co.	(OTC)	NAFC
Microsoft Corp.	(OTC)	MSFT	Nashua Corp.		NSH
Midlantic Corp.	(OTC)	MIDL	Nat'l Bank of Canada	(TSE)	NA.TO
			National City Corp.		NCC
MidSouth Corp.	(OTC)	MSRR	National Computer	(OTC)	NLCS

Name of Stock		Ticker Symbol	Name of Stock		Ticker Symbol
National Convenience Str		NCS	Northern States Power		NSP
National Data Corp.	(OTC)	NDTA	Northern Telecom Ltd		NT
National Education		NEC			
National Fuel Gas		NFG	Northern Trust Corp.	(OTC)	NTRS
Nationsl Intergroup		NII	Northrop Corp.		NOC
			Northw'n Pub. Serv.		NPS
National Medical Entpr		NME	Northwest Nat. Gas	(OTC)	NWNG
National Patent Dev.	(ASE)	NPD	Norwest Corp.		NOB
National Pizza 'A'	(OTC)	PIZA			
National Presto Ind.		NPK	Nova Corp.		NVA
National Semiconductor		NSM	Novell, Inc.	(OTC)	NOVL
			Novellus Sys.	(OTC)	NVLS
National Service Ind.		NSI	Novo-Nordisk (ADR)(g)		NVO
National-Standard Co.		NSD	Nucor Corp.		NUE
Navistar Int'l		NAV			
Neiman-Marcus		NMG	Numac Oil & Gas	(ASE)	NMC
NERCO, Inc.		NER	Nuveen Muni Value Fund		NUV
			NYNEX Corp.		NYN
Neutrogena Corp.	(OTC)	NGNA	OHM Corp.		OHM
Nevada Power		NVP	OMI Corp.	(ASE)	AHM
Newell Co.		NWL			
New England Bus.	(OTC)	NEBS	Oakwood Homes		OH
New England Elec		NES	Occidental Petroleum		OXY
			Ocean Drill & Expl		ODR
Newhall Land & Farming		NHL	Office Depot	(OTC)	ODEP
New Jersey Resources		NJR	Ogden Corp.		OG
New Jersey Steel	(OTC)	NJST			
New Line Cinema	(ASE)	NLN	Ogden Projects		OPI
Newmont Mining		NEM	Ohio Casualty	(OTC)	OCAS
			Ohio Edison		OEC
New Plan Rlty Trust		NPR	Oklahoma Gas & Elec		OGE
Newport Corp.	(OTC)	NEWP	Old Kent Financial	(OTC)	OKEN
News Corp. Ltd. (ADR)		NWS			
N.Y. State Elec. &Gas		NGE	Olin Corp.		OLN
N.Y. Times	(ASE)	NYTA	Olsten Corp.	(ASE)	OLS
			Omnicare, Inc.		OCR
Niagara Mohawk		NMK	Omnicom Group		OMC
Niagara Share		NGS	Oneida, Ltd.		OCQ
Nichols Institute 'C'	(ASE)	LABC			
Nichols Research	(OTC)	NRES	ONEOK, Inc.		OKE
Nicolet Instrument		NIC	Optical Radiation	(OTC)	ORCO
			Oracle Systems	(OTC)	ORCL
NICOR, Inc.		GAS	Orange & Rockland Util		ORU
NIKE, Inc. 'B'		NKE	Orange-Co.		OJ
Nissan Motor ADR(g)	(OTC)	NSANY			
Noble Affiliates		NBL	Oregon Metallurgical	(OTC)	OREM
Noranda, Inc.	(TSE)	NOR.TO	Oregon Steel Mills		OS
			Orion Capital		OC
Norcen Energy Res.	(TSE)	NCN.TO	Orion Pictures		OPC
Nord Resources		NRD	Oryx Energy Co.		ORX
Nordson Corp.	(OTC)	NDSN			
Nordstrom, Inc.	(OTC)	NOBE	Oshawa Group 'A'	(TSE)	OSHA.TO
Norfolk Southern		NSC	Oshkosh B'Gosh 'A'	(OTC)	GOSHA
			Otter Tail Power	(OTC)	OTTR
Norsk Hydro (ADR)(g)		NHY	Outboard Marine		OM
Nortek, Inc.		NTK	Overseas Shipholding		OSG
Northeast Utilities		NU	Owens & Minor		OMI

Name of Stock		Ticker Symbol	Name of Stock		Ticker Symbol
Owens-Corning		OCF	Phila Suburban		PSC
Oxford Indus		OXM	Philip Morris Cos		MO
PHH Corp.		PHH	Philips Elec (NY Shs)(g)		PHG
PHM Corp.		PHM	Phillips Petroleum		P
PNC Financial		PNC	Phililps-Van Heusen		PVH
PPG Inds.		PPG	Piccadily Cafeterias	(OTC)	PICC
PS Group Inc.		PSG	Pic N'Save	(OTC)	PICN
PSI Resources, Inc.		PIN	Piedmont Natural Gas		PHY
PACCAR Inc.	(OTC)	PCAR	Pier One Imports		PIR
Pacific Dunlop (ADR)(g)	(OTC)	PDLPY	Pinnacle West Capital		PNW
Pacific Enterprises		PET	Pioneer Elec. (ADR)(g)		PIO
Pacific Gas & Elec		PCG	Pioneer Fin'l Svcs		PFS
Pacific Scientific		PSX	Pioneer Hi-Bred	(OTC)	PHYB
Pacific Telesis		PAC	Pioneer-Standard	(OTC)	PIOS
PacifiCare Health Sys	(OTC)	PHSY	Pitney Bowes		PBI
PacifiCorp.		PPW	Pittston Co.		PCO
PW CI Regional Fin'l Fd	(MF)	PREAX	Pittway Corp. 'A'	(ASE)	PRYA
PaineWebber Group		PWJ	Placer Dome		PDG
Pall Corp.		PLL	Plains Petroleum		PLP
Pan Am Corp.		PN	Playboy Enterprises 'B'		PLA
PanCanadian Petr.	(TSE)	PCP.TO	Ply-Gem Inds.	(ASE)	PGI
Panhandle Eastern		PEL	Pogo Producing		PPP
Paramount Communic		PCI	Polaroid Corp.		PRD
Park Electrochemical		PKE	Policy Mgmt. Sys.		PMS
Park-Ohio Inds.	(OTC)	PKOH	PolyGram NV (NY Sgs)		PLG
Parker Drilling		PKD	Pope & Talbot		POP
Parker-Hannifin		PH	Porta Systems	(ASE)	PSI
Pathe Communications		PCC	Portec, Inc.		
Patriot Premium Div'd		PDF	Portland General		PGN
Pegasus Gold	(ASE)	PGU	Portugal Fund		PGF
Penn Central Corp.		PC	Potlatch Corp.		PCH
Penney (J. C.)		JCP	Potomac Elec. Power		POM
Penn. Power & Lt		PPL	Power Corp. of Canada	(TSE)	POW.TO
Pennzoil Co.		PZL	Pratt & Lambert	(ASE)	PM
			Precision Castparts		PCP
Pentair, Incs.	(OTC)	PNTA	Premark Int'l		PMI
PENWEST Ltd.	(OTC)	PENW	Premier Industrial		PRE
Peoples Energy		PGL	Preston Corp.	(OTC)	PTRK
Pep Boys		PBY	Price Co.	(OTB)	PCLB
PepsiCo, Inc.		PEP	Primark Corp.		PMK
Perini Corp.	(ASE)	PCR	Primerica Corp.		PA
Perkin-Elmer		PKN	Proctor & Gamble		PG
Perkins Family Rest		PFR	Progressive (Ohio)		PGR
Perry Drug Stores		PDS	Proler Int'l		PS
Petrie Stores		PST	Promus Cos.		PRI
Petroleum & Resources		PEO	Property Capital Trust	(ASE)	PCT
Petrollite Corp.	(OTC)	PLIT	Providence Energy	(ASE)	PVY
Pfizer, Inc.		PFE	Provident Life 'B'	(OTC)	PACCB
Phelps Dodge		PD			
Phila. Electric		PE			

Name of Stock	Ticker Symbol		Name of Stock	Ticker Symbol	
Provigo Ind.	(TSE)	PGI.TO	Rochester Gas & Elec		RGS
Public Serv. Enterprises		PEG	Rochester Tel.		RTC
			Rockwell Int'l		ROK
Public Serv. (Colo.)		PSR	Rogers Corp.	(ASE)	ROG
Public Serv. (N.H.)		PNH			
Public Serv. (N.Mex.)		PNM	Rohm & Haas		ROH
Puget Sound Power & Lt		PSD	Rohr Indus		RHR
Pultizer Publishing	(OTC)	PLTZ	Rollins Environmental		REN
			Rollins, Inc.		ROL
Puritan Bennet	(OTC)	PBEN	Rollins Truck Leasing		RLC
QMS, Inc.		AQM			
QVC Network	(OTC)	QVCN	Rose's Stores 'B'	(OTC)	RSTOB
Quaker Chemical	(OTC)	QCHM	Ross Stores	(OTC)	ROST
Quaker Oats		OAT	Rouse Co.	(OTC)	ROUS
			Rowan Cos.		RDC
Quaker State Corp.		KSF	Royal Bank of Canada	(TSE)	RY.TO
Quality Food Centers	(OTC)	QFCI			
Quanex Corp.		NX	Royal Dutch Petr.		RD
Quantum Chemical		CUE	Royal Trustco Ltd.	(TSE)	RYL.TO
Quantum Corp.	(OTC)	QNTM	Royce Value Trust		RVT
			Rubbermaid, Inc.		RBD
Questar Corp.		STR	Ruddick Corp.		RDK
Quick & Reilly Group		BQR			
Quixote Corp.	(OTC)	QUIX	Russell Corp.		RML
RJM Nabisco Holdings		RN	Russ Togs		RTS
RPM, Inc.	(OTC)	RPOW	Ryan's Family	(OTC)	RYAN
			Ryder System		R
Racal Telecom (ADR)(g)		RTG	Rykoff-Sexton		RYK
Ralston Purina		RAL			
Ranger Oil Ltd		RGO	Ryland Group		RYL
Rank Organ (ADR)(g)	(OTC)	RANKY	Rymer Foods		RYR
Raychem Corp.		RYC	SCEcorp	(OTC)	SCIS
			SHL Systemhouse	(OTC)	SHKIF
Raymond Corp.	(OTC)	RAYM			
Raytheon Co.		RTN	S-K-I Ltd.	(OTC)	SKII
Reader's Digest		RDA	SPS Technologies		ST
Reading & Bates		RB	SPX Corp.		SPW
Recognition Equip		REC	Saatchi (ADR)		SAA
			SafeCard Services		SSI
Reebok Int'l		RBK			
Reliance Group Hldgs		REL	SAFECO Corp.	(OTC)	SAFC
Renaissance Energy	(TSE)	RES.TO	Safeguard Scientifics		SFE
Repsol (ADR)(g)		REP	Safety-Kleen		SK
Republic Automotive	(OTC)	RAUT	Safeway, Inc.		SWY
			St Joseph Lt & Power		SAJ
Republic Gypsum		RGC			
Reuters (ADR)(g)	(OTC)	RTRSY	St. Jude Medical	(OTC)	STJM
Reynolds & Reynolds		REY	St. Paul Bancorp	(OTC)	SPBC
Reynolds Metals		RLM	Str. Paul Cos.	(OTC)	STPL
Rhone Poulenc (ADR)(g)		RPPRA	Salomon Bros Fund		SBF
			Salomon, Inc.		SB
Rhone-Poulenc Rorer		RPR			
Richardson Electr.	(OTC)	RELL	Southwest Gas		SWX
Rite Aid Corp.		RAD	Spain Fund		SNF
Roadway Services	(OTC)	ROAD	Sparton Corp.		SPA
Robertson-Ceco		RHH	Spiegel, Inc. 'A'	(OTC)	SPGLA
Rochester Community	(OTC)	RCSB	Sprague Technologies		SPG

Name of Stock	Ticker Symbol	Name of Stock	Ticker Symbol
Springs Inds.	SMI	Sysco Corp.	SYY
Square D	SQD	System Software (OTC)	SSAX
Standard Brand Paint	SBP		
Standard Commercial	STW	TCBY Enterprises	TBY
Standard Motor Prod	SMP	TCW Conv. Sec. Fund	CVT
		TDK Corp. (ADR)(g)	TDK
Standard-Pacific L.P.	SPF	TECO Energy	TE
Standard Products	SPD	TJ International (OTC)	TJCO
Standard Register (OTC)	SREG		
Standex Int'l	SXI	TJX Companies	TJX
Stanhome, Inc.	STH	TNP Enterprises	TNP
		TRW Inc.	TRW
Stanley Works	SWK	Tab Products (ASE)	TBP
Staples, Inc. (OTC)	SPLS	Taiwan Fund	TWN
Star Banc Corp. (OTC)	STRZ		
Starrett (L.S.)	SCX	Talley Inds.	TAL
State Street Boston (OTC)	STBK	Tambrands, Inc.	TMB
		Tandem Computers	TDM
Steel Technologies (OTC)	STTX	Tandy Corp.	TAN
Stelco Inc. 'A' (TSE)	STEA.TO	Tandycrafts, Inc.	TAC
Sterling Bancorp	STL		
Sterling Chemicals	STX	Teck Corp. 'B' (TSE)	TEKB.TO
Sterling Optical	EYE	Tecumseh Products (OTC)	TECU
		Tektronix, Inc.	TEK
Sterling Software	SSW	Tele Communic. 'A' (OTC)	TCOMA
Stewart & Stevenson (OTC)	SSSS	Teledyne, Inc.	TDY
Stolt Tankers (OTC)	STLTF		
Stone Container	STO	Teleflex, Inc. (ASE)	TFX
Stone & Webster	SW	Telefonica Espana (ADR)(g)	TEF
		Telefonos de Chile (ADR)(g)	TCH
Stoneridge Resources	SRE	Telefonos de Mexico (ADR)	TMX
Storage Technology	STK	Telephone & Data	TDS
Stratus Computer	SRA		
Stride Rite Corp.	SRR	Telxon (OTC)	TLXN
Stryker Corp. (OTC)	STRY	Temple-Inland	TIN
		Templeton Emerg'g	EMF
Student Loan Marketing	SLM	Tennant Co. (OTC)	TANT
Sun Company	SUN	Tenneco, Inc.	TGT
Sun Distributors 'B'	SDPB		
Sundstrand Corp.	SNS	Teradyne, Inc.	TER
Sun Electric	SE	Terex Corp.	TEX
		Tesoro Petroleum	TSO
Sun Energy Partners	SLP	Texaco, Inc.	TX
Sun Microsystems (OTC)	SUNW	Texas Inds	TXI
Sunrise Medical (OTC)	SNMD		
Sunshine Mining	SSC	Texas Instruments	TXN
SunTrust Banks	STI	Texas Pacific Land Trust	TPL
		Texas Utilities	TXU
Super Food Services	SFS	Textron, Inc.	TXT
Superior Inds. Int'l	SUP	Thai Fund	TTF
Super Valu Stores	SVU		
Swiss Helvetia Fund	SWZ	Thermo Electron	TMO
Symbol Technologies	SBL	Thermo Instrument (ASE)	THI
		Thiokol Corp.	TKC
Syms Corp.	SYM	Thomas & Betts	TNB
Synovus Financial	SNV	Thomas Inds	TII
Syntex	SYN	Thomson Corp. (TSE)	TOC.TO

Name of Stock		Ticker Symbol	Name of Stock		Ticker Symbol
Thor Inds.		THO	USX-Marathon Group		MRO
3Com Corp.	(OTC)	COMS	USX-U.S. Steel Group		X
Tidewater, Inc.		TDW	Unifi, Inc.		UFI
Tiffany & Co.		TIF	UniFirst Corp.		UNF
Times Mirror Co.		TMC	Uniforce	(OTC)	UNFR
Time Warner		TWX	Unilever NV (NY Shs)(g)		UN
Timken Co.		TKR	Unilever PLC (ADR)(g)		UL
Titan Corp.		TTN	Union Camp		UCC
Tokheim Corp.		TOK	Union Carbide		UK
Toll Brothers		TOL	Union Corp.		UCO
Tootsie Roll Inds		TR	Union Electric		UEP
Torchmark Corp.		TMK	Union Pacific		UNP
Toro Co.		TTC	Union Texas Petr		UTH
Toronto-Dominion	(TSE)	TD.TO	Unisys Corp.		UIS
Tosco Corp.		TTL	United Dominion	(TSE)	UDI.TO
Total Petroleum	(ASE)	TPN	United Dominion Rlty		UDR
Town & Country 'A'		TNC	United HealthCare	(OTC)	UNIH
Toyota Motor ADR(g)	(OTC)	TOYOY	United Illuminating		UIL
Toys R Us		TOY	United Industrial Corp.		UIC
TransAlta Utilities	(TSE)	TAU.TO	United Inns		UI
Transamerica		TA	United Kingdom Fund		UKM
TransCanada Pipelines		TRP	U.S. Bankcorp	(OTC)	USBC
TransCapital Financial		TFC	U.S. Cellular	(ASE)	USM
Transco Energy		E	U.S. Healthcare	(OTC)	USHC
TransTechnology		TT	U.S. Shoe		USR
Trans World Music	(OTC)	TWMC	U.S. Surgical		USS
Travelers Corp.		TIC	U.S. Trust	(OTC)	USTC
Triad Systems	(OTC)	TRSC	United Stationers	(OTC)	USTR
Tribune Co.		TRB	United Technologies		UTX
Tri-Continental		TY	United Telecom		UT
Trinity Inds.		TRN	United Water Res		UWR
TRINOVA Corp.		TNV	Unitrode Corp.		UTR
Triton Energy		OIL	Univar Corp.		UVX
Tucson Elec Power		TEP	Universal Corp.		UVV
Tultex Corp.		TTX	Universal Foods		UFC
Turner Broadcast 'B'		TBSB	Unocal Corp.		UCL
Tyco Labs		TYC	Unocal Exploration Corp.		UXC
Tyco Toys	(OTC)	TTOY	Upjohn Co.		UPJ
Tyler Corp.		TYL	USAir Group		U
Tyson Foods 'A'	(OTC)	TYSNA	USLIFE Corp.		USH
UAL Corp.		UAL			
UGI Corp.		UGI	U.S. West Inc.		USW
UJB Financial Corp.		UJB	U.S. West NewVector		
UNC Inc.		UNC	UtiliCorp United		UCU
			V.F. Corp.		VFC
UNUM Corp.		UNM	VLSI Technology	(OTC)	VLSI
USF&G Corp.		FG			
USG Corp.		USG	VWR Corp.	(OTC)	VWRX
USLICO Corp.		USC	Valero Energy		VLO
UST Inc.		UST	Valhi, Inc.		VHI

Name of Stock	Ticker Symbol		Name of Stock	Ticker Symbol	
Valley National	(OTC)	VNCP	Westcoast Energy		WE
Valmont Inds.	(OTC)	VALM	Western Co. No Amer		WSN
			Western Deep Lev.	(OTC)	WDEPY
Valspar (The) Corp.	(ASE)	VAL	Western Digital		WDC
Van Dorn		VDC	Western Publishing	(OTC)	WPGI
Varco Int'l		VRC			
Varian Associates		VAR	Westinghouse Electric		WX
Varity Corp.		VAT	Westmark Int'l	(OTC)	WMRK
			Westmoreland Coal	(OTC)	WMOR
Varien Corp.	(OTC)	VRLN	Weston (George)	(TSE)	WN.TO
Viacom, Inc.	(ASE)	VIA	Westvaco Corp.		W
VICORP Restaurants	(OTC)	VRES			
Vishay Intertechn'gy		VSH	Wetterau Inc.	(OTC)	WETT
Vista Chemical		VC	Weyerhaeuser Co.		WY
			Wheelabrator Tech		WTI
Volt Info. Sciences	(OTC)	VOLT	Wheeling Pitt Steel		WHX
Volvo AB (ADR)(g)	(OTC)	VOLVY	Whirlpool Corp.		WHR
Vons Cos		VON			
Vulcan Materials		VMC	Whitehall Corp.		WHT
WD-40 Co.	(OTC)	WDFC	Whitman Co.		WH
			Whittaker Corp.		WKR
WMS Industries		WMS	WICOR, Inc.		WIC
WPL Holdings, Inc.		WPH	Willamette Ind.	(OTC)	WMTT
WPP Group (ADR)	(OTC)	WPPGY			
Wachovia Corp.		WB	Willcox & Gibbs		WG
Wackenhut		WAK	Williams Cos.		WMB
			Willis Corroon (ADR)(g)		WCG
Wainoco Oil		WOL	Windmere Corp.		WND
Walbro Corp.	(OTC)	WALB	Winn-Dixie Stores		WIN
Walgreen Co.		WAG			
Wallace Computer Svs		WCS	Winnebago		WGO
Wal-Mart Stores		WMT	Wisconsin Energy		WEC
			Wisconsin Pub. Serv		WPS
Wang Labs 'B'	(ASE)	WANB	Witco Corp.		WIT
Warner-Lambert		WLA	Wolohan Lumber	(OTC)	WLHN
Washington Energy	(OTC)	WECO			
Washington Fed'l S&L	(OTC)	WFSL	Wolverine World Wide		WWW
Washington Gas Light		WGL	Woolworth Corp.		Z
			Worthington Inds.	(OTC)	WTHG
Washington Mutual	(OTC)	WAMU	Wrigley (Wm.) Jr.		WWY
Washington National		WNT	Wyle Labs		WYL
Washington Post		WPO			
Washington REIT	(ASE)	WRE	Wyman-Gordon	(OTC)	WWW
Washington Water Pwr		WWP	Wynn's Int'l		WN
			Xerox Corp.		XRX
Waste Management		WMX	XTRA Corp.		XTR
Watkins-Johnson		WJ	Yellow Freight Sys.	(OTC)	YELL
Wausau Paper	(OTC)	WSAU			
Webb (Del) Corp.		WBB	Zenith Electronics		ZE
Weis Markets		WMK	Zero Corp.		ZRO
			Zions Bancorp	(OTC)	ZION
Wellman, Inc.		WLM	Zurn Inds.		ZRN
Wells Fargo		WFC			
Wendy's Int'l		WEN			
Werner Enterprises	(OTC)	WERN			
West Co.		WST			

3.7 COMPONENTS OF THE DOW JONES STOCK AVERAGES AND OTHER STOCK MARKET INDEXES

This section provides a description of the most widely used stock market averages and the components of the three Dow Jones stock averages. Note that Barron's *provides weekly performance data for most of these averages.*

3.7.1 Dow Jones Industrial Average

The Dow Jones Industrial Average (DJIA) is an average of the prices of the following 30 well-known, predominantly blue-chip, industrial stocks. The continuity of this average is maintained by changing the divisor whenever there is a substitution, stock split, or stock dividend that would change the average by five points or more.

AT&T
Allied-Signal
Aluminum Company of
   America
American Express
Bethlehem Steel

Boeing
Caterpillar
Chevron
Coca-Cola
Disney (Walt)

Du Pont
East Kodak
Exxon
General Electric
General Motors

Goodyear
IBM
International Paper
McDonald's
Merck & Co.

Minnesota Mining and
   Manufacturing
Morgan (J. P.)
Philip Morris
Procter & Gamble
Sears, Roebuck

Texaco
Union Carbide
United Technology
Westinghouse
Woolworth

3.7.2 Dow Jones Transportation Average

The Dow Jones Transportation Average is an average of the prices of the following 20 transportation stocks.

AMR Corporation
Airborne Freight
Alaska Air
American President Companies
Burlington North

CSX Corporation
Carolina Freight

Consolidated Freight
Consolidated Rail Corporation
Delta Air

Federal Express
Norfolk Southern
Roadway
Ryder System
Santa Fe Pacific

Southwest Airlines
UAL Corporation
USAir Group

Union Pacific
XTRA Corp.

3.7.3 Dow Jones Utility Average

The Dow Jones Utilitly Average is an average of the prices of the following 15 utility stocks.

American Electric Power
Arkla, Inc.
Centerior
Commonwealth Edison
Consolidated Edison
Consolidated Natural Gas
Detroit Edison
Houston Ind

Niagara Mohawk Power
Pacific Gas & Electric
Panhandle EPL
Peoples Energy
Philadelphia Electric
Public Service Enterprises
SCEcorp

3.7.4 The Standard & Poor's 500 Stock Index (Composite Index)

The S&P 500, broader than the Dow Jones 30 Industrial, is a more scientifically constructed index, which includes 425 industrial stocks, 50 utilities, and 25 railroads. Each stock is weighted according to the total number of shares outstanding.

3.7.5 The New York Stock Exchange Index

The NYSE Index includes all of the 2,000-plus stocks listed on the NYSE. The stocks are weighted by the number of shares listed.

3.7.6 The American Stock Exchange Index

The AMEX Index includes more than 1,000 companies, most of them smaller than those listed on the NYSE.

3.7.7 National Association of Securities Dealers Automated Quotations Index

The NASDAQ Index includes over 4,500 stocks traded over the counter; these are smaller companies than those listed on the NYSE or AMEX.

3.7.8 Wilshire 5000 Index

The Wilshire 5000 Index is produced by Wilshire Associates and is a blend of all exchanges and over-the-counter markets. It includes 5,000 stocks.

3.8 STATISTICS ON THE YEARLY DOW JONES INDUSTRIAL AVERAGES

Table 3.6 provides a summary of year-to-year performance data for the Dow Jones Industrial Average since 1963. Although there have been turbulent periods in the stock market, the DJIA rose in 20 out of the 28 years shown.

Table 3.6 Statistics on the Yearly Dow Jones Industrial Averages, 1963–1991

Year	High	Date	Low	Date	Close	% Change for the Year	P/E[1] Ratio	% Yield
1991	3168.83	Dec. 31	2470.30	Jan. 9	3168.83	+20.32	64.3	3.00%
1990	2999.75	July 16	2365.10	Oct. 11	2633.66	–4.34	15.3	3.94
1989	2791.41	Oct. 9	2144.64	Jan. 3	2753.20	+26.96	12.4	3.74
1988	2183.50	Oct. 21	1879.14	Jan. 20	2168.57	+11.85	10.1	3.67
1987	2722.42	Aug. 25	1738.74	Oct. 19	1938.83	+2.26	14.6	3.67
1986	1955.57	Dec. 2	1502.29	Jan. 22	1895.95	+22.58	16.4	3.54
1985	1553.10	Dec. 16	1184.96	Jan. 4	1546.67	+27.66	16.1	4.01
1984	1286.64	Jan. 6	1086.57	July 24	1211.57	–3.74	10.7	5.00
1983	1287.20	Nov. 29	1027.04	Jan. 3	1258.64	+20.27	17.4	4.47
1982	1070.55	Dec. 27	776.92	Aug. 12	1046.54	+19.60	114.4	5.17
1981	1024.05	Apr. 27	824.01	Sept. 25	875.00	–9.23	7.7	6.42
1980	1000.17	Nov. 20	759.13	Apr. 21	963.99	+14.93	7.9	5.64
1979	897.61	Oct. 5	796.67	Nov. 7	838.74	+4.19	6.7	6.08
1978	907.74	Sept. 8	742.12	Feb. 28	805.01	–3.15	7.1	6.03
1977	1014.79	Jan. 3	800.85	Nov. 2	831.17	–17.27	9.3	5.51
1976	1014.79	Sept. 21	858.71	Jan. 2	1004.65	+17.86	10.4	4.12
1975	881.81	July 15	632.04	Jan. 2	852.41	+38.32	11.3	4.39
1974	891.66	Mar. 13	577.60	Dec. 6	616.24	–27.57	6.2	6.12
1973	1051.70	Jan. 11	788.31	Dec. 5	850.86	–16.58	9.9	4.15
1972	1036.27	Dec. 11	889.15	Jan. 26	1020.02	+14.58	15.2	3.16
1971	950.82	Apr. 28	797.97	Nov. 23	890.20	+6.11	16.2	3.47
1970	842.00	Dec. 29	631.15	May 26	838.92	+4.82	16.4	3.76
1969	968.85	May 14	769.93	Dec. 17	800.36	–15.19	14.0	4.24
1968	985.21	Dec. 3	825.13	Mar. 21	943.75	+4.27	16.3	3.32
1967	943.08	Sept. 25	786.41	Jan. 3	905.11	+15.20	16.8	3.33
1966	995.15	Feb. 9	744.32	Oct. 7	785.69	–18.94	13.6	4.06
1965	969.26	Dec. 31	840.59	June 28	969.26	+10.88	18.1	2.95
1964	891.71	Nov. 18	766.08	Jan. 2	874.13	+14.57	18.8	3.57
1963	767.21	Dec. 18	646.79	Jan. 2	762.95	+17.00	18.5	3.07

[1]Price/earnings ration as of year end.

3.9 RETURNS AND YIELDS ON COMMON STOCKS

Figure 3.2 shows the cumulative total returns and capital appreciation of common stocks from 1926 to 1990, total annual returns (in percent), and dividend yields (in percent). As the first graph depicts, a dollar invested in common stocks at year-end 1925, with dividends reinvested, grew to $517.50 at year-end 1990, a compound

FIGURE 3.2 RETURNS AND YIELDS ON COMMON STOCK, 1925–1990

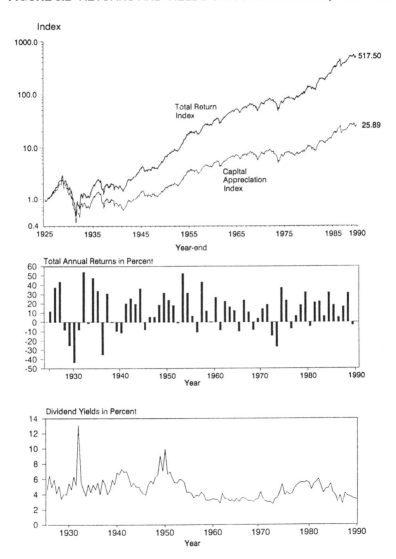

Source: Ibbotson Associates, *Stocks, Bonds, Bills, and Inflation, 1991 Yearbook,* (Chicago: Ibbotson Associates, 1991).

annual growth rate of 9.8 percent. The basis of this data is common stocks represented by the Standard & Poor's 500 Stock Composite Index. (Prior to March 1957, the S & P Composite consisted of 90 stocks.)

3.10 SECURITY PRICES

Table 3.7 shows annual average stock and bond market indexes from 1970.

Table 3.7 Security Prices, 1970–1990

CLASS OR ITEM	1970	1980	1983	1984	1985	1986	1987	1988	1989	1990
Bond prices (dollars per $100 bond):										
Standard & Poor's: Municipal [1] [2] . .	72.3	57.4	51.4	47.9	53.0	65.1	62.7	62.0	66.1	66.0
Dow Jones and Co., Inc.: [3]										
Yearly high.	69.7	76.6	77.8	72.9	83.7	93.7	95.5	91.3	94.2	(NA)
Yearly low	64.4	61.0	69.4	64.8	72.3	83.7	81.3	86.9	87.4	(NA)
Stock prices:										
Standard & Poor's common index										
(500 stocks)(1941-43 = 10) [4] . .	83.2	118.7	160.4	160.5	186.8	236.3	268.8	265.9	323.1	334.6
Industrial	91.3	134.5	180.5	181.3	207.8	262.2	330.5	306.5	392.9	(NA)
N.Y. Stock Exchange common										
stock index										
(Dec. 31, 1965 = 50):										
Composite	45.7	68.1	92.6	92.5	108.1	136.0	161.7	150.0	180.1	183.5
Yearly high [5]	52.4	81.0	99.6	98.1	121.9	145.8	188.0	159.4	199.3	(NA)
Yearly low [5]	37.7	55.3	79.8	85.1	94.6	117.8	125.9	136.7	155.0	(NA)
Industrial.	48.0	78.6	107.5	108.0	123.8	155.9	195.3	180.8	228.0	225.8
Transportation	32.1	60.5	89.4	85.6	104.1	119.9	140.4	134.0	174.9	158.6
Utility	37.2	37.3	47.0	46.4	56.8	71.4	74.3	72.2	94.3	90.6
Finance	54.6	64.3	95.3	89.3	114.2	147.2	146.5	127.4	162.0	133.2
American Stock Exchange										
Market Value Index (Aug. 31,										
1973 = 50)	48.3	150.6	216.5	208.0	229.1	264.4	316.4	295.1	356.7	338.4
NASDAQ OTC composite [6]	(NA)	202.3	278.6	247.4	324.9	348.8	330.5	381.4	454.8	(NA)
Industrial	(NA)	261.4	323.7	260.7	330.2	349.3	338.9	379.0	448.0	(NA)
Insurance.	(NA)	166.8	257.6	283.1	382.1	404.1	351.1	429.1	546.0	(NA)
Banks	(NA)	118.4	203.8	229.8	349.4	412.5	390.7	435.3	391.0	(NA)
Dow Jones and Co., Inc.:										
Composite (65 stocks) [1] [7]	243.9	328.2	472.2	463.1	541.6	702.5	849.5	772.2	966.9	965.2
Industrial (30 stocks).	753.2	891.4	1,190.3	1,178.5	1,328.2	1,792.8	2,276.0	2,060.8	2,508.9	2,678.9
Transportation (20 stocks) . . .	152.4	307.2	544.6	513.8	645.1	785.4	929.2	863.8	1,194.3	1,040.2
Utility (15 stocks)	108.8	110.4	130.0	131.8	157.6	195.2	201.7	179.7	205.7	211.5
Wilshire 5000 equity index										
(Dec. 31, 1980 = 1404.596) [8] . . .	[9]830.3	1,220.7	1,691.5	1,644.6	1,923.8	2,418.8	2,843.7	2,636.9	3,172.6	(NA)
Standard & Poor's:										
Dividend-price ratio (percent). . .	3.83	5.26	4.40	4.64	4.25	3.48	3.08	3.64	3.45	3.61
Earnings-price ratio (percent). . .	6.45	12.66	8.02	10.02	8.12	8.12	6.09	5.48	8.00	7.41	(NA)

NA Not available. [1] Source: U.S. Bureau of Economic Analysis. [2] Derived from average yields on basis of assumed 4 percent, 20-year bond; Wednesday closing prices. [3] Source: Dow Jones and Co., Inc., New York, NY. Effective June 30, 1976, the Dow Jones averages of 20 income railroad bonds were discontinued. With the dropping of the rail averages, which had been part of the Dow-Jones 40-bond average, the 40-bond average became a 20-bond average consisting of 10 utility bonds and 10 industrial bonds. [4] Effective July 1976, the index includes 400 industrial stocks (formerly 425), 20 transportation (formerly 15 rail), 40 public utility (formerly 60), and 40 financial stocks, not previously covered. [5] Source: New York Stock Exchange, Inc., New York, NY, Fact Book, annual. [6] Source: National Association of Securities Dealers, Washington, DC, Fact Book, annual. OTC = over-the-counter. December monthly closing values. [7] Based on stocks listed on the New York Stock Exchange. [8] Represents return on the market value of all common equity securities for which daily pricing is available. Beginning 1980, annual average of daily figures. Source: Wilshire Associates, Santa Monica, CA, releases. [9] Represents Dec. 31, 1970.

Source: Except as noted, Board of Governors of the Federal Reserve System, Federal Reserve Bulletin, monthly and unpublished data.

3.11 SALES OF STOCKS AND OPTIONS ON REGISTERED EXCHANGES

Table 3.8 shows the dramatic growth from 1970 until 1987 of domestic stock and options exchanges. The after effects of the October 1987 stock market crash resulted in a decline in activity in 1988.

Table 3.8 Sales of Stocks and Options on Registered Exchanges, 1970–1989

EXCHANGE	Unit	1970	1980	1982	1983	1984	1985	1986	1987	1988	1989
Market value of all sales,											
all exchanges [1][2]	Bil. dol	136	522	657	1,023	1,004	1,260	1,868	2,492	1,702	2,004
New York	Bil. dol	108	398	515	816	815	1,024	1,453	1,987	1,380	1,581
American..............	Bil. dol	15	47	34	48	32	38	63	102	59	80
Midwest	Bil. dol	5	21	35	60	62	79	102	122	87	101
Chicago	Bil. dol	-	28	32	39	35	38	56	124	64	88
Pacific................	Bil. dol	5	13	21	31	31	40	55	71	49	64
Philadelphia	Bil. dol	3	11	14	20	19	23	35	48	34	50
STOCKS [3]											
Shares sold, all exchanges [2] ...	Million	4,539	15,488	22,414	30,146	30,456	37,046	48,338	63,771	52,533	54,239
New York	Million	3,213	12,390	18,211	24,253	25,150	30,222	39,258	53,038	44,018	44,140
American..............	Million	879	1,659	1,550	2,209	1,584	2,115	2,999	3,496	2,576	3,248
Midwest	Million	149	598	1,144	1,662	1,843	2,274	2,784	3,329	2,771	2,960
Pacific................	Million	165	435	810	1,070	1,006	1,352	1,750	2,034	1,576	1,791
Market value. all exchanges[2] ...	Bil. dol	131	476	603	957	951	1,200	1,705	2,284	1,587	1,845
New York	Bil. dol	103	398	514	815	814	1,023	1,450	1,983	1,378	1,577
American..............	Bil. dol	14	35	20	31	21	26	43	53	31	43
Midwest	Bil. dol	5	21	35	60	62	79	102	122	87	101
Pacific................	Bil. dol	5	11	18	27	28	37	51	57	41	52
OPTIONS [4]											
Contracts traded, all exchanges [2]	Million	(NA)	97	137	149	197	233	289	305	196	227
Chicago	Million	(NA)	53	76	82	123	149	180	182	112	127
American..............	Million	(NA)	29	39	39	40	49	65	71	45	50
Market value of contracts traded,											
all exchanges [2]	Bil. dol	(NA)	45.8	53.7	64.2	53.0	59.1	87.9	118.9	62.6	76.8
Chicago	Bil. dol	(NA)	27.9	32.3	39.4	34.9	38.4	55.9	76.9	39.7	47.3
American..............	Bil. dol	(NA)	12.5	14.3	15.8	10.5	11.6	19.0	25.7	12.4	15.1
Options exercised:											
Number of contracts	Million	(NA)	4.9	9.2	13.6	11.9	10.5	14.5	17.0	11.4	14.6
Value	Bil. dol	(NA)	20.4	37.1	65.1	55.6	49.2	72.8	85.9	51.5	79.5

- Represents zero   NA Not available.   [1] Includes market value of rights and warrants and, for 1970, bond sales. Excludes the value of options exercised.   [2] Includes other registered exchanges, not shown separately.   [3] Includes voting trust certificates, American Depository Receipts, and certificate of deposit for stocks.   [4] Includes non-equity options as of October 1982.

Source: U.S. Securities and Exchange Commission, *SEC Monthly Statistical Review* (discontinued Feb. 1989) and unpublished data.

3.12 VOLUME OF TRADING ON THE NEW YORK STOCK EXCHANGE

Table 3.9 shows the volume and dollar value of shares traded on the New York Stock

Table 3.9 Volume of Trading on New York Stock Exchange, 1970–1989

ITEM	Unit	1970	1980	1981	1982	1983	1984	1985	1986	1987	1988	1989
Shares traded.	Million .	3,124	11,562	12,049	16,669	21,846	23,309	27,774	36,009	48,143	41,118	42,022
Round lots	Million .	2,937	11,352	11,854	16,458	21,590	23,071	27,511	35,680	47,801	40,850	41,699
Average daily shares	Million . .	11.6	44.9	46.9	65.1	85.3	91.2	109.2	141.0	189.0	161.5	165.5
High day	Million .	21.3	84.3	92.9	149.4	129.4	236.6	181.0	244.3	608.1	343.9	416.4
Low day.	Million . .	6.7	16.1	23.9	36.8	53.0	46.4	62.1	48.9	86.7	72.1	68.9
By size: [1]												
100-900 shares [2]	Percent .	(NA)	24.7	21.1	16.2	14.6	11.3	10.6	10.8	13.6	12.6	13.4
1,000-4,900 shares [3] ...	Percent .	(NA)	32.2	31.0	28.5	26.7	25.1	24.1	25.7	21.1	19.8	20.7
5,000-9,900 shares. . . .	Percent .	(NA)	11.4	12.1	12.8	12.7	13.8	13.8	13.9	65.3	67.6	65.9
10,000 or more shares [4]	Percent .	(NA)	31.7	35.8	42.5	46.0	49.8	51.5	49.6			
Odd lots	Million . .	186	209	196	211	256	238	263	329	342	268	324
Value of shares traded .	Bil. dol .	103	382	396	495	775	773	981	1,389	1,889	1,366	1,556
Round lots	Bil. dol .	95	375	389	488	765	765	971	1,374	1,874	1,356	1,543
Odd lots	Bil. dol.	7	8	7	7	10	9	10	15	15	10	13
Bond volume [5]	Mil. dol .	4,495	5,190	5,733	7,155	7,572	6,982	9,046	10,464	9,727	7,702	8,836
Daily average	Mil. dol .	17.7	20.5	22.7	28.3	29.9	27.6	35.9	41.4	38.4	30.4	35.1

NA Not available.   [1] Share volume of reported trades by size (percent of total) on New York Stock Exchange.   [2] Beginning 1988, at 100-1,000 shares.   [3] Beginning 1988, at 1,100-4,900 shares.   [4] Includes bunched orders at the opening and re-opening of trading.   [5] Par value.

Source: New York Stock Exchange, Inc., New York, NY, *Fact Book*, annual.

Exchange since 1970. The higher percentage of large trades in recent years points to the increased dominance of institutional investors in the marketplace.

3.13 NASDAQ SECURITIES STATISTICS

Table 3.10 shows the over-the-counter market has experienced enormous growth since 1980.

Table 3.10 Securities Listed and Volume of Trading on NASDAQ, 1980–1990

ITEM	Unit	1980	1981	1982	1983	1984	1985	1986	1987	1988	1989	1990
Companies listed	Number.	2,894	3,353	3,264	3,901	4,097	4,136	4,417	4,706	4,451	4,293	4,132
Issues	Number.	3,050	3,687	3,664	4,467	4,728	4,784	5,189	5,537	5,144	4,963	4,706
Shares traded	Million	6,692	7,823	8,432	15,909	15,159	20,699	28,737	37,890	31,070	33,530	33,380
Average daily volume. . .	Million	26.5	30.9	33.3	62.9	59.9	82.1	113.6	149.8	122.8	133.1	131.9
Value of shares traded. . . .	Bil. dol.	68.7	71.1	84.2	188.3	153.5	233.5	378.2	499.9	347.1	431.4	452.4

Source: *Nasdaq Fact Book & Company Directory*, National Association of Securities Dealers, Inc., Washington, D.C.

3.14 INVESTING IN FOREIGN STOCKS

Foreign stock markets have consistently outperformed U.S. markets, so a well-diversified stock portfolio should include foreign stocks. International mutual funds and American depository receipts (ADRs) make foreign investing easy and convenient.

The abundance of foreign securities and investment products that have appeared in the United States in the last few years has succeeded in bringing both Main Street and Wall Street dollars to Paris, Tokyo, London, and Malaysia—and that participation has helped to tip the scales of world stock market dominance in favor of companies based abroad. Today, foreign companies account for over 70 percent of the world's stock market capitalization, compared with 50 percent just 10 years ago.

Investors find foreign stocks appealing because they often perform better than U.S. issues. According to Frank Russell Company, the U.S. stock market had an average annualized return of 15.4 percent between 1979 and 1988, ranking it only thirteenth among nations with established stock markets.

The direction of the U.S. dollar has a substantial impact on how foreign securities perform. When the dollar rises against foreign currencies, earnings of overseas companies translate into fewer U.S. dollars, and overseas holdings are worth less to U.S.investors. On the other hand, when the dollar declines, foreign earnings are enhanced when translated into U.S. currency and foreign holdings are worth more to U.S. investors.

3.14.1 International Mutual Funds

Because foreign stocks can buffer losses in the American stock maket and provide a hedge against currency swings, it is generally a good idea to keep a portion of investment capital in international stocks. There are many mutual funds that specialize in investing in foreign stocks. Funds with the word "global" in their names have the option of investing in both the United States and abroad. International or foreign funds usually have no investments in U.S. securities. Global funds may be advantageous if you want a portfolio manager to shift among foreign and domestic companies based on currency fluctuations and the outlooks for various markets. Single-country and single-region international funds have become very popular, although the investor is usually better advised to opt for a broad-based international fund that lets the portfolio manager decide which countries offer the best investment opportunities.

3.14.2 American Depository Receipts

Those who prefer to own individual foreign stocks may want to consider American depository receipts. While a few foreign companies trade directly on the stock exchange, hundreds of others are available via ADRs. An ADR is a negotiable receipt issued by a U.S. bank that represents the holder's interest in the underlying foreign shares. All transactions, including dividends, are made in U.S. dollars. ADRs are traded on the New York and American stock exchanges and on the over-the-counter market.

3.15 PERFORMANCE OF FOREIGN STOCK MARKETS

The following indexes, compiled by Morgan Stanley Capital International, show the annual and cumulative performance from 1969 of world stock markets. Tables 3.11 through 3.15 summarize the performance of the following markets:

3.15.1 Morgan Stanley World Equities Market Index

The World Index, in Table 3.11 (without dividends, year end, in U.S. dollars) consists of 20 countries: Australia, Austria, Belgium, Canada, Denmark, Finland, France, Germany, Hong Kong, Italy, Japan, Netherlands, New Zealand, Norway, Singapore/Malaysia, Spain, Sweden, Switzerland, United Kingdom, and the United States.

Table 3.11 Morgan Stanley International World Index, 1969–1990

Year	Index Value	Index Growth	Year	Index Value	Index Growth
1990	461.53	-18.65%	1979	131.10	7.21
1989	567.34	14.75	1978	122.28	12.68
1988	494.43	21.19	1977	108.52	-2.46
1987	407.99	14.34	1976	111.26	10.31
1986	356.83	39.11	1975	100.86	28.91
1985	256.51	37.02	1974	78.24	-27.83
1984	187.21	1.77	1973	108.41	-17.08
1983	183.95	18.56	1972	130.74	19.96
1982	155.16	5.82	1971	108.99	15.59
1981	146.62	-7.92	1970	94.29	-5.71
1980	159.23	21.46	1969	100.00	

Source: Morgan Stanley Capital International

3.15.2 Morgan Stanley EAFE Index

The EAFE (Europe, Australia, and the Far East) Index (without dividends, year-end, in U.S. dollars), consists of 18 countries: Australia, Austria, Belgium, Denmark, Finland, France, Germany, Hong Kong, Italy, Japan, Netherlands, New Zealand, Norway, Singapore/Malaysia, Spain, Sweden, Switzerland, and the United Kingdom.

Table 3.12 Morgan Stanley International EAFE Index, 1969–1990

Year	Index Value	Index Growth	Year	Index Value	Index Growth
1990	788.98	-24.71%	1979	175.72	1.81
1989	1047.86	9.22	1978	172.59	28.91
1988	963.93	27.26	1977	133.88	14.61
1987	757.45	23.18	1976	116.81	-0.37
1986	614.89	66.80	1975	117.24	31.21
1985	370.09	53.57	1974	89.35	-25.60
1984	240.99	5.02	1973	120.09	-16.82
1983	229.47	20.91	1972	144.37	33.28
1982	190.97	-4.03	1971	108.32	26.14
1981	198.99	-4.85	1970	85.87	-14.13
1980	209.13	19.01	1969	100.00	

Source: Morgan Stanley Capital International

3.15.3 Morgan Stanley Europe Index

The Europe Index, in Table 3.13 (without dividends, year-end, in U.S. dollars), consists of 13 countries: Austria, Belgium, Denmark, Finland, France, Germany, Italy, Netherlands, Norway, Spain, Sweden, Switzerland, and the United Kingdom.

Table 3.13 Morgan Stanley International Europe Index, 1969–1990

Year	Index Value	Index Growth	Year	Index Value	Index Growth
1990	478.69	–6.46%	1979	142.10	8.39
1989	511.75	25.40	1978	131.10	17.64
1988	408.09	12.74	1977	111.44	17.64
1987	361.99	1.42	1976	94.73	–10.84
1986	356.91	40.27	1975	106.25	36.69
1985	254.45	73.31	1974	77.73	–26.86
1984	146.82	–2.77	1973	106.27	–11.09
1983	151.00	17.33	1972	119.53	11.71
1982	128.70	0.02	1971	107.00	23.06
1981	128.67	–15.79	1970	86.95	–13.05
1980	152.80	7.53	1969	100.00	

Source: Morgan Stanley Capital International

3.15.4 Morgan Stanley Pacific Index

The Pacific Index in Table 3.14 (without dividends, year-end, in U.S. dollars), consists of five countries: Australia, Hong Kong, Japan, New Zealand, and Singapore/Malaysia.

Table 3.14 Morgan Stanley International Pacific Index, 1969–1990

Year	Index Value	Index Growth	Year	Index Value	Index Growth
1990	1735.19	–34.95%	1979	297.13	–5.79
1989	2667.68	1.95	1978	315.40	45.06
1988	2616.74	34.20	1977	217.42	10.61
1987	1949.85	38.85	1976	196.56	18.34
1986	1404.28	91.84	1975	166.10	22.84
1985	732.02	37.46	1974	135.22	–23.38
1984	532.55	11.66	1973	176.49	–22.68
1983	476.92	24.01	1972	228.25	102.31
1982	384.59	–8.43	1971	112.82	33.48
1981	420.00	6.03	1970	84.52	–15.48
1980	396.10	33.31	1969	100.00	

Source: Morgan Stanley Capital International

3.15.5 Morgan Stanley North America Index

The North America Index, in Table 3.15 (without dividends, year end; in U.S. dollars), consists of two countries: Canada and the United States.

Table 3.15 Morgan Stanley International North America Index, 1969–1990

Year	Index Value	Index Growth	Year	Index Value	Index Growth
1990	338.81	–6.39%	1979	121.02	17.85
1989	361.93	26.48	1978	102.69	6.08
1988	286.16	11.82	1977	96.80	–11.31
1987	255.91	1.31	1976	109.15	15.90
1986	252.59	13.18	1975	94.18	27.96
1985	223.18	26.12	1974	73.60	–29.86
1984	176.96	0.12	1973	104.93	–17.60
1983	176.75	17.54	1972	127.34	14.20
1982	150.37	13.04	1971	111.51	9.71
1981	133.02	–10.10	1970	101.64	1.64
1980	147.96	22.26	1969	100.00	

Source: Morgan Stanley Capital International

3.16 LIST OF OPTIONABLE STOCKS

Table 3.16 lists stocks that are optionable, identifies the exchange where the options are traded, and lists these options' expiration cycles. Table 3.17 lists index options, Table 3.18 lists foreign currency options, and Table 3.19 lists Treasury options.

Table 3.16 List of Optionable Stocks[1]

symbol[2]	name[3]	cycle[4]
AIR	AAR Corporation	1
ABT	Abbott Laboratories	2
ACN/ACZ	Acuson Corp.	1
AEQ/ADBE	Adobe Systems, Inc.	1
AMD	Advanced Micro Devices, Inc.	1
AET	Aetna Life & Casualty Company	1
ARQ/AGNC	Agency Rent-A-Car, Inc.	1
AHM	Ahmanson (H.F.) & Company	1
ABF	**Airborne Freight Corporation**	**2**
APD	Air Products & Chemicals, Inc.	3
ALK	Alaska Air Group, Inc.	1
ABS	Albertson's Inc.	3
AL	Alcan Aluminium Limited	3
ASN	Alco Standard Corporation	3
AA	ALCOA (Alum. Co. of America)	1
AUQ/ALDC	Aldus Corporation	1
AAL	Alexander & Alexander Services, Inc.	2
ALQ/ALEX	Alexander & Baldwin, Inc.	1
AGN	Allergan Inc.	1
ATK	**Alliant Techsystems**	**2**
ALD	Allied Signal, Inc.	3
AT	Alltel Corporation	1
AWQ/ALWS	Allwaste, Inc.	2
AZA	ALZA Corporation	1
AMX	AMAX Inc.	3
AMH	Amdahl Corporation	2
AHC	Amerada Hess Corporation	2
ABX	American Barrick Resources Corp.	1
AMB	American Brands, Inc.	3
ACY	American Cyanamid Company	1
AEP	American Electric Power Company, Inc.	2
AXP	American Express Company	1
LAX	**American Express Co. (July-92)**	**1**
ZAX	**American Express Co. (Dec-93)**	**1**
AFL	American Family Corporation	2
AGC	American General Corporation	1
AGQ/AGREA	American Greetings Corp. (Class A)	1
AHP	American Home Products Corp.	1
LAH	**American Home Products Corp. (July-92)**	**1**
ZAH	**American Home Products Corp. (Dec-93)**	**1**
AIG	American International Group, Inc.	2
APS	American President Companies, Ltd.	1

1. All options added since September 1990 are indicated in bold face type

2. Over-the-counter stocks are listed with two symbols. The first symbol represents the option code and the second symbol represents the National Association of Securities Dealers (NASD) code.

3. Long-term equity options are noted by expiration month and year.

4. Expiration cycles are 1 = January sequential, 2 = February sequential, 3 = March sequential. (See Table 3.20.)

5. A = American Stock Exchange, C = Chicago Board Options Exchange, N = New York Stock Exchange, P = Pacific Stock Exchange, X = Philadelphia Stock Exchange.

Source: The Options Clearing Corporations, *Directory of Exchange Listed Options*, (Chicago: The Options Clearing Corporation, April 1991).

Table 3.16 continued

exchange[5]	industry group	position limit
X	Wholesale Trade/Durable Goods	3000
X	Drugs	8000
P	Medical Instruments & Supplies	4500
P	Computer/Data Processing Services	8000
P	Electronic Components/Accessories	8000
A	Insurance Carriers	8000
A	Auto Repair/Services/Parking	3000
A	Depository Institutions	8000
C,X	**Air Transportation**	**3000**
X	Chemicals & Allied Products	5500
A	Air Transportation	3000
X	Food Stores	5500
A	Primary Metal Industries	8000
N	Wholesale Trade/Nondurable Goods	3000
C	Primary Metal Industries	8000
P	Computer/Data Processing Services	5500
C	Insurance Agents/Brokers/Service	8000
A	Water Transportation/Cruises	5500
X	Drugs	5500
C,N,X	**Fabricated Metal Products**	**3000**
X	Transportation Equipment	5500
P	Telephone Communications	3000
A,X	Electric/Gas/Sanitary Services	5500
P	Engineering/Management Services	3000
A	Primary Metal Industries	8000
C	Computer/Office Equipment	8000
X	Petroleum/Coal Products	5500
A	Metal Mining	8000
A	Tobacco Products	8000
A	Chemicals/Allied Products	8000
C	Electric/Gas/Sanitary Services	8000
A,C	Security Brokers/Dealers	8000
A	**Security Brokers/Dealers**	**8000**
A	**Security Brokers/Dealers**	**8000**
A	Insurance Carriers	5500
C	Insurance Carriers	8000
C	Printing/Publishing	5500
A	Drugs	8000
A	**Drugs**	**8000**
A	**Drugs**	**8000**
C	Insurance Carriers	8000
P	Water Transportation/Cruises	3000

Table 3.16 continued

symbol[2]	name[3]	cycle[4]
SWQ/AMSWA	American Software, Inc. (Class A)	1
ASC	American Stores Company	1
ATQ/ATCMA	American Television and Comm. Corp. (Class A)	1
AIT	Ameritech	1
AME	Ametek Inc.	1
AMQ/AMGN	Amgen Inc.	1
AN	Amoco Corporation	2
AMP	AMP Incorporated	2
AMR	AMR Corporation	2
LAR	**AMR Corporation (Dec-92)**	**2**
ZAR	**AMR Corporation (Dec-93)**	**2**
APC	Anadarko Petroleum Corporation	2
ADI	Analog Devices, Inc.	3
BUD	Anheuser-Busch Companies, Inc.	3
ATM	Anthem Electronics Inc.	1
AOC	**AON Corporation**	**1**
APA	Apache Corporation	1
AAQ/AAPL	Apple Computer, Inc.	1
LAA	**Apple Computer, Inc. (Dec-92)**	**1**
ZAA	**Apple Computer, Inc. (Dec-93)**	**1**
ABQ/ABIO	Applied Biosystems, Inc.	1
APM	Applied Magnetics Corporation	3
ANQ/AMAT	Applied Materials	1
ADM	Archer-Daniels-Midland Company	3
RCM	ARCO Chemical Company	1
ALG	Arkla, Inc.	2
AS	Armco Inc.	2
ACK	Armstrong World Industries, Inc.	3
ASA	ASA Limited	2
LSL	**ASA Limited (Dec-92)**	**2**
ZSL	**ASA Limited (Dec-93)**	**2**
AR	ASARCO Incorporated	3
ASH	Ashland Oil Inc.	1
TAQ/TATE	Ashton Tate, Inc.	1
ASQ/ASTA	AST Research, Inc.	2
T	AT&T	1
LT	**AT&T (July-92)**	**1**
ZT	**AT&T (Jan-93)**	**1**
ARC	Atlantic Richfield Company (ARCO)	1
ADQ/ACAD	Autodesk	1
AUD	Automatic Data Processing Inc.	2
AVY	Avery Dennison Corp.	1
AVT	Avnet, Inc.	2
AVP	Avon Products, Inc.	1
BHI	Baker Hughes, Inc.	1
LBH	**Baker Hughes, Inc. (July-92)**	**1**

Table 3.16 continued

exchange[5]	industry group	position limit
X	Computer/Data Processing Services	3000
C	Drug/Proprietary Stores	3000
A,C	Cable/Pay TV Services	3000
C	Telephone Communications	8000
X	Electronic/Electric Equipment	3000
A	Drugs	8000
C	Petroleum/Coal Products	8000
C	Electronic Components/Accessories	5500
A	Air Transportation	8000
A	**Air Transportation**	**8000**
A	**Air Transportation**	**8000**
C	Oil/Gas Extraction	5500
X	Electronic Components/Accessories	3000
X	Beverage Products	8000
N,X	Wholesale Trade/Durable Goods	3000
P	**Insurance Carriers**	**3000**
N,X	Oil/Gas Extraction	5500
A,C	Computer/Office Equipment	8000
A	**Computer/Office Equipment**	**8000**
A	**Computer/Office Equipment**	**8000**
P	Instruments & Related Products	3000
C	Electronic Components/Accessories	3000
P	Industrial/Commercial Machinery	5500
X	Food Products	8000
A	Chemicals & Allied Products	3000
A	Electric/Gas/Sanitary Services	5500
X	Primary Metal Industries	5500
X	Stone/Clay/Glass Products	3000
A	Holding/Investment Offices	5500
A	**Holding/Investment Offices**	**5500**
A	**Holding/Investment Offices**	**5500**
A	Primary Metal Industries	3000
X	Petroleum/Coal Products	5500
P	Computer/Data Processing Services	5500
A	Computer/Office Equipment	8000
C	Telephone Communications	8000
C	**Telephone Communications**	**8000**
C	**Telephone Communications**	**8000**
C	Petroleum/Coal Products	8000
P	Computer/Data Processing Services	8000
X	Computer/Data Processing Services	5500
X	Paper & Allied Products	5500
A	Wholesale Trade/Durable Goods	3000
C	Chemicals & Allied Products	5500
P	Industrial/Commercial Machinery	8000
P	**Industrial/Commercial Machinery**	**8000**

Table 3.16 continued

symbol[2]	name[3]	cycle[4]
ZBH	**Baker Hughes, Inc. (Jan-93)**	**1**
BLY	Bally Manufacturing Corporation	2
BGE	**Baltimore Gas & Electric Co.**	**3**
ONE	Banc One Corporation	2
BAC	BankAmerica Corporation	1
BT	Bankers Trust New York Corporation	1
BKB	Bank of Boston Corporation	2
BK	Bank of New York Company, Inc.	1
BCR	Bard (C.R.) Inc.	1
BBI	Barnett Banks, Inc.	1
BTI	B.A.T Industries p.l.c.	1
BMG	Battle Mountain Gold Company	1
BOL	Bausch & Lomb Incorporated	1
BAX	Baxter International Inc.	2
BBQ/BBNK	Bay Banks Inc.	3
BCE	**BCE Inc.**	**1**
BSC	Bear Stearns Companies Inc.	1
BEC	Beckman Instruments, Inc.	1
BDX	Becton Dickinson & Company	3
BEL	Bell Atlantic Corporation	1
BLS	BellSouth Corporation	1
BNL	Beneficial Corporation	1
BBC	Bergen Brunswig Corporation	3
BS	Bethlehem Steel Corporation	1
BEQ/BETZ	Betz Laboratories, Inc.	1
BEV	Beverly Enterprises Inc.	3
BHC	BHC Communications, Inc.	2
BGQ/BGEN	Biogen, Inc.	1
BIQ/BMET	Biomet Inc.	1
BDK	Black & Decker Corporation	2
BV	Blockbuster Entertainment Corp.	3
BTQ/BOAT	**Boatmen's Bancshares, Inc.**	**1**
BA	Boeing Company	2
LBO	**Boeing Company (Aug-92)**	**2**
ZBO	**Boeing Company (Feb-93)**	**2**
BCC	Boise Cascade Corporation	2
BLR	Bolar Pharmaceutical Corporation	1
BCP	Borden Chemicals & Plastics L.P.	2
BN	Borden Inc.	1
BLQ/BORL	Borland International, Inc.	1
BOW	Bowater Inc.	3
BGG	Briggs and Stratton Corp.	1
BMY	Bristol-Myers Squibb Company	3
LBM	**Bristol-Myers Squibb Co. (Sept-92)**	**3**
ZBM	**Bristol-Myers Squibb Co. (Mar-93)**	**3**

104

Table 3.16 continued

exchange[5]	industry group	position limit
P	**Industrial/Commercial Machinery**	**8000**
A,C	Amusement/Recreation Facilities	5500
P	**Electric/Gas/Sanitary Services**	**5500**
P	Depository Institutions	8000
C	Depository Institutions	8000
P	Depository Institutions	5500
X	Depository Institutions	8000
C	Depository Institutions	5500
X	Medical Instruments & Supplies	5500
A	Depository Institutions	5500
C	Tobacco Products	8000
A,C	Metal Mining	8000
A	Instruments & Related Products	3000
C	Drugs	8000
C	Depository Institutions	5500
C	**Telephone Communications**	**5500**
C	Security Brokers/Dealers	5500
C	Instruments & Related Products	3000
X	Medical Instruments & Supplies	3000
C	Telephone Communications	8000
A	Telephone Communications	8000
P	Depository Institutions	3000
C	Wholesale Trade/Nondurable Goods	3000
C	Primary Metal Industries	5500
P	Chemicals & Allied Products	3000
P	Nursing/Personal Care Facilities	8000
C	Radio/Television Broadcasting	3000
A,C,P	Holding Investment Offices	5500
C	Medical Instruments & Supplies	5500
C	Industrial/Commercial Machinery	5500
A,C	Motion Pictures	8000
C	**Depository Institutions**	**3000**
C	Transportation Equipment	8000
C	**Transportation Equipment**	**8000**
C	**Transportation Equipment**	**8000**
C	Paper & Allied Products	3000
C	Drugs	5500
N	Chemicals & Allied Products	3000
P	Food Products	8000
C	Computer/Data Processing Services	5500
P	Paper & Allied Products	3000
X	Industrial/Commercial Machinery	3000
C	Drugs	8000
C	**Drugs**	**8000**
C	**Drugs**	**8000**

Table 3.16 continued

symbol[2]	name[3]	cycle[4]
BAB	**British Airways, PLC**	**1**
BP	British Petroleum Ltd.	1
BST	**British Steel PLC**	**1**
BRO	Broad Inc.	3
BFI	Browning-Ferris Industries, Inc.	3
BRQ/BRNO	Bruno's Inc.	2
BC	Brunswick Corporation	3
BNI	Burlington Northern Inc.	1
BR	Burlington Resources Inc.	2
CVN	C&S/Sovran Corporation	2
CDN	Cadence Design Systems, Inc.	1
CAW	Caesars World, Inc.	2
CAL	CalFed, Inc.	1
RNQ/CRBN	**Calgon Carbon Corp.**	**2**
CPB	Campbell Soup Company	2
CP	Canadian Pacific Limited	1
CCB	Capital Cities/ABC, Inc.	2
CPH	Capital Holding Corporation	3
CCL	Carnival Cruise Lines, Inc.	1
CKE	Castle & Cooke, Inc.	3
CAT	Caterpillar Inc.	2
CBH	CBI Industries, Inc.	3
CBS	CBS Inc.	2
CMQ/COMM	Cellular Communications, Inc.	1
CNT	Centel Corporation	1
CX	Centerior Energy Corporation	2
COQ/CNTO	Centocor Inc.	1
CSR	**Central & Southwest Corp.**	**2**
CTL	Century Telephone Enterprises Inc.	1
CTQ/CTUS	Cetus Corporation	1
CDV/CDVA	Chambers Development Co., Class A	1
CHA	Champion International Corporation	3
CSQ/CHRS	Charming Shoppes, Inc.	1
CMB	Chase Manhattan Corporation	3
LCM	**Chase Manhattan Corp. (Dec-92)**	**3**
ZCM	**Chase Manhattan Corp. (Dec-93)**	**3**
CHQ/CHEK	Checkpoint Systems, Inc.	2
CHL	Chemical Banking Corporation	3
CHW	Chemical Waste Management, Inc.	3
CHV	Chevron Corporation	3
LCH	**Chevron Corporation (Dec-92)**	**3**
ZCH	**Chevron Corporation (Dec-93)**	**3**
CLQ/CHPS	Chips & Technologies, Inc.	1
CQB	Chiquita Brands International, Inc.	3
CCN	Chris-Craft Industries Inc.	1
C	Chrysler Corporation	1
CB	Chubb Corporation	1

Table 3.16 continued

exchange[5]	industry group	position limit
X	**Air Transportation**	**3000**
P	Petroleum/Coal Products	8000
N	**Primary Metal Industries**	**5500**
X	Real Estate	3000
A	Electric/Gas/Sanitary Services	8000
C	Food Stores	5500
C	Industrial/Commercial Machinery	5500
C	Railroad Transportation	5500
X	Oil/Gas Extraction	8000
A,P	Depository Institutions	8000
A,C	Computer/Data Processing Services	5500
A	Amusement/Recreation Facilities	5500
P	Depository Institutions	5500
X	**Chemicals & Allied Products**	**3000**
N	Food Products	5500
X	Railroad Transportation	8000
C	Radio/Television Broadcasting	3000
N	Insurance Carriers	5500
C	Water Transportation/Cruises	3000
P	Agriculture/Field Crops	5500
A	Industrial/Commercial Machinery	8000
X	Fabricated Metal Products	3000
C	Radio/Television Broadcasting	3000
A,C	Telephone Communications	5500
A	Telephone Communications	5500
P	Electric/Gas/Sanitary Services	8000
C	Engineering/Management Services	5500
P	**Electric/Gas/Sanitary Services**	**5500**
P	Telephone Communications	3000
A	Engineering/Management Services	8000
C	Electric/Gas/Sanitary Services	3000
C	Paper & Allied Products	5500
X	Apparel/Accessory Stores	5500
A	Depository Institutions	8000
A	**Depository Institutions**	**8000**
A	**Depository Institutions**	**8000**
P	Electronic/Electric Equipment	3000
A	Depository Institutions	8000
A	Electric/Gas/Sanitary Services	8000
A	Petroleum/Coal Products	8000
A	**Petroleum/Coal Products**	**8000**
A	**Petroleum/Coal Products**	**8000**
A	Electronic Components/Accessories	5500
X	Food Products	3000
C	Radio/Television Broadcasting	3000
C	Transportation Equipment	8000
N	Insurance Carriers	5500

Table 3.16 continued

symbol[2]	name[3]	cycle[4]
CI	CIGNA Corporation	1
CSN	Cincinnati Bell Inc.	1
CDQ/CINF	**Cincinnati Financial Corporation**	**1**
CMZ	Cincinnati Milacron Inc.	2
CPX	Cineplex Odeon Corporation	1
CC	Circuit City Stores	1
CIR	Circus Circus Enterprises, Inc.	3
CCI	Citicorp	1
CLE	Claire's Stores, Inc.	2
CKL	Clark Equipment Co.	2
CLX	Clorox Company	1
CMS	CMS Energy Corporation	3
CNA	CNA Financial Corporation	2
CGP	Coastal Corporation	3
KO	Coca-Cola Company	2
LKO	**Coca-Cola Company (Aug-92)**	**2**
ZKO	**Coca-Cola Company (Feb-93)**	**2**
CCE	Coca-Cola Enterprises Inc.	2
CL	Colgate-Palmolive Company	2
CAQ/CGEN	Collagen Corporation	2
CF	**Collins Foods Inc.**	**1**
CG	Columbia Gas System, Inc.	2
CCQ/CMCSA	Comcast Corp. (Class A)	1
CDO	Comdisco Inc.	1
CBU	Commodore International Ltd.	2
CWE	Commonwealth Edison Company	2
CQ	Communications Satellite Corp.	1
CMY	Community Psychiatric Centers	1
CPQ	Compaq Computer Corp.	1
LCP	**Compaq Computer Corp. (July-92)**	**1**
ZCP	**Compaq Computer Corp. (Jan-93)**	**1**
CA	Computer Associates International, Inc.	1
CSC	Computer Sciences Corporation	3
CAG	ConAgra, Inc.	3
CNR	Conner Peripherals Inc.	1
ED	Consolidated Edison Co. of New York	2
CNF	Consolidated Freightways, Inc.	3
CNG	Consolidated Natural Gas Company	1
CNQ/CPER	Consolidated Papers, Inc.	1
CRR	Consolidated Rail Corporation	1
CTZ	Contel Corporation	1
CBK	Continental Bank Corporation	3
CIC	Continental Corporation	2
CDA	Control Data Corporation	2
CNX	Convex Computer Corp.	3

Table 3.16 continued

exchange[5]	industry group	position limit
C	Insurance Carriers	5500
C	Telephone Communications	3000
A	**Insurance Carriers**	**3000**
X	Industrial/Commercial Machinery	3000
X	Motion Pictures	3000
P	Radio/Television/Computer Stores	5500
A	Amusement/Recreation Facilities	3000
C	Depository Institutions	8000
N	Apparel/Accessory Stores	3000
X	Industrial/Commercial Machinery	3000
X	Chemicals & Allied Products	3000
N	Electric/Gas/Sanitary Services	5500
A	Insurance Carriers	3000
A,C	Electric/Gas/Sanitary Services	5500
C	Beverage Products	8000
C	**Beverage Products**	**8000**
C	**Beverage Products**	**8000**
C	Beverage Products	3000
C	Chemicals & Allied Products	5500
A	Drugs	3000
C	**Eating/Drinking Places**	**3000**
A	Electric/Gas/Sanitary Services	5500
X	Cable/Pay TV Services	5500
P	Computer/Data Processing Services	5500
X	Computer/Office Equipment	3000
C	Electric/Gas/Sanitary Services	8000
X	Communications	3000
X	Hospitals	5500
P	Computer/Office Equipment	8000
P	**Computer/Office Equipment**	**8000**
P	**Computer/Office Equipment**	**8000**
C	Computer/Data Processing Services	8000
C	Computer/Data Processing Services	3000
A	Food Products	5500
P	Computer/Office Equipment	8000
A	Electric/Gas/Sanitary Services	8000
N	Trucking/Courier Services (Ex Air)	5500
A	Electric/Gas/Sanitary Services	3000
P	Paper & Allied Products	3000
X	Railroad Transportation	5500
A	Telephone Communications	8000
C	Depository Institutions	5500
X	Insurance Carriers	5500
C	Computer/Office Equipment	5500
X	Computer/Office Equipment	3000

Table 3.16 continued

symbol[2]	name[3]	cycle[4]
CBE	Cooper Industries, Inc.	1
CTB	Cooper Tire & Rubber Company	2
ACQ/ACCOB	Coors (Adolph) Co., Class B	1
CQQ	**Cordis Corporation**	**1**
CFQ/CSFN	CoreStates Financial Corporation	1
GLW	Corning Incorporated	2
CGQ/COST	Costco Wholesale Corporation	1
CPC	CPC International, Inc.	1
CBQ/CBRL	Craker Barrel Old Country Store Inc.	3
CR	Crane Company	1
CYR	Cray Research, Inc.	3
KSQ/CRFC	**Crestar Financial Corp.**	**3**
CCK	Crown Cork & Seal Company, Inc.	1
CSX	CSX Corporation	2
CY	Cypress Semiconductor Corporation	3
CYM	Cyprus Minerals Company	1
DCN	Dana Corporation	1
DHR	Danaher Corporation	3
DGN	Data General Corporation	3
DH	Dayton Hudson Corporation	1
DF	**Dean Foods Company**	**2**
DE	Deere & Company	3
DLQ/DELL	Dell Computer Corp.	2
DAL	Delta Air Lines, Inc.	1
DLX	Deluxe Corporation	1
DTE	Detroit Edison Company	1
DEX	Dexter Corporation	1
DRM	Diamond Shamrock Inc.	1
DBD	Diebold, Incorporated	2
DCA	Digital Communications Assoc., Inc.	2
DEC	Digital Equipment Corporation	1
LDC	**Digital Equipment Corp. (July-92)**	**1**
ZDC	**Digital Equipment Corp. (Dec-93)**	**1**
DDS	Dillard Department Stores, Class A	2
DIS	Disney (Walt) Company	1
LWD	**Disney (Walt) Company (July-92)**	**1**
ZDS	**Disney (Walt) Company (Dec-93)**	**1**
D	Dominion Resources, Inc.	1
DNY	Donnelley (R.R.) and Sons Company	3
DOV	Dover Corporation	3
DOW	Dow Chemical Company	3
LDO	**Dow Chemical Co. (Sept-92)**	**3**
ZDO	**Dow Chemical Co. (Jan-93)**	**3**
DJ	Dow Jones & Company, Inc.	3
DBQ/DBRN	Dress Barn, Inc.	1
DI	Dresser Industries, Inc.	1
DRY	Dreyfus Corporation	1

Table 3.16 continued

exchange[5]	industry group	position limit
A	Electronic/Electric Equipment	5500
X	Rubber/Plastics Products	3000
P	Beverage Products	5500
X	**Medical Instruments & Supplies**	**3000**
A	Depository Institutions	8000
C	Stone/Clay/Glass Products	5500
A	General Merchandise Stores	5500
P	Food Products	5500
P	Eating/Drinking Places	3000
X	Fabricated Metal Products	3000
P	Computer/Office Equipment	5500
X	**Depository Institutions**	**3000**
X	Fabricated Metal Products	3000
P	Railroad Transportation	5500
C	Electronic/Electric Equipment	5500
C	Metal Mining	3000
N	Transportation Equipment	3000
X	Industrial/Commercial Machinery	3000
P	Computer/Office Equipment	3000
P	General Merchandise Stores	5500
P	**Food Products**	**3000**
A	Industrial/Commercial Machinery	8000
X	Computer/Office Equipment	5500
C	Air Transportation	5500
P	Printing/Publishing	3000
X	Electric/Gas/Sanitary Services	8000
A	Chemicals & Allied Products	3000
C	Petroleum/Coal Products	3000
C	Computer/Office Equipment	3000
N	Computer/Office Equipment	3000
A,C	Computer/Office Equipment	8000
A	**Computer/Office Equipment**	**8000**
A	**Computer/Office Equipment**	**8000**
P	General Merchandise Stores	3000
A,C	Amusement/Recreation Facilities	8000
A	**Amusement/Recreation Facilities**	**8000**
A	**Amusement/Recreation Facilities**	**8000**
X	Electric/Gas/Sanitary Services	5500
A	Printing/Publishing	3000
A	Industrial/Commercial Machinery	3000
C	Chemicals & Allied Products	8000
C	**Chemicals & Allied Products**	**8000**
C	**Chemicals & Allied Products**	**8000**
X	Printing/Publishing	3000
C	Apparel/Accessory Stores	3000
X	Industrial/Commercial Machinery	5500
C	Security/Commodity Services	5500

Table 3.16 continued

symbol[2]	name[3]	cycle[4]
DIQ/DIGI	DSC Communications Corporation	1
DUK	Duke Power Company	1
DNB	Dun & Bradstreet Corporation	2
DD	du Pont (E.I.) de Nemours & Co.	1
LDD	**du Pont (E.I.) de Nemours & Co. (July-92)**	**1**
ZDD	**du Pont (E.I.) de Nemours & Co. (Dec-93)**	**1**
DWG	DWG Corporation	1
EFU	Eastern Enterprises	1
EK	Eastman Kodak Company	1
LEK	**Eastman Kodak Co. (July-92)**	**1**
ZEK	**Eastman Kodak Co. (Jan-93)**	**1**
ETN	Eaton Corporation	1
ECH	Echlin Corporation	3
ECO	Echo Bay Mines, Ltd.	1
ECL	Ecolab Inc.	1
EBS	Edison Brothers Stores Inc.	2
AGE	Edwards (A.G.) Inc.	2
EGG	EG&G Inc.	3
ELN	Elan Corporation, PLC	1
EMR	Emerson Electric Co.	3
EC	Engelhard Corporation	1
ENE	Enron Corp.	1
ENS/ENY	ENSERCH Corporation	2
ETR	Entergy Corporation	3
EFX	Equifax Inc.	1
ESY	E-Systems, Inc.	2
EY	Ethyl Corporation	1
EVQ/EVRX	Everex Systems, Inc.	1
XON	Exxon Corporation	1
LXO	**Exxon Corporation (July-92)**	**1**
ZXO	**Exxon Corporation (Jan-93)**	**1**
FNM	Fannie Mae (Fed. Nat. Mort. Assn.)	3
FJQ	Fedders Corporation	1
FDX	Federal Express Corporation	1
FMO	Federal-Mogul Corporation	1
FBO	Federal Paper Board Company	1
FOE	Ferro Corporation	1
FBS	**First Bank System, Inc.**	**3**
FNB	First Chicago Corporation	1
FFB	First Fidelity Bancorporation	3
FFM	**First Financial Management Corp.**	**1**
I	First Interstate Bancorp	1
FRM	First Mississippi Corporation	1
FOA	**First Of America Bank Corp.**	**2**
FTU	First Union Corporation	1

Table 3.16 continued

exchange[5]	industry group	position limit
A	Electronic/Electric Equipment	8000
X	Electric/Gas/Sanitary Services	5500
A	Engineering/Management Services	8000
A,C	Chemicals & Allied Products	8000
A	**Chemicals & Allied Products**	**8000**
A	**Chemicals & Allied Products**	**8000**
A	Textile Mill Products	3000
X	Electric/Gas/Sanitary Services	3000
C	Photographic Equipment/Supplies	8000
C	**Photographic Equipment/Supplies**	**8000**
C	**Photographic Equipment/Supplies**	**8000**
C	Transportation Equipment	5500
P	Transportation Equipment	3000
P	Metal Mining	8000
N	Chemicals & Allied Products	3000
N	Apparel/Accessory Stores	3000
C	Security Brokers/Dealers	3000
X	Engineering/Management Services	3000
C	Drugs	3000
A	Electronic/Electric Equipment	8000
C	Primary Metal Industries	3000
C	Electric/Gas/Sanitary Services	3000
P	Electric/Gas/Sanitary Services	5500
C	Electric/Gas/Sanitary Services	8000
P	Insurance Agents/Brokers/Service	3000
P	Instruments & Related Products	3000
P	Chemicals & Allied Products	5500
C	Computer/Office Equipment	5500
C	Petroleum/Coal Products	8000
C	**Petroleum/Coal Products**	**8000**
C	**Petroleum/Coal Products**	**8000**
X	Nondepository Credit Institutions	8000
N	Industrial/Commercial Machinery	3000
C	Air Transportation	5500
P	Transportation Equipment	3000
P	Paper & Allied Products	3000
X	Chemicals & Allied Products	3000
A,C	**Depository Institutions**	**5500**
C	Depository Institutions	8000
C	Depository Institutions	5500
N	**Depository Institutions**	**3000**
C	Depository Institutions	8000
P	Chemicals & Allied Products	3000
X	**Depository Institutions**	**3000**
P	Depository Institutions	5500

Table 3.16 continued

symbol[2]	name[3]	cycle[4]
FW	First Wachovia Corporation	1
FNG	Fleet/Norstar Financial Group, Inc.	1
FLE	Fleetwood Enterprises, Inc.	2
FLM	Fleming Companies, Inc.	2
FSI	**Flightsafety International Corp.**	**3**
FLO	**Flowers Industries Inc.**	**1**
FLR	Fluor Corporation	1
FMC	FMC Corporation	2
FAQ/FDLNA	Food Lion, Inc., Class A (non-voting)	1
FBQ/FDLNB	Food Lion, Inc., Class B	1
F	Ford Motor Company	3
FRX	Forest Laboratories, Inc.	2
FWC	Foster Wheeler Corporation	1
FPL	FPL Group (Florida P & L)	3
BEN	Franklin Resources, Inc.	1
FRE	Freddie Mac (FHLMC)	1
FTX	Freeport-McMoRan Inc.	2
FCX	Freeport-McMoRan Copper Co., Inc.	3
FRP	Freeport-McMoRan Resource Partners, L.P.	3
FTL	Fruit of the Loom, Inc.	2
FFC	The Fund American Companies	3
FQA	Fuqua Industries, Inc.	3
GAL	Galoob (Lewis) Toys, Inc.	1
GCI	Gannett Company, Inc.	1
GPS	Gap Inc.	3
GMT	**GATX Corporation**	**3**
GY	GenCorp Inc.	3
GNE/GNZ	Genentech Inc.	1
GCN	General Cinema Corporation	2
GD	General Dynamics Corporation	2
GE	General Electric Company	3
LGR	**General Electric Co. (Sept-92)**	**3**
ZGR	**General Electric Co. (Mar-93)**	**3**
GIS	General Mills, Inc.	1
LMI	**General Mills, Inc. (July-92)**	**1**
ZMI	**General Mills, Inc. (Jan-93)**	**1**
GM	General Motors Corporation	3
LGM	**General Motors Corp. (Sept-92)**	**3**
ZGM	**General Motors Corp. (Mar-93)**	**3**
GME	General Motors Corp. (Class E)	3
GPU	General Public Utilities Corp.	2
GRN	General Re Corporation	3
GSX	General Signal Corporation	2
GPC	Genuine Parts Company	2
GGC	Georgia Gulf Corporation	2
GP	Georgia-Pacific Corporation	1

Table 3.16 continued

exchange[5]	industry group	position limit
P	Depository Institutions	3000
A	Depository Institutions	5500
A	Transportation Equipment	3000
P	Food Stores	3000
X	**Educational Services**	**3000**
X	**Food Products**	**3000**
C	Heavy Construction (Ex Building)	5500
N	Chemicals & Allied Products	3000
A	Food Stores	5500
A	Food Stores	3000
C	Transportation Equipment	8000
C	Drugs	3000
P	Heavy Construction (Ex Building)	5500
X	Electric/Gas/Sanitary Services	8000
P	Security/Commodity Services	3000
A	Nondepository Credit Institutions	8000
C	Chemicals & Allied Products	5500
X	Metal Mining	3000
A	Chemicals & Allied Products	3000
N	Textile Mill Products	5500
C	Insurance Carriers	5500
C	Business Services	3000
P	Toys/Sporting Goods	3000
P	Printing/Publishing	8000
C	Apparel/Accessory Stores	8000
X	**Transportation Services**	**3000**
C	Transportation Equipment	3000
C,P	Drugs	8000
C	General Merchandise Stores	3000
C	Transportation Equipment	3000
C	Electronic/Electric Equipment	8000
C	**Electronic/Electric Equipment**	**8000**
C	**Electronic/Electric Equipment**	**8000**
P	Food Products	8000
P	**Food Products**	**8000**
P	**Food Products**	**8000**
C	Transportation Equipment	8000
C	**Transportation Equipment**	**8000**
C	**Transportation Equipment**	**8000**
X	Computer/Data Processing Services	5500
N	Electric/Gas/Sanitary Services	5500
A	Insurance Carriers	5500
X	Industrial/Commercial Machinery	3000
P	Wholesale Trade/Durable Goods	5500
X	Chemicals & Allied Products	5500
X	Lumber/Wood Products	5500

Table 3.16 continued

symbol[2]	name[3]	cycle[4]
GEB	Gerber Products Company	1
GRB	Gerber Scientific, Inc.	3
GFS	Giant Food, Inc. (Class A)	3
GIQ/GIBG	Gibson Greetings, Inc.	3
GS	Gillette Company	3
GLX	Glaxo Holdings p.l.c.	2
GLN	GLENFED, Inc.	1
GNG	Golden Nugget, Inc.	2
GVF	Golden Valley Microwave Foods, Inc.	1
GDW	Golden West Financial Corp.	2
GR	Goodrich (B.F.) Company	2
GT	Goodyear Tire & Rubber Company	1
GUQ/GULD	Goulds Pumps, Inc.	3
GRA	Grace (W.R.) & Co.	2
GWW	Grainger (W.W.), Inc.	1
GRM	**Grand Metropolitan PLC**	**1**
GSQ/GSCC	Graphic Scanning Corp.	1
GAP	Great Atlantic & Pacific Tea Co., Inc.	1
GLK	Great Lakes Chemical Corporation	3
GWF	Great Western Financial Corporation	1
G	Greyhound Dial Corporation	1
GWQ/GWTI	**Groundwater Technology Inc.**	**1**
GRO	Grow Group, Inc.	2
GQ	Grumman Corporation	1
GTE	GTE Corporation	3
LGT	**GTE Corporation (Sept-92)**	**3**
ZGT	**GTE Corporation (Dec-93)**	**3**
HRB	H & R Block, Inc.	1
HAL	Halliburton Company	1
HDL	Handleman Company	3
MAH	Hanna (M.A.) Company	3
HAN	Hanson Industries PLC	3
JH	Harland (John H.) Co.	3
HDI	Harley-Davidson, Inc.	2
HPH	Harnischfeger Industries, Inc.	2
HRS	Harris Corporation	2
HSC	Harsco Corporation	1
HAS	Hasbro Inc.	1
HBQ/HBOC	HBO & Company	1
HCQ/HECHA	Hechinger Co., Class A	3
HL	Hecla Mining Company	3
HNZ	Heinz (H.J.) Company	3
HP	Helmerich & Payne, Incorporated	3
HPC	Hercules Incorporated	3
HSY	Hershey Foods Corporation	2
HWP	Hewlett-Packard Company	2
HLT	Hilton Hotels Corporation	1

Table 3.16 continued

exchange[5]	industry group	position limit
A	Food Products	3000
X	Computer/Data Processing Services	3000
A	Food Stores	3000
X	Printing/Publishing	3000
A	Fabricated Metal Products	8000
A	Drugs	8000
A	Depository Institutions	5500
A	Amusement/Recreation Facilities	5500
A	Food Products	3000
X	Depository Institutions	5500
C	Chemicals & Allied Products	3000
A	Rubber/Plastics Products	5500
N	Industrial/Commercial Machinery	5500
A	Chemicals & Allied Products	5500
A	Wholesale Trade/Durable Goods	3000
A	**Food Products**	**5500**
C	Telephone Communications	3000
A	Food Stores	3000
C	Chemicals & Allied Products	3000
C	Depository Institutions	8000
A	Eating & Drinking Places	3000
N	**Engineering/Management Services**	**3000**
P	Chemicals & Allied Products	3000
C	Transportation Equipment	3000
A	Telephone Communications	8000
A	**Telephone Communications**	**8000**
A	**Telephone Communications**	**8000**
A	Personal Services	3000
C	Oil/Gas Extraction	8000
C	Wholesale Trade/Durable Goods	3000
N	Rubber/Plastics Products	3000
C	Tobacco Products	8000
N	Printing/Publishing	3000
X	Transportation Equipment	3000
X	Industrial/Commercial Machinery	3000
C	Electronic/Electric Equipment	5500
C	Fabricated Metal Products	3000
P	Toys/Sporting Goods	5500
P	Computer/Data Processing Services	3000
X	Building/Hardware/Garden Stores	3000
A	Metal Mining	3000
C	Food Products	8000
N	Oil/Gas Extraction	3000
A	Chemicals & Allied Products	5500
A	Food Products	5500
C	Computer/Office Equipment	8000
P	Hotels/Lodging Places	8000

Table 3.16 continued

symbol[2]	name[3]	cycle[4]
LHT	**Hilton Hotels Corp. (July-92)**	**1**
ZHT	**Hilton Hotels Corp. (Jan-93)**	**1**
HIT	Hitachi, Ltd.	1
HD	Home Depot, Inc.	2
HFD	HomeFed Corporation	1
HM	Homestake Mining Company	1
HMC	Honda Motor Co., Ltd.	1
HON	Honeywell Inc.	2
HTN	Houghton Mifflin Company	1
HI	Household International, Inc.	1
HOU	Houston Industries Incorporated	3
HUM	Humana Inc.	2
IBP	IBP Inc.	2
ITW	Illinois Tool Works, Inc.	3
IMA	IMCERA Group Inc.	1
ICI	Imperial Chemical Industries PLC	1
IMO	**Imperial Oil Ltd.**	**1**
N	Inco Limited	1
IRQ/IRIC	Information Resources, Inc.	2
IR	Ingersoll-Rand Company	3
IAD	Inland Steel Industries, Inc.	3
INQ/INTC	Intel Corporation	1
LNL	**Intel Corporation (Dec-92)**	**1**
ZNL	**Intel Corporation (Dec-93)**	**1**
IGQ/INGR	Intergraph Corporation	1
IMQ/INTR	Intermec Corporation	1
IBM	International Business Machines Corp.	1
LIB	**International Business Machines (July-92)**	**1**
ZIB	**International Business Machines (Jan-93)**	**1**
IFF	International Flavors & Fragrances Inc.	2
GTQ/IGAM	International Game Technology	1
IP	International Paper Company	1
IPG	The Interpublic Grp. of Companies, Inc.	1
ITL	Itel Corporation	1
ITT	ITT Corporation	3
JR	James River Corporation of Virginia	3
JBM	Jan Bell Marketing, Inc.	1
JP	**Jefferson Pilot Corporation**	**1**
JNJ	Johnson & Johnson	1
LJN	**Johnson & Johnson (July-92)**	**1**
ZJN	**Johnson & Johnson (Jan-93)**	**1**
JCI	Johnson Controls, Inc.	1
JOS	Jostens Inc.	3
JWP	JWP, Inc.	1
KM	K Mart Corporation	3

Table 3.16 continued

exchange[5]	industry group	position limit
P	**Hotels/Lodging Places**	**8000**
P	**Hotels/Lodging Places**	**8000**
C	Electronic/Electric Equipment	3000
X	Building/Hardware/Garden Stores	8000
C	Depository Institutions	5500
C	Metal Mining	8000
X	Transportation Equipment	3000
C	Instruments & Related Products	5500
P	Printing/Publishing	3000
A	Nondepository Credit Institutions	5500
N	Electric/Gas/Sanitary Services	8000
C	Hospitals	5500
A,X	Food Products	5500
X	Rubber/Plastics Products	3000
C	Chemicals & Allied Products	3000
N	Chemicals & Allied Products	3000
C	**Petroleum/Coal Products**	**3000**
A	Primary Metal Industries	5500
C	Computer/Data Processing Services	3000
N	Industrial/Commercial Machinery	5500
X	Primary Metal Industries	3000
A	Electronic Components/Accessories	8000
A	**Electronic Components/Accessories**	**8000**
A	**Electronic Components/Accessories**	**8000**
A	Computer/Office Equipment	8000
C	Computer/Office Equipment	5500
C	Computer/Office Equipment	8000
C	**Computer/Office Equipment**	**8000**
C	**Computer/Office Equipment**	**8000**
C	Chemicals & Allied Products	3000
A	Misc. Manufacturing	3000
C	Paper & Allied Products	8000
N	Advertising	3000
C	Wholesale Trade/Durable Goods	3000
C	Electronic/Electric Equipment	8000
N	Paper & Allied Products	5500
A,C	Jewelry/Silverware	5500
A	**Insurance Carriers**	**3000**
C	Drugs	8000
C	**Drugs**	**8000**
C	**Drugs**	**8000**
X	Instruments & Related Products	3000
N	Jewelry/Silverware	3000
A	Special Trade Contractors	5500
C	General Merchandise Stores	8000

Table 3.16 continued

symbol[2]	name[3]	cycle[4]
KBH	Kaufman and Broad Home Corp.	1
K	Kellogg Company	3
KEM	Kemper Corporation	1
KMG	Kerr-McGee Corporation	1
KII	**Keystone International Inc.**	**3**
KMB	Kimberly-Clark Corporation	1
KWP	King World Productions	2
KLM	**KLM Royal Dutch Airlines**	**3**
KRI	Knight-Ridder Inc.	1
KR	Kroger Co.	1
LAC	LAC Minerals Ltd.	1
LA	L.A. Gear, Inc.	1
LDW	Laidlaw Inc., Class B	3
LKQ/LMRK	Landmark Graphics Corporation	1
LE	Lands' End Inc.	3
LAW	**Lawter International**	**3**
LGQ/LGNT	Legent Corp.	1
LLY	Lilly (Eli) and Company	1
LTD	Limited Inc.	2
LNQ/LINB	LIN Broadcasting Corporation	2
LNC	**Lincoln National Corporation**	**1**
LIT	Litton Industries, Inc.	3
LIQ/LIZC	Liz Claiborne, Inc.	1
LK	Lockheed Corporation	3
LTR	Loews Corporation	3
LCE	Lone Star Industries, Inc.	3
LIL	**Long Island Lighting Company**	**N**
LFB	Longview Fibre Company	3
LOR	Loral Corporation	1
LOQ/LOTS	Lotus Development Corporation	1
LLX	Louisiana Land & Exploration	2
LPX	Louisiana-Pacific Corporation	2
LOW	Lowe's Companies, Inc.	1
LSI	LSI Logic Corporation	1
LZ	Lubrizol Corporation	2
LUB	**Luby's Cafeterias, Inc.**	**1**
LYO	Lyondell Petrochemical Company	3
MNR	Manor Care, Inc.	1
MHC	Manufacturers Hanover Corporation	1
MDA	Mapco, Inc.	1
MKC	Marion Merrill Dow, Inc.	1
MHS	Marriott Corporation	1
MMC	Marsh & McLennan Companies, Inc.	1
ML	Martin Marietta Corporation	3
MAS	Masco Corporation	1
MAQ/MASX	Masco Industries	1
MAT	Mattel, Inc.	1

Table 3.16 continued

exchange[5]	industry group	position limit
X	Real Estate	3000
A	Food Products	5500
X	Insurance Carriers	3000
C	Petroleum/Coal Products	5500
P	**Fabricated Metal Products**	**3000**
A	Paper & Allied Products	5500
P	Motion Pictures	3000
C	**Air Transportation**	**3000**
X	Printing/Publishing	3000
A	Food Stores	5500
C	Metal Mining	5500
C	Rubber/Plastics Products	8000
A	Electric/Gas/Sanitary Services	8000
A	Computer/Data Processing Services	3000
C	Non-store Retailers	3000
X	**Chemicals & Allied Products**	**3000**
C	Computer/Data Processing Services	5500
A	Drugs	8000
C	Apparel/Accessory Stores	8000
X	Radio/Television Broadcasting	5500
A	**Insurance Carriers**	**3000**
C	Instruments & Related Products	3000
C	Apparel & Other Textile Products	8000
P	Transportation Equipment	5500
C	Nondepository Credit Institutions	5500
X	Stone/Clay/Glass Products	3000
3	**Electric/Gas/Sanitary Services**	**5500**
C	Paper & Allied Products	3000
C	Instruments & Related Products	3000
A	Computer/Data Processing Services	8000
X	Oil/Gas Extraction	3000
A	Lumber & Wood Products	3000
X	Building/Hardware/Garden Stores	5500
C	Electronic Components/Accesories	3000
X	Chemicals & Allied Products	3000
C	**Eating/Drinking Places**	**3000**
N	Chemicals & Allied Products	3000
X	Nursing/Personal Care Facilities	3000
A	Depository Institutions	8000
P	Petroleum/Coal Products	3000
P	Drugs	5500
X	Eating/Drinking Places	8000
P	Insurance Agents/Brokers/Service	5500
X	Transportation Equipment	3000
A	Furniture/Fixtures	8000
P	Transportation Equipment	3000
A	Toys/Sporting Goods	5500

Table 3.16 continued

symbol[2]	name[3]	cycle[4]
MXQ/MXTR	Maxtor Corporation	1
MXS	Maxus Energy Corporation	1
MA	May Department Stores Company	3
MYG	Maytag Corporation	1
MWQ/MCAWA	McCaw Cellular Comm., Inc. (Class A)	3
MKQ/MCCRK	McCormick and Company, Inc.	3
MDR	McDermott International, Inc.	2
MCD	McDonald's Corporation	3
LMC	**McDonald's Corp. (Sept-92)**	**3**
ZMC	**McDonald's Corp. (Mar-93)**	**3**
MD	McDonnell Douglas Corporation	2
MHP	McGraw-Hill Inc.	2
MCQ/MCIC	MCI Communications Corporation	1
MCK	McKesson Corporation	2
MEA	Mead Corporation	1
MDQ/MCCS	Medco Containment Services	1
MEQ/MEDC	**Medical Care International, Inc.**	**1**
MDT	Medtronic Inc.	2
MEL	Mellon Bank Corporation	3
MES	Melville Corporation	2
MNQ/MNTR	Mentor Corporation	1
MGQ/MENT	Mentor Graphics Corporation	1
MST	Mercantile Stores Co., Inc.	3
MRK	Merck & Co., Inc.	1
LMK	**Merck & Co., Inc. (July-92)**	**1**
ZMK	**Merck & Co., Inc. (Jan-93)**	**1**
MDP	**Meredith Corporation**	**2**
MER	Merrill Lynch & Co., Inc.	1
MGR	**Merry-Go-Round Enterprises, Inc.**	**1**
MLP	Mesa Limited Partnership (Depository Units)	1
MO	**Michigan National Corporation**	**1**
DRQ/MCRN	Micron Technology, Inc.	1
MSQ/MSFT	Microsoft Corporation	1
LMT	**Microsoft Corporation (July-92)**	**1**
ZMT	**Microsoft Corporation (Jan-93)**	**1**
MLQ/MIDL	Midlantic Corporation	1
MDW	Midway Airlines, Inc.	1
MHQ/MLHR	Miller (Herman),Inc.	2
MIL	Millipore Corporation	1
MMM	Minnesota Mining & Manufacturing	1
MPQ/MIPS	MIPS Computer Systems, Inc.	1
MND	Mitchell Energy & Development Corp.	3
MNC	MNC Financial Inc.	1
MOB	Mobil Corporation	2
MB	Molecular Biosystems, Inc.	1
MOQ/MOLX	Molex Incorporated	1

Table 3.16 continued

exchange[5]	industry group	position limit
P	Computer/Office Equipment	8000
P	Oil/Gas Extraction	5500
C	General Merchandise Stores	8000
N	Household Appliances	5500
A,C	Telephone Communications	8000
X	Food Products	3000
X	Fabricated Metal Products	5500
C	Eating/Drinking Places	8000
C	**Eating/Drinking Places**	**8000**
C	**Eating/Drinking Places**	**8000**
P	Transportation Equipment	5500
X	Printing/Publishing	5500
C	Telephone Communications	8000
P	Wholesale Trade/Nondurable Goods	3000
C	Paper & Allied Products	5500
P	Non-store Retailers	8000
C,P	**Health Services**	**5500**
C	Medical Instruments & Supplies	3000
N	Depository Institutions	3000
P	Apparel/Accessory Stores	5500
A,P	Medical Instruments & Supplies	5500
A	Computer/Data Processing Services	8000
X	General Merchandise Stores	3000
C	Drugs	8000
C	**Drugs**	**8000**
C	**Drugs**	**8000**
X	**Printing/Publishing**	**3000**
A,C	Security Brokers/Dealers	5500
A,C,N,X	**Apparel/Accessory Stores**	**3000**
A	Oil/Gas Extraction	5500
A	**Depository Institutions**	**3000**
A,C,P	Electronic Components/Accessories	8000
A,P	Computer/Data Processing Services	8000
P	**Computer/Data Processing Services**	**8000**
P	**Computer/Data Processing Services**	**8000**
A	Depository Institutions	8000
C	Air Transportation	3000
N	Furniture/Fixtures	3000
A	Instruments & Related Products	3000
C	Paper & Allied Products	8000
A,C	Computer/Data Processing Services	5500
P	Oil/Gas Extraction	3000
A	Depository Institutions	8000
C	Petroleum/Coal Products	8000
A	Engineering/Management Services	3000
C	Electronic Components/Accesories	3000

Table 3.16 continued

symbol[2]	name[3]	cycle[4]
MTC	Monsanto Company	1
JPM	Morgan (J.P.)& Co., Inc.	3
MS	Morgan Stanley Group, Inc.	2
MRQ/MORR	Morrison Inc.	1
MRN	**Morrison Knudsen Corp.**	**1**
MII	Morton International, Inc.	2
MOT	Motorola, Inc.	1
LMA	**Motorola, Inc. (Dec-92)**	**1**
ZMA	**Motorola, Inc. (Dec-93)**	**1**
MUR	Murphy Oil Corporation	2
MYL	Mylan Laboratories Inc.	1
NLC	Nalco Chemical Company	3
NSH	Nashua Corporation	1
NCC	**National City Corporation**	**1**
NTQ/NDTA	National Data Corporation	2
NME	National Medical Enterprises, Inc.	2
NSM	National Semiconductor Corporation	2
NSI	**National Service Industries Inc.**	**3**
NBD	**NBD Bancorp, Inc.**	**1**
NCB	NCNB Corporation	2
NCR	NCR Corporation	3
NMG	**Neiman Marcus Group Inc.**	**1**
NSQ/NSCO	Network Systems Corporation	1
NGQ/NGNA	**Neutrogena Corporation**	**1**
NEQ/NECC	**New England Critical Care Inc.**	**2**
NYT	New York Times (Class A)	1
NWL	Newell Co.	3
NGC	Newmont Gold Company	2
NEM	Newmont Mining Corporation	3
NMK	Niagara Mohawk Power Corporation	3
GAS	NICOR, Inc.	1
NKE	NIKE Inc. (Class B)	1
NL	NL Industries, Inc.	1
NBL	Noble Affiliates, Inc.	2
NRD	Nord Resources Corporation	1
NOQ/NOBE	Nordstrom, Inc.	1
NSC	Norfolk Southern Corporation	3
NT	Northern Telecom Limited	3
NRQ/NTRS	**Northern Trust Corporation**	**1**
NOC	Northrop Corporation	2
NOB	Norwest Corporation	1
NVQ/NOVL	Novell, Inc.	2
NUE	**Nucor Corporation**	**1**
NWN	**NWNL Companies, Inc.**	**1**
NYN	NYNEX Corporation	1
OXY	Occidental Petroleum Corporation	2
ODR	Ocean Drilling & Exploration Co.	2

Table 3.16 continued

exchange[5]	industry group	position limit
C	Chemicals & Allied Products	8000
X	Depository Institutions	8000
X	Security Brokers/Dealers	8000
N	Eating/Drinking Places	3000
X	**Building Construction**	**3000**
X	Chemicals & Allied Products	5500
A	Electronic/Electric Equipment	8000
A	**Electronic/Electric Equipment**	**8000**
A	**Electronic/Electric Equipment**	**8000**
P	Petroleum/Coal Products	3000
A	Drugs	5500
X	Chemicals & Allied Products	3000
A	Paper & Allied Products	3000
A	**Depository Institutions**	**3000**
X	Computer/Data Processing Services	3000
A	Hospitals	5500
A,C	Electronic Components/Accesories	8000
X	**Electronic/Electric Equipment**	**3000**
X	**Depository Institutions**	**3000**
X	Depository Institutions	8000
C	Computer/Office Equipment	8000
N	**General Merchandise Stores**	**3000**
A	Computer/Office Equipment	8000
X	**Chemicals & Allied Products**	**3000**
C,P	**Health Services**	**5500**
P	Printing/Publishing	5500
N	Stone/Clay/Glass Products	5500
X	Metal Mining	3000
X	Metal Mining	5500
A	Electric/Gas/Sanitary Services	8000
P	Electric/Gas/Sanitary Services	3000
P	Rubber/Plastics Products	8000
P	Chemicals & Allied Products	3000
A	Oil/Gas Extraction	3000
X	Metal Mining	3000
A	Apparel/Accessory Stores	8000
C	Railroad Transportation	8000
C	Electronic/Electric Equipment	8000
C	**Depository Institutions**	**3000**
C	Transportation Equipment	5500
P	Depository Institutions	5500
A	Computer/Data Processing Services	8000
C	**Primary Metal Industries**	**3000**
A,C	**Insurance Carriers**	**3000**
N	Telephone Communications	8000
C	Oil/Gas Extraction	8000
A	Oil/Gas Extraction	3000

Table 3.16 continued

symbol[2]	name[3]	cycle[4]
OEQ/OCER	Oceaneering International Inc.	1
OTQ/OCTL	Octel Communications Corp.	1
ODQ/ODEP	Office Depot Inc.	1
OG	Ogden Corporation	2
OHQ/OCAS	**Ohio Casualty Corporation**	**1**
OEC	Ohio Edison Company	1
ORI	Old Republic International Corp.	1
OLN	Olin Corporation	2
OMC	Omnicom Group, Inc.	1
OKE	ONEOK Inc.	2
ORQ/ORCL	Oracle Systems Corporation	3
ORX	Oryx Energy Company	1
GOQ/GOSHA	Oshkosh B'Gosh, Inc.	2
OM	Outboard Marine Corp.	3
OCF	Owens-Corning Fiberglas Corp.	3
PAQ/PCAR	PACCAR Inc.	2
PET	Pacific Enterprises	1
PCG	Pacific Gas & Electric Company	3
PAC	Pacific Telesis Group	1
LPC	**Pacific Telesis Group (July-92)**	**1**
ZPC	**Pacific Telesis Group (Jan-93)**	**1**
PPW	Pacificorp	2
PWJ	PaineWebber Group Inc.	1
PLL	Pall Corporation	3
PEL	Panhandle Eastern Corporation	1
PNS	Pansophic Systems, Incorporated	2
PCI	Paramount Communications Inc.	3
PH	Parker-Hannifin Corporation	2
PGU	Pegasus Gold Inc.	2
PC	Penn Central Corporation	3
JCP	Penney (J.C.) Company, Inc.	2
PZL	Pennzoil Company	1
PBY	Pep Boys—Manny, Moe, & Jack	1
PEP	PepsiCo Inc.	1
PKN	Perkin-Elmer Corporation	3
PST	Petrie Stores Corporation	3
PFE	Pfizer Inc.	3
LPE	**Pfizer Inc. (Dec-92)**	**3**
ZPE	**Pfizer Inc. (Dec-93)**	**3**
PD	Phelps Dodge Corporation	1
PE	Philadelphia Electric Co.	1
MO	Philip Morris Companies, Inc.	3
LMO	**Philip Morris Companies, Inc. (Sept-92)**	**3**
ZMO	**Philip Morris Companies, Inc. (Dec-93)**	**3**
PHG	Philips NV	1

Table 3.16 continued

exchange[5]	industry group	position limit
P	Oil/Gas Extraction	5500
P	Electronic/Electric Equipment	5500
A	Wholesale Trade/Nondurable Goods	3000
C	Engineering/Management Services	3000
A	**Insurance Carriers**	**3000**
P	Electric/Gas/Sanitary Services	8000
X	Insurance Carriers	3000
A	Chemicals & Allied Products	3000
P	Advertising	3000
X	Electric/Gas/Sanitary Services	3000
C	Computer/Data Processing Services	8000
A,C,X	Oil/Gas Extraction	5500
A,C	Apparel & Other Textile Products	3000
C	Industrial/Commercial Machinery	3000
X	Stone/Clay/Glass Products	3000
N	Transportation Equipment	3000
A	Electric/Gas/Sanitary Services	3000
A	Electric/Gas/Sanitary Services	8000
P	Telephone Communications	8000
P	**Telephone Communications**	**8000**
P	**Telephone Communications**	**8000**
P	Electric/Gas/Sanitary Services	8000
C	Security Brokers/Dealers	3000
C	Industrial/Commercial Machinery	3000
X	Electric/Gas/Sanitary Services	8000
C	Computer/Data Processing Services	3000
C	Motion Pictures	8000
X	Transportation Equipment	3000
C	Metal Mining	3000
X	Primary Metal Industries	5500
A	General Merchandise Stores	8000
C	Petroleum/Coal Products	3000
N	Auto Dealers/Gas & Service Stations	5500
C	Beverage Products	8000
P	Instruments & Related Products	5500
X	Apparel/Accessory Stores	3000
A	Drugs	8000
A	**Drugs**	**8000**
A	**Drugs**	**8000**
A	Primary Metal Industries	5500
P	Electric/Gas/Sanitary Services	8000
A	Tobacco Products	8000
A	**Tobacco Products**	**8000**
A	**Tobacco Products**	**8000**
N	Electronic/Electric Equipment	5500

Table 3.16 continued

symbol[2]	name[3]	cycle[4]
P	Phillips Petroleum Corporation	2
PIQ/PICN	Pic 'N' Save Corporation	1
PIR	Pier 1 Imports, Inc.	3
PNW	Pinnacle West Capital Corp.	1
PHQ/PHYB	Pioneer Hi-Bred International, Inc.	3
PBI	Pitney Bowes, Inc.	1
PCO	Pittston Company	2
PDG	Placer Dome Inc.	3
PNC	PNC Financial Corporation	2
PRD	Polaroid Corporation	1
PCH	Potlatch Corporation	3
PPG	PPG Industries, Inc.	2
PCP	Precision Castparts Corp.	2
PMI	Premark International, Inc.	1
PCQ/PCLB	Price Company	1
PDQ	Prime Motor Inns, Inc.	1
PA	Primerica Corporation	3
PG	Procter & Gamble Company	1
LPG	**Procter & Gamble Co. (July-92)**	**1**
ZPG	**Procter & Gamble Co. (Dec-93)**	**1**
PGR	**Progressive Corporation**	**2**
PRI	Promus Companies Incorporated	2
PEG	Public Service Enterprise Group Inc.	3
AQM	QMS, Inc.	2
OAT	Quaker Oats Company	1
KSF	Quaker State Corporation	3
CUE	Quantum Chemical Corporation	2
QNQ/QNTM	Quantum Corporation	2
QVQ/QVCN	QVC Network, Inc.	1
RTG	Racal Telecom plc	1
RAL	Ralston Purina Company	3
RYC	Raychem Corporation	1
RTN	Raytheon Company	2
RDA	Reader's Digest Association, Inc.	1
RBK	Reebok International Ltd.	1
LRK	**Reebok International Ltd. (Dec-92)**	**1**
ZRK	**Reebok International Ltd. (Dec-93)**	**1**
RTQ/RTRSY	Reuters Holdings PLC	2
RLM	Reynolds Metals Company	2
LRM	**Reynolds Metals Co. (Aug-92)**	**2**
ZRM	**Reynolds Metals Co. (Feb-93)**	**2**
RPR	Rhone-Poulenc Rorer, Inc.	1
RAD	Rite Aid Corporation	1
RSQ/ROAD	Roadway Services, Inc.	1
RCQ/RCSB	Rochester Community Savings Bank	1

Table 3.16 continued

exchange[5]	industry group	position limit
A	Petroleum/Coal Products	8000
P	General Merchandise Stores	8000
N	Home Furnishings Stores	3000
P	Electric/Gas/Sanitary Services	8000
A	Agriculture/Field Crops	3000
A	Computer/Office Equipment	5500
X	Air Transportation	3000
X	Metal Mining	8000
X	Depository Institutions	5500
C,P	Photographic Equipment/Supplies	5500
N	Paper & Allied Products	3000
X	Chemicals & Allied Products	5500
C	Primary Metal Industries	3000
C	Rubber/Plastics Products	3000
P	General Merchandise Stores	8000
P	Hotels/Lodging Places	8000
X	Nondepository Credit Institutions	8000
A	Chemicals & Allied Products	8000
A	**Chemicals & Allied Products**	**8000**
A	**Chemicals & Allied Products**	**8000**
X	**Insurance Carriers**	**3000**
C	Hotels/Lodging Places	5500
A	Electric/Gas/Sanitary Services	8000
N,X	Computer/Office Equipment	3000
X	Food Products	5500
A	Petroleum/Coal Products	3000
A	Chemicals & Allied Products	3000
N	Computer/Office Equipment	8000
A,X	Non-store Retailers	3000
A,C	Telephone Communications	3000
C	Food Products	5500
P	Electronic/Electric Equipment	3000
C	Instruments & Related Products	5500
A,C	Printing/Publishing	5500
A,P	Rubber/Plastics Products	8000
A	**Rubber/Plastics Products**	**8000**
A	**Rubber/Plastics Products**	**8000**
A,C	Business Services	8000
P	Primary Metal Industries	8000
P	**Primary Metal Industries**	**8000**
P	**Primary Metal Industries**	**8000**
A	Chemicals & Allied Products	8000
X	Drug/Proprietary Stores	3000
P	Trucking/Courier Services (Ex Air)	3000
A	Nondepository Credit Institutions	3000

Table 3.16 continued

symbol[2]	name[3]	cycle[4]
ROK	Rockwell International Corporation	1
ROH	Rohm and Haas Company	1
RHR	Rohr Industries, Inc.	3
REN	Rollins Environmental Services, Inc.	1
ROQ/ROUS	Rouse Company	C
RD	Royal Dutch Petroleum Company	1
RPQ/RPOW	RPM, Inc.	3
RBD	Rubbermaid, Inc.	2
RML	**Russell Corporation**	**1**
R	Ryder Systems, Inc.	2
SSI	SafeCard Services	1
SAQ/SAFC	SAFECO Corporation	2
SK	Safety-Kleen Corporation	3
SWY	Safeway, Inc.	3
SJQ/STJM	St. Jude Medical, Inc.	1
SPQ/STPL	Saint Paul Companies, Inc.	1
SLM	Sallie Mae (Student Loan Assn.)	1
SBF	Salomon Brothers Fund Inc.	2
SB	Salomon, Inc.	1
SFR	**Sante Fe Energy Resources, Inc.**	**1**
SFX	Sante Fe Pacific Corporation	3
SLE	Sara Lee Corporation	1
SCE	SCE Corp.	1
SGP	Schering-Plough Corporation	2
LSG	**Schering-Plough Corp. (Aug-92)**	**2**
ZSG	**Schering-Plough Corp. (Feb-93)**	**2**
SLB	Schlumberger Limited	2
SCH	Charles Schwab Corporation	3
SSQ/SCIS	SCI Systems, Inc.	1
SFA	Scientific-Atlanta, Inc.	3
SMQ/SMLS	SciMed Life Systems, Inc.	1
SXQ/SCIXF	Scitex Corporation Ltd.	1
SPP	Scott Paper Company	1
SGQ/SGAT	Seagate Technology, Inc.	3
VO	Seagram Company, Ltd.	2
SGO	**Seagull Energy Corp.**	**2**
S	Sears, Roebuck and Co.	1
LS	**Sears, Roebuck and Co. (July-92)**	**1**
ZS	**Sears, Roebuck and Co. (Jan-93)**	**1**
SPC	Security Pacific Corporation	3
SRQ/SNSR	Sensormatic Electronics Corporation	1
SQQ/SQNT	Sequent Computer Services, Inc.	1
SRV	Service Corporation International	2
SME	Service Merchandise Company, Inc.	1
SDQ/SMED	Shared Medical Systems Corporation	1
SHX	Shaw Industries Inc.	2
SNC	Shawmut National Corporation	3

Table 3.16 continued

exchange[5]	industry group	position limit
C	Transportation Equipment	8000
A	Chemicals & Allied Products	3000
X	Transportation Equipment	3000
P	Electric/Gas/Sanitary Services	5500
1	Real Estate	5500
A	Petroleum/Coal Products	8000
C	Chemicals & Allied Products	3000
P	Rubber/Plastics Products	3000
A	**Textile Mill Products**	**3000**
P	Auto Repair/Services/Parking	5500
P	Business Services	3000
N	Insurance Carriers	5500
X	Electric/Gas/Sanitary Services	3000
A,C,P	Food Stores	3000
C	Medical Instruments & Supplies	8000
C	Insurance Carriers	5500
C	Nondepository Credit Institutions	8000
X	Holding/Investment Offices	3000
X	Security Brokers/Dealers	8000
A,C	**Oil/Gas Extraction**	**3000**
A	Railroad Transportation	8000
A	Food Products	8000
P	Electric/Gas/Sanitary Services	8000
P	Drugs	8000
P	**Drugs**	**8000**
P	**Drugs**	**8000**
C	Oil/Gas Extraction	8000
C	Security Brokers/Dealers	3000
C	Instruments & Related Products	3000
P	Electronic/Electric Equipment	3000
C	Medical Instruments & Supplies	8000
A	Computer/Data Processing Services	5500
X	Paper & Allied Products	5500
A	Computer/Office Equipment	8000
P	Beverage Products	5500
X	**Electric/Gas/Sanitary Services**	**3000**
C	General Merchandise Stores	8000
C	**General Merchandise Stores**	**8000**
C	**General Merchandise Stores**	**8000**
X	Nondepository Credit Institutions	8000
A	Electronic/Electric Equipment	5500
A	Computer/Office Equipment	5500
X	Personal Services	5500
X	General Merchandise Stores	5500
P	Computer/Data Processing Services	3000
C	Textile Mill Products	3000
A	Depository Institutions	5500

Table 3.16 continued

symbol[2]	name[3]	cycle[4]
SC	Shell Transport & Trading Co., p.l.c.	2
SHW	Sherwin-Williams Company	3
SHN	Shoney's Inc.	1
IAQ/SIAL	**Sigma-Aldrich Corporation**	**1**
SBK	**Signet Banking Corp.**	**3**
SGI	Silicon Graphics, Inc.	2
SKY	Skyline Corporation	2
SCO	Smith Corona Corporation	1
SII	**Smith International Inc.**	**1**
SBE	SmithKline-Beecham, PLC	3
SNA	Snap-On Tools Corporation	3
SCQ/SPCO	Software Publishing Corp.	3
TWQ/TWRX	Software Toolworks, Inc.	1
SNT	Sonat Inc.	1
SOQ/SONO	Sonoco Products Company	1
BID	Sotheby's Holdings, Inc.	1
STB	Southeast Banking Corporation	2
SO	Southern Company	2
SNG	Southern New England Telecommunications	1
LUV	Southwest Airlines Co.	3
SBC	Southwestern Bell Corporation	1
SOZ	Sovran Financial Corporation	1
SPW	SPX Corp.	3
SQD	Square D Company	1
STH	Stanhome Inc.	2
SWK	Stanley Works	1
SKQ/STBK	State Street Boston Corp.	2
STO	Stone Container Corp.	3
STK	Storage Technology Corporation	3
SRA	Stratus Computer, Inc.	1
SRR	Stride Rite Corporation	1
SIQ/STRY	**Stryker Corporation**	**3**
SUN	Sun Company, Inc.	2
SUQ/SUNW	Sun Microsystems Inc.	1
SNS	Sundstrand Corporation	3
STI	SunTrust Banks, Inc.	1
SVU	Super Valu Stores Inc.	1
SFQ/SCAF	**Surgical Care Affiliates Inc.**	**1**
STQ/SLTI	**Surgical Laser Technologies, Inc.**	**2**
SBL	Symbol Technologies, Inc.	1
SYN	Syntex Corporation	3
SYY	Sysco Corporation	2
TMB	Tambrands Inc.	1
TDM	Tandem Computers Incorporated	1
TAN	Tandy Corporation	1
TBY	TCBY Enterprises Inc.	1

Table 3.16 continued

exchange[5]	industry group	position limit
C	Petroleum/Coal Products	3000
C	Chemicals & Allied Products	3000
P	Eating/Drinking Places	3000
C	**Wholesale Trade/Nondurable Goods**	**3000**
P	**Depository Institutions**	**5500**
A	Computer/Office Equipment	5500
C	Lumber/Wood Products	3000
N	Computer/Office Equipment	3000
X	**Industrial/Commercial Machinery**	**3000**
P	Drugs	8000
A	Fabricated Metal Products	3000
P,X	Computer/Data Processing Services	5500
A	Computer/Data Processing Services	8000
A	Electric/Gas/Sanitary Services	5500
P	Paper & Allied Products	3000
A,C,P	Business Services	5500
C	Depository Institutions	5500
C	Electric/Gas/Sanitary Services	8000
N	Telephone Communications	3000
C	Air Transportation	3000
P	Telephone Communications	8000
P	Depository Institutions	3000
N	Industrial/Commercial Machinery	3000
P	Electronic/Electric Equipment	3000
A	Chemicals & Allied Products	3000
P	Fabricated Metal Products	3000
X	Depository Institutions	5500
P	Paper & Allied Products	5500
C	Computer/Office Equipment	5500
P	Computer/Data Processing Services	5500
P	Leather & Leather Products	3000
X	**Medical Instruments & Supplies**	**3000**
X	Petroleum/Coal Products	3000
P	Computer/Data Processing Services	8000
N,P	Transportation Equipment	3000
P	Depository Institutions	5500
X	Wholesale Trade/Nondurable Goods	5500
N	**Health Services**	**3000**
A	**Medical Instruments & Supplies**	**5500**
A	Computer/Office Equipment	5500
C	Drugs	8000
N	Wholesale Trade/Nondurable Goods	5500
N	Paper & Allied Products	6000
A	Computer/Office Equipment	8000
A,C	Computer/Office Equipment	5500
P	Eating/Drinking Places	5500

Table 3.16 continued

symbol[2]	name[3]	cycle[4]
TEK	Tektronix Inc.	3
TCQ/TCOMA	Tele-Communications, Inc.	1
TDY	Teledyne Inc.	1
TEF	Telefonica de Espana, S.A.	3
TDS	Telephone & Data Systems, Inc.	2
TNQ/TLXN	Telxon Corporation	3
TIN	Temple-Inland, Inc.	2
TGT	Tenneco Inc.	2
TDQ/TDAT	Teradata Corporation	1
TER	Teradyne Inc.	1
TSO	Tesoro Petroleum Corporation	2
TX	Texaco Inc.	1
LTC	**Texaco Inc. (July-92)**	**1**
ZTC	**Texaco Inc. (Dec-93)**	**1**
TXN	Texas Instruments Incorporated	1
TXU	Texas Utilities Company	1
TXT	Textron Inc.	3
TMO	Thermo Electron Corp.	3
TKC	Thiokol Corporation	1
THQ/COMS	3Com Corporation	1
TDW	**Tidewater Inc.**	**1**
TIF	Tiffany & Co.	2
TWX	Time Warner Inc.	3
TMC	Times Mirror Company	3
TKR	Timken Company	3
TJX	TJX Companies Inc.	1
TKA	Tonka Corporation	1
TOQ/TOPPC	The Topps Company	2
TMK	Torchmark Corporation	2
TOS	Tosco Corporation	1
TOY	Toys 'R' Us, Inc.	3
TA	Transamerica Corporation	2
E	Transco Energy Company	2
TIC	Travelers Corporation	2
TRB	Tribune Company	2
TY	Tri-Continental Corporation	3
TRN	Trinity Industries, Inc.	1
TNV	Trinova Corporation	2
TRW	TRW Inc.	1
TEP	Tucson Electric Power Company	1
TYC	Tyco Laboratories, Inc.	1
TYQ/TYSNA	Tyson Foods, Inc.	1
UAL	UAL Corporation	2
UJB	UJB Financial Corp.	1
UN	Unilever N.V.	2
UCC	Union Camp Corporation	3
UK	Union Carbide Corporation	1

Table 3.16 continued

exchange[5]	industry group	position limit
C	Instruments & Related Products	3000
A	Cable/Pay TV Services	8000
C,P	Transportation Equipment	3000
A	Telephone Communications	8000
P	Telephone Communications	3000
C	Computer/Data Processing Services	3000
A	Paper & Allied Products	3000
A	Industrial/Commercial Machinery	8000
C	Computer/Office Equipment	5500
P	Instruments & Related Products	3000
X	Petroleum/Coal Products	3000
A	Petroleum/Coal Products	8000
A	**Petroleum/Coal Products**	**8000**
A	**Petroleum/Coal Products**	**8000**
C	Electronic/Electric Equipment	8000
P	Electric/Gas/Sanitary Services	8000
X	Transportation Equipment	5500
N	Heavy Construction (Ex Building)	3000
X	Chemicals & Allied Products	3000
P	Computer/Office Equipment	8000
N,X	**Water Transportation/Cruises**	**3000**
X	Miscellaneous Retail	3000
X	Printing/Publishing	5500
N	Printing/Publishing	5500
N	Industrial/Commercial Machinery	3000
C	General Merchandise Stores	5500
A,X	Toys/Sporting Goods	3000
X	Printing/Publishing	5500
A	Insurance Carriers	3000
A	Petroleum/Coal Products	5500
C	Miscellaneous Retail	8000
X	Nondepository Credit Institutions	3000
N	Electric/Gas/Sanitary Services	3000
P	Insurance Carriers	8000
C	Printing/Publishing	5500
X	Holding/Investment Offices	3000
A	Transportation Equipment	3000
X	Industrial/Commercial Machinery	3000
A	Transportation Equipment	3000
A	Electric/Gas/Sanitary Services	3000
X	Primary Metal Industries	5500
P	Food Products	5500
C	Air Transportation	5500
C	Depository Institutions	3000
A	Food Products	5500
C	Paper & Allied Products	5500
A	Chemicals & Allied Products	8000

Table 3.16 continued

symbol[2]	name[3]	cycle[4]
LCB	**Union Carbide Corp. (July-92)**	**1**
ZCB	**Union Carbide Corp. (Dec-93)**	**1**
UNP	Union Pacific Corporation	2
UIS	Unisys Corporation	1
UHQ/UNIH	**United HealthCare Corporation**	**3**
USR	United States Shoe Corporation	1
USS	United States Surgical Corporation	1
UTX	United Technologies Corporation	2
UT	United Telecommunications, Inc.	2
UNQ/UNIT	Unitrin, Inc.	1
UFC	Universal Foods Corp.	3
UCL	Unocal Corporation	1
LUL	**Unocal Corporation (July-92)**	**1**
ZUL	**Unocal Corporation (Jan-93)**	**1**
UXC	Unocal Exploration Corporation	1
UNM	UNUM Corporation	3
UPJ	Upjohn Company	1
U	USAir Group Inc.	3
UBQ/USBC	**U.S. Bancorp**	**1**
FG	USF&G Corp.	1
USQ/USHC	U.S. HealthCare, Inc.	1
UST	UST Inc.	2
USW	US WEST, Inc.	1
X	USX Corporation	1
LX	**USX Corporation (Dec-92)**	**1**
ZX	**USX Corporation (Dec-93)**	**1**
VLO	Valero Energy Corporation	3
VHI	Valhi Inc.	3
VNQ/VNCP	Valley National Corporation	3
VAR	Varian Associates, Inc.	2
VFC	V.F. Corporation	2
VIA	Viacom, Inc.	2
VC	Vista Chemical Co.	3
VON	**Vons Companies Inc.**	**3**
WBN	Waban Inc.	3
WAG	Walgreen Company	1
WCS	**Wallace Computer Services Inc.**	**3**
WMT	Wal-Mart Stores, Inc.	3
WLA	Warner-Lambert Company	1
WAQ/WAMU	Washington Mutual Savings Bank	1
WMX	Waste Management, Inc.	2
WLM	Wellman Inc.	3
WFC	Wells Fargo & Company	1
WEN	Wendy's International, Inc.	3
WDC	Western Digital Corporation	1
WPQ/WPGI	Western Publishing Group, Inc.	3
WX	Westinghouse Electric Corporation	1

Table 3.16 continued

exchange[5]	industry group	position limit
A	**Chemicals & Allied Products**	**8000**
A	**Chemicals & Allied Products**	**8000**
X	Railroad Transportation	5500
A,C	Computer/Office Equipment	8000
A,C,N,X	**Insurance Carriers**	**8000**
X	Apparel/Accessory Stores	5500
A	Medical Instruments & Supplies	3000
C	Transportation Equipment	8000
X	Telephone Communications	8000
C	Insurance Carriers	5500
X	Food Products	3000
P	Petroleum/Coal Products	8000
P	**Petroleum/Coal Products**	**8000**
P	**Petroleum/Coal Products**	**8000**
C	Oil/Gas Extraction	3000
A	Insurance Carriers	3000
C	Drugs	8000
P	Air Transportation	5500
A,P	**Depository Institutions**	**8000**
X	Insurance Carriers	8000
A	Insurance Carriers	8000
C	Tobacco Products	5500
A	Telephone Communications	8000
A	Petroleum/Coal Products	8000
A	**Petroleum/Coal Products**	**8000**
A	**Petroleum/Coal Products**	**8000**
A	Petroleum/Coal Products	5500
X	Chemicals & Allied Products	3000
A	Depository Institutions	5500
A	Electronic Components/Accessories	3000
N	Apparel & Other Textile Products	5500
X	Cable/Pay TV Services	3000
P	Chemicals & Allied Products	3000
N,P	**Food Stores**	**3000**
C	General Merchandise Stores	5500
A	Drug/Proprietary Stores	5500
X	**Printing/Publishing**	**3000**
C	General Merchandise Stores	8000
A	Drugs	8000
A	Nondepository Credit Institutions	3000
X	Electric/Gas/Sanitary Services	8000
N	Chemicals & Allied Products	5500
A	Depository Institutions	8000
P	Eating/Drinking Places	8000
P	Electronic/Electric Equipment	5500
X	Printing/Publishing	3000
A	Electronic/Electric Equipment	8000

Table 3.16 continued

symbol[2]	name[3]	cycle[4]
WRQ/WMRK	Westmark International, Inc.	1
W	Westvaco Corporation	1
WY	Weyerhaeuser Company	1
WTI	Wheelabrator Technologies Inc.	1
WHR	Whirlpool Corporation	3
WH	Whitman Corporation	3
WMQ/WMTT	Willamette Industries, Inc.	2
WMB	Williams Companies, Inc.	2
WND	Windmere Corporation	1
WIN	**Winn-Dixie Stores Incorporated**	**1**
WIT	**Witco Corporation**	**1**
Z	Woolworth Corporation	2
WTQ/WTHG	Worthington Industries Inc.	3
WWY	Wrigley (Wm.) Jr. Company	3
XRX	Xerox Corporation	1
YLQ/YELL	Yellow Freight Systems, Inc.	3
ZE	Zenith Electronics Corporation	2
ZRN	Zurn Industries, Inc.	1

Table 3.16 continued

exchange[5]	industry group	position limit
X	Medical Instruments & Supplies	5500
P	Paper & Allied Products	3000
C	Lumber/Wood Products	8000
A	Instruments & Related Products	3000
C	Household Appliances	5500
C	Food Products	5500
N	Paper & Allied Products	3000
C	Electric/Gas/Sanitary Services	5500
P	Household Appliances	3000
C	**Food Stores**	**3000**
N	**Petroleum/Coal Products**	**3000**
X	General Merchandise Stores	8000
X	Primary Metal Industries	3000
A	Food Products	3000
C,P	Photographic Equipment/Supplies	5500
C	Trucking/Courier Services (Ex Air)	3000
A	Household Audio/Video Equipment	3000
A	Industrial/Commercial Machinery	3000

Table 3.17 Index Options[1]

symbol	name	exchange
ADR	International Market Index	A
FNC	Financial News Network Composite Index	P
JPN	**Japan Index**	**A**
LSX	**SPX LEAPS (underlying index value/Dec-1992 exp.)**	**C**
LSW	**SPX LEAPS (Dec-1993 exp.)**	**C**
NSX	S&P 500 Index – Settle On Open	C
NYA	NYSE Composite Index®	N
OEX	S&P 100 Index	C
OLX	**OEX LEAPS (underlying index value/Dec-1992 exp.)**	**C**
OAX	**OEX LEAPS (Dec-1993 exp.)**	**C**
SPL	S&P 500 Index – Long Term	C
SPX	S&P 500 Index	C
UTY	Utility Index	X
VLE	Value Line Composite Index	X
XAU	Gold and Silver Index	X
XCI	Computer Technology Index	A
XII	Institutional Index	A
XIV	Institutional Index – Long Term (Two-Year)	A
XIX	Institutional Index – Long Term (Three-Year)	A
XLT	**LT-20 Index (underlying index value/Dec-1992 exp.)**	**A**
LTA	**LT-20 Index (Dec-1993 exp.)**	**A**
XMI	Major Market Index	A
XOC	National Over-The-Counter Index	X
XOI	Oil Index	A

Source: The Options Clearing Corporations, *Directory of Exchange Listed Options*, (Chicago: The Options Clearing Corporation, April 1991).

1. All options added since September 1990 are indicated in bold face type

2. Over-the-counter stocks are listed with two symbols. The first symbol represents the option code and the second symbol represents the National Association of Securities Dealers (NASD) code.

3. Long-term equity options are noted by expiration month and year.

4. Expiration cycles are 1 = January sequential, 2 = February sequential, 3 = March sequential. (See Table 3.20.)

5. A = American Stock Exchange, C = Chicago Board Options Exchange, N = New York Stock Exchange, P = Pacific Stock Exchange, X = Philadelphia Stock Exchange.

Source: The Options Clearing Corporations, *Directory of Exchange Listed Options*, (Chicago: The Options Clearing Corporation, April 1991).

Table 3.18 Foreign Currency Options[1]

symbol	name	exchange
CAD	Australian Dollar – European-Style	X
CBP	British Pound – European-Style	X
CCD	Canadian Dollar – European-Style	X
CDM	Deutsche Mark – European-Style	X
CFF	French Franc – European-Style	X
CJY	Japanese Yen – European-Style	X
CSF	Swiss Franc – European-Style	X
ECU	European Currency Unit – American-Style	X
XAD	Australian Dollar – American-Style	X
XBP	British Pound – American-Style	X
XCD	Canadian Dollar – American-Style	X
XDM	Deutsche Mark – American-Style	X
XFF	French Franc – American-Style	X
XJY	Japanese Yen – American-Style	X
XSF	Swiss Franc – American-Style	X

Table 3.19 Treasury Options

symbol	name	exchange
YBE	$100,000 T-Bond – 8.75 %	C
YBF	**$100,000 T-Bond – 7.875 %**	**C**
IRX	Short Term Interest Rate Composite Index	C
LTX	Long Term Interest Rate Composite Index	C

Source: The Options Clearing Corporations, *Directory of Exchange Listed Options*, (Chicago: The Options Clearing Corporation, April 1991).

1. All options added since September 1990 are indicated in bold face type

2. Over-the-counter stocks are listed with two symbols. The first symbol represents the option code and the second symbol represents the National Association of Securities Dealers (NASD) code.

3. Long-term equity options are noted by expiration month and year.

4. Expiration cycles are 1 = January sequential, 2 = February sequential, 3 = March sequential. (See Table 3.20.)

5. A = American Stock Exchange, C = Chicago Board Options Exchange, N = New York Stock Exchange, P = Pacific Stock Exchange, X = Philadelphia Stock Exchange.

Table 3.20 Sequential Cycles

JANUARY SEQUENTIAL CYCLE

Expiring Month	Available Months			
Jan	Feb	Mar	Apr	Jul
Feb	Mar	Apr	Jul	Oct
Mar	Apr	May	Jul	Oct
Apr	May	Jun	Jul	Oct
May	Jun	Jul	Oct	Jan
Jun	Jul	Aug	Oct	Jan
Jul	Aug	Sep	Oct	Jan
Aug	Sep	Oct	Jan	Apr
Sep	Oct	Nov	Jan	Apr
Oct	Nov	Dec	Jan	Apr
Nov	Dec	Jan	Apr	Jul
Dec	Jan	Feb	Apr	Jul

FEBRUARY SEQUENTIAL CYCLE

Expiring Month	Available Months			
Jan	Feb	Mar	May	Aug
Feb	Mar	Apr	May	Aug
Mar	Apr	May	Aug	Nov
Apr	May	Jun	Aug	Nov
May	Jun	Jul	Aug	Nov
Jun	Jul	Aug	Nov	Feb
Jul	Aug	Sep	Nov	Feb
Aug	Sep	Oct	Nov	Feb
Sep	Oct	Nov	Feb	May
Oct	Nov	Dec	Feb	May
Nov	Dec	Jan	Feb	May
Dec	Jan	Feb	May	Aug

MARCH SEQUENTIAL CYCLE

Expiring Month	Available Months			
Jan	Feb	Mar	Jun	Sep
Feb	Mar	Apr	Jun	Sep
Mar	Apr	May	Jun	Sep
Apr	May	Jun	Sep	Dec
May	Jun	Jul	Sep	Dec
Jun	Jul	Aug	Sep	Dec
Jul	Aug	Sep	Dec	Mar
Aug	Sep	Oct	Dec	Mar
Sep	Oct	Nov	Dec	Mar
Oct	Nov	Dec	Mar	Jun
Nov	Dec	Jan	Mar	Jun
Dec	Jan	Feb	Mar	Jun

3.17 COMMODITY EXCHANGES: WHAT'S EXCHANGED WHERE

Table 3.21 contains a list of commodities, including the exchange(s) where they are traded.

Table 3.21 Commodities and Their Exchanges

Commodity	Exchange*	Commodity	Exchange
Barley	WCE	Lumber, random length	CME
Boneless beef	CME	Lumber, stud	CME
Broilers, iced	CBOT	Milo	CME
Broilers	CME	Oats	CBOT, WCE
Butter	CME	Oil, No. 2 heating	NYME
Cattle, feeder	CME	Oil, No. 6 industrial fuel	NYME
Cattle, live	CME	Orange juice	NYCE
Cocoa	CSCE	Palladium	NYME
Coffee "C"	CSCE	Platinum	NYME
Coffee "B"	CSCE	Plywood	CBOT
Commercial paper (90-day)	CBOT	Pork bellies	CME
Commercial paper (30-day)	CBOT	Potatoes	NYME
Copper	COMEX	Potatoes, russet burbank	CME
Corn	CBOT	Propane, liquid	NYCE
Cotton no. 2	NYCE	Rapeseed	WCE
Crude oil	NYCE	Rye	WCE
Currencies		Silver	CBOT, COMEX
British pound	IMM, NYFE	Silver coins, U.S.	IMM, NYME
Canadian dollar	IMM, NYFE	Soybeans	CBOT
Dutch guilder	IMM	Soybean meal	CBOT
French franc	IMM	Soybean oil	CBOT
Deutsche mark	IMM, NYFE	Sugar no. 11	CSCE
Japanese yen	IMM, NYFE	Sugar no. 12	CSCE
Mexican peso	IMM	Sunflower seeds	MGE
Swiss franc	IMM, NYFE	Treasury bills (13-week)	IMM
Eggs, fresh	CME	Treasury bills (1-year)	IMM
Eggs, frozen	CME	Treasury bills (90-day)	COMEX
Eggs, nest run	CME	Treasury bills (91-day)	NYFE
GNMA CD	CBOT	Treasury bonds	CBOT, NYFE
GNMA CDR	CBOT	Treasury notes	CBOT, IMM
GNMA	COMEX	Turkeys	CME
Gold	CMOT, IMM, COMEX	Wheat	CBOT, KCBOT, WCE
Gold, centum	WCE		
Hams, skinned	CME	Wheat, durum	MGE
Hogs, live	CME	Wheat, spring	MGE
Imported lean beef	NYME	Zinc	COMEX

*CBOT = Chicago Board of Trade; CME = Chicago Mercantile Exchange; COMEX = Commodity Exchange, Inc.; CSCE = New York Coffee, Sugar, and Cocoa Exchange; IMM = International Money Market; KOBOT = Kansas City Board of Trade; MGE = Minneapolis Grain Exchange; NYCE = New York Curb Exchange; NYFE = New York Futures Exchange; NYME = New York Mercantile Exchange; WCE = Winnipeg Commodity Exchange.

3.18 PRICE TRENDS OF SELECTED METALS AND MINERALS

Table 3.22 shows the average prices of selected metals and minerals since 1975.

Table 3.22 Average Prices of Selected Mineral Products, 1975–1989

MINERAL	Unit	1975	1979	1980	1981	1982	1983	1984	1985	1986	1987	1988	1989, prel.
Aluminum [1]	Cents/lb.	39.8	61.0	71.6	76.0	76.0	77.8	81.0	81.0	81.0	72.3	110.1	87.8
Bituminous coal [2][3]	Dol./sh. ton	19.2	23.7	24.5	26.3	27.1	25.9	25.5	25.1	23.7	23.0	22.0	21.0
Cobalt [4]	Dol./lb.	4.0	24.6	25.0	14.6	8.6	5.8	10.4	11.4	7.5	6.6	7.1	7.6
Copper, electrolytic	Cents/lb.	64.2	93.3	101.3	84.2	72.8	76.5	66.8	67.0	66.1	82.5	120.5	130.9
Gold	Dol./fine oz	161.0	308.0	613.0	460.0	376.0	424.0	361.0	318.0	368.0	448.0	438.0	382.6
Lead (NY) [2][5]	Cents/lb.	21.5	52.6	42.5	36.5	25.5	21.7	25.6	19.1	22.1	35.9	37.1	39.4
Natural gas [2][5]	Dol./1,000 cu. ft	0.5	1.2	1.6	2.0	2.5	2.6	2.7	2.5	1.9	1.7	1.7	1.7
Nickel [6]	Dol./lb.	2.2	3.2	3.0	2.7	2.2	2.2	2.2	2.3	1.8	2.2	6.3	6.1
Petroleum, crude [2]	Dol./bbl	7.7	12.6	21.6	31.8	28.5	26.2	25.9	24.1	12.5	15.4	12.6	15.9
Platinum [7]	Dol./troy oz	164.0	352.0	439.0	475.0	475.0	475.0	475.0	475.0	519.0	600.0	600.0	600.0
Silver	Dol./fine oz	4.4	11.1	20.6	10.5	8.0	11.4	8.1	6.1	5.5	7.0	6.5	5.5
Tungsten concentrate [8]	Dol./lb.	5.3	8.4	8.4	8.0	6.4	4.7	5.2	4.2	3.2	2.9	(NA)	(NA)
Zinc [9]	Cents/lb.	39.0	37.3	37.4	44.6	38.5	41.4	48.6	40.4	38.0	41.9	60.2	82.1

NA Not available. [1] 99.5 percent primary aluminum ingot. [2] Average value at point of production; includes Alaska. Source: U.S. Energy Information Administration, *Annual Energy Review* and *Monthly Energy Review*. [3] Includes subbituminous coal and lignite. [4] Weighted average based on the market price quoted by a major U.S. cobalt dealer, otherwise based on range of prices. [5] Average value of marketed production. [6] 1975 and 1979, peak price quoted U.S. buyers by International Nickel Co., Inc., for electrolytic nickel, includes U.S. duty f.o.b. Port Colborne, Ontario; thereafter, from New York dealer. [7] Producer prices. [8] Average value of shipments. [9] Delivered price.

Source: Except as noted, U.S. Bureau of Mines, *Minerals Yearbook*.

3.19 SOTHEBY'S ART INDEX

Sotheby's Art Index (see Table 3.23) tracks price trends in different sectors of the art market. It does not predict prices or indicate what a particular piece is "worth," but it does provide historical perspective on art and collectible prices. The works of art that have been selected for inclusion in each sector are good quality from the middle range of the market.

Table 3.23 Sotheby's Art Index, 1975–1990[1-5]

Category	1975	1976	1977	1978	1979	1980	1981	1982	1983	1984	1985	1986	1987	1988	1989	1990
Old master paintings	100	105	131	173	224	255	201	205	239	278	289	303	373	469	754	865
19th-century European paintings	100	99	118	160	215	225	179	184	201	230	249	279	323	421	575	634
Impressionist art	100	107	114	133	175	206	248	267	307	356	380	490	723	1255	1845	1471
Modern paintings	100	105	108	132	178	204	249	245	282	336	364	512	757	1138	1684	1600
Contemporary art	100	105	127	159	197	239	285	342	392	444	497	551	609	856	1627	1456
American paintings	100	129	171	255	315	350	450	450	556	589	667	698	871	958	1371	1174
Continental ceramics	100	121	154	213	261	336	293	266	284	284	284	290	331	467	505	572
Chinese ceramics	100	159	181	241	353	462	445	436	459	486	486	526	581	815	875	997
English Silver	100	89	95	124	165	205	175	189	219	261	306	343	381	388	420	453
Continental silver	100	89	92	113	146	179	140	139	156	175	181	201	220	296	367	395
American furniture	100	109	120	134	150	172	209	213	239	289	330	404	459	484	510	510
French and continental furniture	100	104	121	148	197	232	228	234	257	272	273	299	319	409	500	564
English furniture	100	125	156	195	244	256	279	267	328	382	419	517	634	822	822	867
Aggregate	100	111	128	164	217	253	249	252	286	324	344	403	512	737	1038	983

Source: Sotheby's 1991 All rights expressly reserved.

1. In each case, the figures are shown in absolute terms, without making any allowances for inflation.
2. All figures are expressed in terms of the U.S. dollar.
3. The basis for the series is September 1975 = 100.
4. Up to and including 1980, the figures were calculated yearly only, in September of each year. From 1981, the figures quoted are calculated in December of each year.
5. The aggregate index is a weighted figure

Sotheby's Art Index reflects subjective analyses and opinions of Sotheby's art experts, based on auction sales and other information deemed relevant. Sotheby's does not warrant the accuracy of the data contained therein. Nothing in Sotheby's Art Index is intended or should be relied upon as investment advice or as a prediction or guarantee of future performance or otherwise.

144

Chapter 4

FIXED-INCOME INVESTMENTS

While the attention of many investors was riveted to the stock market during the latter half of the 1980s, bonds were undergoing revolutionary changes that would make them more complex, more volatile, and at the same time, often more attractive as an investment vehicle. Today, investors can choose from a wide array of taxable, tax-exempt, and tax-deferred fixed-income investments which can either be purchased directly or indirectly through such vehicles as mutual funds, closed-end bond funds, and unit trusts. Common stocks have long been viewed as offering superior hedges against inflation. Yet fixed-income investments also have a place in the portfolios of many investors seeking attractive real rates of return while assuming a prudent amount of risk. Until the 1970s, when interest rates moved slowly, bonds were considered a safe, stable haven for income-oriented investors. Today, when interest rates can fluctuate several percentage points within the course of a year, price volatility is a factor that must be taken into account in the investment planning equation.

The responsibility of the financial professional is to evaluate how fixed-income vehicles fit into an individual's portfolio and to identify suitable investment types. It is safe to say that except for the very wealthy, perhaps, fixed-income investments belong in every portfolio. Naturally, the actual proportion of fixed-income securities to a particular portfolio, as well as the vehicles belonging in that portfolio, will vary considerably from individual to individual. Obviously, someone who is retired or is nearing retirement will in all likelihood require a larger proportion of fixed-income investments in his or her portfolio than a younger individual who is starting to save for retirement.

Many considerations must be taken into account when selecting an appropriate fixed-income vehicle. One is the tax treatment of interest and capital gains or losses from a bond or bond-based investment product.

Maturity, quality, relative yield, liquidity, and minimum investment required are other important factors in the selection process.

During the 1990s, fixed-income investing will almost certainly continue to be a complex yet potentially rewarding investment area. The popularity of the myriad fixed-income investments which have come on the scene in the last decade will prompt a new, even more diverse crop of bond-based products. Changes in tax laws will continue to play a major role in evaluating the relative attractiveness of tax-exempt and tax deferred bonds as an investment vehicle.

Clearly, investing in fixed-income securities both today and in the future will require thorough, ongoing study of the products available and consistent monitoring of interest rate trends. Timing will be more crucial for investors in securities fixed-income as the days of double-digit Treasury returns are largely over. Fixed-income securities, for the most part, should be purchased with the expectation that they will be held until maturity or call. Municipals will continue to offer more attractive after-tax returns to most investors than taxable fixed-income investments. Although higher-quality and insured issues are preferable during times of economic uncertainty, investors may also find opportunities in foreign fixed-income securities and high yield (junk) bonds. However, investment in these types of securities should usually be accomplished through professionally managed mutual funds whose principals have expertise in these areas.

4.1   FIXED-INCOME INVESTMENT STRATEGIES

Volatile interest rates combined with the proliferation of many different kinds of fixed-income securities have complicated the process of analyzing, selecting, and monitoring these investments. The following suggestions will provide some guidance to the financial professional in dealing effectively with the always changing fixed-income investment markets.

1. *Become familiar with the many interest-earning securities that are currently available.* The following list of the many commonly available securities provides a quick summary of fixed-income vehicles available for investment. Most can be purchased either directly or through a mutual fund for as little as $1,000.

U.S. Treasury notes	Uninsured municipal bonds
U.S. Treasury bonds	Insured municipal bonds
U.S. savings bonds	Certificates of deposit
U.S. government agency debt	Zero-coupon bonds,
Mortgage-backed (pass-	corporate
through) certificates	Zero-coupon bonds,
Municipal notes	municipal

Zero-coupon bonds,	High-grade corporate bonds
U.S. Treasury	Medium-grade corporate
High-yield (junk) bonds	bonds
Convertible bonds	High-yield (junk) corporate
Foreign bonds	bond fund
U.S. government bond mutual	Uninsured municipal bond fund
fund, long term	Insured municipal bond fund
U.S. government bond mutual	International bond mutual fund
fund, intermediate term	Unit investment trust
Ginnie Mae mutual fund	Closed-end bond fund
Investment-grade corporate	
bond fund	

Almost all financial professionals will work with at least some of the investment vehicles listed at some point in their careers. Like all investments products, these fixed-income securities are characterized by varying rates of risk and volatility.

2. *Monitor prevailing interest rates.* The fixed-income investor pays close attention to the movement and behavior of interest rates. The financial professional would do well to develop some rules of thumb that would help him or her to decide when interest rates are "high." For example, a fixed-income investor may find that interest-earning securities are attractive when they pay a rate of interest that exceeds inflation by a couple of percentage points on an after-tax basis. Many successful individual investors, for instance, monitor the yield on the bellwether long-term Treasury bonds to get an idea of the level of interest rates.

The key to investing successfully in fixed-income investments is to purchase longer-maturity securities when interest rates appear to be so high that a downturn seems to be approaching. Purchasing fixed-income securities when rates are peaking enables the investor to "lock in" high returns. Conversely, purchasing shorter maturity securities (or cash equivalent investments) is a sensible tactic if prevailing interest rates look likely to rise.

3. *Don't speculate on interest-rate changes.* While it is very important that the fixed-income investor track interest rates and act according to his or her observations, this process should never lead to interest-rate speculation. Many investors underestimate the volatility of interest-earning investments until they find that their bond or bond mutual fund, for example, has lost value. Fixed-income security prices can in fact be more volatile than stock prices. This risk, which is shared by all long-term fixed- income securities, is called "interest-rate risk." Simply stated, interest-rate risk means that the principal value of a fixed-income investment will decline if interest rates in general rise.

Fixed-income mutual funds have this risk, although many fund managers are adept at handling interest-rate risk over the long run. Some individual investors fancy themselves experts in predicting the direction of interest rates, and, therefore, they buy individual interest-earning securities with the intention of selling them before they mature. Many such armchair speculators end up losing a lot of money on a supposedly safe investment. The only way to avoid this risk is to hold onto these securities until they mature.

On the whole, then, the fixed-income investor is better off buying with the intention of holding to maturity, even though personal circumstances may make some early redemptions necessary. Selling early is a good idea if it enables the investor to take advantage of an increase in the value of his or her fixed-income investments due to a decline in interest rates.

4. *Ladder the maturities of your fixed-income investments.* Investors should avoid taking a large position in one maturity. Instead, the investor should "ladder" or "stagger" the investments in his or her fixed-income portfolio. The investor should opt for a variety of maturities—some short term, some intermediate term, and some long term. If interest rates change significantly, laddered maturities will reduce the risk in a fixed income securities portfolio. Financial professionals should also encourage clients to time some of the maturities to coincide with occasions when they may need funds to meet college tuition bills or to provide a boost to retirement income.

5. *Compare interest rates on various types of securities.* Just as there is a wide variety of products within the fixed-income field, so is there a wide range of interest rates offered by these investment vehicles. Over the past several years, interest rates on tax-exempt bonds have been very attractive compared with the after-tax returns on Treasury securities and corporate bonds. Rates on medium-grade bonds are sometimes much higher than on high grade bonds even though the risk of default on medium-grade bonds is not much higher than the "blue chips."

6. *Make mutual funds a part of your fixed-income investment portfolio.* Fixed-income mutual funds are an excellent way to participate in the many attractive interest-earning investment opportunities. The funds encompass a wide variety of objectives and investment styles. The panoply of fixed-income mutual funds includes Treasury funds, mortgage-backed securities funds, tax-exempt bond funds, corporate bond funds, even foreign bond funds. Within most of those categories, the investor can select funds that invest in high-quality issues, medium-quality issues, or lower-quality issues. Finally, the

investor can often select funds that concentrate on securities with particular maturities.

7. *Consider the tax effects of each investment.* The investor can probably increase his or her investment returns by carefully examining the tax effects of alternative fixed-income investments. Some are fully taxable, Treasury securities are federally taxable but exempt from state taxes, and municipal obligations are usually exempt from federal taxes and may be exempt from your state taxes. The financial professional should encourage clients to place the most heavily taxed (and usually higher yielding) securities into tax-deferred retirement accounts. On the other hand, tax-favored investments should be placed in taxable portfolios.

8. *Don't chase yield.* Many investors erroneously think that the higher the yield, the more attractive the investment. This is not so. As many junk bond devotees found out to their dismay, a number of issues of high-yielding bonds have eroded significantly in value. For most investors, chasing yield can be just as much of a mistake as interest rate speculation. This is not to say that junk bonds are an entirely inappropriate investment. They actually may have a place, albeit a small one, in more aggressive portfolios.

9. *Make fixed-income investments one part of a well-balanced portfolio.* Some people invest too much money in fixed-income securities because they are afraid of stocks. Others think stocks are the only worthwhile investment available and have too little invested in interest-earning securities. The financial professional should be acutely aware that all investors need *balance.* Ideally, the well-balanced portfolio consists of about equal portions of stocks, interest-earning investments, and, if the investor wishes, some income-producing real estate.

4.2 TREASURY SECURITY SUMMARY

Table 4.1 provides information on the three types of marketable securities issued by the Treasury Department—bills, notes, and bonds—including sales procedures, purchase alternatives, forms of payment, and income tax information. See also section 4.3, Treasury Security Issue Date Calendar.

Table 4.1 Treasury Security Summary

	Bills	*Notes*	*Bonds*
Description	Book-entry form through Treasury, Federal Reserve banks, or financial institution. Always discounted.	Currently book entry, as this type of security can be obtained only through financial institution. Definitive form, registered only, through Treasury, Federal Reserve banks, or financial institution. Sometimes discounted but can sell at a premium.	Currently book entry, as this type of security can be obtained only through financial institution. Definitive form, registered only, through Treasury, Federal Reserve banks, or financial institution. Sometimes discounted but can sell at a premium.
Denomination	$10,000 minimum; multiples of $5,000 thereafter.	$1,000, $5,000, $10,000, $100,000, $1 million; minimum denomination varies with each issue.	$1,000, $5,000, $10,000, $100,000, $1 million; minimum denomination is $1,000.
Maturity	3 months (13 weeks). 6 months (26 weeks). 1 year (52 weeks).	Two to 10 years; varies with each issue.	Over 10 years; varies with each issue.
Sale or auction	Three and 6-month bills sold every Monday (Tuesday if Monday is holiday); 1-year bills sold once every 4 weeks on Thursday. (Tenders received too late for 1-year bill auction are automatically held for next scheduled auction and do not earn interest for time held). Call local Federal Reserve office for information for 1-year bills. 1:00 P.M. deadline (auction day); tenders (orders) may be submitted prior to auction day.	Two-year notes usually sold monthly approximately 10 days prior to end of month. Other notes sold less frequently. Call local Federal Reserve office for available offerings. 1:00 P.M. deadline (auction day); tenders (orders) may be submitted prior to auction day.	Sold several times a year, usually quarterly in February, August, and November. Call local Federal Reserve office for available offerings. 1:00 P.M. deadline (auction day); tenders (orders) may be submitted prior to auction day.

	Bills	*Notes*	*Bonds*
Payment	Full payment required if purchased through a Federal Reserve bank or Treasury. Checks must be made payable to Federal Reserve bank, cannot be endorsed over to Federal Reserve bank; however, U.S. Treasury check issued in payment of maturing security is acceptable. Personal checks not acceptable unless certified.	Full payment plus accrued interest, if any, must accompany tender. Checks must be made payable to Federal Reserve bank; however, U.S. Treasury check issued in payment of maturing security is acceptable. Personal checks acceptable. Money market share drafts acceptable.	Full payment plus accrued interest, if any, must accompany tender. Checks must be made payable to Federal Reserve bank; cannot be endorsed to Federal Reserve bank; however, U.S. Treasury check issued in payment of maturing security is acceptable. Personal checks acceptable. Money market share drafts acceptable.
Interest	Refund (discount check) mailed after issued date. If purchased through a Federal Reserve bank, bank mails check. If purchased directly through Treasury, Treasury mails check. If purchased through financial institution or broker, broker will explain payment method. Interest not considered earned until bill matures or is sold prior to maturity.	Semiannually. Book-entry interest paid by financial institution; ask financial institution about method. Registered, semiannual interest check mailed out automatically from Treasury. Interest considered earned each year.	Semiannually. Book-entry interest paid by member bank; ask financial institution about method. Registered semiannually interest check mailed out automatically from Treasury. Interest considered earned each year.

	Bills	*Notes*	*Bonds*
Forms	Three months (13 weeks)— FA 16. Six months (26 weeks)— FA 19. One year (52 weeks)— FA 21 Payer's Request for Taxpayer Identification Number—W-9.	Registered—FA 733. Payer's Request for Taxpayer Identification Number—W-9.	Registered—FA 733. Payer's Request for Taxpayer Identification Number—W-9.
Letter	Contents 1. Type of security (3-mo., 6-mo., 1-year) 2. Dollar amount 3. Name(s), printed 4. Social Security number(s) required for owner and co-owner (two-name limit) 5. Address 6. Telephone number (business and home) 7. Signature 8. Check 9. Certification of taxpayer identification[1] Letter must state that customer is requesting bills to be held in book-entry form; otherwise, customer will be sent a tender for signature. Statement of account is sent as soon as possible after issued date by Treasury.	Contents 1. Security to be purchased 2. Dollar amount 3. Name(s), printed 4. Social Security number(s) required for owner and co-owner 5. Address 6. Telephone number (business and home) 7. Signature 8. Check 9. Certification of taxpayer identification[1]	Contents 1. Security to be purchased 2. Dollar amount 3. Name(s), printed 4. Social Security number (s) required for owner and co-owner 5. Address 6. Telephone number (business and home) 7. Signature 8. Check 9. Certification of taxpayer identification[1]

	Bills	*Notes*	*Bonds*
Transaction	Recorded in financial institution's book-entry account at Federal Reserve bank (fee). Federal Reserve bank opens book-entry account at Treasury in subscriber's name (no fee). Treasury opens book-entry account at Treasury in subscriber's name (no fee). Treasury address: Bureau of Public Debt Department X Washington, D.C. 20226	Financial institution (fee) Federal Reserve bank requests issuance of registered security from Treasury (no fee). Treasury address: Bureau of Public Debt Department A Washington, D.C. 20226	Financial institution (fee). Federal Reserve bank requests issuance of registered security from Treasury (no fee). Treasury address: Bureau of Public Debt Department A Washington D.C. 20226
Redemption	Bills automatically redeemed at maturity and check for proceeds mailed unless reinvestment instructions given at time of purchase or sent to Treasury at least 20 business days prior to maturity.	Maturing notes may be delivered or mailed to Federal Reserve bank (registered and insured) at least 10 days before maturity; check for proceeds mailed on maturity date unless specified that check will be picked up on maturity date. All Treasury securities must be redeemed by a Federal Reserve bank;[2] however, they may be presented for payment through commercial bank.	Maturing bonds may be delivered or mailed to Federal Reserve bank (registered and insured) at least 10 days before maturity; check for proceeds mailed on maturity date unless specified that check will be picked up on maturity date. All Treasury securities must be redeemed by a Federal Reserve bank;[2] however, they may be presented for payment through commercial bank.

	Bills	*Notes*	*Bonds*
Reinvest or rollover	Reinvestment or rollover for bills held in Treasury book-entry account may be made on tender form at time of initial purchase or if request is received by Treasury no later than 20 business days prior to maturity. If Treasury is instructed to roll over bills at time of initial purchase, instruction applies only to initial rollover of these bills. Treasure requires supplemental instructions on subsequent rollover request. To revoke previous instruction to reinvest or redeem, submit notarized Form PD 4633 to Treasury. If no instructions are given, bill is automatically redeemed at maturity and redemption check is mailed from Treasury one day prior to maturity date.	Reinvestment or rollover may be made if note's maturity date falls on or before issued date of security being purchased. Securities must be presented before auction deadline of new issued to be purchased, along with W-9 form or acceptable substitute.	Reinvestment or rollover may be made if bond's maturity date falls on or before issue date of security being purchased. Securities must be presented before auction deadline of new issue to be purchased, along with W-9 form or acceptable substitute.
Taxes	Exempt from state and local taxes. Must pay federal taxes.	Exempt from state and local taxes. Must pay federal taxes.	Exempt from state and local taxes. Must pay federal taxes.
Loss or theft	Book-extry method is safe. Dollar amount cannot be lost if statement is lost or stolen. Bank or Treasury provides duplicate upon request.	Notification of lost registered notes should be communicated directly to Treasury. Interest payments (checks) will continue from Treasury.	Notification of lost registered bond should be communicated directly to Treasury. Interest payments (checks) will continue from Treasury.

	Bills	Notes	Bonds
Forms of ownership or recordation	One or two names. Only one Social Security number required for person assuming tax liability. Trust registrations require name of trustee, name of trust, type of trust instrument, and date of trust. Registration not permitted in the name of minor (under age 18).	One or two names. Only one Social Security number required for person assuming tax liability. Trust registrations require name of trustee, name oftrust, type of trust instrument, and date of trust. Registration not permitted in name of minor (under age 18).	One or two names. Only one Social Security number required for person assuming tax liability. Trust registrations require name of trustee, name of trust, type of trust instrument, and date of trust. Registration not permitted in name of minor (under age 18).
Sale before maturity	If purchased through financial institution, see it for sale or transfer securities. If purchased through Federal Reserve bank or Treasury, account must be transferred to book-entry account maintained by a financial institution before sale can take place.	All notes must be sold through broker or financial institution that handles securities. Federal Reserve bank will not accept notes before 10 business days prior to maturity.	All bonds must be sold through broker or financial institution that handles securities. Federal Reserve bank will not accept bonds before 10 business days prior to maturity.
Addresses	Bureau of the Public Dept Department X Washington, D.C. 20226 (Public information; problems such as those with receiving statement of accounts or statements not received.)	Bureau of the Pubic Debt Department W Washington D.C. 20226 (Problems such as those regarding money, interest checks, payments.)	Bureau of the Public Dept Registered Securities Payment Section Room 644 U.S. Treasury Department Washington, D.C. 20226 (Problems with receiving interest.)

(1) The necessary certification is printed on all tenders mailed by the Federal Reserve Bank of Boston after June 1, 1984. All other forms or requests for securities must be accompanied by IRS Form W-9 or they will not be accepted. Certification may also be accomplished by including the following three statements in the purchase request:
1. "My Social Security number is [...]."
2. "I am not subject to backup withholding under the provisions of Section 3406 of the Internal Revenue Code."
3. "Under the penalties of perjury, I certify that the above information is true, correct, and complete. [signature and date]"
(2) A W-9 form must accompany securities presented for redemption.
Source: Federal Reserve Board.

4.3 TREASURY SECURITY ISSUE DATE CALENDAR

Table 4.2 lists the anticipated auction dates for various maturities of Treasury issues. This data can help the financial professional plan future purchases. Updated auction announcements and times may be found in the major financial press.

Table 4.2 Issue Dates of Treasury Bills, Notes, and Bonds

Treasury Bills	
13-week	Every Monday
26-week	Every Monday
52-week	Every fourth Thursday
Treasury Notes	
2-year	Monthly; on a Wednesday late in the month
3-year	Quarterly; on the 15th day of February, May, August, and November
4-year	Quarterly; late in March, June, September, and December
7-year	Quarterly; early in January, April, July, and October
10-year	Quarterly; on the 15th day of February, May, August, and November
Treasury Bonds	
30-year	Quarterly; on the 15th day of February, May, August, and November

4.4 U.S. SAVINGS BOND SUMMARY

The following is a summary of the regulations and features pertaining to U.S. savings bonds. Savings bonds are often overlooked as an investment vehicle, yet the floating rate interest-rate feature of EE bonds combined with certain tax advantages, that is, deferral of federal income taxes and exemption of state/local income taxes, often make these securities an appropriate investment for many individuals. See also Section 4.5, Savings Bond—Series E and H Extended Maturities, and Section 4.6, Series EE Savings Bond Redemption Values.

U.S. savings bonds were first issued in 1935. During World War II, they became an important medium for absorbing the large increase in personal income. Since then, the Treasury Department has promoted the sale of savings bonds, particularly through payroll savings plans, as an important part of its debt-management operations.

The bonds are designed to provide individuals a savings medium with a relatively attractive guaranteed yield, protection against market fluctuations, ease of purchase and redemption, assurance of replacement in the event of loss, low minimum purchase price, and unique tax features.

In 1980, several major changes occurred with the Savings Bond Program. The new Series EE and HH bonds were introduced and their predecessors, the Series E and H bonds, were withdrawn from sale. A new Series HH exchange offering replaced the Series H exchange.

The Treasury, effective November 1, 1982, set the interest paid on Series EE bonds at 85 percent or rates paid on five-year Treasury marketable securities over the bonds' lifetime, compounded semiannually. The market-based rate changes each May and November. Savings bonds must be held at least five years to earn this rate or the guaranteed minimum return current at the time the bond is purchased. Bonds purchased from November 1, 1982 through October 31, 1986 received a minimum rate of 7.5 percent. Bonds purchased from November 1, 1986 on have a 6 percent minimum rate.

Older Series EE bonds, along with Series E bonds and savings notes (Freedom Shares), which are still outstanding and earning interest, may also earn the market-based rate if it is higher than their currently guaranteed rates. New bonds held less than five years earn interest on a fixed, graduated scale.

When bonds are redeemed after the five-year holding period, the interest received is the average yield of rates for all the periods in which the bond was held. The average yield changes as each new six-month rate is averaged in with previous semiannual rates earned from November 1, 1982 or the issue date of the bond, whichever is later.

At the same time the market-based rate for EE bonds was announced, the Treasury also removed Series HH bonds from cash sale. HH bonds continue, however, to be available in exchange for eligible Series E and EE bonds and savings notes.

4.4.1 Regulations Pertaining to Series EE and HH Bonds

Series EE bonds are accrual-type securities sold at one-half their face amount. Denominations range from $50 to $10,000. There is an annual purchase limitation of $30,000 (face amount) per person. Series EE bonds may be purchased over the counter individually, through the "Bond-a-Month" plan offered by some financial institutions, or through payroll savings plans offered by employers. Most banks and other financial institutions are qualified to issue and redeem Series EE bonds.

Interest accrues through periodic increases in redemption value and is paid at the time a bond is cashed. All EE bonds purchased on or after November 1, 1982 and held five years receive interest at 85 percent of the average return during that time on marketable Treasury securities with five years remaining to maturity or the guaranteed minimum rate prevailing at purchase, whichever is higher. Interest is compounded semiannually. Thereafter, the variable rate will be determined in the same manner for the period from issue date to the end of each additional six-month period. Bonds cashed in before being held five years earn slightly over 4 percent after one year, rising gradually to the 6 percent minimum rate after five years.

Series EE bonds may be redeemed, at purchase price plus accrued interest, any time after six months from the issue date.

Series HH bonds are current income bonds in denominations ranging from $500 to $10,000. They are available only through an exchange of accrual-type savings bonds and savings notes. Series HH bonds are issued and redeemed only by Federal Reserve banks and branches and the Bureau of the Public Debt (Treasury).

Interest is paid semiannually by Treasury check. HH bonds issued from November 1, 1992 through October 31, 1986 earn interest at the rate of 7.5 percent per annum. HH bonds issued from November 1, 1986 to the present earn interest at the rate of 6 percent per annum. Series HH bonds are eligible for redemption six months after issue.

Series HH bonds issued on exchange are not subject to the annual purchase limitation or to any interest adjustment for early redemption. Any combination of eligible Series E and EE bonds and savings notes may be presented for exchange, provided they have a total current redemption value of at least $500. Series E bonds are eligible for exchange until one year after final maturity; Series EE bonds are eligible six months after issue. Owners making such an exchange may continue to defer federal income tax reporting of accrued E and/or EE savings note interest until the HH bonds reach final maturity, are redeemed, or are disposed of otherwise, whichever comes first.

Series EE and HH savings bonds are nontransferable securities that may be registered in single-ownership, co-ownership, or beneficiary form. They may not be pledged as collateral. The bonds may be issued under conditions specified in the governing regulations.

The interest on all savings bonds is subject to federal income tax, but is exempt from state and local income taxes. For federal income tax purposes, interest on Series EE bonds may be reported each year as it accrues, or reporting may be deferred until the bonds are cashed, reach final maturity, or are disposed of otherwise, whichever occurs first. Interest on Series HH bonds must be reported annually for the year in which it is paid. Series EE and HH bonds are subject to estate, inheritance, and gift taxes—both federal and state.

4.4.2 The College Break

Interest on bonds purchased in January 1990 and after may be free of taxes when they are used to pay for college tuition and educational fees for a dependant child, spouse, or self. However, the tax break is phased out gradually for families with adjusted gross incomes of $60,000 to $90,000 ($40,000 to $55,000 for single filers) when the bonds are redeemed. These income levels are adjusted for inflation, and parents earning over the maximum adjusted gross income when the bonds are redeemed will be ineligible for this favorable tax treatment. The bonds must be purchased by the parents and held in one or both of their names to qualify.

Even parents who don't qualify for the tax break because their income is too high, however, can still reap tax benefits from Series EE bonds. The so-called kiddie tax makes all net unearned income over $1,000 taxable at the parent's rate if the child is under age 14. After age 14, all income, regardless of the amount, is taxed at the child's generally lower rate. Because taxes on accrued interest need not be paid until redemption, Series EE bonds can help parents circumvent the kiddie tax if they hold off cashing in the bonds until the child reaches age 14.

4.5 SAVINGS BONDS—SERIES E AND H EXTENDED MATURITIES

Table 4.3 provides information on the length of time U.S. savings bonds of varying issue dates will continue to earn interest. It is important for investment professionals to review their clients' U.S. savings bond holdings to make sure these bonds are still producing income.

Table 4.3 Length of Time U.S. Savings Bonds of Varying Issue Dates Will Continue to Earn Interest.

Series E Bond Extended Maturities

Date of Issue	Date of Maturity	Term of Bond
May 1941–Apr. 1952	May 1981–Apr. 1992	40 years*
May 1952–Jan. 1957	Jan. 1992–Sept. 1996	39 years, 8 months
Feb. 1957–May 1959	Jan. 1996–Apr. 1998	38 years, 11 months
June 1959–Nov. 1965	Mar. 1997–Aug. 2003	37 years, 9 months
Dec. 1965–May 1969	Dec. 1992–May 1996	27 years
June 1969–Nov. 1973	Apr. 1995–Sept. 1999	25 years, 10 months
Dec. 1973–June 1980	Dec. 1998–June 2005	25 years

Series H Extended Maturities

Date of Issue	Date of Maturity	Term of Bond
June 1952–Jan. 1957	Feb. 1982–Sept. 1986	29 years, 8 months*
Feb. 1957–May 1959	Feb. 1987–May 1989	30 years*
June 1959–Dec. 1979	June 1989–Dec. 2009	30 years

Savings Notes Extended Maturities

Date of Issue	Date of Maturity	Term of Bond
May 1967–Oct. 1970	Nov. 1991–Apr. 1995	24 years, 6 months

*Maturity dates of these Bonds will not be extended further.

4.6 SERIES EE SAVINGS BOND REDEMPTION VALUES

Table 4.4 provides U.S. Treasury tables that show the redemption value of cumulative interest earned on Series E and Series EE U.S. savings bonds as of December 1991. These tables can be used to approximate the redemption value and accrued interest on savings bonds. If exact redemption values are needed, most banks can provide this information, or monthly tables may be purchased from the Department of the Treasury.

Table 4.4 U.S. Savings Bonds, Series EE Redemption Values and Interest Earned

U.S. SAVINGS BONDS, SERIES E-REDEMPTION VALUES AND INTEREST EARNED AMOUNTS BY DENOMINATION-APRIL 1992

ISSUE YEAR	ISSUE MONTHS	$10		$25		$50		$75		$100		$200		$500		$1,000	
		REDEMP. VALUE	INTEREST EARNED	REDEMP. VALUE	INTEREST EARNED	REDEMP. VALUE	INTEREST EARNED	REDEMP. VALUE	INTEREST EARNED	REDEMP. VALUE	INTEREST EARNED	REDEMP. VALUE	INTEREST EARNED	REDEMP. VALUE	INTEREST EARNED	REDEMP. VALUE	INTEREST EARNED
1945 A B	Dec.	46.91	39.41	117.28	98.53	234.56	197.06			469.12	394.12	938.24	788.24	2,345.60	1,970.60	4,691.20	3,941.20
A B	Nov.	45.77	38.27	114.43	95.68	228.86	191.36			457.72	382.72	915.44	765.44	2,288.60	1,913.60	4,577.20	3,827.20
A B	June thru Oct.	45.33	37.83	113.33	94.58	226.66	189.16			453.32	378.32	906.64	756.64	2,266.60	1,891.60	4,533.20	3,783.20
A B	May	44.62	37.12	111.54	92.79	223.08	185.58			446.16	371.16			2,230.80	1,855.80	4,461.60	3,711.60
A B	Jan. thru Apr.	44.19	36.69	110.47	91.72	220.94	183.44			441.88	366.88			2,209.40	1,834.40	4,418.80	3,668.80
1944 A B	Dec.	44.19	36.69	110.47	91.72	220.94	183.44			441.88	366.88			2,209.40	1,834.40	4,418.80	3,668.80
A B	Nov.	43.50	36.00	108.75	90.00	217.50	180.00			435.00	360.00			2,175.00	1,800.00	4,350.00	3,600.00
A B	June thru Oct.	43.08	35.58	107.70	88.95	215.40	177.90			430.80	355.80			2,154.00	1,779.00	4,308.00	3,558.00
A B	May			106.11	87.36	212.22	174.72			424.44	349.44			2,122.20	1,747.20	4,244.40	3,494.40
A B	Jan. thru Apr.			105.09	86.34	210.18	172.68			420.36	345.36			2,101.80	1,726.80	4,203.60	3,453.60
1943 A B	Dec.			105.09	86.34	210.18	172.68			420.36	345.36			2,101.80	1,726.80	4,203.60	3,453.60
A B	Nov.			103.48	84.73	206.96	169.46			413.92	338.92			2,069.60	1,694.60	4,139.20	3,389.20
A B	June thru Oct.			102.48	83.73	204.96	167.46			409.92	334.92			2,049.60	1,674.60	4,099.20	3,349.20
A B	May			100.91	82.16	201.82	164.32			403.64	328.64			2,018.20	1,643.20	4,036.40	3,286.40
A B	Jan. thru Apr.			99.95	81.20	199.90	162.40			399.80	324.80			1,999.00	1,624.00	3,998.00	3,248.00
1942 A B	Dec.			99.95	81.20	199.90	162.40			399.80	324.80			1,999.00	1,624.00	3,998.00	3,248.00
A B	Nov.			98.40	79.65	196.80	159.30			393.60	318.60			1,968.00	1,593.00	3,936.00	3,186.00
A B	June thru Oct.			97.45	78.70	194.90	157.40			389.80	314.80			1,949.00	1,574.00	3,898.00	3,148.00
A B	May			96.00	77.25	192.00	154.50			384.00	309.00			1,920.00	1,545.00	3,840.00	3,090.00
A B	Jan. thru Apr.			94.35	75.60	188.70	151.20			377.40	302.40			1,887.00	1,512.00	3,774.00	3,024.00
1941 A B	Dec.			94.35	75.60	188.70	151.20			377.40	302.40			1,887.00	1,512.00	3,774.00	3,024.00
A B	Nov.			92.86	74.11	185.72	148.22			371.44	296.44			1,857.20	1,482.20	3,714.40	2,964.40
A B	June thru Oct.			91.96	73.21	183.92	146.42			367.84	292.84			1,839.20	1,464.20	3,678.40	2,928.40
A B	May			90.59	71.84	181.18	143.68			362.36	287.36			1,811.80	1,436.80	3,623.60	2,873.60

A BONDS WITH THESE ISSUE DATES HAVE REACHED FINAL MATURITY AND WILL EARN NO ADDITIONAL INTEREST
B BONDS WITH ISSUE DATES OF MARCH 1951 AND PRIOR ARE NOT ELIGIBLE FOR EXCHANGE TO SERIES HH BONDS

Table 4.4 (continued)

U.S. SAVINGS BONDS, SERIES E-REDEMPTION VALUES AND INTEREST EARNED AMOUNTS BY DENOMINATION-APRIL 1992

ISSUE YEAR	ISSUE MONTHS	$10		$25		$50		$75		$100		$200		$500		$1,000	
		REDEMP. VALUE	INTEREST EARNED	REDEMP. VALUE	INTEREST EARNED	REDEMP. VALUE	INTEREST EARNED	REDEMP. VALUE	INTEREST EARNED	REDEMP. VALUE	INTEREST EARNED	REDEMP. VALUE	INTEREST EARNED	REDEMP. VALUE	INTEREST EARNED	REDEMP. VALUE	INTEREST EARNED
1952	Dec.			167.54	148.79	335.08	297.58			670.16	595.16	1,340.32	1,190.32	3,350.80	2,975.80	6,701.60	5,951.60
	Nov.			167.09	148.34	334.18	296.68			668.36	593.36	1,336.72	1,186.72	3,341.80	2,966.80	6,683.60	5,933.60
	Oct.			167.11	148.36	334.22	296.72			668.44	593.44	1,336.88	1,186.88	3,342.20	2,967.20	6,684.40	5,934.40
	Sep.			165.03	146.28	330.06	292.56			660.12	585.12	1,320.24	1,170.24	3,300.60	2,925.60	6,601.20	5,851.20
	June thru Aug.			170.39	151.64	340.78	303.28			681.56	606.56	1,363.12	1,213.12	3,407.80	3,032.80	6,815.60	6,065.60
	May			170.00	151.25	340.00	302.50			680.00	605.00	1,360.00	1,210.00	3,400.00	3,025.00	6,800.00	6,050.00
	A Jan. thru Apr.			170.66	151.91	341.32	303.82			682.64	607.64	1,365.28	1,215.28	3,413.20	3,038.20	6,826.40	6,076.40
1951 A	Dec.			170.65	151.90	341.30	303.80			682.60	607.60	1,365.20	1,215.20	3,413.00	3,038.00	6,826.00	6,076.00
	Nov.			168.23	149.48	336.46	298.96			672.92	597.92	1,345.84	1,195.84	3,364.60	2,989.60	6,729.20	5,979.20
	A July thru Oct.			166.60	147.85	333.20	295.70			666.40	591.40	1,332.80	1,182.80	3,332.00	2,957.00	6,664.00	5,914.00
	A June			166.61	147.86	333.22	295.72			666.44	591.44	1,332.88	1,182.88	3,332.20	2,957.20	6,664.40	5,914.40
	A May			164.16	145.41	328.32	290.82			656.64	581.64	1,313.28	1,163.28	3,283.20	2,908.20	6,566.40	5,816.40
	A B Jan. thru Apr.			162.60	143.85	325.20	287.70			650.40	575.40	1,300.80	1,150.80	3,252.00	2,877.00	6,504.00	5,754.00
1950 A B	Dec.			154.26	135.51	308.52	271.02			617.04	542.04	1,234.08	1,084.08	3,085.20	2,710.20	6,170.40	5,420.40
	Nov.			151.99	133.24	303.98	266.48			607.96	532.96	1,215.92	1,065.92	3,039.80	2,664.80	6,079.60	5,329.60
	A B June thru Oct.			150.53	131.78	301.06	263.56			602.12	527.12	1,204.24	1,054.24	3,010.60	2,635.60	6,021.20	5,271.20
	A B May			148.48	129.73	296.96	259.46			593.92	518.92	1,187.84	1,037.84	2,969.60	2,594.60	5,939.20	5,189.20
	A B Jan. thru Apr.	58.82	51.32	147.06	128.31	294.12	256.62			588.24	513.24	1,176.48	1,026.48	2,941.20	2,566.20	5,882.40	5,132.40
1949 A B	Dec.	58.82	51.32	147.06	128.31	294.12	256.62			588.24	513.24	1,176.48	1,026.48	2,941.20	2,566.20	5,882.40	5,132.40
	Nov.	58.09	50.59	145.23	126.48	290.46	252.96			580.92	505.92	1,161.84	1,011.84	2,904.60	2,529.60	5,809.20	5,059.20
	A B June thru Oct.	57.53	50.03	143.83	125.08	287.66	250.16			575.32	500.32	1,150.64	1,000.64	2,876.60	2,501.60	5,753.20	5,003.20
	A B May	55.21	47.71	138.02	119.27	276.04	238.54			552.08	477.08	1,104.16	954.16	2,760.40	2,385.40	5,520.80	4,770.80
	A B Jan. thru Apr.	54.68	47.18	136.69	117.94	273.38	235.88			546.76	471.76	1,093.52	943.52	2,733.80	2,358.80	5,467.60	4,717.60
1948 A B	Dec.	54.68	47.18	136.69	117.94	273.38	235.88			546.76	471.76	1,093.52	943.52	2,733.80	2,358.80	5,467.60	4,717.60
	Nov.	53.80	46.30	134.51	115.76	269.02	231.52			538.04	463.04	1,076.08	926.08	2,690.20	2,315.20	5,380.40	4,630.40
	A B June thru Oct.	53.29	45.79	133.23	114.48	266.46	228.96			532.92	457.92	1,065.84	915.84	2,664.60	2,289.60	5,329.20	4,579.20
	A B May	52.44	44.94	131.09	112.34	262.18	224.68			524.36	449.36	1,048.72	898.72	2,621.80	2,246.80	5,243.60	4,493.60
	A B Jan. thru Apr.	52.56	45.06	131.41	112.66	262.82	225.32			525.64	450.64	1,051.28	901.28	2,628.20	2,253.20	5,256.40	4,506.40
1947 A B	Dec.	52.56	45.06	131.41	112.66	262.82	225.32			525.64	450.64	1,051.28	901.28	2,628.20	2,253.20	5,256.40	4,506.40
	Nov.	51.74	44.24	129.34	110.59	258.68	221.18			517.36	442.36	1,034.72	884.72	2,586.80	2,211.80	5,173.60	4,423.60
	A B June thru Oct.	50.63	43.13	126.57	107.82	253.14	215.64			506.28	431.28	1,012.56	862.56	2,531.40	2,156.40	5,062.80	4,312.80
	A B May	49.83	42.33	124.57	105.82	249.14	211.64			498.28	423.28	996.56	846.56	2,491.40	2,116.40	4,982.80	4,232.80
	A B Jan. thru Apr.	49.35	41.85	123.38	104.63	246.76	209.26			493.52	418.52	987.04	837.04	2,467.60	2,092.60	4,935.20	4,185.20
1946 A B	Dec.	49.35	41.85	123.38	104.63	246.76	209.26			493.52	418.52	987.04	837.04	2,467.60	2,092.60	4,935.20	4,185.20
	Nov.	48.57	41.07	121.42	102.67	242.84	205.34			485.68	410.68	971.36	821.36	2,428.40	2,053.40	4,856.80	4,106.80
	A B June thru Oct.	48.10	40.60	120.25	101.50	240.50	203.00			481.00	406.00	962.00	812.00	2,405.00	2,030.00	4,810.00	4,060.00
	A B May	47.36	39.86	118.41	99.66	236.82	199.32			473.64	398.64	947.28	797.28	2,368.20	1,993.20	4,736.40	3,986.40
	A B Jan. thru Apr.	46.91	39.41	117.28	98.53	234.56	197.06			469.12	394.12	938.24	788.24	2,345.60	1,970.60	4,691.20	3,941.20

APRIL 1992
INSIST ON PROPER IDENTIFICATION.

6

Table 4.4 (continued)

U.S. SAVINGS BONDS, SERIES E-REDEMPTION VALUES AND INTEREST EARNED AMOUNTS BY DENOMINATION-APRIL 1992

ISSUE YEAR	ISSUE MONTHS	$10 REDEMP VALUE	$10 INTEREST EARNED	$25 REDEMP VALUE	$25 INTEREST EARNED	$50 REDEMP VALUE	$50 INTEREST EARNED	$75 REDEMP VALUE	$75 INTEREST EARNED	$100 REDEMP VALUE	$100 INTEREST EARNED	$200 REDEMP VALUE	$200 INTEREST EARNED	$500 REDEMP VALUE	$500 INTEREST EARNED	$1,000 REDEMP VALUE	$1,000 INTEREST EARNED
1957	Dec.	131.39	112.64	262.78	225.28					525.56	450.56	1,051.12	901.12	2,627.80	2,252.80	5,255.60	4,505.60
	Aug. thru Nov.	141.05	122.30	282.10	244.60					564.20	489.20	1,128.40	978.40	2,821.00	2,446.00	5,642.00	4,892.00
	July	141.06	122.31	282.12	244.62					564.24	489.24	1,128.48	978.48	2,821.20	2,446.20	5,642.40	4,892.40
	June	139.44	120.69	278.88	241.38					557.76	482.76	1,115.52	965.52	2,788.80	2,413.80	5,577.60	4,827.60
	Feb. thru May	142.65	123.90	285.30	247.80					570.60	495.60	1,141.20	991.20	2,853.00	2,478.00	5,706.00	4,956.00
	Jan.	141.40	122.65	282.80	245.30					565.60	490.60	1,131.20	981.20	2,828.00	2,453.00	5,656.00	4,906.00
1956	Dec.	141.40	122.65	282.80	245.30					565.60	490.60	1,131.20	981.20	2,828.00	2,453.00	5,656.00	4,906.00
	Oct. thru Nov.	140.63	121.88	281.26	243.76					562.52	487.52	1,125.04	975.04	2,812.60	2,437.60	5,625.20	4,875.20
	Sep.	139.01	120.26	278.02	240.52					556.04	481.04	1,112.08	962.08	2,780.20	2,405.20	5,560.40	4,810.40
	June thru Aug.	142.83	124.08	285.66	248.16					571.32	496.32	1,142.64	992.64	2,856.60	2,481.60	5,713.20	4,963.20
	Apr. thru May	142.49	123.74	284.98	247.48					569.96	494.96	1,139.92	989.92	2,849.80	2,474.80	5,699.60	4,949.60
	Mar.	138.64	119.89	277.28	239.78					554.56	479.56	1,109.12	959.12	2,772.80	2,397.80	5,545.60	4,795.60
	Jan. thru Feb.	142.46	123.71	284.92	247.42					569.84	494.84	1,139.68	989.68	2,849.20	2,474.20	5,698.40	4,948.40
1955	Dec.	142.46	123.71	284.92	247.42					569.84	494.84	1,139.68	989.68	2,849.20	2,474.20	5,698.40	4,948.40
	Oct. thru Nov.	142.09	123.34	284.18	246.68					568.36	493.36	1,136.72	986.72	2,841.80	2,466.80	5,683.60	4,933.60
	Sep.	140.20	121.45	280.40	242.90					560.80	485.80	1,121.60	971.60	2,804.00	2,429.00	5,608.00	4,858.00
	June thru Aug.	144.06	125.31	288.12	250.62					576.24	501.24	1,152.48	1,002.48	2,881.20	2,506.20	5,762.40	5,012.40
	May	143.68	124.93	287.36	249.86					574.72	499.72	1,149.44	999.44	2,873.60	2,498.60	5,747.20	4,997.20
	Apr.	143.67	124.92	287.34	249.84					574.68	499.68	1,149.36	999.36	2,873.40	2,498.40	5,746.80	4,996.80
	Mar.	141.85	123.10	283.70	246.20					567.40	492.40	1,134.80	984.80	2,837.00	2,462.00	5,674.00	4,924.00
	Jan. thru Feb.	145.75	127.00	291.50	254.00					583.00	508.00	1,166.00	1,016.00	2,915.00	2,540.00	5,830.00	5,080.00
1954	Dec.	145.75	127.00	291.50	254.00					583.00	508.00	1,166.00	1,016.00	2,915.00	2,540.00	5,830.00	5,080.00
	Oct. thru Nov.	145.45	126.70	290.90	253.40					581.80	506.80	1,163.60	1,013.60	2,909.00	2,534.00	5,818.00	5,068.00
	Sep.	143.52	124.77	287.04	249.54					574.08	499.08	1,148.16	998.16	2,870.40	2,495.40	5,740.80	4,990.80
	June thru Aug.	147.46	128.71	294.92	257.42					589.84	514.84	1,179.68	1,029.68	2,949.20	2,574.20	5,898.40	5,148.40
	May	147.09	128.34	294.18	256.68					588.36	513.36	1,176.72	1,026.72	2,941.80	2,566.80	5,883.60	5,133.60
	Apr.	147.10	128.35	294.20	256.70					588.40	513.40	1,176.80	1,026.80	2,942.00	2,567.00	5,884.00	5,134.00
	Mar.	145.23	126.48	290.46	252.96					580.92	505.92	1,161.84	1,011.84	2,904.60	2,529.60	5,809.20	5,059.20
	Jan. thru Feb.	149.22	130.47	298.44	260.94					596.88	521.88	1,193.76	1,043.76	2,984.40	2,609.40	5,968.80	5,218.80
1953	Dec.	149.22	130.47	298.44	260.94					596.88	521.88	1,193.76	1,043.76	2,984.40	2,609.40	5,968.80	5,218.80
	Nov.	148.85	130.10	297.70	260.20					595.40	520.40	1,190.80	1,040.80	2,977.00	2,602.00	5,954.00	5,204.00
	Oct.	148.84	130.09	297.68	260.18					595.36	520.36	1,190.72	1,040.72	2,976.80	2,601.80	5,953.60	5,203.60
	Sep.	146.98	128.23	293.96	256.46					587.92	512.92	1,175.84	1,025.84	2,939.60	2,564.60	5,879.20	5,129.20
	June thru Aug.	151.03	132.28	302.06	264.56					604.12	529.12	1,208.24	1,058.24	3,020.60	2,645.60	6,041.20	5,291.20
	May	150.66	131.91	301.32	263.82					602.64	527.64	1,205.28	1,055.28	3,013.20	2,638.20	6,026.40	5,276.40
	Apr.	150.67	131.92	301.34	263.84					602.68	527.68	1,205.36	1,055.36	3,013.40	2,638.40	6,026.80	5,276.80
	Mar.	148.82	130.07	297.64	260.14					595.28	520.28	1,190.56	1,040.56	2,976.40	2,601.40	5,952.80	5,202.80
	Jan. thru Feb.	167.54	148.79	335.08	297.58					670.16	595.16	1,340.32	1,190.32	3,350.80	2,975.80	6,701.60	5,951.60

APRIL 1992
INSIST ON PROPER IDENTIFICATION.

Table 4.4 (continued)

U.S. SAVINGS BONDS, SERIES E-REDEMPTION VALUES AND INTEREST EARNED AMOUNTS BY DENOMINATION-APRIL 1992

ISSUE YEAR	ISSUE MONTHS	$10 REDEMP. VALUE	$10 INTEREST EARNED	$25 REDEMP. VALUE	$25 INTEREST EARNED	$50 REDEMP. VALUE	$50 INTEREST EARNED	$75 REDEMP. VALUE	$75 INTEREST EARNED	$100 REDEMP. VALUE	$100 INTEREST EARNED	$200 REDEMP. VALUE	$200 INTEREST EARNED	$500 REDEMP. VALUE	$500 INTEREST EARNED	$1,000 REDEMP. VALUE	$1,000 INTEREST EARNED
1962	Dec.			119.11	100.36	238.22	200.72			476.44	401.44	952.88	802.88	2,382.20	2,007.20	4,764.40	4,014.40
	Oct. thru Nov.			118.62	99.87	237.24	199.74			474.48	399.48	948.96	798.96	2,372.40	1,997.40	4,744.80	3,994.80
	Sep.			118.61	99.86	237.22	199.72			474.44	399.44	948.88	798.88	2,372.20	1,997.20	4,744.40	3,994.40
	Aug.			117.78	99.03	235.56	198.06			471.12	396.12	942.24	792.24	2,355.60	1,980.60	4,711.20	3,961.20
	June thru July			120.16	101.41	240.32	202.82			480.64	405.64	961.28	811.28	2,403.20	2,028.20	4,806.40	4,056.40
	Apr. thru May			119.85	101.10	239.70	202.20			479.40	404.40	958.80	808.80	2,397.00	2,022.00	4,794.00	4,044.00
	Mar.			119.86	101.11	239.72	202.22			479.44	404.44	958.88	808.88	2,397.20	2,022.20	4,794.40	4,044.40
	Feb.			119.00	100.25	238.00	200.50			476.00	401.00	952.00	802.00	2,380.00	2,005.00	4,760.00	4,010.00
	Jan.			121.39	102.64	242.78	205.28			485.56	410.56	971.12	821.12	2,427.80	2,052.80	4,855.60	4,105.60
1961	Dec.			121.39	102.64	242.78	205.28			485.56	410.56	971.12	821.12	2,427.80	2,052.80	4,855.60	4,105.60
	Oct. thru Nov.			121.04	102.29	242.08	204.58			484.16	409.16	968.32	818.32	2,420.80	2,045.80	4,841.60	4,091.60
	Sep.			121.05	102.30	242.10	204.60			484.20	409.20	968.40	818.40	2,421.00	2,046.00	4,842.00	4,092.00
	Aug.			119.71	100.96	239.42	201.92			478.84	403.84	957.68	807.68	2,394.20	2,019.20	4,788.40	4,038.40
	June thru July			122.13	103.38	244.26	206.76			488.52	413.52	977.04	827.04	2,442.60	2,067.60	4,885.20	4,135.20
	Apr. thru May			121.77	103.02	243.54	206.04			487.08	412.08	974.16	824.16	2,435.40	2,060.40	4,870.80	4,120.80
	Mar.			121.78	103.03	243.56	206.06			487.12	412.12	974.24	824.24	2,435.60	2,060.60	4,871.20	4,121.20
	Feb.			120.39	101.64	240.78	203.28			481.56	406.56	963.12	813.12	2,407.80	2,032.80	4,815.60	4,065.60
	Jan.			122.82	104.07	245.64	208.14			491.28	416.28	982.56	832.56	2,456.40	2,081.40	4,912.80	4,162.80
1960	Dec.			122.82	104.07	245.64	208.14			491.28	416.28	982.56	832.56	2,456.40	2,081.40	4,912.80	4,162.80
	Oct. thru Nov.			122.58	103.83	245.16	207.66			490.32	415.32	980.64	830.64	2,451.60	2,076.60	4,903.20	4,153.20
	Sep.			122.57	103.82	245.14	207.64			490.28	415.28	980.56	830.56	2,451.40	2,076.40	4,902.80	4,152.80
	Aug.			121.17	102.42	242.34	204.84			484.68	409.68	969.36	819.36	2,423.40	2,048.40	4,846.80	4,096.80
	June thru July			123.66	104.91	247.32	209.82			494.64	419.64	989.28	839.28	2,473.20	2,098.20	4,946.40	4,196.40
	Mar. thru May			123.45	104.70	246.90	209.40			493.80	418.80	987.60	837.60	2,469.00	2,094.00	4,938.00	4,188.00
	Feb.			122.06	103.31	244.12	206.62			488.24	413.24	976.48	826.48	2,441.20	2,066.20	4,882.40	4,132.40
	Jan.			126.01	107.26	252.02	214.52			504.04	429.04	1,008.08	858.08	2,520.20	2,145.20	5,040.40	4,290.40
1959	Dec.			126.01	107.26	252.02	214.52			504.04	429.04	1,008.08	858.08	2,520.20	2,145.20	5,040.40	4,290.40
	Sep. thru Nov.			125.74	106.99	251.48	213.98			502.96	427.96	1,005.92	855.92	2,514.80	2,139.80	5,029.60	4,279.60
	Aug.			124.34	105.59	248.68	211.18			497.36	422.36	994.72	844.72	2,486.80	2,111.80	4,973.60	4,223.60
	June thru July			128.40	109.65	256.80	219.30			513.60	438.60	1,027.20	877.20	2,568.00	2,193.00	5,136.00	4,386.00
	Jan. thru May			128.76	110.01	257.52	220.02			515.04	440.04	1,030.08	880.08	2,575.20	2,200.20	5,150.40	4,400.40
1958	Dec.			127.24	108.49	254.48	216.98			508.96	433.96	1,017.92	867.92	2,544.80	2,169.80	5,089.60	4,339.60
	July thru Nov.			130.81	112.06	261.62	224.12			523.24	448.24	1,046.48	896.48	2,616.20	2,241.20	5,232.40	4,482.40
	June			129.31	110.56	258.62	221.12			517.24	442.24	1,034.48	884.48	2,586.20	2,211.20	5,172.40	4,422.40
	Jan. thru May			132.95	114.20	265.90	228.40			531.80	456.80	1,063.60	913.60	2,659.00	2,284.00	5,318.00	4,568.00

Table 4.4 (continued)

U.S. SAVINGS BONDS, SERIES E-REDEMPTION VALUES AND INTEREST EARNED AMOUNTS BY DENOMINATION–APRIL 1992

ISSUE YEAR	ISSUE MONTHS	$10 REDEMP. VALUE	$10 INTEREST EARNED	$25 REDEMP. VALUE	$25 INTEREST EARNED	$50 REDEMP. VALUE	$50 INTEREST EARNED	$75 REDEMP. VALUE	$75 INTEREST EARNED	$100 REDEMP. VALUE	$100 INTEREST EARNED	$200 REDEMP. VALUE	$200 INTEREST EARNED	$500 REDEMP. VALUE	$500 INTEREST EARNED	$1,000 REDEMP. VALUE	$1,000 INTEREST EARNED
1967	Dec.			93.47	74.72	186.94	149.44	280.41	224.16	373.88	298.88	747.76	597.76	1,869.40	1,494.40	3,738.80	2,988.80
	Nov.			92.35	73.60	184.70	147.20	277.05	220.80	369.40	294.40	738.80	588.80	1,847.00	1,472.00	3,694.00	2,944.00
	June thru Oct.			94.89	76.14	189.78	152.28	284.67	228.42	379.56	304.56	759.12	609.12	1,897.80	1,522.80	3,795.60	3,045.60
	May			93.86	75.11	187.72	150.22	281.58	225.33	375.44	300.44	750.88	600.88	1,877.20	1,502.20	3,754.40	3,004.40
	Jan. thru Apr.			96.46	77.71	192.92	155.42	289.38	233.13	385.84	310.84	771.68	621.68	1,929.20	1,554.20	3,858.40	3,108.40
1966	Dec.			96.45	77.70	192.90	155.40	289.35	233.10	385.80	310.80	771.60	621.60	1,929.00	1,554.00	3,858.00	3,108.00
	Nov.			95.39	76.64	190.78	153.28	286.17	229.92	381.56	306.56	763.12	613.12	1,907.80	1,532.80	3,815.60	3,065.60
	June thru Oct.			98.02	79.27	196.04	158.54	294.06	237.81	392.08	317.08	784.16	634.16	1,960.40	1,585.40	3,920.80	3,170.80
	May			97.02	78.27	194.04	156.54	291.06	234.81	388.08	313.08	776.16	626.16	1,940.40	1,565.40	3,880.80	3,130.80
	Jan. thru Apr.			99.70	80.95	199.40	161.90	299.10	242.85	398.80	323.80	797.60	647.60	1,994.00	1,619.00	3,988.00	3,238.00
1965	Dec.			99.68	80.93	199.36	161.86	299.04	242.79	398.72	323.72	797.44	647.44	1,993.60	1,618.60	3,987.20	3,237.20
	Sep. thru Nov.			99.85	81.10	199.70	162.20	299.55	243.30	399.40	324.40	798.80	648.80	1,997.00	1,622.00	3,994.00	3,244.00
	Aug.			99.36	80.61	198.72	161.22	298.08	241.83	397.44	322.44	794.88	644.88	1,987.20	1,612.20	3,974.40	3,224.40
	June thru July			102.09	83.34	204.18	166.68	306.27	250.02	408.36	333.36	816.72	666.72	2,041.80	1,666.80	4,083.60	3,333.60
	Mar. thru May			101.53	82.78	203.06	165.56	304.59	248.34	406.12	331.12	812.24	662.24	2,030.60	1,655.60	4,061.20	3,311.20
	Feb.			101.04	82.29	202.08	164.58	303.12	246.87	404.16	329.16	808.32	658.32	2,020.80	1,645.80	4,041.60	3,291.60
	Jan.			113.73	94.98	227.46	189.96	341.19	284.94	454.92	379.92	909.84	759.84	2,274.60	1,899.60	4,549.20	3,799.20
1964	Dec.			113.73	94.98	227.46	189.96	341.19	284.94	454.92	379.92	909.84	759.84	2,274.60	1,899.60	4,549.20	3,799.20
	Sep. thru Nov.			113.01	94.26	226.02	188.52	339.03	282.78	452.04	377.04	904.08	754.08	2,260.20	1,885.20	4,520.40	3,770.40
	Aug.			112.48	93.73	224.96	187.46	337.44	281.19	449.92	374.92	899.84	749.84	2,249.60	1,874.60	4,499.20	3,749.20
	June thru July			116.13	97.38	232.26	194.76	348.39	292.14	464.52	389.52	929.04	779.04	2,322.60	1,947.60	4,645.20	3,895.20
	Apr. thru May			115.36	96.61	230.72	193.22	346.08	289.83	461.44	386.44	922.88	772.88	2,307.20	1,932.20	4,614.40	3,864.40
	Mar.			115.37	96.62	230.74	193.24			461.48	386.48	922.96	772.96	2,307.40	1,932.40	4,614.80	3,864.80
	Feb.			114.82	96.07	229.64	192.14			459.28	384.28	918.56	768.56	2,296.40	1,921.40	4,592.80	3,842.80
	Jan.			117.14	98.39	234.28	196.78			468.56	393.56	937.12	787.12	2,342.80	1,967.80	4,685.60	3,935.60
1963	Dec.			117.14	98.39	234.28	196.78			468.56	393.56	937.12	787.12	2,342.80	1,967.80	4,685.60	3,935.60
	Sep. thru Nov.			116.42	97.67	232.84	195.34			465.68	390.68	931.36	781.36	2,328.40	1,953.40	4,656.80	3,906.80
	Aug.			115.86	97.11	231.72	194.22			463.44	388.44	926.88	776.88	2,317.20	1,942.20	4,634.40	3,884.40
	June thru July			118.18	99.43	236.36	198.86			472.72	397.72	945.44	795.44	2,363.60	1,988.60	4,727.20	3,977.20
	Apr. thru May			117.29	98.54	234.58	197.08			469.16	394.16	938.32	788.32	2,345.80	1,970.80	4,691.60	3,941.60
	Mar.			117.31	98.56	234.62	197.12			469.24	394.24	938.48	788.48	2,346.20	1,971.20	4,692.40	3,942.40
	Feb.			116.76	98.01	233.52	196.02			467.04	392.04	934.08	784.08	2,335.20	1,960.20	4,670.40	3,920.40
	Jan.			119.11	100.36	238.22	200.72			476.44	401.44	952.88	802.88	2,382.20	2,007.20	4,764.40	4,014.40

APRIL 1992
INSIST ON PROPER IDENTIFICATION.

Table 4.4 (continued)
U.S. SAVINGS BONDS, SERIES E-REDEMPTION VALUES AND INTEREST EARNED AMOUNTS BY DENOMINATION-APRIL 1992

ISSUE YEAR	ISSUE MONTHS	$10 REDEMP. VALUE	$10 INTEREST EARNED	$25 REDEMP. VALUE	$25 INTEREST EARNED	$50 REDEMP. VALUE	$50 INTEREST EARNED	$75 REDEMP. VALUE	$75 INTEREST EARNED	$100 REDEMP. VALUE	$100 INTEREST EARNED	$200 REDEMP. VALUE	$200 INTEREST EARNED	$500 REDEMP. VALUE	$500 INTEREST EARNED	$1,000 REDEMP. VALUE	$1,000 INTEREST EARNED
1973	Dec.			69.68	50.93	139.36	101.86	209.04	152.79	278.72	203.72	557.44	407.44	1,393.60	1,018.60	2,787.20	2,037.20
	Sep. thru Nov.			71.71	52.96	143.42	105.92	215.13	158.88	286.84	211.84	573.68	423.68	1,434.20	1,059.20	2,868.40	2,118.40
	Aug.			71.70	52.95	143.40	105.90	215.10	158.85	286.80	211.80	573.60	423.60	1,434.00	1,059.00	2,868.00	2,118.00
	July			71.54	52.79	143.08	105.58	214.62	158.37	286.16	211.16	572.32	422.32	1,430.80	1,055.80	2,861.60	2,111.60
	June			72.98	54.23	145.96	108.46	218.94	162.69	291.92	216.92	583.84	433.84	1,459.60	1,084.60	2,919.20	2,169.20
	Feb. thru May			72.81	54.06	145.62	108.12	218.43	162.18	291.24	216.24	582.48	432.48	1,456.20	1,081.20	2,912.40	2,162.40
	Jan.			72.63	53.88	145.26	107.76	217.89	161.64	290.52	215.52	581.04	431.04	1,452.60	1,077.60	2,905.20	2,155.20
1972	Dec.			74.09	55.34	148.18	110.68	222.27	166.02	296.36	221.36	592.72	442.72	1,481.80	1,106.80	2,963.60	2,213.60
	Aug. thru Nov.			73.93	55.18	147.86	110.36	221.79	165.54	295.72	220.72	591.44	441.44	1,478.60	1,103.60	2,957.20	2,207.20
	July			73.77	55.02	147.54	110.04	221.31	165.06	295.08	220.08	590.16	440.16	1,475.40	1,100.40	2,950.80	2,200.80
	June			75.28	56.53	150.56	113.06	225.84	169.59	301.12	226.12	602.24	452.24	1,505.60	1,130.60	3,011.20	2,261.20
	Feb. thru May			75.08	56.33	150.16	112.66	225.24	168.99	300.32	225.32	600.64	450.64	1,501.60	1,126.60	3,003.20	2,253.20
	Jan.			74.89	56.14	149.78	112.28	224.67	168.42	299.56	224.56	599.12	449.12	1,497.80	1,122.80	2,995.60	2,245.60
1971	Dec.			77.33	58.58	154.66	117.16	231.99	175.74	309.32	234.32	618.64	468.64	1,546.60	1,171.60	3,093.20	2,343.20
	Aug. thru Nov.			77.14	58.39	154.28	116.78	231.42	175.17	308.56	233.56	617.12	467.12	1,542.80	1,167.80	3,085.60	2,335.60
	July			76.96	58.21	153.92	116.42	230.88	174.63	307.84	232.84	615.68	465.68	1,539.20	1,164.20	3,078.40	2,328.40
	June			79.47	60.72	158.94	121.44	238.41	182.16	317.88	242.88	635.76	485.76	1,589.40	1,214.40	3,178.80	2,428.80
	Feb. thru May			79.25	60.50	158.50	121.00	237.75	181.50	317.00	242.00	634.00	484.00	1,585.00	1,210.00	3,170.00	2,420.00
	Jan.			79.07	60.32	158.14	120.64	237.21	180.96	316.28	241.28	632.56	482.56	1,581.40	1,206.40	3,162.80	2,412.80
1970	Dec.			85.23	66.48	170.46	132.96	255.69	199.44	340.92	265.92	681.84	531.84	1,704.60	1,329.60	3,409.20	2,659.20
	Sep. thru Nov.			85.04	66.29	170.08	132.58	255.12	198.87	340.16	265.16	680.32	530.32	1,700.80	1,325.80	3,401.60	2,651.60
	Aug.			85.03	66.28	170.06	132.56	255.09	198.84	340.12	265.12	680.24	530.24	1,700.60	1,325.60	3,401.20	2,651.20
	July			84.84	66.09	169.68	132.18	254.52	198.27	339.36	264.36	678.72	528.72	1,696.80	1,321.80	3,393.60	2,643.60
	June			87.16	68.41	174.32	136.82	261.48	205.23	348.64	273.64	697.28	547.28	1,743.20	1,368.20	3,486.40	2,736.40
	Feb. thru May			86.75	68.00	173.50	136.00	260.25	204.00	347.00	272.00	694.00	544.00	1,735.00	1,360.00	3,470.00	2,720.00
	Jan.			86.53	67.78	173.06	135.56	259.59	203.34	346.12	271.12	692.24	542.24	1,730.60	1,355.60	3,461.20	2,711.20
1969	Dec.			88.93	70.18	177.86	140.36	266.79	210.54	355.72	280.72	711.44	561.44	1,778.60	1,403.60	3,557.20	2,807.20
	Aug. thru Nov.			88.47	69.72	176.94	139.44	265.41	209.16	353.88	278.88	707.76	557.76	1,769.40	1,394.40	3,538.80	2,788.80
	July			88.27	69.52	176.54	139.04	264.81	208.56	353.08	278.08	706.16	556.16	1,765.40	1,390.40	3,530.80	2,780.80
	June			90.70	71.95	181.40	143.90	272.10	215.85	362.80	287.80	725.60	575.60	1,814.00	1,439.00	3,628.00	2,878.00
	May			88.36	69.61	176.72	139.22	265.08	208.83	353.44	278.44	706.88	556.88	1,767.20	1,392.20	3,534.40	2,784.40
	Jan. thru Apr.			90.79	72.04	181.58	144.08	272.37	216.12	363.16	288.16	726.32	576.32	1,815.80	1,440.80	3,631.60	2,881.60
1968	Dec.			90.80	72.05	181.60	144.10	272.40	216.15	363.20	288.20	726.40	576.40	1,816.00	1,441.00	3,632.00	2,882.00
	Nov.			89.59	70.84	179.18	141.68	268.77	212.52	358.36	283.36	716.72	566.72	1,791.80	1,416.80	3,583.60	2,833.60
	July thru Oct.			92.05	73.30	184.10	146.60	276.15	219.90	368.20	293.20	736.40	586.40	1,841.00	1,466.00	3,682.00	2,932.00
	June			92.07	73.32	184.14	146.64	276.21	219.96	368.28	293.28	736.56	586.56	1,841.40	1,466.40	3,682.80	2,932.80
	May			90.98	72.23	181.96	144.46	272.94	216.69	363.92	288.92	727.84	577.84	1,819.60	1,444.60	3,639.20	2,889.20
	Jan. thru Apr.			93.46	74.71	186.92	149.42	280.38	224.13	373.84	298.84	747.68	597.68	1,869.20	1,494.20	3,738.40	2,988.40

APRIL 1992
INSIST ON PROPER IDENTIFICATION.

Table 4.4 (continued)

U.S. SAVINGS BONDS, SERIES E-REDEMPTION VALUES AND INTEREST EARNED AMOUNTS BY DENOMINATION-APRIL 1992

ISSUE YEAR	ISSUE MONTHS	$10 REDEMP. VALUE	$10 INTEREST EARNED	$25 REDEMP. VALUE	$25 INTEREST EARNED	$50 REDEMP. VALUE	$50 INTEREST EARNED	$75 REDEMP. VALUE	$75 INTEREST EARNED	$100 REDEMP. VALUE	$100 INTEREST EARNED	$200 REDEMP. VALUE	$200 INTEREST EARNED	$500 REDEMP. VALUE	$500 INTEREST EARNED	$1,000 REDEMP. VALUE	$1,000 INTEREST EARNED
1980	May thru June			47.67	28.92	95.34	57.84	143.01	86.76	190.68	115.68	381.36	231.36	953.40	578.40	1,906.80	1,156.80
	Jan. thru Apr.			48.97	30.22	97.94	60.44	146.91	90.66	195.88	120.88	391.76	241.76	979.40	604.40	1,958.80	1,208.80
1979	Nov. thru Dec.			48.97	30.22	97.94	60.44	146.91	90.66	195.88	120.88	391.76	241.76	979.40	604.40	1,958.80	1,208.80
	June thru Oct.			50.33	31.58	100.66	63.16	150.99	94.74	201.32	126.32	402.64	252.64	1,006.60	631.60	2,013.20	1,263.20
	May			50.21	31.46	100.42	62.92	150.63	94.38	200.84	125.84	401.68	251.68	1,004.20	629.20	2,008.40	1,258.40
	Jan. thru Apr.			51.59	32.84	103.18	65.68	154.77	98.52	206.36	131.36	412.72	262.72	1,031.80	656.80	2,063.60	1,313.60
1978	Dec.			51.58	32.83	103.16	65.66	154.74	98.49	206.32	131.32	412.64	262.64	1,031.60	656.60	2,063.20	1,313.20
	Nov.			51.45	32.70	102.90	65.40	154.35	98.10	205.80	130.80	411.60	261.60	1,029.00	654.00	2,058.00	1,308.00
	June thru Oct.			52.87	34.12	105.74	68.24	158.61	102.36	211.48	136.48	422.96	272.96	1,057.40	682.40	2,114.80	1,364.80
	May			52.74	33.99	105.48	67.98	158.22	101.97	210.96	135.96	421.92	271.92	1,054.80	679.80	2,109.60	1,359.60
	Jan. thru Apr.			54.20	35.45	108.40	70.90	162.60	106.35	216.80	141.80	433.60	283.60	1,084.00	709.00	2,168.00	1,418.00
1977	Dec.			54.20	35.45	108.40	70.90	162.60	106.35	216.80	141.80	433.60	283.60	1,084.00	709.00	2,168.00	1,418.00
	Nov.			54.05	35.30	108.10	70.60	162.15	105.90	216.20	141.20	432.40	282.40	1,081.00	706.00	2,162.00	1,412.00
	July thru Oct.			60.85	42.10	121.70	84.20	182.55	126.30	243.40	168.40	486.80	336.80	1,217.00	842.00	2,434.00	1,684.00
	June			60.86	42.11	121.72	84.22	182.58	126.33	243.44	168.44	486.88	336.88	1,217.20	842.20	2,434.40	1,684.40
	May			60.74	41.99	121.48	83.98	182.22	125.97	242.96	167.96	485.92	335.92	1,214.80	839.80	2,429.60	1,679.60
	Jan. thru Apr.			62.70	43.95	125.40	87.90	188.10	131.85	250.80	175.80	501.60	351.60	1,254.00	879.00	2,508.00	1,758.00
1976	Dec.			62.70	43.95	125.40	87.90	188.10	131.85	250.80	175.80	501.60	351.60	1,254.00	879.00	2,508.00	1,758.00
	Nov.			62.52	43.77	125.04	87.54	187.56	131.31	250.08	175.08	500.16	350.16	1,250.40	875.40	2,500.80	1,750.80
	July thru Oct.			63.78	45.03	127.56	90.06	191.34	135.09	255.12	180.12	510.24	360.24	1,275.60	900.60	2,551.20	1,801.20
	June			63.79	45.04	127.58	90.08	191.37	135.12	255.16	180.16	510.32	360.32	1,275.80	900.80	2,551.60	1,801.60
	May			63.64	44.89	127.28	89.78	190.92	134.67	254.56	179.56	509.12	359.12	1,272.80	897.80	2,545.60	1,795.60
	Jan. thru Apr.			64.94	46.19	129.88	92.38	194.82	138.57	259.76	184.76	519.52	369.52	1,298.80	923.80	2,597.60	1,847.60
1975	Dec.			64.93	46.18	129.86	92.36	194.79	138.54	259.72	184.72	519.44	369.44	1,298.60	923.60	2,597.20	1,847.20
	Nov.			64.79	46.04	129.58	92.08	194.37	138.12	259.16	184.16	518.32	368.32	1,295.80	920.80	2,591.60	1,841.60
	June thru Oct.			66.08	47.33	132.16	94.66	198.24	141.99	264.32	189.32	528.64	378.64	1,321.60	946.60	2,643.20	1,893.20
	May			65.93	47.18	131.86	94.36	197.79	141.54	263.72	188.72	527.44	377.44	1,318.60	943.60	2,637.20	1,887.20
	Jan. thru Apr.			67.26	48.51	134.52	97.02	201.78	145.53	269.04	194.04	538.08	388.08	1,345.20	970.20	2,690.40	1,940.40
1974	Dec.			67.27	48.52	134.54	97.04	201.81	145.56	269.08	194.08	538.16	388.16	1,345.40	970.40	2,690.80	1,940.80
	Nov.			67.10	48.35	134.20	96.70	201.30	145.05	268.40	193.40	536.80	386.80	1,342.00	967.00	2,684.00	1,934.00
	June thru Oct.			68.46	49.71	136.92	99.42	205.38	149.13	273.84	198.84	547.68	397.68	1,369.20	994.20	2,738.40	1,988.40
	May			68.30	49.55	136.60	99.10	204.90	148.65	273.20	198.20	546.40	396.40	1,366.00	991.00	2,732.00	1,982.00
	Jan. thru Apr.			69.68	50.93	139.36	101.86	209.04	152.79	278.72	203.72	557.44	407.44	1,393.60	1,018.60	2,787.20	2,037.20

APRIL 1992
INSIST ON PROPER IDENTIFICATION.

Table 4.4 (continued)

U.S. SAVINGS BONDS, SERIES EE-REDEMPTION VALUES AND INTEREST EARNED AMOUNTS BY DENOMINATION-APRIL 1992

ISSUE YEAR	ISSUE MONTHS	$50 REDEMP. VALUE	$50 INTEREST EARNED	$75 REDEMP. VALUE	$75 INTEREST EARNED	$100 REDEMP. VALUE	$100 INTEREST EARNED	$200 REDEMP. VALUE	$200 INTEREST EARNED	$500 REDEMP. VALUE	$500 INTEREST EARNED	$1,000 REDEMP. VALUE	$1,000 INTEREST EARNED	$5,000 REDEMP. VALUE	$5,000 INTEREST EARNED	$10,000 REDEMP. VALUE	$10,000 INTEREST EARNED
1988	Nov. thru Dec.	29.00	4.00	43.50	6.00	58.00	8.00	116.00	16.00	290.00	40.00	580.00	80.00	2,900.00	400.00	5,800.00	800.00
	May thru Oct.	29.98	4.98	44.97	7.47	59.96	9.96	119.92	19.92	299.80	49.80	599.60	99.60	2,998.00	498.00	5,996.00	996.00
	Jan. thru Apr.	31.06	6.06	46.59	9.09	62.12	12.12	124.24	24.24	310.60	60.60	621.20	121.20	3,106.00	606.00	6,212.00	1,212.00
1987	Nov. thru Dec.	31.06	6.06	46.59	9.09	62.12	12.12	124.24	24.24	310.60	60.60	621.20	121.20	3,106.00	606.00	6,212.00	1,212.00
	May thru Oct.	32.28	7.28	48.42	10.92	64.56	14.56	129.12	29.12	322.80	72.80	645.60	145.60	3,228.00	728.00	6,456.00	1,456.00
	Jan. thru Apr.	35.28	10.28	52.92	15.42	70.56	20.56	141.12	41.12	352.80	102.80	705.60	205.60	3,528.00	1,028.00	7,056.00	2,056.00
1986	Nov. thru Dec.	35.28	10.28	52.92	15.42	70.56	20.56	141.12	41.12	352.80	102.80	705.60	205.60	3,528.00	1,028.00	7,056.00	2,056.00
	May thru Oct.	37.50	12.50	56.25	18.75	75.00	25.00	150.00	50.00	375.00	125.00	750.00	250.00	3,750.00	1,250.00	7,500.00	2,500.00
	Jan. thru Apr.	38.90	13.90	58.35	20.85	77.80	27.80	155.60	55.60	389.00	139.00	778.00	278.00	3,890.00	1,390.00	7,780.00	2,780.00
1985	Nov. thru Dec.	38.90	13.90	58.35	20.85	77.80	27.80	155.60	55.60	389.00	139.00	778.00	278.00	3,890.00	1,390.00	7,780.00	2,780.00
	May thru Oct.	40.36	15.36	60.54	23.04	80.72	30.72	161.44	61.44	403.60	153.60	807.20	307.20	4,036.00	1,536.00	8,072.00	3,072.00
	Jan. thru Apr.	41.86	16.86	62.79	25.29	83.72	33.72	167.44	67.44	418.60	168.60	837.20	337.20	4,186.00	1,686.00	8,372.00	3,372.00
1984	Nov. thru Dec.	41.86	16.86	62.79	25.29	83.72	33.72	167.44	67.44	418.60	168.60	837.20	337.20	4,186.00	1,686.00	8,372.00	3,372.00
	May thru Oct.	44.22	19.22	66.33	28.83	88.44	38.44	176.88	76.88	442.20	192.20	884.40	384.40	4,422.00	1,922.00	8,844.00	3,844.00
	Jan. thru Apr.	45.94	20.94	68.91	31.41	91.88	41.88	183.76	83.76	459.40	209.40	918.80	418.80	4,594.00	2,094.00	9,188.00	4,188.00
1983	Nov. thru Dec.	45.94	20.94	68.91	31.41	91.88	41.88	183.76	83.76	459.40	209.40	918.80	418.80	4,594.00	2,094.00	9,188.00	4,188.00
	May thru Oct.	47.72	22.72	71.58	34.08	95.44	45.44	190.88	90.88	477.20	227.20	954.40	454.40	4,772.00	2,272.00	9,544.00	4,544.00
	Jan. thru Apr.	50.66	25.66	75.99	38.49	101.32	51.32	202.64	102.64	506.60	256.60	1,013.20	513.20	5,066.00	2,566.00	10,132.00	5,132.00
1982	Nov. thru Dec.	50.66	25.66	75.99	38.49	101.32	51.32	202.64	102.64	506.60	256.60	1,013.20	513.20	5,066.00	2,566.00	10,132.00	5,132.00
	May thru Oct.	55.26	30.26	82.89	45.39	110.52	60.52	221.04	121.04	552.60	302.60	1,105.20	605.20	5,526.00	3,026.00	11,052.00	6,052.00
	Jan. thru Apr.	56.92	31.92	85.38	47.88	113.84	63.84	227.68	127.68	569.20	319.20	1,138.40	638.40	5,692.00	3,192.00	11,384.00	6,384.00
1981	Nov. thru Dec.	56.92	31.92	85.38	47.88	113.84	63.84	227.68	127.68	569.20	319.20	1,138.40	638.40	5,692.00	3,192.00	11,384.00	6,384.00
	May thru Oct.	58.62	33.62	87.93	50.43	117.24	67.24	234.48	134.48	586.20	336.20	1,172.40	672.40	5,862.00	3,362.00	11,724.00	6,724.00
	Jan. thru Apr.	61.84	36.84	92.76	55.26	123.68	73.68	247.36	147.36	618.40	368.40	1,236.80	736.80	6,184.00	3,684.00	12,368.00	7,368.00
1980	Nov. thru Dec.	61.84	36.84	92.76	55.26	123.68	73.68	247.36	147.36	618.40	368.40	1,236.80	736.80	6,184.00	3,684.00	12,368.00	7,368.00
	May thru Oct.	66.84	41.84	100.26	62.76	133.68	83.68	267.36	167.36	668.40	418.40	1,336.80	836.80	6,684.00	4,184.00	13,368.00	8,368.00
	Jan. thru Apr.	68.16	43.16	102.24	64.74	136.32	86.32	272.64	172.64	681.60	431.60	1,363.20	863.20	6,816.00	4,316.00	13,632.00	8,632.00

APRIL 1992
INSIST ON PROPER IDENTIFICATION.

Table 4.4 (continued)

U.S. SAVINGS BONDS, SERIES EE-REDEMPTION VALUES AND INTEREST EARNED AMOUNTS BY DENOMINATION-APRIL 1992

ISSUE YEAR	ISSUE MONTHS	$50 REDEMP. VALUE	$50 INTEREST EARNED	$75 REDEMP. VALUE	$75 INTEREST EARNED	$100 REDEMP. VALUE	$100 INTEREST EARNED	$200 REDEMP. VALUE	$200 INTEREST EARNED	$500 REDEMP. VALUE	$500 INTEREST EARNED	$1,000 REDEMP. VALUE	$1,000 INTEREST EARNED	$5,000 REDEMP. VALUE	$5,000 INTEREST EARNED	$10,000 REDEMP. VALUE	$10,000 INTEREST EARNED
1992	Jan. thru Apr.	Not eligible for payment															
1991	Nov. thru Dec.	Not eligible for payment															
	Oct.	25.52	.52	38.28	.78	51.04	1.04	102.08	2.08	255.20	5.20	510.40	10.40	2,552.00	52.00	5,104.00	104.00
	Sep.	25.60	.60	38.40	.90	51.20	1.20	102.40	2.40	256.00	6.00	512.00	12.00	2,560.00	60.00	5,120.00	120.00
	Aug.	25.70	.70	38.55	1.05	51.40	1.40	102.80	2.80	257.00	7.00	514.00	14.00	2,570.00	70.00	5,140.00	140.00
	July	25.78	.78	38.67	1.17	51.56	1.56	103.12	3.12	257.80	7.80	515.60	15.60	2,578.00	78.00	5,156.00	156.00
	June	25.88	.88	38.82	1.32	51.76	1.76	103.52	3.52	258.80	8.80	517.60	17.60	2,588.00	88.00	5,176.00	176.00
	May	25.98	.98	38.97	1.47	51.96	1.96	103.92	3.92	259.80	9.80	519.60	19.60	2,598.00	98.00	5,196.00	196.00
	Apr.	26.08	1.08	39.12	1.62	52.16	2.16	104.32	4.32	260.80	10.80	521.60	21.60	2,608.00	108.00	5,216.00	216.00
	Mar.	26.18	1.18	39.27	1.77	52.36	2.36	104.72	4.72	261.80	11.80	523.60	23.60	2,618.00	118.00	5,236.00	236.00
	Feb.	26.28	1.28	39.42	1.92	52.56	2.56	105.12	5.12	262.80	12.80	525.60	25.60	2,628.00	128.00	5,256.00	256.00
	Jan.	26.38	1.38	39.57	2.07	52.76	2.76	105.52	5.52	263.80	13.80	527.60	27.60	2,638.00	138.00	5,276.00	276.00
1990	Dec.	26.48	1.48	39.72	2.22	52.96	2.96	105.92	5.92	264.80	14.80	529.60	29.60	2,648.00	148.00	5,296.00	296.00
	Nov.	26.58	1.58	39.87	2.37	53.16	3.16	106.32	6.32	265.80	15.80	531.60	31.60	2,658.00	158.00	5,316.00	316.00
	Oct.	26.70	1.70	40.05	2.55	53.40	3.40	106.80	6.80	267.00	17.00	534.00	34.00	2,670.00	170.00	5,340.00	340.00
	Sep.	26.80	1.80	40.20	2.70	53.60	3.60	107.20	7.20	268.00	18.00	536.00	36.00	2,680.00	180.00	5,360.00	360.00
	Aug.	26.92	1.92	40.38	2.88	53.84	3.84	107.68	7.68	269.20	19.20	538.40	38.40	2,692.00	192.00	5,384.00	384.00
	July	27.04	2.04	40.56	3.06	54.08	4.08	108.16	8.16	270.40	20.40	540.80	40.80	2,704.00	204.00	5,408.00	408.00
	June	27.16	2.16	40.74	3.24	54.32	4.32	108.64	8.64	271.60	21.60	543.20	43.20	2,716.00	216.00	5,432.00	432.00
	May	27.28	2.28	40.92	3.42	54.56	4.56	109.12	9.12	272.80	22.80	545.60	45.60	2,728.00	228.00	5,456.00	456.00
	Apr.	27.40	2.40	41.10	3.60	54.80	4.80	109.60	9.60	274.00	24.00	548.00	48.00	2,740.00	240.00	5,480.00	480.00
	Mar.	27.52	2.52	41.28	3.78	55.04	5.04	110.08	10.08	275.20	25.20	550.40	50.40	2,752.00	252.00	5,504.00	504.00
	Feb.	27.64	2.64	41.46	3.96	55.28	5.28	110.56	10.56	276.40	26.40	552.80	52.80	2,764.00	264.00	5,528.00	528.00
	Jan.	27.76	2.76	41.64	4.14	55.52	5.52	111.04	11.04	277.60	27.60	555.20	55.20	2,776.00	276.00	5,552.00	552.00
1989	Dec.	27.90	2.90	41.85	4.35	55.80	5.80	111.60	11.60	279.00	29.00	558.00	58.00	2,790.00	290.00	5,580.00	580.00
	Nov.	28.02	3.02	42.03	4.53	56.04	6.04	112.08	12.08	280.20	30.20	560.40	60.40	2,802.00	302.00	5,604.00	604.00
	May thru Oct.	28.16	3.16	42.24	4.74	56.32	6.32	112.64	12.64	281.60	31.60	563.20	63.20	2,816.00	316.00	5,632.00	632.00
	Jan. thru Apr.	29.00	4.00	43.50	6.00	58.00	8.00	116.00	16.00	290.00	40.00	580.00	80.00	2,900.00	400.00	5,800.00	800.00

PROCEEDS FROM SERIES EE SAVINGS BONDS WITH ISSUE DATES BEGINNING JANUARY 1990 MAY BE ELIGIBLE FOR SPECIAL TAX EXEMPTION WHEN USED FOR POST SECONDARY EDUCATION - SEE INSIDE FRONT COVER.

APRIL 1992

INSIST ON PROPER IDENTIFICATION.

INTEREST EARNED:

4.7 HISTORICAL RETURNS ON GOVERNMENT AND CORPORATE BONDS

The cumulative annual total returns and annual total returns of long-term government bonds and long-term corporate bonds from 1926 to 1990 and shown in figures 4.1 and 4.2. Yields on long-term government bonds are also shown. One dollar invested in long-term government bonds at year-end 1925 grew to $17.99 at year-end 1990. Over a similar period, long-term corporate bonds grew to $27.18.

FIGURE 4.1 LONG-TERM GOVERNMENT BONDS, 1925–1990

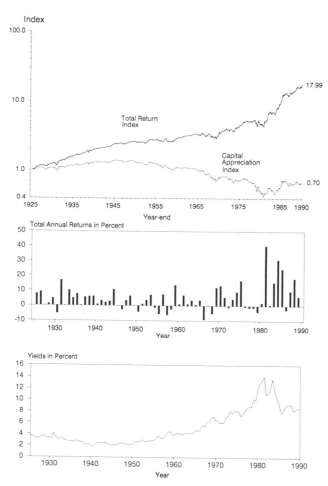

Source: Ibbotson Associates, *Stocks, Bonds, Bills, and Inflation, 1991 Yearbook*, (Chicago: Ibbotson Associates, 1991).

FIGURE 4.2 LONG-TERM CORPORATE BONDS, 1925–1990

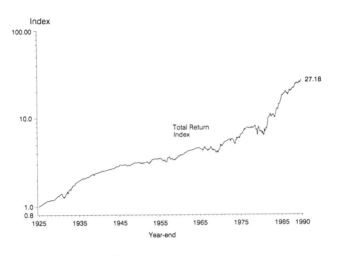

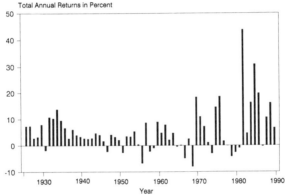

Source: Ibbotson Associates, *Stocks, Bonds, Bills, and Inflation, 1991 Yearbook,* (Chicago: Ibbotson Associates, 1991).

4.8 PRICES OF VARIOUS MATURITY 10 PERCENT COUPON BONDS

Table 4.5 presents the prices of bonds with maturities of 30 years, 10 years, 5 years, and 1 year, with yields-to-maturity levels ranging from 1 percent to 20 percent. The table illustrates the effect on bond prices of changes in prevailing interest rates. Rising interest rates result in declining bond prices, while falling interest rates result in rising bond prices. In addition, the table shows that the longer the maturity of the bond, the greater the volatility in price occasioned by a change in prevailing interest rates. Bond investors who are interested in maximizing capital gains and minimizing capital losses will lengthen maturities if they expect interest rates to fall, and will shorten maturities if they expect interest rates to rise. The effects of such strategies can be seen by examining the table.

Table 4.5 Prices of Various-Maturity 10 Percent Coupon Bonds

Coupon	10 Percent	10 Percent	10 Percent	10 Percent
Yield to Maturity (percent)	30 years	*Maturity* 10 years	5 years	1 year
1	332.765	185.443	143.786	108.932
2	279.820	172.182	137.885	107.881
3	237.830	160.090	132.277	106.845
4	204.282	149.054	126.947	105.824
5	177.271	138.972	121.880	104.818
6	155.351	129.754	117.060	103.826
7	137.417	121.318	112.474	102.849
8	122.623	113.590	108.110	101.886
9	110.319	106.503	103.956	100.936
10	100.000	100.000	100.000	100.000
11	91.275	94.024	96.231	99.076
12	83.838	88.530	92.639	98.166
13	77.450	83.472	89.216	97.269
14	71.921	78.811	85.952	96.383
15	67.101	74.513	82.839	95.511
16	62.870	70.545	79.869	94.650
17	59.131	66.878	77.035	93.801
18	55.808	63.485	74.329	92.963
19	52.836	60.344	71.745	92.137
20	50.164	57.432	69.277	91.322

4.9 PERCENTAGE BOND PRICE DECLINE RESULTING FROM A 100-BASIS-POINT INTEREST RATE RISE FROM VARIOUS YIELD LEVELS

Rising interest rates can have a dramatic negative impact on bond prices. Table 4.6 shows the percentage decline in the price of a bond resulting from a 100-basis-point rise in yield levels.

Table 4.6 Percentage Bond Price Decline Resulting from-100 Basis-Point Interest-Rate Rise from Various Yield Levels

		Percentage Decline in Price Resulting from a 100-Basis-Point Rise in Yield Levels from				
Coupon (percent)	Maturity (years)	2 to 3 Percent	4 to 5 Percent	6 to 7 Percent	8 to 9 Percent	10 to 11 Percent
2%	30	–19.7	–17.8	–15.7	–13.6	–11.6
2	10	–8.6	–8.4	–8.2	–8.0	–7.8
2	5	–4.6	–4.6	–4.5	–4.4	–4.4
2	1	–0.98	–0.97	–0.96	–0.95	–0.94
4	30	–17.4	–15.6	–13.5	–11.6	–9.9
4	10	–8.0	–7.8	–7.6	–7.3	–7.1
4	5	–4.4	–4.4	–4.3	–4.2	–4.2
4	1	–0.97	–0.96	–0.95	–0.94	–0.94
6	30	–16.2	–14.3	–12.5	–10.8	–9.3
6	10	–7.6	–7.4	–7.1	–6.9	–6.6
6	5	–4.3	–4.2	–4.2	–4.1	–4.0
6	1	–0.97	–0.96	–0.95	–0.94	–0.93
8	30	–15.5	–13.7	–11.9	–10.3	–8.9
8	10	–7.3	–7.0	–6.8	–6.5	–6.2
8	5	–4.2	–4.1	–4.0	–4.0	–3.9
8	1	–0.96	–0.95	–0.95	–0.94	–0.93
10	30	–15.0	–13.2	–11.5	–10.0	–8.7
10	10	–7.0	–6.8	–6.5	–6.2	–6.0
10	5	–4.1	–4.0	–3.9	–3.8	–3.8
10	1	–0.96	–0.95	–0.94	–0.93	–0.92

4.10 FEDERAL TAX-EXEMPT YIELDS AND EQUIVALENT TAXABLE YIELDS

Table 4.7 shows the taxable yield required to equal the yield on a tax-exempt investment. For example, a taxable security would have to yield 11.11 percent to equal an 8 percent federally tax-exempt yield for a taxpayer in the 28 percent tax bracket. Where applicable, state income taxes (see section 4.11) and/or alternative minimum tax exposure should also be considered.

Table 4.7 Taxable Yield Equivalents to Federally Tax-Exempt Yields

	Federal Income Tax Bracket		
Tax Exempt Yield*	15%	28%	31%
	Approximate Equivalent Taxable Yield		
5.00	5.88	6.94	7.25
5.25	6.18	7.29	7.61
5.50	6.47	7.64	7.97
5.75	6.76	7.99	8.33
6.00	7.06	8.33	8.70
6.10	7.18	8.47	8.84
6.20	7.29	8.61	8.99
6.25	7.35	8.68	9.06
6.30	7.41	8.75	9.13
6.40	7.53	8.89	9.28
6.50	7.65	9.03	9.42
6.60	7.76	9.17	9.57
6.70	7.88	9.31	9.71
6.75	7.94	9.38	9.78
6.80	8.00	9.44	9.86
6.90	8.12	9.58	10.00
7.00	8.24	9.72	10.14
7.10	8.35	9.86	10.29
7.20	8.47	10.00	10.43
7.25	8.53	10.07	10.51
7.30	8.59	10.14	10.58
7.40	8.71	10.28	10.72
7.50	8.82	10.42	10.87
7.60	8.94	10.56	11.01
7.70	9.06	10.69	11.16
7.75	9.12	10.76	11.23
7.80	9.18	10.83	11.30
7.90	9.29	10.97	11.45
8.00	9.41	11.11	11.59
8.10	9.53	11.25	11.74

*The yield on purchases of tax-exempt securities made at par or above par.

Table 4.7 (continued)

Tax Exempt Yield*	Federal Income Tax Bracket		
	15%	28%	31%
	Approximate Equivalent Taxable Yield		
8.20	9.65	11.39	11.88
8.25	9.71	11.46	11.96
8.30	9.76	11.53	12.03
8.40	9.88	11.67	12.17
8.50	10.00	11.81	12.32
8.60	10.12	11.94	12.46
8.70	10.24	12.08	12.61
8.75	10.29	12.15	12.68
8.80	10.35	12.22	12.75
8.90	10.47	12.36	12.90
9.00	10.59	12.50	13.04
9.10	10.71	12.64	13.19
9.20	10.82	12.78	13.33
9.25	10.88	12.85	13.41
9.30	10.94	12.92	13.48
9.40	11.06	13.06	13.62
9.50	11.18	13.19	13.77
9.60	11.29	13.33	13.91
9.70	11.41	13.47	13.06
9.75	11.47	13.54	14.13
9.80	11.53	13.61	14.20
9.90	11.65	13.75	14.35
10.00	11.76	13.89	14.49

*The yield on purchases of tax-exempt securities made at par or above par.

4.11 DOUBLE TAX-EXEMPT YIELDS AND EQUIVALENT TAXABLE YIELDS

Table 4.8 can be used to compare the yield on a taxable interest-earning security against the yield on a state municipal security or single state municipal security fund that is exempt from both federal and state taxes. In spite of their apparent lower yields, an investor may actually be better off investing in municipal securities in his or her resident state after taxes are considered.

Table 4.8 Comparision Between a Taxable Investment and a Double Tax-Free Investment

State Tax Rate For Your Locale	Multiplier For Investor In: 28% bracket	31% bracket
2%	1.42	1.48
3	1.43	1.49
4	1.45	1.51
5	1.46	1.53
6	1.48	1.54
7	1.49	1.56
8	1.51	1.58
9	1.53	1.59
10	1.54	1.61
11	1.56	1.68
12	1.58	1.70
20% of Federal Tax Liability	1.47	1.61
25% of Federal Tax Liability	1.49	1.63

4.12 DEFINITIONS OF RATINGS BY STANDARD & POOR'S AND MOODY'S

Investors are often confused or uncertain about bond ratings used by the major security rating services. This section describes Standard & Poor's corporate and municipal bond ratings, Moody's corporate bond ratings, Moody's municipal bond ratings, and Moody's short-term loan ratings. Corporate and municipal bonds are rated by both Standard & Poor's and Moody's Investor's Service. Their ratings do not constitute a recommendation to buy, sell, or hold bonds. The ratings assess only the ability of the issuer to meet the obligations of the bond. They do not address considerations such as price of the security or its suitability for a particular investor.

Ratings are based on the most current information available, and they may be changed at any time. One should verify that the rating of any bond under consideration is current.

4.12.1 Standard & Poor's Corporate and Municipal Bond Rating Definitions

AAA Bonds rated AAA have the highest rating assigned by Standard & Poor's to a debt obligation. Capacity to pay interest and repay principal is extremely strong.

AA Bonds rated AA have a very strong capacity to pay interest and repay principal and differ from the highest-rated issues only in small degree.

A Bonds rated A have a strong capacity to pay interest and repay principal, although they are somewhat more susceptible to the adverse effects of changes in circumstances and economic conditions than bonds in higher-rated categories.

BBB Bonds rated BBB are regarded as having an adequate capacity to pay interest and repay principal. Whereas they normally exhibit adequate protection parameters, adverse economic conditions or changing circumstances are more likely to lead to a weakened capacity to pay interest and repay principal for bonds in this category than for bonds in higher-rated categories.

BB, B, CCC, CC Bonds rated BB, B, CCC, and CC are regarded, on balance, as predominantly speculative with respect to capacity to pay interest and repay principal in accordance with the terms of the obligation. BB indicates the lowest degree of speculation and CC the highest degree of speculation. While such bonds will likely have some quality and protective characteristics, these are outweighed by large uncertainties or major risk exposures to adverse conditions.

C The rating C is reserved for income bonds on which no interest is being paid.

D Bonds rated D are in default, and payment of interest and/or repayment of principal is in arrears.

Plus (+) or Minus (-) The ratings from AA to B may be modified by the addition of a plus or minus sign to show relative standing within the major rating categories.

Provisional Ratings The letter "p" indicates that the rating is provisional. A provisional rating assumes the successful completion of the project being financed by the bonds being rated and indicates that payment of debt service requirements is largely or entirely dependent upon the successful and timely completion of the project. This rating, however, while addressing credit quality subsequent to completion of the project, makes no comment on the likelihood of, or the risk of default upon failure of, such completion. The investor should exercise his own judgment with respect to such likelihood and risk.

NR Indicates that no rating has been requested, that there is insufficient information on which to base a rating, or that S&P does not rate a particular type of obligation as a matter of policy.

4.12.2 Moody's Corporate Bond Rating Definitions

AAA Bonds which are rated AAA are judged to be of the best quality. They carry the smallest degree of investment risk and are generally referred to as "gilt edged." Interest payments are protected by a large or an exceptionally stable margin, and principal is secure. While the various protective elements are likely to change, such changes as can be visualized are most unlikely to impair the fundamentally strong position of such issues.

AA Bonds which are rated AA are judged to be of high quality by all standards. Together with the AAA group, they comprise what are generally known as high grade bonds. They are rated lower than the best bonds because margins of protection may not be as large as in AAA securities or fluctuation of protective elements may be of greater amplitude, or there may be other elements present which make the long-term risks appear somewhat larger than in AAA securities.

A Bonds which are rated A possess many favorable investment attributes and are to be considered as upper-medium-grade obligations. Factors giving security to principal and interest are considered adequate, but elements may be present which suggest a susceptibility to impairment sometime in the future.

Baa Bonds which are rated Baa are considered as medium grade obligations; that is, they are neither highly protected nor poorly secured. Interest payments and principal security appear adequate for the present, but certain protective elements may be lacking or may be characteristically unreliable over any great length of time. Such bonds lack outstanding investment characteristics and in fact have speculative characteristics as well.

Ba Bonds which are rated Ba are judged to have speculative elements; their future cannot be considered as well assured. Often the protection of interest and principal payments may be very moderate, and thereby not well safeguarded during both good and bad times over the future. Uncertainty of position characterizes bonds in this class.

B Bonds which are rated B generally lack characteristics of the desirable investment. Assurance of interest and principal payments or of maintenance of other terms of the contract over any long period of time may be small.

Caa Bonds which are rated Caa are of poor standing. Such issues may be in default, of there may be present elements of danger with respect to principal or interest.

Ca Bonds which are rated Ca represent obligations which are speculative in a high degree. Such issues are often in default or have other marked shortcomings.

C Bonds which are rated C are the lowest rated class of bonds, and issues so rated can be regarded as having extremely poor prospects of ever attaining any real investment standing.

4.12.3 Moody's Municipal Bond Rating Definitions

AAA Bonds which are rated AAA are judged to be of the best quality. They carry the smallest degree of investment risk and are generally referred to as "gilt edged." Interest payments are protected by a large or an exceptionally stable margin and principal is secure. While the various protective elements are likely to change, such changes as can be visualized are most unlikely to impair the fundamentally strong position of such issues.

AA Bonds which are rated AA are judged to be of high quality by all standards. Together with the AAA group they comprise what are generally known as high-grade bonds. They are rated lower than the best bonds because margins of protection may not be as large as in AAA securities or fluctuation of protective elements may be of greater amplitude or there may be other elements present which make the long-term risks appear somewhat larger than in AAA securities.

A Bonds which are rated A possess many favorable investment attributes and are to be considered as upper-medium-grade obligations. Factors giving security to principal and interest are considered adequate, but elements may be present which suggest a susceptibility to impairment sometime in the future.

Baa Bonds which are rated Baa are considered as medium grade obligations; that is, they are neither highly protected nor poorly secured. Interest payments and principal security appear adequate for the present, but certain protective elements may be lacking or may be characteristically unreliable over any great length of time. Such bonds lack outstanding investment characteristics and in fact have speculative characteristics as well.

Ba Bonds which are rated Ba are judged to have speculative elements; their future cannot be considered as well assured. Often the protection of interest and principal payments may be very moderate, and thereby not well safeguarded during both good and bad times over the future. Uncertainty of position characterizes bonds in this class.

B Bonds which are rated B generally lack characteristics of the desirable investment. Assurance of interest and principal payments or of maintenance of other terms of the contract over any long period of time may be small.

Caa Bonds which are rated Caa are of poor standing. Such issues may be in default, of there may be present elements of danger with respect to principal or interest.

Ca Bonds which are rated Ca represent obligations which are speculative in a high degree. Such issues are often in default or have other marked shortcomings.

C   Bonds which are rated C are the lowest rated class of bonds, and issues so rated can be regarded as having extremely poor prospects of ever attaining any real investment standing.

CON.(...) These are bonds for which the security depends upon the completion of some act or the fulfillment of some condition are rated conditionally. These are bonds secured by (1) earnings of projects under construction, (2) earnings of projects unseasoned in operating experience, (3) rentals which begin when facilities are completed, or (4) payments to which some other limiting condition attaches. Parenthetical rating denotes probable credit stature upon completion of construction or elimination of basis of condition.

Those bonds in the A and Baa groups which Moody's believes possess the strongest investment attributes are designated by the symbols A 1 and Baa 1.

4.12.4 Moody's Short-Term Loan Rating Definitions

MIG 1   Loans bearing this designation are of the best quality, enjoying strong protection from established cash flows of funds for their servicing or from established and broad-based access to the market for refinancing, or both.

MIG 2   Loans bearing this designation are of high quality, with margins of protection ample although not so large as in the preceding group.

MIG 3   Loans bearing this designation are of favorable quality, with all security elements accounted for but lacking the undeniable strength of the preceding grades. Market access for refinancing, in particular, is likely to be less well established.

MIG 4   Loans bearing this designation are of adequate quality, carrying specific risk but having protection commonly regarded as required of an investment security and not distinctly or predominantly speculative.

Chapter 5 _____

MUTUAL FUNDS

To many investment professionals, it's no surprise that mutual funds have experienced explosive growth in recent years. They are an excellent investment for those with small- to medium-sized portfolios as well as wealthier individuals or institutions that do not want to be burdened with evaluating and selecting individual securities.

Basically, a mutual fund is a pool of investors' money which is used to purchase a professionally managed, diversified portfolio of stocks, bonds, or money market instruments. Each share in a mutual fund represents a small slice of this large portfolio pie.

The first open-end mutual fund, the Massachusetts Investors Trust, was started in 1924. Industry growth remained relatively sluggish until the 1950s and 1960s, when the stock market enjoyed boom times. Then in the late 1960s and early 1970s, a succession of bear markets caused a decline in popularity. Sales picked up again in the late 1970s and have flourished in recent years with a bullish stock market and the introduction of a variety of fixed-income funds.

For the average investor, the advantages that mutual funds offer outweigh their disadvantages. On the plus side,

- Owning mutual fund shares is a low-cost way to diversify one's investment portfolio, thereby reducing investment risk.

- Bookkeeping tasks such as depositing dividend checks and keeping track of a large number of securities are avoided.

- Investors have access to a number of convenient services, such as an option to reinvest dividends and capital gains automatically and regular, automatic investment plans. These features are useful for individuals who can benefit from a systematic, forced savings plan. They also allow investors to switch from one type of fund to another with a minimum of paperwork, although many funds now have restrictions on the number of trades investors can make during the year.

- Readily available current and past performance records are listed in newspapers, magazines and other publications.

The main drawback of mutual funds is that, like the securities in which they invest, their value will fluctuate with changing market conditions. Another drawback is the increasingly confusing array of fee structures for mutual funds. These include no-loads, which carry no sales commission and are sold directly to the public; load funds, which carry a commission of up to 8.5 percent to invest; and low-load funds, which have a lower commission of 1 to 2 percent. Some newer funds have contingent deferred sales charges, which are deducted from investors' accounts if they redeem their shares before a specified period of time. Investment professionals should carefully explain these fees to investors.

Mutual funds will play an increasingly important role in individual and institutional investment management; and as mutual funds begin to demonstrate consistency of performance, more investors will see the benefit of this investment method. To capture investment dollars, mutual funds will offer even more attractive and convenient features, as well as a broader range of funds, particularly in the area of international and global stock or fixed-income funds. The continued proliferation of mutual funds will make fund selection that much more difficult, but a more sophisticated investing public will opt for those funds with superior long-term track records.

5.1 CHOOSING A MUTUAL FUND

The mistakes that individual investors tend to make when investing in the stock market constitute a sound argument for the value of investment companies, which take on the responsibility of choosing which stocks to purchase. Although the range of mutual funds from which an investor must choose is almost as large as individual stocks, funds offer the advantage of requiring less investor attention after purchase than would individually owned securities. The following section highlights matters of importance in choosing a mutual fund.

5.1.1 Focus on Income or Growth

In deciding what kind of fund to buy, an investor needs to determine what degree of current income, if any, he or she will require. Certain funds are designed specifically to provide substantial current income, while others forgo income for potential capital gains. Funds whose objective is growth of capital and future income may be most suitable unless present income is needed. An investor who wishes to minimize current income taxes would choose a fund that held tax-free municipal securities or a low-turnover fund that holds mostly low-yielding growth stocks.

5.1.2 Track Record

Investors should generally only consider funds which have a proven record of success. Often investors rely too heavily on funds' recent performance—in fact, any given top performer over the last year may very likely not prove so successful over a longer period of time. Sector funds, for example, whose assets are concentrated in just one industry, will often perform spectacularly in one year and then turn in a spectacularly poor performance in the next. For the purposes of the long-term investor, then, funds which have performed well over a long period of time, say 5 to 10 years, should be emphasized. There will always be relatively new funds which will prove to be successful, but a wise investor will restrict his or her investment to funds that have proved their value over time.

"Performance," as an attribute of mutual funds, refers to the fund's total return. This figure is the sum of the increase or decrease of a fund's net asset value (NAV) per share during a given period, and the total of dividend distributions per share and capital gains for the same period of time. Many publications publish a wide variety of current mutual fund statistics, including the top performing funds over several time periods. The first step in selecting a fund should be to check in these tables for funds which were well-above-average performers in their respective fund categories over several time periods.

Once the investor has selected several funds that have passed the performance hurdles, he or she should consider how well those same funds performed in a year in which the stock market as a whole declined: a down year. Down-year performance is a crucial indicator of the fund's ability not only to make money when markets are rising, but to keep the portfolio from being too badly hit when prices are falling. For the same reason that an investor may wish to stay away from sector funds, which may perform wonderfully in the right circumstances but which will probably be disastrous as a long-term investment, the investor should avoid funds which did not perform adequately in a bad year. In some ways this is the truest test of a fund's overall worth—precious few fund managers will be able to weather foul investment climates as well as fair ones.

5.1.3 Fund Management

Although a fund's investment policy may be determined by its charter and its board of directors, it is a fund's manager who performs the actual operation of the fund, and when a new manager takes on a fund, that fund's past performance history becomes in large part irrelevant. For this reason it is crucial that an investor find out for how long the portfolio manager has been managing the fund. A fund is not required to provide a portfolio manager's identity in its reports, so an investor may need to ask the fund for this information. A manager determines what sectors of the economy will be most heavily represented in the portfolio, and within these sectors, which companies will be included. A potential investor should scrutinize the fund's current investments to get some idea of how well diversified they are and how consistent they are with the investor's own opinions and preferences.

5.1.4 Fund Prospectus

An investor can obtain a considerable amount of information about a particular fund from its prospectus, for example, the affiliations and aims of the fund's directors, as well as detailed, up-to-date listings of portfolio holdings. Other useful information which might be included in a prospectus (or in supplementary reports) are expense breakdowns, sales and redemptions of fund shares, the extent of portfolio turnover, and the management's view on current and future developments.

There are a few matters discussed in the fund prospectus concerning fund operations that can affect a fund's performance. Funds that use leverage—investing with borrowed money—and inherently more volatile and risky, but may be a good feature for more aggressive investors. The ratio of operating expense to average net assets (the expense ratio), although in most cases not significant, may be problematic if it is excessively high (over 1.5 percent for most stock fund categories, less for bond funds). Redemption fees are another feature that may nonetheless be a problem if too high. Many funds charge a temporary redemption to discourage excessive trading, with the fee reduced or eliminated after a specified period of time. If the fees or operating expenses on a fund are especially high, an investor want to avoid the fund.

5.2 ASSEMBLING AND EVALUATING A MUTUAL FUND PORTFOLIO

Mutual funds should be an essential investment tool for most investors. As discussed in Section 5.1, because there are thousands of funds currently available, choosing the right fund can be a formidable task, and assembling a well-balanced portfolio of funds can prove to be an even greater challenge. This section will assist the financial professional in advising clients on assembling and evaluating a mutual fund portfolio that will meet investment objectives.

5.2.1 Assembling a Fund Portfolio

The task of assembling a portfolio of mutual funds may seem daunting at first, given the wide variety of available funds. Individual investors will find that with a little effort they can construct a very suitable group of funds that will help them achieve their financial objectives. Funds have a wide variety of investment objectives, such as maximum capital gains, growth and income, or income. Many investors are well served by investing a part of their money in several different fund categories. There are three levels of analysis that are necessary prior actually to selecting individual funds.

1. **Determine investment objectives**
   Before individual investors start to acquire appropriate investments, they will need to specify clearly their investment objectives. How much risk can the investor afford to take? What major future financial hurdles, such as college education costs, will investors need to overcome and when? What are future income prospects? By realistically assessing the current situation and future needs, individual investors can begin to identify what they want to accomplish. From there, they can begin to identify the kinds of mutual funds that will help them meet their investment objectives.

2. **Determine an appropriate portfolio allocation**
   The portfolio allocation process involves assigning appropriate percentages of total investment portfolio (no matter how small or large it might be) to interest-earning investments and stock investments. Virtually everyone should have stock investments, and many experts suggest that stocks comprise 50 to 60 percent of a portfolio for younger people and 40 to 50 percent for people who are less than 10 years from retirement.

3. **Identify appropriate categories of mutual funds**
   After the individual investor has decided on a suitable portfolio allocation, the specific categories within both the stock portion and interest-earning portion must be determined. Investors need to consider several factors, including overall investment objectives, current financial status, the current investment climate, and their familiarity with the various mutual fund categories. Funds provide an ideal means for individual investors to participate in certain investment markets. For example, mutual funds are an excellent way to participate in the attractive international stock markets. Mutual funds also provide broad diversification in the interest-earning side of a portfolio. While mutual funds are an excellent way for investors to assemble an appropriate portfolio with modest resources they are also useful to and widely used by, more substantial individual and institutional investors.

5.2.2 Evaluating a Fund Portfolio

Once the individual investor has put together a mutual fund portfolio, he or she will need to evaluate it periodically from the standpoint of the allocation of the total portfolio and individual fund performance. With respect to the portfolio as a whole, the investor will need to determine how the total fund assets are allocated. Is the allocation in line with his or her parameters? If not, perhaps some reallocation is necessary. If stock prices have risen sharply, the proportion of stocks in relation to the total portfolio is probably higher than the investor had originally determined was appropriate. If so, he or she should sell some stock funds and buy additional interest-earning funds. Note that the investor would follow the opposite course should stock prices fall. The disciplined approach to fund evaluation forces the investor to sell stock funds when prices are high and buy stock funds when prices have dropped. This is exactly the approach that most investors should take, but few have the discipline, and most do the opposite. How often should the investor reallocate? Certainly no more frequently than once per quarter and probably less frequently unless there has been a precipitous change in stock or bond prices.

Beyond having to sell certain funds as part of a portfolio reallocation, the individual investor also needs to make an objective evaluation periodically of each fund in the portfolio. If he or she selected good funds in the first place, the investor is probably better off holding onto the funds even if they post a few disappointing months or quarters. If a particular fund consistently turns in below-average results for its fund category, the investor should consider replacing it with a better performing fund. This shouldn't happen too often, however. Most important, the investor shouldn't fret over short-term fluctuations in either market conditions or in performance of funds in his or her investment "stable."

5.3   MUTUAL FUND INVESTMENT CATEGORIES

Many investors tend to concentrate their mutual funds in one or very few fund categories. Yet there are many types of mutual funds that are currently available that can help most investors achieve a well-diversified, well-balanced portfolio. Brief descriptions of each of the many categories of mutual funds are provided for in this section. The funds are organized into four sectors: stock funds, bond funds, money market funds, and specialized funds.

5.3.1 Stock Funds

Maximum capital gains funds (also called *aggressive growth funds*) attempt to achieve very high returns by investing in more speculative stocks, maximizing capital gains income at the expense of income from dividends. For these funds, the potential for rapid growth is the primary criterion for investment. In addition, techniques such as leveraged buying, option writing, and short-term trading further increase possible yields. Of course, the potential for greater rewards means that these funds are risky; they tend to do very well in bull markets and very poorly in bear markets. *Small company growth funds* (also called *emerging growth funds*) are a type of maximum capital gains funds specializing in stocks of promising small companies.

Growth funds seek capital gains from companies that have realized steady growth in earnings. Growth companies aim to grow at a steady rate; they generally do not employ speculative investing techniques, and are more stable, less volatile, and more consistent than maximum capital gains funds. Growth funds aim to achieve a rate of growth that beats inflation without taking the risks necessary to achieve occasional spectacular success.

Growth and income funds seek a balanced stock portfolio that will achieve capital appreciation as well as current income from dividends. These funds are less risky than growth funds, because the dividend income may offset at least some of the periodic losses in stock prices. In times of high market volatility—either in an up or down direction—growth and income funds are slower to respond. *Income funds,* or *equity-income funds,* generally invest about half their portfolio in dividend-paying stocks and the rest in convertible securities and straight debt instruments. Income funds may have capital growth as a secondary objective.

International stock funds take advantage of the fact that foreign stock markets have been fairly consistent in outperforming the U.S. stock market. Moreover, there are many excellent companies that trade only on foreign stock exchanges. Therefore, many investors wish to turn to international investments, which also provide additional diversification to a portfolio. A U.S. investor will have difficulty finding adequate information of foreign companies, many of which are not governed by the kinds of regulatory bodies that protect American investments, so an international fund is the best means for an investor to enter the international market. Some international funds invest only in one country or region. *Global stock funds* differ from international stock funds only insofar as the global fund may also invest in U.S. securities.

5.3.2 Bond Funds

For many years, especially during the period of high inflation in the 1970s, bond funds were poor investments, but if inflation stays low, they will continue to be the oustanding investments they have been in recent years. Except for funds that invest solely in government bonds, all bond funds have some degree of risk of default; however, the real risks of holding bonds or bond funds is that high inflation will outpace the returns and/or rising interest rates will reduce the principal value of the investment. You should also note that within each bond fund category, there are usually several funds that specialize in investments of short-term duration, inter-mediate-term duration, and long-term duration.

Corporate bond funds seek a high level of income by buying bonds of corporations.

Government bond funds, backed by the "full faith and credit" of the U.S. government, offer total credit safety, although they do fluctuate with interest rates like all bonds and bond funds. One variety of government bond funds are those which invest a majority of their portfolio in mortgage-backed securities issued by the Government National Mortgage Association

(*GNMA* or *Ginnie Mae Funds*). Holders of GNMA certificates receive both interest and partial return of principal. A GNMA fund reinvests the capital distributions. Different types of GNMA funds—holding either premium or discount certificates—can vary in their total return according to the stability or volatility of interest rates.

Convertible bond funds are a third alternative. Convertible securities are bonds or preferred stock that can be exchanged for a fixed number of shares in the common stock of the underlying company. The conversion feature is inteded to induce investors to accept a lower interest rate in the hopes that the accompanying stock will rise in value and bring up the convertible's value. When stocks rise, convertibles will rise as well—albeit at a slower rate—while when stocks fall, convertibles tend to fall less because of the benefit of their yield. Convertibles thus combine, in diluted form, features of both stocks and bonds.

International bond funds' returns depend in part on the relative strength of the U.S. dollar. An international bond fund typically invests in high-quality government or corporate bonds and enters into currency hedges in countries whose currency is expected to appreciate against the dollar. These funds can provide a portfolio with an additional degree of diversification.

Municipal bond funds, introduced in 1976, provide investors with a means for tax-free income with liquidity, convenience, and professional management. Since municipal bond prices do not appear in the daily papers, and the market for municipals is less attractive than for other kinds of securities, muni bond funds are a useful way for an individual investor to avoid these inconveniences. Interest earned from bonds not issued in the investor's own state is fully taxable in his or her own state, so in order to produce maximum tax-free income, funds have been developed that hold bonds only from one state. A New York investor owning the New York muni fund will avoid state taxes and increase after-tax return. However, single-state funds generally have slightly lower yields than multistate municipal bond funds.

High-yield bond funds (junk bond funds) specialize in low-quality, high-yield bonds that may offer substantial profits but that also carry higher risk. High-yield funds invest either in corporate bonds or municipal bonds. They can be very volatile, and investors in corporate high-yield bond funds in recent years have been surprised to find their principal eroding from time to time, sometimes significantly.

5.3.3 Money Market Funds

Money market funds, first created in 1972, have become the most widely held mutual fund category. They hold a variety of short-term money market instruments and have as their three main objectives preservation of capital, liquidity, and the highest income that can be achieved without sacrificing the first two objectives. Money market funds offer excellent liquidity: an investor need only write a check to transfer money. These funds are commonly used as an account in which funds can be stored until new stock or bond investment opportunities arise. *U.S. government money market funds* and *tax-exempt money market funds* invest in short-term instruments of the U.S. government and states/municipalities, respectively. As with municipal bond funds, there are also some single-state tax-exempt money funds.

5.3.4 Specialized Funds

Balanced funds maintain a conbination of common stocks, bonds, and perhaps preferred stocks. Balanced funds may have income, growth, or growth and income as an objective. Balanced funds provide diversification between stocks and bonds in the same fund with a low minimum investment and are thus a good investment for someone with a small amount to invest.

Specialized industry funds (sector funds) invest only in the stocks of a single industry, like biotechnology, waste management, or energy. Sector funds, unlike well-diversified funds, zero in on a particular area of the stock market that may or may not have attractive prospects. The lack of diversity across industries means that sector funds can rapidly switch from excellent to abysmal performance. Sector funds behave more like individual stocks than diversified funds, and their erratic behavior cannot be predicted by the same criteria (such as past track record and management skill) that usually guide purchase of funds.

Asset allocation funds go in the opposite extreme as sector funds, providing extremely broad diversification. They generally invest in up to five or six different markets, so that any one market's losses may be offset by another's gain.

Variable funds (market timing funds) may shift allocation according to large economic trends and are thus more flexible.

Precious metals funds (gold funds) usually invest in stocks of gold-mining firms and other companies engaged in the business of precious metals. Some funds may actually purchase and store the metal itself. These funds tend to move in synchronization with precious metal prices. Historically, precious metals funds have been considered an inflation hedge, but lackluster performance in recent years has brought this into question.

Option funds and the stock options they represent are so complex an investment that a well-managed fund is a very effective way of entering the market. Most option funds are conservative and income oriented. In a long-term bull market, option funds tend to perform poorly; they achieve their best payoff in a flat market.

Index funds own all the stocks in an index, the Standard & Poor's 500, for example. These "unmanaged" funds have attracted the attention of institutional investors who have had a very difficult time beating the market. By simply duplicating a broad section of the market, an institution can save substantial amounts on management and research and trading fees. Individual investors can do the same through an index fund.

5.4 DIRECTORY OF INVESTMENT COMPANY MANAGERS/ADVISORS

Table 5.1 lists the names and telephone numbers of investment company managers/advisors who had at least $1 billion of fund assets under management in 1991.

Table 5.1 Directory of Investment Company Managers/Advisors (Minimum of $1 Billion of Fund Assets Under Management)

AIM Advisors, Inc. (800) 347-1919	Delaware Management Co. (215) 988-1200
Alliance Capital Management L.P. (800) 221-5872	Dimensional Fund Advisors, Inc. (DFA Funds) (213) 395-8005
American Cap Asset Management (800) 421-5666	Dreyfus Corporation (800) 645-6561
Back Bay Advisors (New England Funds) (800) 283-1155	Eaton Vance Management, Inc. (800) 225-6265
Barlow, Hanley, Newhinney & Strauss/INVESCO (Windsor II) (800) 662-7447	Federated Management Company (800) 245-2423 Fidelity Management & Research Corp (800) 544-6666
Benham Management Corp. (800) 321-8321	First Fidelity Bank, National Association, New Jersey (FFB Funds)
Boston Co. Advisors (800) 225-5267	(800) 845-8406
Calvert Asset Management Co. (800) 368-2748	First Investors Management Co. (800) 423-4026
Capital Research & Management Co. (800)421-0180	Flag Investors Management Corp. (800) 767-3524
Carnegie Capital Management Co. (800) 321-2322	Franklin Advisers (800) 342-5236
CIGNA Investments, Inc. (800) 572-4462	Freedom Capital Management Corp. (800) 225-6258
Citibank N.A. (Landmark Funds) (212) 559-7823	Gabelli Funds, Inc. (800) 422-3554 General Electric Investment Corp.
Colonial Management Associates (617) 426-3750	(800) 242-0134 Goldman Sachs & Co.
Columbia Funds Management Co. (800) 547-1707	(800) 621-2550 IDS Financial Corp.
Common Sense Investment Advisors (800) 544-5445	(800) 222-9700 INVESCO Fund Group Inc.
Dean Witter Reynolds InterCapital (800) 869-3863	(Financial Funds) (800) 525-8085

Investors Research Corp.
(Twentieth Century Funds)
(800) 345-2021

Jones & Babson, Inc.
(800) 422-2766

Kemper Financial Services,Inc.
(800) 621-1048

Keystone Custodian Funds, Inc.
(800) 343-2898

Loomis-Sayles & Co., Inc.
(800) 343-7104

Lord Abbett & Co.
(800) 426-1130

Massachusetts Financial Services
(800) 343-2829

Merrill Lynch Asset Management, Inc.
(800) 637-3863

Mitchell Hutchins Asset Management, Inc.
(PaineWebber Funds)
(800) 647-1568

National Securities & Research
(800) 223-7757

Neuberger and Berman Management
(800) 877-9700

Phoenix Investment Counsel
(203) 253-1000

Pilgrim Management Corporation
(800) 334-3444

Pioneering Management Corporation
(Pioneer Funds)
(800) 821-1239

Price (T. Rowe) Associates
(800) 638-5660

Provident Institutional Management Corp.
(800) 441-7762

Putnam Management Co.
(800) 225-1581

Reich & Tang L.P.
(212) 370-1110

Reserve Management Company
(800) 223-2213

Rodney Square Management Corp.
(800) 225-5084

Rushmore Services, Inc.
(800) 343-3355

Scudder Stevens & Clark
(800) 225-2470 (Boston)
(800) 854-8525 (NYC)

SEI Financial Management Corp.
(800) 345-1151

Selected Financial Services, Inc.
(800) 553-5533

Seligman (J. & W.) & Co., Inc.
(800) 221-2450

Shearson/Lehman Advisors
(Boston Company Advisors, Inc.)
(800) 451-2010

Smith Barney Harris Upham
(Smith Barney Advisors, Inc.)
(800) 544-7835

SteinRoe & Farnham, Inc.
(800) 338-2550

Strong/Corneliuson Capital Management
(800) 368-3863

Templeton, Galbraith & Hansberger
(800) 237-0738

Thomson Advisory Group
(800) 628-1237

Transamerica Fund Management Co.
(800) 343-6840

USAA Investment Management Co.
(800) 531-8181

Value Line, Inc.
(800) 223-0818

Van Kampen Merrit Inv. Advisory Corp.
(800) 225-2222

Vanguard Group, Inc.
(800) 662-7447

Waddell & Reed
(United Funds)
(913) 236-1303

Webster Management Corp.
(Kidder Peabody Funds)
(215) 510-5041

Wellington Management Co.
(Various Vanguard Funds)
(800) 662-7447

5.5 TOP-PERFORMING MUTUAL FUNDS

Every day that the markets are open, the financial press lists the pennies per share won or lost by the mutual funds. Every week, month, and quarter, the papers are full of news the top-performing mutual funds over that small period of time. The press isn't so forthcoming with longer-term statistics, however. For investors who care more about selection than timing, and who plan to hold on to any shares they buy for at least a few quarters, Tables 5.2 to 5.15 present lists of the top ten funds in each fund category for the last 1-, 5- and 10-year periods. Although these funds' past records indicate that they'll do well in the long run, many of these funds have not appeared on the winner's list for many of the shorter time periods.

Table 5.2 Maximum Capital Gains Funds

1-Year	*Total Return (6/30/91)*
1. Twentieth Century Ultra	30.1
2. Fidelity Contrafund	21.0
3. Founders Special Fund	17.9
4. Flex Fund—Growth	17.3
5. Pru-Bache Flexi-Strategy (B)	15.7
6. Pacific Horizon Agg. Growth	14.7
7. Crabbe Huson Growth Fund	14.7
8. Fidelity Specl Sit (Initial)	14.0
9. Strong Discovery Fund	13.8
10. Fidelity Specl Sit (Plymouth)	13.4
Total number of funds	91

5-Years	*Total Returns (7/1/86–6/30/91)*
1. Delaware Grp DelCap—Concpt I	138.6
2. Fidelity Contrafund	117.8
3. Twentieth Century Ultra	110.7
4. Keystone America Omega	87.9
5. AIM Equity—Constellation	86.9
6. Fidelity Magellan Fund	82.1
7. Founders Special Fund	77.8
8. Putnam Voyager Fund	76.5
9. Columbia Special Fund	74.5
10. Twentieth Century Growth	74.3
Total number of funds	68

Table 5.2 (continued)

10-Years	Total Returns (7/1/81–6/30/91)
1. Fidelity Magellan Fund	583.6
2. Sequoia Fund	418.3
3. Phoenix Stock Fund	366.4
4. Quest for Value Fund	365.6
5. Putnam Voyager Fund	323.2
6. WPG Tudor Fund	311.2
7. Neuberger Berman Partners	295.7
8. Fidelity Contrafund	293.5
9. Seliglman Capital Fund	282.2
10. Oppenheimer Time Fund	279.9
Total number of funds	45

Table 5.3 Small Company Growth Funds

1-Year	Total Returns (6/30/91)
1. Wasatch Growth Fund	15.1
2. Nicholas Limited Edition Fd	14.8
3. Legg Mason Special Invest	14.4
4. Wasatch Aggressive Equity	14.2
5. Sit New Beginning Growth	14.1
6. Fidelity OTC Portfolio	13.4
7. Quest for Value Small Cap	13.1
8. ABT Emerging Growth Fund	12.4
9. Janus Venture Fund	11.9
10. American Capital Emerg Gth	10.3
Total number of funds	44

5-Years	Total Returns (7/1/86–6/30/91)
1. Janus Venture Fund	93.2
2. Hartwell Emerging Growth Fund	81.2
3. Twentieth Century Gift Trust	74.9
4. Kaufmann Fund	70.3
5. Sit New Beginning Growth	67.5
6. Fidelity OTC Portfolio	65.8
7. Acorn Fund	60.2
8. Legg Mason Special Invest	53.7
9. Pennsylvania Mutual Fund	50.6
10. Twentieth Century Vista	50.2
Total number of funds	24

Table 5.3 (continued)

10-Years	*Total Returns* *(7/1/81–6/30/91)*
1. Pennsylvania Mutual Fund	272.3
2. Acorn Fund	252.9
3. American Capital Emerg Gth	216.0
4. Over-the-Counter Securities	168.4
5. Hartwell Emerging Growth	158.9
6. Price (T. Rowe) New Horizons	123.4
7. Vanguard Explorer Fund	94.9
8. Lord Abbett Devel Growth	86.9
9. Vanguard Small Cap Stock	79.9
Total number of funds	9

Table 5.4 Long-Term Growth Funds

1-Year	*Total Returns* *(6/30/91)*
1. Phoenix Capital Appreciation	27.5
2. American Express Equity Gth	26.2
3. United New Concepts Fund	23.7
4. CGM Capital Development	22.4
5. Westcore Midco Growth	22.5
6. Portico Fds-Special Growth	21.7
7. Vista Growth & Income	21.3
8. Axe-Houghton Growth Fund	19.1
9. Mairs & Power Growth Fund	18.9
10. Berger One Hundred	18.6
Total number of funds	309

5-Years	*Total Returns* *(7/1/86–6/30/91)*
1. IDEX Fund II	123.7
2. IDEX Fund	114.6
3. Equitable Growth (B)	105.7
4. Gabelli Asset Fund	104.2
5. Fidelity Destiny Fund II	97.2
6. Kemper Growth Fund	95.3
7. CIGNA Value Fund	94.8
8. Janus Fund	92.0
9. Berger One Hundred	91.4
10. Price (T. Rowe) Cap Apprec	90.3
Total number of funds	217

Table 5.4 (continued)

10-Years	*Total Returns (7/1/81–6/30/91)*
1. CGM Capital Development	540.8
2. Phoenix Growth Fund Series	491.6
3. Fidelity Destiny Fund I	423.8
4. AIM Equity—Weingarten Fund	419.8
5. IAI Regional Fund	402.4
6. New England Growth Fund	401.8
7. IDS New Dimensions Fund	381.5
8. New York Venture Fund	377.7
9. Mutual Benefit Fund	354.9
10. SteinRoe Special Fund	352.6
Total number of funds	122

Table 5.5 Growth and Current Income Funds

1-Year	*Total Returns (6/30/91)*
1. Fam Value Fund	20.9
2. Franklin Managed—Rising Div	19.9
3. Royce Fund—Total Return	17.6
4. Dreman High Return Port	16.8
5. Fidelity Asset Manager	16.7
6. Selected American Shares	16.7
7. Rightime Blue Chip Fund	16.4
8. Plymouth Income & Growth	15.9
9. Principal Pres—Div Achvrs	15.6
10. Monetta Fund	15.4
Total number of funds	205

5-Years	*Total Returns (7/1/86–6/30/91)*
1. FPA Paramount Fund	116.7
2. Fidelity Growth & Income	90.8
3. Monetta Fund	90.4
4. Financial Industrial Income	82.9
5. US Boston Inv—Grth & Inc	80.5
6. Nationwide Fund	77.8
7. IDS Managed Retirement	76.4
8. Dodge & Cox Stock Fund	75.4
9. Mass Investors Trust	74.5
10. Investment Co. of America	74.4
Total number of funds	108

Table 5.5 (continued)

10-Years	Total Returns (7/1/81–6/30/91)
1. FPA Paramount Fund	464.1
2. Financial Industrial Income	405.4
3. Selected American Shares	374.3
4. Washington Mutual Investors	373.9
5. Investment Co. of America	361.4
6. Sentinel Common Stock Fund	344.7
7. Dodge & Cox Stock Fund	343.8
8. Fundamental Investors Fund	338.1
9. Elfun Trusts	326.1
10. Dean Witter Dividend Growth	325.4
Total number of funds	70

Table 5.6 Balanced Funds

1-Year	Total Returns (6/30/91)
1. State Farm Balanced Fund	16.1
2. Pax World Fund	14.8
3. Phoenix Balanced Fund	14.2
4. Axe-Houghton Fund B	14.0
5. Fidelity Balanced Fund	13.6
6. CGM Mutual Fund	12.2
7. Composite Bond & Stock Fd	10.9
8. Bascom Hill Balanced Fd	9.9
9. Putnam George Fund	9.6
10. SafeGuard Balanced Port	9.6
Total number of funds	38

5-Years	Total Returns (7/1/86–6/30/91)
1. State Farm Balanced Fund	89.4
2. Dodge & Cox Balanced Fund	68.5
3. Phoenix Balanced Fund	68.5
4. Equitable Balanced	67.9
5. USAA Cornerstone Fund	66.1
6. CGM Mutual Fund	65.6
7. Pax World Fund	63.9
8. Putnam George Fund	61.3
9. IDS Mutual Fund	60.3
10. American Balanced Fund	59.1
Total number of funds	24

Table 5.6 (continued)

10-Years	Total Returns (7/1/81–6/30/91)
1. Phoenix Balanced Fund	401.2
2. CGM Mutual Fund	352.2
3. State Farm Balanced Fund	321.7
4. Wellington Fund	305.2
5. Massachusetts Financial Total Ret	301.1
6. Sentinel Balanced Fund	300.0
7. IDS Mutual Fund	297.6
8. United Continental Income	283.1
9. Dodge & Cox Balanced Fund	290.5
10. American Balanced Fund	282.8
Total number of funds	18

Table 5.7 Equity Income Funds

1-Year	Total Returns (6/30/91)
1. Capital Income Builder	14.8
2. Shearson Option Income	12.3
3. Stratton Monthly Dividend	12.3
4. Fidelity Qualified Dividend	12.3
5. Vanguard Preferred Stock	11.6
6. USAA Mutual—Income Stock	11.5
7. Dean Witter Option Income	11.4
8. Colonial Corp Cash I	11.3
9. Mairs & Power Income Fund	11.3
10. American National Income	11.1
Total number of funds	44

5-Years	Total Returns (7/1/86–6/30/91)
1. United Income Fund	78.2
2. Oppenheimer Premium Income	75.8
3. Price (T. Rowe) Equity, Inc	71.9
4. State Bond Diversified Fd	66.5
5. Oppenheimer Equity Income	57.4
6. American National Income	56.6
7. Shearson Option Income	55.5
8. Mairs & Power Income Fund	55.1
9. Sit New Beginning Inc & Gth	54.3
10. Smith Barney Fds—Inc & Gth	53.5
Total number of funds	27

Table 5.7 (continued)

10-Years	Total Returns (7/1/81–6/30/91)
1. United Income Fund	424.4
2. Oppenheimer Equity Income	320.1
3. Fidelity Equity Income	296.2
4. State Bond Diversified Fd	271.4
5. SAFECO Income Fund	258.3
6. American National Income	252.6
7. Vanguard Preferred Stock	251.3
8. Mairs & Power Income Fund	247.9
9. Smith Barney Fds—Inc & Gth	246.2
10. Stratton Monthly Dividend	232.8
Total number of funds	13

Table 5.8 Flexible Income Fund

1-Year	Total Returns (6/30/91)
1. Fidelity Capital & Income	12.7
2. Janus Flexible Income Fund	12.5
3. Fidelity Convertible Sec	11.6
4. USAA Mutual—Income Fund	11.5
5. Concord Inc Tr—Covertible	11.4
6. Value Line Income Fund	11.3
7. Franklin Income Fund	11.3
8. SBSF Convertible Secs	11.1
9. Convertible Sec & Income	10.8
10. MainStay Convertible Fund	10.8
Total number of funds	52

5-Years	Total Returns (7/1/86–6/30/91)
1. First Prairie Divers Asset	65.8
2. USAA Mutual—Income Fund	60.4
3. Income Fund of America	57.1
4. Wellesley Income Fund	56.8
5. Phoenix Convertible Fund	56.1
6. Fidelity Puritan Fund	55.8
7. Franklin Income Fund	54.7
8. Lindner Dividend Fund	54.6
9. Mutual of Omaha Income	52.9
10. Founders Equity Income Fund	51.1
Total number of funds	35

5.8 (continued)

10-Years	Total Returns (7/1/81–6/30/91)
1. Lindner Dividend Fund	365.5
2. Fidelity Puritan Fund	314.0
3. Income Fund of America	306.0
4. National Total Income	294.0
5. Wellesley Income Fund	293.6
6. Phoenix Convertible Fund	287.4
7. Franklin Income Fund	254.9
8. United Retirement Shares	251.0
9. Keystone K-1	249.8
10. USAA Mutual—Income Fund	242.9
Total number of funds	26

Table 5.9 Corporate Bond Funds

1-Year	Total Returns (6/30/91)
1. Franklin Managed-Corp Cash	14.3
2. FPA New Income Fund	14.0
3. Dean Witter Tax Advantage	13.5
4. Scudder Short-Term Bond	12.6
5. Pimit Total Return	12.5
6. IDS Bond Fund	12.2
7. Paine Webber Master Income	11.6
8. GE S&S Long Term Interest	11.5
9. Transamerica Invest Qual Bd	11.0
10. Forum Investors Bond Fund	11.0
Total number of funds	129

5-Years	Total Returns (7/1/86–6/30/91)
1. UST Master—Managed Income	63.9
2. FPA New Income Fund	61.7
3. Mackenzie Series—Fixed Inc	53.3
4. Elfun Income Fund	52.6
5. Scudder Short-Term Bond	52.2
6. Fidelity Intermediate Bond	52.0
7. Vanguard Fixed—Inv Grade	52.0
8. Columbia Fixed Income Secs	51.6
9. Lutheran Brotherhood Income	51.5
10. Guardian Bond Fund	50.0
Total number of funds	68

Table 5.9 (continued)

10-Years	Total Returns (7/1/81–6/30/91)
1. GE S&S Long Term Interest	277.5
2. IDS Selective Fund	263.3
3. IDS Bond Fund	257.5
4. United Bond Fund	252.9
5. Putnam Income Fund	252.2
6. Massachusetts Financial Bond Fund	247.1
7. Bond Fund of America	246.0
8. Alliance Bond—Monthly Income 1987	245.3
9. JP Income Fund	242.8
10. Bond Port. for Endowments	239.2
Total number of funds	40

Table 5.10 Corporate High Yield Funds

1-Year	Total Returns (6/30/91)
1. Plymouth High Yield Port	20.0
2. Liberty High Income Bond	18.7
3. Paine Webber High Income	17.9
4. American Investors Income	17.4
5. Oppenheimer Champion H/Y	16.5
6. AMEV Advantage—High Yield	16.4
7. Putnam High Yield Trust II	16.2
8. Massachusetts Financial High Income II	16.0
9. MFS Lifetime High Income Tr	15.4
10. Federated High Yield Trust	15.0
Total number of funds	82

5-Years	Total Returns (7/1/86–6/30/91)
1. Van Kampen High Yield	64.1
2. Merrill Lynch Corp—H/Inc (A)	51.4
3. Kemper High Yield Fund	48.6
4. Aegon USA—High Yield	48.3
5. Oppenheimer High Yield	45.2
6. Delaware Grp Delchester I	43.5
7. Liberty High Income Bond	42.2
8. Federated High Yield Trust	41.7
9. CIGNA High Yield Fund	41.6
10. Putnam High Yield Trust	39.0
Total number of funds	51

Table 5.10 (continued)

10-Years	Total Returns (7/1/81–6/30/91)
1. Kemper High Yield Fund	281.4
2. CIGNA High Yield Fund	242.1
3. Delaware Grp Delchester I	241.8
4. Merrill Lynch Corp—H/Inc (A)	224.6
5. Liberty High Income Bond	221.0
6. Putnam High Yield Trust	220.7
7. Massachusetts Financial High Income	213.7
8. Vanguard Fixed—High Yield	206.7
9. Northeast Investors Trust	206.2
10. Eaton Vance Inc Fd of Boston 1982	205.5
Total number of funds	29

Table 5.11 Government Securities Funds

1-Year	Total Returns (6/30/91)
1. Institutional Gov't Income	12.7
2. American Capital Gov't Sec	12.0
3. Franklin US Gov't Series	11.9
4. Kemper US Gov't Sec	11.8
5. Voyageur US Gov't Secs	11.6
6. Premier Income Fund	11.2
7. Smith Barney Fds—US Gov't	11.2
8. Merrill Lynch Federal Sec	11.2
9. Composite US Gov't Sec	11.2
10. First Trust US Government	11.1
Total number of funds	169

5-Years	Total Returns (7/1/86–6/30/91)
1. Benham Target Mat.—2005	62.7
2. Smith Barney Fds—US Gov't	57.4
3. Conn Mutual—Gov't	55.5
4. Franklin US Gov't Series	55.3
5. Putnam US Gov't Income	55.2
6. Fund for U.S. Gov't Sec	55.1
7. Federated Income Trust	54.7
8. Government Income Secs	54.4
9. Van Kampen US Govt	53.4
10. State Bond US Gov't Secs	53.2
Total number of funds	80

Table 5.11 (continued)

10-Years	Total Returns (7/1/81–6/30/91)
1. Fund for U.S. Govt Sec	234.0
2. Kemper US Gov't Sec	232.2
3. Franklin US Gov't Series	224.1
4. State Farm Interim Fund	195.5
5. Fidelity Gov't Securities	193.7
6. AMA-US Gov't Secs.—Inc Plus 1989	178.7
7. Benham Treasury Note Trust	171.2
8. Mutual of Omaha America	169.9
9. Midwest Income—Interm Govt	150.4
Total number of funds	9

Table 5.12 Government Mortgage-Backed Funds

1-Year	Total Returns (6/30/91)
1. Alliance Mortgage Securities	12.9
2. American Capital Fed Mtg	12.3
3. Vanguard Fixed—GNMA	11.7
4. Cardinal Gov't Obligations	11.6
5. Federated GNMA Trust	11.6
6. Dreyfus GNMA Fund	11.5
7. Fidelity GNMA Fund	11.5
8. Benham Gov't Income—GNMA	11.4
9. Pacific Horizon US Gov't	11.4
10. Fidelity Mortgage Securities	11.4
Total number of funds	42

5-Years	Total Returns (7/1/86–6/30/91)
1. Federated GNMA Trust	58.7
2. Vanguard Fixed—GNMA	58.5
3. Benham Gov't Income—GNMA	57.0
4. Princor Gov't Sec Income	56.2
5. Alliance Mortgage Securities	55.5
6. Mimlic Mortgage Securities	54.8
7. Lexington GNMA Income Fund	54.4
8. IDS Federal Income Fund	53.7
9. Cardinal Gov't Obligations	53.4
10. Fidelity GNMA Fund	52.3
Total number of funds	26

Table 5.12 (continued)

10-Years	Total Returns (7/1/81–6/30/91)
1. Vanguard Fixed—GNMA	250.2
2. Lexington GNMA Income Fund	204.3
Total number of funds	2

Table 5.13 Municipal Bond Funds

1-Year	Total Return (6/30/91)
1. First Prairie T/E—Insured	9.9
2. General Municipal Bond Fund	9.9
3. Lord Abbett T/T Income—Nat'l	9.6
4. Premier Municipal Bond	9.5
5. First Prairie T/E—Interm	9.4
6. ND Tax-Free Fund, Inc.	9.4
7. Vanguard Muni—Intermediate	9.3
8. Vista Tax-Free Income	9.3
9. Fidelity Limited Term Muni	9.3
10. Nuveen Insured T/F—National	9.3
Total number of funds	152

5-Years	Total Return (7/1/86–6/30/91)
1. UST Master—T/E Long Term	67.2
2. SAFECO Municipal Bond Fund	54.3
3. Lord Abbett T/F Income—Nat'l	54.1
4. State Farm Muni Bond Fund	53.2
5. Scudder Managed Muni Bond	52.8
6. Nuveen Municipal Bond Fund	52.2
7. Kemper Municipal Bond Fund	52.0
8. United Muni Bond Fund	51.8
9. Eaton Vance Municipal Bond	51.6
10. Mutual of Omaha T/F Income	51.2
Total number of funds	96

Table 5.13 (continued)

10-Years	Total Return (7/1/81–6/30/91)
1. Elfun T/E Income Fund	278.7
2. SteinRoe Managed Munis	233.0
3. Putnam Tax Exempt Income	232.2
4. MFS Mgd Municipal Bond	227.9
5. Oppenheimer T/F Bond Fund	215.1
6. Kemper Municipal Bond Fund	214.6
7. Eaton Vance Municipal Bond	214.1
8. Shearson Managed Munis	209.5
9. New England T/E Income	209.2
10. Dean Witter T/E Sec	205.2
Total number of funds	42

Table 5.14 Gold and Precious Metals Funds

1-Year	Total Return (6/30/91)
1. Enterprise—Precious Metals	3.7
2. Vanguard Specialzed—Gold	2.7
3. Fidelity Select—Prec Met	1.7
4. International Investors	1.3
5. Keystone Precious Metals	0.8
6. Franklin Gold Fund	0.3
7. Strategic Investments Fund	–0.2
8. United Gold & Gov't Fund	–0.2
9. Lexington Goldfund	–1.9
10. Scudder Gold Fund	–3.1
Total number of funds	33

5-Years	Total Return (7/1/86–6/30/91)
1. Oppenheimer Gold/Spec Min	151.1
2. Franklin Gold Fund	122.5
3. Vanguard Specialized—Gold	88.1
4. IDS Precious Metals	71.4
5. International Investors	66.5
6. Keystone Precious Metals	65.5
7. Lexington Goldfund	59.2
8. Shearson Prec Metals Port	55.7
9. Fidelity Select—Prec Met	55.1
10. United Gold & Gov't Fund	54.7
Total number of funds	22

Table 5.14 (continued)

10-Years	Total Return (7/1/86–6/30/91)
1. Franklin Gold Fund	140.8
2. International Investors	121.7
3. Lexington Goldfund	85.4
4. US Gold Shares	35.9
5. Bull & Bear Gold Investors	12.5
6. Keystone Precious Metals	7.0
7. Strategic Investments Fund	–19.7
Total number of funds	7

Table 5.15 International Equity Funds

1-Year	Total Return (6/30/91)
1. Fidelity Canada Fund	16.8
2. Merrill Lynch Pacific (A)	12.6
3. Merrill Lynch Pacific (B)	11.9
4. Merrill Lynch Global All (A)	11.8
5. Merrill Lynch Global All (B)	10.7
6. Dreyfus Strategic World Inv	7.0
7. Founders Worldwide Growth	6.8
8. SoGen International Fund	3.5
9. Templeton Smaller Co's Gth	3.3
10. Nomura Pacific Basin Fund	2.2
Total number of funds	109

5-Years	Total Return (7/1/86–6/30/91)
1. G.T. Japan Growth Fund	168.4
2. G.T. Pacific Growth	130.9
3. First Inv Global Fund	130.1
4. Nomura Pacific Basin Fund	119.2
5. Templeton Foreign Fund	118.9
6. Ivy Fund—International	112.0
7. Merrill Lynch Pacific (A)	106.5
8. Trustees' Commingled—Int'l Eq	90.6
9. EuroPacific Growth Fund	90.3
10. G.T. International Growth	89.8
Total number of funds	43

Table 5.15 (continued)

10-Years	Total Return (7/1/81–6/30/91)
1. Merrill Lynch Pacific (A)	513.5
2. SoGen International Fund	368.1
3. Putnam Global Growth	330.5
4. Scudder International Fund	323.2
5. Templeton Smaller Co's Gth	321.0
6. Price (T. Rowe) Int'l Stock	320.3
7. G.T. Pacific Growth	294.0
8. Kemper International	281.9
9. Oppenheimer Global Fund	275.8
10. United Int'l Growth Fund	268.7
Total number of funds	18

5.6   MUTUAL FUND PERFORMANCE SUMMARY

Table 5.16 summarizes mutual fund total return performance by category over the 1, 3, 5, and 10 years ending June 1991. Total return performance assumes that all capital gains and income dividends were reinvested in additional shares. While they constitute only a small portion of total mutual fund assets, balanced funds, which invest in both stocks and fixed-income securities, posted excellent 5- and 10-year performance compared with other mutual fund categories. If nothing else, this shows the efficacy of taking a balanced approach to investing.

Table 5.16 Total Return Performance of Mutual Funds by Investment Objective (through June 1991)

Objective	1 Year	3 Years	5 Years	10 Years
Stock Funds				
Maximum capital gain	4.5%	36.2%	47.7%	214.5%
Small-company growth	4.2	40.0	43.5	161.5
Long-term growth	5.1	39.1	51.5	242.5
Growth and current income	5.9	35.2	53.7	258.4
Balanced	8.1	32.1	52.1	284.1
Equity Income	5.7	28.4	46.3	255.5
Flexible Income	6.5	25.6	39.6	226.1
Fixed-Income Funds				
Corporate bond	9.4	28.3	44.0	224.3
Corporate high yield	8.1	10.6	24.8	173.6
Government securities	9.2	28.6	43.3	194.4
Government mortgage	10.6	30.8	49.8	227.2
Municipal bond	7.9	26.3	43.4	180.7

Table 5.16 (continued)

Objective	1 Year	3 Years	5 Years	10 Years
Municipal high yield	7.4	26.9	45.6	202.0
Municipal single state	8.0	27.6	43.9	172.6
Specialized Funds				
Energy/natural resources	–0.7	24.7	71.3	120.8
Financial services	11.4	36.9	26.8	292.6
Gold and precious funds	–6.4	–11.9	46.6	54.8
Health care	31.8	122.3	114.9	
International bond	8.2	23.4	64.9	
International equity	–8.2	20.4	63.3	261.0
Technology	–0.6	32.3	50.3	196.1
Utilities	4.9	36.2	42.6	249.2
Other	3.8	32.2	51.0	
Market Indicators				
Dow Jones Industrial Average	4.7	64.8	99.5	397.5
S&P 500 Stock Index	7.4	50.5	75.2	322.8

Source: *Management Results*, Wiesenberger Investment Companies Service, Rockville, MD.

5.7 WIESENBERGER MUTUAL FUND PORTFOLIO INDEX

While it is periodically necessary to review the performance of an investor's mutual funds, it is also critical to review how the total investment portfolio (mutual funds and directly owned investments) has performed. One convenient basis of comparison is the Wiesenberger Mutual Fund Portfolios Index, which consists of four diversified portfolios of mutual funds with different policies—aggressive, moderate, conservative, and income-oriented—and is based upon average mutual fund performance. Another use of the index is to compare relative returns of various diversified portfolios. As Table 5.17 shows, aggressive portfolios, in spite of their higher risk, provided superior returns over the five-year period surveyed. The composition of each of the four portfolios is shown in Table 5.18.

Table 5.17 Wiesenberger Mutual Fund Portfolios Index, 1986–1991[1]

Portfolio	1991 Total Return Second Quarter	1990 First Half	12-Mo. Yield	3-Year Total Return $10,000 Invested in July 1988 Would Be Worth	5-Year Total Return $10,000 Invested in July 1986 Would Be Worth
Aggressive	–0.5%	10.8%	3.7%	$14,517	$16,298
Moderate	0.3	8.7	5.0	14,136	16,087
Conservative	0.8	6.7	6.0	13,749	15,686
Income oriented	1.1	5.6	7.1	13,376	15,089

[1]The figures in this table assume that the portfolios are reweighted quarterly.

Table 5.18 Allocation of Portfolio Assets[1]

	% of Assets in Portfolio			
Fund Category	Aggressive	Moderate	Conservative	Income Oriented
Maximum capital gain	20%	10%	5%	—
Long-term growth/income secondary	20	10	5	—
Growth and current income	10	20	15	20
International equity	20	10	5	—
Subtotal equity oriented	70%	50%	30%	20%
U.S. government securities	10	20	30	45
Corporate bond	10	15	20	35
Municipal bond	10	15	20	—
Subtotal fixed-income oriented	30%	50%	70%	80%
Total	100%	100%	100%	100%

[1]Total return for each portfolio is based upon the average performance of mutual funds over the periods indicated. The composition of each portfolio is aggressive: 70% equity funds, 30% fixed-income funds; moderate: 50% equity funds, 50% fixed-income funds; conservative: 30% equity funds, 70% fixed-income funds; income-oriented: 20% equity funds, 80% fixed-income funds. This index can be used to compare the performance of a managed portfolio against a diversified portfolio of average-performing mutual funds. The Wiesenberger Mutual Fund Portfolios Index is a service of the Wiesenberger Investment Companies Service.

5.8 CLOSED-END FUNDS

A closed-end fund issues a limited number of shares which are purchased and sold on the open market. Open-end funds, however, issue and redeem shares directly to/from the fund shareholders. The value of closed-end fund shares is determined by the market in those shares, not the value of the securities held by the fund. Therefore, closed-end fund shares usually trade at a discount from or premium over the net asset value of the funds' portfolios.

Table 5.19 provides a list of closed-end funds which were compiled by the Investment Company Institute and Lipper Analytical Services. Closed-end stock funds invest in diversified portfolios although some concentrate on one or a few industry groups or a particular country or region. Closed-end bond funds usually have diversified portfolios of debt issues. Closed-end convertible funds invest in preferred stock that is convertible into common shares.

Table 5.19 Closed-End Funds and the Exchanges They are Traded On

Fund Name	Stock Exchange	Fund Name	Stock Exchange
Diversified Common Stock Funds		American Capital Conv	NYSE
Adams Express	NYSE	ASA Ltd	NYSE
Allmon Trust	NYSE	Asia Pacific	NYSE
Baker Fentress	NYSE	Austria Fund	NYSE
Blue Chip Value	NYSE	Bancroft Convertible	AMEX
Clemente Global Gro	NYSE	Bergstrom Capital	AMEX
Gemini II Capital	NYSE	BGR Precious Metals	TOR
Gemini II Income	NYSE	Brazil	NYSE
General Amer Invest	NYSE	CNV Holdings Capital	NYSE
Liberty All-Star Eqty	NYSE	CNV Holdings Income	NYSE
Niagara Share Corp.	NYSE	Castle Convertible	AMEX
Quest For Value Cap	NYSE	Central Fund Canada	AMEX
Quest For Value Inco	NYSE	Central Securities	AMEX
Royce Value Trust	NYSE	Chile Fund	NYSE
Salomon Fd	NYSE	Couns Tandem Secs	NYSE
Source Capital	NYSE	Cypress Fund	AMEX
Tri-Continental Corp	NYSE	Duff&Phelps Sel Utils	NYSE
Worldwide Value	NYSE	Ellsw Conv Gr&Inc	AMEX
Zweig Fund	NYSE	Emerging Ger Fd	NYSE
Closed End Bond Funds		Emerging Mexico Fd	NYSE
CIM High Yield Secs	AMEX	Engex	AMEX
Franklin Multi Inc Tr	NYSE	Europe Fund	NYSE
Franklin Prin Mat Tr	NYSE	1stAustralia	AMEX
Franklin Universal Tr	NYSE	First Financial Fund	NYSE
Municipal High Inco	NYSE	First Iberian	AMEX
Zenix Income Fund	NYSE	First Phillippine Fund	NYSE
Flexible Portfolio Funds		France Growth Fund	NYSE
America's All Seasn	OTC	Future Germany Fund	NYSE
European Warrant Fd	NYSE	Gabelli Equity Trust	NYSE
Zweig Total Return Fd	NYSE	Germany Fund	NYSE
Specialized Equity and Convertible Funds		Growth Fund Spain	NYSE
		GT Greater Europe FD	NYSE
		H&Q Healthcare Inv	NYSE
Alliance Global Env Fd	NYSE	Hampton Utils Tr Cap	AMEX

Table 5.19 (continued)

Fund Name	Stock Exchange	Fund Name	Stock Exchange
Hampton Utils TR Pref	AMEX	ACM Mdg Inco	NYSE
India Growth Fund	NYSE	ACM Mdg Multi-Market	NYSE
Indonesia Fund	NYSE	AIM Strategic Inco	AMEX
Inefficient Market Fund	AMEX	AMEV Securities	NYSE
Irish Investment Fd	NYSE	American Adj Rate '95	NYSE
Italy Fund	NYSE	American Adj Rate '96	NYSE
Jakarta Growth Fd	NYSE	American Adj Rate '97	NYSE
Japan OTC Equity Fund	NYSE	American Capital Bond	NYSE
Korean Fund	NYSE	American Capital Inco	NYSE
Latin America Inv Fd	NYSE	American Govt Income	NYSE
Malaysia Fund	NYSE	American Govt Portif	NYSE
Mexico Equity Inc Fd	NYSE	American Govt Term	NYSE
Mexico Fund	NYSE	American Opp Inco Fund	NYSE
Morgan Grenf SmCap	NYSE	Blackstone Advtg Trm	NYSE
New Germany Fund	NYSE	Blackstone Income	NYSE
Patriot Prem Div Fd	NYSE	Blackstone 1988 Term	NYSE
Patriot Prem Div Fd II	NYSE	Blackstone Strat Trm	NYSE
Patriot Select Div Trust	NYSE	Blackstone Target Trm	NYSE
Petrol & Resources	NYSE	Bunker Hill Income	NYSE
Portugal Fund	NYSE	CIGNA High Income	NYSE
Preferred Income Fd	NYSE	CNA Income Shares	NYSE
Putnam Dividend Inco	NYSE	Circle Income Shares	OTC
RI Estate Sec Inco Fd	AMEX	Colonial Intrmkt Inco I	NYSE
ROC Taiwan Fund	NYSE	Current Income Shares	NYSE
Scudder New Asia	NYSE	Dean Witter Govt Inco	NYSE
Scudder New Europe	NYSE	Dreyfus Strt Gov Inco	NYSE
SE Savings Inst Fd	OTC	1838 Bond-Deb Trad	NYSE
Singapore Fd	NYSE	Excelsior Inco Shares	NYSE
Spain Fund	NYSE	First Boston Inco Fd	NYSE
Swiss Helvetia Fd	NYSE	First Boston Strategic	NYSE
Taiwan Fund	NYSE	Ft Dearborn Income	NYSE
TCW Convertible Secs	NYSE	John Hancock Income	NYSE
Templeton Em Mkts	AMEX	John Hancock Invest	NYSE
Templeton Global Util	AMEX	Hatteras Income Secs	NYSE
Thai Capital Fund	NYSE	High Income Adv Tr	NYSE
Thai Fund	NYSE	High Income Adv II	NYSE
Turkish Inv Fund	NYSE	High Income Adv III	NYSE
United Kingdom Fund	NYSE	High Yield Income Fd	NYSE
Z-Seven	OTC	High Yield Plus Fund	NYSE
Bond Funds		Hyperion Total Ret	NYSE
		INA Investments	NYSE
ACM Govt IncoFund	NYSE	Independence Sq	OTC
ACM Govt Oppor Fd	NYSE	Intercapital Income	NYSE
ACM Govt Securities	NYSE	Kemper High Inco Tr	NYSE
ACM Govt Spectrum	NYSE		

Table 5.19 (continued)

Fund Name	Stock Exchange	Fund Name	Stock Exchange
Kemper Inter Govt Tr	NYSE	**Municipal Bond Funds**	
Kemper Multi Inco Tr	NYSE	Allstate Mun Inc Op	NYSE
Lincoln Natl Inco	NYSE	Allstate Mun Inc Op II	NYSE
MFS Charter Inco	NYSE	Allstate Mun Inc Op III	NYSE
MFS Govt Mkts Inco	NYSE	Allstate Muni Inco	NYSE
MFS Intermed Inco Tr	NYSE	Allstate Muni Inco II	NYSE
MFS Multimkt Inco Tr	NYSE	Allstate Muni Inco III	NYSE
MFS Multimkt Ttl Ret	NYSE	Allstate Muni Pr Inco M	NYSE
MFS Special Value Tr	NYSE	Amer Muni Term Tr	NYSE
Montgomery Street	NYSE	Apex Muni Fund	NYSE
Mutual Omaha Int Shs	NYSE	Colonial Hi Inco Muni	NYSE
New America Hi Inco	NYSE	Colonial Inv Gr Muni	NYSE
Oppenhmr Multi-Govt	NYSE	Colonial Muni Inco Tr	NYSE
Oppenhmr Multi-Sectr	NYSE	Dreyfus Cal Muni Inco	AMEX
Pacific Amer Inco Shs	NYSE	Dreyfus Muni Inco	AMEX
Prospect St Hi Inco Fd	NYSE	Dreyfus NY Muni Inco	AMEX
Prudential Interm Inco	NYSE	Drefus Strategic Muni	NYSE
Putnam Div Prem Inco	NYSE	Dreyfus Strategic Munis	NYSE
Putnam Int Govt Inco	NYSE	InterCap Insured Munis	NYSE
Putnam Mstr Inco Tr	NYSE	Kemper Muni Inco Tr	NYSE
Putnam Mstr Int Inco	NYSE	Kemper Strategic Inco	NYSE
Putnam Prem Inco Tr	NYSE	MFS Muni Inco Tr	NYSE
RAC Income Fund	NYSE	MuniEnhanced Fund	NSYE
State Mutual Securities	NYSE	MuniInsured Fd Inc	AMEX
Transameria Income	NYSE	Muni Vest Fund Inc	AMEX
Tyler Cabot Mort Sec Fd	NYSE	New York Tax-Exempt	AMEX
USF&G Pacholder Fd	AMEX	Nuveen CA Inv Qual Muni	NYSE
USLife Income Fund	NYSE	Nuveen CA Muni Inco	NYSE
VanKmpn Merr Inter	NYSE	Nuveen CA Muni Mkt Opp	NYSE
VanKmpn Mer Hi Inco	NYSE	Nuveen CA Muni Val	NYSE
Vestaur Securities	NYSE	Nuveen CA Perf Plus	NYSE
Convertible Bond Funds		Nuveen CA Sel Qual	NYSE
Lincoln Natl Conver	NYSE	Nuveen FL Inv Qual Muni	NYSE
Putnam Hi Inco Conv	NYSE	Nuveen Ins Quality Muni	NYSE
International Bond Funds		Nuveen Inv Quality Muni	NYSE
		Nuveen Muni Adv	NYSE
First Australia Prime	AMEX	Nuveen Muni Inco	NYSE
Global Government	NYSE	Nuveen Muni Mkt Opp	NYSE
Global Income Plus	NYSE	Nuveen Muni Value	NYSE
Global Yield Fund	NYSE	Nuveen NJ Inv Qual Muni	NYSE
Kleinwort Benson Aust	NYSE	Nuveen NY Muni Inco	AMEX
Templeton Glbl Gov Inco	NYSE	Nuveen NY Muni Mkt Opp	NYSE
Templeton Global Inco	NYSE	Nuveen NY Muni Val	NYSE
World Income Fund	AMEX	Nuveen NY Perf Plus	NYSE

Table 5.19 (continued)

Fund Name	Stock Exchange	Fund Name	Stock Exchange
Nuveen NY Sel Qual	NYSE	Putnam Mgd Mun Inco	NYSE
Nuveen PA Inv Qual Muni	NYSE	Seligman Select Muni	NYSE
Nuveen Perf Plus	NYSE	Taurus Muni CA Hldgs	NYSE
Nuveen Prem Inco	NYSE	Taurus Muni Ny Hldgs	NYSE
Nuveen Qual Inco Muni	NYSE	VanKmpn M CA Muni	AMEX
Nuveen Sel Qual Muni	NYSE	VanKmpn M Inv GR	NYSE
Putnam HI Yld Muni	NYSE	VanKmpn M Muni	NYSE
Putnam Inv Grade Muni	NYSE		

Source: Investment Company Institute, Washington, DC.
Source: Lipper Analytical Services, Denver Colorado.

5.9 MUTUAL FUNDS WITH MINIMUM INITIAL PURCHASE REQUIREMENTS OF $200 OR LESS

Many mutual funds are available with low initial minimum purchase requirements. These funds may be of interest to new investors and/or investors who are considering a gift, perhaps to a child or grandchild. Mutual funds are an excellent way for new and inexperienced investors to learn about investing without subjecting their money to undue risk. Table 5.20 lists many of the mutual funds with their minimum initial purchase of $200 or less.

Table 5.20 Mutual Funds with Minimum Initial Purchases of $200 or Less

Fund[1]	Minimum Initial Purchase	
Amana Mutual Fund Tr-Income (IEQ)	$100	(No load)
American National Growth (MCG)	20	
American National Income (IEQ)	100	
A. T. Ohio T/F Money Fund (TFM)	No minimum	(No load)
Beacon Hill Mutual Fund F(LTG)	No minimum	(No load)
Caldwell Fund, Inc. (GCI)	No minimum	(No load)
Cashman Farrell Value Fund (LTG)	No minimum	
Charter Cap Blue Chip Growth (LTG)	No minimum	(No load)
Country Capital Growth (LTG)	100	
Country Capital Income Fund (CBD)	100	
Country Capital T/E Bond Fund (MBD)	100	
Declaration Cash Account (MMF)	No minimum	(No load)
Deleware Grp. Decatur Fund I (GCI)	25	
Dupree KY T/F Short/Medium (MSS)	100	(No load)
Eagle Growth Shares (LTG)	No minimum	
Elfun Income Fund (CBD)	No minimum	(No load)
Elfun Trusts (GCI)	No minimum	(No load)

Table 5.20 (continued)

Fund[1]	Minimum Initial Purchase	
Elfun T/E Income Fund (MBD)	No minimum	(No load)
European Plus Fund (INT)	200	
Evergreen American Retirement (BAL)	No minimum	(No load)
Excel Midas Gold Shares (GPM)	100	
Excel Value Fund (LTG)	100	
Financial Reserves Fund (MMF)	No minimum	(No load)
First Hawaii Muni Bond (MSS)	100	(No load)
First Inv Global Fund (INT)	200	
Franklin Calif Insured T/F Inc (MSS)	100	
Franklin Calif T/F Income Fund (MSS)	100	
Franklin Dynatech Series (TCH)	100	
Franklin Equity Fund (MCG)	100	
Franklin Federal T/F Inc (MBD)	100	
Franklin Gold Fund (GPM)	100	
Franklin Growth Series (LTG)	100	
Franklin Income Fund (IFL)	100	
Franklin Insured T/F Inc (MBD)	100	
Franklin Inv—Adj. US Govt. (MTG)	100	
Franklin Inv—Convert Secs (IFL)	100	
Franklin Inv—Global Opp Inc (IBD)	100	
Franklin Inv—Special Eq. Incm (IEQ)	100	
Franklin Managed—Inv Grade (CBD)	100	
Franklin Managed—Rising Div (GCI)	100	
Franklin Massachusetts Insured T/F Inc (MSS)	100	
Franklin Michigan Insured T/F Inc (MSS)	100	
Franklin Minnesota Insured T/F Inc (MSS)	100	
Franklin New York T/F Inc (MSS)	100	
Franklin Ohio Insured T/F Inc (MSS)	100	
Franklin Option Fund (IEQ)	100	
Franklin Pennsylvania Investors Equity (LTG)	100	
Franklin Pennsylvania T/F Tr Inc (MSS)	100	
Franklin Puerto Rico T/F Tr Inc (MSS)	100	
Franklin T/F Tr—Alabama T/F Inc (MSS)	100	
Franklin T/F Tr—Arizona T/F Inc (MSS)	100	
Franklin T/F Tr—Colorado T/F Inc (MSS)	100	
Franklin T/F Tr—Connecticut T/F Inc (MSS)	100	
Franklin T/F Tr—Florida T/F Inc (MSS)	100	
Franklin T/F Tr—Georgia T/F Inc (MSS)	100	
Franklin T/F Tr—High Yield T/F (MSS)	100	
Franklin T/F Tr—Indiana T/F Inc (MSS)	100	
Franklin T/F Tr—Louisiana T/F Inc (MSS)	100	
Franklin T/F Tr—Maryland T/F Inc (MSS)	100	
Franklin T/F Tr—Missouri T/F Inc (MSS)	100	
Franklin T/F Tr—New Jersey T/F Inc (MSS)	100	

Table 5.20 (continued)

Fund[1]	Minimum Initial Purchase	
Franklin T/F Tr—North Carolina T/F Income (MSS)	100	
Franklin T/F Tr—Oregon T/F Inc (MSS)	100	
Franklin T/F Tr—Texas T/F Inc (MSS)	100	
Franklin T/F Tr—Virginia T/F Inc (MSS)	100	
Franklin T/F US Gov't Series (GOV)	100	
Franklin Utilities Series (UTL)	100	
Fund of the Southwest (LTG)	200	
GE S&S Long Term Interest (CBD)	No minimum	(No load)
GE S&S Program Mutual Fund (GCI)	No minimum	(No load)
IDEX Fund (LTG)	50	
IDEX Fund II (LTG)	50	
IDEX Fund III (LTG)	50	
IDS Managed Retirement (GCI)	50	
Investors Research Fund (LTG)	No minimum	
Janus Flexible Income Fund (IFL)	No minimum	(No load)
Janus Fund (LTG)	No minimum	(No load)
Janus Twenty Fund (LTG)	No minimum	(No load)
Janus Venture Fund (SCG)	No minimum	(No load)
Kidder Peabody Premium Acct (MMF)	No minimum	(No load)
Medical Research Investment (HLT)	No minimum	(No load)
Merrill Lynch Retirement Reserves (MMF)	No minimum	(No load)
Mimlic Cash Fund Inc (MMF)	No minimum	(No load)
Monetta Fund (GCI)	100	(No load)
Muhlenkamp Fund (GCI)	200	(No load)
Pacific American Fund—MM (MMF)	No minimum	(No load)
Pacific American Fd—US Trea (MMF)	No minimum	(No load)
Paine Webber Master Money (MMF)	25	(No load)
Paine Webber RMA CA Muni Money Fd (TFM)	No minimum	(No load)
Paine Webber RMA Retirement Money Fd (MMF)	25	(No load)
Paine Webber Rma Ny Muni Money Fd (TFM)	No minimum	(No load)
Paine Webber RMA Tax-Free Fd (TFM)	25	(No load)
PBHG Growth Fund Inc. (LTG)	200	
Pioneer Fund (GCI)	50	
Pioneer II (GCI)	50	
ProvidentMutual Convertible (IFL)	No minimum	
ProvidentMutual Growth Fund (LTG)	No minimum	
ProvidentMutual Investment (GCI)	No minimum	
ProvidentMutual Pennsylvania Tax-Free (MSS)	No minimum	
ProvidentMutual Tax-Free Bd (MBD)	No minimum	
ProvidentMutual Total Return (GCI)	No minimum	
ProvidentMutual US Gov't (GOV)	No minimum	
ProvidentMutual Value (LTG)	No minimum	
ProvidentMutual World (INT)	No minimum	
Ray Equity—Income (GCI)	No minimum	

Table 5.20 (continued)

Fund[1]	Minimum Initial Purchase	
Rodney Square—Gov't (MMF)	100	
Rodney Square—T/F Fund (TFM)	100	(No load)
Security Action Plan (LTG)	50	
Security Cash Fund (MMF)	100	(No load)
Security Equity Fund (LTG)	100	
Security Income—High Yield (CHY)	100	
Security Income—US Gov't (MTG)	100	
Security Investment Fund (IFL)	100	
Security Omni (MCG)	100	
Security T/E Fund (MBD)	100	
Security Ultra Fund (MCG)	100	
SEI Cash + Plus Tr—Fed Secs (MMF)	No minimum	(No load)
SEI Cash + Plus Tr—GNMA (MTG)	No minimum	(No load)
SEI Cash + Plus Tr—Interm Gov't (GOV)	No minimum	(No load)
SEI Cash + Plus Tr—Money Market (MMF)	No minimum	(No load)
SEI Cash + Plus Tr—S/T Gov't (GOV)	No minimum	(No load)
SEI Cash + Plus Tr—Treasury (TFM)	No minimum	(No load)
SEI Index Funds—Bond Index (CBD)	No minimum	(No load)
SEI Index Funds—S&P 500 (GCI)	No minimum	(No load)
SEI Inst'l Managed—Bond (CBD)	No minimum	(No load)
SEI Inst'l Managed—Cap Appr (LTG)	No minimum	(No load)
SEI Inst'l Managed—Cap Growth (LTG)	No minimum	(No load)
SEI Inst'l Managed—Eqty Inc (IEQ)	No minimum	(No load)
SEI Inst'l Managed—Ltd Vol (CBD)	No minimum	(No load)
SEI Inst'l Managed—Value (GCI)	No minimum	(No load)
SEI International Tr—Int'l (INT)	No minimum	(No load)
SEI Liquid Asset Tr—Commercial (MMF)	No minimum	(No load)
SEI Liquid Asset Tr—Gov't (MMF)	No minimum	(No load)
SEI Liquid Asset Tr—Pr Oblg (MMF)	No minimum	(No load)
SEI Liquid Asset Tr—Treas II (MMF)	No minimum	(No load)
SEI Liquid Asset Tr—Treasury (MMF)	No minimum	(No load)
SEI T/E Tr—Inst'l Tax-Free (TFM)	No minimum	(No load)
SEI T/E Tr—Pennsylvania Muni (MSS)	No minimum	(No load)
SEI T/E Tr—Tax-Free (TFM)	No minimum	(No load)
Sentry Fund (LTG)	200	(No load)
Sovereign Investors (GCI)	30	
State Farm Balanced Fund (BAL)	50	(No load)
State Farm Growth Fund (LTG)	50	(No load)
State Farm Interim Fund (GOV)	50	(No load)
Stralem Fund (LTG)	100	(No load)
Transamerica Growth & Income (GCI)	100	
Transamerica Invest Qual Bd (CBD)	100	
Transamerica Sunbelt Growth (LTG)	100	
Transamerica Technology (TCH)	100	

Table 5.20 (continued)

Fund[1]	Minimum Initial Purchase	
Twentieth Century Balanced (BAL)	No minimum	(No load)
Twentieth Century Cash Reserves (MMF)	No minimum	(No load)
Twentieth Century Growth (MCG)	No minimum	(No load)
Twentieth Century Heritage (LTG)	No minimum	(No load)
Twentieth Century Long Term Bond (CBD)	No minimum	(No load)
Twentieth Century Select (LTG)	No minimum	(No load)
Twentieth Century T/E—Intermediate (MBD)	No minimum	(No load)
Twentieth Century T/E—Long Term (MBD)	No minimum	(No load)
Twentieth Century Ultra (MCG)	No minimum	(No load)
Twentieth Century U.S. Gov't (GOV)	No minimum	(No load)
Twentieth Century Vista Fund (SCG)	No minimum	(No load)
US All American Equity (LTG)	100	(No load)
US Gold Shares (GPM)	100	(No load)
US Growth Fund (LTG)	100	(No load)
US Income Fund (IEQ)	100	(No load)
US Real Estate Fund (OTH)	100	(No load)
US Treasury Securities Cash Fund (MMF)	100	(No load)
US Trend Fund (LTG)	200	(No load)
US T/F Fund (MBD)	100	(No load)
US World Gold Fund(s) (GPM)	100	(No load)
Variable Stock Fund (LTG)	50	(No load)

[1]Fund Investment Objectives: BAL - balanced; CBD - corporate bond; CHY - corporate high yield; GCI - growth and current income; GOV - government securities; GPM - gold and precious metals; HLT - health care; IBD - international bond; IEQ - equity income; IFL - flexible income; INT - international stock; LTG - long-term growth; MBD - municipal bond; MCG - maximum capital gains; MMF - money market fund; MTG - government mortgage; MSS - municipal single state; TCH - technology; TFM - tax-free money market; UTL - utilities.

5.10 MUTUAL FUND INDUSTRY STATISTICS

The following tables, compiled by the Investment Company Institute, show trends in the total number of mutual funds (Table 5.21), industry net assets (Table 5.22), the percentage distribution of total net assets by type of fund (Table 5.23), and number of shareholder accounts (Table 5.24). Growth in the mutual fund industry slowed somewhat in 1990 after a decade of tremendous growth. Table 5.25 shows the relative proportion of total fund sales during 1990 made by sales force and direct marketers.

Table 5.21 Number of Mutual Funds

Year	Money market and Short-Term Municipal Bond Funds	Stock Bond and Income Funds	Total
1950	—	98	98
1960	—	161	161
1970	—	361	361
1975	36	390	426
1980	106	458	564
1981	179	486	665
1982	318	539	857
1983	373	653	1,026
1984	421	820	1,241
1985	457	1,071	1,528
1986	485	1,355	1,840
1987	541	1,776	2,317
1988	605	2,110	2,715
1989	664	2,253	2,917
1990	746	2,362	3,108

Source: Investment Company Institute, *Mutual Fund Fact Book*, (Washington, D.C.: Investment Company Institute, annual).

Table 5.22 Total Industry Net Assets, 1975–1990
(billions of dollars)

Year	Equity Funds	Bond and Income Funds	Money Market Funds	Short-Term Municipal Bond Funds	Total
1975	$ 32.4	$ 9.8	$ 3.7	—	$ 45.9
1976	34.3	13.3	3.7	—	51.3
1977	30.0	15.0	3.9	—	48.9
1978	29.0	16.0	10.9	—	55.9
1979	32.5	16.5	45.2	0.3	94.5
1980	41.0	17.4	74.5	1.9	134.8
1981	38.4	16.9	181.9	4.2	241.4
1982	50.6	26.3	206.6	13.2	296.7
1983	73.9	39.7	162.6	16.8	293.0
1984	83.1	54.0	209.7	23.8	370.6
1985	116.9	134.8	207.5	36.3	495.5
1986	161.5	262.6	228.3	63.8	716.2
1987	180.7	273.1	254.7	61.4	769.9
1988	194.8	277.5	272.3	65.7	810.3
1989	249.1	304.8	358.7	69.4	982.0
1990	245.8	325.0	414.7	83.6	1,069.1

Source: Investment Company Institute, *Mutual Fund Fact Book*, (Washington, D.C.: Investment Company Institute, annual).

Table 5.23 Distribution of Total Net Assets by Type of Fund, 1980–1990

	1980	1990
Money market funds	55.3%	38.8%
Equity funds	30.4	23.0
Bond and income funds	12.9	30.4
Short-term municipal bond funds	1.4	7.8

Source: Investment Company Institute, *Mutual Fund Fact Book*, (Washington, D.C.: Investment Company Institute, annual).

Table 5.24 Total Industry Shareholder Accounts, 1976–1990 (millions)

Year	Equity Funds[1]	Bond and Income Funds	Money Market Funds	Short-Term Municipal Bond Funds	Total
1976	8.9		0.2	—	9.1
1977	8.5		0.2	—	8.7
1978	7.4	0.8	0.5	—	8.7
1979	5.6	1.9	2.3	—	9.8
1980	5.8	1.5	4.8	—	12.1
1981	5.7	1.5	10.3	—	17.5
1982	6.2	2.0	13.1	0.1	21.4
1983	8.9	3.2	12.3	0.2	24.6
1984	10.0	4.4	13.6	0.3	28.3
1985	11.5	8.3	14.5	0.5	34.8
1986	16.6	13.2	15.6	0.7	46.1
1987	21.4	15.5	16.8	0.8	54.5
1988	20.6	15.4	17.8	0.9	54.7
1989	21.5R	15.4R	20.2	1.1	58.2
1990	23.0	16.6	21.6	1.4	62.6

[1]Equity funds could not be counted separately from bond and income funds before 1978.
Source: Investment Company Institute, *Mutual Fund Fact Book*, (Washington, D.C.: Investment Company Institute, annual).

Table 5.25 Sales of Sales Force and Direct Marketing Funds by Investment Objective, 1990

Type of Fund	Direct Marketing	Sales Force
Aggressive growth	74.3%	25.7%
Growth	48.8	51.2
Growth and income	46.2	53.8
Precious metals	74.6	25.4
International	32.8	67.2
Global equity	9.7	90.3
Income equity	51.6	48.4
Option/income	0	100

Table 5.25 (continued)

Type of Fund	Direct Marketing	Sales Force
Flexible portfolio	33.2	66.8
Balanced	56.3	43.7
Income—mixed	15.6	84.4
Income—bond	23.4	76.6
U.S. government income	17.9	82.1
Ginnie Mae	24.5	75.5
Global bond	16.8	83.2
Corporate bond	49.9	50.1
High-yield bond	14.9	85.1
Long-term municipal bond	34.1	65.9
State municipal bond, long term	30.2	69.8

Source: Investment Company Institute, *Mutual Fund Fact Book*, (Washington, D.C.: Investment Company Institute, annual).

5.11 INCOME TAX TREATMENT OF MUTUAL FUND DIVIDENDS

Mutual fund investors are often confused about the income tax treatment of their mutual fund's capital gain and dividend distributions. Table 5.26 provides a summary of the tax treatment of the more commonly encountered mutual fund distributions.

Table 5.26 How Mutual Fund Dividends Are Taxed

Fund Distribution	Tax Treatment
Ordinary dividends	Ordinary dividends from a mutual fund are fully taxable.
Capital gain dividends	Capital gain dividends are reported as long-term capital gains no matter how long the investor has held the mutual fund shares. A few mutual funds retain their long-term capital gains and pay capital gains tax on those amounts. The investor includes as a capital gain dividend on his or her return the amount of the undistributed capital gain dividend allocated to him or her by the fund. The investor is entitled to a credit if the mutual fund paid a tax on the undistributed capital gain. A loss on the sale of mutual fund shares held for one year or less is treated as a long-term capital loss to the extent of the capital gain dividend received before the sale. This restriction does not apply to dispositions under periodic redemption plans.

Nontaxable distributions	The mutual fund designates amounts representing return of capital as nontaxable distributions, thus reducing the cost basis of the mutual fund shares. A return of capital is not taxed unless the distribution (when added to past such distributions) exceeds the investment in the fund. Exempt-interest dividends are nontaxable as well and do not reduce the investor's basis in the mutual fund shares. Exempt-interest dividends are not included by the fund on Form 1099-DIV but are reported separately. The investor must report them on Form 1040 with other tax-exempt interest.
Dividends from foreign investments	The dividends are taxable, but the investor may be able to claim a foreign tax credit (on Form 1116) or a deduction on Schedule A for his share of the fund's foreign taxes. The fund should give the investor instructions for claiming the foreign tax credit or deduction and report the investor's share of the foreign taxes on Form 1099-DIV.
Reinvested dividends	If the investor does not take the dividends in cash and participates in a dividend reinvestment plan instead, he or she should keep a record of the dividends and of the shares purchased with the reinvestment. Records of reinvestments should also be maintained to be able to determine cost basis when some or all of the shares are sold.

5.12 MUTUAL FUND INVESTOR PROFILES

Investors choose mutual funds over other financial products for a variety of reasons as indicated in Table 5.27. Table 5.28 shows that retirement is by far the most commonly cited financial goal of mutual fund buyers. The importance of saving and investing for retirement is not likely to subside in the 1990s as an aging population emerges from a financially painful recession. Both these tables are based upon statistics compiled by the Investment Company Institute.

Table 5.27 Why Investors Choose Mutual Funds over Other Financial Products

Funds are more diversified:	60%
Funds are more professionally managed:	45%
Funds have higher investment returns:	44%
I prefer funds to picking my own investments:	37%
Funds are easier to invest in:	23%

Source: Investment Company Institute, *Mutual Fund Fact Book*, (Washington, D.C.: Investment Company Institute, annual).

Table 5.28 Financial Goals Rated as Very Important by Mutual Fund Buyers

Retirement:	73%
More money now:	42%
Children's education:	32%
Major purchases:	24%
Providing inheritance:	23%

Source: Investment Company Institute, *Mutual Fund Fact Book*, (Washington, D.C.: Investment Company Institute, annual).

Chapter 6

REAL ESTATE INVESTMENTS

During much of the 1980s, real estate was widely considered a "can't lose" investment. Today, cooling markets in many areas of the country, combined with less attractive tax incentives, have made real estate investments somewhat less alluring, at least in the short term. Yet real estate remains a worthwhile component in a well-balanced investment portfolio and, if chosen properly, can create opportunities for capital accumulation and tax deferral.

The Tax Reform Act of 1986 had a dramatic impact on the entire arena of real estate investment. Less generous depreciation schedules, as well as the inability to use real estate tax losses to offset ordinary income, have severely curtailed investment in loss-generating properties. Now, investors must look for real estate investments that can stand on economic merit alone, that is, properties that generate positive or close to positive cash flow.

In addition to helping individuals choose properties that will produce a stable and high level of income, the financial professional may also be asked to recommend the form which such an investment should take. For example, an affluent young person might consider investing in a small apartment building as the first in a series of direct real estate investments. In fact, direct ownership can be the most desirable way to own real estate, although maintaining and managing a property can often require a greater time commitment than people may be willing to make.

The financial professional should not overlook other forms of real estate ownership for individuals who have neither the time nor the capital required for direct ownership. In a limited partnership, money that is put up by individuals is invested in office buildings, shopping centers, mortgages, or other properties. The loss liability of these individuals is limited to the amount of their investment. The general partner, who usually organizes the partnership, receives a share of the profits, plus fees and commissions. Most of the real estate limited partnerships on the market today stress income and capital gains because of decreased tax incentives for investing in nonincome-producing properties.

Limited partnerships are generally not advisable for investors who may need access to their money in the near future, since selling the shares on the secondary market before the partnership is liquidated can result in substantial losses, if it can be sold at all. Such investors may want to consider real estate investment trusts (REITs). These closed-end mutual funds, which invest in real estate-related securities, trade on the major stock exchanges and are therefore highly liquid.

Whatever form a real estate investment takes, its return will depend, to a large extent, on the overall health of the real estate market. Many regions of the country will continue to suffer from a severe and protracted downturn in the real estate market; and while opportunities for direct investment in depressed real estate will present themselves, only investors with considerable staying power should consider them. On a more positive note, housing in many locales has become more affordable, particularly for first-time homebuyers. And, offerings by real estate limited partnerships could become more attractive as the industry begins to emerge from the ashes to reattract wary investors. In short, real estate will be a more sensible, less frenzied area of investment than it was during the 1980s.

6.1 INVENTORY OF REAL ESTATE INVESTMENT ALTERNATIVES

In this section a description of the characteristics of various real estate investment alternatives is provided. Important characteristics of each category of real esate investment are highlighted to assist investors either in evaluating a specific investment or in considering real estate investing in general. Also see Section 6.2, Real Estate Investment Evaluation Formulas. Investors generally have three different ways to invest in real estate: directly, indirectly via limited partnerships, and indirectly via shares of real estate investment trusts. Within each of those three categories, there is a range of alternative types of real estate.

Many investors overlook real estate as an investment candidate, yet real estate has proven to be an attractive wealth-creating component of many investment portfolios. Real estate investments, however, are difficult to evaluate and can prove to be financially penalizing. Moreover, direct investment in real estate, particularly income-producing real estate, can be very time consuming. Yet the advantages of owning real estate, either directly or indirectly, merit investor attention.

6.1.1 Direct Real Estate Investment

6.1.1.1 Undeveloped Land Undeveloped land is the most speculative type of real estate investment. It has both the greatest potential for development and appreciation and the greatest risk. An investor should try to purchase land that is currently of low value but that seems likely to increase in value. The most important factors determining raw land value are physical conditions and governmental, economic, and sociologic considerations. A poor drainage system or water supply might be a problem, as could undesirable subsoil foundations. A piece of land that is too small or irregularly shaped could also discourage development. Just as basic to the possibility of development as physical conditions are governmental rules and regulations: restrictive building codes and zoning could prohibit development and limit profit. Local tax laws and environmental regulations may also have significant implications for development.

Economic factors such as local employment rates, interest rates, and inflation are all important considerations. The more employment growth and diversification evident in a community, the more promising an adjacent raw land purchase might be. Growing populations with shrinking household sizes are favorable demographic trends, indicating a need for more residential housing. In order to understand the effect of all these various forces on a potential raw land purchase, an investor should deal with a local broker, attorney, and perhaps an engineer or land surveyor.

The chief advantages to raw land are the possibility of a relatively low purchase price and the potential for sizable appreciation. Disadvantages include the lack of any current income and an accompanying reluctance on the part of bank lenders to finance raw land investment (since, without any income, the bank has no guarantee against default). Also, since few comparative appraisals are available for raw land, and industry standards are not well established, some land may be overpriced. Often the lowest-priced land is located in areas where values are unlikely to increase substantially or at all in the near future.

6.1.1.2 Residential Rental Property Residential property's greatest benefit as an investment is that it produces income, which lessens out-of-pocket costs while the property increases in value. Location, structure type, and available utilities all may affect the property's value as can local population movement and zoning changes. The primary categories of residential property are single-family homes, condominiums, multifamily houses, and apartment buildings.

Single-Family Units. Single-family homes offer the smaller investor two advantages: they require little equity, and they provide rental income. A single-family unit does require active management however. The most important factor in determining value is the neighborhood—availability of recreational facilities, transportation, and shopping are all important. A potentially profitable approach to investment is to purchase at low cost in an undesirable neighborhood that seems ready to improve. This technique is, of course, very speculative and is not advisable for an inexperienced investor.

The potential for capital appreciation with single-family units is great.

Such residences have been good insulators against inflation. In addition, small investments for cosmetic purposes can substantially improve the residence's selling price.

However, single-family residences provide relatively low cash flow, and they tend not to be self-supporting—most return potential through value appreciation. Probably the most important factor in single-family residential investment is location, because even the most desirable house is unlikely to appreciate in declining neighborhoods. Also, prospective tenants must be carefully screened for ability to pay rent reliably.

Condominiums and Cooperatives. Condominiums offer lower prices than single-family homes and often have collectively owned amenities, such as a swimming pool and parking facilities, that would otherwise be out of range to a tenant. Cooperatives differ from condominiums primarily in the effects of an owner's default. Since a condominium's apartment units are individually financed, remaining tenants only need assume a defaulting owner's share of operating expenses. A cooperative usually takes out a blanket mortgage on an entire building, so if an owner defaults, remaining tenants must assume the extra share of real estate taxes and other expenses.

Condominiums and cooperatives are a viable investment in areas where rents can be significantly increased over time. In recent years, however, many areas of the country were overbuilt with condos and co-ops, which subsequently have actually declined in value.

Vacation Homes. A second home offers some of the tax benefits of a primary residence (although recently the IRS has severely restricted the tax shelter benefits of vacation homes), as well as economic advantages through rent-producing potential. Rents provide solid returns but may entail hidden costs; also, in most areas of the country, prime rental season is limited to a few months of the year.

Time-sharing. Time-sharing, or interval ownership, is particularly suited to resort areas because owners can pay a smaller price for a piece of a more expensive property. Time-sharing property is marketed very heavily, since developers need to find many owners for each unit. While many owners have been pleased with their investment, most of these projects are of dubious quality. The time-share resale market is almost nonexistent, and therefore, the vast majority of these investments should not be considered investment quality. However, as larger, well-established companies begin to enter this business, time-sharing may become a more viable investment.

Multifamily Units and Apartments. Multifamily units offer an investor greater opportunities for tax shelter and positive cash flow than do single-family structures. Although large units require a greater initial investment, the cost per dwelling unit is lower. Multifamily units are relatively easy to finance, as lenders see the potential rental income as protection on their loans. A major problem with large apartment units is rent control restrictions (either present or potential). Other drawbacks include the possibility of overbuilding and the illiquidity of the investment. As with any other real estate investment, the property's location can make or break the investor; a prospective buyer should avoid areas of depreciating property values. Proximity to main avenues of transportation, as well as to shopping, recreation, and work, is particularly important to the apartment house dweller. If the physical condition of the property has been neglected, the costs of repair could erode profits. Unexpected expenses such as reroofing or replacing the electrical or heating systems may arise, so an investor who assumes an apartment complex must have adequate reserves.

6.1.1.3 Commercial Property Office buildings, shopping centers, other retail property, and industrial real estate all offer a high-income investor an opportunity for substantial appreciation. However, as potential rewards increase, buying and managing become more complicated, so the investor should be especially well informed about the specifics of the purchase.

Office Buildings. A successful office building should be located in a convenient area with easy access to major transportation routes, shopping areas, and restaurants. An investor who buys a property outright may choose either to manage it himself or herself—requiring a staff—or else may contract with a professional firm to manage it, usually for 2 to 5 percent of gross revenues. An investor who is not quite committed to acquisition of the property may choose to lend money through a convertible mortgage, with the option to convert that sum of money into equity against the property at some future date.

An investor should attempt to forecast the income and operating expenses of the property in question. The latter can be difficult. The investor should list basic expenses: real estate taxes, payrolls, insurance premiums for fire and liability coverage, maintenance and repairs, utilities, and replacement reserves.

A well-constructed and well-located office building can appreciate over 10 percent per year. Cash returns and the safety and preservation of capital are two other advantages. With 95 percent of a building occupied, the investor should expect a total return of about 12 to 13 percent. Most of the cash flow is generated by the last 20 percent of a building's occupancy, so the investor must make great efforts to fill the building. In most cases the hiring of an experienced realtor will be well worth the price.

Because each office building is unique, such property is particularly illiquid; it may take several months, if not years, to find a buyer. Therefore, if an investor is losing money, he or she may have difficulty divesting of the property. Functional obsolesence and difficult city regulations can be another problem. Physical weaknesses such as insufficient floor space or an aging elevator, heating, air conditioning, or electrical system can seriously affect the profitability of office space.

If the investor desires a more fixed, continuous cash flow, the building can be leased to a single tenant, with rent thus paid to the owner on a net basis.

Shopping Centers. Shopping centers provide the same advantages and disadvantages as office real estate. The value of a property is usually derived from its ability to generate income. Since the end of World War II, numerous kinds of shopping centers have evolved. Community shopping centers of 400,000 square feet are presently having trouble competing against the largest kind, the regional or superregional, encompassing up to 1 million square feet and generally possessing at least one large department store as an anchor. Smaller neighborhood shopping centers can be successful on a local level by renting to supermarkets, drugstores, banks, and other small retail stores. Other types of shopping centers include the discount center and specialty center.

As with all real estate, good location is crucial to success in investment in shopping center property, and an investor should check predicted population growth, trade development, and transportation accessibility in the surrounding area. The investor should also consider costs for management, repairs, maintenance, and other expenditures. An investor will want to establish a good tenant mix between recognizable national retail stores and local merchants. A major department store or other prestige store usually pays very low rent because the business it generates for the entire center more than compensates for the reduced revenue. Local tenants, since they have little influence in the development of the center, pay much higher rent.

An investor should attempt to establish favorable leasing arrangements so that most business risk is passed on to the tenants. The lease should include expense escalation clauses, which protect the investor against inflation by guaranteeing that all increases in fixed costs will be absorbed by the tenant. The investor will want to make sure that tenants maintain a high sales volume, since increased overhead means greater rental profit.

Shopping centers, depending in large part on their location, tend to be either great successes or unmitigated disasters, so an investor should enter this enterprise with caution.

Industrial Real Estate. Industrial property, including warehouses, wholesale and assembly sites, and manufacturing plants, is an area of real estate that has become dominated by industrial firms. However, excellent prospects for appreciation, consistent demand, and limited management make industrial property an attractive investment. The spiraling growth of high-technology and electronic industries promises a great need for industrial space. Even during periods of economic slowdown, firms constantly move resources to increase productivity.

The two most popular kinds of industrial real estate are incubator buildings and industrial parks. An incubator building, a multipurpose structure combining storage and work space with offices, is ideal for small, new firms that lack the resources for separate office and warehouse facilities. An industrial park houses a number of tenants and provides utilities, roads, railroad sidings, and other facilities.

The structure of industrial buildings—which are generally merely shells—results in minimal necessary maintenance. Tenants tend to pay rent on a net basis, which further frees the owner from management responsibilities. Most industrial properties are in areas with low land costs. All these factors provide good potential for appreciation.

Before purchase, an investor should consider the site location with an eye toward availability of utilities, taxes, and any city ordinances that might complicate development of the site. An investor may simply purchase property without plans for development—which is very risky—or may choose to involve himself or herself in a sale-leaseback program, in which the former owner obtains an unofficial 100 percent mortgage on his or her property by selling it and simultaneously leasing it back.

6.1.2 Indirect Real Estate Investment

6.1.2.1 Limited Partnerships In a real estate limited partnership, a group of individual investors pools its money to invest in either new construction or existing commercial or residential property. Shares in this partnership are offered to potential limited partners by a general partner in order to attract additional capital. Limited partners are liable only to the extent of the amount they invest. The general partner arranges the deal and is typically involved in the day-to-day management of the investment.

The various types of programs available allow an individual investor to shop for a real estate partnership that best suits hir or her financial situation. A potential investor should carefully examine the offering memorandum or prospectus for information about risks and returns of the investment and about the general partner's background and experience; the investor should also look for independent sources of information about similar limited partnerships.

Advantages to investment in real estate limited partnership include the following:

- *Ease of buying in.* While direct ownership requires a complex system of transfer, an investor in a limited partnership need only send a check to the general partner. The partnership's prospectus give an investor access to information necessary to make a quick decision.

- *Fixed cash requirements.* After an investor makes the initial payment, he or she will usually not be responsible for financing any further cost overruns.

- *No management responsibility.* The general partner is responsible for construction, maintenance, bookkeeping, and all other management duties.

- *Limited legal liability.* An investor's other assets are not at risk.

- *Smaller initial investment.* A partner may need to invest as little as $5,000 to receive the benefits of a large real estate project.

- *Lower overall risk.* Diversification and professional management can make limited partnership investments less risky than direct ownership.

Disadvantages include the following:

- *No acquaintance with manager and restricted knowledge of the deal.* The investor usually must base his or her knowledge of the general partner on secondary sources, and an investor might, despite the information available in the prospectus, fail to identify hidden risks associated with the deal. The limited partner's best interests will not always be served by those of the real estate syndicate.
- *Less control.* A limited partner has no say in the investment policy.
- *Lower overall return.* Fees for participating in partnership narrow profit margin.
- *Tax risks.* Under the 1986 Tax Reform Act, tax shelter opportunities are either severely restricted or are eliminated with limited partnerships.
- *Illiquidity.* With no organized secondary market for limited partnership investment units, the units often cannot be sold for a good price.

The risk connected with real estate limited partnership deals is affected by three different factors: the amount of leverage used, the percentage specified, and the type of property and investment.

- *Leverage.* Highly leveraged investments—those financed with a large amount of borrowed cash—require larger cash flows to make payments on the debt and are thus riskier.
- *Percentage specified.* A general partner may offer limited partners shares before selecting or specifying all specific properties. A deal with 0 percent specified—a "blind pool"—is the riskiest kind, since the investor cannot examine and evaluate the investment beforehand (although a general partner with a strong track record might not present too high a risk even with a blind pool). A further risk connected with blind pools is the possibility that the sponsor might be forced to lower his or her standards and make riskier investments, in a robust real estate market, in order to produce the promised yields.
- *Type of property.* Investments in existing property will have more information available, because of the property's operating history. Commercial property and established residential property will probably be more secure investments than hotels or undeveloped land.

The current tax laws are particularly stringent in tightening restrictions on real estate tax shelters for limited partnerships. An individual who holds a limited partnership interest cannot meet the "active participation" requirement for limited deductible rental loss to the extent of his or her limited partnership interest. The current tax laws make limited partnerships much less attractive, so that many now offer little more yield than a long-term bond but with far less liquidity. In response to the new laws, several alternative kinds of partnerships, such as income-producting partnerships and "master limited partnerships," have been created to varying degrees of sucees.

6.1.2.2 Real Estate Investment Trusts REITs, like mutual funds, provide a way for an investor to acquire real estate with a minimal outlay. Small investors pool their funds to be placed into real estate ownership or loaned to real estate borrowers backed by mortgages. Several REITs are traded on the stock market; minimum investments are as low as $20 to $30 per share. A REIT that meets certain criteria (such as proper size and distribution of membership and a large enough percentage of investments and assets related to real estate) qualifies for tax exemption.

REITs can be excellent investment vehicles for small investors: all capital gains realized through the trust go directly to the shareholders, the diversified portfolio minimizes risks, and the ability to trade provides greater liquidity than other real estate investments. REITs, like mutual funds, bring the advantages of centralized, professional management to a negotiable investor; finally, REITs are subject to strict regulations and thus tend to be well managed.

The potential investor should realize, however, that REITs are very vulnerable to fluctuations in the real estate market and at certain times in the recent past have performed very poorly. Today, many REITs are suffering from major cash flow problems as a result of overbuilding and recent low inflation. Under these circumstances an investor may want to consider another means of real estate investment, such as investing in companies with substantial undervalued real estate holdings on their balance sheets. Investment professionals often cite the large paper companies and retailers as attractive "real estate rich" companies.

6.2 REAL ESTATE INVESTMENT EVALUATION FORMULAS

Real estate investments require careful evaluation. Experienced real estate investors use a variety of formulas to assist in the evaluation of an available property. In order to do a quick initial evaluation of a property, investors typically use simple formulas which compare selling price to expected income from the property. The "rent multiplier" and "capitalization rate" are two commonly used formulas for an initial evaluation. If the price-income relationship seems reasonable, investors will then conduct a more rigorous analysis based on return on investment and/or discounted cash flow. All these formulas may be useful whether the investor is considering the purchase of a specific property or a real estate limited partnership.

6.2.1 Rent Multiplier

The simplest formula involves comparing the total selling price with the current gross annual rental:

$$\text{Rent multiplier} = \frac{\text{Selling price}}{\text{Gross annual rental}}$$

For example, say a duplex selling for $180,000 generates $15,000 in annual rent. The rent multiplier is calculated as follows:

$$\text{Rent multiplier} = \frac{\text{Selling price}}{\text{Gross annual rental}} = \frac{\$180,000}{\$15,000} = 12$$

In other words, the property is selling for 12 times its annual rental. A property that is selling for much more than 7 times the gross annual rental is likely to yield a negative cash flow. In the example, until rents can be raised significantly, which may take years, the investor is probably going to be pouring more cash into the investment. If an investor put a sizable cash down payment into the property to assure a positive cash flow, he or she should realize there's an opportunity cost associated with tying up a lot of cash that could otherwise be earning interest.

Similarly, if a general partnership pays more than 7 times the gross annual rental to buy a property, the partnership is probably paying too much, unless it can reasonably expect a dramatic increase in the value of the property (for example, immediate condo conversion).

6.2.2 Capitalization Rate

A second real estate evaluation formula is the capitalization rate, usually referred to as the "cap rate." The formula is simple:

$$\text{Capitalization rate} = \frac{\text{Net operating income}}{\text{Total amount invested}}$$

For example, a limited partnership in an apartment building requiring a total investment of $3.5 million has an estimated net operating income of (NOI) $300,000. The cap rate is calculated as follows:

$$\text{Capitalization rate} = \frac{\text{Net operating income}}{\text{Total amount invested}} = \frac{\$3,500,00}{\$300,000} = 8.6\%$$

A cap rate of 8 percent or greater is considered desirable. Whether investing in real estate individually or through a limited partnership, make sure the amounts that go into the cap rate formula are realistic:

"Total amount invested" includes both the downpayment and the borrowed money necessary to buy the property.

"Net operating income" is the total rental income (allowing for vacancies) less all the expenses except debt service. A common practice of real estate agents and general partners is known as "bumping to market," which means raising rent projections from what they currently are to a supposed market level in order to make the deal look more attractive.

These formulas are simply rules of thumb and are just two of a multiplicity of relevant considerations that go into making real estate investments. In some instances, a promising location may outweigh a low cap rate, or tax advantages may compensate for a high rent multiplier. Those who are most successful in real estate investing, whether they do it themselves or through limited partnerships, share one characteristic—patience. When they find that real estate is overpriced, they are happy to wait until market conditions meet their criteria.

6.2.3 Return on Investment

Traditional methods of calculating return on investment (ROI) are basically quick and simple. Although the usual ROI analyses do not consider the time value of money, they do provide a quick preliminary analysis and make it relatively easy to compare one investment with another. One such technique is the free-and-clear method, whereby return is calculated by dividing NOI by the total cost of the investment (equity plus all mortgages on the investment). This technique is especially useful in making a comparison of properties, but it does not accurately calculate actual return. Return is calculated by use of the following formulas:

Rental income – Operating expenses and reserves = NOI

$$\frac{NOI}{\text{Total cost of investment}} = \text{Free–and–clear ROI}$$

The following table illustrates the free-and-clear method. A rental income of $83,000 less operating expenses and reserves of $24,000 gives an NOI of $59,000. NOI divided by the total cost of the investment ($500,000) provides the investor with a free-and-clear ROI of 11.8 percent.

Rental income	$ 83,000
Less: Operating expenses and reserves	24,000
NOI	$ 59,000
Total cost of investment	$500,000

$$\frac{NOI}{\text{Total cost of investment}} = \frac{\$59,00}{\$500,000}$$
$$= 11.8\% \text{ Free–and–clear ROI}$$

To compute actual return, the cash flow method is the technique most frequently used. Cash flow is divided by equity (the actual amount of cash paid for the investment). Debt-service charges are assumed to equal zero so that specific financing terms do not affect the cash flow. Cash flow ROI is determined by applying the following formulas:

Rental income – Operating expenses and reserves + Debt service on mortgage = Cash flow

$$\frac{\text{Cash flow}}{\text{Equity investment}} = \text{Cash flow ROI}$$

In the next table, cash flow is found by subtracting operating expenses and reserves ($24,000) and debt service on the mortgage ($50,000) from the rental income ($83,000). The $9,000 cash flow is then divided by the actual equity investment ($125,000) to provide a cash flow ROI of 7.2 percent.

Rental income	$ 83,000
Less: Operating expenses and reserves	24,000
Less: Debt service on mortgage ($375,000 mortgage at 13% interest for 25 years)	50,000
Cash flow	$ 9,000

Equity investment		
Investment cost	$500,000	
Less: Mortgage	375,000	
		$125,000

$$\frac{\text{Cash flow}}{\text{Equity investment}} = \frac{\$9,000}{\$125,000}$$
$$= 7.2\% \text{ Cash flow ROI}$$

Using the same investment as an example, the investor can add tax savings to cash flow and divide by equity to calculate tax-adjusted cash flow ROI, illustrated in the next table. Similarly, including the amount of equity buildup and appreciation before dividing provides the most inclusive traditional method of evaluation. However, equity buildup and appreciation should be added only if the investor expects to hold property over a long period of time.

Cash flow	
Rental income	$ 83,000
Less: Operating expenses and reserves	24,000
Less: Debt service on mortgage ($375,000 mortgage at 13% interest for 25 years)	50,000
Total	$ 9,000
Tax savings	
Cash flow	$ 9,000
Mortgage principal amortization (not tax deductible)	2,000

Less: Depreciation on building
    ($400,000/27.5 years)   (14,500)
Tax loss $ (3,500)
Tax savings (28% tax bracket)[1] $ 1,000
Equity investment $125,000

$$\frac{\text{Cash flow} + \text{tax savings}}{\text{Equity}} = \frac{\$9,000 + \$1,000}{\$125,000}$$
$$= 8\% \text{ Tax–adjusted cash flow ROI}$$

[1]Assumes owner qualifies for deduction of real estate losses.

6.2.4 Net Present Value

An investor who has a good idea about the appropriate ROI must also consider its relationship to the discount rate. The net present value (NPV) approach can help an investor to analyze these two figures and to determine if the projected ROI will meet his or her objectives. The cost of the investment is compared with the present value of all future cash flows. All investments made are listed for comparison with the sum of after-tax dollars returned, adjusted for present value and assuming some percentage return. This percentage return is the investment goal previously chosen. If the NPV equals or exceeds zero, the investment goal has been achieved or exceeded. The advantage of this analysis is that comparisons can be made between investments with incomes that differ widely in timing. However, selecting a realistic discount rate to be used in the present value adjustments can be difficult. Sound judgment is critical in accurately predicting a discount rate appropriate to the degree of risk, liquidity, and amount of management involved in a particular property.

EXAMPLE. An investor is considering a $1 million real estate investment that will require $300,000 in cash. He intends to hold it for five years and has set an after-tax requirement of 12 percent. After-tax dollar returns are expected to be as follows:

Year	After-Tax Dollar Return
1	$20,000[2]
2	30,000
3	33,000
4	35,000
5	38,000

[2]Substantial repairs required.

The investor estimates a 5 percent annual rate of appreciation; after selling costs, this will bring a $1.2 million selling price. After paying the mortgage and taxes, the investor will receive $400,000.

Appreciation	After-Tax Dollar Return	Present Value Factor (12%)	Present Value of Return
Year 1	$20,000	.893	$ 17,860
Year 2	30,000	.797	23,910
Year 3	33,000	.712	23,496
Year 4	35,000	.636	22,260
Year 5	38,000	.567	21,546
Sale (end of year 5)	400,000	.567	$226,800
Net present value			$335,872

Compared with the investor's initial $300,000 outlay, the proposed investment exceeds his 12 percent requirements, since the NPV is greater than $300,000.

6.3 REAL ESTATE LIMITED PARTNERSHIP DUE DILIGENCE CONSIDERATIONS

The following items should be considered as part of the due diligence process in evaluating a real estate limited partnership investment. The spate of failed real estate limited partnerships reinforces the need to evaluate thoroughly any potential real estate limited partnership investment. In spite of their sullied reputation, many investors should still consider sound, economically viable real estate partnership investments as a component of their long-term investment portfolios—but only after a thorough evaluation of the following matters.

Investor suitability

1. Does the investor meet network suitability standards set forth in the offering memorandum?

2. Is the investor's current and future tax bracket appropriate for this investment?

3. Does the investor have sufficient cash reserves to make the minimum initial investments?

4. Is the investor's net worth suitable for the purchase of multiple limited partnership units (if this is being considered)?

5. If the investment requires future payments, will the investor be able to afford making them out of cash reserves, or will funds have to be borrowed?

6. Can the investor afford to go without the required resources for a period at least as long as the estimated life of the partnership?

7. Can the investor afford to lose his or her entire investment?

8. Is the investment appropriate in terms of the investor's overall investment objectives?

Economic Risks

1. Are the business risks reasonable for the particular type of investment?
2. Are the risks appropriate when compared to the potential awards?
3. Does the investor understand the risks of the investment?

Use of Proceeds

1. How much of the investor's dollar will go toward
   a. Purchase of partnership assets?
   b. Fees to the general partner and affiliates?
   c. Sales, costs, and commissions?
   d. Fees to other parties?
   e. Cost of rehabilitating the project?
   f. Cost of covering projected negative cash flow from operations?
   g. Amount to be held for reserves?
2. Are the expenses associated with the investment reasonable, in light of this particular investment as well as in comparison to alternative investments?

Allocation of benefits between general partner and limited partners:

1. How are the following allocated between the general partner and the limited partners:
   a. Tax benefits?
   b. Cash flow from operations?
   c. Sale or refinancing of partnership assets?
2. Are the limited partners entitled to the return of their capital contributions plus the preference on any money invested, prior to the time the general partner receives any proceeds?
3. Do the allocation arrangements provide enough incentive to the general partner to maximize the performance of partnership assets during:
   a. The operational phase?
   b. The liquidation phase?
4. Are the overall allocation arrangements reasonable to all parties?

Partnership assets

1. Does the real estate parcel have the potential to appreciate in value?
2. Are current economic conditions conducive to this type of real estate investment?
3. Are local real estate market conditions favorable to this kind of invest-

ment, including current and projected competition in the area and vacancy rates?

4. Is the purchase price of the real estate reasonable in relation to appraisal value, current market data, and so on?

5. Will reasonable amounts of money be set aside to improve or rehabilitate the project?

6. Are the projections reasonable considering
   a. Historical operating performance?
   b. Historical occupancy rates?
   c. Previous rate of increase in rent and expenses?
   d. Rents in the local market?

7. Are terms of the mortgage, if any, appropriate to the structure of the partnership?

8. If a negative cash flow is projected, are there enough reserves in the partnership to cover same?

9. Is the projected sales price of the asset at the time the partnership is expected to be liquidated reasonable?

General Partner Compensation

1. Is the compensation of the general partner adequately disclosed?

2. What percentage of the total equity to be raised from all limited partners are to be paid to the general partner? Are these fees reasonable for the industry?

3. Are the fees received by the general partner for performing services during the operational phase of the investment reasonable?

The General Partner's Track Record

1. How long has the general partner been in the real estate business?

2. How much experience does the general partner have in investing in and managing similar real estate projects?

3. Is the general partner's track record of all past projects satisfactory?

6.4   REAL ESTATE INVESTMENT TRUSTS

Real estate investment trusts (REITs) allow investors to participate in real estate investing with a smaller cash commitment than is required for direct real estate investments and real estate limited partnerships. REITs are organizations, usually corporations, established for the accumulation of funds for investing in real estate holdings, or the extension of credit on real estate. Table 6.1 provides a list of some of the major REITs, all of which trade on either the New York Stock Exchange or American Stock Exchange. Publicly traded REITs are very liquid in contrast to other real estate investment alternatives. There are three different REIT industry sectors: property owners, mortgage makers, and hybrids. Within each sector, investors can select REITs that invest in or finance particular categories of real estate. For example, property owner REITs may invest in such properties as shopping centers, office space, multi family rental housing, distribution/service facilities, even a racetrack (Santa Anita Realty). Therefore, the REIT selection process may not only focus on the value of the security per se, but also on the nature of the REIT's business. Just like any real estate investment, REIT stocks should generally be considered longer-term investments.

Table 6.1 Major Publicly Traded REITs

Name	Description
BRE Properties	Emphasizes income producing real estate
Federal Realty	Emphasizes the ownership and renovation of shopping malls nationwide
First Union	Nationwide, emphasizes income-producing properties
HRE Properties	Invests in retail, office, and distribution/service facilities throughout the United States.
L&N Housing	Invests in multifamily rental housing with a view toward conversion into condominiums; has diversified into apartment, retail, and office properties
L&N Mortgage	Emphasizes short-term mortgages on a nationwide basis
MGI Properties	Engages in geographically diverse real estate investments
New Plan Realty	Specializes in the ownership of income-producing shopping malls
Property Capital	Specializes in making equity participation loans on real estate properties
Santa Anita Realty	Owns Santa Anita racetrack and other real estate properties
Washington REIT	Emphasizes investing in and developing income-producing properties

6.5 EXISTING ONE-FAMILY HOUSES SOLD AND PRICED, BY REGION

Table 6.2 shows the regional trends in sales and sales prices of existing one-family homes. The sales price data illustrates the long-term appreciation potential of home ownership. The table shows the median sales price of new one-family houses dating from 1970. A comparison of this table with Table 6.5, Median Sales Price of New Privately Owned One-Family Houses Sold, by Region, shows the difference in selling prices of new versus existing housing. On a national basis, and in each region, with the exception of the West, new one-family homes are considerably more expensive than existing homes. Nevertheless, while dramatic year-to-year appreciation in housing costs has been largely a phenomenon of the mid- and late 1980s, home ownership remains an attractive long-term investment.

Table 6.2 Existing One-Family Houses Sold and Price, by Region, 1970–1989

YEAR	HOUSES SOLD (1,000)					MEDIAN SALES PRICE (dol.)				
	Total	North-east	Mid-west	South	West	Total	North-east	Mid-west	South	West
1970	1,612	251	501	568	292	23,000	25,200	20,100	22,200	24,300
1971	2,018	311	583	735	389	24,800	27,100	22,100	24,300	26,500
1972	2,252	361	630	788	473	26,700	29,800	23,900	26,400	28,400
1973	2,334	367	674	847	446	28,900	32,800	25,300	29,000	31,000
1974	2,272	354	645	839	434	32,000	35,800	27,700	32,300	34,800
1975	2,476	370	701	862	543	35,300	39,300	30,100	34,800	39,600
1976	3,064	439	881	1,033	712	38,100	41,800	32,900	36,500	46,100
1977	3,650	515	1,101	1,231	803	42,900	44,400	36,700	39,800	57,300
1978	3,986	516	1,144	1,416	911	48,700	47,900	42,200	45,100	66,700
1979	3,827	526	1,061	1,353	887	55,700	53,600	47,800	51,300	77,400
1980	2,973	403	806	1,092	672	62,200	60,800	51,900	58,300	89,300
1981	2,419	353	632	917	516	66,400	63,700	54,300	64,400	96,200
1982	1,990	354	490	780	366	67,800	63,500	55,100	67,100	98,900
1983	2,719	493	709	1,035	481	70,300	72,200	56,600	69,200	94,900
1984	2,868	511	755	1,073	529	72,400	78,700	57,100	71,300	95,800
1985	3,214	622	866	1,172	554	75,500	88,900	58,900	75,200	95,400
1986	3,565	703	991	1,261	610	80,300	104,800	63,500	78,200	100,900
1987	3,526	685	959	1,282	600	85,600	133,300	66,000	80,400	113,200
1988	3,594	673	929	1,350	642	89,300	143,000	68,400	82,200	124,900
1989	3,440	589	919	1,307	610	93,100	145,200	71,300	84,500	139,900

Source: National Association of Realtors, *Existing Home Sales*, (Washington, D.C.: The Association, monthly)

6.6 MEDIAN PURCHASE PRICE OF EXISTING ONE-FAMILY HOMES, BY METROPOLITAN AREA

Table 6.3 shows the median sales price of existing one-family homes by metropolitan area from 1985. Caution should be exercised when considering average sales prices because widely divergent averages have been published by various sources. Nevertheless, this table provides a reasonable assessment of the appreciation, and in some instances depreciation, in the value of existing single-family houses in major metropolitan areas.

Table 6.3 Median Prices Existing One-Family Homes, by Metropolitan Area, 1985–1990

METROPOLITAN AREA	1985	1988	1989	1990, 2d qtr.	METROPOLITAN AREA	1985	1988	1989	1990, 2d qtr.
U.S., all areas	75.5	89.3	93.1	96.9	Louisville, KY-IN	50.6	54.5	58.4	59.7
Akron, OH PMSA	52.7	59.9	64.5	67.0	Memphis, TN-AR-MS	64.6	76.3	78.1	78.1
Albany-Schenectady-Troy, NY ..	60.3	92.2	104.9	106.9	Miami-Hialeah, FL PMSA	80.5	82.9	86.9	89.0
Albuquerque, NM	76.8	80.4	83.0	86.1	Milwaukee, WI PMSA........	67.5	74.5	79.6	86.6
Anaheim-Santa Ana, CA PMSA .	136.2	206.9	241.6	248.9	Minneapolis-St. Paul, MN-WI ...	75.2	85.2	87.2	90.3
Baltimore, MD............	72.6	88.7	96.3	100.9	Nashville, TN	66.1	77.6	79.9	82.4
Baton Rouge, LA	74.6	64.7	63.8	66.5	New York-Northern New Jersey-				
Birmingham, AL	64.5	75.7	78.5	82.6	Long Island, NY-NJ-CT CMSA .	134.0	183.8	183.2	175.0
Boston, MA PMSA.........	134.2	181.2	181.9	176.2	Oklahoma City, OK	64.7	56.2	53.5	54.1
Buffalo-Niagara Falls, NY					Omaha, NE-IA	58.3	59.5	60.6	61.4
CMSA	46.7	65.6	72.5	77.3	Orlando, FL	70.3	79.1	79.8	83.3
Chicago, IL PMSA.........	81.1	98.9	107.0	116.6	Philadelphia, PA-NJ PMSA	74.0	102.4	103.9	110.8
Cincinnati, OH-KY-IN PMSA ...	60.2	69.7	75.8	81.4	Phoenix, AZ	74.7	80.0	78.8	84.0
Cleveland, OH PMSA.......	64.4	69.2	75.2	81.5	Portland, OR PMSA.........	61.5	64.4	70.1	79.7
Columbus, OH	62.2	72.6	77.9	82.4	Providence, RI PMSA........	67.5	130.6	130.2	130.5
Dallas, TX PMSA..........	94.0	90.8	92.4	92.0	Riverside/San Bernardino, CA				
Denver, CO PMSA.........	84.3	81.8	85.5	87.0	PMSA	(NA)	106.7	123.8	133.2
Des Moines, IA...........	52.5	55.8	57.5	58.1	Rochester, NY	64.2	75.7	78.5	79.9
Detroit, MI PMSA..........	51.7	73.1	73.7	77.9	St. Louis, MO-IL	65.7	78.1	76.9	82.0
Ft. Lauderdale-Hollywood-					Salt Lake City-Ogden, UT	66.7	67.7	69.4	69.2
Pompano Beach, FL PMSA...	74.6	81.1	83.9	92.2	San Antonio, TX	67.7	65.0	64.2	62.8
Ft. Worth, TX PMSA	74.9	73.3	79.9	74.6	San Diego, CA	106.4	147.8	181.8	183.7
Hartford, CT PMSA	99.6	167.6	165.9	159.3	San Francisco-Oakland-				
Honolulu, HI..............	162.1	215.1	267.6	345.0	San Jose, CA CMSA	(NA)	212.6	260.2	263.6
Houston, TX PMSA	78.6	61.8	66.7	71.4	Seattle/Tacoma, WA CMSA ...	(NA)	88.7	115.0	147.6
Indianapolis, IN...........	55.0	66.1	71.2	82.3	Syracuse, NY	58.8	74.6	79.3	80.5
Jacksonville, FL	58.4	67.7	69.3	73.0	Tampa-St. Petersburg-				
Kansas City, MO-KS	61.4	70.5	71.6	73.2	Clearwater, FL	58.4	65.6	71.9	70.4
Las Vegas, NV	75.1	78.8	85.7	93.3	Tulsa, OK	66.7	65.0	62.6	64.4
Los Angeles-Long Beach, CA					Washington, DC-MD-VA	97.1	132.5	144.4	150.9
PMSA	118.7	179.4	214.1	216.9	West Palm Beach-Boca Raton-				
					Delray Beach, FL..........	88.3	99.0	102.6	108.2

Source: National Association of Realtors, *Existing Home Sales*, (Washington, D.C.: The Association, monthly)

6.7 MEDIAN SALES PRICE OF NEW PRIVATELY OWNED ONE-FAMILY HOUSES SOLD, BY REGION

Table 6.4 shows the median sales price, by region, of *new* privately owned one-family houses. Table 6.3 shows comparable statistics for sales of existing houses.

Table 6.4 Median Sales Price of New Privately Owned One-Family Houses Sold, by Region, 1970–1990

YEAR	U.S.	North-east	Midwest	South	West	YEAR	U.S.	North-east	Midwest	South	West
1970.....	23,400	30,300	24,400	20,300	24,000	1981.....	68,900	76,000	65,900	64,400	77,800
1971.....	25,200	30,600	27,200	22,500	25,500	1982.....	69,300	78,200	68,900	66,100	75,000
1972.....	27,600	31,400	29,300	25,800	27,500	1983.....	75,300	82,200	79,500	70,900	80,100
1973.....	32,500	37,100	32,900	30,900	32,400	1984.....	79,900	88,600	85,400	72,000	87,300
1974.....	35,900	40,100	36,100	34,500	35,800	1985.....	84,300	103,300	80,300	75,000	92,600
1975.....	39,300	44,000	39,600	37,300	40,600	1986.....	92,000	125,000	88,300	80,200	95,700
1976.....	44,200	47,300	44,800	40,500	47,200	1987.....	104,500	140,000	95,000	88,000	111,000
1977.....	48,800	51,600	51,500	44,100	53,500	1988.....	112,500	149,000	101,600	92,000	126,500
1978.....	55,700	58,100	59,200	50,300	61,300	1989.....	120,000	159,600	108,800	96,400	139,000
1979.....	62,900	65,500	63,900	57,300	69,600						
1980.....	64,600	69,500	63,400	59,600	72,300	1990, prel..	123,000	157,500	108,000	99,000	148,000

Source: U.S. Bureau of the Census and U.S. Dept. of Housing and Urban Development, *Construction Reports*, series C25, *Characteristics of New Housing*, annual; and *New One-Family Houses Sold and For Sale*, monthly.

6.8 RECENT HOME-BUYERS—GENERAL CHARACTERISTICS AND DOWN PAYMENTS

Table 6.5 shows the trends in home purchase activity dating from 1976. Steady, and in many areas dramatic increases in home prices and average monthly mortgage payments are evident.

Table 6.5 Recent Home Buyers—General Characteristics, 1976–1989

ITEM	Unit	1976	1980	1983	1984	1985	1986	1987	1988	1989
Median purchase price ..	Dollars ...	43,340	68,714	90,000	89,400	90,400	93,680	99,260	121,910	129,800
First-time buyers	Dollars ...	37,670	61,450	73,100	81,500	75,100	74,700	84,730	97,100	105,200
Repeat buyers [1]	Dollars ...	50,090	75,750	101,800	100,400	106,200	114,860	115,430	141,400	144,700
Average monthly mortgage										
payment	Dollars ...	329	599	794	868	896	852	939	1,008	1,054
Percent of income....	Percent ...	24.0	32.4	32.5	30.3	30.0	28.6	29.3	32.8	31.8
Percent buying—										
New houses	Percent ...	15.1	22.4	26.4	22.3	23.8	25.7	23.8	26.2	21.8
Existing houses.......	Percent ...	84.9	77.6	73.6	77.7	76.2	74.3	76.2	73.8	78.2
Single-family houses ..	Percent ...	88.8	82.4	87.8	89.9	87.0	85.1	87.3	83.3	84.8
Condominiums [2]	Percent ...	11.2	17.6	12.2	10.1	10.6	14.2	12.5	12.4	13.5
For the first time	Percent ...	44.8	32.9	40.5	37.7	36.6	35.5	36.8	37.8	40.2
Average age:										
First-time buyers	Years	28.1	28.3	28.9	29.1	28.4	30.9	29.6	30.3	29.6
Repeat buyers [1]	Years	35.9	36.4	37.3	37.8	38.4	39.5	39.1	38.9	39.4
Downpayment/sales price	Percent ...	25.2	28.0	22.9	20.9	24.8	23.4	27.2	24.0	24.4
First-time buyers	Percent ...	18.0	20.5	15.7	13.2	11.4	13.4	20.4	14.6	15.8
Repeat buyers [1]	Percent ...	30.8	32.7	27.8	25.6	32.7	28.9	31.3	29.7	30.3

[1] Buyers who previously owned a home. [2] Includes multiple-family houses.
Source: Chicago Title Insurance Company, Chicago, IL, *The Guarantor*, bimonthly. (Copyright.)

Source: Chicago Title Insurance Company, *The Guarantor*, (Chicago: Chicago Title Insurance Company, bimonthly).

6.9   HOME OWNERSHIP RATES BY AGE OF HOUSEHOLD HEAD

Table 6.6 shows the percentage of home ownership by age. The increased costs of owning a home have forced many households to delay or abandon the effort to become homeowners. The national homeownership rate stood at 63.9% in 1988, well below the 1980 figure of 65.6%. The drop-off in home ownership rates is most dramatic for younger households. Between 1980 and 1988, the homeownership among 25-29 year-olds fell from 43.3% to 36.2%, while that for 30-34 year-olds fell from 61.1% to 52.6%. Nationwide, some 2 million more young households would own homes today if ownership rates had remained steady since 1980.

Table 6.6   Homeownership Rates by Age of Household Head (Percent)

Age	*1973*	*1976*	*1980*	*1983*	*1988*
Under 25	23.4%	21.0%	21.3%	19.3%	15.5%
25-29	43.6	43.2	43.3	38.2	36.2
30-34	60.2	62.4	61.1	55.7	52.6
35-39	68.5	69.0	70.8	65.8	63.2
40-44	72.9	73.9	74.2	74.2	71.4
45-54	76.1	77.4	77.7	77.1	76.0
55-64	75.7	77.2	79.3	80.5	79.6
65-74	71.3	72.7	75.2	76.9	78.2
75+	64.4	64.8	65.6	64.9	63.9
Total	**64.4%**	**64.8%**	**65.6%**	**64.9%**	**63.9%**

Chapter 7

INSURANCE

Having the appropriate insurance coverage can mean the difference between successfully coping with a financial emergency or being desperately ill-prepared for one. Yet few areas are as little understood, and inappropriately utilized, as insurance protection.

Reduced to its simplest terms, insurance is a means of minimizing the losses of a few by spreading the cost among many. Insurance protection can be broadly divided into two categories: (1) property and casualty, which insures possessions such as a home, a car, and other personal and business property; and (2) life and health which covers loss of life, injury, or illness.

Beyond these basic definitions, however, lies a world of premiums, forms, deductibles, policy exceptions, and tax ramifications that is likely to confound the majority of individuals. As a result, many people are underinsured, while others are overinsured or covered at much higher costs than necessary. Moreover, investment professionals are increasingly being asked to evaluate an expanded array of tax-advantaged insurance products such as single premium, variable, and universal life insurance. Since policy features vary so widely, this task has become very difficult, if not impossible. Yet the popularity of these insurance-based investment products as tax-deferred retirement savings vehicles is likely to increase.

Despite these roadblocks, the financial professional must have the knowledge required to help the individual evaluate his or her insurance needs, for without proper insurance, coverage assets and future earnings could be severely jeopardized.

During their working years, most people will need the following basic forms of insurance:

- *Life insurance.* The main purpose of life insurance is to provide for dependents after the policyholder's death and ideally should replace most, if not all, of an individual's wages for several years after his death.

242

Life insurance also helps provide liquidity for the estate. As the size of family estates grow, the market for life insurance to fund estate taxes will probably increase.

- *Health insurance.* Although many peoples' health insurance is provided by an employer, self-employed individuals and retirees who are no longer covered by a company plan must be particularly careful about selecting appropriate coverage.

  As employers and health insurance companies search for ways to control health insurance costs, employees, too, will become increasingly diligent in seeking ways to monitor and reduce personal health care costs.

- *Disability insurance.* This replaces all or part of an individual's wage income if a disabling accident occurs. Disability is often the most overlooked area of insurance coverage and should be examined closely.

- *Homeowners' and renters' insurance.* Theft, fire, or natural catastrophes can befall homeowners and apartment dwellers. Policy provisions should be carefully noted, since some policies cover the depreciated cash value of an individual's possessions, while others provide replacement value coverage.

- *Automobile insurance.* Financial professionals should pay particular attention to the adequacy of bodily injury liability protection, since jury awards in some accident cases are very high.

- *Personal liability insurance.* Extended personal liability (umbrella) insurance takes over where the liability portion of homeowner'-renters' and automobile insurance leaves off. It also covers the insured for potential personal (not job-related) liability not related to one's domicile or the operation of an automobile. Persons whose occupations put them at risk for professional liability should also consider acquiring professional liability or malpractice insurance.

Since few people are totally insured, one of the first steps to take when examining insurance coverage or responding to client inquiries about insurance is to look for any gaps. For example, an individual may be adequately covered if his or her home is burglarized, but inadequate life insurance could leave his or her family financially strapped in the event of his death.

However, it is also important to guard against wasted premium dollars that are being spent on unnecessary coverage. A retiree with little debt and adequate savings and outside sources of income, or a single individual with no dependents, is probably wasting money if extensive life insurance coverage is purchased.

The deterioration of the investment portfolios of many insurance companies combined with several well-publicized bankruptcies of large life insurance companies has understandably increased policyholders' concern over the safety of their insurers. In addition to the troubling financial problems of many insurance companies, several trends in the insurance industry, combined with demographic changes, will likely affect the insurance planning process in 1992 and beyond. Continued competition in the marketplace will breed new policies that have features that are novel, but not necessarily superior. As the population ages and as many individuals and families join the ranks of the affluent, insurance needs will change, although this will not necessarily be readily apparent. For example, the role of life insurance in estate planning will become more widely understood once affluent clients understand its efficacy. Finally, the aging population will increase interest in retirement-oriented savings programs such as cash-value life insurance and annuities.

7.1 RISK CATEGORIES AND THEIR APPROPRIATE INSURANCE COVERAGE

Most people are overinsured in some areas and underinsured in others. Underinsurance or lack of insurance can wipe out years of accumulated capital and may also jeopardize future earnings. Table 7.1 describes important areas of risk along with the appropriate categories of insurance to protect against such risks.

7.2 INVENTORY OF LIFE INSURANCE POLICY CLASSIFICATIONS AND PROVISIONS

The many varieties of life insurance policies combined with a bewildering array of policy provisions make the decision of which policy to buy a difficult and confusing one. It is important, however, for individuals to make informed life insurance purchase decisions. The two basic categories of insurance are (1) term insurance, which provides insurance protection only, and (2) cash-value insurance, which has a savings component. Within these two categories are many subspecies of insurance. This section explains and comments on the more commonly used types of life insurance policies.

7.2.1 Term Policies

Term life insurance is fairly straightforward. The policyholder pays an annual premium, and in exchange the insurance company pays a sum of money to the policyholder's beneficiaries if he or she dies within the time covered. Most term policies are renewable, meaning that when the policy expires (generally every 1 or 5 years), the policyholder may have the policy renewed, no matter what change in health he or she has undergone. The premium rises each term as the policyholder's age increases. The option to

Table 7.1 Risk Categories and Their Appropriate Insurance Coverage

Risk Category	Appropriate Insurance Coverage
Loss of Income	
During your life	Disability insurance
After your death	Life insurance
Death of spouse	Life Insurance
Short-term disability	Short-term disability insurance
Long-Term disability	Long-term disability insurance
Permanent disability	Long-term disability insurance
Loss of Property	
Total loss	Homeowner's/renter's and automotive insurance
Loss of use	Homeowner's/renter's and automotive insurance
Repairs/Replacements	Homeowner's/renter's and automotive insurance
Loss of valuables	Floater policy on homeowner's/renter's and automotive insurance
Injury to Others	
Damage to property	Homeowner's/renter's, automotive, and umbrella liability insurance
Damage to person	Homeowner's/renter's, automotive, and umbrella liability insurance
Libel	Umbrella liability insurance
Illness/Injury	
Routine	Medical insurance
Catastrophic	Medical insurance
Old-age	Medicare gap and nursing home insurance
Occupational	
Professional liability	Professional liability insurance
Inflation	
Loss of income	Disability insurance with inflation provision
Loss of property	Homeowner's/renter's insurance with replacement cost provision
Estate Liquidity	
Final expenses	Life insurance
Estate taxes	Life insurance
Estate administration	Life insurance

renew continues up to a specified age, usually 65 years or so. Renewability is a very important feature. Specific kinds of term insurance include the following:

7.2.1.1 *Level Renewable Term Insurance.* This policy maintains a fixed annual premium which increases each time the policy is renewed. A policyholder generally may reduce the amount of coverage when he or she renews, but may have to undergo a medical examination in order to increase coverage.

7.2.1.2 *Level Nonrenewable Term Insurance.* Thsi policy maintains a fixed face amount and annual premium throughout the term of coverage—which might be 5, 10, or 20 years—and may not be renewed thereafter.

7.2.1.3 *Decreasing or Declining Term Insurance.* This policy's annual premium remains fixed, but its face amount gradually decreases. These policies, usually purchased for 10 to 25 or more years, are often used to provide for payment of an outstanding debt. Mortgage life insurance is a variety of decreasing term insurance that is specifically designed to pay off the balance of a mortgage upon the policyholder's death. Mortgage life insurance or credit life insurance (designed to pay off a loan) are both somewhat restrictive in that the policyholder's dependents will not have any option with the policy funds other than to pay the mortgage or loan. A term insurance policy that is large enough to cover a mortgage or debt has the advantages of greater flexibility and usually much lower cost than these targeted programs.

7.2.1.4 *Group Term Insurance.* Many Americans are covered by some form of group life insurance, through their employers, unions, professional and fraternal organizations, alumni associations, and so on. Group life insurance is generally less expensive than individual insurance and does not require a medical examination; eligibility for group coverage usually ends if the policyholder leaves the sponsoring group.

7.2.2 Cash-Value Policies

These more complicated policies combine life insurance coverage with a savings plan. Like a savings account, a cash-value insurance policy gradually builds up a cash-value which the policyholder can borrow against or cash in. Cash-value insurance thus enforces a regimented savings plan. It is much more expensive than term insurance, so that most people can't afford to obtain all of their life insurance needs with a cash-value policy.

A cash-value policy usually remains in effect for a holder's entire life, and a fixed annual premium is paid throughout. The policy's death benefit remains fixed even as the cash-value rises with annual payments; when the policyholder dies, the beneficiary receives only the policy's face value. The savings component of a cash-value policy is, thus, largely for the benefit of the policyholder, who may cash in the policy at any time, or may borrow against the cash-value. Alternatively, the cash-value can be used to pay premiums in later years of the policy's life or to purchase additional insurance.

A cash-value policy may be participating or nonparticipating. With a "par" policy, a policyholder receives annual dividends representing whatever portion of his or her premium the insurance company did not use to pay death benefits and other expenses. Dividends may be received in cash, reinvested in insurance, or held by the company to reduce future premium payments.

7.2.2.1 Whole Life Insurance. As its name suggests, this policy covers a policyholder until death. The high annual premiums in a whole life policy will eventually begin to accumulate a substantial cash-value, but only after several years, since in a policy's early years sales commissions and administrative costs absorb much of the premium payments. Only a total withdrawal of funds, canceling the policy, is permitted, but a holder may borrow against the cash-value, generally at a low interest rate. Whole life policies, as well as other kinds of cash-value insurance, have been treated as a tax-deferred investment up to the time of withdrawal (at which point part of the cash-value is taxed).

7.2.2.2 Universal Life Insurance. While the company administering a whole life policy is not required to inform policyholders about the effective rate of interest that is being paid on a policy, universal life insurance allows a policyholder to see what percentage of premiums go respectively toward company expenses, protecting the client, and the savings component. The policyholder is also advised of the interest rate that the savings are earning. Universal life holders are permitted to withdraw a portion of the cash-value account without terminating the policy. One form of universal life policy—which is for obvious reasons, more expensive—allows the policy's beneficiaries to receive the policy's accumulated cash-value as well as its face value.

Many universal life insurance policies allow holders some flexibility in paying premiums; as long as they pay a minimum premium, they may pay more or less than usual, increasing or reducing the speed with which their cash-value grows. Companies guarantee that they will credit a certain minimum interest rate to a policyholder's cash-value, the rate sometimes increasing with higher cash-values.

7.2.2.3 Variable Life Insurance. This kind of policy is similar to universal life insurance except that each policyholder is permitted to decide how his or her money is to be invested. He or she has a choice between various different investment vehicles—stocks, bonds, money market funds—from the company's portfolio and can therefore tailor their own investment portfolio.

7.3 DISABILITY INSURANCE POLICY PROVISIONS

Lack of adequate long-term disability insurance coverage is one of the most common gaps in insurance coverage. Yet a working person is far more likely to suffer a long-term disability than to die before retirement. Many people think that since they are covered for disability at their place of employment, they have adequate coverage. Employer-provided disability insurance coverage, however, may lack important policy features or provide insufficient benefits. Therefore, it is important to examine any existing or contemplated disability insurance policies for adequacy of coverage.

Disability insurance policies differ widely in features and benefits. For example, some policies terminate coverage when the disabled individual can perform any occupation, while others continue coverage until the disabled individual can perform his or her "usual and customary" occupation. Some policies offer the same benefits throughout the period of disability, while others adjust for inflation. Table 7.2 provides a list of questions that highlight various features and standard limitations of disability insurance policies. Employer-provided disability coverage will lack many of these features. However, a comprehensive individually purchased disability policy will be quite expensive.

Table 7.2 Features and Standard Limitations of Disability Insurance Policies

1. What is the definition of total disability:
   • During initial period?
   • After initial period?

2. Is the contract noncancellable and guaranteed renewable to age 65 with guaranteed level premium?

3. Can total disability coverage be continued on a conditionally renewable basis to age 75 if the insured is employed full time?

4. Is a proportionate benefit for partial disability automatically included?

5. Is the contract participating?

6. Does the contract state that the number of days to satisfy the beginning date need not be continuous?

7. Does the contract have a presumptive total disability clause that starts on the day of a specified loss and provides for lifetime payments whether the insured is working or not?

8. What, if any, are the waiver of premium provisions?

9. What are the standard exclusions?

10. Is the policy incontestable after two years from date of issue?

11. Is a rehabilitation benefit automatically included?

12. Are lifetime benefits for total disability available?

13. Is a nonsmoker discount available?

14. Does the policy provide for inflation indexation of benefits?

15. Does the policy pay Social Security substitute benefits?

16. Does the policy offer additional regular disability coverage on an annually renewable, increasing premium basis?

7.4 HOMEOWNERS' AND RENTERS' INSURANCE POLICY COVERAGE OPTIONS

Everyone should have homeowners' or renters' insurance coverage, but individual needs vary across a wide spectrum. For example, those who have valuable possessions, whether they are kept in the home or in a safe deposit box, need an endorsement on their homeowners' or renters' policy to assure adequate coverage.

Tables 7.3 and 7.4 summarize the various kinds of coverage that are available. Table 7.3, "Comparison of Risks Covered Under Various Homeowners' Insurance Plans," shows the extent of coverage available under the various homeowners' insurance plans and can be used to identify the appropriate level of coverage to meet a client's home insurance needs as well as to note risks that are not covered. Table 7.4, "Frequently Used Homeowners' Insurance Endorsements," can be used to identify risks and/or coverage modifications that can be added to a basic insurance plan to ensure that coverage is comprehensive.

7.5 BEST'S RATING CLASSIFICATIONS AND MODIFIERS

A .M. Best Company provides a rating service of life and property/casualty insurance companies. These ratings are designed to reflect the company's strengths and weaknesses in four areas: underwriting, expense control, reserve adequacy, and sound investments. Best's ratings are often used by financial services professionals as one of several criteria to gauge the ability of an insurance company to meet its obligations. Table 7.5 contains explanations of the Best's ratings and modifiers. [Note that many insurance companies are not eligible for a Best's rating, in which case these companies are placed in a "not assigned" (NA) classification.] In addition, the table includes explanations of the 10 classifications used by A. M. Best to identify the reason why the company was not eligible for a Best's rating.

Table 7.3 Comparison of Risks Covered Under Various Homeowners' Insurance Plans

Risks	Basic HO-1	Broad HO-2	Special HO-3[1]	Renters HO-4	Unit Owners HO-6	Older Home HO-8
Fire or lightning	A,B	A,B	A,B	B	B	A,B
Windstorm or hail	A,B	A,B	A,B	B	B	A,B
Explosion	A,B	A,B	A,B	B	B	A,B
Riot or civil commotion	A,B	A,B	A,B	B	B	A,B
Damage from aircraft	A,B	A,B	A,B	B	B	A,B
Damage from vehicles	A,B	A,B	A,B	B	B	A,B
Damage from smoke	A,B	A,B	A,B	B	B	A,B
Vandalism and malicious mischief	A,B	A,B	A,B	B	B	A,B
Theft	A,B	A,B	A,B	B	B	A,B
Damage by glass or safety glazing material which is a part of a building	A,B	A,B	A,B	B	B	A,B
Volcanic eruption	A,B	A,B	A,B	B	B	A,B
Falling objects		A,B	A,B	B	B	
Weight of ice, snow, or sleet		A,B	A,B	B	B	
Accidental discharge or overflow of water or steam from within a plumbing, heating,						

Table 7.3 (continued)

Peril			
air-conditioning or automatic fire protective sprinkler system or from within a household appliance	A,B	A,B	B
Sudden and accidental tearing apart, cracking, burning, or bulging of a steam or hot water heating system, an air-conditioning, automatic fire protective sprinkler system or an appliance for hot water	A,B	A,B	B
Freezing of a plumbing, heating, air-conditioning or automatic fire protective sprinkler system or household appliance	A,B	A,B	B
Sudden and accidental damage from artificially generated electrical current	A,B	A,B	B
All perils except flood, earthquake, war, nuclear accident, and others specified in policy	A,B		

[1]Under new homeowners program, comprehensive coverage is available by endorsement to the HO-3 special policy, which otherwise covers only personal property.

A = Dwelling

B = Personal Property

Table 7.4 Frequently Used Homeowners Insurance Endorsements

Program	Endorsement
HO-40	Appurtenant Structures—Rented to Others
HO-41	Additional Insured—Designated Premises Only
HO-42	Office, Professional, Private School, or Studio Occupancy. Described Residence Premises Only
HO-43	Office, Professional, Private School, or Studio Occupancy. Additional Residence Premises (Section II only)
HO-45	Change Endorsement
HO-46	Theft Coverage Extension (Form HO-2, HO-3, or HO-4 only—Section I)
HO-47	Inflation Guard Endorsement
HO-48	Appurtenant Structures (Section I only)
HO-49	Secondary Residence Premises, Building Additions and Alterations. Increased Limit of Liability (Form HO-5 only—Section I)
HO-50	Additional Amount on Unscheduled Personal Property. In Secondary Residence (Form HO-5 only—Section I)
HO-53	Credit Card Forgery and Depositors Forgery Coverage Endorsement (Section I only)
HO-54, HO-54A, HO-54C	Earthquake Damage Assumption Endorsements (Form HO-1, HO-2, HO-3, or HO-4 only—Section I—variable in coverage for earthquake and/or volcanic eruption and deductibles)
HO-55, HO-55A, HO-55C	Earthquake Damage Assumption Endorsements (Form HO-5 only—Section I— variable in coverage for earthquake and/or volcanic eruption and deductibles)
HO-56	$100 Special Loss Deductible Clause (Form HO-1, HO-2, HO-3, or HO-4 only—Section I)
HO-57	$50 Loss Deductible Clause (Form HO-5 only—Section I)
HO-58	$250 Special Loss Deductible Clause (Section I only)
HO-59	$500 Special Loss Deductible Clause (Section I only)
HO-61	Scheduled Personal Property Endorsement
HO-65	Increased Limits on Money and Securities (Section I only)

Table 7.4 (continued)

Program	Endorsement
HO-66	Additional Amount on Unscheduled Personal Property—Away From Premises (Form HO-1, HO-2, HO-3, or HO-4 only—Section I)
HO-67	Secondary Residence Premises Endorsement
HO-68	Scheduled Glass Endorsement (Section I only)
HO-69	Physicians, Surgeons, Dentists and Veterinarians— Away From Premises Endorsement (Form HO-2, HO-3, or HO-4 only—Section I)
HO-70	Additional Residence Premises—Rented to Others (1 or 2 families—Section II only)
HO-71	Business Pursuits Endorsement (Section II only)
HO-72	Farmers Comprehensive Personal Liability Endorsement
HO-75	Watercraft Endorsement (Section II only)
HO-114	$50 Loss Deductible Clause No. 1 and No. 2 (Form HO-5 only—Section I)
HO-122	Loss Deductible Clause No. 1—Windstorm or Hail (Form HO-1, HO-2, HO-3, or HO-4 only— Section I)
HO-148	$50 Modified Loss Deductible Clause No. 2 (Form HO-2, HO-3, or HO-4 only—Section I)
HO-162	Credit for Existing Insurance Endorsement (for those states where permitted)
HO-164	Snowmobile Endorsement (Section II)
HO-171	Unscheduled Jewelry, Watches, and Furs Increased Limits of Liability (Form HO-1, HO-2, HO-3, or HO-4 only—Section I)
HO-172	Unscheduled Jewelry, Watches, and Furs Increased Limits of Liability (Form HO-5 only—Section I)
HO-174	$100 Loss Deductible Clause (Form HO-1, HO-2, HO-3, or HO-4 only—Section I)
HO-175	$100 Loss Deductible Clause No. 1—Windstorm or Hail (Form HO-1, HO-2, HO-3, or HO-4 only— Section I)
HO-192	Condominium Unit—Owner's Endorsement (Form HO-4 only—Section I)

Table 7.5 Best's Rating Classification and Modifiers

Rating	Application	Explanation
A+ (Superior)	Life and Property/Casualty	Assigned to those companies which in Best's opinion have achieved superior overall performance when compared to the norms of the insurance industry. A+ (Superior)-rated insurers generally have demonstrated the strongest ability to meet their respective policyholder and other contractual obligations.
A and A– (Excellent)	Life and Property/Casualty	Assigned to those companies which in Best's opinion have achieved excellent overall performance when compared to the norms of the insurance industry. A and A– (Excellent)-rated insurers generally have demonstrated a strong ability to meet their respective policyholder and other contractual obligations.
B+ (Very Good)	Life and Property/Casualty	Assigned to those companies which in Best's opinion have achieved very good overall performance when compared to the norms of the insurance industry. B+ (Very Good)-rated insurers generally have demonstrated a very good ability to meet their policyholder and other contractual obligations.
B and B– (Good)	Life and Property/Casualty	Assigned to those companies which in Best's opinion have achieved good overall performance when compared to the norms of the insurance industry. B and B– (Good)-rated insurers generally have demonstrated a good ability to meet their policyholder and other contractual obligations.
C+ (Fairly Good)	Life and Property/Casualty	Assigned to those companies which in Best's opinion have achieved fairly good overall performance when compared to the norms of the insurance industry. C+ (Fairly Good)-rated insurers generally have demonstrated a fairly good ability to meet their respective policyholder and other contractual obligations.
C and C– (Fair)	Life and Property/Casualty	Assigned to those companies which in Best's opinion have achieved fair overall performance when compared to the norms of the insurance industry. C and C– (Fair)-rated insurers generally have demonstrated a fair ability to meet their policyholder and other contractual obligations.

Table 7.5 (continued)

Rating	Application	Explanation
c (Contingent Rating)	Life and Property/Casualty	Temporarily assigned to a company when there has been a decline in performance in its profitability, leverage, and/or liquidity but the decline has not been significant enough to warrant an actual reduction in the company's previously assigned rating. Best's evaluation may be based on the availability of more current information and/or be contingent on the successful execution by management of a program of corrective action.
q (Qualified Rating)	Property/Casualty	Indicates the company's assigned rating has been qualified to recognize that it has payments due from state-mandated funding programs which were equal to or exceed its policyholders' surplus.
w (Watch List)	Life and Property/Casualty	Indicates the company was placed on Best's rating "Watch List" during the year because it experienced a downward trend in profitability, leverage, and/or liquidity performance, but the decline was not significant enough to warrant an actual reduction in the assigned rating.
x (Revised Rating)	Life and Property/Casualty	Indicates the company's assigned rating was revised during the year to the rating shown.
s (Consolidated Rating)	Property/Casualty	Indicates the rating is assigned to a parent company and is based on the consolidated performance of the company and its domestic property/casualty subsidiaries in which ownership exceeds 50%. The rating applies only to the parent company, as subsidiaries are normally rated on the basis of their own financial condition and performance.
e (Parent Rating)	Life and Property/Casualty	Indicates the rating assigned is that of the parent of a domestic subsidiary in which ownership exceeds 50% and is based on the consolidatd performance of the parent and subsidiary. To qualify, the subsidiary must be eligible for a rating based on its own performance after attaining five consecutive years of representative experience; have common management with the parent; underwrite similar classes of business; and have interim leverage and liquidity performance comparable to that of its parent.

Table 7.5 (continued)

Rating	Application	Explanation
r (Reinsured Rating)	Life and Property/Casualty	Indicates that the rating and financial size category assigned to the company are those of an affiliated carrier which reinsures 100% of the company's written net business.
p (Pooled Rating)	Life and Property/Casualty	Assigned to companies under common management or ownership which pool 100% of their net business. All premiums, expenses, and losses are prorated in accordance with specified percentages that reasonably relate to the distribution of the policyholders' surplus of each member in the group. All members participating in the pooling arrangement are assigned the same rating and financial size category, based on the consolidated performance of the group.
g (Group Rating)	Property/Casualty	To qualify for a "Group" rating, the companies in the group must be affiliated via common management and/or ownership, pool a substantial portion of their net business, and have only minor differences in their underwriting and operating performance. All members are assigned the same rating and financial size category, based on the consolidated performance of the group.

"Not Assigned" Ratings Classifications

NA-1 Special Data Filing	Life and Property/Casualty	Assigned primarily to small mutuals, exempt from the requirement to file the standard NAIC Fire & Casualty Annual Statement blank. Their report is based on selected financial information requested by the A. M. Best Company and submitted via a cooperative program with the National Association of Mutual Insurance Companies. The data for each company has been reviewed by a certified public accountant auditor for compliance with NAIC annual statement instructions. While the information obtained from these sources is believed to be reliable, its accuracy is not guaranteed by either the A. M. Best Company or the National Association of Mutual Insurance Companies.

Table 7.5 (continued)

Rating	Application	Explanation
NA-2 Less than Minimum Size	Life and Property/Casualty	Assigned to a company whose admitted assets or annual gross premiums written do not meet Best's minimum size requirement of $3.5 million. It is also assigned to a company which is virtually dormant or has no net insurance business in force. Exceptions are a company that is 100% reinsured by a rated company, or is a member of a group participating in a business pooling arrangement, or was formerly assigned a rating.
NA-3 Insufficient Experience	Life and Property/Casualty	Assigned to a company which has not accumulated at least five consecutive years of representative operating experience. Additional years of experience may be required if the company is principally engaged in "long tail" casualty lines (such as professional malpractice liability) whereby the development and payment pattern of the loss reserves may not be sufficiently mature at the end of five years to permit a satisfactory evaluation of their adequacy.
NA-4 Rating Procedure Inapplicable	Life and Property/Casualty	Assigned to a company when the nature of its operations and/or mix of business are such that Best's normal rating procedures for insurers do not properly apply. Examples are companies which have discontinued writing new business and are in a run-off position; or companies whose sole insurance operation is the acceptance of business written directly by a parent, subsidiary, or affiliated insurance company; or companies retaining only a small portion of their premiums written; or companies not soliciting business in the United States.
NA-5 Significant Change	Life and Property/Casualty	Assigned to a previously rated company which experiences a significant change in ownership, management, or book of business whereby its operating experience may be interrupted or subject to change. Depending on the nature of the change, Best's procedure may require a period of one to five years to elapse before the company is eligible for a rating.

Table 7.5 (continued)

Rating	Application	Explanation
NA-6 Reinsured by Unrated Reinsurer	Life and Property/Casualty	Assigned to a company which has a substantial portion of its book of business reinsured by unrated reinsurers and/or has reinsurance recoverables which exceed its policyholders' surplus due from unrated reinsurers. Exceptions are unrated foreign reinsurers that comply with Best's reporting requirements and satisfy Best's financial performance standards.
NA-7 Below Minimum Standards	Life and Property/Casualty	Assigned to a company that meets Best's minimum size and experience requirements, but does not meet the minimum standards for a Best's rating of C–.
NA-8 Incomplete Financial Information	Life and Property/Casualty	Assigned to a company which fails to submit, prior to Best's rating deadline, complete financial information for the current five-year period under review. This requirement also includes all domestic subsidiaries in which the company's ownership exceeds 50%.
NA-9 Company Request	Life and Property/Casualty	Assigned when a company is eligible for a rating but disputes Best's rating assignment or procedure. If company subsequently requests a rating assignment, Best's policy normally requires a minimum period of three years to elapse before the company is eligible for a rating.
NA-10 Under State Supervision	Life and Property/Casualty	Assigned when a company is under conservatorship, rehabilitation, receivership, or any other form of supervision, control, or restraint by state regulatory authorities.

7.6 TRENDS IN LIFE INSURANCE PURCHASES

Table 7.6 shows trends in the purchase of life insurance policies since 1970. While the total amount purchased annually shows a steady upward trend, the mix of ordinary insurance purchases between whole life and term changed dramatically in 1988 from previous years. The total number of life insurance policies purchased increased steadily over the period surveyed until 1986 and then declined in each of the following two years.

Table 7.6 Life Insurance Purchasers in the United States, 1970–1989

YEAR	NUMBER OF POLICIES PURCHASED (1,000)						AMOUNT PURCHASED (bil. dol.)					
	Total	Ordinary			Group	Indus-trial	Total [3]	Ordinary			Group [3]	Indus-trial
		Total	Percent—					Total	Percent—			
			Whole life [1]	Term [2]					Whole life [1]	Term [2]		
1970	23,769	10,968	90	10	5,219	7,582	193.1	122.8	59	41	63.7	6.6
1980	29,007	14,750	78	22	11,379	2,878	572.6	385.6	43	57	183.4	3.6
1981	29,552	15,838	77	23	11,923	1,791	831.1	481.9	41	59	346.7	2.5
1982	28,894	15,614	76	24	11,930	1,350	837.9	585.4	40	60	250.5	1.9
1983	32,021	17,737	77	23	13,450	834	1,026.4	753.4	47	53	271.6	1.4
1984	33,012	17,695	77	23	14,605	712	1,114.8	820.3	55	45	293.5	0.9
1985	33,880	17,104	78	22	16,243	533	1,231.2	910.9	62	38	319.5	0.7
1986	34,623	16,811	77	23	17,507	305	1,308.8	933.6	61	39	374.7	0.4
1987	33,153	16,225	75	25	16,698	230	1,352.5	986.7	57	43	365.5	0.3
1988	31,589	15,579	81	19	15,793	217	1,406.9	995.7	61	39	410.8	0.3
1989	29,960	14,694	80	20	15,110	156	1,441.7	1,020.7	59	41	420.7	0.3

[1] Life insurance payable to a beneficiary at the death of the insured whenever that occurs. Premiums may be payable for a specified number of years or for life. Includes a small number of endowment and retirement income policies. [2] Life insurance payable to a beneficiary only when an insured dies within a specified period. [3] Includes Servicemen's Group Life Insurance: $17.1 billion in 1970, $45.6 billion in 1981, and $51.0 billion in 1986; as well as Federal Employees' Group Life Insurance: $84.4 billion in 1981 and $10.8 billion in 1986.

Source: American Council of Life Insurance, *Life Insurance Fact Book*, (Washington, D.C.: American Council of Life Insurance, biennial).

7.7 TRENDS IN LIFE INSURANCE IN FORCE

Table 7.7 shows trends from 1970 in life insurance in force, including average policy sizes and average amounts per household. Average amount of coverage per insured household has more than quadrupled since 1970 while disposable personal income per household increased at a somewhat lower rate. Average policy size for ordinary, group, and credit life insurance in force increased in each year surveyed.

7.8 AVERAGE DAILY HOSPITAL ROOM CHARGES

Table 7.8 shows the trends in average daily hospital room charge, average cost per day, and average cost per stay by state. Clearly, hospital costs are rising dramatically, thus underscoring the need for comprehensive and continuous health insurance coverage.

Table 7.7 Life Insurance in Force in the United States, 1970–1989

YEAR	LIFE INSURANCE IN FORCE						AVERAGE SIZE POLICY IN FORCE (dollars)				AVERAGE AMOUNT ($1,000)		Disposable personal income per household ($1,000)
	Number of policies, total (mil.)	Value (bil. dol.)					Ordinary	Group	Industrial	Credit [1]	Per household	Per insured household	
		Total	Ordinary	Group	Industrial	Credit [1]							
1970	355	1,402	731	545	39	88	6,110	6,910	500	1,000	22.1	26.6	11.3
1980	402	3,541	1,761	1,579	36	165	11,920	13,410	620	2,110	43.8	53.5	23.7
1981	400	4,064	1,978	1,889	35	162	13,310	15,400	630	2,220	49.3	60.2	25.8
1982	390	4,477	2,217	2,066	33	161	15,140	16,630	630	2,410	53.6	66.2	27.1
1983	387	4,966	2,544	2,220	31	171	17,380	17,530	630	2,650	59.2	73.1	28.9
1984	385	5,500	2,888	2,392	30	190	19,970	18,780	630	2,880	64.5	79.6	31.3
1985	386	6,053	3,247	2,562	28	216	22,780	19,720	640	3,100	69.7	86.1	32.7
1986	391	6,720	3,658	2,801	27	234	25,540	20,720	650	3,310	76.0	93.8	34.1
1987	395	7,452	4,139	3,043	27	243	28,510	22,380	650	3,330	82.8	102.2	35.6
1988	391	8,020	4,512	3,232	26	251	31,390	23,410	660	3,570	87.6	108.2	38.0
1989	394	8,694	4,940	3,469	24	260	34,410	24,510	670	3,600	93.6	115.5	40.7

[1] Insures borrower to cover consumer loan in case of death.

Source: American Council of Life Insurance, *Life Insurance Fact Book*, (Washington, D.C.: American Council of Life Insurance, biennial).

7.9 INDEXES OF MEDICAL CARE PRICES

Table 7.9 reflects, both in terms of an index and annual percentage changes, the increases in medical care services from 1970. Of the components shown, hospital room costs have risen most dramatically, although the rate of annual increases of these costs as well as the other has begun to slow somewhat but still outpaces inflation.

7.10 TAXATION OF LIFE INSURANCE

Careful planning of a client's life insurance program can minimize both income and estate taxation. This section provides a summary of key tax considerations pertaining to life insurance.

7.10.1 Life Insurance Premiums

7.10.1.1 Employer-paid group term An employee must include in his or her taxable income the cost of any group term life insurance over $50,000 provided by his employer. If, for example, an employee received $80,000 worth of insurance coverage, $30,000 of insurance coverage would be

Table 7.8 Indexes of Medical Care Prices, 1970–1990

YEAR	Index, total	MEDICAL CARE SERVICES					Medical care commodities [2]	ANNUAL PERCENT CHANGE					Medical care commodities [2]
		Total [1]	Professional services			Hospital room		Total [1]	Medical care services				
			Total [1]	Physicians	Dental				Total [1]	Physicians	Dental	Hospital room	
1970	34.0	32.3	37.0	34.5	39.2	23.6	46.5	[3]6.6	[3]7.0	[3]7.5	[3]5.7	[3]12.9	[3]2.4
1975	47.5	46.6	50.8	48.1	53.2	38.3	53.3	12.0	12.6	12.1	10.4	17.1	8.3
1977	57.0	56.4	60.0	58.5	60.8	48.6	60.2	9.6	9.9	9.3	7.6	11.5	6.5
1978	61.8	61.2	64.5	63.4	65.1	54.0	64.4	8.4	8.5	8.4	7.1	11.1	7.0
1979	67.5	67.2	70.1	69.2	70.5	60.1	69.0	9.2	9.8	9.1	8.3	11.3	0.1
1980	74.9	74.8	77.9	76.5	78.9	68.0	75.4	11.0	11.3	10.5	11.9	13.1	9.3
1981	82.9	82.8	85.9	84.9	86.5	78.1	83.7	10.7	10.7	11.0	9.6	14.9	11.0
1982	92.5	92.6	93.2	92.9	93.1	90.4	92.3	11.6	11.8	9.4	7.6	15.7	10.3
1983	100.6	100.7	99.8	100.1	99.4	100.6	100.2	8.8	8.7	7.8	6.8	11.3	8.6
1984	106.8	106.7	107.0	107.0	107.5	109.0	107.5	6.2	6.0	6.9	8.1	8.3	7.3
1985	113.5	113.2	113.5	113.3	114.2	115.4	115.2	6.3	6.1	5.9	6.2	5.9	7.2
1986	122.0	121.9	120.8	121.5	120.6	122.3	122.8	7.5	7.7	7.2	5.6	6.0	6.6
1987	130.1	130.0	128.8	130.4	128.8	131.1	131.0	6.6	6.6	7.3	6.8	7.2	6.7
1988	138.6	138.3	137.5	139.8	137.5	143.3	139.9	6.5	6.4	7.2	6.8	9.3	6.8
1989	149.3	148.9	146.4	150.1	146.1	158.1	150.8	7.7	7.7	7.4	6.3	10.3	7.8
1990	162.8	162.7	156.1	160.8	155.8	175.4	163.4	9.0	9.3	7.1	6.6	10.9	8.4

[1] As of January. Source: Health Insurance Association of America, Washington, DC, *Source Book of Health Insurance Data*, (Washington, D.C.: Health Insurance Association of America, 1989), and *Survey of Hospital Semi-Private Room Changes*, (Washington, D.C.: Health Insurance Association of America, annual).

Source: Except as noted, American Hospital Association, *Hospital Statistics* (Chicago: American Hospital Association, annual), and unpublished data.

subject to tax. If the annual cost for this policy were $5 per $1,000 coverage, then $150 (30 × $5) would be includable in the employee's taxable income. This $50,000 limit applies to group term life insurance coverage which an employee receives during any part of the tax year.

7.10.1.2 Split-dollar insurance An employee receiving split-dollar insurance coverage must report as taxable income an amount equal to the one-year term cost of the insurance protection to which he or she is entitled, less any portion of the premium provided by the employee. If the term cost of $80,000 insurance provided by the employer is $590, the employee pays tax on $590, less his or her premium payment (if the employee paid $210 premium, he/she would pay tax on $590 − $210 = $380).

7.10.2 Life Insurance Proceeds

7.10.2.1 Lump Sum Life insurance proceeds paid because of the death of an insured person are generally not taxable. This exclusion applies to death

Table 7.9 Average Daily Hospital Room Charges, 1980–1988

STATE	AVERAGE DAILY ROOM CHARGE [1]			AVERAGE COST PER DAY		AVERAGE COST PER STAY		STATE	AVERAGE DAILY ROOM CHARGE [1]			AVERAGE COST PER DAY		AVERAGE COST PER STAY	
	1980	1985	1990	1980	1988	1980	1988		1980	1985	1990	1980	1988	1980	1988
U.S.	127	212	315	245	586	1,851	4,207	MO	107	185	259	230	578	1,848	4,288
AL	96	161	225	209	506	1,459	3,471	MT	113	201	294	160	354	1,321	3,312
AK	189	295	407	408	961	2,276	5,616	NE	100	155	208	194	414	1,526	4,093
AZ	106	191	296	290	760	2,013	4,527	NV	125	243	285	343	763	2,201	4,840
AR	86	140	180	185	463	1,172	2,994	NH	125	200	321	203	546	1,432	3,685
CA	161	281	452	362	804	2,395	5,061	NJ	146	183	271	212	510	1,850	3,774
CO	124	211	326	247	627	1,760	4,432	NM	115	193	252	263	670	1,549	3,793
CT	127	206	434	271	685	2,039	5,065	NY	157	228	415	257	530	2,469	5,070
DE	125	214	385	238	628	1,937	4,391	NC	87	139	215	187	487	1,397	3,538
DC	170	274	325	358	811	3,189	6,150	ND	93	173	236	177	377	1,528	3,869
FL	109	181	277	247	646	1,803	4,506	OH	139	228	307	241	612	1,907	4,173
GA	92	150	197	218	516	1,380	3,488	OK	101	162	224	239	547	1,527	3,632
HI	127	231	349	245	517	1,868	4,651	OR	133	225	375	277	703	1,671	3,833
ID	110	197	259	208	457	1,251	3,151	PA	132	255	408	234	583	1,947	4,370
IL	144	248	326	277	633	2,183	4,646	RI	138	206	365	260	546	2,162	4,396
IN	107	184	271	214	572	1,620	3,750	SC	80	145	212	186	474	1,367	3,347
IA	107	179	220	199	432	1,465	3,547	SD	96	161	206	189	360	1,265	3,214
KS	104	183	267	207	448	1,592	3,498	TN	91	140	196	204	517	1,427	3,545
KY	92	175	266	189	485	1,268	3,108	TX	91	159	228	226	628	1,491	3,884
LA	89	154	220	233	605	1,492	3,784	UT	112	173	338	271	737	1,462	3,879
ME	124	208	330	217	475	1,707	3,808	VT	116	209	374	183	491	1,472	3,588
MD	119	186	277	251	579	2,136	3,997	VA	101	165	228	211	529	1,647	3,690
MA	151	229	404	294	671	2,578	5,225	WA	125	229	346	262	708	1,502	3,984
MI	151	267	338	267	644	2,087	4,712	WV	110	166	240	195	494	1,393	3,319
MN	105	187	281	203	458	1,818	4,103	WI	104	166	223	218	484	1,765	3,583
MS	67	113	162	174	375	1,178	2,593	WY	98	173	242	242	416	1,189	3,107

[1] As of January. Source: Health Insurance Association of America, Washington, DC, *Source Book of Health Insurance Data*, 1990, and *Survey of Hospital Semi-Private Room Charges*, annual.
Source: Except as noted, American Hospital Association, Chicago, IL, *Hospital Statistics*, annual (coypright); and unpublished data.

benefits under worker's compensation insurance and employers' group insurance plans, but not to a policy combined with a nonrefund life annuity contract for which a single premium equal to the insurance's face value is paid.

7.10.2.2 Installment Payments Life insurance proceeds received in installments are tax free for the amount that does not include interest income. To determine the excludable part of an insurance payment, divide the face value of the policy by the number of years the installments are to be paid. For example, if a policy beneficiary elects to take annual installment payments for 10 years on a $150,000 policy, each year $15,000 could be received tax free. If the beneficiary is the surviving spouse of a policy holder who died before October 23, 1986, an additional $1,000 of interest paid with an annual installment may be received tax free (so in the example, the beneficiary could receive $16,000 tax free).

7.10.2.3 Interest Option If a life insurance beneficiary chooses to leave the proceeds with an insurance company under an agreement to pay interest only, then the interest paid to the beneficiary is taxable. The $1,000 exclusion for the spouse for a policyholder who died before October 23, 1986 does not apply to the interest option.

7.10.2.4 Payments to Beneficiaries of Deceased Beneficiaries of a deceased employee can exclude from income the first $5,000 of death benefits paid by or for an employer. The amount cannot be greater than $5,000, regardless of the number of employers or beneficiaries. This exclusion does not apply to amounts to which the employee had a guaranteed right to receive had death not occurred. If the deceased employee was receiving a retirement annuity which will be continued to be paid to a beneficiary under a joint and survivor annuity option, these payments are taxable. However, the exclusion does apply where a lump-sum distribution of an employee's interest payable from an exempt pension, profit-sharing, or stock bonus trust is paid to a beneficiary within one of his or her tax years. Whether or not payments received by a surviving spouse from the deceased spouse's employer are treated as excludable gifts or taxable income has been a subject of controversy; if the payments are income, then the $5,000 exclusion applies.

7.10.3 Estate Tax Planning

When the holder of an insurance policy pays premiums, the value of his or her contract increases tax free at compound interest rates, and when the policy is paid at death, its proceeds are not subject to income tax. These features mean that insurance provides a tax-free accumulation of cash that can be valuable for estate tax planning. In order to shelter life insurance proceeds from estate tax, the policyholder must not have ownership rights—the right to change beneficiaries, to surrender or cancel the policy, or to borrow against it must all be assigned to someone else more than three years before the policyholder's death. Irrevocable life insurance trusts can be used to prevent life insurance proceeds from being subject to estate taxation.

If a taxpayer creates a trust to carry a policy on his or her life by transferring property, the income from which is used to pay the premiums, the trust income is taxable. If the taxpayer's spouse creates the trust to carry the policy on the taxpayer's life, the spouse is taxable on the income as well. This rule does not apply on the trust funding of life insurance covering a third party other than a spouse.

7.11   STATE INSURANCE DEPARTMENTS

Each state has its own laws and regulations governing all types of insurance. The offices listed in Table 7.10 are responsible for enforcing these laws, as well as providing the public with information about insurance.

Table 7.10 State Insurance Department

Alabama
Alabama Insurance Department
135 South Union Street
Montgomery, AL 36130-3401
(205) 269-3550

Alaska
Alaska Insurance Department
3601 C Street, Suite 722
Anchorage, AK 99503
(907) 562-3626

American Samoma
American Samoa Insurance
    Department
Office of the Governor
Pago Pago, AS 96797
(011-684) 633-4116

Arizona
Arizona Insurance Department
Consumer Affairs and
Investigation Division
3030 N. Third Street
Phoenix, AZ 85012
(602) 255-4783

Arkansas
Arkansas Insurance Department
Consumer Service Division
400 University Tower Bldg.
12th and University Streets
Little Rock, AR 72204
(501) 371-1813

California
California Insurance Department
Consumer Services Division
100 Van Ness Avenue
San Francisco, CA 94102
1-(800) 233-9045
        or
600 S. Commonwealth Avenue
Los Angeles, CA 90005
1-(800) 233-9045

Colorado
Colorado Insurance Division
303 West Colfax Avenue

5th Floor
Denver, CO 80204
(303) 620-4300

Connecticut
Connecticut Insurance
    Department
165 Capitol Avenue
State Office Building
Room 425
Hartford, CT 06106
(203)566-5275

Delaware
Delaware Insurance Department
841 Silver Lake Boulevard
Dover, DE 19901
(302) 736-4251

District of Columbia
District of Columbia Insurance
614 H Street, NW
Suite 512
Washington, DC 20001
(202) 783-3191

Florida
Florida Department of Insurance
State Capitol
Plaza Level Eleven (11)
Tallahassee, FL 32399-0300
(904) 488-0030

Georgia
Georgia Insurance Department
2 Martin L. King, Jr., Dr.
7th Floor West Tower
Atlanta, GA 30334
(404) 656-2056

Guam
Guam Insurance Department
P.O. Box 2796
Agana, Guam 96910 or
855 West Marine Drive
(011-671) 477-1040

Hawaii
Hawaii Department of Commerce
and Consumer Affairs

Insurance Division
P.O. Box 3614
Honolulu, HI 96811
(808) 548-5450

Idaho
Idaho Insurance Department
Public Service Department
500 South 10th Street
Boise, ID 83720
(208) 334-2250

Illinois
Illinois Insurance Department
320 West Washington Street
4th Floor
Springfield, IL 62767
(217) 782-4515

Indiana
Indiana Insurance Department
311 West Washington Street
Suite 300
Indianapolis, IN 46204
(317) 232-2395

Iowa
Iowa Insurance Division
Lucas State Office Bldg.
E. 12 & Walnut Sts.
6th Floor
Des Moines, IA 50319
(515) 281-5705

Kansas
Kansas Insurance Department
420 S.W. 9th Street
Topeka, KS 66612
(913) 296-3071

Kentucky
Kentucky Insurance Department
229 West Main Street
P.O. Box 517
Frankfort, KY 40602
(502) 564-3630

Louisiana
Louisiana Insurance Department
P.O. Box 94214
Baton Rouge, LA 70804-9214
(504) 342-5900

Maine
Maine Bureau of Insurance
Consumer Division
State House, Station 34
Augusta, ME 04333
(207) 582-8707

Maryland
Maryland Insurance Department
Complaints and Investigation Unit
501 St. Paul Place
Baltimore, MD 21202-2272
(301) 333-2792

Massachusetts
Massachusetts Insurance Division
Consumer Services Section
280 Friend Street
Boston, MA 02114
(617) 727-3357

Michigan
Michigan Insurance Department
P.O. Box 30220
Lansing, MI 48909
(517) 373-0220

Minnesota
Minnesota Insurance Department
Department of Commerce
500 Metro Square Building
Junction of 7th & Roberts Sts.
St. Paul, MN 55101
(612) 296-4026

Mississippi
Mississippi Insurance Department
Consumer Assistance Division
P.O. Box 79
Jackson, MS 39205
(601) 359-3569

Missouri
Missouri Division of Insurance
Consumer Services Section
P.O. Box 690
Jefferson City, MO 65102-0690
(314) 751-2640

Montana
Montana Insurance Department
126 North Sanders

Mitchell Building
P.O. Box 4009, Room 270
Helena, MT 59604
(406) 444-2040

Nebraska
Nebraska Insurance Department
Terminal Building
941 O Street, Suite 400
Lincoln, NE 68508
(402) 471-2201

Nevada
Nevada Department of Commerce
Insurance Division
Consumer Section
201 South Fall Street,
Room 316
Carson City, NV 89701
(702) 885-4270

New Hampshire
New Hampshire Insurance
Department
Life and Health Division
169 Manchester Street
Concord, NH 03301
(603) 271-2261

New Jersey
New Jersey Insurance Department
20 West State Street
Roebling Building
Trenton, NJ 08625
(609) 292-4757

New Mexico
New Mexico Insurance Department
P.O. Box 1269
Santa Fe, NM 87504-1269
(505) 827-4500

New York
New York Insurance Department
160 West Broadway
New York, NY 10013
New York City
(212) 602-0203
Toll Free
(within State outside of NYC)
1-(800) 342-3736

North Carolina
North Carolina Insurance
Department
Consumer Insurance Information
Dobbs Building
P.O. Box 26387
Raleigh, NC 27611
(919) 733-2004

North Dakota
North Dakota Insurance Department
Capitol Building
Fifth Floor
Bismarck, ND 58505
(701) 224-2440

Ohio
Ohio Insurance Department
Consumer Services Division
2100 Stella Court
Columbus, OH 43215
(614) 644-2673

Oklahoma
Oklahoma Insurance Department
P.O. Box 53408
Oklahoma City, OK
73152-3408
(405) 521-2828

Oregon
Oregon Department of Insurance
and Finance
Insurance Division/Consumer
Advocate
21 Labor and Industry Bldg.
Salem, OR 93710
(503) 378-4484

Pennsylvania
Pennsylvania Insurance
Department
1326 Strawberry Square
Harrisburg, PA 17120
(717) 787-3289

Puerto Rico
Puerto Rico Insurance Department
Fernandez Juncos Station
P.O. Box 8330

Santurce, PR 00910
(809) 722-8686

Rhode Island
Rhode Island Insurance Division
233 Richmond Street
Suite 233
Providence, RI 02903-4233
(401) 277-2223

South Carolina
South Carolina Insurance
  Department
Consumer Assistance Section
P.O. Box 100105
Columbia, SC 29202-3105
(803) 737-6140

South Dakota
South Dakota Insurance
  Department Enforcement
500 E. Capitol
Pierre, SD 57501
(605) 773-3563

Tennessee
Tennessee Insurance Department
Department of Commerce and
  Insurance
Policyholders Service Section
1880 West End Avenue
14th Floor
Nashville, TN 37219-5318
1-(800) 342-4031

Texas
Texas Board of Insurance
Complaints Division
1110 San Jacinto Blvd.
Austin, TX 78701-1998
(512) 463-6501

Utah
Utah Insurance Department
Consumer Services
P.O. Box 45803
Salt Lake City, UT 84145
(801) 530-6400

Vermont
Vermont Department of Banking
  and Insurance
Consumer Complaint Division
120 State Street
Montpelier, VT 05602
(802) 828-3301

Virgin Islands
Virgin Islands Insurance
  Department
Kongens Garde No. 18
St. Thomas, VI 00802
(809) 774-2991

Virginia
Virginia Insurance Department
Consumer Services Division
700 Jefferson Building
P.O. Box 1157
Richmond, VA 23209
(804) 786-7691

Washington
Washington Insurance Department
Insurance Building AQ21
Olympia, WA 98504
(206) 753-7300

West Virginia
West Virginia Insurance
  Department
2019 Washington Street, E
Charleston, WV 25305
(304) 348-3386

Wisconsin
Wisconsin Insurance Department
Complaints Department
P.O. Box 7873
Madison, WI 53707
(608) 266-0103

Wyoming
Wyoming Insurance Department
Herschler Building
122 West 25th Street
Cheyenne, WY 82002
(307) 777-7401

Chapter 8_____

CREDIT MANAGEMENT

Credit is a double-edged sword. On the one hand, it enables individuals to pursue wealth building strategies such as investing in real estate, borrowing on margin, or starting and expanding a business. It permits people to pay gradually for goods and services. And equally important, it allows individuals to deal promptly with financial emergencies without draining their savings and other personal resources.

On the other hand, its easy availability, along with the high interest rates on some forms of consumer credit, makes overextension a problem that is being seen with increasing frequency. In fact, the tightening of credit and the rise in loan delinquency rates in 1991 will, in all likelihood, spill over into 1992. This rising delinquency rate will result in negative credit ratings, repossessions, and bankruptcies and will severely restrict the use of credit by many individuals in the future.

The role of the financial professional in the area of personal credit management is to advise the client on the amount and type of credit that are best suited for his or her needs. The first step in this process is a review of current debts, including mortgages, installment loans, and outstanding credit card balances. By doing this, the professional can ascertain approximate debt service burden and detect signs of overextension.

After the initial review, investment professionals should also project short-term borrowing requirements such as large tax liabilities and annual bills, as well as longer-term ones such as contemplated home improvements.

The sound use of credit involves knowing not only how much to borrow, but which type of loan to utilize and how to evaluate its terms. This is especially true today, because of the limitations on the deductibility of certain types of interest, for example, consumer interest.

The popularity of home equity loans has increased enormously over the last several years because the interest on them remains deductible in most instances. While home equity loans can be a cost-effective, tax-advantaged source of credit, the financial professional should guard against their overuse by individuals. The most serious potential problem is that if a borrower falls behind in payments, the home is at risk. The variable interest rates attached to many of these loans can lead to an unanticipated rise in payments. Finally, the application fees and other costs associated with such loans, combined with the lower tax rates, may make the resulting tax savings of marginal benefit to the borrower. For these reasons, the terms and interest rates available on home equity loans should be compared with other sources of credit to best determine the most cost-effective method of borrowing.

The 1990s are likely to bear witness to a much more prudent approach to personal credit management—something that was lacking in the previous decade. Whether they were overextended or not, many people will strive to eliminate or at least reduce their personal indebtedness in order to prepare better for a more secure financial future.

8.1   PREPARING A PERSONAL BALANCE SHEET

Prospective borrowers are usually required to prepare a personal balance sheet, sometimes referred to as a net worth statement, which lists assets and liabilities in dollar terms as of a specific time. Personal balance sheets should also be prepared periodically for the purpose of evaluating a client's current financial position. This section includes a sample personal balance sheet (Figure 8.1) as well as suggestions on how to prepare it.

Personal balance sheets are almost identical to business balance sheets. Balance sheets list *assets* and *liabilities*. *Net worth* is found by subtracting total liabilities from total assets. The following explanations will help the client fill out a reasonably accurate personal balance sheet which will not only be helpful when applying for a loan, but will also assist in monitoring financial progress. By periodically preparing a personal balance sheet, say, once per year, the client will be able to gauge his or her progress as indicated by the change in net worth.

Figure 8.1 provides a typical personal balance sheet used by many lenders. It includes a personal balance sheet and supplementary financial data.

Assets should be realistically valued. Any overstatement of their actual market value will result in a corresponding overstatement of net worth. The most difficult assets to value are real estate, including the home, and automobiles and other personal property. Many people tend to think that their home is worth more than it actually is, particularly since housing prices have been flat or declining in many areas of the country. Also, remember that personal property such as furniture and clothing is not worth very much if it has to be sold.

Liabilities include debt outstanding on a home mortgage, automobile, credit cards, and so forth. Be sure to remind the client to list *all* liabilities.

Just as many people tend to overstate the value of their assets, others fail to remember all of their liabilities.

Net worth is simply the difference between total assets and total liabilities. Over time, of course, client net worth should rise. One additional step that is often useful is to analyze the cause of changes in client net worth over time. For example, an increase in net worth caused solely by the (perceived) increase in the value of the family home is far different from an increase in net worth caused by interest and capital gains income and additional personal savings.

8.2   CREDIT BUREAU REPORTS

Before they apply for credit, prospective borrowers should review their credit reports. This record of the borrower's bill paying history also takes into account factors like an individual's age and type—and duration—of employment. Recent studies have shown that a significant percentage of credit bureau reports contain erroneous information. The sooner that any errors are discovered and corrected, the better. Information on obtaining, evaluating, and, if necessary, correcting a credit bureau report is discussed in this section.

When an individual applies for credit, the first step the lender usually takes is to check that individual's credit rating to determine whether he or she poses a credit risk. Unfortunately, credit ratings—which many borrowers never see—don't always fairly reflect the borrower's true credit-worthiness. While borrowers' promptness in paying the rent, and in settling utility, medical, and American Express bills may not affect their credit ratings, mismanaged MasterCard or Visa accounts or unpaid department store bills could have damaging effects.

Recently, the media has focused attention on issues of credit agency accuracy, and as a number of investigations of certain industry heavyweights have shown, credit reports may well contain erroneous information. Furthermore, credit agencies sometimes break the law by including debtor information in credit reports that should not be used in calculating credit ratings. For example, despite regulations governing the industry, borrowers who have withheld payment on a bill over a dispute with a creditor over goods or services purchased may find that their credit reports state that they have defaulted on a legitimate obligation. Married women—despite the Equal Credit Opportunity Act—may have their credit performances reported under their husbands' names, leaving them with no credit history.

8.2.1 How to Request a Report

As the preceding discussion shows all too well, it is important that individuals periodically check their credit reports. Even if the borrower has

FIGURE 8.1 PERSONAL BALANCE SHEET

If you are applying for credit jointly with another person, or securing credit through another's assets or income, fill in all information for yourself as applicant and for the other person as co-applicant. Co-applicants will be asked to sign documents in evidence of liability for credit extended. You need not include information about your spouse unless he or she is the co-applicant. We are not always required to consider the full value of jointly-held assets in our evaluation of individual requests for credit.

Personal Financial Statement as of |___|___|___| **(date).**

I. PERSONAL INFORMATION (Type or print)

Name

Residence Address

City, State, Zip

Residence Phone (   )

Social Security #   Date of Birth

Position or Occupation

Business Name

Business Address

City, State, Zip

Business Phone (   )

II. JOINT APPLICATION INFORMATION

Name

Residence Address

City, State, Zip

Residence Phone (   )

Social Security #   Date of Birth

Position or Occupation

Business Name

Business Address

City, State, Zip

Business Phone (   )

III. PERSONAL FINANCIAL INFORMATION

Assets (Do not include Assets of doubtful value)	In Dollars (Omit Cents)	Liabilities	In Dollars (Omit Cents)
Cash on hand and in banks - see Schedule A		Notes payable to banks (secured) - see Schedule F	
U.S. Gov't. & Marketable Securities - see Schedule B		Notes payable to banks (unsecured) - see Schedule F	
Non-Marketable Securities - see Schedule C		Due to brokers - see Schedule F	
Securities held by broker in margin accounts		Amounts payable to others - secured - see Schedule F	
Restricted or control stocks		Amounts payable to others - unsecured - see Schedule F	
Partial Interest in Real Estate Equities - see Schedule D		Accounts and bills due	
Real Estate Owned - see Schedule D		Unpaid income tax	
Loans Receivable		Other unpaid taxes and interest	
Automobiles and other personal property		Real estate mortgages payable - see Schedule D	
Cash value - life insurance - see Schedule E		Other debts - itemize	
Other assets - itemize			
		TOTAL LIABILITIES	
		NET WORTH	
TOTAL ASSETS		TOTAL LIABILITIES AND NET WORTH	

IV. PERSONAL INCOME AND CONTINGENT LIABILITIES

Salary, bonuses & commissions $

Dividends $

Real estate income $

Other income (Alimony, child support, or separate maintenance income need $
not be revealed if you do not wish to have it considered as a basis for repaying
this obligation)

TOTAL $

Contingent Liabilities

Do you have any contingent liabilities? ☐ Yes ☐ No   If so, describe

As endorser, co-maker or guarantor? ☐ Yes ☐ No $

On leases or contracts? ☐ Yes ☐ No $

Legal claims? ☐ Yes ☐ No $

Other special debt? ☐ Yes ☐ No $

Contested income tax liens? ☐ Yes ☐ No $

V. MISCELLANEOUS INFORMATION

Do you have a will? ☐ Yes ☐ No   If so, name of executor

Are you a partner or officer in any other venture? ☐ Yes ☐ No   If so, describe

Are you obligated to pay alimony, child support, or separate maintenance payments? ☐ Yes ☐ No   If so, describe

Are any assets pledged other than as described on schedules? ☐ Yes ☐ No   If so, describe

Income tax settled through (date)

Are you a defendant in any suits or legal actions? ☐ Yes ☐ No   If so, describe

Personal bank accounts carried at:

Have you ever been declared bankrupt? ☐ Yes ☐ No   If so, describe

FIGURE 8.1 (continued)

SCHEDULE A: Cash

| | | | Any outstanding loans secured by this cash | |
Name of Bank/Money Market Fund	Legal Owner(s)	Deposit Balance	Loan Balance	Bank

---

SCHEDULE B: U.S. Governments and Marketable Securities

Number of Shares or Face Value (Bonds)	Description	In Name Of	Market Value Per Share	Total Market Value	Are these Assets Pledged?

SCHEDULE C: Non-Marketable Securities

Number of Shares	Description	In Name Of	% Ownership	Value	Source of Value	Are these Assets Pledged?

SCHEDULE D: Real Estate Equity

	Address Street, City or Town	Title in Name Of	% Ownership	Cost	Market Value
Primary residence					
Property					
Property					

	Monthly Payment	Mortgage Amount Outstanding	Mortgage Maturity	Financial Institution
Primary residence				
Property				
Property				

SCHEDULE E: Life Insurance, including N.S.L.I. and Group Insurance

Name of Insurance Company	Owner of Policy	Beneficiary	Face Amount	Policy Loans	Cash Surrender Value

---

SCHEDULE F: Loan Relationships (Exclusive of Real Estate Loans)

Lender	Original Amount of Loan	Date of Loan	Monthly Payment	Secured or unsecured?	Current Balance Outstanding

---

The information contained in this statement is provided for the purpose of obtaining, or maintaining credit with you on behalf of the undersigned, or persons, firms or corporations in whose behalf the undersigned may either severally or jointly with others, execute a guaranty in your favor. Each undersigned understands that you are relying on the information provided herein (including the designation made as to ownership of property) in deciding to grant or continue credit. Each undersigned represents and warrants that the information provided is true and complete and that you may consider this statement as continuing to be true and correct until a written notice of a change is given to you by the undersigned. You are authorized to make all inquiries you deem necessary to verify the accuracy of the statements made herein, and to determine my/our creditworthiness. You are authorized to answer questions about your credit experience with me/us.

Signature (Individual) _____

Date Signed _____ 19 ___   Signature (Joint Applicant) _____ not yet encountered difficulty in securing credit or a loan, he or she should obtain a copy of the credit report (at a nominal cost) in order to catch any potential problems. The borrower's first step should be to ask his or her bank for the names of the major credit bureaus servicing the area. These companies are also listed in the Yellow Pages under "Credit Bureaus." Once the borrower has located the bureau or bureaus that maintain a report on his or her credit, he or she should write them a letter requesting a copy. This letter should include the borrower's address for the past five years, Social Security number, and a check for the credit agency report fee.

8.2.2 How to Interpret a Report

A credit report, designed for computer processing rather than for reading by the layperson, cannot be easily deciphered unless the reader becomes familiar with the codes and abbreviations useds in these reports. The typical credit report includes a column called "Account Performance," containing the three categories "POS" (positive), "NEG" (negative), and "NON" (not evaluated). Every account that the debtor has had (with a credit card company or department store, for example) will be rated with one of these three codes. An account for which the debtor has always paid bills promptly will, of course, be rated as "POS." Accounts characterized by late payments or nonpayments may be labeled "NON" or "NEG." An occasional month-late payment will not generally affect an account's rating. The report will also include the date when the debtor opened each account, what types of charge accounts the debtor has and the credit lines authorized for these accounts, and the current balance for each account. If the debtor has ever been late in paying a particular account, the report will include the amount owed.

8.2.3 How to Correct Errors

If the borrower finds an error in a report, he or she must contact the particular creditor involved, rather than the credit bureau. Credit bureaus will not correct an error simply because a borrower claims an error exists. When contacting a creditor about an error, the borrower may find it advisable to state that he or she is writing under the provisions of the Fair Credit Reporting Act or the Fair Credit Billing Act.

8.2.4 Debtor Rights

Under the Fair Credit Reporting Act, a debtor has the following rights:

1. To learn the name and address of the consumer reporting agency whose report has adversely affected the debtor's credit or job application.

2. To discover upon request the nature and substance of all information, except medical, that a credit agency has collected about the debtor.

3. To know the sources of such information, except investigative sources.

4. To get the names of all people who have received reports about the debtor within the previous six months or within the previous year if the report was furnished for employment reasons.

5. To have all incomplete or incorrect information investigated and, if any information cannot be verified, to have that information deleted from the file.

6. To have the credit bureau notify—free of charge—all agencies that the debtor requests that the bureau has made an error on the debtor's credit report.

7. To have the debtor's side of any controversy included in a creditor's report, if differences with that creditor cannot be resolved.

8. To have no information sent out that is more than 7 years old (10 years if the debtor has declared bankruptcy), with some exceptions if the individual is applying for an insurance policy or a job.

8.3 INVENTORY OF MORTGAGE LOAN ALTERNATIVES

Table 8.1 summarizes various types of mortgage loans, including advantages and drawbacks. Clients who are contemplating taking out or refinancing a mortgage should be encouraged to review the many available alternatives in order to select the one that best meets their needs.

8.4 INCOME TAX TREATMENT OF INTEREST EXPENSE

A review of the tax treatment of mortgage, investment, and personal interest expenses is presented in this section. Taxpayers are often unsure about the deductibility of the interest on their various debt obligations.

8.4.1 Mortgage Interest

Interest paid on mortgages for up to two residences remains fully deductible subject to some limits. If the taxpayer owns more than two residences, he or she may designate for tax purposes which two are the primary and secondary residences.

The law now distinguishes between mortgages taken out before and after October 14, 1987: on mortgages incurred before that date, all interest taken out on mortgages for up to two residences is deductible; on mortgages incurred after that date, interest may be deductible for debt of up to $1,100,000 on two residences.

Table 8.1 Types of Mortgage Loans

Technique	Description	Considerations
Fixed-rate mortgage	• Fixed Interest rate, usually long term. • Equal monthly payments of principal and interest until debt is paid in full.	• Offers stability and long-term tax advantages. • Limited availability. • Interest rates may be higher than other types of financing. • New fixed rates are rarely assumable.
Variable-rate mortgage	• Interest rate changes based on a financial index, resulting in possible changes in monthly payments, loan term, and/or principal. • May have rate or payment caps.	• Readily available. • Starting interest rate is slightly below market, but payments can increase sharply and frequently if index increases. • Payment caps prevent wide fluctuations in payments but may cause negative amortization. • Rate caps, while rare, limit amount total debt can expand.
Renegotiable rate mortgage (rollover)	• Interest rate and monthly payments are constant for several years; changes possible thereafter. • Long term.	• Less frequent changes in interest rate offer some stability.
Balloon mortgage	• Monthly payments based on fixed interest rate. • Usually short term.	• Offers low monthly payments but possibly no equity until loan is fully paid.

Table 8.1 (continued)

Technique	Description	Considerations
Balloon mortgage	• Payments may cover interest only with principal due in full at term end.	• When due, loan must be paid off or refinanced. • Refinancing poses high risk if rates climb.
Graduated payment mortgage	• Lower monthly payments rise gradually (usually over 5 to 10 years), then level off for duration of term. • With variable interest rate, additional payment changes possible if index changes.	• Easier to qualify for. • Buyer's income must be able to keep pace with scheduled payment increases. • With a variable rate, payment increases beyond the graduated payments can result in additional negative amortization.
Shared-appreciation mortgage	• Below-market interest rate and lower monthly payments, in exchange for a share of profits when property is sold or on a specified date. • Many variations.	• If home appreciates greatly, total cost of loan jumps. • If home fails to appreciate, projected increase in value may still be due, requiring refinancing at possibly higher rates.
Assumable mortgage	• Buyer takes over seller's original, below-market rate mortgage.	• Lowers monthly payments. • May be prohibited if there is "due on sale" clause in original mortgage. • Not permitted on most new fixed-rate mortgages.

Table 8.1 (continued)

Technique	Description	Considerations
Seller take-back	• Seller provides all or part of financing with a first or second mortgage.	• May offer below-market interest rate. • May have a balloon payment requiring full payment in a few years or refinancing at market rates, which could sharply increase debt.
Wrap-around mortgage	• Seller keeps original low-rate mortgage; buyer makes payments to seller, who forwards a portion to the lender holding original mortgage. • Offers lower effective interest rate on total transaction.	• Lender may call in old mortgage and require higher rate. • If buyer defaults, seller must take legal action to collect debt.
Growing equity mortgage (rapid payoff mortgage)	• Fixed interest rate but monthly payments may vary according to agreed-on schedule or index.	• Permits rapid payoff of debt because payment increases reduce principal. • Buyer's income must be able to keep up with payment increases.
Land contract	• Seller retains original mortgage. • No transfer of title until loan is fully paid. • Equal monthly payments based on below-market interest rate with unpaid principal due at loan end.	• May offer no equity until loan is fully paid. • Buyer has few protections if conflict arises during loan.
Buy-down	• Developer (or third party) provides an interest subsidy which lowers monthly payments during the first few years of the loan.	• Offers a break from higher payments during early years. • Enables buyer with lower income to qualify.

Table 8.1 (continued)

Technique	Description	Considerations
Buy-down	• Can have fixed or variable interest rate.	• With variable-rate mortgage, payments may jump substantially at end of subsidy. • Developer may increase selling price.
Rent with option to buy	• Renter pays "option fee" for right to purchase property at specified time and agreed-on price. • Rent may or may not be applied to sales price.	• Enables renter to buy time to obtain down payment and decide whether to purchase. • Locks in price during inflationary times. • Failure to take option means loss of option fee and rental payments.
Reverse annuity mortgage (equity conversion)	• Borrower, who owns mortgage-free property and needs income, receives monthly payments from lender, using property as collateral.	• Can provide homeowners with needed cash. • At end of term, borrower must have money available to avoid selling property or refinancing.
Zero-rate and low-rate mortgage	• Appears to be completely or almost interest free. • Large down payment and one-time finance charge, then loan is repaid in fixed monthly payments over short term.	• Permits quick ownership. • May not lower total cost (because of possibly increased sales price). • Does not offer long-term tax deductions.

Source: Federal Trade Commission, *The Mortgage Money Guide.*

The tax rules distinguish between

- Debt incurred to buy, construct, and improve a residence
- Debt secured by a residence where the proceeds from the loan are used for other purposes.

Debt secured by a first or second residence and used to buy, construct, or improve a residence is called *acquisition debt.* Up to $1 million debt of this kind is fully deductible (and is therefore said to be "qualifying debt").

Home equity debt is defined as any debt secured by a personal residence provided the debt does not exceed the fair market value of the residence minus the acquisition debt on the residence. That is to say, if the fair market value on a house is $200,000 and the current acquisition debt is $150,000, then interest on a home equity loan of up to $50,000 ($200,000 minus $150,000) is fully deductible. Up to $100,000 of home equity debt may be fully deducted, no matter what the money from the loan in question is to be used for. In the previous example, if the value of the house was $250,000 or more, interest on a home equity loan of no more than $100,000 would be deductible.

A loan for the purpose of home construction (on a primary or secondary residence) is considered acquisition debt, subject to the following limitations:

- Interest is fully deductible from the time construction begins and for a period of 24 months during construction. Interest incurred on a loan previous to construction is treated as personal interest (see Section 8.4.3, "Personal Interest"), as is interest during construction exceeding the 24-month limit.

- Interest on loans made within 90 days after construction is completed qualifies as acquisition debt, as long as the loan is used to reimburse construction expenses incurred within the last 24 months of construction.

8.4.2 Mortgage Payments

Not all mortgage payments may count as acquisition or home equity debt. Although payments to the institution holding a taxpayer's home mortgage may include principal payments and fire insurance premiums, only the payments of interest and taxes are deductible.

Lenders may charge "points" above the regular interest rate when granting a mortgage. These points are interest paid in advance, and they are generally deductible only over the period of time covered by the mortgage. The exception to this rule is when the loan on which the points are applied is used to buy or improve the borrower's *primary* home. In this case the amount paid as points may be deducted in the year of payment, subject to the following limitations:

- The payment of points must be an established business practice in the area where the loan was made.
- The points paid must not exceed the number generally charged in the area.
- The points may not be paid from funds obtained from the lender.

8.4.3 Personal Interest

Beginning in 1991, personal interest is no longer deductible. Personal interest is any interest other than

- Trade or business interest
- Investment interest
- Passive activity interest
- Interest on the deferral of certain estate taxes
- Fully deductible home mortgage interest.

The following are considered personal interest:

- Interest payments on an installment plan, if the payments are separately stated or can be determined and proved
- Credit card finance charges added to a taxpayer's monthly statements
- Finance charges on a bank credit card account balance (if no part of the charge is a service charge, loan fee, or other similar charge)
- Interest on income tax
- One-time charges for each cash, check, or overdraft advance added to a bank credit card account balance
- Separately stated finance charges figured under an annual percentage rate shown in a retail installment contract—also any fee charged for prepayment in such a contract
- Finance charges on a revolving charge account
- "Unstated interest" on installment payments

8.4.4 Investment Interest

Interest paid on debts to buy or carry investments is deductible up to the amount of the borrower's net investment income.

For example, if

- A taxpayer's investment interest expense is $10,000,
- His or her investment income is $12,000, and investment expenses are $4,000—his or her net investment income is therefore $8,000.
- Then he or she can deduct $8,000 as investment interest expense.

8.5 TRENDS IN CONSUMER FINANCES

Consumer indebtedness increased substantially during the 1980s, leading to record numbers of bankruptcies in the early 1990s. The following tables show trends in consumer financial status. Table 8.2 presents trends in consumer credit which, as a percentage of disposable personal income, increased during the mid- and late-1980s. Delinquency rates on bank installment loans are shown in Table 8.3.

Table 8.2 Consumer Credit Outstanding, 1970–1990

TYPE OF CREDIT	1970	1975	1980	1981	1982	1983	1984	1985	1986	1987	1988	1989	1990
Credit outstanding	**131.6**	**204.9**	**350.3**	**366.9**	**383.1**	**431.2**	**511.3**	**592.1**	**649.1**	**681.9**	**731.5**	**778.0**	**(NA)**
Ratio to disposable personal income [1] (percent)	18.3	17.9	18.3	17.2	16.9	17.8	19.2	20.9	21.5	21.3	21.0	20.6	(NA)
Installment.	103.9	167.0	298.2	311.3	325.8	369.0	442.6	518.3	573.0	610.5	664.7	716.6	739.0
Automobile paper	36.3	56.9	112.0	119.0	125.9	143.6	173.6	210.2	247.4	265.9	284.6	290.8	285.3
Revolving	4.9	14.5	55.1	61.1	66.5	79.1	100.3	121.8	135.9	153.1	174.1	197.1	218.2
Mobile home paper	2.4	15.3	18.7	20.1	22.6	23.6	25.9	26.8	27.1	25.9	25.2	22.3	21.8
All other loans	60.2	80.1	112.3	111.1	110.8	122.8	142.9	159.4	162.6	165.6	180.9	206.4	213.6
Noninstallment	27.7	37.9	52.1	55.6	57.3	62.2	68.7	73.8	76.1	71.4	66.8	61.4	(NA)
FINANCE RATES (percent)													
Commercial banks:													
New automobiles (48 months) [2] . . .	(NA)	11.36	14.30	16.54	16.83	13.92	13.71	12.91	11.33	10.46	10.85	12.07	11.78
Mobile homes (120 months) [2]	(NA)	11.82	14.99	17.45	18.05	15.91	15.58	14.96	13.99	13.38	13.54	14.11	14.02
Other consumer goods (24 months)	(NA)	13.08	15.47	18.09	18.65	16.68	16.47	15.94	14.82	14.23	14.68	15.44	15.46
Credit-card plans	(NA)	17.16	17.31	17.78	18.51	18.78	18.77	18.69	18.26	17.93	17.78	18.02	18.17
Finance companies:													
New automobiles	(NA)	13.12	14.82	16.17	16.15	12.58	14.62	11.98	9.44	10.73	12.60	12.62	12.54
Used automobiles	(NA)	17.63	19.10	20.00	20.75	18.74	17.85	17.59	15.95	14.61	15.11	16.18	15.99

NA Not available.   [1] Based on fourth quarter seasonally adjusted disposable personal income at annual rates as published by the U.S. Bureau of Economic Analysis in sources listed in table 708.   [2] For 1975-1982, maturities were 36 months for new car loans and 84 months for mobile home loans.

Source: Board of Governors of the Federal Reserve System, *Federal Reserve Bulletin*, monthly; *Annual Statistical Digest*, and unpublished data.

Table 8.3 Deliquency Rates on Bank Installment Loans, 1970–1989

TYPE OF CREDIT	1970	1980	1981	1982	1983	1984	1985	1986	1987	1988	1989
DELINQUENCY RATES											
Closed-end installment loans, total	2.14	2.82	2.61	2.39	1.94	2.09	2.32	2.26	2.47	2.49	2.64
Personal loans [1]	2.39	3.53	3.20	3.04	2.84	3.16	3.63	3.11	3.66	3.34	3.52
Automobile, direct loans [2]	1.43	1.81	1.80	1.68	1.53	1.47	1.64	1.80	1.59	1.92	2.03
Automobile, indirect loans [3]	1.94	2.29	2.03	1.73	1.50	1.77	2.02	2.09	2.20	2.46	2.61
Property improvement [4]	1.96	1.93	1.98	1.98	2.14	2.00	1.91	1.77	1.88	2.06	2.25
Home equity and second mortgage loans [5] . .	(NA)	(NA)	(NA)	(NA)	(NA)	1.94	1.77	2.06	1.85	2.01	1.86
Mobile home loans	2.59	3.14	3.37	2.69	2.44	2.56	2.39	3.04	2.57	3.12	2.51
Recreational vehicle loans	(NA)	1.94	2.05	1.88	1.58	1.87	1.84	1.92	1.99	2.07	1.85
Bank card loans	(NA)	2.72	2.53	2.38	2.08	2.81	2.95	3.15	2.33	2.19	2.24
Revolving credit loans	(NA)	2.70	2.86	2.16	1.44	1.50	1.96	1.53	2.33	2.87	2.92
Home equity lines of credit loans (open-end) [5] .	(NA)	(NA)	(NA)	(NA)	(NA)	(NA)	(NA)	(NA)	0.74	0.68	0.78
REPOSSESSIONS PER 1,000 LOANS OUTSTANDING											
Mobile home	3.59	1.57	1.47	1.14	1.23	1.29	1.21	2.50	1.58	1.77	1.63
Automobile, direct loans [2]	1.52	1.10	0.99	0.90	0.70	0.72	1.11	1.15	0.86	1.03	1.03
Automobile, indirect loans [3]	4.88	2.75	2.40	2.13	1.56	1.58	2.08	1.95	2.04	1.86	1.70

NA Not available.   [1] Beginning 1983, includes home appliance loans.   [2] Made directly by bank's lending function.   [3] Made by automobile dealerships; loans in bank's portfolio.   [4] Beginning 1983, own plan and FHA Title I loans.   [5] Seasonally not adjusted.

Source: American Bankers Association, Washington, DC, *Consumer Credit Delinquency Bulletin*, quarterly.

Chapter 9

EDUCATION PLANNING

Meeting the cost of four years of college has always put some financial strain on the coffers of many middle- and even upper-income families. With college costs continuing to soar far in excess of the rate of inflation, paying for college is likely to become an even more difficult challenge in the years ahead. Financial professionals are often called upon to advise parents in planning for meeting the costs of college and, perhaps, private primary and secondary schools.

The amount needed to pay educational costs indeed appears daunting. Universities estimate a 6.5 percent compound annual increase in tuition costs. This means that by the year 2000, the average public school's total four-year cost will exceed $51,400. The cost of the average private school will top $92,000, with total costs of top-tier schools such as Harvard touching the $160,000 level.

Yet with careful planning, meeting a sizable portion of these expenses is possible for the average family. Indeed, widespread publicity about the rising cost of an education has resulted in an increased awareness among the general public of the need for a well thought out college savings plan.

Several tax regulations will almost certainly influence decisions on how to invest college-earmarked savings for many years to come. For children under age 14, unearned income under $500 is not taxed, unearned income between $500 and $1,000 is taxed at the child's tax rate, and unearned income over $1,000 is taxed at the parent's rate. If a child is age 14 or older, unearned income is taxed at the child's rate, regardless of the amount.

Many people are taking advantage of income-shifting devices such as trust accounts set up under the Uniform Gift to Minors Act (UGMA) or the Uniform Transfer to Minors Act (UTMA). These accounts are set up to allow a parent or other individual to give money to a child while keeping it in the hands of an adult custodian. The assets usually revert to the child when he or she reaches the age of majority. Other, more individualized types of trusts are also available for wealthier families. Before embarking upon any income-shifting programs, however, parents should weigh the tax-saving benefits against, in effect, giving the money to a child (who may opt not to go to college).

Certain parents whose income falls under specified, inflation-adjusted levels may also benefit from the tax-exempt status of interest on Series EE bonds if these bonds are used to pay for certain college expenses such as tuition. This tax break is available for bonds purchased after December 31, 1989.

Of course, investment as well as tax considerations must be taken into account. If parents have a relatively long time horizon for accumulating college savings, a portion of these portfolios should be earmarked for stock investments, which have historically performed better than other types of securities over the long term. However, as children approach college age, parents may want to consider moving a greater portion of their college funds into less volatile investments.

Even the most diligent college savings plan, however, may need to be augmented by financial aid in the form of loans or scholarships, such as those detailed in this chapter. This aid is available from a number of sources, including the state or federal government, schools, or private foundations, and may be based on merit as well as financial need.

Because legislative initiatives as well as individual college aid programs change rapidly, it is important to keep abreast of them both before and during college. Although federal and state fiscal belt-tightening will almost certainly make obtaining financial aid more difficult except for the most needy of families, diligent parents and students will continue to benefit from uncovering the many sources of grants, scholarships, and loans that are available.

9.1 COLLEGE EDUCATION COST FORECASTER

Table 9.1 projects current average four-year education costs compiled by The College Board, assuming a 6 percent annual increase in costs. These figures can be used as a guide in estimating the future costs of college for a student entering in a given year. Costs included in these figures are tuition, fees, room, and board. The costs of books and supplies, transportation, and miscellaneous expenses are not included.

**Table 9.1 Current Average Four-Year Education Costs,
1991–2010**

Year Entering	Public School	Private School	Selective Private School
1991	$24,405	$62,104	$87,690
1992	25,870	65,831	92,951
1993	27,422	69,780	98,528
1994	29,067	73,967	104,440
1995	30,811	78,405	110,706
1996	32,660	83,110	117,348
1997	34,620	88,096	124,389
1998	36,697	93,382	131,853
1999	38,899	98,985	139,764
2000	41,232	104,923	148,150
2001	43,706	111,219	157,039
2002	46,329	117,893	166,461
2003	49,109	124,966	176,449
2004	52,055	132,464	187,036
2005	55,178	140,412	198,258
2006	58,489	148,837	210,153
2007	61,998	157,767	222,762
2008	65,718	167,233	236,127
2009	69,661	177,267	250,295
2010	73,841	187,903	265,313

Source: The College Board

9.2 SUMMARY OF COLLEGE FINANCIAL AID PARAMETERS

Increasingly limited resources for college grants and scholarships preclude many families from qualifying for much, if any financial aid. Table 9.2 approximates the expected parents' annual contribution toward their children's education costs depending on available assets (including equity in home) and pretax income. For example, the expected parents' annual contribution for a family with income of $50,000 and assets of $100,000 is $10,220.

Table 9.2 Estimated Parental Contribution for One Year of College,
1991–1992

1990 income	Net Family Assets (1n 1990)					
	$20,000	$40,000	$60,000	$80,000	$100,000	$120,000
$20,000	$ 41	$ 370	$ 898	$ 1,426	$ 1,960	$ 2,575
$30,000	1,648	1,896	2,498	3,210	4,057	5,068
$40,000	3,679	3,951	4,943	6,071	7,199	8,327
$50,000	6,509	6,836	7,964	9,092	10,220	11,348
$60,000	9,470	9,798	10,926	12,054	13,182	14,310
$70,000	12,478	12,806	13,934	15,062	16,190	17,318

Source: The College Board

9.3   EDUCATION FUNDING ALTERNATIVES

While colleges and most student aid sponsors expect parents or students to be the primary funding source for meeting college costs, a host of financial aid alternatives, such as those summarized in this section, are also available. For more information, the finanial professional should advise parents or students to contact their guidance counselor or the financial aid administrator of the school in which they are interested.

9.3.1 Grants and Scholarships

Grants are often awarded on the basis of need alone, while scholarships may be based on need as well as demonstrated athletic or academic achievement. Because federal funding has lagged the rise in college costs and the federal budget deficit has become increasingly burdensome, federal grants are becoming quite scarce and are usually available only to families of relatively limited resources. The largest federal need-based student aid program is the Pell Grant Program.

Scholarships from the Natinal Honor Society and National Merit Scholarships are available to students with high grades who qualify. Foundations, religious organizations, and civic or trade groups may also offer sources of scholarship funding.

Individuals should keep in mind that scholarship awards will not necessarily lessen a family's financial burden. Because colleges and universities base their grant aid on financial need, the amount of such aid received may be reduced because of scholarship availability.

Some scholarships, most notably those offered by the Reserve Officers' Training Corps (ROTC) pay virtually all college costs. However, students must agree to serve in the military as commissioned officers after graduation.

9.3.2 Loans

As the cost of college rises, more students will find it necessary to turn to loans for financial assistance. Student loans, which usually bear low rates of interest compared to most other forms of commercial debt, are subsidized by the state or federal government, or by the colleges themselves. Common types of loans available from the federal government include PLUS loans for parents who want to borrow to help pay for a child's college education and Supplemental Loans for Students (SLS) for student borrowers. Both carry variable interest rates which are lower than most commercial loans, but generally higher than some other types of student loans such as Stafford Student Loans.

Perkins Loans, available through college financial aid offices, have an interest rate of just 5 percent. In addition, some banks, credit unions, and other organizations have special loan programs that may carry more favorable rates than other consumer borrowing options.

If a student uses more than one student loan, he or she may be able to pay them all back using one repayment plan. A loan consolidation program, available from certain eligible lenders, is available to students who have loans totaling at least $5,000. The repayment period is 10 to 25 years, depending on the amount to be repaid.

Both parents and students should review key loan provisions, including loan deferment, repayment terms, and refinancing and consolidation options. Of course, both students and their parents should be counseled on the responsible use of credit and how much they can realistically afford to borrow. Lenders should be kept informed of a change of address or any problems with loan repayment.

Also keep in mind that the interest on student loans will no longer be deductible beginning in 1991. For this reason, parents may want to consider using a home equity loan to help pay college costs, since interest on these loans generally remains fully deductible.

9.3.3 Work-Study Programs

Many students work part-time to help defray college expenses. The College Work-Study Program (CWS) provides jobs on and off campus for undergraduate and graduate students who need financial aid. Pay is at least minimum wage, but may be higher, depending on the type of work. Those whose jobs are on campus usually work for the school. Off-campus jobs generally involve work that is in the public interest, and the employer is usually a nonprofit organization or a local state or federal agency.

Many colleges have internship programs which offer part-time work for students, and at the same time, give them a chance to gain experience in their chosen fields. Others have instituted special programs which help match students with area employers.

Since a student's aid is determined largely by financial need, investment professionals should investigate ways in which an institution's estimate of the family's portion of the contribution may be reduced. First, it is important to avoid overstating the value of family assets, particularly the home. Second, if there is any possibility that a family might qualify for financial aid, parents should generally not transfer assets to their children because schools require a much higher percentage of assets in the student's name to be considered in meeting college expenses than they do assets in the parents' name. Finally, it is beneficial if a student can declare himself or herself financially independent, since the student's income and assets will generally be lower than that of his or her parents.

9.4 INVENTORY OF COLLEGE FUNDING SOURCES

Most families end up funding college education costs from a variety of sources, including grants, scholarships, and fellowships; education loans; personal loans; and personal resources. Table 9.3 illustrates the commonly used sources of money to pay for higher education.

Table 9.3 Sources for College Funding

Grants, scholarships, and fellowships:
Pell Grant
Supplemental Education Opportunity Grant
State financial assistance
School financial assistance
School scholarship/fellowship
Private aid programs
Military benefits or officer-training program
Social Security benefits

Education loans
Perkins Loan (formerly National Direct Student Loan)
Stafford Student Loan (formerly Guaranteed Student Loan)
Parent Loans for Undergraduate Students
School loan programs
State loan programs
Private education loan programs

Personal loans
Home equity loan
Other secured financing
Unsecured loans

Personal resources allocable to funding education costs
Income of parents
Income of student—school jobs
Income of student—summer jobs
Parents' savings/investments
Student's savings/investments
Gifts from relatives

9.5 STATE EDUCATIONAL AGENCIES

Table 9.4 is a list of state agencies that coordinate state college financial aid programs. These agencies can supply information on and applications for state programs and can provide guidance on where to go for information on federal student aid programs.

Table 9.4 State Agencies that Coordinate State College Financial Aid Programs

Alabama: Alabama Commission on Higher Education; One Court Square, Suite 221, Montgomery, AL 36197; (205) 269-2700

Alaska: Alaska Commission on Postsecondary Education, Box FP, Juneau, AK 99811; (907) 465-2962

Arizona has no central aid agency, but information on state programs is available from the financial aid office of any college in the state.

Arkansas: Arkansas Department of Higher Education; 1220 West Third Street, Little Rock, AR 72201; (501) 371-1441

California: California Student Aid Commission; Box 942845; Sacramento, CA 94245; (916) 445-0880

Colorado: Colorado Commission on Higher Education; Colorado Heritage Center; 1300 Broadway, 2nd Floor; Denver, CO 80203; (303) 866-2723

Connecticut: Connecticut Department of Higher Education; 61 Woodland Street; Hartford, CT 06105; (203) 566-2618

Delaware: Delaware Postsecondary Education Commission; Carvel State Office Building; 820 North French Street, 4th Floor; Wilmington, DE 19801; (302) 571-3240

District of Columbia: Office of Postsecondary Education; D.C. Department of Human Services; 1331 H Street N.W., Suite 600; Washington, D.C. 20005; (202) 727-3688

Florida: Office of Student Financial Assistance; Department of Education; Knott Building; Tallahassee, FL 32399; (904) 488-4095

Georgia: Georgia Student Financial Authority; 2082 East Exchange Place, Suite 200; Tucker, GA 30084; (404) 493-5444

Hawaii has no central aid authority, but information on state programs is available from the financial aid office of any college in the state.

Idaho: Idaho Scholarship Program; Office of the State Board of Education; 650 West State Street, Room 307; Boise, ID 83720; (208) 334-2270

Illinois: Illinois State Scholarship Commission; 106 Wilmot Road; Deerfield, IL 60015; (312) 948-8550

Indiana: State Student Assistance Commission; 964 North Pennsylvania Avenue; Indianapolis, IN 46204; (317) 232-2350

Iowa: Iowa College Aid Commission; 201 Jewett Building; Ninth and Grand Avenues; Des Moines, IA 50309; (515) 281-3501

Kansas: Kansas Board of Regents; Capitol Tower, Suite 609; 400 Southwest 8th Street; Topeka, KS 66603; (913) 296-3517

Kentucky: Kentucky Higher Education Assistance Authority; 1050 U.S. 127 South; West Frankfort Office Complex; Frankfort, KY 40601; (502) 564-8121

Louisiana: Louisiana Governor's Special Commission on Educational Services; Box 91202; Baton Rouge, LA 70821; (800) 626-0115 (in Louisiana only); (504) 922-1038

Maine: Higher Education Services; State House Station 119; Augusta, ME 04333; (207) 289-2183

Maryland: Maryland State Scholarship Administration; 2100 Guilford Avenue; Baltimore, MD 21218; (301) 333-6420

Massachusetts: Board of Regents Scholarship Office; 150 Causeway Street, Room 600; Boston, MA 02114; (617) 727-9420

Michigan: Michigan Department of Education; Student Financial Assistance Services; Box 30008; Lansing, MI 48909; (517) 373-3394

Minnesota: Minnesota Higher Education Coordinating Board; Capital Square, Suite 400; 550 Cedar Street; St. Paul, MN 55101; (612) 296-5715

Mississippi: Board of Trustees of State Institutions of Higher Learning; Box 2336; Jackson, MS 39225; (601) 982-6570

Missouri: Missouri Coordinating Board of Higher Education; Box 1438; 101 Adams Street; Jefferson City, MO 65102; (314) 751-3940

Montana has no central aid agency, but information on state programs is available from the financial aid office of any college in the state.

Nebraska has no central aid agency, but information on state programs is available from the financial aid office of any college in the state.

Nevada has no central aid agency, but information on state programs is available from the financial aid office of any college in the state.

New Hampshire: New Hampshire Postsecondary Education Commission; 2 1/2 Beacon Street; Concord, NH 03301; (603) 271-2555

New Jersey: New Jersey Department of Higher Education; Office of Student Assistance; 4 Quakerbridge Plaza, C.N. 540; Trenton, NJ 08625; (800) 962-4636 (in New Jersey only); (609) 586-5092

New Mexico: New Mexico Educational Assistance Foundation; Box 27020; 3900 Osuna Avenue, N.E.; Albuquerque, NM 87109; (505) 345-3371

New York: New York State Higher Education Services Corporation; Student Information; 99 Washington Avenue; Albany, NY 12255; (800) 642-6234 or 6238 (in New York only; out of state inquiries must be made by mail).

North Carolina: North Carolina State Education Assistance Authority; Box 2688; Chapel Hill, NC 27515; (919) 549-8614

North Dakota: North Dakota Student Financial Assistance Program; State Capitol, 10th Floor; Bismarck, ND 58505; (701) 224-4114

Ohio: Ohio Board of Regents; Student Assistance Office; 3600 State Office Tower; 30 East Broad Street; Columbus, OH 43266; (614) 466-7420

Oklahoma: Oklahoma State Regents for Higher Education; 500 Education Building; State Capitol Complex; Oklahoma City, OK 73105; (405) 525-8180

Oregon: Oregon State Scholarship

Commission; 1445 Willamette Street; Eugene, OR 97401; (800) 452-8807 (in Oregon only); (503) 686-4166

Pennsylvania: Pennsylvania Higher Education Assistance Authority; 660 Boas Street; Harrisburg, PA 17102; (800) 692-7435 (in Pennsylvania only); (717) 257-2800

Rhode Island: Rhode Island Higher Education Assistance Authority; 560 Jefferson Boulevard; Warwick, RI 02886; (401) 277-2050

South Carolina has no central aid agency, but information on state programs is available from the financial aid office of any college in the state.

South Dakota: Office of the Secretary; South Dakota Department of Education and Cultural Affairs; 700 Governors Drive; Pierre, SD 57501; (605) 773-3134

Tennessee: Tennessee Student Assistance Corporation; 1950 Parkway Towers; 404 James Robertson Parkway; Nashville, TN 37219; (800) 342-1663 (in Tennessee only); (615) 741-1346

Texas: Coordinating Board; Texas College and University System; Box 12788, Capitol Station; Austin, TX 78711; (512) 462-6325

Utah: Utah System of Higher Education; Utah State Board of Regents; 355 West North Temple; 3 Triad Center, Suite 550; Salt Lake City, UT 84180; (801) 538-5247

Vermont: Vermont Student Assistance Corporation; Champlain Mill; Box 2000; Winooski, VT 05404; (802) 655-9602

Virginia: State Council of Higher Education; James Monroe Building; 101 North 14th Street; Richmond, VA 23219; (804) 225-2141

Washington: Higher Education Coordinating Board; 917 Lakeridge Way; Mail Stop 6V-11; Olympia, WA 98504; (206) 753-3571

West Virginia: West Virginia Board of Regents; Higher Education Grant Program; Box 4007; Charleston, WV 25364; (304) 347-1227

Wisconsin: Wisconsin Higher Education Aids Board; Box 7885; Madison, WI 53707; (608) 266-2578

Wyoming has no central aid agency, but information on state programs is available from the financial aid office of any college in the state.

Puerto Rico: Council on Higher Education; Box F, UPR Station; San Juan, PR 00931; (809) 758-3356 or -3328

Guam: University of Guam; UOG Station; Mangilao, GU 96913; (671) 734-2921

Virgin Islands: Virgin Islands Board of Education; Box 11900; St. Thomas, VI 00801; (809) 774-4546

American Samoa: American Samoa Community College; Box 2609; Pago Pago, AS 96799; (684) 699-9155

Northern Mariana Islands: Northern Marianas College; Board of Regents; Box 1250; Saipan, Central Mariana 96950; Saipan (670) 234-7642/5498/5499

Federated States of Micronesia/Marshall Islands/Palau: Community College of Micronesia; Box 159, Kolonia; Ponape, Federated States of Micronesia 94941; phone: Ponape 480 or 479; *or* Micronesian Occupational College; Box 9; Koror, Palau 96940; phone: Ponape 471

9.6 SCHOLARSHIPS AND GRANTS ORGANIZED BY VOCATION

Table 9.5 provides a list of scholarships and grants organized according to vocational goal. *Parents and students should be advised to seek out possible scholarships and grants diligently, many of which are not based upon financial need.* *For further information, refer to* Scholarships, Fellowships and Loans *(Bellman Publishing).*

Table 9.5 Scholarships and Grants According to Vocational Goal

Vocational Goal and Name of Administering Agency	Level of Study[1]	Residency Requirement?	Affiliation Requirement?[2]
Accounting			
AIESEC-United States, Inc.	U, MS	No	Yes
American Institute of Certified Public Accountants	U, D, R	No	Yes[3]
Administration			
American Home Economics Association Foundation	MS	No	Yes
Minnesota Association of School Administrators	O	No	Yes
Advertising			
The Meriden Record Company	U, MS	Yes	No
Aeronautics			
Zonta International	MS	No	No
Aerospace Sciences			
Hughes Aircraft Company	D, P, MS	Yes	No
Tailhook Association	U	No	Yes
Whirly-Girls, Inc.	P	No	No
Zonta International	MS	No	No

[1]D = Ph.D., Ed.D, ScD., etc.; DDS = doctor of dentistry; HS = secondary school level; JR = two-year college or two-year vocational technical institute that awards an associate degree; LLB = law degree; LPN = licensed practical nurse; MD = doctor of medicine; MS = master's degree; O = not formal study; anything that is not one of the above categories; P = professional; PD = postdoctoral; R = research; RN = registered nurse; U = undergraduate college, or technical institute leading to a bachelor's degree; VT = associate degree or non-degree vocational-technical course work at high school or post-secondary school levels.

[2]Affiliation categories may be associations, employers, ethnicities, fraternal organizations, the military, minorities, religious groups, unions, and veterans' organizations.

[3]Some of the administering agency's offerings have residence requirements whereas others do not.

Vocational Goal and Name of Administering Agency	Level of Study[1]	Residency Requirement?	Affilication Requirement?[2]
Agribusiness			
American Home Economics Association			
Foundation	D, R	No	Yes
Abbie Sargent Memorial Scholarship,			
Inc.	U	Yes	No
Agriculture			
Association of Official Analytical			
Chemists	U	No	No
The Bush Foundation	O	Yes	No
The Farm Foundation	O	No	No
New York State Grange	JR, U, VT	Yes	Yes[3]
Abbie Sargent Memorial Scholarship,			
Inc.	U	Yes	No
Agronomy			
Abbie Sargent Memorial Scholarship,			
Inc.	U	Yes	No
American Indian Studies			
The Newberry Library	PD, R, D	Yes	Yes[3]
Animal Science/Behavior			
Rob and Bessie Welder Wildlife			
Foundation	MS, D, R	Yes	No
Anthropology			
Fondation Fyssen	P	Yes	No
The George A. and Eliza Gardner			
Howard Foundation	O	No	No
National Geographic Society	R	No	No
Wenner-Gren Foundation for			
Anthropological Research, Inc.	D, PD, R	No	No
Applied Arts			
The George A. And Eliza Gardner			
Howard Foundation	O	No	No
Spoleto Festival U.S.A	O	Yes	No
Archaeology			
Archaeological Institute of America	O	Yes	No
Fondation Fyssen	P	Yes	No
The George A. And Eliza Gardner			
Howard Foundation	O	No	No
National Geographic Society	R	No	No
Architecture			
American Academy and Institute of			
Arts and Letters	O	No	No
American Association of University Women			
Educational Foundation	D, PD, R	No	No
American Hospital Association	U, MS	No	No

Vocational Goal and Name of Administering Agency	Level of Study[1]	Residency Requirement?	Affilication Requirement?[2]
Architecture (continued)			
American Institute of Architects	U, MS	No	Yes[3]
American Society of Interior Designers Educational Foundation, Inc.	U, O	No	No
The Bush Foundation	O	Yes	No
Graham Foundation for Advanced Studies in the Fine Arts	R, MS, O	No	No
The Alfred T. Granger Student Art Scholarship	JR, U, VT, O	Yes	No
National Institute for Architectural Education	P	Yes	No
New Jersey Society of Architects	U, P	Yes	No
New York Foundation for the Arts	O	Yes	No
Virginia Museum of Fine Arts	U, MS, P	Yes	No
Western Interstate Commission for Higher Education	DDS, P, JD	No	No
Art			
American Academy and Institute of Arts and Letters	O	No	No
Florida Department of State	P, O	Yes	No
The Alfred T. Granger Student Art Scholarship	JR, U, VT, O	Yes	No
The MacDowell Colony	O	Yes	No
The National League of American Pen Women, Inc	O	No	No
Pollock-Krasner Foundation, Inc.	O	No	No
Ragdale Foundation	O	Yes	No
Scholastic Inc.	U, O	No	No
Two/Ten National Foundation	JR, U, RN, LPN, VT, O	Yes	Yes
Veterans of Foreign Wars of the United States Ladies Auxiliary	HS	No	No
Art History			
The Metropolitan Museum of Art	O	Yes	No
National Gallery of Art	D	Yes	No
Virginia Museum of Fine Arts	U, MS, P	Yes	No
Woodrow Wilson National Fellowship Foundation	PD	No	No
Arts Administration			
The Bush Foundation	O	Yes	No
Spoleto Festival U.S.A.	O	Yes	No
Asian Studies			
Gannett Fellowship Committee	P	Yes	No

Vocational Goal and Name of Administering Agency	Level of Study[1]	Residency Requirement?	Affiliation Requirement?[2]
Astronomy/Astronomical Sciences			
Mount Wilson and Las Campanas Observatories of the Carnegie Institution of Washington	PD, R	Yes	No
National Geographic Society	R	No	No
Atmospheric Science			
American Meteorological Society	U	No	No
National Center for Atmospheric Research	PD	Yes	No
Southeastern Center for Electrical Engineering Education	PD, R	Yes	No
Audiology			
Easter Seal Society of Iowa, Inc.	U, MS	Yes	No
Automobile Mechanics			
Plymouth-AAA Trouble Shooting Contest	VT	No	No
Aviation			
AOPA Air Safety Foundation	U	No	No
Banking			
The Kosciuszko Foundation	U, MS, MD, DDS	Yes	Yes
Behavioral Sciences			
The Journal of Applied Behavioral Science	O	No	No
National Academy of Education	PD, R	No	No
Science Service	U	No	No
Biochemistry			
The Chemical Institute of Canada	MS, D	Yes	No
The Camille and Henry Dreyfus Foundation, Inc.	PD, R	No	Yes
Biological Sciences			
Marshall H. and Nellie Alworth Memorial Fund	U	Yes	No
Oak Ridge Associated Universities	U, MS, D, PD	No	Yes
Science Service	U	No	No
Whitehall Foundation, Inc.	R	No	No
Biology			
Associated Western Universities, Inc.	O, D, R, MS, PD, U	Yes[3]	No
Los Alamos National Laboratory	PD, R	Yes	No
Lucille P. Market Charitable Trust	R	No	No
National Center for Atmospheric Research	PD	Yes	No

Vocational Goal and Name of Administering Agency	Level of Study[1]	Residency Requirement?	Affiliation Requirement?[2]
Biology (continued)			
National Geographic Society	R	No	No
Rob and Bessie Welder Wildlife Foundation	MS, D, R	Yes	No
Biomedical Sciences			
Lucille P. Market Charitable Trust	R	No	No
United Cerebral Palsey Research and Educational Foundation, Inc.	MS, D, MD	Yes	No
Blood Banking			
American Association of Blood Banks	P	No	No
Botany			
National Geographic Society	R	No	No
The New York Botanical Garden	D	Yes	No
Rob and Bessie Welder Wildlife Foundation	MS, D, R	Yes	No
Broadcasting			
The Canadian Association of Broadcasters	U, MS	Yes	No
International Thespian Society	Jr, U, O	No	Yes
National Association of Broadcasters	R	No	No
Business			
The Bush Foundation	O	Yes	No
Business and Professional Women's Foundation	JR, U, O LLB, MS, MD, VT	No	No
Civitan International Foundation	MS	No	No
International Foundation of Employee Benefit Plans	MS, D, PD, R	No	No
Richard D. Irwin Foundation	D	No	No
Phi Gamma Nu Fraternity	U	No	Yes
Svenska Handelsbanken Foundations for Social Science Research	MS, D, R	Yes	No
Business Administration			
AIESEC-United States, Inc.	U, MS	No	Yes
American Assembly of Collegiate Schools of Business	D	No	No
American Association of University Women Educational Foundation	D, PD, R	No	No
The Robert Bosch Foundation	P	Yes	No
Consortium for Graduate Study in Management	MS	Yes	Yes

Vocational Goal and Name of Administering Agency	Level of Study[1]	Residency Requirement?	Affiliation Requirement?[2]
Business Administration (continued)			
The Kosciuszko Foundation	U, MS, MD, DDS	Yes	Yes
National Association of Plumbing- Heating-Cooling Contractors	U	No	No
National Black MBA Association, Inc	MS	No	Yes
Business Technology			
National Scholarship Trust Fund	MS, D, R	No	No
Byzantine Studies			
Dumbarton Oaks	D, PD	Yes	No
Cartography/surveying			
American Congress on Surveying and Mapping	U, MS, D	No	No
The Newberry Library	PD, R, P	Yes	Yes[3]
Chemistry			
Marshall H. and Nellie Alworth Memorial Fund	U	Yes	No
Associated Western Universities, Inc.	O, D, R, MS, PD, U	Yes[3]	No
Association of Official Analytical Chemists	U	No	No
AT&T Bell Laboratories	D, U	Yes	Yes[3]
The Chemical Institute of Canada	MS, D	Yes	No
The Camille and Henry Dreyfus Foundation, Inc.	PD	No	Yes
The Kosciuszko Foundation	U, MS, MD, DDS	Yes	Yes
Los Alamos National Laboratory	PD, R	Yes	No
National Center for Atmospheric Research	PD	Yes	No
National Scholarship Trust Fund	MS, D, R	No	No
Society for the Advancement of Material and Process Engineering (SAMPE)	MS, D, U	No	No
Southeastern Center for Electrical Engineering Education	PD, R	Yes	No
Chinese Language/Studies			
Republic of China	U, MS, D, O	Yes	No
The Yale-China Association	U, MS, D, R	Yes	No
Chiropractic Medicine			
Foundation for Chiropractice Education and Research	P, R	No	No

Vocational Goal and Name of Administering Agency	Level of Study[1]	Residency Requirement?	Affiliation Requirement?[2]
Choreography			
New York Foundation for the Arts	O	Yes	No
Church Related Occupations			
Lutheran Church in America	P, O, MS	Yes[3]	Yes
William H. Nelson Educational Foundation	U, MS	Yes	Yes
Presbytery of Chicago	U, MS, D, P	No	Yes
Classical Languages/Literature Studies			
National Junior Classical League	U	No	Yes
Clinical Laboratory Sciences			
American Society for Medical Technology Education & Research Fund, Inc.	MS, D, O, R, P	No	No
Communications			
AT&T Bell Laboratories	D, U	Yes	Yes[3]
Women in Communications, Inc.	JR, U, MS	Yes	No
Computer Science			
AIESEC-United States, Inc.	U, MS	No	Yes
Argonne National Laboratory	D, R, U, MS	Yes	Yes[3]
AT&T Bell Laboratories	U, D	Yes[3]	Yes[3]
AT&T Foundation	D	No	No
Hughes Aircraft Company	D, P, MS	Yes	No
Los Alamos National Laboratory	PD, R	Yes	No
Oak Ridge Associated Universities	U, D, R, MS, PD	Yes[3]	Yes[3]
Southeastern Center for Electrical Engineering Education	PD, R	Yes	No
Conservation			
American Fishing Tackle Manufacturers Association	MS, D, R	No	No
Argonne National Laboratory	MS, D, R	Yes	Yes[3]
The Metropolitan Museum of Art	O	Yes	No
National Campers and Hikers Association	JR, U	No	Yes
Rob and Bessie Welder Wildlife Foundation	MS, D, R	Yes	No
Construction			
AGC Education and Research Foundation	U, MS	No	No
Merit Shop Foundation, Ltd.	JR, U	No	No
National Association of Plumbing-Heating-Cooling Contractors	U	No	No
Counseling/guidance			
Arkansas Department of Education	U, MS	Yes	No

Vocational Goal and Name of Administering Agency	Level of Study[1]	Residency Requirement?	Affiliation Requirement?[2]
Counseling/guidance (continued)			
Association of Eastern College			
Personnel Officers	R	No	Yes
Council on Career Development for			
Minorities, Inc.	MS	Yes	Yes
Marland Association for Multicultural			
Counseling and Development	MS	Yes	No
Crafts			
New York Foundation for the Arts	O	Yes	No
Virginia Museum of Fine Arts	U, MS, P	Yes	No
Criminal Justice			
Boy Scouts of America	U	No	Yes
Critic (Art, Drama, Literary)			
American Academy and Institute of Arts			
and Letters	O	No	No
The George A. and Eliza Gardner Howard			
Foundation	O	No	No
Culinary Arts			
The National Institute for the Foodservice			
Industry	JR, U	No	No
Dairy Science			
Dairy Shrine	U, MS	No	No
Dance			
Florida Department of State	P, O	Yes	No
International Thespian Society	JR, U, O	No	Yes
Two/Ten National Foundation	JR, U, RN, LPN, VT,		
	O	Yes	Yes
Dental Hygiene			
American Dental Hygienists' Association			
Foundation	JR, U, MS, D	No	No
Dentistry			
American Association of University			
Women Educational Foundation	D, PD, R	No	No
Fresno-Madera Medical Society Scholarship			
Foundation	MD, DDS, P, RN	Yes	No
The Kosciuszko Foundation	U, MS, MD, DDS	Yes	Yes
Westchester Community Service			
Council, Inc.	MS, DDS, D, MD, RN	Yes	No

Vocational Goal and Name of Administering Agency	Level of Study[1]	Residency Requirement?	Affiliation Requirement?[2]
Dentistry (continued)			
Western Interstate Commission for	DDS, JD, U		
Higher Education	MS, MD, P	Yes	No
Design			
National Scholarship Trust Fund	JR, U	No	No
Dietetics			
American Dietetic Association	JR, VT,		
	MS, O, U	No	Yes[3]
American Dietetic Association			
Foundation	O	No	No
Drawing			
The John F. and Anna Lee Stacey			
Scholarship Fund for Art Education	P	No	No
Earth Sciences			
Oak Ridge Associated Universities	U, MS, D,		
	PD	No	Yes
Ecology			
The Garden Club of America	O	No	No
National Campers and Hikers			
Association	JR, U	No	Yes
National Geographic Society	R	No	No
Smithsonian Environmental Research			
Center	U, MS, D	Yes	No
Rob and Bessie Welder Wildlife			
Foundation	MS, D, R	Yes	No
Economics			
American Defense Institute	D	Yes	No
The Robert Bosch Foundation	P	Yes	No
The Brookings Institution	R, P, D	Yes	Yes
Civitan International Foundation	MS	No	No
Earhart Foundation	R, MS, D	No	No
Economic Development Institute of the			
World Bank	R	Yes	No
The Farm Foundation	O	No	No
International Foundation of Employee			
Benefit Plans	MS, D,		
	PD, R	No	No
Richard D. Irwin Foundation	D	No	No
National Association of Broadcasters	R	No	No
Svenska Handelsbanken Foundations			
for Social Science Research	MS, D, R	Yes	No
Education			
American Foundation for the Blind,			
Inc.	MS	No	No

Vocational Goal and Name of Administering Agency	Level of Study[1]	Residency Requirement?	Affiliation Requirement?[2]
Education (continued)			
Association for the Study of Higher Education	D	No	No
First National Bank	U	Yes	No
The Kosciuszko Foundation	U, MS, MD, DDS	Yes	Yes
National Academy of Education	PD, R	No	No
National Scholarship Trust Fund	JR, U	No	No
Phi Delta Kappa, George Washington University Chapter	U	Yes	No
Educational Administration			
The Bush Foundation	O	Yes	No
Electronics			
American Vacuum Society	MS, D	Yes	No
Energy-Related Areas			
Argonne National Laboratory	MS, D, R, U	Yes	Yes[3]
Associated Western Universities, Inc.	D, R, U, O, MS, PD	Yes[3]	No
Oak Ridge Associated Universities	PD, R, MS, U, D	Yes	No
Engineering			
AGC Education and Research Foundation	U, MS	No	No
Marshall H. and Nellie Alworth Memorial Fund	U	Yes	No
American Association of University Women Educational Foundation	D, PD, R	No	No
American Public Works Association	U, MS	No	No
The American Society of Mechanical Engineers Auxiliary, Inc.	MS, U	No	Yes[3]
Argonne National Laboratory	MS, D, R, U	Yes	Yes[3]
Associated Western Uiversities, Inc.	O, D, R, PD, MS, U	Yes[3]	No
AT&T Bell Laboratories	U, D	Yes[3]	Yes[3]
The Bush Foundation	O	Yes	No
Committee on Institutional Cooperation (CIC)	D	Yes	Yes
The Camille and Henry Dreyfus Foundation	PD, R	Yes	Yes
The Glass, Pottery, Plastic and Allied Workers International Union (AFL-CIO, CLC)	U	No	Yes
Hughes Aircraft Company	D, P, MS	Yes	No

Vocational Goal and Name of Administering Agency	Level of Study[1]	Residency Requirement?	Affilication Requirement?[2]
Engineering (continued)			
The Kosciuszko Foundation	U, MS, MD, DDS	Yes	Yes
Los Alamos National Laboratory	PD, R	Yes	No
Massachusetts Institute of Technology (MIT)	PD, R	Yes	No
National Associatin of Plumbing-Heating- Cooling Contractors	U	No	No
National Center for Atmospheric Research	PD	Yes	No
National Scholarship Trust Fund	D, R, U, MS, JR	No	No
National Space Club	U, MS	No	No
NSPE Educational Foundation	MS, U	No	No
Oak Ridge Associated Universities	R, U, D, PD, MS	Yes[3]	Yes[3]
Oakland Scottish Rite Scholarship Foundations	JR, U	Yes	No
Royal Norwegian Council for Scientific and Industrial Research (NTNF)	PD, R	Yes	No
Science Service	U	No	No
Society for the Advancement of Material and Process Engineering (SAMPE)	MS, D, U	No	No
Society of Women Engineers	U	No	No
Southeastern Center for Electrical Engineering Education	PD, R	Yes	No
Tau Beta Pi Association	MS, D	No	Yes
Watertown Foundation Inc.	U	Yes	No
Zonta International	MS	No	No
Entomology			
National Geographic Society	R	No	No
Environmental Conservation			
The Charles A. Lindbergh Fund, Inc.	O	No	No
National Wildlife Federation	MS, D, R	No	No
Environmental Design			
American Society of Interior Designers Educational Foundation, Inc.	U, O	No	No
Graham Foundation for Advanced Studies in the Fine Arts	R, MS, O	No	No
Argonne National Laboratory	MS, D, R	Yes	Yes[3]
Associated Western Universities, Inc.	O, D, R, MS, PD, U	Yes	No
Association of Official Analytical Chemists	U	No	No

Vocational Goal and Name of Administering Agency	Level of Study[1]	Residency Requirement?	Affilication Requirement?[2]
Environmental Design (continued)			
Cooperative Institute for Research in Environmental Sciences	PD, R	Yes	No
Smithsonian Environmental Research Center	U, MS, D	Yes	No
Ethnology			
National Geographic Society	R	No	No
Ethology			
Fondation Fyssen	P	Yes	No
National Geographic Society	R	No	No
Fashion/Fashion Related			
Washington Fashion Group, Inc.	JR, U, MS	Yes	No
Filmmaking			
The American Film Institute	O, P	No	No
The MacDowell Colony	O	Yes	No
New York Foundation for the Arts	O	Yes	No
Virginia Museum of Fine Arts	U, MS, P	Yes	No
Finance			
AIESEC-United States, Inc.	U, MS	No	Yes
International Foundation of Employee Benefits Plans	MS, D, PD, R	No	No
The Kosciuszko Foundation	U, MS, MD, DDS	Yes	Yes
National Commercial Finance Association	U, MS	No	No
Fine Arts			
Graham Foundation for Advanced Studies in the Fine Arts	R, MS, O	No	No
John Simon Guggenheim Memorial Foundation	R, O	No	No
The George A. and Eliza Gardner Howard Foundation	O	No	No
Fisheries Sciences/Management			
Rob and Bessie Welder Wildlife Foundation	MS, D, R	Yes	No
Food Science/Technology			
Institute of Food Technologists	U, MS, R	No	No
Food Service Careers			
International Food Service Executives Association	JR, U, VT, O	No	No

Vocational Goal and Name of Administering Agency	Level of Study[1]	Residency Requirement?	Affiliation Requirement?[2]
Food Service Careers (continued)			
The National Institute for the Food-service Industry	JR, U	No	No
NFBA Education Foundation	U, MS	Yes	No
Foreign Policy			
The Brookings Institution	R, P, D	No	Yes[3]
Forestry			
The Bush Foundation	O	Yes	No
The Northeastern Loggers' Association, Inc.	U	Yes	No
Western Interstate Commission for Higher Education	U, MS, MD, DDS, P, JD	Yes	No
French Studies/History/Language/Literature			
The United Chapters of Phi Beta Kappa	D, R	No	No
Funeral Service Education			
American Board of Funeral Service Education	U, MS	No	No
Fusion Technology			
American Vacuum Society	MS, D	Yes	No
General Education			
AFTRA (American Federation of Television and Radio Artists) Memorial Foundation, Inc.	U, MS	No	Yes
Air Line Pilots Association	U	No	Yes
Alameda Naval Air Station Officers' Wives' Club	JR, U	Yes	Yes
Alcoa Foundation	U	No	Yes
All Indian Pueblo Council	U	No	Yes
American Association of University Women Educational Foundation	D, PD, R	No	No
American Business Women's Association	U, MS	No	No
American Can Company Foundation	U	No	Yes
American Council of the Blind	JR, U, MS, VT	No	No
American Foundation for the Blind, Inc.	JR, U	No	No
The American Legion	HS	No	No
American Postal Workers Union AFL-CIO	U	No	Yes
American School	JR, U, VT	No	Yes

Vocational Goal and Name of Administering Agency	Level of Study[1]	Residency Requirement?	Affiliation Requirement?[2]
General Education (continued)			
The American-Scandinavian Foundation	R	Yes	No
AMVETS	JR, U, VT	No	Yes
Army Emergency Relief	JR, U	Yes	Yes
Association of the Sons of Poland, Incorporated	U	No	Yes
Astraea Foundation, Inc.	O	No	No
Athena Civic Memorial Association	JR, U	Yes	No
Avon Products Foundation	U	Yes	Yes
The Bailey Foundation	U	Yes	No
Bank of America National Trust and Savings Association	U	Yes	Yes
Bank of New England-West	U, MS	Yes	No
Baptist Life Association	JR, U, MS	No	Yes
Belgian American Education Foundation, Inc.	D	Yes	No
Alexander Graham Bell Association for the Deaf	U, MS	No	No
Beta Theta Pi	U, MS	No	Yes
Blinded Veterans Association	JR, U, VT	No	Yes
B'nai B'rith Career and Counseling Services	U	Yes	No
Boettcher Foundation	U	Yes	No
The Boston Globe	JR, U, VT, O	Yes	No
Ethel N. Bowen Foundation	U	Yes	No
Boy Scouts of America	U, O, JR, VT, HS	Yes[3]	Yes
Otto Bremer Foundation	JR, U, VT	Yes	Yes
Bristol Volunteer Fire Department, Ladies Auxiliary	LPN, VT, JR, U, RN	No	Yes
Burlington Northern Railroad Company	JR, U	Yes	Yes
Business and Professional Women's Foundation	JR, LLB, MS, MD, VT, O, U	No	No
The James F. Byrnes Foundation	U	Yes	No
Fuller E. Callaway Foundation	U	Yes	No
Carolina Freight Carriers Corporation	JR, U, VT	Yes	Yes
Marjorie S. Carter Boy Scout Scholarship Trust	U	Yes	Yes
Charleston Evening Post The News and Courier	U	No	Yes
Cheyenne-Arapaho Tribal Offices	U, MS	Yes	Yes

Vocational Goal and Name of Administering Agency	Level of Study[1]	Residency Requirement?	Affilication Requirement?[2]
General Education (continued)			
Chicago Boys and Girls Clubs	U	Yes	Yes
Citizens' Scholarship Foundation of America, Inc.	JR, RN, U, O, VT, LPN	No	Yes[3]
City Volunteer Corps	JR, VT, U, O	Yes	No
Ty Cobb Educational Foundation	U, DDS, MD, LLB	Yes	No
The College Board	U	No	Yes
College Scholarship Service	JR, U	No	Yes
Colorado AFL-CIO	JR, U	No	Yes
Communications Workers of America-Georgia	U	No	Yes
Carle C. Conway Scholarship Foundation, Inc.	U	No	Yes
Council on International Educational Exchange	U, HS	No	No
Cummins Engine Foundation, Inc.	U	No	Yes
Dane County Labor Council AFL-CIO	JR, U, VT	No	Yes
Daniel International Corporation	U	No	Yes
Daughters of the Cincinnati	U	No	Yes
Lady Davis Fellowship Trust	D, PD, R	Yes	No
Deep Springs College	JR, U, HS	Yes	No
The Delta Gamma Foundation	MS, U	No	Yes
DeMolay Foundation, Inc.	JR, U	No	Yes
Denver Area Labor Federation, AFL-CIO	JR, U, VT	Yes	Yes
Des Moines Register	U	No	Yes
Disabled American Veterans	U	No	Yes
Duke Power Company	U	Yes	No
Duracell Scholarship Competition	JR, U	No	No
Eagle Scout Association	U	Yes	Yes
East Providence Senior High School	JR, U, VT	Yes	No
The Ebell of Los Angeles	U	Yes	No
James H. and Minnie M. Edmonds Educational Foundation	U	Yes	No
Educational Communications Scholarship Foundation	U	No	No
Edwards Scholarship Fund	U, MS	Yes	No
The English-Speaking Union	O	Yes	No
Fifth Marine Division Association Scholarship Fund	JR, LPN, U, RN, VT	No	Yes
Fina Oil and Chemical Company	U	Yes	No

Vocational Goal and Name of Administering Agency	Level of Study[1]	Residency Requirement?	Affiliation Requirement?[2]
General Education (continued)			
The Firestone Tire and Rubber Company	U	Yes	Yes
First Marine Division Association, Inc.	JR, U, VT	No	Yes
First National Bank of Akron	U, MS	Yes	No
Fourteenth Air Force Association, Inc.	U	No	Yes
Fourth Marine Division Association	JR, U, VT	No	Yes
Charles W. Frees, Jr. Educational Fund	U	Yes	No
The Glass, Pottery, Plastic and Allied Workers International Union (AFL-CIO, CLC)	U	No	Yes
Graphic Communications International Union	JR, LPN, U, VT, RN	No	Yes
Guideposts	U	No	No
Hammermill Paper Company	U, D, R, MS	No	Yes
The Hauss-Helms Foundation, Inc.	JR, U, MS, VT	Yes	No
Hawaiian Trust Company Limited	U, MS	Yes	Yes
Health and Community Services Council of Hawaii	JR, U, MS	Yes	No
HIAS	U, MS	No	No
Honeywell Inc.	U, MS	No	No
Hotel Restaurant & Club Employees and Bartenders Union Local 6	U	No	Yes
Illinois AMVETS	JR, U	Yes	Yes[3]
Inland Steel-Ryerson Foundation, Inc.	JR, U, VT, O	No	Yes
Institute of International Education	MS, O	Yes	No
International Association of Fire Fighters	U	No	Yes
International Association of Machinists and Aerospace Workers-Local 733	U	Yes	Yes
International Brotherhood of Electrical Workers Local 426	JR, U, RN, VT	No	Yes
International Chemical Workers Union	JR, U, RN, VT	No	Yes
International Union of Bricklayers and Allied Craftsmen	U	No	Yes
International Union of Electronic, Electrical, Technical, Salaried and Machine Workers, AFL-CIO	JR, LPN, U, RN, VT	No	Yes

Vocational Goal and Name of Administering Agency	Level of Study[1]	Residency Requirement?	Affiliation Requirement?[2]
General Education (continued)			
International Union of Operating			
Engineers	U	No	Yes
Iowa Federation of Labor, AFL-CIO	JR, U	Yes	No
Ishizaka Foundation	U, MS	Yes	No
JANGO, Inc.	JR, U, RN	No	Yes
Japanese American Citizens League	JR, RN,		
	VT, MS	No	Yes
Jewish Children's Regional Service of			
Jewish Children's Home	JR, MS, U,		
	D, VT	Yes	Yes
Jewish Foundation for Education of			
Women	JR, U,		
	MD, VT	Yes	No
Kappa Kappa Gamma Fraternity	U, O, P, MS,		
	JR, VT	No	Yes
Edward Bangs Kelley and Alza Kelley			
Foundation, Inc.	U, MS	Yes	No
Richard C. Knight Insurance Agency	JR, U, D,		
	MS HS	No	No
Knights of Columbus	U	No	Yes
Ladies Auxiliary to the Veterans of			
Foreign Wars	JR, U	No	Yes
Lee County Labor Council AFL-CIO	U	Yes	No
Lido Civic Club	U	Yes	Yes
The Lincoln-Lane Foundation	U	Yes	No
Lorain City Schools	JR, U, VT	Yes	No
Lutheran Church in America	U, D, P,		
	MS	No	Yes
Marin Educational Foundation	JR, U,		
	VT, O	Yes	No
Marine Corps Scholarship Foundation,			
Inc.	U	No	Yes
Ernestine Matthews Trust	U	Yes	No
Oscar Mayer Foods Corporation	U	No	Yes
Mayor's Scholarship Program	U, MS	Yes	No
James G.K. McClure Educational and			
Development Fund, Inc.	JR, U,		
	VT, RN	Yes	No
McCormick & Company, Inc.	U	No	Yes
The Meriden Record Company	JR, U	Yes	Yes
Merrill Lynch & Co. Inc.	U	No	Yes
The Metropolitan Museum of Art	HS	Yes	No
Minnesota American Federation of Labor			
and Congress of Industrial Organizations	JR,		
	U, VT	Yes	Yes

Vocational Goal and Name of Administering Agency	Level of Study[1]	Residency Requirement?	Affiliation Requirement?[2]
General Education (continued)			
Miss America Pageant Scholarship			
Foundation	U	No	No
Miss Teenage America	JR, U	No	No
Modern Woodmen of America	U, JR, VT	No	Yes[3]
The National Association of Secondary			
School Principals	U	No	No
National Bowling Council	U	No	No
National Campers and Hikers			
Association	JR, U	No	Yes
National Catholic Society of Foresters	U, JR, VT	No	Yes
National Center for American Indian			
Alternative Education	U	Yes	Yes
National Council of Jewish Women	U	Yes	Yes
National Federation of the Blind	JR, U, MS, VT	No	Yes
National History Day	HS	Yes	No
National Merit Scholarship			
Corporation	U	No	Yes[3]
National Office Products Association	JR, U, VT	No	Yes
National Twenty and Four	JR, U, MS, VT	No	Yes
New England Board of Higher			
Education	JR, U, MS, D, VT	Yes	No
New Jersey State Federation of Women's			
Clubs	MS, D	Yes	No
New York State Senate	MS, U	Yes	No
Newspaper Guild of New York—New York			
News Pension and Welfare Fund	JR, U	No	Yes
The Noble Educational Fund	JR, U, VT, O	No	Yes
Northern California Joint Council of Service			
Employees of the Service Employees			
International Union	U	No	Yes
Oakland Scottish Rite Scholarship			
Foundations	JR, U	Yes	No
Optimist International	JR, U	No	No
Order of Ahepa	U	Yes	Yes
Pacific Gas and Electric Company	JR, U	Yes	No
Arthur C. and Lucia S. Palmer			
Foundation, Inc.	U	Yes	No
The Pantagraph	JR, U, VT	Yes	Yes

Vocational Goal and Name of Administering Agency	Level of Study[1]	Residency Requirement?	Affiliation Requirement?[2]
General Education (continued)			
Pearl Harbor-Honolulu Branch 46	JR, U	No	Yes
Phi Eta Sigma National Honor Society	MS, P	No	Yes
The Pillsbury Company Foundation	JR, U, VT	No	Yes
Minnie Stevens Piper Foundation	U	Yes	No
Plumbers Union No. 15	JR, U, VT	No	Yes
Portuguese Continental Union of the United States of America	U	No	Yes
Presbyterian Church (U.S.A.)—New York	U, MS, D, P	Yes[3]	Yes
President's Committee on Employment of the Handicapped	JR, U, VT, HS	No	No
Herschel C. Price Educational Foundation	U	Yes	No
Jeannette Rankin Foundation, Inc.	O	No	Yes
Republic of China	U, MS, D, O	Yes	No
Reserve Officers Association of the United States	U	No	Yes
The Rhodes Scholarship Trust	MS	Yes	No
Sid Richardson Memorial Fund	U	No	Yes
Jackie Robinson Foundation	U	No	Yes
The Roothbert Fund	U	Yes	No
Rotary Foundation of Rotary International	U, MS	Yes	No
The S&H Foundation, Inc.	U	No	Yes
Abbie Sargent Memorial Scholarship, Inc.	U	Yes	No
Seafarers Welfare Plan	U, JR, VT	No	Yes
Society of the Daughters of the United States Army	JR, U, VT	No	Yes
Society of the First Division	U	No	Yes
Society of the First Division Foundation	JR, U, VT	No	Yes
Soroptimist International of the Americas, Inc.	JR, U, VT, O	No	No
The Southland Corporation	U	No	Yes
Southwestern Ohio Council for Higher Education	JR, U, MS	Yes	Yes
The Stop & Shop Companies, Inc.	U	No	Yes
Surflant Scholarship Foundation	U	No	Yes
Swiss Relief Society	U	Yes	Yes
Taft Broadcasting Company	U	No	Yes

Vocational Goal and Name of Administering Agency	Level of Study[1]	Residency Requirement?	Affilication Requirement?[2]
General Education (continued)			
The Teagle Foundation	U, D, P, LLB, MD, MS, DDS	No	Yes
Telluride Association	HS	Yes	No
Texas AFL-CIO	JR, U, VT	No	Yes
Third Marine Division Association, Inc.	U	No	Yes
37th Division Veterans Association	U	No	Yes
Transport Workers Union of America	U	No	Yes
Twin City Carpenters District Council of United Brotherhood of Carpenters and Joiners of America	U	No	Yes
Two/Ten National Foundation	JR, LPN, U, RN, VT, O	Yes	Yes
Unitarian Universalist Association	JR, U, P	No	Yes
United Food and Commercial Workers International Untion, AFL-CIO, CLC	U	Yes	Yes
United Jewish Endowment Fund	U, MS, D	Yes	No
United Steelworkers of America	U	No	Yes
United Steelworkers of America, District 28	U	No	Yes
Urann Foundation Scholarship Program	JR, U, RN, VT	Yes	Yes
U.S. Department of Education	JR, U, MS, VT	No	No
U.S. Naval Academy Class of 1963 Foundation	JR, U, VT	No	Yes
Utah State AFL-CIO	U	Yes	No
Utility Workers Union of America, AFL-CIO	U	No	Yes
Veterans of Foreign Wars of the United States and Ladies Auxiliary to the V.F.W.	U	No	No
Richard F. Walsh Foundation	U	No	Yes
The Washington Center	U	Yes	No
The Washington Post	JR, U, VT	No	Yes
Watertown Foundation, Inc.	U	Yes	No
The Windham Foundation, Inc.	U	Yes	No
The Women Marines Associatin	JR, U	No	Yes
Woonsocket Kiwanis Education Fund	JR, U, VT	Yes	No
Youth for Understanding	HS, O	No	No

Vocational Goal and Name of Administering Agency	Level of Study[1]	Residency Requirement?	Affiliation Requirement?[2]
Genetics			
Rob and Bessie Welder Wildlife Foundation	MS, D, R	Yes	No
Geodesy			
American Congress on Surveying and Mapping	U, MS, D	No	No
Geography			
The Association of American Geographers	R, D	No	Yes
The Farm Foundation	O	No	No
National Geographic Society	R	No	No
Geology/Geophysics/Geosciences			
Marshall H. and Nellie Alworth Memorial Fund	U	Yes	No
Associated Western Universities, Inc.	O, D, R, MS, PD, U	Yes	No
The Geological Society of America	MS, D, R	Yes	No
Los Alamos National Laboratory	PD, R	Yes	No
National Center for Atmospheric Research	PD	Yes	No
Southeastern Center for Electrical Engineering Educatin	PD, R	Yes	No
German Studies			
American Association of Teachers of German	HS	Yes	No
German Academic Exchange Service (DAAD)	U, MS, D, PD	Yes	No
Institute of International Education	O	Yes	No
Gerontology			
The Gerontological Society of America	R	Yes	No
Glaciology			
National Geographic Society	R	No	No
Government			
American Political Science Association	O	Yes	Yes
The American Political Science Association	D, PD, O	Yes	No
The Brookings Institution	R, P, D	Yes	Yes[3]
The Bush Foundation	O	Yes	No
The James A. Finnegan Fellowship Foundation	U	Yes	No

Vocational Goal and Name of Administering Agency	Level of Study[1]	Residency Requirement?	Affiliation Requirement?[2]
Government (continued)			
New York State Senate	MS, U	Yes	No
Washington Crossing Foundation	U	No	No
Graphics/Graphic Art/Graphic Communication			
The Meriden Record Company	U, MS	Yes	No
National Scholarship Trust Fund	MS, D, R, JR, U	No	No
New York Foundation for the Arts	O	Yes	No
Pollock-Krasner Foundation, Inc.	O	No	No
Two/Ten National Foundation	JR, LPN, U, O, VT, RN	Yes	Yes
Greek Archeology/Classical Studies/History/Language/Literature			
Center for Hellenic Studies	PD, R	Yes	No
Eta Sigma Phi	MS, D	Yes	No
The United Chapters of Phi Beta Kappa	D, R	No	No
Health Professions/Careers			
American Respiratory Therapy Foundation	R	No	Yes
Arthritis Foundation	R, D	No	No
Business and Professional Women's Foundation	U, P, O, VT	No	No
Civitan International Foundation	U, MS	No	No
East Providence Senior High School	JR, LPN, U, RN, VT	Yes	No
Institute of Medicine	O	No	Yes
South Dakota State Medical Association and Auxiliary	JR, U, VT	Yes	No
Health Sciences			
American Heart Association	U	Yes	No
International Foundation of Employee Benefit Plans	MS, D, PD, R	No	No
Los Alamos National Laboratory	PD, R	Yes	No
Oak Ridge Associated Universities	MS, D, PD, U	No	Yes[3]
Watertown Foundation Inc.	U	Yes	No
Health Services Administration			
The Bush Foundation	O	Yes	No
Foundation of the American College of Healthcare Executives	MS	No	Yes
The Foundation of the American College of Healthcare Executives	MS	No	No
History			
American Antiquarian Society	D, R	Yes	No

Vocational Goal and Name of Administering Agency	Level of Study[1]	Residency Requirement?	Affiliation Requirement?[2]
History (continued)			
American Defense Institute	D	Yes	No
American Historical Association	R, PD	Yes[3]	Yes[3]
Civitan International Foundation	U, MS	No	No
Earhart Foundation	R, MS, D	No	Yes[3]
The George A. and Eliza Gardner Howard Foundation	O	No	No
Institute of Early American Culture	O	No	No
National History Day	HS	Yes	No
The National Society of the Sons of the American Revolution	HS	No	No
The Newberry Library	PD, R, D	Yes	Yes[3]
Phi Alpha Theta International Honor Society in History	MS, D	No	Yes
Sourisseau Academy	R	No	No
The Harry S. Truman Library Institute	U, D, R, S, PD	Yes	No
Home Economics			
American Home Economics Association Foundation	O, MS, D, R	Yes[3]	Yes[3]
Abbie Sargent Memorial Scholarship, Inc.	U	Yes	No
Horticulture			
Horticultural Research Institute, Inc.	R	No	No
National Junior Horticultural Association	O	Yes	No
Hotel/Institutional/Restaurant Management			
American Dietetic Association	U	No	No
David Rubenstein Memorial Scholarship Foundation	U	Yes	No
Human Services			
Astraea Foundation, Inc.	O	No	No
Humanities			
Earhart Foundation	R, MS, D	No	Yes[3]
The Kosciuszko Foundation	U, MS, MD, DDS	Yes	Yes
Massachusetts Institute of Technology (MIT)	PD, R	Yes[3]	No
National Academy of Education	PD, R	No	No
National Junior Classical League	U	No	Yes
The Newberry Library	PD, R	Yes	Yes
Woodrow Wilson National Fellowship Foundation	PD, D	Yes	No

Vocational Goal and Name of Administering Agency	Level of Study[1]	Residency Requirement?	Affiliation Requirement?[2]
Hydrology			
Our World-Underwater Scholarship Society	P	No	No
Iberian Studies			
The Tinker Foundation	PD, R	Yes	No
Industrial Education			
National Scholarship Trust Fund	MS, D, R	No	No
Industrial/Labor Relations			
AFTRA (American Federation of Television and Radio Artists) Memorial Foundation, Inc.	U, MS	No	Yes
Educational and Cultural Fund of the Electrical Industry	U	Yes	Yes
The Glass, Pottery, Plastic and Allied Workers International Union (AFL-CIO, CLC)	U	No	Yes
International Foundation of Employee Benefit Plans	MS, D, PD, R	No	No
Information Science/Technology			
AT&T Bell Laboratories	D, U	Yes	Yes[3]
Insurance/Insurance Related Fields			
The S.S. Huebner Foundation for Insurance Education	D, PD	Yes	No
Interdisciplinary Studies			
Northwood Institute Alden B. Dow Creativity Center	O	Yes	No
Interior Design			
American Society of Interior Designers Educational Foundation, Inc.	U, O	No	No
International Affairs/Relations			
American Jewish Committee	MS	Yes	No
Commission of the European Communities	R	No	No
Earhart Foundation	R, MS, D	No	Yes[3]
The Experiment in International Living	O	No	No
Institute of Current World Affairs	O	No	No
The Tinker Foundation	PD, R	Yes	No
Youth for Understanding	HS, O	No	No
Italian/Italian-American Studies			
American Association of Teachers of Italian	JR, U, HS	No	No
Order Sons of Italy in America	JR, U, HS	Yes	No

Vocational Goal and Name of Administering Agency	Level of Study[1]	Residency Requirement?	Affiliation Requirement?[2]
Japanese Studies			
Ishizaka Foundation	U, MS	Yes	No
Journalism			
American Medical Association	PD	Yes	No
The American Political Science			
Association	O	Yes	No
Asian American Journalists Association	JR, U	No	Yes
The Robert Bosch Foundation	P	Yes	No
The Bush Foundation	O	Yes	No
The Dow Jones Newspaper Fund, Inc.	MS, U	No	Yes[3]
Sidney Hillman Foundation, Inc.	O	No	No
Inter American Press Association			
Scholarship Fund, Inc.	P, O	Yes	No
Kansas State University	U	Yes	No
The Kosciuszko Foundation	U, MS, MD, DDS	Yes	Yes
The Ralph McGill Scholarship Fund	U	Yes	No
The Meriden Record Company	U, MS	Yes	No
New York State Senate	MS	Yes	No
Quill and Scroll	U, HS	No	No
The Scripps-Howard Foundation	U, MS, P	No	No
Women in Communications, Inc.	JR, U, MS	Yes	No
Landscape Architecture/Design			
Dumbarton Oaks	D, PD	Yes	No
Landscape Architecture Foundation	P, U, R, MS	No	No
Languages			
American Classical League	HS	No	No
Eta Sigma Phi	MS D	Yes	No
The George A. and Eliza Gardner Howard			
Foundation	O	No	No
Kappa Kappa Gamma Fraternity	MS	Yes	Yes
Latin American Studies			
Inter American Press Association			
Scholarship Fund, Inc.	P, O	Yes	No
The Tinker Foundation	PD, R	Yes	No
Law			
American Association of University			
Women Educational Foundation	D, PD, R	No	No
American Defense Institute	D	Yes	No
AT&T Bell Laboratories	U	Yes	Yes
The Robert Bosch Foundation	P	Yes	No
Boy Scouts of America	U	No	Yes
The Bush Foundation	O	Yes	No
Fuller E. Callaway Foundation	LLB, JD	Yes	No

Vocational Goal and Name of Administering Agency	Level of Study[1]	Residency Requirement?	Affiliation Requirement?[2]
Law (continued)			
Council on Legal Education Opportunity	LLB	No	Yes
International Foundation of Employee Benefit Plans	MS, D, PD, R	No	No
The Kosciuszko Foundation	U, MS, MD, DDS	Yes	Yes
Law School Admission Council/Law School Admission Services	LLB	No	No
Puerto Rican Legal Defense and Education Fund, Inc.	LLB	No	Yes
The Teagle Foundation	U, D, P, DDS, MD, LLB, MS	No	Yes
Earl Warren Legal Training Program, Inc.	LLB	No	Yes
Western Interstate Commission for Higher Education	U, DDS, MS, MD, P, JD	Yes	No
Law Enforcement			
Association of Former Agents of the U.S. Secret Service, Inc.	U, MS	No	No
Boy Scouts of America	U	No	Yes
The Bush Foundation	O	Yes	No
Leadership, Institutional/Community			
W.K. Kellogg Foundation	O	No	No
Library Science/Library Technician			
Akron-Summit County Public Library	MS	Yes	No
Hartford Public Library	MS	No	Yes
Mountain Plains Library Association	P, O	Yes	Yes
New Jersey Library Association	MS	Yes	No
North Carolina Library Association	MS	Yes	No
Oregon Library Association	P	Yes	No
Pennsylvania Library Association	U, R, P, MS, O	Yes[3]	Yes[3]
Special Libraries Association	MS	Yes	No
Western Interstate Commission for Higher Education	U, DDS, MS, MD, P, JD	Yes	No
Licensed Practical Nursing			
Bristol Volunteer Fire Department Ladies Auxiliary	JR, LPN, U, RN, VT	No	Yes

Vocational Goal and Name of Administering Agency	Level of Study[1]	Residency Requirement?	Affiliation Requirement?[2]
Licensed Practical Nursing (continued)			
Citizens' Scholarship Foundation of America, Inc.	JR, LPN, U, RN, O, VT	No	Yes
National Black Nurses' Association, Inc.	U, RN, LPN	No	Yes
Life Sciences			
Argonne National Laboratory	MS, D, R, U	Yes	Yes[3]
Oak Ridge Associated Universities	U, D, R, MS, PD	Yes	No
Whitehall Foundation, Inc.	R	No	No
Linguistics			
The George A. and Eliza Gardner Howard Foundation	O	No	No
The Newberry Library	PD, R	Yes	Yes
Literature			
Florida Department of State	P, O	Yes	No
The George A. and Eliza Gardner Howard Foundation	O	No	No
The Newberry Library	PD, R	Yes	Yes
Mammology			
National Geographic Society	R	No	No
Rob and Bessie Welder Wildlife Foundation	MS, D, R	Yes	No
Management			
American Assembly of Collegiate Schools of Business	D	No	No
American Society for Medical Technology Education & Research Fund, Inc.	MS, D, O	No	No
National Scholarship Trust Fund	JR, U	No	No
NSPE Educational Foundation	MS	No	No
W.E. Upjohn Institute for Employment Research	R	No	No
Manufacturing			
National Scholarship Trust Fund	JR, U	No	No
Marine Biology/Policy/Science			
American Fishing Tackle Manufacturers Association	MS, D, R	No	No
National Geographic Society	R	No	No
Our World—Underwater Scholarship Society	P	No	No
The Tinker Foundation	PD, R	Yes	No

Vocational Goal and Name of Administering Agency	Level of Study[1]	Residency Requirement?	Affiliation Requirement?[2]
Marine Engineering			
The Society of Naval Architects and Marine Engineers	MS, D	No	No
Marketing/Distribution			
AIESEC-United States, Inc.	U, MS	No	Yes
Civitan International Foundation	MS	No	No
Materials Research/Science			
AT&T Bell Laboratories	D, U	Yes	Yes[3]
Los Alamos National Laboratory	PD, R	Yes	No
Mathematics/Mathematical Sciences			
Marshall H. and Nellie Alworth Memorial Fund	U	Yes	No
Argonne National Laboratory	MS, D, R, U	Yes	No
Associated Western Universities, Inc.	O, D, R, MS, PD, U	Yes	No
AT&T Bell Laboratories	D, U	Yes	Yes[3]
Committee on Institutional Cooperation (CIC)	D	Yes	Yes
Hughes Aircraft Company	D, P, MS	Yes	No
IBM Thomas J. Watson Research Center	PD, R	Yes	No
The Kosciuszko Foundation	U, MS, MD, DDS	Yes	Yes
Los Alamos National Laboratory	PD, R	Yes	No
National Center for Atmospheric Research	PD	Yes	No
National Scholarship Trust Fund	MS, D, R	No	No
Oak Ridge Associated Universities	MS, D, U, PD, R	Yes[3]	Yes[3]
Science Service	U	No	No
Southeastern Center for Electrical Engineering Education	PD, R	Yes	No
Mechanical Drawing			
The Alfred T. Granger Student Art Scholarship	JR, U, VT, O	Yes	No
Media Arts			
Florida Department of State	P, O	Yes	No
Medical Assisting			
American Medical Technologists	JR, U, VT	No	No
Medical Laboratory Technology			
International Society for Clinical Laboratory Technology (ISCLT)	VT, O	Yes	No
Medical Research			
The American Academy for Cerebral Palsy and Developmental Medicine	R	No	No

Vocational Goal and Name of Administering Agency	Level of Study[1]	Residency Requirement?	Affiliation Requirement?[2]
Medical Research (continued)			
American Cancer Society, Inc.	R, PD	Yes[3]	No
American College of Preventive Medicine	PD, R	No	No
American Heart Association	PD, R	Yes[3]	No
Arthritis Foundation	PD, R	No	No
The Burroughs Wellcome Fund	R	Yes[3]	No
The Jane Coffin Childs Memorial Fund for Medical Research	PD, R	No	No
Cystic Fibrosis Foundation	PD, R	Yes[3]	No
Damon Runyon-Walter Winchell Cancer Fund	PD, R	No	No
Epilepsy Foundation of America	R	No	No
Foundation for Chiropractic Education and Research	R, P	No	No
The Anna Fuller Fund	R, PD	No	No
Ruth Estrin Goldberg Memorial for Cancer Research	R	No	No
The Grass Foundation	D, MD, PD	Yes	No
The John A. Hartford Foundation, Inc.	PD, R	No	No
The Heiser Program for Research in Leprosy	R	Yes[3]	No
International Brain Research Organization	O	No	No
Leukemia Society of America	P	No	No
Lucille P. Markey Charitable Trust	R	No	No
Muscular Dystrophy Association	PD, R	No	No
The Myasthenia Gravis Foundation, Inc.	PD, R	No	No
National Kidney Foundation	R	No	No
Orthopaedic Research and Education Foundation	PD, R	No	No
Society of Biological Psychiatry	P	No	No
United Cerebral Palsy Research and Educational Foundation, Inc.	R	No	No
The Helen Hay Whitney Foundation	PD, R	No	No
Medical Sciences And Allied Fields			
The American Academy for Cerebral Palsy and Developmental Medicine	R	No	No
American Heart Association	U, MD	Yes	No
American Medical Association	PD	Yes	No
Medical Technology			
American Medical Technologists	JR, U, VT	No	No
American Society for Medical Technology Education & Research Fund, Inc.	D, O, R, U, P, MS	No	No

Vocational Goal and Name of Administering Agency	Level of Study[1]	Residency Requirement?	Affiliation Requirement?[2]
Medicine			
Marshall H. and Nellie Alworth Memorial Fund	U	Yes	No
American Association of University Women Educational Foundation	D, PD, R	No	No
American College of Physicians	PD	Yes	Yes
American Heart Association	U, MD	Yes	No
Arthritis Foundation	PD	No	No
Joseph Collins Foundation	MD	No	No
Cystic Fibrosis Foundation	PD, R	Yes	No
Easter Seal Society of Iowa, Inc.	U, MS	Yes	No
Epilepsy Foundation of America	MD	No	No
Fresno-Madera Medical Society Scholarship Foundation	MD, DDS, P, RN	Yes	No
Jewish Foundation for Education of Women	F	Yes	No
The Kosciuszko Foundation	U, D, R, MS, MD, DDS, PD	Yes	Yes
National Council on the Aging, Inc.	MD	No	No
National Medical Fellowships, Inc.	MD	No	Yes
Sacramento-El Dorado Medical Society	MD, PD	Yes	No
The Teagle Foundation	U, D, P, LLB, MS, MD, DDS	No	Yes
United Cerebral Palsy Research and Educational Foundation, Inc.	PD, MS, D, MD	Yes[3]	No
Westchester Community Service Council, Inc.	MS, D, MD, DDS, RN	Yes	No
Western Interstate Commission for Higher Education	U, DDS, MS, MD, P, JD	Yes	No
Metallurgy			
American Vacuum Society	MS, D	Yes	No
Los Alamos National Laboratory	PD, R	Yes	No
Society for the Advancement of Material and Process Engineering (SAMPE)	MS, D, U	No	No
Meteorology			
American Meteorological Society	U	No	No
Southeastern Center for Electrical Engineering Education	PD, R	Yes	No

Vocational Goal and Name of Administering Agency	Level of Study[1]	Residency Requirement?	Affiliation Requirement?[2]
Middle/Near Eastern Studies			
Center for Arabic Study Abroad	U, MS, D, PD	Yes	No
Military Education			
The Falcon Foundation	O	Yes	No
Mineralogy			
National Geographic Society	R	No	No
Museum Careers			
The Metropolitan Museum of Art	HS	Yes	No
Metropolitan Museum of Art	U, O, MS	Yes	No
Virginia Museum of Fine Arts	MS, D	Yes	No
Music			
American Acedemy and Institute of Arts and Letters	O	No	No
American College of Musicians	U, O	No	Yes
American Foundation for the Blind, Inc.	U, MS	No	No
Associated Male Choruses of America, Inc.	U	No	No
Baldwin Piano and Organ Company	O	No	No
Florida Department of State	P, O	Yes	No
Fondation des Etats-Unis	MS, O	Yes	No
International Piano Recording Competition of the Piano Guild, USA	O	No	Yes
International Thespian Society	JR, U, O	No	Yes
The Kosciuszko Foundation	O	No	No
Music Assistance Fund	P	No	Yes
National Federation of Music Clubs	O	Yes[3]	Yes[3]
National Institute for Music Theater	P	No	No
The National League of American Pen Women, Inc.	O	No	No
National Symphony Orchestra	O, HS	Yes	No
Mary and Edith Pillsbury Foundation	O	Yes	No
Sigma Alpha Iota Philanthropies, Inc.	O	Yes	No
Van Cliburn International Quadrennial Piano Competition	O	No	No
Women's Association Minnesota Orchestra (WAMSO)	U, O	Yes	No
Music Composition			
Edward F. Albee Foundation, Inc.	O	Yes	No
American College Theatre Festival	U, MS	No	No
Dorland Mountain Colony	O	Yes	No
The Fargo-Moorhead Symphony Orchestral Association	O	No	No
John Simon Guggenheim Memorial Foundation	R, O	No	No
The MacDowell Colony	O	Yes	No

Vocational Goal and Name of Administering Agency	Level of Study[1]	Residency Requirement?	Affiliation Requirement?[2]
Music Composition (continued)			
The Millay Colony for the Arts, Inc.	O	Yes	No
New York Foundation for the Arts	O	Yes	No
"Queen Marie Jose"	O	No	No
Yaddo	O	Yes	No
Musicology			
John Simon Guggenheim Memorial Foundation	R, O	No	No
The Newberry Library	PD, R	Yes	No
Mycology			
The Mycological Society of America	D	Yes	No
Natural Sciences			
The Kosciuszko Foundation	U, MS, MD, DDS	Yes	Yes
Naval Architecture			
The Society of Naval Architects and Marine Engineers	MS, D	No	No
Neuroscience			
Fondation Fyssen	P	Yes	No
The Grass Foundation	D, MD, PD	Yes	No
Nuclear Science			
Argonne National Laboratory	U, D, R, MS	Yes	Yes[3]
Oak Ridge Associated Universities	U, MS, D, PD	No	Yes
Nursing			
Aid Association for Lutherans	JR, U, RN	No	Yes
American Association of Critical- Care Nurses	U	No	Yes
American Legion	P	No	No
American Nurses' Foundation, Inc.	R	No	No
Association of Operating Room Nurses, Inc. (AORN)	U, MS, RN	No	Yes
Bristol Volunteer Fire Department, Ladies Auxiliary	JR, LPN, U, RN, VT	No	Yes
Citizens' Scholarship Foundation of America, Inc.	JR, LPN, U, RN, O, VT	No	Yes
Cleveland Area Citizens League for Nursing	RN	Yes	No
East Providence Senior High School	JR, LPN, U, RN, VT	Yes	No
Fifth Marine Division Association Scholarship Fund	JR, LPN, RN, U, VT	No	Yes

Vocational Goal and Name of Administering Agency	Level of Study[1]	Residency Requirement?	Affiliation Requirement?[2]
Nursing (continued)			
Fresno-Madera Medical Society Scholarship Foundation	MD, DDS, P, RN	Yes	No
Graphic Communications International Union	JR, LPN, U, RN, VT	No	Yes
Illinois AMVETS	JR, U, RN	Yes	No
International Association for Enterostomal Therapy	O	No	Yes
International Brotherhood of Electrical Workers Local 426	JR, U, RN, VT	No	Yes
International Chemical Workers Union	JR, U, RN, VT	No	Yes
International Union of Electronic, Electrical, Technical, Salaried and Machine Workers, AFL-CIO	JR, LPN, U, RN, VT	No	Yes
JANGO, Inc.	JR, U, RN	No	Yes
Japanese American Citizens League	JR, U, RN, VT	No	Yes
Robert Wood Johnson Foundation	PD	Yes	No
Massachusetts/Rhode Island League for Nursing	U, RN, LPN	Yes	No
Maternity Center Association	P	No	No
James G. K. McClure Educational and Development Fund, Inc.	JR, U, VT, RN	Yes	No
Methodist Hospitals Foundation	RN	No	No
Missouri League for Nursing, Inc.	JR, LPN, U, MS, RN, VT	Yes	No
Mountain States Health Corporation	P	Yes	No
NAPNAP Foundation	R	No	No
National Association of Pediatric Nurse Associates and Practitioners	P	No	No
National Association of School Nurses, Inc.	R	No	Yes
National Black Nurses' Association, Inc.	U, RN, LPN	No	Yes
North Dakota Nursing Scholarship Loan Committee	U, MS, RN, LPN	Yes	No
The Nurses' Association of the American College of Obstetricians and Gynecologists	RN, LPN, U, MS, D	No	Yes
Nurses' Educational Funds, Inc.	U, MS, D, RN	No	Yes

Vocational Goal and Name of Administering Agency	Level of Study[1]	Residency Requirement?	Affiliation Requirement?[2]
Nursing (continued)			
Oregon League for Nursing	P, RN, O	Yes	No
Sigma Theta Tau	R	No	No
Suburban Hospital Board of Trustees	RN	Yes	No
Two/Ten National Foundation	JR, LPN, U, O, RN, VT	Yes	Yes
Westchester Community Service Council, Inc.	MS, DDS, D, MD, RN	Yes	No
Western Interstate Commission for Higher Education	MS, DDS, U, MD, P, JD	Yes	No
Nutrition			
American Dietetic Association	U	No	No
American Home Economics Association Foundation	O, D, R	Yes[3]	Yes[3]
Lucille P. Market Charitable Trust	R	No	No
Occupational Therapy			
American Occupational Therapy Foundation, Inc.	PD	No	Yes
Easter Seal Society of Iowa, Inc.	U, MS	Yes	No
Excalibur Foundation	U	No	No
Western Interstate Commission for Higher Education	MS, DDS, U, MD, P, JD	Yes	No
Ocean Engineering			
The Society of Naval Architects and Marine Engineers	MS, D	No	No
Ocean Management			
Western Interstate Commission for Higher Education	U, DDS, MS, MD, P, JD	Yes	No
Ocean Sciences			
Our World-Underwater Scholarship Society	P	No	No
Oceanography			
National Center for Atmospheric Research	MS, D, R, PD	Yes	No
National Geographic Society	R	No	No
Operations Research			
AT&T Bell Laboratories	D, U	Yes	Yes[3]
Optometry			
American Academy of Optometry	P	No	No

Vocational Goal and Name of Administering Agency	Level of Study[1]	Residency Requirement?	Affiliation Requirement?[2]
Optometry (continued)			
American Optometric Foundation	R, P	No	No
The Auxiliary to the Washington Optometric Association	P	Yes	No
Western Interstate Commission for Higher Education	U, DDS, MS, MD, P, JD	Yes	No
Ornithology			
National Geographic Society	R	No	No
Rob and Bessie Welder Wildlife Foundation	MS, D, R	Yes	No
Osteopathic Medicine			
American Association of University Women Educational Foundation	D, PD, R	No	No
Auxiliary to the American Osteopathic Association	DO	No	No
Western Interstate Commission for Higher Education	U, DDS, MS, MD, P, JD	Yes	No
Packaging			
National Scholarship Trust Fund	MS, JR, D, R, U	No	No
Painting			
Edward F. Albee Foundation, Inc.	O	Yes	No
American Academy and Institute of Arts and Letters	O	No	No
Dorland Mountain Colony	O	Yes	No
Fondation des Estats-Unis	MS, O	Yes	No
The MacDowell Colony	O	No	Yes
New York Foundation for the Arts	O	Yes	No
Pollock-Krasner Foundation, Inc.	O	No	No
The John F. and Anna Lee Stacey Scholarship Fund for Art Education	P	No	No
Virginia Museum of Fine Arts	U, MS, P	Yes	No
Yaddo	O	Yes	No
Paleontology			
Fondation Fyssen	P	Yes	No
National Geographic Society	R	No	No
Performing Arts			
AFTRA (American Federation of Television and Radio Artists) Memorial Foundation, Inc.	U, MS	No	Yes
The Bush Foundation	D	Yes	No
Georgetown Workshop Theatre	JR, U, O	Yes	No

Vocational Goal and Name of Administering Agency	Level of Study[1]	Residency Requirement?	Affiliation Requirement?[2]
Performing Arts (continued)			
The George A. and Eliza Gardner			
Howard Foundation	O	No	No
International Thespian Society	JR, U, O	No	Yes
National Association of Teachers of			
Singing, Inc.	O	No	Yes
Personnel Administration			
International Foundation of Employee			
Benefit Plans	MS, D, PD, R	No	No
Pharmaceutical Sciences			
Lambda Kappa Sigma	U, MS, D	No	Yes
Pharmacology			
American Foundation for Pharmaceutical			
Engineering	D, PD	No	No
Fresno-Madera Medical Society			
Scholarship Foundation	MD, DDS, P, RN	Yes	No
Lambda Kappa Sigma	U, MS, D	No	Yes
Western Interstate Commission for			
Higher Education	U, DDS, MS, MD, P, JD	Yes	No
Philosophy			
The George A. and Eliza Gardner			
Howard Foundation	O	No	No
Photogrammetry			
American Congress on Surveying and			
Mapping	U, MS, D	No	No
Photography			
The Friends of Photography	O	No	No
Kansas State University	U	Yes	No
The MacDowell Colony	O	Yes	No
The Meriden Record Company	U, MS	Yes	No
New York Foundation for the Arts	O	Yes	No
The Photographic Society of America, Inc.	U	Yes	No
Scholastic, Inc.	U	Yes	No
Virginia Museum of Fine Arts	U, MS, P	Yes	No
Yaddo	O	Yes	No
Physical Sciences			
Argonne National Laboratory	MS, D, R, U	Yes	Yes[3]
Fannie and John Hertz Foundation	MS, D	Yes	No
Oak Ridge Associated Universities	MS, D, U, PD, R	Yes[3]	Yes[3]
Science Service	U	No	No

Vocational Goal and Name of Administering Agency	Level of Study[1]	Residency Requirement?	Affiliation Requirement?[2]
Physical Therapy			
Easter Seal Society of Iowa, Inc.	U, MS	Yes	No
Excalibur Foundation	U	No	No
Western Interstate Commission for Higher Education	MS, DDS, U, MD, P, JD	Yes	No
Physics			
Marshall H. and Nellie Alworth Memorial Fund	U	Yes	No
American Association of Physics Teachers	U	Yes	No
American Vacuum Society	MS, D	Yes	No
Associated Western Universities, Inc.	MS, D, U, R, O, PD	Yes	No
AT&T Bell Laboratories	D, U	Yes	Yes[3]
Hughes Aircraft Company	D, P, MS	Yes	No
Los Alamos National Laboratory	PD, R	Yes	No
National Center for Atmospheric Research	MS, D, R, PD	Yes	No
National Scholarship Trust Fund	MS, D, R	No	No
Society for the Advancement of Material and Process Engineering (SAMPE)	MS, D, U	No	No
Placement			
Council on Career Development for Minorities, Inc.	MS	Yes	Yes
Play Writing			
Actors Theatre of Louisville	O	No	No
American College Theatre Festival	U, MS, JR	No	No
Court Theatre	O	No	No
The Foundation of the Dramatists Guild	O	Yes	No
Jacksonville University	O	No	No
New York Foundation for the Arts	O	Yes	No
The Playwriters' Center	P	Yes	No
Podiatry			
Western Interstate Commission for Higher Education	U, MS, MD, DDS, P, JD	Yes	No
Poetry			
The Academy of American Poets	O	No	No
Edward F. Albee Foundation, Inc.	O	Yes	No
American Academy and Institute of Arts and Letters	O	No	No
Dorland Mountain Colony	O	Yes	No
Lincoln College	O	No	No
New York Foundation for the Arts	O	Yes	No

Vocational Goal and Name of Administering Agency	Level of Study[1]	Residency Requirement?	Affiliation Requirement?[2]
Polish Studies			
The Kosciuszko Foundation	MS, PD, D, U, MD, R, DDS	Yes[3]	Yes[3]
Political Science			
American Defense Institute	D	Yes	No
The American Political Science Association	D, PD, O	Yes	No
American Political Science Association	D	No	Yes
The Robert Bosch Foundation	P	Yes	No
Civitan International Foundation	U, MS	No	No
Earhart Foundation	R, MS, D	No	Yes[3]
The Farm Foundation	O	No	No
The George A. and Eliza Gardner Howard Foundation	O	No	No
National Association of Broadcasters	R	No	No
Portuguese Studies			
The Newberry Library	PD, R	Yes	Yes
Pre-Columbian Studies			
Dumbarton Oaks	D, PD	Yes	No
Pre-Medicine/-Optometry/-Veterinary Medicine/-Dentistry/-Law			
Abbie Sargent Memorial Scholarship, Inc.	U	Yes	No
Primatology			
National Geographic Society	R	No	No
Printing			
National Scholarship Trust Fund	MS, D, JR, R, U	No	No
The Newberry Library	PD, R	Yes	Yes
Printmaking			
Fondation des Etats-Unis	MS, O	Yes	No
Virginia Museum of Fine Arts	U, MS, P	Yes	No
Psychiatry			
The John Frederick Steinman Fellowship Fund	MS, D, PD	No	No
Psychology			
American Psychological Association	D	No	Yes
AT&T Bell Laboratories	U	Yes	Yes
James McKeen Cattell Fund	P	No	Yes
Excalibur Foundation	U	No	No
The Farm Foundation	O	No	No
Fondation Fyssen	P	Yes	No
The Journal of Applied Behavioral Science	O	No	No

329

Vocational Goal and Name of Administering Agency	Level of Study[1]	Residency Requirement?	Affiliation Requirement?[2]
Psychology (continued)			
The John Frederick Steinman Fellowship Fund	MS, D, PD	No	No
Public Administration			
American Public Works Association	U, MS	No	No
Citizens Research Council of Michigan	MS	Yes	No
Public Affairs			
The Robert Bosch Foundation	P	Yes	No
Coro Foundation	O	Yes	No
Public Health			
Association of Official Analytical Chemists	U	No	No
Westchester Community Service Council, Inc.	MS, DDS, D, MD, RN	Yes	No
Western Interstate Commission for Higher Education	MS, DDS, U, MD, P, JD	Yes	No
Public Service			
New York State Senate	MS	Yes	No
Washington Crossing Foundation	U	No	No
Publishing			
National Scholarship Trust Fund	MS, D, JR, U, R	No	No
Pupil Personnel Services			
Arkansas Department of Education	U, MS	Yes	No
Quality Control			
Association of Official Analytical Chemists	U	No	No
Radio/Radio Science			
Citizens' Scholarship Foundation of America	JR, VT, U, O, MS	Yes	No
Foundation for Amateur Radio, Inc.	O	No	No
Sidney Hillman Foundation, Inc.	O	No	No
The Scripps-Howard Foundation	P	No	No
Real Estate			
American Institute of Real Estate Appraisers	U, MS, D	No	No
Regulatory Work			
Association of Official Analytical Chemists	U	No	No
Rehabilitation Counseling			
American Foundation for the Blind, Inc.	MS	No	No
Epilepsy Foundation for America	P	No	No

Vocational Goal and Name of Administering Agency	Level of Study[1]	Residency Requirement?	Affiliation Requirement?[2]
Rehabilitation, Physical/Psychological			
The American Academy for Cerebral Palsy and Developmental Medicine	R	No	No
Easter Seal Society of Iowa, Inc.	U, MS	Yes	No
Kappa Kappa Gamma Fraternity	U, MS	No	No
Religion			
The Bush Foundation	O	Yes	No
Church of the Brethren	P	No	Yes
The Community Church of New York	P	No	Yes
The Episcopal Church Foundation	D	No	Yes
The First National Bank and Trust Company of Tulsa	P	No	Yes
Hawaiian Trust Company Limited	U, MS	Yes	No
The George A. and Eliza Gardner Howard Foundation	O	No	No
Lutheran Church in America	P, O, MS	Yes[3]	Yes
Munderloh Ministerial Scholarship Foundation	P	No	Yes
William H. Nelson Educational Foundation	U, MS	Yes	Yes
The Order of the Daughters of the King	U, MS	No	Yes
Presbyterian Church (U.S.A.)-New York	P, MS	No	Yes
Presbytery of Chicago	U, MS, D, P	No	Yes
Unitarian Universalist Association	JR, U, P	No	Yes
The United Methodist Church	P, MS, D	No	Yes
Religious Education			
The Community Church of New York	P	No	Yes
William H. Nelson Educational Foundation	U, MS	Yes	Yes
Presbyterian Church (U.S.A.)-New York	P, MS	No	Yes
Renaissance Studies			
The Newberry Library	MS, D, PD, R	Yes	No
Research			
American Nurses' Foundation, Inc.	R	No	No
Association of Eastern College Personnel Officers	R	No	Yes
Association of Official Analytical Chemists	U	No	No
Business and Professional Women's Foundation	R	No	Yes
Council for International Exchange of Scholars	PD, P	Yes	No
Lady Davis Fellowship Trust	PD, R, P	Yes	No
Economic Development Institute of the World Bank	R	Yes	No
The Folger Shakespeare Library	R	Yes	No
The Geontological Society of America	R	Yes	No

Vocational Goal and Name of Administering Agency	Level of Study[1]	Residency Requirement?	Affilication Requirement?[2]
Research (continued)			
John Simon Guggenheim Memorial Foundation	R, O	No	No
Huntington Library and Art Gallery	R, P	Yes	No
The Lyndon Baines Johnson Foundation	R	Yes	No
The Kosciuszko Foundation	U, MS, D, MD, PD, R	Yes	Yes
The Henry A. Murray Research Center of Radcliffe College	D, R	Yes	No
The Newberry Library	PD, R, MS, D	Yes	Yes[3]
North Atlantic Treaty Organization (NATO)	R, O	Yes	Yes
Organization of American States General Secretariat	MS, D, R	Yes	No
The United Chapters of Phi Beta Kappa	D, R	No	No
Sigma Xi The Scientific Research Society	R	No	No
Vatican Film Library	O, PD, R	Yes	No
Respiratory Therapy			
American Respiratory Therapy Foundation	JR, VT, O, P	No	Yes[3]
Science			
Marshall H. and Nellie Alworth Memorial Fund	U	Yes	No
Argonne National Laboratory	U, MS	Yes	No
AT&T Bell Laboratories	D, U	Yes	Yes[3]
AT&T Foundation	D	No	No
The Bush Foundation	O	Yes	No
Committee on Institutional Cooperation (CIC)	D	Yes	Yes
The Kosciuszko Foundation	U, MS, MD, DDS	Yes	Yes
Massachusetts Institute of Technology (MIT)	PD, R	Yes	No
The Metropolitan Museum of Art	O	Yes	No
National Scholarship Trust Fund	MS, D, R, JR, U	No	No
National Space Club	U, MS	No	No
New Jersey Academy of Science	R, HS	Yes	No
Oak Ridge Associated Universities	U, D, R, MS, PD	Yes	No
Royal Norwegian Council for Scientific and Industrial Research (NTNF)	PD, R	Yes	No
Sigma Xi The Scientific Research Society	R	No	No
Watertown Foundation, Inc.	U	Yes	No
Scouting, Professional			
Boy Scouts of America	U	Yes	No

Vocational Goal and Name of Administering Agency	Level of Study[1]	Residency Requirement?	Affiliation Requirement?[2]
Sculpture			
Edward F. Albee Foundation, Inc.	O	Yes	No
American Academy and Institute of Arts and Letters	O	No	No
Dorland Mountain Colony	O	Yes	No
Fondation des Etats-Unis	MS, O	Yes	No
The MacDowell Colony	O	Yes	No
New York Foundation for the Arts	O	Yes	No
Pollock-Krasner Foundation, Inc.	O	No	No
Virginia Museum of Fine Arts	U, MS, P	Yes	No
Yaddo	O	Yes	No
Social Sciences			
Earhart Foundation	R, MS, D	No	Yes[3]
Epilepsy Foundation of America	P	No	No
The Farm Foundation	O	No	No
The George A. and Eliza Gardner Howard Foundation	O	No	No
Human Relations Area Files	U, MS, D	No	No
International Foundation of Employee Benefit Plans	MS, D, PD, R	No	No
Richard D. Irwin Foundation	D	No	No
The Kosciuszko Foundation	U, MS, MD, DDS	Yes	Yes
Massachusetts Institute of Technology (MIT)	PD, R	Yes	No
National Academy of Education	PD, R	No	Yes
The Newberry Library	U, D, R	Yes	Yes
Oak Ridge Associated Universities	U, D, R, MS, PD	Yes[3]	Yes[3]
Science Service	U	No	No
The Tinker Foundation	PD, R	Yes	No
Social Studies			
Civitan International Foundation	U, MS	No	No
Social Work			
B'nai B'rith Youth Organization	MS	No	No
The Bush Foundation	O	Yes	No
Easter Seal Society of Iowa, Inc.	U, MS	Yes	No
The John Frederick Steinman Fellowship Fund	MS, D, PD	No	No
Westchester Community Service Council, Inc.	MS DDS, D, MD, RN	Yes	No
Sociology			
American Sociological Association	D	No	Yes

Vocational Goal and Name of Administering Agency	Level of Study[1]	Residency Requirement?	Affiliation Requirement?[2]
Sociology (continued)			
The Farm Foundation	O	No	No
The George A. and Eliza Gardner Howard Foundation	O	No	No
The Journal of Applied Behavioral Science	O	No	No
National Association of Broadcasters	R	No	No
W.E. Upjohn Institute for Employment Research	R	No	No
Solar Energy			
Argonne National Laboratory	MS, D, R	Yes	Yes[3]
Space and Planetary Sciences			
The Planetary Society	U	No	Yes
Special Education			
Civitan International Foundation	U, MS	No	No
Easter Seal Society of Iowa, Inc.	U, MS	Yes	No
Excalibur Foundation	U	No	No
Knights of Columbus	MS	No	Yes
Speech, Hearing/Pathology/Therapy			
Communication Skill Builders	MS, R	No	No
Excalibur Foundation	U	No	No
Kappa Kappa Gamma Fraternity	O	Yes	No
Statistics			
AT&T Bell Laboratories	MS, R, U, O	Yes[3]	No
Surgical Technology			
Association of Surgical Technologists, Inc.	P	No	No
Teaching			
Arkansas Department of Education	U, MS	Yes	No
Arkansas Education Association	MS	No	Yes
Association of Official Analytical Chemists	U	No	No
Baldwin Piano and Organ Company	O	No	No
Civitan International Foundation	U, MS	No	No
Lady Davis Fellowship Trust	PD, R, P	Yes	No
The Episcopal Church Foundation	D	No	Yes
Eta Sigma Phi	MS, D	Yes	No
Knights of Columbus	MS	No	Yes
New York State Congress of Parents and Teachers, Inc.	MS, D, U	Yes[3]	Yes[3]
Oregon PTA	U	Yes	No
The Roothbert Fund	U	Yes	No
Rotary Foundation of Rotary International	P	Yes	No
Woodrow Wilson National Fellowship Foundation	D	Yes	No
Technology			
The Charles A. Linbergh Fund, Inc.	O	No	No

Vocational Goal and Name of Administering Agency	Level of Study[1]	Residency Requirement?	Affiliation Requirement?[2]
Technology (continued)			
Massachusetts Institute of Technology(MIT)	PD, R	Yes	No
Watertown Foundation, Inc.	U	Yes	No
Telecommunication Systems			
AT&T Foundation	D	No	No
Television			
Citizens' Scholarship Foundation of	JR, VT, U,		
America	O, MS	Yes	No
Sidney Hillman Foundation, Inc.	O	No	No
International Thespian Society	JR, U, O	No	Yes
The Scripps-Howard Foundation	P	No	No
Theatre Arts			
Florida Department of State	P, O	Yes	No
International Thespian Society	JR, U, O	No	Yes
National Institute for Music Theater	P	No	No
Toxicology			
Lucille P. Markey Charitable Trust	R	No	No
Trade Unionism			
The Bush Foundation	O	Yes	No
The Regina V. Polk Scholarship Fund for			
Labor Leadership	JR, U	No	No
Translating			
The Academy of American Poets	O	No	No
Travel			
American Association of University			
Women Educational Foundation	O	No	Yes
The English-Speaking Union	O	Yes	No
Turf (Golf) Management			
Golf Course Superintendents Association			
of America	JR, U, MS	No	No
Union Leadership			
The Regina V. Polk Scholarship Fund for			
Labor Leadership	JR, U	No	No
Vacuum Science & Technology			
American Vacuum Society	MS, D	Yes[3]	No
Veterinary Medicine/Pathology			
American Association of University			
Women Educational Foundation	D, PD, R	No	No
Rob and Bessie Welder Wildlife			
Foundation	MS, D, R	Yes	No
Western Interstate Commission for			
Higher Education	MS, DDS, U,		
	MD, P, JD	Yes	No

Vocational Goal and Name of Administering Agency	Level of Study[1]	Residency Requirement?	Affilication Requirement?[2]
Video			
New York Foundation for the Arts	O	Yes	No
Virginia Museum of Fine Arts	U, MS, P	Yes	No
Visual Arts			
The Bush Foundation	O	Yes	No
The Dobie-Paisano Project	O	Yes	No
Dorland Mountain Colony	O	Yes	No
Fine Arts Work Center in Provincetown, Inc.	P	Yes	No
Florida Department of State	P, O	Yes	No
The Millay Colony for the Arts, Inc.	O	Yes	No
National Gallery of Art	D, PD, O	Yes	No
New York Foundation for the Arts	O	Yes	No
Vocational-Technical Education			
Aid Association for Lutherans	JR, VT	No	Yes
American Council for the Blind	JR, U, VT, MS	No	No
AMVETS	JR, U, VT	No	Yes
Blinded Veterans Association	JR, U, VT	No	Yes
The Boston Globe	JR, U, VT, O	Yes	No
Bristol Volunteer Fire Department, Ladies Auxiiliary	JR, LPN, U, RN, VT	No	Yes
Business and Professional Women's Foundation	JR, LLB, MS, MD, U, VT, O	No	No
Citizens' Scholarship Foundation of America, Inc.	JR, LPN, U, O, RN, VT	No	Yes
City Volunteer Corps	JR, U, VT, O	Yes	No
Civitan International Foundation	U, MS	No	No
Dane County Labor Council AFL-CIO	JR, U, VT	No	Yes
Fifth Marine Division Association Scholarship Fund	JR, LPN, U, RN, VT	No	Yes
First Marine Division Association, Inc.	JR, U, VT	No	Yes
Fourth Marine Division Association	JR, U, VT	No	Yes
Graphic Communications International Union	JR, LPN, U, RN, VT	No	Yes
The Hauss-Helms Foundation, Inc.	JR, U, MS, VT	Yes	No
Inland Steel-Ryerson Foundation, Inc.	JR, U, VT, O	No	Yes

Vocational Goal and Name of Administering Agency	Level of Study[1]	Residency Requirement?	Affiliation Requirement?[2]
Vocational-Technical Education (continued)			
International Brotherhood of Electrical Workers Local 426	JR, U, RN, VT	No	Yes
International Chemical Workers Union	JR, U, RN, VT	No	Yes
International Union of Electronic, Electrical, Technical, Salaried and Machine Workers, AFL-CIO	JR, LPN, U, RN, VT	No	Yes
Japanese American Citizens League	JR, U, VT, RN	No	Yes
Jewish Children's Regional Service of Jewish Children's Home	JR, MS, U, D, VT	Yes	Yes
Jewish Foundation for Education of Women	JR, MD, U, VT	Yes	No
Kappa Kappa Gamma Fraternity	JR, MS, U, P, O, VT	No	Yes
Lorain City Schools	JR, U, VT	Yes	No
Marin Educational Foundation	JR, U, VT, O	Yes	No
James G.K. McClure Educational and Development Fund, Inc.	JR, U, VT, RN	Yes	No
Minnesota American Federation of Labor and Congress of Industrial Organizations	JR, U, VT	Yes	Yes
Modern Woodmen of America	JR, VT	No	Yes
National Catholic Society of Foresters	JR, U, VT	No	Yes
National Office Products Association	JR, U, VT	No	Yes
New York State Grange	JR, U, VT	Yes	Yes
The Pillsbury Company Foundation	JR, U, VT	No	Yes
Rotary Foundation of Rotary International	VT	Yes	No
Seafarers Welfare Plan	JR, U, VT	No	Yes
Society of the Daughters of the United States Army	JR, U, VT	No	Yes
Society of the First Division Foundation	JR, U, VT	No	Yes
Soroptimist International of the Americas, Inc.	JR, U, VT	Yes	No
Texas AFL-CIO	JR, U, VT	No	Yes
Two/Ten National Foundation	JR, LPN, U, RN, O, VT	Yes	Yes
U.S. Department of Education	JR, U, MS, VT	No	No
The Washington Post	JR, U, VT	Yes	Yes

Vocational Goal and Name of Administering Agency	Level of Study[1]	Residency Requirement?	Affiliation Requirement?[2]
Water Supply Industry			
American Water Works Association	MS, D	No	No
Wildlife Conservation/Management			
Rob and Bessie Welder Wildlife Foundation	MS, D, R	Yes	No
Writing			
Edward F. Albee Foundation, Inc.	O	Yes	No
American Academy and Institute of Arts and Letters	O	No	No
American Foundation for the Blind, Inc.	U	No	No
Appalachian Center	O	No	No
The Bush Foundation	O	Yes	No
Chicago Tribune	O	No	No
The Dobie-Paisano Project	O	Yes	No
Dorland Mountain Colony	O	Yes	No
Doubleday & Company, Inc.	O	Yes	No
Fine Arts Work Center In Privincetown, Inc.	P	Yes	No
Hamilton Prize Competition	O	No	No
Sidney Hillman Foundation, Inc.	O	No	No
Houghton Mifflin Company	O	No	No
The George A. and Eliza Gardner Howard Foundation	O	No	No
Institute of Early American History and Culture	O	No	No
Iowa School of Letters	O	No	No
The MacDowell Colony	O	Yes	No
The Millay Colony for the Arts, Inc.	O	Yes	No
The National League of American Pen Women, Inc.	O	No	No
New York Foundation for the Arts	O	Yes	No
Ragdale Foundation	O	Yes	No
The San Francisco Foundation	O	Yes	No

Chapter 10

TAX PLANNING

Virtually every area of our financial lives is influenced by tax consequences. From setting financial objectives to investing, from insurance planning to estate planning, tax considerations are often important. Affluent taxpayers not only should understand the tax effect of a proposed action but also must develop a sound and comprehensive strategy to address tax reduction opportunities. The objective of tax planning is to pay the lowest tax legally allowable, consistent with overall personal financial planning objectives.

The sweeping tax reform of the 1980s has required financial professionals and clients to think about taxes in a new manner. Lower marginal income tax rates decreased the importance of tax effects on clients' financial lives. However, higher taxation rates on capital gains have increased the significance of taxes on investment decisions. Despite Presidesnt Bush's "read my lips" campaign promise of no new taxes, federal fiscal woes will no doubt prompt a new round of federal tax "complification." States, too, are facing financial difficulties and are increasingly turning to taxpayers to help overcome financial difficulties. These developments are making it more important than ever for the financial professional to keep attuned to new developments and legislation and to advise individuals about tax planning and investment options that can help minimize the potentially onerous impact of taxes.

Many clients remain preoccupied with reducing income taxes in spite of the lower marginal level of taxation compared with pre-1987 rates. Income tax considerations remain important, but they should generally not be the sole or even a major determinant of a tax-relevant decision.

While capital gains tax rates may be reduced further in the 1990s, tax rates on both passive income and capital gains will remain high enough to make tax-deferred investing particularly attractive. Also, tax legislation will probably further encourage savings, particularly for retirement, by expanding the number of tax-favored investment programs, including a return of the fully tax-deductible individual retirement account (IRA). However, in order to pay for these incentives, many loopholes will be closed as the tax rules will become even more befuddling. Financial professionals will have to become accustomed to keeping up with an ever-changing federal income tax landscape. Estate tax regulations may also come under increased congressional scrutiny during the 1990s.

Sound tax planning is a year-round process. Over the short term, clients should be encouraged to establish and maintain an effective tax record-keeping system as part of the broader process of developing client "tax awareness." Longer-term tax planning helps clients minimize future income taxes. Many effective tax-saving strategies require a time horizon of several years—there are no quick fixes.

10.1   YEAR-END TAX PLANNING IDEAS

The following guidelines can be used to assist the client in year-end tax planning.

1. Consider making year-end charitable contributions of personal property such as clothing and furniture.

2. Consider making a contribution of appreciated securities to avoid paying capital gains tax, but be wary of possible adverse alternative minimum tax (AMT) consequences.

3. Consider bunching miscellaneous expenses, including professional dues, tax preparation fees, and unreimbursed employee business expenses, into the current year so that the total exceeds 2 percent of adjusted gross income.

4. If the 2 percent threshold will not be exceeded even through bunching, consider postponing as many of these expenses as possible until next year.

5. If enough money has not been withheld to meet the current year's tax liability, consider increasing the amount withheld from pay late in the year.

6. Make the maximum possible deductible IRA contribution.

7. Increase participation in employer's 401 (k) plan.

8. If there is any income from self-employment, consider opening a Keogh account on or before December 31.

9. If taxable income is likely to push the taxpayer into a higher tax bracket, consider deferring income, to the extent permissible, until the succeeding year.

10. Consider paying the last installment of estimated state income tax payments in December rather than January.

11. Determine AMT liability and shift itemized deductions that are treated as exclusion items for AMT purposes into years in which no AMT liability will be incurred. Theses include personal interest, state and local taxes, and most miscellaneous itemized deductions.

12. Determine whether medical expenses are likely to exceed the 7.5 percent of the adjusted gross income (AGI) hurdle; if so, bunch them in current year. If not, defer them.

13. Consider realizing capital losses to offset capital gains and investment interest or vice versa if taxpayer will be in a lower tax bracket in later years.

14. Use installment sales method to defer capital gain recognition, particularly if it is likely that taxpayer will be in a lower tax bracket in later years.

15. If a change in filing status is expected in the succeeding year, defer current income and accelerate deductions if the change in status will lower tax rates. If higher rates are expected, reverse the strategy.

10.2 FEDERAL INCOME TAX RATES

Table 10.1 presents federal income tax rates for taxable years beginning 1992. Note that the income tax brackets are adjusted for inflation each year.

Table 10.1 Federal Income Tax Rates for Tax Years Beginning in 1992

Single Taxpayers

If taxable income is: Over—	*but not over—*	*The tax is:*	*of the amount over—*
$ 0	$21,450	15%	$ 0
21,450	51,900	$3,217.50 + 28%	21,450
51,900	—	11,743.50 + 31%	51,900

Spouses Filing Separate Returns

If taxable income is: Over—	*but not over—*	*The tax is:*	*of the amount over—*
$ 0	$17,900	15%	$ 0
17,900	43,250	$2,685 + 28%	17,900
43,250	—	9,783 + 31%	43,250

Table 10.1 (continued)

Spouses Filing Joint Returns and Surviving Spouses

If taxable income is: Over—	but not over—	*The tax is:*	of the amount over—
$ 0	$35,800	15%	$ 0
35,800	86,500	$5,370 + 28%	35,800
86,500	—	19,566 + 31%	86,500

Heads of Households

If taxable income is: Over—	but not over—	*The tax is:*	of the amount over—
$ 0	$28,750	15%	$ 0
28,750	74,150	$4,312.50 + 28%	28,750
74,150	—	17,024.50 + 31%	74,150

10.3 STATE INCOME TAX RATES

Table 10.2 summarizes state income tax rates and rules. This table may be used whenever preliminary information is needed as to the personal income tax regulations for any state. If more detailed information is needed, the financial services professional can refer to any of several state income tax loose-leaf services.

Table 10.2 State Government Individual Income Taxes, 1989

[**As of October 1989.** Only basic rates, brackets and exemptions are shown. Local income tax rates, even those mandated by the State, are not included. Taxable income rates and brackets listed below apply to single individuals and married taxpayers filing "combined separate" returns (in States where this is permitted). Alaska, Florida, Nevada, South Dakota, Texas, Washington, and Wyoming have no State income tax]

STATE	Taxable income rates (range in percent)	TAXABLE INCOME BRACKETS		PERSONAL EXEMPTIONS			SIZE OF STANDARD DEDUCTION [1]			Federal income tax deductible [2]
		Lowest: amount under	Highest: amount over	Single	Married-joint return	Dependents	Percent	Single	Married-joint return	
AL [3][4]	2.0-5.0	$500	$3,000	$1,500	$3,000	$300	20	$2,000	$4,000	Yes
AZ [5]	2.0-8.0	1,290	7,740	2,229	4,458	1,337	22.29	1,115	2,229	Yes [6]
AR	1.0-7.0	3,000	25,000	[7]20	[7]40	[7]20	10	1,000	1,000	No
CA [5]	1.0-9.3	4,020	26,380	[7]55	[7]110	[7]55	(X)	2,070	4,140	No
CO				5% of modified Federal taxable income						No
CT				Limited income tax [8]						No
DE [3]	3.2-7.7	1,000	40,000	1,250	2,500	1,250	10	1,300	1,600	No
DC	6.0-9.5	10,000	20,000	1,160	2,320	1,160	(X)	2,000	2,000	No
GA	1.0-6.0	750	7,000	1,500	3,000	1,500	(X)	2,300	3,000	No
HI [3]	2.0-10.0	1,500	20,500	1,040	2,080	1,040	(X)	1,500	1,900	No
ID	2.0-8.2	1,000	20,000			Same as Federal [9]				No
IL	3.0	Flat rate		1,000	2,000	1,000	(X)	(X)	(X)	No
IN [3]	3.4	Flat rate		1,000	2,000	1,000	(X)	(X)	(X)	No
IA [3][5]	.4-9.98	[10]1,016	[10]45,720	[7]20	[7]40	[7]15	(X)	1,230	3,030	Yes
KS	[11]4.5-5.95	[11]27,500	[11]27,500	2,000	4,000	2,000	(X)	Same as Federal [9]		Yes
KY [3]	2.0-6.0	3,000	8,000	[7]20	[7]40	[7]20	(X)	650	650	Yes
LA	2.0-6.0	10,000	50,000	[12]4,500	[12]9,000	[12]1,000	Combined with exemptions [12]			Yes
ME	2.0-8.5	4,000	16,000	2,000	4,000	2,000	(X)	3,100	5,200	No
MD [3][13]	2.0-5.0	1,000	3,000	1,100	2,200	1,100	15	2,000	4,000	No
MA	5.0-10.0	Flat rate [14]		2,200	4,400	1,000	(X)	(X)	(X)	No
MI [3]	4.6	Flat rate		2,000	4,000	2,000	(X)	(X)	(X)	No
MN [5]	6.0-8.0	13,000	13,000			Same as Federal [9]				No
MS [3]	3.0-5.0	5,000	10,000	6,000	9,500	1,500	15	2,300	3,400	No
MO [3][15]	1.5-6.0	1,000	9,000	1,200	2,400	400	(X)	Same as Federal [9]		Yes
MT [5]	2.0-11.0	1,500	52,500	1,200	2,400	1,200	20	2,250	4,500	Yes
NE	2.0-5.9	1,800	27,000	1,180	2,360	1,180	(X)	Same as Federal [9]		Yes
NH				Limited income tax [16]						No
NJ	[17]2.0-3.5	20,000	50,000	1,000	2,000	1,000	(X)	(X)	(X)	No
NM [3]	1.8-8.5	5,200	64,000	2,000	4,000	2,000	(X)	Same as Federal [9]		No
NY [3]	4.0-7.5	5,500	13,000	-	-	1,000	(X)	6,000	9,500	No
NC	[18]6.0-7.0	12,750	12,750	2,000	4,000	2,000	(X)	Same as Federal [9]		No
ND	[19]2.6-12.0	[19]3,000	[19]50,000			Same as Federal [9]				Yes
OH [3]	.743-6.9	5,000	100,000	650	1,300	650	(X)	(X)	(X)	No [20]
OK	[20].5-6.0	[20]1,000	[20]7,500	1,000	2,000	1,000	15	2,000	2,000	Yes [20]
OR [3][5]	5.0-9.0	2,000	5,000	94	188	94	(X)	1,800	3,000	Yes [21]
PA [3]	2.1	Flat rate		(X)	(X)	(X)	(X)	(X)	(X)	No
RI				22.96% of Federal income tax liability						No
SC	3.0-7.0	4,000	10,000			Same as Federal [9]				No
TN				Limited income tax [22]						No
UT	2.55-7.22	750	3,750		75% of Federal exemption		Same as Federal [9]			Yes [23]
VT				25% of Federal income tax liability						No
VA	2.0-5.75	3,000	16,000	800	1,600	800	(X)	Same as Federal [9]		No
WV	3.0-6.5	10,000	60,000	2,000	4,000	2,000	(X)	(X)	(X)	No
WI	4.9-6.93	7,500	15,000	-	-	[7]50	(X)	5,200	8,900	No

- Represents zero. X Not applicable. [1] The lesser of either (a) the percentage indicated, multiplied by adjusted gross income or (b) the dollar value listed. [2] A State provision that allows the taxpayer to deduct fully the Federal income tax payment reduces the effective marginal tax rate for persons in the highest State and Federal tax brackets by approximately one-half the nominal tax rate—the deduction is of a lesser benefit to other taxpayers. [3] States in which one or more local governments levy a local income tax. [4] Social Security (FICA) taxes are included in itemized deductions. [5] Indexed by an inflation factor. [6] An additional deduction from income is allowed in the amount of 65% of federal income tax liability or $600, whichever is greater, but not to exceed $10,000 for married filing joint or $5,000 for all other filers. [7] Tax credit. [8] There is an income tax on interest and dividend income only. The rate of this tax ranges from 1% of interest and dividend income for taxpayers with an AGI of $54,000 to $57,999 to 12% of such income of taxpayers with an AGI over $100,000. Capital gains are taxed at 7% after an exemption of $100 is applied. [9] Personal exemptions on the 1989 return are $2,000 each; standard deduction for single is $3,000 and for those filing joint returns, $5,000 (single or $7,500 (married-joint return). [10] Tax cannot reduce after-tax income of taxpayer to below $5,000. [11] Income below $27,500 taxed at 4.5% rate, income above $27,500 taxed at 5.95% rate. [12] Personal exemption and standard deduction are combined. [13] All counties have a local income tax surcharge of at least 20% of State tax liability; most counties have a surcharge of 50%. [14] 10% (flat rate) imposed on capital gains, interest, and dividends of residents, and Massachusetts business income of nonresidents. All other net income taxed at 5%. No taxes are imposed on a single persons with gross income of $8,000 or less ($12,000 married). [15] FICA taxes deductible when itemizing deductions. [16] There is a 5% tax on dividend and interest income (excluding income from savings bank deposits) in excess of $1,200 ($2,400 married). [17] No taxpayer is subject to tax if gross income is $3,000 or less ($1,500 married, filing separately). [18] Taxable income brackets are for single taxpayers. Breaking point for higher marginal tax rate varies according to filing status. [19] Taxpayers have the option of paying a tax of 14% of the taxpayers adjusted Federal income tax liability or using the long form with a separate schedule; taxpayers using the long form may deduct Federal income tax paid. [20] These tax rates and brackets apply to single persons not deducting Federal income tax. For individuals deducting Federal income tax, rates range from .5% of the first $1,000 to 10% on income over $15,250. [21] Federal tax deduction limited to $3,000 ($1,500 married, filing separately). [22] Interest and dividends taxed at 6%. [23] One-half of federal tax liability is deductible.

Source: Advisory Commission on Intergovernmental Relations, *Significant Features of Fiscal Federalism*, (Washington, D.C.: Advisory Commission on Intergovernmental Relations, 1989).

10.4   FEDERAL TAX RETURN FORMS

Table 10.3 provides a list of the more commonly used federal income tax forms.

Table 10.3   Common Federal Income Tax Forms

706	United States Estate Tax Return
709	United States Gift Tax Return
709A	U.S. Short Form Gift Tax Return
1040	U.S. Individual Income Tax Return
	☐ Schedule A—Itemized Deductions
	☐ Schedule B—Interest and Dividend Income
	☐ Schedule C—Profit (Loss) From Business or Profession (Sole Proprietorship)
	☐ Schedule D—Capital Gains and Losses
	☐ Schedule E—Supplemental Income Schedule
	☐ Schedule F—Farm Income and Expenses
	☐ Schedule R—Credit for the Elderly and the Permanently and Totally Disabled
	☐ Schedule SE—Computation of Social Security Self-Employment Tax
1040A	U.S. Individual Income Tax Return (Short Form)
1040ES	Payment-Voucher for Estimated Tax by Individuals
1040EZ	U.S. Income Tax Return (Short Form for Single Filers With No Dependents)
1040X	Amended U.S. Individual Income Tax Return
1041	U.S. Fiduciary Income Tax Return
	☐ Schedule D—Capital Gains and Losses
	☐ Schedule J—Trust Allocation of an Accumulation Distribution
	☐ Schedule K-1—Beneficiary's Shares of Income, Deductions, Credits, etc.
1065	U.S. Partnership Return of Income
	☐ Schedule D—Capital Gains and Losses
	☐ Schedule K—Partner's Share of Income, Credits, Deductions, etc. [*required only when there are more than 10 schedules*]
	☐ Schedule K-1—Partners' Shares of Income, Credits, Deductions, etc. [*filed with Form 1065*]
1096	Annual Summary and Transmittal of Certain Information Returns
1098	Mortgage Interest Statement
1099-B	Statement for Recipients of Proceeds From Broker and Barter Exchange Transactions
1099-DIV	Statement for Recipients of Dividends and Distributions
1099-G	Statement for Recipients of Certain Government Payments
1099INT	Statement for Recipients of Interest Income
1099MISC	Statement for Recipients of Miscellaneous Income
1099OID	Statement for Recipients of Original Issue Discount

Table 10.3 (continued)

1099R	Statement for Recipients of Total Distributions From Profit-Sharing, Retirement Plans, Individual Retirement Arrangements, Insurance Contracts, etc.
1099S	Statement for Recipients of Proceeds From Real Estate Transactions
1116	Computation of Foreign Tax Credit
	☐ Schedule A—Schedule of Foreign Taxable Income and Foreign Taxes Paid or Accrued
1120S	Income Tax Return, S Corporation
	☐ Schedule D—Capital Gains and Losses
	☐ Schedule K-1—Shareholder's Share of Undistributed Taxable Income, etc.
1310	Statement of Person Claiming Refund Due to a Deceased Taxpayer
2106	Employee Business Expenses
2119	Sale or Exchange of Personal Residence
2120	Multiple Support Declaration
2210	Underpayment of Estimated Tax by Individuals
2439	Notice to Shareholder of Undistributed Long-Term Capital Gains
2440	Disability Income Exclusion
2441	Credit for Child Care and Dependent Care Expenses
2688	Application for Extension of Time to File
2848	Power of Attorney and Declaration of Representative
3468	Computation of Investment Credit
3559	Alimony or Separate Maintenance Statement
3903	Moving Expenses Adjustment
4136	Computation of Credit for Federal Tax on Gasoline, Special Fuels, and Lubricating Oils
4137	Computation of Social Security Tax on Unreported Tax Income
4469	Computation of Excess Medicare Tax Credit
4562	Depreciation
4684	Casualties and Thefts
4768	Application for Extension of Time to File U.S. Estate Tax Return and/or Pay Estate Tax
4782	Employee Moving Expense Information
4797	Supplemental Schedule of Gains and Losses
4835	Farm Rental Income and Expenses
4868	Automatic Extension to File
4952	Investment Interest Expense Deduction
4970	Tax on Accumulation Distribution of Trusts
4972	Special Ten-Year Averaging Method

Table 10.3 (continued)

5329	Return for Individual Retirement Arrangement Taxes
5498	Individual Retirement Arrangement Information
5544	Multiple Recipient Special Ten-Year Averaging
5695	Residential Energy Credits
5884	Job Credit (and WIN Credit Carry-over)
6251	Alternative Minimum Tax Computation
6252	Computations of Installment Sale Income
6781	Gains and Losses From Regulated Futures Contracts and Straddles
8027	Employer's Annual Information Return of Tip Income and Allocated Tips
8283	Noncash Charitable Contributions
8332	Release of Claim to Exemption for Child of Divorced or Separated Parents
8582	Passive Activity Loss Limitations
8598	Home Mortgage Interest
8606	Nondeductible IRA Contributions, IRA Basis, and Nontaxable IRA Distributions
8615	Computation of Tax for Children Under Age 14 Who Have Investment Income of More than $1,000
8801	Credit for Prior Year Minimum Tax
SSA-1099	Social Security Benefit Statement
W-2	Wage and Tax Statement
W-2c	Statement of Corrected Income and Tax Amounts
W-2P	Statement for Recipients of Annuities, Pensions, Retired Pay, or IRA Payments
W-3	Transmittal of Income and Tax Amounts
W-4	Employee's Withholding Allowance Certificate
W-4P	Withholding Certificate for Pension or Annuity Payments
W-4S	Request for Federal Income Tax Withholding From Sick Pay
W-5	Earned Income Credit Advance Payment Certificate
W-9	Payer's Request for Taxpayer Identification Number

10.5 DIRECTORY OF FEDERAL TAX PUBLICATIONS

The publications listed in Table 10.4, available at no cost from the Internal Revenue Service, can assist in tax planning and tax return preparation. They may be ordered by calling the IRS.

Table 10.4 Internal Revenue Service Publications

Publication Number	Title
1	Your Rights as a Taxpayer
15	Circular E, Employer's Tax Guide
17	Your Federal Income Tax
51	Circular A, Agricultural Employer's Tax Guide
54	Tax Guide for U.S. Citizens and Resident Aliens Abroad
80	Circular SS, Federal Tax Guide for Employers in the Virgin Islands, Guam, and American Samoa
179	Federal Tax Guide for Employers in Puerto Rico (in Spanish)
225	Farmer's Tax Guide
334	Tax Guide for Small Businesses
349	Federal Highway Use Tax on Heavy Vehicles
378	Fuel Tax Credits and Refunds
448	Federal Estate and Gift Taxes
463	Travel, Entertainment, and Gift Expenses
501	Exemptions, Standard Deduction, and Filing Information
502	Medical and Dental Expenses
503	Child and Dependent Care Credit
504	Tax Information for Divorced or Separated Individuals
505	Tax Withholding and Estimated Tax
508	Educational Expenses
509	Tax Calendars
510	Excise Taxes
513	Tax Information for Visitors to the United States
514	Foreign Tax Credit for Individuals
515	Withholding of Tax on Nonresident Aliens and Foreign Corporations
516	Tax Information for U.S. Government Civilian Employees Stationed Abroad
517	Social Security for Members of the Clergy and Religious Workers
519	U.S. Tax Guide for Aliens
520	Scholarships and Fellowships
521	Moving Expenses
523	Tax Information on Selling Your Home
524	Credit for the Elderly or the Disabled
525	Taxable and Nontaxable Income
526	Charitable Contributions
527	Residential Rental Property
529	Miscellaneous Deductions
530	Tax Information for Homeowners (Including Owners of Condominiums and Cooperative Apartments)
531	Reporting Income From Tips

Table 10.4 (continued)

Publication Number	Title
533	Self-Employment Tax
534	Depreciation
535	Business Expenses
536	Net Operating Losses
537	Installment Sales
538	Accounting Periods and Methods
539	Employment Taxes
541	Tax Information on Partnerships
542	Tax Information on Corporations
544	Sales and Other Dispositions of Assets
545	Interest Expense
547	Nonbusiness Disasters, Casualties, and Thefts
548	Deduction for Bad Debts
549	Condemnations and Business Casualties and Thefts
550	Investment Income and Expenses
551	Basis of Assets
552	Recordkeeping for Individuals and a List of Tax Publications
554	Tax Information for Older Americans
555	Community Property and the Federal Income Tax
556	Examination of Returns, Appeal Rights, and Claims for Refund (also available in Spanish; Publication 556S)
557	Tax-Exempt Status for Your Organization
559	Tax Information for Survivors, Executors, and Administrators
560	Self-Employed Retirement Plans
561	Determining the Value of Donated Property
564	Mutual Fund Distributions
570	Tax Guide for Individuals in U.S. Possessions
571	Tax-Sheltered Annuity Programs for Employees of Public Schools and Certain Tax-Exempt Organizations
572	General Business Credit
575	Pension and Annuity Income
579S	How to Prepare the Federal Income Tax Return (in Spanish)
583	Information for Business Taxpayers
584	Nonbusiness Disaster, Casualty, and Theft Loss Workbook
586A	The Collection Process (Income Tax Accounts) (also available in Spanish; Publication 586S)
587	Business Use of Your Home
588	Tax Information for Homeowners Associations
589	Tax Information on S Corporations

Table 10.4 (continued)

Publication Number	Title
590	Individual Retirement Arrangements (IRAs)
593	Tax Highlights for U.S. Citizens and Residents Going Abroad
594	The Collection Process (Employment Tax Accounts)
595	Tax Guide for Commercial Fishermen
596	Earned Income Credit
597	Information on the United States-Canada Income Tax Treaty
598	Tax on Unrelated Business Income of Exempt Organizations
686	Certification for Reduced Tax Rates in Tax Treaty Countries
721	Comprehensive Tax Guide to U.S. Civil Service Retirement Benefits
794	Favorable Determination Letter
850	English-Speaking Glossary of Words and Phrases Used in Publications Issued by the Internal Revenue Service
901	U.S. Tax Treaties
904	Interrelated Computations for Estate and Gift Taxes
907	Tax Information for Handicapped and Disabled Individuals
908	Bankruptcy and Other Debt Cancellation
909	Alternative Minimum Tax for Individuals
910	Guide to Free Tax Services
911	Tax Information for Direct Sellers
915	Social Security Benefits and Equivalent Railroad Retirement Benefits
916	Information Returns
918	Business Use of a Car
919	Is My Withholding Correct?
924	Reporting of Real Estate Transactions to IRS
925	Passive Activity and At-Risk Rules
926	Employment Taxes for Household Employers
927	Tax Obligations of Legalized Aliens
929	Tax Rules for Children and Dependents
934	Supplemental Medicare Premium
936	Limits on Home Mortgage Interest Deduction
1004	Identification Numbers Under ERISA
1045	Information for Tax Practitioners
1048	Filing Requirements for Employee Benefit Plans
1212	List of Original Issue Discount Instruments
1244	Employee's Daily Record of Tips (Form 4070A) and Employee's Report of Tips to Employer (Form 4070)

10.6 INCOME TAX DUE-DATE CALENDAR

Table 10.5 shows the annual due dates for filing a return or making the payment of tax indicated. Each date shown is the prescribed last day for filing. For income tax returns, the due dates apply to calendar year taxpayers only. If such a day falls on a Saturday, Sunday, or legal holiday, the due date is the next succeeding date that is not a Saturday, Sunday, or legal holiday. Legal holidays include national holidays or statewide (or District of Columbia) holidays in the state where the return is filed.

Table 10.5 Calendar for 1992 Tax Returns

Date	
Jan. 15	Final installment of 1991 estimated tax by individuals due, unless income tax return is filed with final payment by January 31, 1992 (Form 1040-ES).
	Farmers and fishermen must pay estimated tax in full unless income tax return filed with payment by March 1, 1992 (Form 1040-ES).
Jan. 31	Individuals (other than farmers or fishermen) who owed, but did not pay, estimated tax on January 15 must pay tax in full to avoid penalty (Form 1040).
Mar 2	Last day for farmers and fishermen who owed, but did not pay, estimated tax on January 15 to file 1991 calendar year income tax return to avoid late payment penalty.
Apr 15	Last date for filing income tax and self-employment tax returns of individuals for the calendar year 1991 and income tax returns of calendar year decedents who died in 1991 (Form 1040, 1040A, or 1040EZ).
	Last day for calendar year individuals to file application for automatic four-month extension to file 1991 income tax return (Form 4868).
	Payment of first installment of 1992 estimated income taxes by calendar year individuals (other than farmers and fishermen) (Form 1040ES).
June 15	Last day for nonresident alien individuals not subject to withholding, as well as U.S. citizens and resident aliens who were abroad on April 15, to file income tax return for calendar year 1991.
	Payment of second installment of 1992 estimated tax by individuals other than farmers and fishermen. Nonresident aliens who have no wages subject to U.S. withholding must make first payment.

Table 10.5 (continued)

July 31	Last day for pension, profit-sharing, stock bonus, or other employee benefit plans that use a calendar year to file for calendar year 1991 (Form 5500, Form 5500EZ, Form 5500-C or Form 5500-R).
Aug 7	Last day for filing 1991 income tax return by calendar year individuals who obtained an automatic four-month filing extension.
Sept. 15	Payment of third installment of 1992 estimated tax by individuals other than farmers and fishermen.

10.7 ESTIMATED STATE AND LOCAL TAXES PAID BY A FAMILY OF FOUR IN SELECTED LARGE CITIES

Table 10.6 shows total taxes paid in 1988 by a family of four in each of 30 cities in dollars and a percentage of income, at various income levels. In most cities, the rate of state and local taxation is mildly progressive, although some are regressive as a percentage of income. The amounts are based upon a family of four, two wage earners and two school-aged children, who own their own home. The amounts are composed of state and local sales, income, auto, and real estate taxes. The median amounts consist of 51 cities (21 in addition to the 30 listed in this table).

10.8 HOW TO DETERMINE TAX BASIS OF SECURITIES

One of the most vexing problems that investors must confront when filling out their tax returns is determining the tax basis of investments that they have sold. Good record keeping can avoid many of these problems. The following information will assist in dealing with the confusion surrounding tax basis.

The cost basis of stocks or bonds is the purchase price plus the various costs of purchase such as commissions and transfer fees. If stocks or bonds are purchased in another way, the basis is determined by the fair market value or the donor's adjusted basis. After the purchase is made, the basis may be adjusted for certain events that may occur. For example, if an investor receives additional shares from nontaxable dividends or stock splits, he or she has to reduce the basis of the original stock. Investors must also reduce their basis when receiving nontaxable distributions, because these are a return of capital.

Depending upon how an investor acquires stocks and bonds, there are varying ways of determining their bases: Automatic investment programs, dividend reinvestment plans and stock rights are different ways to acquire stocks and bonds, each of which requires special record keeping.

Table 10.6 Estimated State and Local Taxes Paid by a Family of Four in Selected Large Cities, by Income Level, 1989

CITY	TOTAL TAXES PAID BY GROSS FAMILY INCOME LEVEL (dol.)				PERCENT OF INCOME BY INCOME LEVEL			
	$25,000	$50,000	$75,000	$100,000	$25,000	$50,000	$75,000	$100,000
Albuquerque, NM	2,074	4,116	6,880	9,679	8.3	8.2	9.2	9.7
Atlanta, GA	2,651	5,181	8,478	11,202	10.6	10.4	11.3	11.2
Baltimore, MD	2,861	5,758	8,832	11,701	11.4	11.5	11.8	11.7
Bridgeport, CT	2,754	4,484	7,653	9,717	11.0	9.0	10.2	9.7
Burlington, VT	2,024	4,075	6,888	9,446	8.1	8.1	9.2	9.4
Charleston, WV	1,877	3,560	6,514	8,834	7.5	7.1	8.7	8.8
Charlotte, NC	2,309	4,558	7,416	9,909	9.2	9.1	9.9	9.9
Chicago, IL	1,931	3,791	5,910	7,772	7.7	7.6	7.9	7.8
Cleveland, OH	2,429	5,049	8,051	11,126	9.7	10.1	10.7	11.1
Columbia, SC	2,352	4,928	8,226	10,862	9.4	9.9	11.0	10.9
Des Moines, IA	2,610	5,331	8,287	10,951	10.4	10.7	11.0	11.0
Detroit, MI	3,016	6,091	9,363	12,478	12.1	12.2	12.5	12.5
Honolulu, HI	2,282	5,002	8,200	11,222	9.1	10.0	10.9	11.2
Indianapolis, IN	2,197	3,834	6,361	8,202	8.8	7.7	8.5	8.2
Jackson, MS	1,988	3,951	7,010	9,178	8.0	7.9	9.3	9.2
Louisville, KY	2,380	4,696	7,110	9,288	9.5	9.4	9.5	9.3
Memphis, TN	1,849	3,036	4,546	5,840	7.4	6.1	6.1	5.8
Milwaukee, WI	3,546	7,409	11,405	15,063	14.2	14.8	15.2	15.1
Newark, NJ	2,418	4,878	7,636	10,117	9.7	9.8	10.2	10.1
New York City, NY	2,654	6,154	10,272	14,001	10.6	12.3	13.7	14.0
Norfolk, VA	2,120	4,317	7,396	9,618	8.5	8.6	9.9	9.6
Omaha, NE	2,306	4,351	7,377	9,856	9.2	8.7	9.8	9.9
Philadelphia, PA	3,067	5,803	8,529	11,135	12.3	11.6	11.4	11.1
Portland, ME	2,047	4,622	8,455	11,409	8.2	9.2	11.3	11.4
Portland, OR	3,496	7,288	11,429	15,139	14.0	14.6	15.2	15.1
Providence, RI	2,595	4,904	8,364	11,125	10.4	9.8	11.2	11.1
St. Louis, MO	2,164	4,303	6,804	8,883	8.7	8.6	9.1	8.9
Salt Lake City, UT	2,313	4,784	7,593	10,083	9.3	9.6	10.1	10.1
Sioux Falls, SD	2,312	3,869	5,790	7,396	9.2	7.7	7.7	7.4
Washington, DC	2,602	5,381	8,732	11,941	10.4	10.8	11.6	11.9
Median [1]	2,195	4,484	7,375	9,446	8.8	9.0	9.8	9.4

Source: Government of the District of Columbia, Department of Finance and Revenue, *Tax Rates and Tax Burdens in the District of Columbia, a Nationwide Comparison*, (Washington, D.C.: Government of the District of Columbia, annual).

10.8.1 Stock Splits

Suppose that in 1988, an investor purchased 100 shares of stock XYZ at $10 a share, thus paying a total amount of $1,000. Then the next year, in 1989, the same investor purchased 100 more shares of XYZ at a price of $16 a share, or $1,600 in total. Then, in 1990, a 2-for-1 stock split is declared. The investor now owns 200 shares of XYZ with a basis of $5 per share and 200 shares with a basis of $8 per share.

10.8.2 Selecting Securities To Be Sold

If a stock portfolio contains various lots of the same stock acquired at different times and at different costs, the portfolio holder must exercise caution when considering the sale of a portion of these shares. For example, assume an investor owns five different lots of stock XXX, acquired at different times, which range in cost from $50 to $100 per share. If the stock is currently selling for $70 per share and the investor sells a lot with a basis of $50 per share, he or she recognizes a gain, but, if the investor sells a lot with a basis of $100 per share, he or she sustains a loss. The situation could end up being more complicated if the company has paid stock dividends or if it has split its stock one or more times. The best way to simplify this situation is for the stockholder to take the shares received as a result of a stock dividend or a stock split and consolidate them with the shares from which they originated. In other words, the broker should make all related stock certificates into one certificate. Thus, each block of stock with a distinguishable cost basis is separately maintained. This simplifies record keeping and keeps portfolios better organized as well.

It is considered an adequate identification for investors to deliver to their brokers or agents certificates for securities purchased on a certain date or for a specific price. If certificates have been left in the possession of a broker or agent, or if an investor has one certificate for securities bought in different lots at different times, then the investor has made an adequate identification if you inform the broker of the security to be sold or transferred.

10.8.3 FIFO Basis

It may be difficult for you to identify securities bought or sold in varying quantities at different times. if an investor cannot identify the basis of a particular block of securities that he or she sold, the basis is figured by the first-in first-out (FIFO) method. This means that the first securities that the investor acquired are the first sold.

10.8.4 Incentive Stock Options

If a stockholder acquired the shares being sold through an incentive stock option (ISO), with previously owned employer shares, special rules will apply in determining the basis of those shares. For instance, what is known as a "disqualifying disposition" is the sale or transfer of stock acquired through the exercise of an incentive stock option within one year of the option's exercise date. If the sale constitutes a disqualifying disposition" of the ISO shares, the lowest basis shares are considered to be sold first, regardless of the stockholder's effort to identify and sell specific shares.

10.8.5 Charitable Contributions of Appreciated Securities

Charitable contributions of blocks of appreciated stocks with the lowest tax basis are generally to the donor's advantage if he or she is not subject to the alternative minimum tax in the year the contribution is made. At the time a contribution is made, the donor should be sure to be clear in designating which shares are to be contributed and should inform his or her broker or agent the date on which donated shares were purchased.

Current tax rules treat the untaxed appreciation deducted as a charitable contribution as a preference item for the purpose of calculating the AMT. Depending upon an individual's tax situation, the effect of this may be to limit deductions to his or her tax basis. Thus, prior to deciding whether or not to donate appreciated property, individuals should carefully consider the effect of a donation on their regular taxes and the AMT.

10.8.6 Other Matters Pertaining to Tax Basis

When an investor purchases a taxable bond at a premium and chooses to amortize the premium paid, he or she must reduce the basis of the bond by the amount of the amortized premium (despite the fact that a deduction may not be taken for the premium on tax-exempt bonds).

In an original issue discount (OID) bond instrument, bondholders must increase their basis by the amount of OID included in income for that instrument. OID on tax-exempt bonds is not taxable. However, there are special rules for determining basis on tax-exempt original issue discount bonds issued after September 3, 1982 and acquired after March 1, 1984.

10.9 TAX DEDUCTIBLE ITEMS

Table 10.7 can be used to identify the more commonly used tax deductible items for individual taxpayers. Of course, more detailed explanations should be sought in considering any single item as a tax deduction. Note that many of the items listed are deductible only under certain circumstances and/or are subject to limitations. More detailed checklists are available in many of the popular tax preparation guides as well as in IRS publications. Following the alphabetical list of tax deductible items are a list of miscellaneous deductions subject to the 2 percent of adjusted gross income limit and a list of nondeductible expenses.

Table 10.7 Common Tax-Deductible Items

Accelerated cost recovery on business equipment

Accounting and auditing expenses paid for keeping your business books and accounts and preparation of tax returns

Alimony, if it meets certain tax tests

Alternations and repairs on business or income-producing property

Amortization of bond premiums, with some exceptions

Apppraisal costs for tax and business purposes

Attorney fees related to

 Your job or business

 Estate planning

 Libel suits, business reputation

 Obtaining taxable alimony

 Tax advice

Table 10.7 (continued)

Automobile expenses incurred during business trips, job-related moving, trips for charitable organizations, and trips for medical care

Back pay, expenses to collect

Bad debts

Bank deposit loss by failure of bank

Burglary losses

Business expense and losses

Capital asset loss

Capital loss carry-over

Casualty losses

Charitable contributions paid to religious, charitable, scientific, literary, educational, and other organizations (including family foundations) which qualify under the tax law

Christmas presents and other holiday gifts paid to employees, customers or prospects up to $25 per person

Clothing—uniforms, costumes, and working clothes—cost, laundering, and cleaning if required by job and not adaptable to regular wear

Collection of income and business debts, expenses connected with

Commissions paid to agents (press agents, literary agents, booking agents, etc.)

Commissions paid in connection with rented property

Condominium owners' interest and realty taxes

Contributions to IRAs, subject to limits and restrictions

Contributions to disability insurance funds in certain states

Convention expenses

Custodian fees paid to banks or investment counsel, fees incurred in the management of your investments where they produce taxable income

Damage to property held for personal use, as a result of a casualty such as a fire and storm

Debts, uncollectible

Depreciation on business or income-producing property

Directors' expenses

Disability insurance deductions in certain states

Disaster losses

Donations to qualified charities

Drugs and medicines, subject to limitations

Dues to

    Clubs and associations which employer requires you to belong to in order to hold your job

    Membership in organized labor unions

    Professional societies

    Trade associations

Education—tuition fees, books, traveling expenses, etc.—if required to keep your employment or professional standards; carrying charges on installment payments of tuition

Employment agency fees

Entertainment of customers

Table 10.7 (continued)

Estate tax paid on income reported by heirs

Expenses paid for the production and collection of income, and expenses to maintain, manage, and conserve property held for investment

Farm expenses, if operated for profit

Fees paid
  To bank acting as dividend agent in automatic dividend reinvestment plan
  To secure employment, within limits of
  To secure readmission to organized labor union
  For passports on a business trip

Finance charges

Fire insurance premiums (on business or income-producing property)

Flood losses

Food and drinks (for business entertainment)

Forced sales, losses

Foreign taxes paid

Gambling losses (only to the extent of gambling gains)

Gifts for business purposes up to certain limits

Home office expenses, subject to limitations

Household or personal assets stolen or destroyed by fire or other casualty

Housing costs while working abroad if self-employed or costs not employer financed

Hurricane losses

Income tax return, fees for preparation

Income tax, state or city

Individual retirement account (IRA) contributions, subject to limits

Information, cost of obtaining, including cost of standard services for business, tax, or investment use

Injury benefits to employees (not compensated by insurance)

Interest paid or imputed (subject to limits)

Interest, prepaid, must be allocated over life of loan

Interest, although not stated, on tuition installment plans or personal property purchases

Interest paid in form of dividends from stock pledged for your loan

Investment counsel fees

Involuntary conversion, loss

Job expenses

Joint venture losses

Keogh plan contributions

Labor union dues

Library expenses used only for business or profession

License and regulatory fees for business

Loans, uncollectible

Lodging on trips to obtain medical care

Table 10.7 (continued)

Losses (except to the extent covered by insurance) arising from
  Abandoned property
  Abandonment of worthless business machinery
  Bad debts
  Bonds sold or exchanged
  Bonds, worthless
  Business operations
  Capital assets, sale of
  Casualties such as fire, theft, storm, shipwreck
  Deposits in closed banks
  Endorser or guarantor compelled to pay for principal when transaction was
    entered into for profit
  Forced sales
  Foreclosures
  Forfeitures
  Futures account closed by broker
  Gambling to the extent of gains
  Goodwill, sale or abandonment
  Investments, worthless
  Joint ventures, syndicates, pools, etc., participation in
  Loans not repaid
  Mortgaged property sold (business or investment)
  Net operating loss carried over and back
  Obsolescence of business asset
  Partnership operations
  Profit-seeking transactions
  Sale of capital assets
  Sale of inherited residence
  Sales and exchanges of property
  Securities, sale or exchange
  Securities, worthless
  Seizures by the government
  Short sales
  Stocks, worthless
  Transactions entered into for profit, even though not connected with a business
  Worthless securities

Magazines, technical or in waiting room of professional

Malpractice, expenses of professional in defense of suit for

Materials and supplies used in your business

Meals and lodging

Medical expenses, subject to limitations

Membership dues

Mortgage foreclosure losses

Moving expense of business property

National Defense Education Act grants under Title IV to graduate students preparing for college teaching careers

Table 10.7 (continued)

Ordinary and necessary business expenses

Penalty paid for prepaying mortgage payments
Periodicals used in your business or profession
Plane fare for business trips
Points paid for loan under certain circumstances
Preparation of tax returns, cost of
Professional dues
Professional's expenses, including books and equipment of short life
Property damage
Property taxes

Real estate, expenses of rental or investment property
Real estate sales losses
Real estate taxes
Religious organizations, contributions to
Rents, including payments for the use of safe deposit box used for business or
    investment purposes
Repairs of business or income-producing property
Repairs to a residence or property which you can rent to others

Safe deposit box costs for records used in your business or for income-producing
    or investment property
Salespersons' expenses
Securities as charitable contributions
Security transactions, cost of
Short sales losses
Short selling costs
Simplified employee pension plan contributions
State income and other taxes
Storm damage
Subscriptions to professional or trade journals
Supplies used in profession or business
Support of a student, unrelated to you, in your home, up to $50 per month

Tax preparation fees
Taxes paid (property, state income)
Teachers' expenses of attending summer school
Technical magazines used in your business
Tenants—payment of real estate taxes, interest or other items for your landlord (if
    property is leased for income-producing purposes)
Theft losses
Trade associations' dues
Traveling and entertaining expenses
Traveling between two jobs
Traveling to professional convention, subject to limits
Traveling to get medical care
Traveling to look after income-producing property
Trustees' expenses, certain commissions

Uncollectible debts

Table 10.7 (continued)

Uniforms, required for your job and not generally adaptable for ordinary wear
Union assessments
Union dues
Unreimbursed volunteer expenses for charity
Unstated interest
Upkeep, care and maintenance of real estate held for investment or rented to others
Worthless bonds or stocks

Miscellaneous Deductions Subject to the 2% of Adjusted Gross Income Limit

Certain appraisal fees
Certain legal fees
Clerical help and office rent in caring for investments
Custodial fees in connection with property held for producing income
Dues to professional societies
Employment-related education
Fees to collect interest and dividends
Hobby expenses, but generally not more than hobby income
Investment counsel fees
Laboratory breakage fees
Liquidated damages paid to former employer for breach of employment contract
Looking for a new job
Malpractice insurance premiums
Medical examinations required by employer
Occupational taxes paid by an employee
Part of home used regularly and exclusively in work
Research expenses of a college professor
Safe deposit box rental
Small tools and supplies used in taxpayer's work
Subscriptions to professional journals and trade magazines related to taxpayer's work
Tax preparation fees
Union dues and expenses
Work clothes and uniforms

Note: The above deductions are subject to the 2% limit even if they are passed through to the taxpayer from certain entities (for example, partnerships, S corporations, and certain mutual funds).

Nondeductible expenses

Adoption expenses for children with special needs
Burial or funeral expenses
Campaign expenses
Capital expenses
Certain fees and licenses
Commuting expenses
Fines and penalties, such as parking tickets
Gifts to influence legislation
Health spa expenses

Table 10.7 (continued)

Nondeductible expenses

Hobby losses
Home repairs, insurance, and rent
Illegal bribes and kickbacks
Life insurance
Losses from the sale of taxpayer's home, furniture, personal car, etc.
Lost or misplaced cash or property
Lunches and meals while working late
Personal legal expenses
Personal, living or family expenses
Political contributions
Professional accreditation fees
Relief fund contributions for fellow employee
Self-improvement expenses
Stockholders' meeting, expenses of attending
Tax-exempt income expenses
Voluntary unemployment benefit fund contributions

10.10 INTERNAL REVENUE SERVICE CENTERS

Table 10.8 provides the mailing addresses for filing income tax returns. The IRS requests that, if an addressed envelope came with the return, the taxpayer should use it. A fiduciary of an estate or trust should generally file form 1041 with the Internal Revenue Service Center for the state in which the fiduciary resides or has his or her principal place of business. Those who moved during the year should mail their returns to the Internal Revenue Service Center serving their current locale.

10.11 FORMULA FOR CALCULATING THE ALTERNATIVE MINIMUM TAX

The alternative minimum tax is designed to ensure that high-income taxpayers who benefit greatly from deductions still pay some minimum tax. Financial professionals should be familiar with the AMT formula (Table 10.9) since some planning opportunities are available to reduce its effects.

Table 10.8 Mailing Addresses for Filing Income Tax Returns

If you are located in:	Use this address:
Florida, Georgia, South Carolina	Atlanta, GA 39901
New Jersey, New York (New York City and counties of Nassau, Rockland, Suffolk, and Westchester)	Holtsville, NY 00501
Connecticut, Maine, Massachusetts, New Hampshire, New York (all other counties), Rhode Island, Vermont	Andover, MA 05501
Illinois, Iowa, Minnesota, Missouri, Wisconsin	Kansas City, MO 64999
Delaware, District of Columbia, Maryland, Pennsylvania, Virginia	Philadelphia, PA 19255
Indiana, Kentucky, Michigan, Ohio, West Virginia	Cincinnati, OH 45999
Kansas, New Mexico, Oklahoma, Texas	Austin, TX 73301
Alaska, Arizona, California (counties of Alpine, Amador, Butte, Calaveras, Colusa, Contra Costa, Del Norte, El Dorado, Glenn, Humboldt, Lake, Lassen, Marin, Mendocino, Modoc, Napa, Nevada, Placer Plumas, Sacramento, San Joaquin, Shasta, Sierra, Siskiyou, Solano, Sonoma, Sutter, Tehama, Trinity, Yolo and Yuba), Colorado, Idaho, Montana, Nebraska, Nevada, North Dakota, Oregon, South Dakota, Utah, Washington, Wyoming	Ogden, UT 84201
California (all other counties), Hawaii	Fresno, CA 93888
Alabama, Arkansas, Louisiana, Mississippi, North Carolina, Tennessee	Memphis, TN 37501
American Samoa	Philadelphia, PA 19255

Table 10.8 (continued)

Guam	Commissioner of Taxes Agana, GU 96910
Puerto Rico (or if excluding income under section 933) Virgin Islands: Nonpermanent residents	Philadelphia, PA 19255
Virgin Islands Permanent residents	V.I. Bureau of Internal Revenue Lockharts Garden No. 1A Charlotte Amalie, St. Thomas, VI 00802
Foreign country: U.S. citizens and those filing form 2555 or Form 4563, even if you have an A.P.O. or F.P.O. address	Philadelphia, PA 19255
A.P.O. or F.P.O. address of:	Miami—Atlanta, GA 39901 New York—Holtsville, NY 00501 San Francisco—Fresno, CA 93888 Seattle—Ogden, UT 84201

Table 10.9 Alternative Minimum Tax Formula

Taxable Income
Plus or minus: Adjustments

• Itemized deductions for taxes, certain interest, and most miscellaneous deductions are not allowed

• Standard deduction is not allowed

• Modified accelerated cost recovery system (MACRS) depreciation is figured under the alternative MACRS system for real estate, using 40-year straight-line recovery, and for personal property, the 150 percent declining balance method is used

• Allowable mining exploration and development costs are allowable costs that must be amortized ratably over 10 years

• For long-term contracts entered into after February 28, 1986 income is figured under the percentage of completion method

• Pollution control facilities amortization is figured under alternative MACRS

• Alternative tax net operating loss is allowed with certain adjustments

• Circulation expenditures must be amortized ratably over three years

Table 10.9 (continued)

- Research and experimentation expenditures must be amortized ratably over 10 years
- Net passive activity losses, including tax shelter farm activities, are not allowed

Plus: Tax preferences

- Depletion—excess of depletion deduction over adjusted basis in property
- Intangible drilling costs—excess of deducted costs over the total of the amount allowable if costs were amortized ratably over 120 months plus 65 percent of net income from the properties
- Incentive stock options—excess of fair market value over option price at date of exercise
- Accelerated depreciation on depreciable real property and depreciable leased personal property placed in service before 1987—excess depreciation or amortization taken over straight-line deduction
- Certain tax-exempt interest on specified private activity bonds
- Unrealized appreciation on donated long-term capital gain property

Equals: AMT taxable income
Less: Exemption amount

- $40,000 if married filing a joint return or qualifying widow(er)
- $30,000 if single or head of household or
- $20,000 if married filing a separate return
- The exemption is reduced by 25 cents for each $1 that AMT taxable income exceeds $150,000 for joint filers or a qualifying surviving spouse, $112,500 for single persons, and $75,000 for married persons filing separately. The exemption is completely phased out at $310,000 on a joint return, $232,500 on a single or head of household return, $155,000 on a married separate return.

Subtotal
Multiplied by 24%
Subtotal
Less: AMT foreign tax credit
Equals Tentative minimum tax
Less: Regular tax
Equals Alternative minimum tax

Chapter 11_____

RETIREMENT PLANNING

Assisting individuals in achieving a comfortable retirement is one of the investment professional's most challenging and important tasks. Indeed, many individuals' first contact with a financial counselor is motivated by concern about having an adequate retirement income. During this decade, retirement planning is likely to become an even more important issue, as the postwar baby boom generation enters their fifties and begins to ponder the prospects of achieving financial security in their "golden years."

Increasingly, both employers and the federal government expect that individuals can and should be prepared to fund a substantial portion of retirement income from personal savings. On the corporate side, pension plans are already under pressure because of the increasing costs associated with funding those plans. Many companies, in fact, are replacing traditional pension plans, which provide a guaranteed income at retirement, with plans that base corporate contributions on annual profits. In addition, many pensions do not provide postretirement cost-of-living increases, and those that do have generally not kept pace with inflation in recent years.

Many experts feel that Social Security benefits—once considered a legislative sacred cow—will eventually be subject to a means-based test. Should this occur, relatively affluent workers may find that their Social Security benefits will be less than they had planned on.

However, the federal government has introduced a number of retirement savings programs to help boost a sagging personal savings rate. Employers, too, now offer tax-advantaged savings plans that often have incentives such as matching contributions. Financial institutions now feature an array of products and services to take advantage of the growing retirement market.

Thus, while it is becoming increasingly important for individuals to save for their own retirement, there is an attractive array of investment and savings alternatives to do so. It is up to the financial professional to acquaint himself or herself with these varied and complex opportunities.

Ideally, retirement planning should be a process that starts when individuals are in their twenties or thirties. While it is difficult to predict retirement income or expenses at this point, younger individuals can begin saving for retirement by taking advantage of an IRA or other tax-advantaged savings plan, determining an appropriate investment strategy, and making regular plan contributions.

Financial professionals are likely to encounter a wide range of individuals, from those who have accumulated a substantial nest egg to those whose resources are clearly inadequate. Unfortunately, because many people have more pressing and immediate concerns in their younger years, retirement planning is often put on hold until individuals are in their fifties, when there is much less time to build personal funds.

The first step in retirement planning is determining how much income will be needed and what its sources will be. Retirement income is often compared to a three-legged stool consisting of Social Security, pension plans, and personal savings, and these resources should be examined carefully to determine if they can adequately meet postretirement life-style expectations. Individuals who are satisfied with only the bare necessities, obviously, will need much less income than will those who plan to travel extensively or to incur expenses close to preretirement levels.

After this initial step, an estimate should be made of anticipated expenses at retirement. If retirement is more than a few years away, it is important to factor inflation into the picture as well. Fortunately, for many retirees, the cost of living falls for several reasons. Senior citizens pay less in taxes than most individuals because their income is lower. Saving for retirement is reduced, but not eliminated, when retirement commences. Work related expenses are lower, and retirees have at their disposal numerous discounts on every-day goods and services such as entertainment or public transportation.

Medical expenses and insurance costs, however, are often higher for retirees than other segments of the population. Individuals who retire before age 65, and who are thus not yet eligible for Medicare, may be particularly vulnerable to unexpected medical expenses and high insurance costs. Therefore, those who are considering early retirement should inquire about their company's policy on providing health insurance for such former workers. Those age 65 or over should examine the features of health insurance policies that supplement Medicare.

With the assistance of a financial professional, individuals in their preretirement years should review their tax planning and estate planning programs to maximize retirement assets and income and ensure smooth transfer of the estate. In addition, appropriate capital accumulation and capital preservation techniques from equities, fixed-income, or real estate investments must be explored.

11.1   RETIREMENT PLAN SUMMARY

The best way for people to prepare for retirement is to make regular contributions to one or more tax-favored retirement plans such as an individual retirement account (IRA), a 401 (k), or a Keogh plan. Whether offered by an employer or self-funded, these plans offer the advantage of tax deferral of investment earnings until the funds are withdrawn, usually during retirement. In addition, contributions to some self-funded plans are also tax deductible. A description of the major tax-deferred retirement plans follows.

11.1.1   Company Qualified Plans

11.1.1.1   General considerations A company qualified pension or profit-sharing plan offers several benefits. First, if the employer makes contributions to the plan on the employee's behalf, they are not included in the employee's current income for tax purposes.

Second, income earned on the funds compounds tax free. Third, the employer may allow the employee to make voluntary contributions. Although these contributions are not tax deductible, income earned on voluntary contributions is not taxed until withdrawn.

11.1.1.2   Tax treatment of distributions If an individual receives a lump sum when he or she retires, taxes on the distribution may be reduced by special averaging rules. Alternatively, the lump-sum payment could be rolled over to an IRA account to postpone taxation further. Distributions from qualified plans before age 59 1/2 are generally subject to penalties, but there are exceptions. IRA rollovers of lump-sum payments may also be elected to defer taxes on the distribution. Finally, a penalty may apply to distributions from a pension plan that exceed specified ceilings.

11.1.2   Keogh Plans

11.1.2.1   General considerations Individuals who have income from self-employment may be eligible to establish a Keogh plan, even if they already participate in a pension plan through their regular employer. Individuals owning Keogh plans may deduct contributions up to a specified limit, and income earned on Keogh plan investments is not taxed until withdrawn. These plans must be set up by the end of tax year, although contributions may be made up to the date of filing tax returns (including extensions). If the individual has employees, they must be included under specified rules.

11.1.2.2   Tax treatment of distributions Self-employed persons may not generally withdraw Keogh plan funds until age 59½ unless they are disabled. Premature withdrawals are subject to penalty. Lump-sum distributions to self-employed person or beneficiaries at death may qualify for favored lump-sum distribution treatment under specified rules.

11.1.3 Deferred Compensation (401(k)) Plans

11.1.3.1 General considerations 401 (k) plans generally involve joint contributions by employees and employers. Contributions are, in effect, deducted from 401 (k) plan holders' salaries so these funds aren't taxed until they are withdrawn during retirement. Income earned on the funds accumulates tax free until it is withdrawn. Many of these plans offer the plan holder choice among a number of investment possibilities. Individuals who work for charitable or educational organizations may find that their employers offer similar deferred compensation arrangements known as *tax-sheltered annuities* or *403 (b) plans*. Because participation in 401(k) or 403(b) plans is so attractive, financial services professionals should encourage their clients to take advantage of these plans if their employers offer them.

11.1.3.2 Tax treatment of distributions Withdrawals are penalized if received before age 59½ with some exceptions although plan holders may be able to borrow from their accounts. At the time of withdrawal, the tax on proceeds may be computed under specified rules.

11.1.4 Simplified Employee Pension (SEP) Plans

11.1.4.1 General considerations Companies may establish simplified employee pension (SEP) plans for their employees. However, if a person is a sole proprietor, he or she may set one up individually. In company-sponsored SEP plans, the employer makes contributions on behalf of the employees—up to specified limits—which are deposited in each employee's IRA account. There is less red tape with SEPs than there is with Keogh plans. Some employers may qualify for SEP plans that allow employees to contribute to the SEP through salary reduction.

11.1.4.2 Tax treatment of distributions Withdrawals are taxable under rules explained for IRAs (see section 11.1.5).

11.1.5 Individual Retirement Accounts

11.1.5.1 General considerations Anyone who has earned income may contribute to an IRA, but the contribution is fully or partially deductible only if certain requirements are met. One criterion for tax-deductible IRA eligibility is income level; another is whether or not an individual already participates in a company pension plan. Whether IRA contributions are deductible or not, income earned on IRA accounts is not taxed until the funds are withdrawn. Whether contributions to these accounts are deductible or not, IRAs continue to be an excellent way for working Americans to build up money for retirement.

11.1.5.2 Tax treatment of distributions Funds may not be withdrawn without incurring a penalty until the account holder is 59½, disabled, or receives distributions in the form of a lifetime annuity. IRA owners who can afford to delay withdrawing from their accounts in order to take full advantage of tax-free compounding must begin withdrawing funds no later than age 70½ according to specified rules.

11.2   EARLY RETIREMENT STRATEGIES

Although early retirement offers many personal advantages to the retiree, such as more years of work-free time to be enjoyed, several financial obstacles must be overcome. Some strategies for, along with the pitfalls of, early retirement are discussed in this section.

11.2.1 Social Security

One obstacle to early retirement which must be considered is a reduction in Social Security benefits. Two factors cause this reduction: (1) more years in retirement and (2) fewer years in which to contribute to Social Security. For Social Security, the normal retirement age is currently set at age 65. A person can receive early retirement benefits no sooner than at age 62, but they will be significantly reduced.

11.2.2 Pension Plans

The preretiree should make sure that his or her personal pension plan has been completely vested. Many pension plans allow workers to retire if they meet certain conditions, such as reaching age 55 and completing at least 10 years of service. Even then, though, pension benefits may be much lower.

For highly compensated persons, current tax regulations limit the maximum benefit that can be provided under defined benefit pension plans for individuals who retire before the Social Security retirement age. A true actuarial reduction is now required for early retirement, and the prior $75,000 floor at age 55 has been removed. These reduction rules do not apply to plans of tax-exempt employers and organizations.

11.2.3 Strategies

Special financial planning strategies may be appropriate for some clients who choose to retire early. Since normal retirement benefits from IRAs, Keogh plans, employer pension plans, and Social Security will either be reduced or penalized significantly if they are withdrawn before standard retirement age, personal savings and investments will consequently play an even greater role for the early retiree.

The individual who wishes to retire early may want to consider less conventional planning strategies to emphasize income and security. Some people's desire for early retirement has led them to sell their assets and property and invest most of the proceeds on low-risk income-producing instruments such as bank certificates of deposit. Any such strategy should be reviewed extensively to assure that it does provide some capital appreciation and protection from inflation. Many people find that being able to quit work is worth a reduction in their standard of living. To this end, moving, especially out of urban areas, may reduce costs considerably. Part-time employment answers the two most frequent complaints of retirees: too much time and too little money, but the client should think twice about this option. Good part-time jobs that are financially and emotionally rewarding are few and far between, especially for older persons. Also, planning for part-time employment should take into account not only the additional income it produces, but also the additional costs it may incur, such as higher income taxes and reduced Social Security benefits.

The years between early retirement and normal retirement age pose special perils. Early retirees tend to be in better physical and financial condition and, as a result, less inclined to frugality. When possible, financing for these early years of retirement should come entirely from personal savings. The client should be encouraged to wait to withdraw funds from company pension plans, if this is possible, as well as from IRAs and other tax-advantaged investment plans. Moreover, it may be advisable to defer claiming Social Security benefits until the early retiree is eligible for full benefits.

11.2.4 Early Retirement Incentive Plans

Traditionally, the decision to retire early was made by the employee for personal reasons such as health or the financial ability to leave the work force. Recently, however, many workers have been prompted to consider leaving the workforce prior to age 65 by early retirement incentive programs offered by companies in the midst of mergers, takeovers, or downsizing. These incentive programs are now the most popular means of achieving a reduction in the work force and have been an effective means of reducing layoffs. The financial professional may be called upon to assist someone in evaluating an early retirement, or "window," offer. This must be done as quickly as possible, since such programs are usually one-time offers and the employee must decline or accept within a relatively short period of time (usually one to two months).

At first glance, many early retirement incentive programs look appealing. Incentives may include additional or enhanced pension benefits, retiree health insurance, and lump-sum cash benefits. However, the client should keep in mind that the high cost of living and the erosion of purchasing power due to inflation may make such benefits much less attractive in only a few years. It is important for the potential retiree who has been offered an early retirement incentive package to try to determine the likelihood of continued employment should he or she decline such an offer. He or she should consider whether there is a possibility of being laid off in the future; whether the company appears vulnerable to a merger or takeover. If future layoffs appear likely, there may be little choice but to participate in an early retirement program.

11.3   RETIREMENT PLANNING TIMETABLE

The financial professional can play an important role in helping clients plan wisely for their retirement. As clients pass through the various stages of their working lives, there are a number of concrete steps that they can take to ensure that their retirements are as secure and as pleasant as possible. The timetable in Table 11.1 describes the retirement-oriented steps that clients should take at each stage in their careers. This timetable will help the financial professional guide his or her clients toward well planned retirements.

Table 11.1   Retirement-Oriented Steps

During All Working Years

1. Clients should make sure that their insurance coverage is adequate and continuous.

2. Employees contemplating job changes should consider its ramifications on future pension benefits. "Job hopping" can severely curtail pension benefits.

3. Employees who have changed jobs should roll over any vested pension benefits into an IRA or other tax-deferred retirement plan.

Before Age 40

1. Clients should regularly contribute to an IRA or other retirement-earmarked savings fund.

2. Clients should consider purchasing a home with the goal of having low or minimal mortgage costs by the time retirement approaches.

3. Employees should discuss the fine points of the pension plan with company benefits officers.

Ages 40-49

1. Clients should periodically determine the status of their Social Security benefits by submitting Form SSA-7004 to the Social Security Administration. Filers of this form will receive a "Personal Earnings and Benefit Estimate Statement" verifying that their wages are being properly credited to their accounts. This statement will enable the recipient to determine how Social Security benefits will affect his or her projected retirement income.

2. Clients should analyze personal assets and work out a plan for funding an adequate retirement income.

3. Holders of IRAs and other retirement funds should actively manage them, placing appropriate emphasis on capital gains-oriented investments.

4. Clients should make a will and review it every three years or when moving to another state.

Ages 50-59

1. Periodically, the preretiree should continue to request his or her Social Security "Personal Earnings and Benefit Estimate Statement."

Table 11.1 (continued)

2. Employees should regularly review their status with company pension plans.

3. Preretirees should periodically revise their retirement income and expense projections in order to take the effects of inflation into consideration.

4. The preretiree should confirm the beneficiary designations on life insurance policies.

5. Holders of IRAs and other retirement-earmarked funds should gradually start shifting assets into lower risk investments with more emphasis on yield.

6. Preretirees should join the American Association of Retired Persons to take advantage of the many sources of information and help that it offers. The address is
   AARP
   1909 K St., N.W.
   Washington, D.C. 20049

Ages 60-64

1. Employees contemplating early retirement should discuss its advantages and disadvantages with company personnel officers and local Social Security offices.

2. Preretirees should collect the documents necessary to process Social Security benefits:
   Both spouses' Social Security cards
   Proof of both spouses' ages
   Marriage certificate
   Copy of latest income tax withholding statement (W-2)

3. Before taking any major actions, such as selling a house, the preretiree should weigh the merits of waiting until age 65, because many special breaks are available to the elderly or retired.

4. The preretiree should determine the status and duration of ongoing financial commitments such as mortgages and loans.

5. The preretiree should prepare detailed cash flow projections from estimated year of retirement until age 85 to 90, taking inflation into consideration.

6. The preretiree should practice living for a month under the planned retirement income.

7. Preretirees should consider different retirement locations. If a location other than the present home is chosen, they should try living there for a while before making the move.

Right Before Retirement

1. The imminent retiree should establish what your retirement income will be and estimate as closely as possible what the retirement costs of living will be.

2. Employees should have company personnel officers determine the level of their pension benefits, what company or bank will send the pension, and when the first check (or lump-sum distribution) will arrive; what can be done about accumulated vacation time; whether there are any special annuity benefits; and whether supplemental medical or hospital insurance is available.

Table 11.1 (continued)

3. Preretirees should register with the Social Security Administration at least three months before retirement.

4. Preretirees should ask about possible entitlements to partial pensions from past jobs.

11.4 SOCIAL SECURITY RETIREMENT BENEFIT PROJECTOR

The computation of Social Security benefits is quite complicated. Fortunately, the Social Security Administration provides a worker with an accounting of his or her yearly salary history; a total of how much has been paid in Social Security taxes to date; estimates of retirement benefits at ages 65, 70, and an age that is designated on the application form; and estimates of survivors and disability benefits. Form SSA-7004 ("Request for Earnings and Benefit Estimate Statement") can be obtained from the local Social Security office or by calling 800-234-5772.

In lieu of requesting information pertaining to a specific individual's Social Security benefit status, Table 11.2 shows the approximate monthly retirement benefits based upon current age and income.

11.5 EFFECT OF OTHER INCOME ON TAXABILITY OF SOCIAL SECURITY BENEFITS

In Table 11.3 the second column lists how much income (including tax-exempt interest) the taxpayer may receive before Social Security benefits become taxable. [The second column includes adjusted gross income without regard to Social Security benefits.] The last column lists the levels at which 50 percent of all Social Security benefits become taxable.

Table 11.2 Approximate Monthly Retirement Benefits If the Worker Retires at Normal Retirement Age and Had Steady Lifetime Earnings

Your Earnings In 1990

Your Age In 1991	Your Family	$20,000	$30,000	$40,000	$50,000	$51,300 Or More
45	You	$ 863	$1,124	$1,263	$1,392	$1,422
	You and your spouse[2]	1,294	1,686	1,894	2,088	2,133
55	You	783	1,014	1,106	1,181	1,195
	You and your spouse[2]	1,174	1,521	1,659	1,771	1,792
65	You	725	926	982	1,021	1,022
	You and your spouse[2]	1,087	1,389	1,473	1,531	1,533

[1] Use this column if you earn more than the maximum Social Security earnings base.
[2] Your spouse is assumed to be the same age as you. Your spouse may qualify for a higher retirement benefit based on his or her own work record.

Note: The accuracy of these estimates depends on the pattern of your actual past earnings, and on your earnings in the future.

Table 11.3 Effect of Other Income on Taxability of Social Security Benefits

Monthly Social Security Benefits	No Benefits Taxed Unless Other Income Exceeds	50 Percent Of Benefits Taxed If Other Income Is At Least
Single filing status		
$ 300	$23,200	$26,800
350	22,900	27,100
400	22,600	27,400
450	22,300	27,700
500	22,000	28,000
550	21,700	28,300
600	21,400	28,600
650	21,100	28,900
700	20,800	29,200
750	20,500	29,500
800	20,200	29,800
850	19,900	30,100
900	19,600	30,400
950	19,300	30,700
1,000	19,000	31,000
Married filing jointly		
$ 700	$27,800	$36,200
750	27,500	36,500
800	27,200	36,800
850	26,900	37,100
900	26,600	37,400
950	26,300	37,700
1,000	26,000	38,000
1,050	25,700	38,300
1,100	25,400	38,600
1,150	25,100	38,900
1,200	24,800	39,200
1,250	24,500	39,500
1,300	24,200	39,800
1,350	23,900	40,100
1,400	23,600	40,400

11.6 HOW EARLY OR LATE RETIREMENT AFFECTS SOCIAL SECURITY BENEFITS

Tables 11.4 and 11.5 show the percentage amounts that Social Security benefits are reduced if payments commence before age 65 or are increased if collection of benefits is postponed until after age 65. Deciding upon when to begin receiving benefits requires careful consideration, particularly for early retirees. The prospect of beginning to collect Social Security at age 62 may seem enticing. On the one hand, by receiving benefits 3 years early, a retiree would need to collect benefits at the full rate for 12 years to make up the difference in total income. On the other hand, once the retiree begins receiving Social Security benefits at a reduced rate, he or she will always receive benefits at a reduced rate.

Table 11.4 Social Security Benefit Reductions for Early Retirees (Multiply estimated benefits at age 65 as provided by the Social Security Administration by the appropriate reduction factor shown.)

Months Before Age 65[1]	Reduction Factor	Months Before Age 65[1]	Reduction Factor
1	.994	19	.894
2	.988	20	.888
3	.983	21	.883
4	.977	22	.877
5	.972	23	.872
6	.966	24	.866
7	.961	25	.861
8	.955	26	.855
9	.950	27	.850
10	.944	28	.844
11	.938	29	.838
12	.933	30	.833
13	.927	31	.827
14	.922	32	.822
15	.916	33	.816
16	.911	34	.811
17	.905	35	.805
18	.900	36	.800

[1]Retiree benefits cannot commence before age 62. Dependent spouses who retire early have a somewhat greater reduction factor. A dependent spouse who retires 36 months before age 65 has a reduction factor of .750 (versus .800 for the early retiree).

Table 11.5 Social Security Benefit Increases for Late Retirees[1]

Year Age 65 Attained[2]	Monthly Percentage (of 1 percent)	Yearly Percentage
1990–91	7/24%	3.5%
1992–93	1/3	4
1994–95	3/8	4.5
1996–97	5/12	5
1998–99	11/24	5.5
2000–2001	1/2	6
2002–2003	13/24	6.5
2004–2005	7/12	7
2006–2007	5/8	7.5
2008 or later	2/3	8

[1]Increase estimated benefits at age 65 as provided by the Social Security Administration by the appropriate percentage factor. For example, assume that an individual who reaches age 65 in 1992 expects to begin collecting Social Security at age 67. In this case, initial Social Security benefits will be 8% higher (yearly percentage of 4% times two years) than they would have been had benefits commenced at age 65.

[2]Normal retirement age will increase to age 66 beginning in 2009 and to age 67 in 2027.

11.7 SUMMARY OF MEDICARE AND OTHER HEALTH CARE ALTERNATIVES FOR RETIRED PERSONS

Most older Americans and their families are justifiably worried about meeting the health care costs of the elderly. Financial professionals should be aware of the different options that are available. These may include

1. *Medicare*
2. *Retiree medical benefits*
3. *Medicare supplemental health insurance*
4. *Health maintenance organizations*
5. *Medicaid*
6. *Long term care insurance*
7. *Continuous care communities*

Each of these health care programs are discussed in this section.

11.7.1 Medicare

Medicare, a health insurance program administered by the federal government, provides hospital and medical insurance for people 65 years of age or older, as well as for disabled people. It consists of

- Part A, or hospital insurance, which helps pay for certain hospital, hospice, skilled nursing facility care, and home health care

- Part B, or medical insurance, which covers certain types of outpatient care, such as visits to a physician, laboratory fees, and certain outpatient prescription drugs

Most people over age 65 have Medicare coverage, and anyone who has worked long enough to receive Social Security is automatically eligible for Part A hospital insurance. Spouses and certain dependents of eligible workers are also eligible, as are certain divorced persons and widows and widowers. Eligible people are covered by Part A without payment, but others who are not eligible may purchase Part A. Almost anyone aged 65 or more may enroll for Medicare Part B, which requires a monthly premium that is automatically deducted from the Social Security check.

Insurance protection starts automatically for some, while others need to apply for Parts A and B about three months before turning 65. A current copy of a handbook explaining Medicare coverage in detail may be obtained at a local Social Security office. Anyone expecting to need Medicare coverage should read this handbook carefully, because Medicare, contrary to common belief, does not provide complete health care coverage: its gaps include deductibles, copayments, limits, or reimbursements for certain services, as well as a lack of coverage for some services, notably, long-term nursing home confinements.

Medicare Part A pays for unlimited number of days of hospitalization, but a Medicare beneficiary who is hospitalized must pay an annual hospital deductible, set once a year at the average national cost for a day of hospitalization. Once the deductible is met, Medicare pays for all medically necessary inpatient hospital care for the remainder of the year, regardless of the cost or frequency of this care.

Part A also covers up to 150 days of skilled nursing facility care each year, with a copayment for each of the first 8 days of care. A skilled nursing facility is a specialized facility—most nursing homes in the United States are not skilled nursing facilities, and many skilled nursing facilities are not certified by Medicare. In addition, Medicare will not pay for a stay even in a certified skilled nursing facility if the services received are mainly personal or custodial services.

Part A pays for the intermittent services of a skilled nurse for a homebound beneficiary, and physical and speech therapist services furnished by a certified home health agency. Part A does not cover, however, full-time nursing care, drugs, meals delivered to a home, or homemaker services. Services such as routine medical examinations and most dental services and hearing and vision testing are also excluded from coverage.

Medicare beneficiaries who are certified as terminally ill may elect to receive hospice care for an unlimited duration in lieu of other benefits. Part A will pay the full cost necessary for the symptom management and pain relief of a terminally ill beneficiary. There are no deductibles or copayments aside from limited cost sharing for outpatient drugs and inpatient respite care.

Anyone enrolled in Medicare Part A is automatically enrolled in Part B unless he or she states the desire not to be enrolled. There is a deductible for outpatient care covered by Part B, after which Medicare pays 80 percent of the amount that Medicare approves for covered services. Medicare sets a rate for doctors' fees based upon the average fee for a geographical area and then reimburses the doctor or patient 80 percent of that amount. If a doctor charges more than the Medicare assignment, then the patient may have to pay the difference. For example, if a doctor charges $100 but Medicare's approved charge is $80, then Medicare will pay $64 (80 percent of $80). Supplemental insurance would probably cover the remaining 20 percent of the $80 ($16), but would likely not cover the difference between the actual charge and the Medicare assignment amount. In some states, doctors are prohibited from charging more than the Medicare-approved charge. Patients should, in any case, check whether or not their doctor accepts Medicare assignment.

Services covered by Part B include

- Physicians' and surgeons' services, whether received at home or at a facility of any kind. Routine physical exams are excluded.
- Home health visits. For a patient who does not have Part A, Part B pays the full cost of medically necessary home health visits for patients requiring skilled care. The only copayment is 20 percent of the cost of durable medical equipment.
- Physical therapy and speech pathology services.
- Certain other services and supplies, such as outpatient hospital services, X rays and laboratory tests, certain ambulance services, and purchase or rental of durable medical equipment (such as wheelchairs).

Medicare coverage of outpatient prescription drugs is presently being phased in. Expenses not covered by Medicare include

- Private duty nursing
- Skilled nursing home care costs beyond 150 days a year
- Custodial care in a nursing home or at home
- Intermediate nursing home care
- Physician charges above Medicare's approved amount
- Most kinds of outpatient drugs
- Care received outside the United States, except under certain circumstances in Mexico and Canada
- Dental care or dentures, checkups, most routine immunizations, cosmetic surgery, routine foot care, and examinations for and the cost of eyeglasses or hearing aids.

Starting in 1990, the upper limit on a Medicare beneficiary's out-of-pocket expenses for Part B benefits will be set at $1,370, due to rise with inflation. Once this limit has been reached, Medicare will pay 100 percent of all reasonable charges, instead of 80 percent.

11.7.1.1 Filing Claims Hospitals and other institutions file Medicare claims directly, and the patient receives notice of such charges and payments. Medicare frequently takes a long time to process these claims. Patients do need to file claims for Part B insurance services. If a doctor accepts Medicare assignments, he or she will file the claim and bill the patient the remaining 20 percent, but if a doctor does not accept the assignment, the patient will be billed directly and will be responsible for submitting a request for payment from Medicare.

If a patient believes Medicare's coverage of a claim is inappropriate, he or she may appeal the decision. Depending on whether the decision is part of Part A or Part B coverage, and on how large an amount the claim is for, this appeal should be addressed to different authorities.

Medicare has introduced a "Prospective Payment System for Hospital Reimbursement," limiting payments to hospitals to a fixed amount per illness. Some patients have complained that this system has forced them to be discharged before they are ready to go. In order to prevent problems, a patient (or his or her family caretaker) should get in touch with the doctor and the hospital's discharge planner at the beginning of a hospital stay. A hospital social worker can make arrangements for services to assist the patient when he or she returns home. The more information the social worker is provided with and the more time he or she has to work on a discharge plan, the more smoothly departure is likely to go.

11.7.2 Retiree Medical Benefits

Retiree medical benefits are provided by some companies to their former employees. These benefit plans fill in some of the gaps in Medicare's coverage, meaning that the retiree may not need to purchase Medicare supplemental health coverage.

11.7.3 Medicare Supplemental Health Coverage

Medicare supplemental health coverage, also known as "Medigap" insurance, can help pay for Medicare deductibles, the remaining 20 percent of a medical bill, or specific items not covered by Medicare. Supplemental insurance rarely covers a service that Medicare determines to be medically unnecessary. Before purchasing a supplemental health plan, the following policy features should be considered:

* *Deductibles.* Many supplemental health plans, while paying for Medicare deductibles, also have their own deductibles.

* *Exclusions.* Possible exclusions are routine physical or eye examinations and podiatric and dental care.

- *Preexisting illness.* Some policies require a waiting period before they will provide coverage for a preexisting illness.

- *Renewability.* Some policies can be canceled on the basis of too many claims.

- *Maximum coverage limits.* A health insurance plan may, for example, limit its coverage to $500 a year for prescription drugs.

- *State regulations.* Insurance regulated by a policyholder's own state may provide more consumer protection.

A new federal law effective 1992 has mandated simplification of Medicare Gap insurance policies, and it should facilitate the selection process.

11.7.4 Health Maintenance Organizations (HMOs)

Health maintenance organizations (HMOs) emphasize a preventive approach to health care, and many cover the cost of a routine physical examination. With some HMOs all out-of-pocket expenses not covered by Medicare are eliminated and are replaced by a single monthly premium paid to the HMO. Advantages of an HMO may include

- A doctor assigned to coordinate all the patient's health care, eliminating fragmentary care

- No deductibles

- Coverage for preventive care

- Convenient 24-hour daily access to health care

- No paperwork

- Many health care services available in one location

- Fully covered office visits (with a small copayment, often $5 or so).

Disadvantages are

- Patient can use only physicians associated with the HMO and may have fewer choices in selecting specialists

- Members must use the hospitals and facilities with which the HMO is affiliated

If an older person using an HMO decides to change health care coverage, the following should be done before making the change:

- Check to make sure the health plan is accepting new members.

- Make sure new coverage is in effect before canceling old coverage.

- Let the HMO know that coverage is being terminated.

11.7.5 Medicaid

Medicaid is funded by the state and federal governments. Unlike Medicare, Medicaid will pay for extended nursing home care for eligible individuals. All older persons receiving Supplemental Security Income (SSI) are eligible. In some states, individuals whose incomes are too high to qualify normally for Medicaid may qualify if their medical expenses are so large that their net income is reduced to a level within state requirements. This process whereby individuals become eligible for Medicaid is called "spending down." Formulas and criteria for spending down vary from state to state. Elderly persons (and their children) should be cautioned about certain techniques that are sometimes used to qualify an elderly person or couple for Medicaid, such as giving all their assets to their children or placing all their assets in an irrevocable trust.

11.7.6 Long Term Care Insurance

Long term care insurance is a relatively new type of insurance policy that is designed to fill the large gaps left by Medicare with respect to nursing home and home health care. The amount of coverage, deductibles, exclusions, and other factors all vary depending on the type of policy. Comprehensive coverage can be very expensive, particularly if the person who obtains the coverage is already quite old. A thorough evaluation of several competing policies is recommended for those who want to purchase this coverage.

11.7.7 Continuous Care Communities

Continuous care communities are also a recent innovation in care for our senior citizens. The individual or couple typically pays a large admission fee in addition to monthly payments in return for lifetime residential accommodations and nursing home care when needed. These communities offer the elderly person the advantages of independent living, long-term security, and affordable nursing home care. However, the financial stability of many continuous care communities is shaky, and therefore, prior to signing up, it is important to evaluate thoroughly the financial strength of the community.

11.8 DETERMINING THE DEDUCTIBILITY OF INDIVIDUAL RETIREMENT ACCOUNT CONTRIBUTIONS

The rules governing the deductibility of individual retirement account (IRA) contributions are confusing to many people. Table 11.6 shows whether a taxpayer can take a full deduction, a partial deduction, or no deduction for his or her IRA contribution.

Table 11.6 Determining the Deductibility of an IRA Contribution

CAN YOU TAKE AN IRA DEDUCTION?

This chart sums up whether you can take a full deduction, a partial deduction, or no deduction as discussed in this chapter.

If Your Modified AGI* Is		If You Are Covered by a Retirement Plan at Work and Your Filing Status Is			If You Are Not Covered by a Retirement Plan at Work and Your Filing Status Is			
At Least	But Less Than	• Single, or • Head of Household	• Married Filing Jointly (even if your spouse *is not* covered by a plan at work) • Qualifying Widow(er)	Married Filing Separately**	• Single, or • Head of Household	• Married Filing Jointly (and your spouse *is* covered by a plan at work) • Qualifying Widow(er)	• Married Filing Jointly or Separately (and your spouse *is not* covered by a plan at work) • Qualifying Widow(er)	Married Filing Separately (even if your spouse *is* covered by a plan at work)***
		You Can Take	You Can Take	You Can Take	You Can Take	You Can Take	You Can Take	You Can Take
$—0—	$10,000	Full deduction	Full deduction	Partial deduction	Full Deduction	Full deduction	Full Deduction	Full Deduction
$10,000	$25,000	Full deduction	Full deduction	No deduction		Full deduction		
$25,000	$35,000	Partial deduction	Full deduction	No deduction		Full deduction		
$35,000	$40,000	No deduction	Full deduction	No deduction		Full deduction		
$40,000	$50,000	No deduction	Partial deduction	No deduction		Partial deduction		
$50,000 or over		No deduction	No deduction	No deduction		No deduction		

Maximum deduction. You can deduct IRA contributions up to the amount of your allowable deduction (full or partial), or 100% of your taxable compensation, whichever is less.

$200 floor. The partial deduction has a $200 floor. For example, if your deduction would have been reduced to less than $200 (but not zero), you can deduct IRA contributions up to $200 or 100% of your taxable compensation, whichever is less. If the deduction is completely phased out (reduced to zero), no deduction is allowed.

*Modified AGI (adjusted gross income) is: (1) for Form 1040A—the amount on line 11, or (2) for Form 1040—the amount on line 31, figured without taking into account any IRA deduction or any foreign earned income exclusion and foreign housing exclusion (deduction).

**If you *did not* live with your spouse *at any time* during the year, your filing status is considered, for this purpose, as Single (therefore your IRA deduction is determined under the "Single" column).

***You are entitled to the full deduction *only if you did not* live with your spouse *at any time* during the year. If you *did* live with your spouse during the year, you are, for this purpose, treated as though you are covered by a retirement plan at work (therefore, your IRA deduction is determined under the "Married Filing Separately" column in the "If You Are Covered by a Retirement Plan . . ." section of the chart).

11.9 IRS SINGLE AND JOINT LIFE EXPECTANCY TABLES

Tables 11.7 and 11.8 show single and joint life expectancy rates as provided by the Internal Revenues Service. They are used to compute the expected return under an annuity contract and to compute the required minimum distributions after age 70½ from all qualified retirement plans, including Keogh plans and individual retirement accounts.

Table 11.7 IRS Single Life Expectancy Table

Age	Multiple	Age	Multiple	Age	Multiple
5	76.6	42	40.6	79	10.0
6	75.6	43	39.6	80	9.5
7	74.7	44	38.7	81	8.9
8	73.7	45	37.7	82	8.4
9	72.7	46	36.8	83	7.9
10	71.7	47	35.9	84	7.4
11	70.7	48	34.9	85	6.9
12	69.7	49	34.0	86	6.5
13	68.8	50	33.1	87	6.1
14	67.8	51	32.2	88	5.7
15	66.8	52	31.3	89	5.3
16	65.8	53	30.4	90	5.0
17	64.8	54	29.5	91	4.7
18	63.9	55	28.6	92	4.4
19	62.9	56	27.7	93	4.1
20	61.9	57	26.8	94	3.9
21	60.9	58	25.9	95	3.7
22	59.9	59	25.0	96	3.4
23	59.0	60	24.2	97	3.2
24	58.0	61	23.3	98	3.0
25	57.0	62	22.5	99	2.8
26	56.0	63	21.6	100	2.7
27	55.1	64	20.8	101	2.5
28	54.1	65	20.0	102	2.3
29	53.1	66	19.2	103	2.1
30	52.2	67	18.4	104	1.9
31	51.2	68	17.6	105	1.8
32	50.2	69	16.8	106	1.6
33	49.3	70	16.0	107	1.4
34	48.3	71	15.3	108	1.3
35	47.3	72	14.6	109	1.1
36	46.4	73	13.9	110	1.0
37	45.4	74	13.2	111	.9
38	44.4	75	12.5	112	.8
39	43.5	76	11.9	113	.7
40	42.5	77	11.2	114	.6
41	41.5	78	10.6	115	.5

Table 11.8 IRS Joint Life Expectancy Table

Ages	45	46	47	48	49	50	51	52	53	54
45	31.4	30.9	30.5	30.0	29.4	28.9	28.3	27.7	27.1	26.5
46	30.9	30.5	30.0	29.6	29.1	28.5	28.0	27.4	26.9	26.3
47	30.5	30.0	29.6	29.2	28.7	28.2	27.7	27.1	26.6	26.0
48	30.0	29.6	29.2	28.7	28.3	27.8	27.3	26.8	26.3	25.7
49	29.4	29.1	28.7	28.3	27.9	27.4	26.9	26.5	25.9	25.4
50	28.9	28.5	28.2	27.4	27.4	27.0	26.5	26.1	25.6	25.1
51	28.3	28.0	27.7	27.3	26.9	26.5	26.1	25.7	25.2	24.7
52	27.7	27.4	27.1	26.8	26.5	26.1	25.7	25.3	24.8	24.4
53	27.1	26.9	26.6	26.3	25.9	25.6	25.2	24.8	24.4	24.0
54	26.5	26.3	26.0	25.7	25.4	25.1	24.7	24.4	24.0	23.6
55	25.9	25.7	25.4	25.1	24.9	24.6	24.2	23.9	23.5	23.2
56	25.2	25.0	24.8	24.6	24.3	24.0	23.7	23.4	23.1	22.7
57	24.6	24.4	24.2	24.0	23.7	23.5	23.2	22.9	22.6	22.2
58	23.9	23.7	23.5	23.3	23.1	22.9	22.6	22.4	22.1	21.7
59	23.2	23.1	22.9	22.7	22.5	22.3	22.1	21.8	21.5	21.2
60	22.5	22.4	22.2	22.1	21.9	21.7	21.5	21.2	21.0	20.7
61	21.8	21.7	21.6	21.4	21.2	21.1	20.9	20.6	20.4	20.2
62	21.1	21.0	20.9	20.7	20.6	20.4	20.2	20.0	19.8	19.6
63	20.4	20.3	20.2	20.1	19.9	19.8	19.6	19.4	19.2	19.0
64	19.7	19.6	19.5	19.4	19.3	19.1	19.0	18.8	18.6	18.5
65	19.0	18.9	18.8	18.7	18.6	18.5	18.3	18.2	18.0	17.9
66	18.3	18.2	18.1	18.0	17.9	17.8	17.7	17.6	17.4	17.3
67	17.6	17.5	17.4	17.3	17.3	17.2	17.1	16.9	16.8	16.7
68	16.9	16.8	16.7	16.7	16.6	16.5	16.4	16.3	16.2	16.1
69	16.2	16.1	16.1	16.0	15.9	15.8	15.8	15.7	15.6	15.4
70	15.5	15.4	15.4	15.3	15.3	15.2	15.1	15.0	14.9	14.8
71	14.8	14.8	14.7	14.7	14.6	14.5	14.5	14.4	14.3	14.2
72	14.1	14.1	14.1	14.0	14.0	13.9	13.9	13.8	13.7	13.6
73	13.5	13.5	13.4	13.4	13.3	13.3	13.2	13.2	13.1	13.0
74	12.8	12.8	12.8	12.7	12.7	12.7	12.6	12.6	12.5	12.4
75	12.2	12.2	12.2	12.1	12.1	12.1	12.0	12.0	11.9	11.9
76	11.6	11.6	11.6	11.5	11.5	11.5	11.4	11.4	11.3	11.3
77	11.0	11.0	11.0	10.9	10.9	10.9	10.8	10.8	10.8	10.7
78	10.4	10.4	10.4	10.4	10.3	10.3	10.3	10.2	10.2	10.2
79	9.9	9.8	9.8	9.8	9.8	9.8	9.7	9.7	9.7	9.6
80	9.3	9.3	9.3	9.3	9.2	9.2	9.2	9.2	9.1	9.1
81	8.8	8.8	8.7	8.7	8.7	8.7	8.7	8.7	8.6	8.6
82	8.3	8.2	8.2	8.2	8.2	8.2	8.2	8.2	8.1	8.1
83	7.8	7.8	7.7	7.7	7.7	7.7	7.7	7.7	7.7	7.6
84	7.3	7.3	7.3	7.3	7.3	7.2	7.2	7.2	7.2	7.2
85	6.8	6.8	6.8	6.8	6.8	6.8	6.8	6.8	6.8	6.7
86	6.4	6.4	6.4	6.4	6.4	6.4	6.4	6.4	6.3	6.3
87	6.0	6.0	6.0	6.0	6.0	6.0	6.0	6.0	6.0	5.9
88	5.6	5.6	5.6	5.6	5.6	5.6	5.6	5.6	5.6	5.6
89	5.3	5.3	5.3	5.3	5.3	5.3	5.3	5.2	5.2	5.2
90	5.0	4.9	4.9	4.9	4.9	4.9	4.9	4.9	4.9	4.9
91	4.6	4.6	4.6	4.6	4.6	4.6	4.6	4.6	4.6	4.6
92	4.4	4.4	4.4	4.3	4.3	4.3	4.3	4.3	4.3	4.3
93	4.1	4.1	4.1	4.1	4.1	4.1	4.1	4.1	4.1	4.1
94	3.9	3.9	3.8	3.8	3.8	3.8	3.8	3.8	3.8	3.8
95	3.6	3.6	3.6	3.6	3.6	3.6	3.6	3.6	3.6	3.6
96	3.4	3.4	3.4	3.4	3.4	3.4	3.4	3.4	3.4	3.4
97	3.2	3.2	3.2	3.2	3.2	3.2	3.2	3.2	3.2	3.2
98	3.0	3.0	3.0	3.0	3.0	3.0	3.0	3.0	3.0	3.0
99	2.8	2.8	2.8	2.8	2.8	2.8	2.8	2.8	2.8	2.8
100	2.6	2.6	2.6	2.6	2.6	2.6	2.6	2.6	2.6	2.6
101	2.5	2.5	2.5	2.5	2.5	2.5	2.5	2.5	2.5	2.5
102	2.3	2.3	2.3	2.3	2.3	2.3	2.3	2.3	2.3	2.3
103	2.1	2.1	2.1	2.1	2.1	2.1	2.1	2.1	2.1	2.1
104	1.9	1.9	1.9	1.9	1.9	1.9	1.9	1.9	1.9	1.9
105	1.8	1.8	1.8	1.8	1.8	1.8	1.8	1.8	1.8	1.8
106	1.6	1.6	1.6	1.6	1.6	1.6	1.6	1.6	1.6	1.6
107	1.4	1.4	1.4	1.4	1.4	1.4	1.4	1.4	1.4	1.4
108	1.3	1.3	1.3	1.3	1.3	1.3	1.3	1.3	1.3	1.3
109	1.1	1.1	1.1	1.1	1.1	1.1	1.1	1.1	1.1	1.1
110	1.0	1.0	1.0	1.0	1.0	1.0	1.0	1.0	1.0	1.0
111	.9	.9	.9	.9	.9	.9	.9	.9	.9	.9
112	.8	.8	.8	.8	.8	.8	.8	.8	.8	.8
113	.7	.7	.7	.7	.7	.7	.7	.7	.7	.7
114	.6	.6	.6	.6	.6	.6	.6	.6	.6	.6
115	.5	.5	.5	.5	.5	.5	.5	.5	.5	.5

Table 11.8 (continued)

Ages	55	56	57	58	59	60	61	62	63	64
55	22.7	22.3	21.9	21.4	20.9	20.4	19.9	19.4	18.8	18.3
56	22.3	21.9	21.5	21.1	20.6	20.1	19.6	19.1	18.6	18.0
57	21.9	21.5	21.1	20.7	20.3	19.8	19.3	18.8	18.3	17.8
58	21.4	21.1	20.7	20.3	19.9	19.5	19.0	18.5	18.0	17.5
59	20.9	20.6	20.3	19.9	19.5	19.1	18.7	18.2	17.7	17.3
60	20.4	20.1	19.8	19.5	19.1	18.7	18.3	17.9	17.4	17.0
61	29.9	19.6	19.3	19.0	18.7	18.3	17.9	17.5	17.1	16.7
62	19.4	19.1	18.8	18.5	18.2	17.9	17.5	17.1	16.8	16.3
63	18.8	18.6	18.3	18.0	17.7	17.4	17.1	16.8	16.4	16.0
64	18.3	18.0	17.8	17.5	17.3	17.0	16.7	16.3	16.0	15.6
65	17.7	17.5	17.3	17.0	16.8	16.5	16.2	15.9	15.6	15.3
66	17.1	16.9	16.7	16.5	16.3	16.0	15.8	15.5	15.2	14.9
67	16.5	16.3	16.2	16.0	15.8	15.5	15.3	15.0	14.7	14.5
68	15.9	15.8	15.6	15.4	15.2	15.0	14.8	14.6	14.3	14.0
69	15.3	15.2	15.0	14.9	14.7	14.5	14.3	14.1	13.9	13.6
70	14.7	14.6	14.5	14.3	14.2	14.0	13.8	13.6	13.4	13.2
71	14.1	14.0	13.9	13.8	13.6	13.5	13.3	13.1	12.9	12.7
72	13.5	13.4	13.3	13.2	13.1	12.9	12.8	12.6	12.4	12.3
73	13.0	12.9	12.8	12.7	12.5	12.4	12.3	12.1	12.0	11.8
74	12.4	12.3	12.2	12.1	12.0	11.9	11.8	11.6	11.5	11.3
75	11.8	11.7	11.7	11.6	11.5	11.4	11.3	11.1	11.0	10.9
76	11.2	11.2	11.1	11.0	11.0	10.9	10.9	10.8	10.6	10.5
77	10.7	10.6	10.6	10.5	10.4	10.3	10.3	10.2	10.0	9.9
78	10.1	10.1	10.0	10.0	9.9	9.8	9.8	9.7	9.6	9.5
79	9.6	9.6	9.5	9.5	9.4	9.3	9.3	9.2	9.1	9.0
80	9.1	9.0	9.0	9.0	8.9	8.9	8.8	8.7	8.7	8.6
81	8.6	8.5	8.5	8.5	8.4	8.4	8.4	8.3	8.3	8.1
82	8.1	8.1	8.0	8.0	8.0	7.9	7.9	7.8	7.8	7.7
83	7.6	7.6	7.6	7.5	7.5	7.5	7.4	7.4	7.3	7.3
84	7.2	7.1	7.1	7.1	7.1	7.0	7.0	7.0	6.9	6.9
85	6.7	6.7	6.7	6.7	6.6	6.6	6.6	6.5	6.5	6.5
86	6.3	6.3	6.3	6.3	6.2	6.2	6.2	6.2	6.1	6.1
87	5.9	5.9	5.9	5.9	5.9	5.8	5.8	5.8	5.8	5.7
88	5.6	5.5	5.5	5.5	5.5	5.5	5.5	5.4	5.4	5.4
89	5.2	5.2	5.2	5.2	5.2	5.2	5.1	5.1	5.1	5.1
90	4.9	4.9	4.9	4.9	4.9	4.9	4.8	4.8	4.8	4.8
91	4.6	4.6	4.6	4.6	4.6	4.6	4.5	4.5	4.5	4.5
92	4.3	4.3	4.3	4.3	4.3	4.3	4.3	4.2	4.2	4.2
93	4.1	4.1	4.0	4.0	4.0	4.0	4.0	4.0	4.0	4.0
94	3.8	3.8	3.8	3.8	3.8	3.8	3.8	3.8	3.8	3.7
95	3.6	3.6	3.6	3.6	3.6	3.6	3.6	3.6	3.6	3.5
96	3.4	3.4	3.4	3.4	3.4	3.4	3.4	3.4	3.3	3.3
97	3.2	3.2	3.2	3.2	3.2	3.2	3.2	3.2	3.1	3.1
98	3.0	3.0	3.0	3.0	3.0	3.0	3.0	3.0	3.0	3.0
99	2.8	2.8	2.8	2.8	2.8	2.8	2.8	2.8	2.8	2.8
100	2.6	2.6	2.6	2.6	2.6	2.6	2.6	2.6	2.6	2.6
101	2.5	2.4	2.4	2.4	2.4	2.4	2.4	2.4	2.4	2.4
102	2.3	2.1	2.3	2.3	2.3	2.3	2.3	2.3	2.3	2.2
103	2.1	2.1	2.1	2.1	2.1	2.1	2.1	2.1	2.1	2.1
104	1.9	1.9	1.9	1.9	1.9	1.9	1.9	1.9	1.9	1.9
105	1.8	1.8	1.8	1.8	1.8	1.8	1.7	1.7	1.7	1.7
106	1.6	1.6	1.6	1.6	1.6	1.6	1.6	1.6	1.6	1.6
107	1.4	1.4	1.4	1.4	1.4	1.4	1.4	1.4	1.4	1.4
108	1.3	1.3	1.3	1.3	1.3	1.3	1.3	1.3	1.3	1.3
109	1.1	1.1	1.1	1.1	1.1	1.1	1.1	1.1	1.1	1.1
110	1.0	1.0	1.0	1.0	1.0	1.0	1.0	1.0	1.0	1.0
111	.9	.9	.9	.9	.9	.9	.9	.9	.9	.9
112	.8	.8	.8	.8	.8	.8	.8	.8	.8	.8
113	.7	.7	.7	.7	.7	.7	.7	.7	.7	.7
114	.6	.6	.6	.6	.6	.6	.6	.6	.6	.6
115	.5	.5	.5	.5	.5	.5	.5	.5	.5	.5

Table 11.8 (continued)

Ages	65	66	67	68	69	70	71	72	73	74
65	14.9	14.5	14.1	13.7	13.3	12.9	12.5	12.0	11.6	11.2
66	14.5	14.2	13.8	13.4	13.1	12.6	12.2	11.8	11.4	11.0
67	14.1	13.8	13.5	13.1	12.8	12.4	12.0	11.6	11.2	10.8
68	13.7	13.4	13.1	12.8	12.5	12.1	11.7	11.4	11.0	10.6
69	13.3	13.1	12.8	12.5	12.1	11.8	11.4	11.1	10.7	10.4
70	12.9	12.6	12.4	12.1	11.8	11.5	11.2	10.8	10.5	10.1
71	12.5	12.2	12.0	11.7	11.4	11.2	10.9	10.5	10.2	9.9
72	12.0	11.8	11.6	11.4	11.1	10.8	10.5	10.2	9.9	9.6
73	11.6	11.4	11.2	11.0	10.7	10.5	10.2	9.9	9.7	9.4
74	11.2	11.0	10.8	10.6	10.4	10.1	9.9	9.6	9.4	9.1
75	10.7	10.5	10.4	10.2	10.0	9.8	9.5	9.3	9.1	8.8
76	10.3	10.1	9.9	9.8	9.6	9.4	9.2	9.0	8.8	8.5
77	9.8	9.7	9.5	9.4	9.2	9.0	8.8	8.6	8.4	8.2
78	9.4	9.2	9.1	9.0	8.8	8.7	8.5	8.3	8.1	7.9
79	8.9	8.8	8.7	8.6	8.4	8.3	8.1	8.0	7.8	7.6
80	8.5	8.4	8.3	8.2	8.0	7.9	7.8	7.6	7.5	7.3
81	8.0	8.0	7.9	7.9	7.7	7.7	7.5	7.4	7.1	7.0
82	7.6	7.5	7.5	7.4	7.3	7.2	7.1	6.9	6.8	6.7
83	7.2	7.1	7.1	7.0	6.9	6.8	6.7	6.6	6.5	6.4
84	6.8	6.7	6.7	6.6	6.5	6.4	6.4	6.3	6.2	6.0
85	6.4	6.4	6.3	6.2	6.2	6.1	6.0	5.9	5.8	5.7
86	6.0	6.0	5.9	5.9	5.8	5.8	5.7	5.6	5.5	5.4
87	5.7	5.6	5.6	5.6	5.5	5.4	5.4	5.3	5.2	5.2
88	5.3	5.3	5.3	5.2	5.2	5.1	5.1	5.0	5.0	4.9
89	5.0	5.0	5.0	4.9	4.9	4.8	4.8	4.7	4.7	4.6
90	4.7	4.7	4.7	4.6	4.6	4.6	4.5	4.5	4.4	4.4
91	4.5	4.4	4.4	4.4	4.3	4.3	4.3	4.2	4.2	4.1
92	4.2	4.2	4.1	4.1	4.1	4.1	4.0	4.0	3.9	3.9
93	3.9	3.9	3.9	3.9	3.9	3.8	3.8	3.8	3.7	3.7
94	3.7	3.7	3.7	3.7	3.6	3.6	3.6	3.6	3.5	3.5
95	3.5	3.5	3.5	3.5	3.4	3.4	3.4	3.4	3.3	3.3
96	3.3	3.3	3.3	3.3	3.3	3.2	3.2	3.2	3.2	3.1
97	3.1	3.1	3.1	3.1	3.1	3.1	3.0	3.0	3.0	3.0
98	2.9	2.9	2.9	2.9	2.9	2.9	2.9	2.9	2.8	2.8
99	2.8	2.8	2.8	2.7	2.7	2.7	2.7	2.7	2.7	2.6
100	2.6	2.6	2.6	2.6	2.6	2.5	2.5	2.5	2.5	2.5
101	2.4	2.4	2.4	2.4	2.4	2.4	2.4	2.4	2.3	2.3
102	2.2	2.2	2.2	2.2	2.2	2.2	2.2	2.2	2.2	2.2
103	2.1	2.1	2.1	2.1	2.1	2.0	2.0	2.0	2.0	2.0
104	1.9	1.9	1.9	1.9	1.9	1.9	1.9	1.9	1.9	1.9
105	1.7	1.7	1.7	1.7	1.7	1.7	1.7	1.7	1.7	1.7
106	1.6	1.6	1.6	1.6	1.6	1.6	1.6	1.6	1.5	1.5
107	1.4	1.4	1.4	1.4	1.4	1.4	1.4	1.4	1.4	1.4
108	1.3	1.3	1.3	1.3	1.3	1.3	1.3	1.3	1.3	1.3
109	1.1	1.1	1.1	1.1	1.1	1.1	1.1	1.1	1.1	1.1
110	1.0	1.0	1.0	1.0	1.0	1.0	1.0	1.0	1.0	1.0
111	.9	.9	.9	.9	.9	.9	.9	.9	.9	.9
112	.8	.8	.8	.8	.8	.8	.8	.8	.8	.8
113	.7	.7	.7	.7	.7	.6	.6	.6	.6	.6
114	.6	.6	.6	.6	.6	.6	.5	.5	.5	.5
115	.5	.5	.5	.5	.5	.5	.5	.5	.5	.5

Table 11.8 (continued)

Ages	75	76	77	78	79	80	81	82	83	84
75	8.6	8.3	8.0	7.7	7.4	7.1	6.6	6.5	6.2	5.9
76	8.3	8.0	7.8	7.5	7.2	6.9	6.7	6.4	6.1	5.8
77	8.0	7.8	7.6	7.3	7.0	6.8	6.5	6.2	5.9	5.7
78	7.7	7.5	7.3	7.0	6.8	6.6	6.3	6.0	5.8	5.5
79	7.4	7.2	7.0	6.8	6.6	6.3	6.1	5.9	5.6	5.4
80	7.1	6.9	6.8	6.6	6.3	6.1	5.9	5.7	5.5	5.2
81	6.8	6.7	6.5	6.3	6.1	5.9	5.7	5.5	5.3	5.1
82	6.5	6.4	6.2	6.0	5.9	5.7	5.5	5.3	5.1	4.9
83	6.2	6.1	5.9	5.8	5.6	5.5	5.3	5.1	4.9	4.7
84	5.9	5.8	5.7	5.5	5.4	5.2	5.1	4.9	4.7	4.6
85	5.6	5.5	5.4	5.3	5.2	5.0	4.9	4.7	4.6	4.4
86	5.4	5.3	5.1	5.0	4.9	4.8	4.7	4.5	4.4	4.2
87	5.1	5.0	4.9	4.8	4.7	4.6	4.4	4.3	4.2	4.1
88	4.8	4.7	4.6	4.5	4.4	4.3	4.2	4.1	4.0	3.9
89	4.5	4.5	4.4	4.3	4.2	4.1	4.0	3.9	3.8	3.7
90	4.3	4.2	4.2	4.1	4.0	3.9	3.8	3.8	3.7	3.5
91	4.1	4.0	4.0	3.9	3.8	3.7	3.7	3.6	3.5	3.4
92	3.9	3.8	3.7	3.7	3.6	3.6	3.5	3.4	3.3	3.2
93	3.7	3.6	3.6	3.5	3.4	3.4	3.3	3.2	3.2	3.1
94	3.5	3.4	3.4	3.3	3.3	3.2	3.2	3.1	3.0	3.0
95	3.3	3.2	3.2	3.2	3.1	3.1	3.0	3.0	2.9	2.8
96	3.1	3.1	3.0	3.0	3.0	2.9	2.9	2.8	2.8	2.7
97	2.9	2.9	2.9	2.9	2.8	2.8	2.7	2.7	2.6	2.6
98	2.8	2.8	2.7	2.7	2.7	2.6	2.6	2.6	2.5	2.5
99	2.6	2.6	2.6	2.6	2.5	2.5	2.5	2.4	2.4	2.3
100	2.5	2.5	2.4	2.4	2.4	2.4	2.3	2.3	2.3	2.2
101	2.3	2.3	2.3	2.3	2.2	2.2	2.2	2.2	2.1	2.1
102	2.2	2.1	2.1	2.1	2.1	2.1	2.0	2.0	2.0	2.0
103	2.0	2.0	2.0	2.0	1.9	1.9	1.9	1.9	1.9	1.8
104	1.8	1.8	1.8	1.8	1.8	1.8	1.8	1.7	1.7	1.7
105	1.7	1.7	1.7	1.7	1.6	1.6	1.6	1.6	1.6	1.6
106	1.5	1.5	1.5	1.5	1.5	1.5	1.5	1.5	1.5	1.4
107	1.4	1.4	1.4	1.4	1.4	1.4	1.3	1.3	1.3	1.3
108	1.3	1.2	1.2	1.2	1.2	1.2	1.2	1.2	1.2	1.2
109	1.1	1.1	1.1	1.1	1.1	1.1	1.1	1.1	1.1	1.1
110	1.0	1.0	1.0	1.0	1.0	1.0	1.0	1.0	1.0	1.0
111	.9	.9	.9	.9	.9	.9	.9	.9	.8	.8
112	.8	.8	.8	.7	.7	.7	.7	.7	.7	.7
113	.6	.6	.6	.6	.6	.6	.6	.6	.6	.6
114	.5	.5	.5	.5	.5	.5	.5	.5	.5	.5
115	.5	.5	.5	.5	.5	.5	.5	.5	.5	.5

Ages	85	86	87	88	89	90	91	92	93	94
85	4.2	4.1	3.9	3.8	3.6	3.4	3.3	3.2	3.0	2.9
86	4.1	3.9	3.8	3.6	3.5	3.3	3.2	3.1	2.9	2.8
87	3.9	3.8	3.6	3.5	3.4	3.2	3.1	3.0	2.8	2.7
88	3.8	3.6	3.5	3.4	3.2	3.1	3.0	2.9	2.8	2.6
89	3.6	3.5	3.4	3.2	3.1	3.0	2.9	2.8	2.7	2.6
90	3.4	3.3	3.2	3.1	3.0	2.9	2.8	2.7	2.6	2.5
91	3.3	3.2	3.1	3.0	2.9	2.8	2.7	2.6	2.5	2.4
92	3.2	3.1	3.0	2.9	2.8	2.7	2.6	2.5	2.4	2.3
93	3.0	2.9	2.8	2.8	2.7	2.6	2.5	2.4	2.3	2.3
94	2.9	2.8	2.7	2.6	2.6	2.5	2.4	2.3	2.3	2.2
95	2.8	2.7	2.6	2.5	2.5	2.4	2.3	2.2	2.2	2.1
96	2.6	2.6	2.5	2.4	2.4	2.3	2.2	2.2	2.1	2.0
97	2.5	2.5	2.4	2.3	2.3	2.2	2.2	2.1	2.0	2.0
98	2.4	2.4	2.3	2.2	2.2	2.1	2.1	2.0	2.0	1.9
99	2.3	2.2	2.2	2.1	2.1	2.0	2.0	1.9	1.9	1.8
100	2.2	2.1	2.1	2.0	2.0	1.9	1.9	1.9	1.8	1.8
101	2.1	2.0	2.0	1.9	1.9	1.9	1.8	1.8	1.7	1.7
102	1.9	1.9	1.9	1.8	1.8	1.8	1.7	1.7	1.6	1.6
103	1.8	1.8	1.8	1.7	1.7	1.7	1.6	1.6	1.5	1.5
104	1.7	1.7	1.6	1.6	1.6	1.5	1.5	1.5	1.5	1.4
105	1.6	1.5	1.5	1.5	1.5	1.4	1.4	1.4	1.4	1.3
106	1.4	1.4	1.4	1.4	1.4	1.3	1.3	1.3	1.3	1.2
107	1.3	1.3	1.3	1.3	1.2	1.2	1.2	1.2	1.2	1.2
108	1.2	1.2	1.2	1.1	1.1	1.1	1.1	1.1	1.1	1.1
109	1.1	1.1	1.0	1.0	1.0	1.0	1.0	1.0	1.0	1.0
110	.9	.9	.9	.9	.9	.9	.9	.9	.9	.9
111	.8	.8	.8	.8	.8	.8	.8	.8	.8	.8
112	.7	.7	.7	.7	.7	.7	.7	.7	.7	.7
113	.6	.6	.6	.6	.6	.6	.6	.6	.6	.6
114	.5	.5	.5	.5	.5	.5	.5	.5	.5	.5
115	.5	.5	.5	.5	.5	.5	.5	.5	.5	.5

Table 11.8 (continued)

Ages	95	96	97	98	99	100	101	102	103	104
95	2.0	2.0	1.9	1.8	1.8	1.7	1.6	1.6	1.5	1.4
96	2.0	1.9	1.9	1.8	1.7	1.7	1.6	1.5	1.5	1.4
97	1.9	1.9	1.8	1.7	1.7	1.6	1.6	1.5	1.4	1.3
98	1.8	1.8	1.7	1.7	1.6	1.6	1.5	1.5	1.4	1.3
99	1.8	1.7	1.7	1.6	1.6	1.5	1.5	1.4	1.4	1.3
100	1.7	1.7	1.6	1.6	1.5	1.5	1.4	1.4	1.3	1.3
101	1.6	1.6	1.6	1.5	1.5	1.4	1.4	1.3	1.3	1.2
102	1.6	1.5	1.5	1.5	1.4	1.4	1.3	1.3	1.2	1.2
103	1.5	1.5	1.4	1.4	1.4	1.3	1.3	1.2	1.2	1.1
104	1.4	1.4	1.3	1.3	1.3	1.3	1.2	1.2	1.1	1.1
105	1.3	1.3	1.3	1.2	1.2	1.2	1.2	1.1	1.1	1.0
106	1.2	1.2	1.2	1.2	1.1	1.1	1.1	1.1	1.0	1.0
107	1.1	1.1	1.1	1.1	1.1	1.0	1.0	1.0	1.0	.9
108	1.0	1.0	1.0	1.0	1.0	1.0	1.0	.9	.9	.9
109	1.0	.9	.9	.9	.9	.9	.9	.9	.8	.8
110	.9	.9	.8	.8	.8	.8	.8	.8	.8	.8
111	.8	.8	.8	.8	.8	.7	.7	.7	.7	.7
112	.7	.7	.7	.7	.7	.7	.7	.7	.6	.6
113	.6	.6	.6	.6	.6	.6	.6	.6	.6	.6
114	.5	.5	.5	.5	.5	.5	.5	.5	.5	.5
115	.5	.5	.5	.5	.5	.5	.5	.5	.5	.5

Ages	105	106	107	108	109	110	111	112	113	114	115
105	1.0	1.0	.9	.9	.8	.7	.7	.6	.6	.5	.5
106	1.0	.9	.9	.8	.8	.7	.7	.6	.6	.5	.5
107	.9	.9	.8	.8	.7	.7	.7	.6	.6	.5	.5
108	.9	.8	.8	.8	.7	.7	.6	.6	.5	.5	.5
109	.8	.8	.7	.7	.7	.7	.6	.6	.5	.5	.5
110	.7	.7	.7	.7	.7	.6	.6	.6	.5	.5	.5
111	.7	.7	.7	.6	.6	.6	.6	.5	.5	.5	.5
112	.6	.6	.6	.6	.6	.6	.5	.5	.5	.5	.5
113	.6	.6	.6	.5	.5	.5	.5	.5	.5	.5	.5
114	.5	.5	.5	.5	.5	.5	.5	.5	.5	.5	.5
115	.5	.5	.5	.5	.5	.5	.5	.5	.5	.5	.5

11.10   ANNUITY CONTRACT PAYMENT OPTIONS

Table 11.9 shows the various payment options that are commonly available for annuitants. Some are designed to provide income for one recipient only, while other options arrange for coverage of both the annuitant and a spouse or other dependent. These options should be reviewed carefully and factors such as age, health, other sources of income, and income tax ramifications must be considered before making the important and usually irreversible decision regarding the form of annuity payment to take. Also, if the client has the option of selecting an annuity from any insurance company, he or she should be encouraged to comparison shop. Benefit levels vary considerably among insurance companies on an otherwise identical policy.

11.11   TAX TREATMENT OF RETIREMENT PLAN DISTRIBUTIONS

An explanation of the various tax and payment options for distributions from a company retirement plan or Keogh plan is presented in this section.
Briefly, these options are

- Transferring the distribution to an IRA or to the qualified plan of a new employer

- Taking the distribution immediately and paying taxes on it

- Receiving the distribution in the form of an annuity. The disposition of a retirement plan distribution requires careful analysis of all possible options.

A taxpayer who receives a qualified lump-sum distribution from a company retirement plan or a Keogh plan may be able to benefit from favorable tax elections:

- If he or she was at least 50 years old on January 1, 1986, special averaging is permitted as are as capital gains treatment for gains realized before 1974 and special averaging on the taxable balance of the distribution.

- Tax-free rollover to an IRA or a qualified company plan is permitted, whether or not the taxpayer was 50 on January 1, 1986.

A rollover of a lump-sum distribution must be made within 60 days of its receipt. Therefore, a taxpayer who is not eligible for special averaging must elect the rollover within 60 days or else his or her distribution will be taxed at regular rates.

A lump-sum distribution received by a taxpayer before he or she is

Table 11.9 Payment Options Available for Annuitants

Annuity	Description
One annuitant annuity	The annuitant receives payments for the rest of his or her life.
Temporary annuity	The annuitant receives payment until death or until the end of a specified limited period, whichever occurs earlier.
Uniform joint and survivor annuity	The annuitant receives payments for the rest of his or her life, and after death, the same amount is paid to another annuitant. The expected return is based on the combined life expectancies of both annuitants.
One annuitant stepped-up annuity	The annuitant receives smaller payments at first, and after reaching a certain age, usually upon retirement, receives larger payments.
One annuitant stepped-down annuity	The annuitant receives larger payments at first, and then, when he or she reaches a certain age, smaller payments commence.
Variable payment joint and survivor annuity with lesser annuity to survivor	The annuitant and spouse receive payments while both are alive, and, on the death of one, a lesser amount is paid to the survivor—regardless of who dies first.
Variable payment joint and survivor annuity with first and second annuitants specified	The annuitant receives payments of a certain amount, and on his or her death another annuitant gets a lesser amount. The exclusion ratio remains the same for both annuitants.

59½ may be subject to a 10 percent penalty. A lump-sum distribution of more than $750,000 may be subject to a 15 percent penalty.

To qualify as a lump-sum distribution, payment must meet the following requirements:

- Payment must be from a pension or profit-sharing or stock bonus plan that is approved by the IRS.
- Payment must include all that is due under the plan. Distribution of only a part of the plan does not qualify as lump-sum distribution.

- Payment must be made within one calendar year of retirement.

- If the taxpayer is an employee, the distribution must be made because he or she has separated from service, reached the age of 59½, or died.

- In order for the recipient to qualify for special averaging, payment of distribution must be made after five years of participation in the plan.

A taxpayer who qualifies for special averaging must try to project whether the largest retirement fund yield will result from using special averaging and investing the funds or from rolling over the distribution and letting earnings accumulate tax free. A rollover must be elected within 60 days after receiving the lump-sum distribution, and once the rollover is made, the IRA fund cannot then be exchanged for special averaging. A taxpayer should not elect a rollover if he or she may wish to withdraw the entire account in a few years, because special averaging is not permitted for distribution from the IRA. In addition, special averaging can be elected only once—if a taxpayer receives special averaging on a distribution and then continues working, a later lump-sum distribution will not qualify for averaging.

A taxpayer who was age 50 on January 1, 1986 may elect either

- A 10-year averaging method based on 1986 tax rates

- A 5-year averaging method based on current 1989 tax rates

If an employee is not 59½ years old, he or she must be "separated from service" in order for his or her distribution to qualify as lump sum. To count as "separated from service," an employee must have retired, resigned, or been discharged. After the age of 59½, an employee does not need to be separated from service in order to qualify. However, if an employee receives lump-sum distribution from a pension plan after 59½ but continues to work for the company, he or she must also reach normal retirement age (as stated in the company plan) in order to receive lump-sum distribution.

A taxpayer may defer tax on a lump-sum distribution by transferring it within 60 days to a qualified plan of a new employer or to an IRA account. However, the amount rolled over may not include the taxpayer's own contributions (after tax) to the plan, and a taxpayer may not make a tax-free rollover of a distribution which a taxpayer is required to make because he or she has retired or reached the age of 70½. To qualify as a tax-free rollover, a lump-sum distribution must meet these tests:

- Distribution must be all that is due to the taxpayer under the plan

- Payments must be made within one of the taxpayer's taxable years

- If taxpayer is an employee, distribution must be made due to separation from service, or having reached age 59½, or termination of plan.

Partial rollovers are allowed—the entire distribution need not be rolled over. But once a rollover is made, the contribution must irrevocably be treated as such. A rollover to an IRA is no longer eligible for averaging (while a withdrawal from a qualified plan is eligible).

If the taxpayer has been married for at least a year, then payments of vested interest must be in a specific annuity form to protect the surviving spouse. Unless the taxpayer, with the written consent of his or her spouse, elects differently, all benefit and money purchase plans must provide benefits in the form of a qualified joint and survivor annuity. A profit-sharing or stock bonus plan also must provide a qualified joint and survivor annuity, unless the taxpayer does not elect a life annuity payment, and the plan provides that the benefit is paid in full upon the taxpayer's death to the surviving spouse (or to a different beneficiary, if the spouse consents).

Under a qualified joint and survivor annuity, the taxpayer's spouse must receive an annuity for his or her life that is no less than 50 percent of the amount paid to both. Spousal consent is required to take a different kind of annuity (such as a lump-sum distribution or a single life annuity).

A preretirement survivor's annuity must be paid to a surviving spouse if the taxpayer dies before vested interests become payable. The preannuity payments must be equal to those under a single life annuity valued at at least 50 percent of the taxpayer's account balances.

Tax-free buildup of a retirement fund increases as retirement distributions are deferred, so most taxpayers will wish to defer distribution for as long as possible. However, tax law requires distribution to begin at a certain date, according to the following guidelines:

- *Taxpayers who reached age 70½ before 1988,* and who do not own more than a 5% ownership interest, need not begin receiving distribution until April 1 of the calendar year following the year of retirement. A taxpayer who was 70½ before 1988 and who retired in 1994, for example, would not have to begin receiving distribution until April 1, 1995.

- *Taxpayers who reach age 70½ after 1987* need to begin receiving distributions (at the latest) on April 1 on the calendar year following the year in which they turn 70½. A 50 percent tax will be applied to required minimum distributions that are not made during the year.

A taxpayer may borrow from an employer retirement plan without incurring tax, if the loan satisfies the following requirements:

- If a taxpayer's accrued benefit is $20,000 or less, then a loan is not taxed if it (when added to other outstanding loans from all plans of the employer) totals $10,000 or less.

- If a taxpayer's accrued benefit exceeds $20,000 then
  -if the taxpayer did not borrow from any employer plan within one year before the day before the date of the new loan, then a loan of $50,000 or 50 percent of the vested benefit—whichever is less—is tax free;
  -if the taxpayer *did* borrow from any employer plan within the year, then the total of the new loan may not exceed $50,000 minus the outstanding loan balance, minus the difference between the highest outstanding loan balance during the one-year period and the outstanding balance on the date of the new loan. (However, if 50 percent of the vested benefit is less than this final total, then 50 percent of the benefit is the maximum total loan).

For example, a taxpayer's vested plan benefit is $150,000 and in February 1992 he borrows $40,000 from the plan. In December 1992, when the balance on the first loan is $30,000, the taxpayer wishes to find out what the maximum amount he can take out on a second loan. That amount is

$50,000
-$30,000 (the present outstanding loan balance)
-$10,000 (the difference between the highest loan balance during the year of $40,000 and the present outstanding loan balance of $30,000)
_____
$10,000

Since $10,000 is less than 50 percent of $150,000, that is the maximum loan limit.

These kinds of loans must be repayable within five years, unless the loan is used for the purpose of purchasing a principal residence, in which case the repayment period may be extended.

Loans from plans subject to joint and survivor rules require spousal consent.

Interest deductions on plan loans are limited under new law restrictions for personal and investment loans, and interest deductions are entirely barred if the taxpayer is a key employee or if he or she borrows his or her own elective deferrals of salary from a 401(k) plan or tax-sheltered annuity plan.

11.12   RETIREMENT FUND WITHDRAWAL CHART

Retirees and people who are planning for retirement must be particularly careful to avoid withdrawing (or planning to withdraw) too much of their personal investments each year. Retirees who either overspend or fail to anticipate a long life risk exhausting their resources. Table 11.10 shows the number of years that retirement savings will last, assuming a given annual withdrawal rate and rate of return. For example, someone who withdraws 8 percent of his or her retirement funds each year and who earns 7 percent on them will deplete those funds in 30 years.

Table 11.10 Number of Years Retirement Funds Can Last

Annual Withdrawal Rate	Return on Retirement Funds				
	5%	6%	7%	8%	9%
10%	14	15	17	20	26
9%	16	18	22	28	
8%	20	23	30		
7%	25	33			
6%	36				

11.13 LIFE EXPECTANCY TABLE

Table 11.11 shows life expectancies and expected deaths by gender, race, and age. Life expectancy tables may be helpful in planning to accumulate sufficient resources to support the retiree and his or her dependents over their estimated lifetimes. These tables are, of course, only approximations, and many specialists suggest using a life expectancy of 85 to 90 years for people who are nearing retirement age and who are in reasonably good health.

Table 11.11 Life Expectancy Table

Age in 1986 (years)	Expectation of Life in Years					Expected Deaths per 1,000 Alive at Specified Age[1]				
	Total	White Male	White Female	Black Male	Black Female	Total	White Male	White Female	Black Male	Black Female
At birth	74.8	72.0	78.8	65.2	73.5	10.36	10.02	7.80	20.04	16.09
1	74.6	71.7	78.4	65.5	73.7	.72	.76	.57	1.16	.96
2	73.6	70.8	77.5	64.6	72.8	.55	.55	.44	.94	.79
3	72.7	69.8	76.5	63.6	71.9	.43	.42	.34	.76	.64
4	71.7	68.8	75.5	62.7	70.9	.35	.34	.27	.62	.52
5	70.7	67.8	74.6	61.7	69.9	.29	.30	.22	.51	.43
6	69.8	66.9	73.6	60.7	69.0	.26	.28	.19	.43	.35
7	68.8	65.9	72.6	59.8	68.0	.23	.26	.17	.37	.29
8	67.8	64.9	71.6	58.8	67.0	.21	.23	.15	.33	.25
9	66.8	63.9	70.6	57.8	66.0	.19	.20	.14	.30	.22
10	65.8	62.9	69.6	56.8	65.0	.17	.18	.13	.30	.20
11	64.8	61.9	68.6	55.8	64.1	.18	.19	.14	.32	.20
12	63.8	61.0	67.7	54.9	63.1	.23	.27	.17	.40	.22
13	62.9	60.0	66.7	53.9	62.1	.34	.43	.23	.52	.25
14	61.9	59.0	65.7	52.9	61.1	.47	.64	.30	.69	.30
15	60.9	58.0	64.7	52.0	60.1	.63	.88	.39	.88	.36
16	59.9	57.1	63.7	51.0	59.1	.78	1.10	.46	1.08	.43
17	59.0	56.1	62.8	50.1	58.2	.90	1.29	.52	1.30	.49
18	58.0	55.2	61.8	49.1	57.2	.99	1.42	.54	1.54	.55
19	57.1	54.3	60.8	48.2	56.2	1.04	1.50	.53	1.80	.60

[1]Based on the proportion of the cohort who are alive at the beginning of an indicated age interval who will die before reaching the end of that interval. For example, out of every 1,000 people alive and exactly 50 years old at the beginning of the period, between 5 and 6 (5.17) will die before reaching their 51st birthday Source: U.S. National Center for Health Statistics, *Vital Statistics of the United States*, (Washington, D.C.: U.S. National Center for Health Statistics, annual).

Table 11.11 (continued)

Age in 1986 (years)	Expectation of Life in Years					Expected Deaths per 1,000 Alive at Specified Age[1]				
		White		Black			White		Black	
	Total	Male	Female	Male	Female	Total	Male	Female	Male	Female
20	56.2	53.4	59.9	47.3	55.3	1.09	1.58	.52	2.07	.66
21	55.2	52.5	58.9	46.4	54.3	1.15	1.66	.52	2.35	.73
22	54.3	51.5	57.9	45.5	53.3	1.18	1.70	.51	2.58	.79
23	53.3	50.6	56.9	44.6	52.4	1.20	1.69	.51	2.74	.86
24	52.4	49.7	56.0	43.7	51.4	1.19	1.66	.52	2.87	.93
25	51.5	48.8	55.0	42.8	50.5	1.18	1.60	.52	2.98	1.00
26	50.5	47.9	54.0	42.0	49.5	1.17	1.55	.53	3.12	1.07
27	49.6	47.0	53.1	41.1	48.6	1.18	1.53	.54	3.28	1.17
28	48.7	46.0	52.1	40.2	47.6	1.21	1.56	.55	3.48	1.28
29	47.7	45.1	51.1	39.4	46.7	1.27	1.62	.57	3.72	1.40
30	46.8	44.2	50.1	38.5	45.7	1.33	1.69	.60	3.98	1.55
31	45.8	43.2	49.2	37.7	44.8	1.39	1.76	.63	4.23	1.69
32	44.9	42.3	48.2	36.8	43.9	1.45	1.82	.67	4.49	1.82
33	44.0	41.4	47.2	36.0	43.0	1.51	1.87	.71	4.75	1.91
34	43.0	40.5	46.3	35.2	42.1	1.56	1.90	.75	5.00	1.99
35	42.1	39.5	45.3	34.3	41.1	1.61	1.95	.79	5.27	2.07
36	41.2	38.6	44.3	33.5	40.2	1.69	2.02	.85	5.55	2.17
37	40.2	37.7	43.4	32.7	39.3	1.78	2.11	.93	5.88	2.32
38	39.3	36.8	42.4	31.9	38.4	1.90	2.22	1.03	6.25	2.53
39	38.4	35.9	41.5	31.1	37.5	2.04	2.37	1.14	6.65	2.79

Table 11.11 (continued)

Age in 1986 (years)	Expectation of Life in Years					Expected Deaths per 1,000 Alive at Specified Age[1]				
		White		Black			White		Black	
	Total	Male	Female	Male	Female	Total	Male	Female	Male	Female
40	37.4	34.9	40.5	30.3	36.6	2.20	2.54	1.27	7.11	3.09
41	36.5	34.0	39.6	29.5	35.7	2.38	2.73	1.42	7.58	3.40
42	35.6	33.1	38.6	28.7	34.8	2.57	2.95	1.57	8.02	3.68
43	34.7	32.2	37.7	28.0	34.0	2.77	3.18	1.71	8.40	3.94
44	33.8	31.3	36.7	27.2	33.1	2.98	3.43	1.86	8.75	4.18
45	32.9	30.4	35.8	26.4	32.2	3.22	3.72	2.03	9.10	4.42
46	32.0	29.5	34.9	25.7	31.4	3.50	4.05	2.22	9.52	4.71
47	31.1	28.7	33.9	24.9	30.5	3.82	4.44	2.45	10.11	5.08
48	30.2	27.8	33.0	24.1	29.7	4.21	4.90	2.72	10.92	5.56
49	29.4	26.9	32.1	23.4	28.8	4.67	5.42	3.04	11.91	6.14
50	28.5	26.1	31.2	22.7	28.0	5.17	6.00	3.39	13.03	6.78
51	27.6	25.2	30.3	22.0	27.2	5.70	6.64	3.77	14.17	7.45
52	26.8	24.4	29.4	21.3	26.4	6.27	7.35	4.15	15.25	8.08
53	26.0	23.6	28.6	20.6	25.6	6.85	8.14	4.53	16.21	8.65
54	25.1	22.7	27.7	19.9	24.8	7.46	9.01	4.93	17.09	9.19
55	24.3	21.9	26.8	19.3	24.0	8.10	9.94	5.35	17.96	9.70
56	23.5	21.2	26.0	18.6	23.3	8.82	10.94	5.83	18.95	10.31
57	22.7	20.4	25.1	18.0	22.5	9.64	12.06	6.39	20.24	11.17
58	21.9	19.6	24.3	17.3	21.8	10.60	13.30	7.07	21.94	12.35
59	21.2	18.9	23.4	16.7	21.0	11.68	14.65	7.85	23.97	13.78

Table 11.11 (continued)

Age in 1986 (years)	Expectation of Life in Years					Expected Deaths per 1,000 Alive at Specified Age[1]				
	Total	White		Black		Total	White		Black	
		Male	Female	Male	Female		Male	Female	Male	Female
60	20.4	18.2	22.6	16.1	20.3	12.87	16.14	8.70	26.24	15.39
61	19.7	17.5	21.8	15.5	19.6	14.11	17.70	9.61	28.54	16.99
62	18.9	16.8	21.0	15.0	19.0	15.36	19.31	10.53	30.68	18.40
63	18.2	16.1	20.2	14.4	18.3	16.58	20.92	11.46	32.52	19.49
64	17.5	15.4	19.5	13.9	17.7	17.82	22.57	12.40	34.13	20.35
65	16.8	14.8	18.7	13.4	17.0	19.10	24.28	13.41	35.69	21.15
70	13.6	11.7	15.1	10.8	13.9	29.01	37.82	20.93	49.25	29.85
75	10.7	9.1	11.8	8.7	11.1	43.45	57.82	32.69	68.36	42.47
80	8.1	6.9	8.8	6.8	8.5	66.00	87.57	52.87	97.05	64.22
85 and over	6.0	5.1	6.4	5.5	6.7	1,000.00	1,000.00	1,000.00	1,000.00	1,000.00

[1]Based on the proportion of the cohort who are alive at the beginning of an indicated age interval who will die before reaching the end of that interval. For example, out of every 1,000 people alive and exactly 50 years old at the beginning of the period, between 5 and 6 (5.17) will die before reaching their 51st birthdays.

Source: U.S. National Center for Health Statistics, *Vital Statistics of the United States*, annual.

Chapter 12_____

ESTATE PLANNING

Effective estate planning need not be complicated, and it has several worth-while objectives: including

- To minimize the problems and expenses of probate; to avoid potential family conflicts, where possible
- To provide a spouse with as much responsibility and flexibility in estate management as desired, consistent with potential tax savings.
- To provide for the conservation of an estate and its effective management following death of either or both spouses.
- To minimize taxes at time of death as well as income taxes after death.
- To avoid leaving the children "too much too soon."
- To provide for adequate liquidity to cover taxes and other expenses at death without the necessity of forced sale of assets.
- To provide for estate management in the event of incapacity of either spouse.
- To coordinate a personal estate plan with all business arrangements, if applicable.
- To organize all important papers affecting an estate plan in a spot known to all family members and to review them at least annually.
- To inform family members about the overall estate plan.

Unfortunately, many adults fail to complete the most basic estate planning documents—even though they realize the importance of doing so. Nevertheless, sound estate planning can provide more than peace of mind. For example, personal records are usually better organized as a result of properly organizing an estate and, once organized, keeping the estate plans up to date. Beyond the basics of a will, durable power of attorney or living trust, living will, and letter of instructions are a plethora of more sophisticated estate planning techniques.

The 1990s will witness an unprecedented transfer of wealth through inheritances as the people who took advantage of the post-World War II economic boom die and pass on their wealth to children and grandchildren. This, combined with a higher savings rate and a general trend toward increasing affluence among middle- and upper-class families, will mean that many families will find themselves with rather large estates that those people who have taken the time to prepare estate planning documents may find that their estate has "outgrown" them. Unfortunately, many will not realize this, and even those who do may be reticent to devote the additional time and expense necessary to assure that their estates have been properly planned.

Finally, Congress is beginning to pay more attention to the estate and gift tax as a means of raising additional revenue. The 1990s may well witness changes in the estate and gift tax laws, and any changes do not bode well even for moderately affluent families. According to many estate tax experts, the tightening of the estate and gift tax laws will probably not affect many of the estate plans already in effect. This is all the more reason to attend to important estate planning matters sooner rather than later.

12.1 INVENTORY OF ESTATE PLANNING TECHNIQUES

Estate planning for many people involves several considerations beyond the basic estate planning documents, that is, a will, a living trust, a durable power of attorney, a letter of instructions, and a living will. Various estate planning techniques that can benefit clients during their lifetimes and/or their heirs after death are discussed in this section.

12.1.1 Property Ownership Designations

Joint ownership of property is common, particularly among married couples, and it can be advantageous from an estate planning standpoint if the estate is fairly small. But jointly held property is not desirable in many instances. It is possible that the property will be subject to estate taxation *twice*. Also, the surviving spouse can ignore the decedent's wishes as to the ultimate disposition of the property. Property that is held jointly with a nonspouse (or severance of joint tenancy between nonspouses) can result in gift taxes. The best person to advise clients on this, as well as other important estate planning matters, is an attorney. Ideally, the attorney should have considerable experience in estate planning.

12.1.2 Lifetime Gifts

The annual gift tax exclusion allows an individual to give up to $10,000 per year per person in gifts, as well as *direct* payments of tuition to educational institutions and of medical expenses. While gifts to children and grandchildren are a convenient way for high net worth families to reduce the size of their taxable estate during their lifetimes, they should be cautioned against being so generous that they end up jeopardizing their own financial well-being. Also, they should be particularly wary of giving money to children with the expectation that they will pay it back. Finally, the often-used practice of the elderly of giving money to relatives so that they can qualify for Medicaid in the event they have to go to a nursing home is full of pitfalls.

12.1.3 Disposition of Family Businesses

Owners of closely held businesses face particularly thorny estate planning problems. Current tax rules (known as "antiestate-freeze" provisions) are especially burdensome on family businesses. Therefore, careful planning is necessary to assure that the business can continue operating successfully without family rancor should the owner die. An additional estate planning consideration involves the eventual sale of the business during the owner's lifetime, whether to family members or outsiders. There are a variety of mechanisms for dealing with these problems including buy-sell agreements, installment sales of company stock, private annuities, life insurance trusts, and employee stock ownership plans.

12.1.4 Selection of an Executor

Although they are not around to witness the problems, many people select an inappropriate estate executor. While close relatives are the natural choice for many people and it usually works out well, sometimes it does not. The reasons why it doesn't work out should guide a client in making sure he or she selects an appropriate executor:

- Inexperience (particularly with complicated estates)
- Lack of time or inclination to devote to proper estate administration
- Inability to get along with relatives
- Conflict of interests between executor and other beneficiaries

12.1.5 Estate Liquidity

Many wage earners fail to consider the fact that their survivors will need access to cash immediately after death. Liquidity needs may include

- Funeral expenses and expenses of final illness
- Federal estate taxes and state death taxes
- Federal and state income taxes
- Probate and administration expenses
- Payment of maturing debts

- Maintenance and welfare of the family
- Payment of specific cash bequests
- Funds to continue running a family business

These needs must be estimated, and one's estate and personal financial planning should provide survivors with timely access to sufficient resources to meet these needs.

12.1.6 Multistate Property Ownership

More and more people divide their time between two states and/or own property in more than one state. Those who do need to be particularly careful as to establishing primary residence in one state. Even so, there may still be problems where property is located in more than one state since each state may attempt to collect death taxes on the property. Sometimes, a living trust can alleviate these problems. Expert legal advice is necessary under any circumstances.

12.1.7 Trusts

Whether they are established during lifetime (living trusts) or take effect upon death (testamentary trusts), trusts can provide a great deal of flexibility as to how you want your estate handled and distributed. For example, many people are very uncomfortable with the thought that their spouses and children will receive their shares of the estate with no strings attached. However, a simple will does just that. Some trusts have the added advantage of saving taxes and/or protecting an estate from creditors. One of the most commonly overlooked estate tax-saving trust arrangements are marital trusts that are designed to take maximum use of the unified credit. See Section 12.3 for a description of many commonly used trusts.

12.2 WILL DRAFTING AND REVIEW CONSIDERATIONS

The following list of questins highlights important points to consider when advising clients on the preparation of a will or when reviewing an existing will.

1. Will the client's surviving family have enough cash to pay ordinary family living expenses while the estate is in probate?
2. Does the client have special directions for the funeral, disposition of the body, or memorials?
3. Does the will identify the sources from which debts of the decedent, funeral expenses, and estate administrative costs will be paid?
4. Does the will reflect the client's current situation and not contain

sections that may be obselete? For example, is the will current for the following:
- State of residence
- Tax law changes
- Executor suitability
- Birth or death of an heir

5. How does the client wish to dispose of tangible personal property?
6. Does the client wish to make any specific bequests or legacies?
7. Are there bequests to charity, either outright or in trust, in order to obtain benefit of the charitable deduction?
8. Does the client want to dispose of real property?
9. Does the will provide for disposition of property if an heir predeceases the client?
10. Does the client wish to provide for periodic payments of income for certain beneficiaries?
11. Does the client want to establish trusts for certain beneficiaries or does he or she want them to receive the assets outright?
12. Does the will take advantage of the unlimited marital deduction to the most effective and practical extent allowed?
13. Does the will provide for a qualified terminable interest property (QTIP) trust as a postmortem planning device? (If the executor makes the QTIP election, the trust property is subject to the marital deduction even though the remainder of the trust passes to someone other than the surviving spouse.)
14. Does the will provide for a nonmarital trust?
15. What arrangements does the client wish to make for minor children or incompetent adult beneficiaries?
16. Is the custody of minors satisfactorily addressed?
17. Does the will specify that any minor beneficiary's share of the estate will be held until he or she reaches maturity?
18. Does the will provide for a guardianship or trust to protect the inheritance of disabled or incompetent beneficiaries?
19. What provision should be made to dispose of the client's business interests?
20. Does the will call for the disposition of a closely held business according to the client's wishes?
21. If a noncorporate executor is named, is there a provision for a co-executor? If not, are there reasons why naming a co-executor might be appropriate?
22. Who should serve as the executor, trustee, or guardian?
23. Do any potential conflicts of interest exist between the named executor and the beneficiaries under the will?

24. Is the individual or institution named as executor competent to carry out the duties of administering the estate?
25. Does the will name an alternate or successor executor?
26. Should any special powers be given to or taken away from the executor?
27. Has the executor's bond requirement been waived in the will?
28. Are specific powers granted to the executor, such as the following:
    a. To retain or sell property
    b. To invest trust and estate assets
    c. To exercise stock options
    d. To manage real estate
    e. To allocate receipts and disbursements to income and principal
    f. To make loans and borrow funds
    g. To settle claims
    h. To make decisions relating to the decedent's business, partnership interest, or stock
    i. To distribute property in kind
    j. To perform other appropriate duties
29. How should federal estate taxes and state death taxes, if any, be paid out of the estate?
30. Does the will state who will receive property if the beneficiary disclaims it? (Disclaimers can be an effective postmortem planning device.)
31. Is there a common disaster provision that indicates which spouse is deemed to have survived the other in the event of simultaneous deaths? (The Uniform Simultaneous Death Act, effective in most states, makes the presumption that the transferor spouse was the survivor, causing loss of the marital deduction in some cases. A common disaster provision can overcome this provision.)
32. Is the ownership of the assets complementary to the provisions of the will (i.e., some assets may pass outside of the will by contract or by type of ownership)?

12.3 TRUST SUMMARY

Trusts can be used in a variety of ways to accomplish many estate planning objectives. Although many people continue to believe that trusts are appropriate only for persons of substantial financial means, several types of trusts can and do play an important role in both the lifetime and estate planning for people of more modest financial circumstances. This section highlights commonly used trusts.

12.3.1 Trusts That Can Protect an Estate

A *minor's testamentary trust* is created in a will. It ensures that if the grantor dies while his or her heirs are still children, their inheritance will be protected and used appropriately. In these trusts, the trustee manages the inheritance for the children's express benefit until they reach their majority or—if the grantor so desires—until they reach a particular age specified in the will. By appointing a trustee who is not also the children's guardian, the grantor can ensure that the children's funds won't be squandered by an incompetent guardian. Also, a minor's testamentary trust can establish limits and control of the heirs' access to their inheritance until the age that the grantor feels they are mature enough to handle the entire sum wisely.

A *testamentary discretionary spendthrift trust* is also created in a will. This type of trust provides security for a disabled beneficiary. It supplements government assistance by allowing for the trustee to distribute income from the fund to the disabled beneficiary. If he or she is unable to handle this money, it is given to the guardian to spend in the best interest of the beneficiary.

A *revocable living trust* is a trust into which assets are usually placed during the settlor's lifetime. In so-called probate-unfriendly states (i.e., states where the probate process is onerous), this type of trust can be used effectively to avoid the publicity, delay, and expense involved with the probate process. The most attractive things about a revocable living trust is that it allows the grantor to act as the trustee, the grantor can keep some or all of the income the trust produces, its provisions can be altered, and it can be terminated. Some other advantages to having this trust are

- It avoids interruption of the settlor's family's income when he or she dies or becomes disabled.

- It allows for an operating business to continue uninterrupted.

- It relieves the settlor of the burdens of investment management.

- It requires less accounting, administration, and judicial supervision than a testamentary trust.

- In some states, it places property beyond the reach of the settlor's creditors.

After the death of the settlor, the trust can remain intact to benefit heirs, or the trust can be dissolved and the property distributed, according to the grantor's instructions, by the successor trustee named in the trust agreement.

Income produced by a revocable living trust is taxable, but, once the settlor has died, it becomes an irrevocable trust and the beneficiaries are therefore entitled to any of the tax savings that an irrevocable trust provides. In general, however, there are no immediate income tax or first-generation estate tax advantages provided by a revocable living trust. Also, the cost of operating this type of trust may be high.

A *revocable standby trust* is established to take over the settlor's asset management when he or she becomes unable to do so. These circumstances could include a long trip or a serious physical or mental disability. A standby trust helps to avoid long legal incompetency proceedings. This type of trust is not created to save taxes. A standby trust is usually revocable, however, if the settlor becomes permanently disabled or incapacitated, there may be a provision included in the trust that makes it irrevocable.

Despite the fact that there are now laws to prevent parents from sheltering money from taxes by putting it in their children's names, there are still reasons to open an *irrevocable 2503(c) trust*. When the grantor establishes this trust, he or she relinquishes control of the trust property and the power to change the trust agreement; thus, the trust's assets are no longer a part of the grantor's taxable estate. With an irrevocable 2503(c) trust, grantors may restrict beneficiaries from obtaining the trust's income and principal until they reach the age of 21 or even older if the beneficiary fails to claim the assets within 30 to 90 days of his 21st birthday. There may also be some income tax reduction possibilities with a 2503(c) trust.

An *irrevocable Crummey trust* has essentially the same income and estate tax benefits as the irrevocable 2503(c) trust. However, one major difference is that the Crummey trust does not have to terminate when the child turns 21. This trust enables grantors to take advantage of the $10,000 annual gift tax exclusion by giving beneficiaries "Crummey powers." This means the beneficiary is allowed to withdraw a portion of the trust's principal each year. Despite these advantages, there can often be large legal and accounting fees associated with both the irrevocable Crummey trust and the irrevocable 2503(c) trust, so a considerable amount of money must be placed in the trust in order to make it cost effective.

12.3.2 Trusts That Can Reduce Estate Taxes

Even married couples whose estates are less than $1 million can take advantage of certain trust arrangements that can end up saving the next generation well over $100,000 in federal estate taxes. So-called unified credit trusts are set up to hold that portion of the estate that is exempt from tax upon the death of the first spouse by reason of the $600,000 unified credit. The unified credit trust is designed to exempt the assets placed in the trust from estate taxation upon the death of the second spouse. In most cases to accomplish this, the choice will be between a power of appointment trust or a "QTIP" trust.

The most distinctive characteristic of a *general power of appointment trust* is that it gives the surviving spouse the power to name (usually in a will) the ultimate beneficiary of the trust's assets, that is, a general power of appointment. If the surviving spouse fails to name a beneficiary of the assets, the assets will go to the beneficiary named by the spouse who died first. Two other essentials for setting up a general power of appointment trust are that it must give the surviving spouse life income interest in the trust property and it must give the trustee or surviving spouse the power to withdraw and use the trust principal for certain purposes. A common provision included in the trust states that the general power of appointment is exercisable only by will. This avoids having the capital gains of the trust taxable to the surviving spouse. If the spouse fails to execute the power of appointment, the trust's assets are included in his or her taxable estate.

A *qualified terminable interest property trust* is a way to ensure that life income interest given to the grantor's spouse will qualify for the marital deduction. The settlor of the QTIP, however, may himself or herself name the ultimate beneficiary of the trust. The financial professional should be aware that there are certain requirements necessary in order for this life income interest to qualify for the marital deduction. First, the executor of the will must choose to have the interest from the trust treated as a QTIP. Also, the surviving spouse must be entitled to all the income the trust produces, payable at least once a year, and no one, including the surviving spouse, can have the power to distribute property to anyone but the spouse. Also, the QTIP interest in property that is not placed in trust must provide the surviving spouse with the rights to that income, which ensures that it satisfies the rules of a marital deduction trust.

To avoid incurring estate taxes on life insurance proceeds, the grantor can place his or her policies in an *irrevocable life insurance trust*. This will ensure that beneficiaries do not incur tax liabilities on monies received from life insurance policies. However, when the grantor sets up a life insurance trust, he or she must forfeit all ownership rights. Rights lost include the ability to borrow against the policies and to change the beneficiaries. Also, if the grantor dies within three years of establishing the trust, life insurance proceeds will be included as part of the taxable estate regardless of the trust's existence.

When the settlor establishes a charitable remainder trust, he or she places property in an irrevocable trust. The income from the trust is distributed to any number of beneficiaries who are selected by the settlor of the trust, including the settlor if he or she so wishes. This trust includes the provision that when the last income recipient dies, the property in the trust is to be given to a qualified charity for unrestricted use. One tax saving benefit that a charitable remainder trust provides is an income tax deduction for the settlor based on the value of the property that the charity will ultimately receive. Another tax saving benefit is that the settlor's estate will not include the value of the property in the trust and, therefore, will not be taxed on it. Last, the transfer of the income from settlor to the trust's beneficiaries may result in income tax savings.

A *charitable lead trust* is an irrevocable trust into which the settlor places property with the provision that the income from the property is to be given to a qualified charity. However, a charitable lead trust also includes the provision that on the occassion of the settlor's death, the property is to be given to any number of specified beneficiaries, typically family members. From the time the trust begins operation, the value of the property in the trust is no longer included in the settlor's taxable estate, but there is no immediate income tax deduction granted to the settlor upon the opening of the trust. At the expense of a lower cash flow, the transfer of income from the settlor to the charity can provide a significant estate tax savings.

12.4   FEDERAL ESTATE TAX RATES

Tables 12.1 and 12.2 present federal estate tax rates for taxable years beginning in 1992. The schedule in Table 12.1 applies to income tax of estates and trusts for 1992. Note that the income tax brackets are adjusted for inflation each year. The schedule in Table 12.2 shows the estate and gift transfer tax rates applicable to the transfer of property from one person to another. This tax applies whether there is a gift made during the transferor's lifetime or upon the transferor's death. State death taxes may be more burdensome than federal transfer taxes, so you should evaluate the impact of state death taxes in conjunction with a client's estate planning.

**Table 12.1 Income Tax of Estates and Trusts For Tax Years
Beginning in 1992**

| *If taxable income is:* | | *The tax is:* | |
Over—	but not over—		of the amount over—
$ 0	$ 3,600	15%	$ 0
3,600	10,900	$540 + 28%	3,600
10,900	—	2,584 + 31%	10,900

Transfer Tax Rate Schedules

Note that each decedent is entitled to a $192,800 "unified credit" against transfer taxes, which, in effect, means that the estate of decedents who did not make major gifts during their lifetime (in excess to the $10,000 annual gift tax exclusion) does not incur federal estate taxes on the first $600,000 of estate value. Such an estate may, however, incur state death taxes.

Table 12.2 Unified Transfer Tax Rate Schedules for Decedents Dying and Gifts Made

1988–1992

Amount		Tentative Tax		
Over	But Not Over	Tax +	Percentage	On Excess Over
$ 0	$ 10,000	$ 0	18%	$ 0
10,000	20,000	1,800	20	10,000
20,000	40,000	3,800	22	20,000
40,000	60,000	8,200	24	40,000
60,000	80,000	13,000	26	60,000
80,000	100,000	18,200	28	80,000
100,000	150,000	23,800	30	100,000
150,000	250,000	38,800	32	150,000
250,000	500,000	70,800	34	250,000
500,000	750,000	155,800	37	500,000
750,000	1,000,000	248,300	39	750,000
1,000,000	1,250,000	345,800	41	1,000,000
1,250,000	1,500,000	448,300	43	1,250,000
1,500,000	2,000,000	555,800	45	1,500,000
2,000,000	2,500,000	780,800	49	2,000,000
2,500,000	3,000,000	1,025,800	53	2,500,000
3,000,000	10,000,000	1,290,800	55	3,000,000
10,000,000	21,040,000	5,140,800	60	10,000,000
21,040,000		11,764,800	55	21,040,000

1993 and Thereafter

Amount		Tentative Tax		
Over	But Not Over	Tax +	Percentage	On Excess Over
$ 0	$ 10,000	$ 0	18%	$ 0
10,000	20,000	1,800	20	10,000
20,000	40,000	3,800	22	20,000
40,000	60,000	8,200	24	40,000
60,000	80,000	13,000	26	60,000
80,000	100,000	18,200	28	80,000
100,000	150,000	23,800	30	100,000
150,000	250,000	38,800	32	150,000
250,000	500,000	70,800	34	250,000
500,000	750,000	155,800	37	500,000
750,000	1,000,000	248,300	39	750,000
1,000,000	1,250,000	345,800	41	1,000,000
1,250,000	1,500,000	448,300	43	1,250,000
1,500,000	2,000,000	555,800	45	1,500,000
2,000,000	2,500,000	780,800	49	2,000,000
2,500,000	10,000,000	1,025,800	50	2,500,000
10,000,000	18,340,000	4,775,800	55	10,000,000
18,340,000		9,362,800	50	18,340,000

12.5 FEDERAL ESTATE AND GIFT TAX RETURN FORMS AND PUBLICATIONS

Table 12.3 is a list of federal estate and gift tax publications and commonly used tax return forms, all of which are available at no cost from the Internal Revenue Service. The publications can be very helpful in handling the many income and estate tax complexities involved in planning and settling an estate.

Table 12.3 Federal Estate and Gift Tax

Publications and Commonly Used Tax Return Forms Publications

Publication Number	Title
448	Federal Estate and Gift Taxes
525	Taxable and Nontaxable Income
559	Tax Information for Survivors, Executors and Administrators
721	Comprehensive Tax Guide to U.S. Civil Service Retirement Benefits
904	Interrelated Computations for Estate and Gift Taxes

Forms

Form	Title
706	U.S. Estate and Generation-Skipping Transfer Tax Return
706-A	U.S. Additional Estate Tax Return
706-B	Generation Skipping Transfer Tax Return
706CE	Certification of Payment of Foreign Death Tax
706NA	Federal Estate (and Generation-Skipping Transfer) Tax Return for Estate of Nonresident Alien
709	U.S. Gift (and Generation-Skipping Transfer) Tax Return
709-A	U.S. Short Form Gift Tax Return
712	Life Insurance Statement
1041	U.S. Fiduciary Income Tax Return
4351	Interest Computation - Estate Tax Deficiency on Installment Basis
4768	Application for Extension of Time to File U.S. Estate Tax Return and/or Pay Estate Tax
4808	Computation of Credit for Gift Tax (No Credit Allowed for Gifts Made After December 31, 1976)
6180	Line adjustment - Estate Tax

12.6 CHARITABLE REMAINDER INTEREST SUMMARY

Charitable remainders offer a variety of benefits to charitably inclined donors. First, there is a partial charitable income tax deduction for the value of the cash, securities, or property that is donated. Second, the donor (and, if he or she chooses, other beneficiaries) receive a lifetime or time certain income from the charity. Finally, the assets that are contributed are removed from the donor's taxable estate. Most larger charitable organizations, including colleges, are well equipped to handle and explain the ramifications of charitable remainder contributions. Characteristics and benefits of commonly used charitable remainder interests are summarized in Table 12.4.

12.7 VALUATION OF ANNUITIES, LIFE ESTATES, AND REMAINDER INTERESTS

Effective May 1, 1989, the Internal Revenue Service (IRS) 10 percent valuation tables that formerly were used to compute limited interests such as reversions, annuities, life estates, and remainder interest were modified. The change applies for gift and estate tax purposes and for the calculation of charitable deductions for charitable remainder trusts, charitable lead trusts, pooled income funds, remainder interests in houses and farms, and charitable gift annuities. This section is a summary of the impact of these changes.

The existing tables that were used to compute limited interests were based on 10 percent interest/discount assumptions. A formula is now used that is based on an interest/discount rate equal to 120 percent of the IRC Sec. 1274(d)(1) monthly federal midterm interest rate, which itself is based on the average market yield of U.S. obligations. Because of the frequency of rate changes, computers may be required to perform these computations.

Donors to charity will have the option of electing to value their gifts by reference to the federal midterm rate in effect for either of the two months preceding the valuation date of the property. That seems to give charitable donors a three-month spread over which to choose an interest rate, but it is actually 4. The rate for a particular month is published on the 20th day of the previous month; therefore, donors on August 21 will know the rates for September, August, July, or June. Or they can wait a few weeks, value the gift in September, and use the September rate, if it is more favorable.

The new system, if the 120 percent rate remains near 10 percent, will not have much effect on deductions. Unitrusts and pooled income fund gifts will not be seriously affected, regardless of where the rates go. Annuity trust gifts and charitable gift annuities will generate greater deductions if 120 percent of the midterm rate goes over 10 percent; deductions will decline if the rate goes below 10 percent. Gift tax, estate tax, and income tax deductions for qualified charitable lead annuity trusts will improve if the 120 percent rate drops below 10 percent; they will worsen if the rate climbs above 10 percent. Charitable lead unitrusts are little affected by variations in the midterm rate. Gifts of remainder interests on homes and farms will improve when the rate goes down and worsen when it goes up.

In addition to creating "floating deductions," Congress has instructed the Treasury to revise, at least once every 10 years, the mortality tables that underlie the formulas the IRS uses for valuing annuities, remainder interests, and life income interests.

Table 12.4 Charitable Remainder Interest

			Type of Charitable Remainder Interest			
	Gift Annuity	Deferred Gift Annuity	Pooled Income Fund	Net Income Unitrust	Basic Unitrust	Annuity Trust
Types of Gifts:						
Cash or unappreciated securities	Yes	Yes	Yes	Yes	Yes	Yes
Appreciated securities	Yes	Yes	Yes	Yes	Yes	Yes
Real property	Yes	Yes	In special cases	Yes	In special cases	In special cases
Annual Income	Fixed	Fixed	Variable	Variable	Variable	Fixed
Taxes[1]:						
Charitable deduction	Yes	Yes	Yes	Yes	Yes	Yes
Annual income	Partly tax-free	Partly tax-free	Fully taxable	May be either	May be either	May be either
Initial capital gains	Partially taxable	Partially taxable	Usually tax-free	Usually tax-free	Usually tax-free	Usually tax-free
Management of Property Donated[2]:	Not held in trust	Not held in trust	Commingled	Separate	Separate	Separate

[1] Gift taxes can generally be precluded in all cases and estate taxes are eliminated except when one of the beneficiaries is a nonspouse.
[2] Some donors prefer that the assets donated be managed separately.

12.8 STAGE AGENCIES ON AGING

Each state has a department devoted to coordinating services for older residents. These agencies can be used, among other things, to obtain information regarding services and programs available to the elderly. Table 12.5 is a list of state agencies on aging.

Table 12.5 State Agencies on Aging

Alabama
Alabama Commission on Aging
136 Catoma Street
Montgomery, AL 36130
Toll Free (within state)
1-(800) 243-5463
(205) 261-5743

Alaska
Older Alaskans Commission
P.O. Box C, MS 0209
Juneau, AK 99811
(907) 465-3250

American Samoa
Territorial Administration on Aging
Government of American Samoa
Pago, Pago, AS 96799
(684) 633-1251

Arizona
Department of Economic Security
Aging and Adult Administration
1400 W. Washington Street
Phoenix, AZ 85007
(602) 254-4446

Arkansas
Division of Aging and Adult Services
Donaghey Plaza South,
Suite 1417
7th and Main Streets
P.O. Box 1437/Slot 1412
Little Rock, AR 72203-1437
(501) 682-2441

California
Department of Aging
1600 K Street
Sacramento, CA 95814
(916) 322-3887

Colorado
Aging and Adult Services
Department of Social Services
1575 Sherman St., 10th Floor
Denver, CO 80203-1714
(303) 866-5905

Commonwealth of the Northern Mariana Islands
Department of Community and
   Cultural Affairs
Civic Center
Commonwealth of the Northern
   Mariana Islands
Saipan, CM 96950
(670) 234-6011

Connecticut
Department on Aging
175 Main Street
Hartford, CT 06106
Toll Free (within state)
1-(800) 443-9946
(203) 566-7772

Delaware
Division of Aging
Department of Health and Social
   Services
1901 N. Dupont Highway
New Castle, DE 19720
(302) 421-6791

District of Columbia
Office on Aging
Executive Office of the Mayor
1424 K Street N.W.
2nd Floor
Washington, D.C. 20005
(202) 724-5626
(202) 724-5622

Federated States of Micronesia
State Agency on Aging
Office of Health Services
Federated States of Micronesia
Ponape, E.C.I. 96941

Florida
Florida Department of Insurance
The Capitol
Tallahassee, FL 32301
Toll Free (within state)
1-(800) 342-2762

Georgia
Office of Aging
Department of Human Resources
878 Peachtree Street, NE., Room 632
Atlanta, GA 30309
(404) 894-5333

Guam
Division of Senior Citizens
Department of Public Health and
    Social Services
P.O. Box 2816
Agana, GU 96910
(671) 734-2942

Hawaii
Executive Office on Aging
335 Merchant Street, Room 241
Honolulu, HI 96813
(808) 548-2593

Idaho
Office on Aging
Statehouse, Room 114
Boise, ID 83720
(208) 334-3833

Illinois
Department on Aging
421 East Capitol Avenue
Springfield, IL 62701
(217) 785-2870

Indiana
Department of Human Services
251 North Illinois
P.O. Box 7083
Indianapolis, IN 46207-7083
(317) 232-1139

Iowa
Department of Elder Affairs
Suite 236, Jewett Building
914 Grand Avenue
Des Moines, IA 50319
(515) 281-5187

Kansas
Department on Aging
122-S, Docking State Office Bldg.
915 SW Harrison
Topeka, KS 66612-1500
(913) 296-4986

Kentucky
Division for Aging Services
Department for Social Services
275 East Main Street
Frankfort, KY 40621
(502) 564-6930

Louisiana
Governor's Office of Elderly Affairs
P.O. Box 80374
Baton Rouge, LA 70898-0374
(504) 925-1700

Maine
Maine Committee of Aging
State House, Station 127
Augusta, ME 04333
(207) 289-3658

Maryland
State Agency on Aging
301 West Preston Street
Baltimore, MD 21201
(301) 225-1102

Massachusetts
Executive Office of Elder Affairs
38 Chauncy Street
Boston, MA 02111
Toll Free (within state)
1-(800) 882-2003
(617) 727-7750

Michigan
Office of Services to the Aging
P.O. Box 30026
Lansing, MI 48909
(517) 373-8230

Minnesota
Minnesota Board on Aging
Metro Square Building, Suite 204
121 East Seventh Street
St. Paul, MN 55101
(612) 296-2770

Mississippi
Council on Aging
301 West Pearl Street
Jackson, MS 39203-3092
Toll Free (within state)
1-(800) 222-7622
(601) 949-2070

Missouri
Missouri Division of Insurance
Truman Building 630
P.O. Box 690
Jefferson, MO 65102-0690
Toll Free (within state)
1-(800) 235-5503

Montana
Department of Family Services
P.O. Box 8005
Helena, MT 59604
(406) 444-5900

Nebraska
Department on Aging
Legal Services Developer
State Office Building
301 Centennial Mall South
Lincoln, NE 68509
(402) 471-2306

Nevada
Department of Human Resources
Division for Aging Services
505 East King Street
Room 101
Carson City, NV 89710
(702) 885-4210

New Hampshire
Department of Health and Human
    Services
Division of Elderly and Adult Services
6 Hazen Drive
Concord, NH 03301
(603) 271-4390

New Jersey
Department of Community Affairs
Division on Aging
South Broad and Front Sts.
CN 807
Trenton, NJ 08625-0807
(609) 292-0920

New Mexico
Agency on Aging
La Villa Rivera Bldg., 4th Floor
224 East Palace Avenue
Santa Fe, NM 87501
Toll Free (within state)
1-(800) 432-2080
(505) 827-7640

New York
State Office for the Aging
Agency Building
#2 Empire State Plaza
Albany, NY 12223-0001
Toll Free (within state)
1-(800) 342-9871
(518) 474-5731

North Carolina
Department of Human Resources
Division of Aging
1985 Umstead Drive
Raleigh, NC 27603
(919) 733-3983

North Dakota
Department of Human Services
Aging Services Division
State Capitol Building
Bismark, ND 58505
(701) 224-2577

Ohio
Department of Aging
50 West Broad Street, 9th Floor
Columbus, OH 43266-0501
(614) 466-1220

Oklahoma
Department of Human Services
Aging Services Division
P.O. Box 25352
Oklahoma City, OK 73125
(405) 521-2327

Oregon
Department of Human Resources
Senior Services Division
313 Public Service Building
Salem, OR 97310
Toll Free (within state)
1-(800) 232-3020
(503) 378-4636

Palau
State Agency on Aging
Department of Social Services
Republic of Palau
Koror, Palau 96940

Pennsylvania
Department of Aging
231 State Street
Batto Building
Harrisburg, PA 17101
(717) 783-1550

Puerto Rico
Governors Office of Elderly
Affairs
Gericulture Commission
Box 11398
Santurce, PR 00910
(809) 722-2429 or 722-0225

Republic of the Marshall Islands
State Agency on Aging
Department of Social Services
Republic of the Marshall Islands
Marjuro, Marshall Islands 96960

Rhode Island
Department of Elderly Affairs
79 Washington Street
Providence, RI 02903
(401) 277-2858

South Carolina
Commission on Aging
400 Arbor Lake Drive
Suite B-500
Columbia, SC 29223
(803) 735-0210

South Dakota
Agency on Aging
Adult Services and Aging

Richard F. Kneip Building
700 Governors Drive
Pierre, SD 57501-2291
(605) 773-3656

Tennessee
Commission on Aging
Commerce and Insurance
Department
Volunteer Plaza
James Robinson Parkway
Nashville, TN 37219-5573
(615) 741-2241

Texas
Department on Aging
P.O. Box 12786
Capitol Station
Austin, TX 78711
(512) 444-2727

Utah
Division of Aging & Adult
Services
120 North 200 West
Post Office Box 45500
Salt Lake City, UT 84145-0500
(801) 538-3910

Vermont
Office on Aging
Waterbury Complex
103 S. Main Street
Waterbury, VT 05676
(802) 241-2400

Virgin Islands
Department of Human Services
Barbel Plaza South
Charlotte Amalie
St. Thomas, VI 00802
(809) 774-0930

Virginia
Department for the Aging
18th Floor
101 North 14th Street
Richmond, VA 23219
Toll Free (within state)
1-(800) 552-4464
(804) 225-2271

Washington
Aging & Adult Services
  Administration
Department of Social & Health
  Services
Mail Stop OB-44-A
Olympia, WA 98504
(206) 586-3768

West Virginia
Commission on Aging
State Capitol Complex
Holly Grove
Charleston, WV 25305
Toll Free (within state)
1-(800) 642-3671
(304) 348-3317

Wisconsin
Bureau on Aging
Department of Health and Social
  Services
P.O. Bop 7851
Madison, WI 53707
Toll Free (within state)
1-(800) 242-1060
(608) 266-2536

Wyoming
Commission on Aging
Hathaway Building
First Floor
Cheyenne, WY 82002
Toll Free (within state)
1-(800) 442-2766
(307) 777-7986

Chapter 13_____

PRACTICE MANAGEMENT AND REGULATION

The financial services industry continues to evolve in response to the needs of an increasingly informed and affluent consumer. Providing financial services requires a competence and style similar to that of other professional consulting businesses. The advisor must be familiar with relevant strategies and products and must have the ability to evaluate each client's situation and unique requirements to recommend suitable courses of action. The financial services professional must have the facility to understand and empathize with clients' needs and desires; furthermore, he or she should impart to clients a growing understanding of the many and varied matters that can affect their financial lives.

Whatever the nature of the financial services professional's business, his or her practice should be structured to meet client needs efficiently and effectively. Every financial professional has a unique approach to providing services, although there are several common elements, including obtaining pertinent information, analyzing the clients' unique circumstances and needs, and presenting appropriate recommendations.

Just as the financial services business is changing rapidly, so is the regulatory environment. Financial services professionals need to keep abreast of changes in the regulatory environment that affect their practices. It seems apparent that stricter regulations will be forthcoming in light of the financial problems that plague many financial services companies and the scandals that have rocked some major financial institutions.

13.1   ENGAGEMENT REMINDER

In this section a reminder list of important matters that may be relevant to a particular financial services engagement is provided. It can be used to help assure that important financial matters are not overlooked when working with a client.

Planning and Record Keeping

1. Obtain the necessary information and supporting documentation to conduct an evaluation.
2. Evaluate the effect of the client's qualitative considerations (e.g., preferences, time constraints, expertise) and external considerations (e.g., the investment environment, the tax environment), as well as the client's quantitative considerations as they relate to financial planning requirements and needs.
3. Obtain and evaluate a list of the client's financial planning goals and objectives.
4. Develop strategies that will assist the client in achieving financial goals and objectives.
5. Assist the client in establishing priorities for achieving financial planning goals and objectives.
6. Consider the effects of inflation on all financial projections.
7. Evaluate the client's personal record-keeping system and make suggestions and/or provide forms to assist the client.

Personal Financial Statements

1. Prepare and analyze a personal statement of financial condition.
2. Prepare and analyze a personal statement of changes in net worth.
3. Prepare a summary of cash receipts and cash disbursements.
4. Prepare projections of financial condition and net worth changes in accordance with overall financial planning recommendations.

Insurance Planning

1. Obtain a summary of the client's current insurance coverage.
2. Determine the appropriate level of life insurance needed by the client and other family members.
3. Evaluate the adequacy and cost-effectiveness of the life insurance coverage of the client and other family members and/or dependents who require coverage.
4. Evaluate the adequacy and continuity of the medical insurance coverage of the client and other family members and/or dependents.
5. Assess the client's long-term disability insurance coverage, including its cost-effectiveness.
6. Review the client's homeowners' or renters' insurance coverage to ensure that it is adequate and all special risks are appropriately covered.

7. Review the adequacy and cost-effectiveness of the client's automobile insurance coverage.

8. Determine whether the client has sufficient extended personal liability (umbrella) insurance.

9. Evaluate, where appropriate, the client's exposure to professional liability and review the adequacy of this coverage.

10. Determine whether the client has sufficiently considered and prepared contingency plans for ensuring continuity of insurance coverage in the event of a sudden change in personal circumstances (e.g., unemployment, disability, death).

Borrowing And Credit

1. Obtain a summary of the client's current total indebtedness.

2. Determine whether the client's current level of debt is appropriate to his or her financial circumstances.

3. Verify that the client's loans are cost-effective with respect to loan terms, interest rates, and tax deductibility.

4. Evaluate the client's overall use of credit, including borrowing for appropriate purposes and repayment of debt over periods consistent with the purpose of the loan.

5. Review, where applicable, the client's plans for funding dependents' education costs.

Capital Accumulation

1. Review the client's capital accumulation program, or assist in its preparation.

2. Obtain a summary of the client's investment portfolio, classified according to type of investment (e.g., equity, fixed-income, real estate).

3. Verify that the risk profile of the client's investment portfolio is consistent with his or her preferences and financial condition.

4. Review the client's capital accumulation program over time to ensure that it is sufficient to achieve overall financial planning objectives.

5. Verify that the client's investment portfolio is properly balanced between equity investments, fixed-income investments, and real estate investments.

6. Determine whether the appropriate portions of the client's investment portfolio are sufficiently liquid to provide for unanticipated emergencies.

7. Review the client's current investment holdings and contemplated future investments in light of current tax regulations.

Equity Investments

1. Analyze the client's current equity investment holdings and, if appropriate, make recommendations for changes in the portfolio.
2. Verify that the equity investment portfolio is appropriately diversified.
3. Advise the client on the effective use of mutual funds.

Fixed-Income Investments

1. Verify that the client's fixed-income investment portfolio is consistent with overall financial planning objectives.
2. Advise the client on the multiplicity of fixed-income vehicles currently available.
3. Verify that the level of risk of the client's fixed-income investments is consistent with objectives and circumstances.
4. Make recommendations to the client regarding possible ways to increase portfolio yield and/or minimize exposure to interest rate risk.

Real Estate Investments

1. If appropriate, advise the client on the desirability of real estate investments as part of a capital accumulation program.
2. Verify that the client's current real estate investment portfolio is consistent with overall financial planning objectives.
3. Evaluate the client's current and contemplated real estate investments in light of current tax regulations.
4. Assist the client in evaluating any contemplated real estate investments.

Tax Planning

1. Review the client's federal, state, and, if applicable, local tax returns to identify any opportunities for tax reduction.
2. Prepare income tax projections for the next three to five years.
3. Assess whether the client is sufficiently knowledgeable about income tax requirements and tax-saving opportunities.
4. Evaluate the client's potential alternative minimum tax exposure.
5. Develop long-term tax planning strategies that are consistent with current tax rules.
6. Coordinate tax planning activities with other related areas of personal financial planning, particularly investments and estate planning.

Retirement Planning

1. Verify that the client has developed an explicit program directed toward securing a financially comfortable retirement.

2. If the client is contemplating early retirement, determine whether the projected level of capital accumulation and pension benefits are sufficient to fund an early retirement.

3. Evaluate the preretiree's investment portfolio to ensure that it is appropriate for impending retirement income needs.

4. Prepare a forecast of retirement income and expenses that accounts for the effects of inflation.

5. Advise the client on the importance of preparing for an active retirement lifestyle as well as a financially secure retirement.

6. Assist the client in evaluating the potential effects of a prolonged, uninsured illness in retirement.

Estate Planning

1. Review wills, letters of instructions, and adult guardianship arrangements to ensure that they are up to date and properly reflect the client's wishes.

2. Estimate the client's combined state and federal estate tax liability.

3. Determine whether provisions have been made to ensure adequate estate liquidity upon the client's death.

4. Review the client's estate plans in light of the applicable estate and income tax regulations.

5. Consider various estate planning techniques, including property ownership designation, gifting/charitable contribution programs, trusts, and disposition of a closely held business.

13.2 COMMONLY ENCOUNTERED FINANCIAL ISSUES

This section provides a list of commonly encountered financial issues. The financial services professional may want to review this list as part of a review of a specific client's financial status.

Planning And Record Keeping

1. Establish realistic short-term and long-term financial goals.

2. Develop a satisfactory record keeping system.

3. Obtain a safe-deposit box for storing valuable papers and possessions.

4. Obtain a comprehensive current inventory of household furnishings and possessions.
5. Prepare periodic balance sheets.
6. Prepare a household budget listing expected income and expenses.

Insurance

1. Establish sufficient life insurance coverage for client and, if applicable, spouse to meet dependents' financial needs in the event of death.
2. Obtain comprehensive and continuous health insurance coverage for entire family.
3. Establish adequate long-term disability insurance coverage.
4. Ensure adequate homeowner's or renter's insurance coverage.
5. Obtain additional insurance protection for valuables.
6. Maintain a personal liability (umbrella) insurance policy.
7. Ensuring sufficient professional liability insurance.

Borrowing And Credit

1. Establish credit through borrowing for worthwhile purposes.
2. Prepare for a major purchase or expenditure that will require borrowing.
3. Secure a home equity loan.
4. Fund education for children or grandchildren.

Savings And Investments

1. Establish regular savings through payroll withholding or other savings programs.
2. Establish an emergency fund equal to at least three months' salary.
3. Establish a proper balance between stocks and savings in the portfolio.
4. Determine appropriate investment objectives.
5. Periodically review the investment portfolio.
6. Reduce risk in the investment portfolio.
7. Participate in an employer's stock purchase plan.
8. Diversify the investment portfolio.
9. Participate in dividend reinvestment plans of stocks or mutual funds.
10. Plan inheritance expectancies.

Real Estate

1. Buy first home or condominium.
2. Make major home improvements.
3. Purchase a second home.
4. Purchase a vacation time-share.
5. Directly invest in income producing real estate.
6. Own real estate through a limited partnership.

Tax Planning

1. Understand current tax laws and tax saving techniques.
2. Maintain adequate tax records.
3. Evaluate the efficacy of tax-advantaged investments.
4. Evaluate the effect of current tax regulations on income tax status.
5. Plan for significant increases in future income.
6. Understand the tax implications of full- or part-time self-employment.

Retirement Planning

1. Make Individual Retirement Account contributions.
2. Participate, if self-employed, in a Keogh plan or SEP (simplified employee pension) plan.
3. Participate in an employer-sponsored thrift plan, savings plan, or salary reduction (401(k)) plan.
4. Retire prior to age 65.
5. Invest in tax-deferred annuities.
6. Estimate income that will be available on retirement.
7. Take action to fund a comfortable retirement.
8. If preretiree, evaluate investment portfolio mix in light of retirement income needs.
9. Evaluate expected pension benefits.
10. Choose between a lump sum pension payment and an annuity at retirement.
11. Ensure that Social Security Administration has accurate records of earnings.
12. Estimate what Social Security retirement benefits will be.

Estate Planning

1. Maintain a valid and up-to-date will.

2. Prepare a letter of instructions.
3. Familiarize immediate family with both the location and contents of will and letter of instructions.
4. Appoint a financial guardian for dependent children.
5. Establish an adult guardianship arrangement in the event that either spouse becomes disabled or mentally incapacitated.
6. Establish trust funds as part of estate planning.
7. Explore alternative methods of ownership of real estate in order to ascertain the most advantageous.
8. Consider the implications of business or real estate interests in more than one state.
9. Evaluate the impact of possible uninsured illness during retirement.

13.3 ORGANIZATIONS OF INTEREST TO FINANCIAL SERVICES PROFESSIONALS

A list of associations that may be of interest to financial services professionals is provided for in this section.

American Association of Personal Financial Planners
21031 Ventura Boulevard, Suite 903
Woodland Hills, CA 91364
(818) 348-5400

American Institute of Certified Public Accountants
1211 Avenue of the Americas
New York, NY 10036
(212) 575-6200

American Society of Chartered Life Underwriters and CHFC
270 Bryn Mawr Avenue
Bryn Mawr, PA 19010
(312) 329-8559

American Institute of Real Estate Appraisers
430 N. Michigan Avenue
Chicago, IL 60611
(215) 526-2500

Bank Administration Institute
60 Gould Center
2550 Golf Road

Rolling Meadows, IL 60008
(312) 228-6200

Consumer Bankers Association
1000 Wilson Boulevard,
30th Floor
Arlington, VA 22209
(703) 276-1750

Consumer Credit Insurance Association
542 S. Dearborn Street,
Suite 400
Chicago, IL 60605
(312) 939-2242

Financial Analysts Federation
Boar's Head Lane, #5
P.O. Box 3726
Charlottesville, VA 22903
(804) 977-8977

Health Insurance Association of America
1025 Connecticut Avenue N.W.,
Suite 1200
Washington, D.C. 20036
(202) 233-7780

Independent Insurance Agents of
America
100 Church Street,
Suite 1901
New York, NY 10007
(212) 285-4250

Institute of Certified Financial
Planners
Two Denver Highlands,
Suite 320
10065 E. Harvard Avenue
Denver, CO 80231
(303) 751-7600

Institute of Chartered Financial
Analysts
P.O. Box 3668
Charlottesville, VA 22903
(804) 977-6600

Institute of Management
Accountants
10 Paragon Drive
Montvale, NJ 07645
(201) 573-9000

International Association for
Financial Planning
Two Concourse Parkway,
Suite 800
Atlanta, GA 30328
(404) 395-1605

Investment Company Institute
1600 M St. N.W.,
Suite 600
Washington, D.C. 20036
(202) 293-7700

Mutual Fund Education Alliance,
the Association of No-Load Funds
520 N. Michigan Avenue, Suite 1632
Chicago, IL 60611
(312) 527-1454

National Association of Estate
Planning Councils
P.O. Box 7314
Athens, GA 30604

National Association of Federal
Credit Unions
P.O. Box 3769
Washington, VA 20007
(703) 522-4770

National Association of Personal
Financial Advisors
3726 Olentangy River Road
Columbus, OH 43214
(614) 457-8200

National Association of Professional Insurance Agents
400 N. Washington Street
Alexandria, VA 22314
(703) 836-9340

National Society of Public
Accountants
1010 N. Fairfax Street
Alexandria, VA 22314
(703) 549-6400

Society of Certified Insurance
Counselors
P.O. Box 27027
Austin, Tex. 78755
(512) 345-7932

13.4 SUMMARY OF THE INVESTMENT ADVISORS ACT OF 1940

Many professionals who offer investment advisory services are concerned about whether their activities fall under the Investment Advisors Act of 1940 (the Act), which requires investment advisors to be registered with the federal government. The definition of an investment advisor, how the planner can determine if he meets that definition, the consequences of registration, and the method of registration are treated in the following discussion. Also included is the Table of Contents of the Act.

The Act was the final measure in a series of six statutes designed to eliminate abuses in the securities industry. (The first five were the Securities Act of 1933, the Securities Exchange Act of 1934, the Public Utility Holding Company Act of 1935, the Trust Indenture Act of 1939, and the Investment Company Act of 1940.) This legislation was passed partly in response to the 1929 stock market crash and the Great Depression that followed. It was felt that the public needed to be protected from unscrupulous individuals seeking their money. It was also argued that bona fide professionals would want the entire profession's reputation protected from deceitful practitioners. In an effort to raise the standards of business ethics in the securities industry, the concepts of full disclosure and fair play were instituted and investment advisors became subject to the mandates of the Act and to registration with the Securities and Exchange Commission (SEC).

13.4.1 Definition of Investment Advisor

The Act, officially Public Law 768 of the 76th Congress, regulates all investment advisors meeting its definition, excluding those who are specifically exempt. Even the latter, however, are subject to its antifraud provisions. (The original Act was amended in 1960 to secure broader enforcement powers in its regulation of investment advisors.) The Act defines an investment advisor as follows:

> any person who, for compensation, engages in the business of advising others, either directly or through publications or writings, as to the value of securities, or as to the advisability of investing in, purchasing or selling securities or who, for compensation and as part of a regular business, issues or promulgates analyses or reports concerning securities...

The following six exemptions are listed specifically in the Act. By definition, any individual or business meeting any one of these exemptions is not deemed an investment advisor:

1. A bank, or any bank holding company as defined in the Bank Holding Company Act of 1956, that is not an investment company.

2. Any lawyer, accountant, engineer, or teacher whose performance of investment services is solely incidental to the practice of his profession.

3. Any broker or dealer whose performance of such services is solely incidental to the conduct of his or her business as a broker or dealer and who receives no special compensation therefor.

4. The publisher of any bona fide newspaper, news magazine, or business or financial publication of general and regular circulation.

5. Any person whose advice, analyses, or reports relate only to securities that are direct obligations of, or obligations guaranteed as to principal or interest by, the United States or to securities issued or guaranteed by corporations in which the United States has a direct or indirect interest that have been designated by the Secretary of the Treasury, pursuant to Section 3(a)(12) of the Securities Exchange Act of 1934, as exempted securities for the purposes of that Act.

6. Others not within the intent of the definition of an investment advisor under the Act as the SEC may determine by rules and regulations or orders.

In addition to these six exemptions, three categories of investment advisors are excepted under the Act:

1. Any investment advisor all of whose clients reside in the state within which he or she maintains his or her principal office and place of business and who does not furnish advice or issue analyses or reports with respect to securities listed or admitted to unlisted trading privileges on any national securities exchange.

2. Any investment advisor whose only clients are insurance companies.

3. Any investment advisor who, during the course of the preceding 12 months, has had fewer than 15 clients and who neither holds himself or herself out generally to the public as an investment advisor nor acts as an investment advisor to any investment company registered under the Investment Company Act of 1940.

13.4.2 Meeting the Definition

To be considered as an investment advisor, the planner must (1) give advice or analyses concerning securities, (2) be in the business of doing such, and (3) receive compensation for it. All three requirements must be met. A planner who is unsure of his or her status may seek assistance from the SEC, which will probably refer him or her to Investment Advisors Release No. 770; or, if the situation is wholly unique, the SEC may take independent action to answer the question. Because many professionals who now offer some financial services may no longer fit into distinct occupational categories, it is difficult to delineate just who qualifies as an investment advisor. Release No. 770 (dated August 13, 1981 and entitled "Applicability of the Investment Advisors Act to Financial Planners, Pension Consultants, and Other Persons Who Provide Investment Advisory Services as an Intregral Component of Other Financial Related Services") provides guidelines that are very useful in determining a planner's status.

13.4.3 Definition of Securities

Under the first element, securities are defined not simply as stocks and bonds but as any investment contract. The latter term has been construed by the Supreme Court to include most instances where a passive investor relies on the skill or advice of an active person who seeks a profit from the transaction; hence, limited partnership interests, syndications, condominium rental pool arrangements, and related activities are investment contracts.

The act of advising is not limited to cases where a planner recommends a specific security to the client. Where a planner gives a general recommendation about holding securities, he or she is considered an investment advisor under the Act, provided he or she meets the other two requirements.

13.4.4 Business Requirement

The planner must also meet the securities business requirement to be labeled an investment advisor. Under this standard, his or her business must consist of advising others concerning securities and their values or of making recommendations regarding the investment in and the purchase or sale of securities. This advice must be the planner's principal business activity, not merely an insignificant or minor portion of the business, and one for which he or she is compensated.

Thus the SEC's position is that a professional who offers financial services including investment advice is an investment advisor unless that advice is incidental to a noninvestment business, is nonspecific, and is not specifically compensated for. Someone whose principal business is providing financial services other than investment advice is not regarded as an investment advisor if he or she discusses in general terms the value of investing in securities or the role of securities in his or her clients' overall financial objectives. Thus, accountants, bankers, lawyers, insurance agents, and financial planners are not investment advisors under the Act if their securities advice is incidental to their primary business. It is the SEC's position, however, that financial planners, pension consultants, sports and entertainment representatives, and others who do provide investment advice as an important component of other financial services should register. An individual may avoid registering in his or her own name if registration is made in the name of a broker-dealer, management company, or other organization. This applies only if all fees for securities transactions are made payable to the registered company and not to the individual. It may be wise to resolve uncertainty concerning status by consulting with an attorney.

A free copy of the Investment Advisors Act may be obtained by writing to The Public Reference Branch, Securities and Exchange Commission, Washington, D.C. 20549. The Rules and Regulations pertaining to this Act can be obtained for a fee from The Superintendent of Documents, Government Printing Office, Washington, D.C. 20402.

13.4.5 Consequences of Registration

The registration procedure is relatively simple and inexpensive ($150 for filing). However, the professional encounters a variety of problems by registering. Most important, registration opens the door to regulation, as the SEC requires a number of disclosure statements, record-keeping procedures, and fee restrictions; prohibits certain transactions; and creates a fiduciary legal relationship between the professional and his or her client. Under Rule 204-3, an investment advisor must provide a written disclosure statement to each of his or her clients. The form, containing appropriate information, is sent to the advisor as Part II of the registration material and includes such matters as fees, the professional's educational level and background, and his or her other current business activities. Records, reports, and brochures must be filed, maintained, and kept up to date for inspection and audit by the SEC. Rule 204-2 requires that records be kept for a minimum of five years in a safe and accessible place. The restrictions the Act places on fees are complex, and a careful reading is in order. In essence, the Act prohibits an investment advisor from basing fees on a share of the capital appreciation of a client's funds except where the client is a registered investment company or where the contract is in excess of $1 million. Several activities are expressly prohibited under the Act.

1. There can be no representation of sponsorship by the United States or any agency thereof, although the planner may state that he or she is registered under the Investment Advisors Act.

2. A registered advisor cannot use the name "investment counsel" unless his principal business consists of investment advising and a substantial part of this business consists of investment supervisory services.

3. An advisor is prohibited from practicing any fraud or deceit upon clients or prospective clients.

4. An advisor cannot purchase from or sell securities to any client without advising the client and obtaining his consent.

5. The advisor may not engage in any fraudulent business.

6. Neither an advisor nor any other person may make a material misrepresentation or fail to make a statement of a required material fact in any registration statement or report filed with the SEC.

13.4.6 How to Register

For information about registration, write or call Office of Applications and Reports Services, 500 N. Capitol St., N.W., Washington, D.C. 20549, (202) 523-5543.

To register, Form ADV must be completed and returned with a $150 filing fee. Investment advisors must file annual Form ADV-S as well.

13.4.7 Table of Contents of the Investment Advisors Act

(b) Disclosure of fact of examination or investigation; exceptions

(c) Disclosure by investment advisor of identity of clients

Section 211 Rules, Regulations, and Orders of Commissions

(a) Powers of Commission under the Act

(b) Effective date of regulation

(c) Orders of Commssion after notice and opportunity for hearing; type of notice

(d) Good faith compliance with rules and regulations

Section 212 Hearings

Section 213 Court Review of Commission Orders

Section 214 Jurisdiction of Offenses and Suits

Section 215 Validity of Contracts

Section 216 Annual Reports of Commission

Section 217 Penalties Under the Act

Section 218 Officers and Employees of Commission

Section 218A State Control of Investment Advisors

Section 219 Separability of Provisions

Section 220 Short Title: "Investment Advisors Act of 1940"

13.5 STATE SECURITIES COMMISSIONERS

The mailing addresses and telephone numbers of the state securities commissioners appear in this section.

Alabama
Securities Commission
Director
66 Commerce Street, 2nd Floor
Montgomery, AL 36130
(205) 261-2984

Alaska
Department of Commerce and
   Economic Development
Division of Banking, Securities,
   and Corporations Commissioner
333 Willoughby Avenue,
   9th Floor
P.O. Box D
Juneau, AK 99811-0800
(907) 465-2521

Arizona
Corporation Commission,
   Securities Division
Director
120 West Washington Street,
   2nd Floor
Phoenix, AZ 85007
(602) 542-4242

Arkansas
Securities Department
Commissioner
Heritage West Building,
   3rd Floor
201 East Markham
Little Rock, AR 72201
(501) 371-1011

California
Department of Corporations
Commissioner
615 S. Flower Street, 19th Floor
Los Angeles, CA 90017
(213) 620-6547

Colorado
Division of Securities
Securities Commissioner
1560 Broadway, Suite 1450
Denver, CO 80202
(303) 894-2320

Connecticut
Department of Banking
Securities and Business
Investments Division
Banking Commissioner
44 Capitol Avenue
Hartford, CT 06106
(203) 566-4560

Delaware
Department of Justice, Division of
Securities
Securities Commissioner
State Office Building
820 North French Street, 8th Floor
Wilmington, DE 19801
(302) 571-2515

District Of Columbia
Public Service Commission,
Division of Securities
Director of Securities
450 5th Street, N.W., Suite 821
Washington, D.C. 20001
(202) 626-5105

Florida
Office of Comptroller, Department
of Banking and Finance
Division of Securities and Investor
Protection
Comptroller and Head of
Department of Banking and
Finance
The Capitol
Tallahassee, FL 32301-8054
(904) 488-0370

Georgia
Office of Secretary of State,
Business Services and Regulation
Secretary of State
Two Martin Luther King Jr. Drive
Suite 315, West Tower
Atlanta, GA 30334
(404) 656-2894

Hawaii
Department of Commerce and
Consumer Affairs
Business Registration Division
Commissioner of Securities
1010 Richards Street
P.O. Box 40
Honolulu, HI 96810
(808) 548-6521

Idaho
Department of Finance, Securities
Bureau
Director
700 West State Street
Boise, ID 83720
(208) 334-3684

Illinois
Office of the Secretary of State,
Securities Department
Director
900 South Spring Street
Springfield, IL 62704
(217) 785-4941

Indiana
Office of the Secretary of State,
Securities Division
Commissioner
One North Capital,
Suite 560
Indianapolis, IN 46204
(317) 232-6690

Iowa
Office of Commissioner of
Insurance, Securities Bureau
Superintendent of Securities
Lucas State Office Building
Des Moines, IA 50319
(515) 281-4441

Kansas
Office of Securities Commissioner
Securities Commissioner
618 South Kansas Avenue,
2nd Floor
Topeka, KS 66603
(913) 296-3307

Kentucky
Department of Financial
Institutions, Division of Securities
Director
911 Leawood Drive
Frankfort, KY 40601
(502) 564-2180

Louisiana
Securities Commission
Commissioner of Financial
Institutions
Louisiana State Office Building,
Suite 315
325 Loyola Avenue
New Orleans, LA 70112
(504) 568-5515

Maine
Department of Professional and
Financial Regulation
Bureau of Banking, Securities
Division
Administrator
State House Station 121
Augusta, ME 04333
(207) 582-8760

Maryland
Office of the Attorney General,
Division of Securities
Securities Commissioner
Munsey Building
7 North Calvert Street,
18th Floor
Baltimore, MD 21202-1918
(301) 576-6360

Massachusetts
Secretary of the Commonwealth,
Securities Division
Director
1719 John W. McCormack
Building, 17th Floor

One Ashburton Place
Boston, MA 02108
(617) 727-3548

Michigan
Department of Commerce,
Corporation and Securities
Bureau
Director
P.O. Box 30222
6546 Mercantile Way
Lansing, MI 48909
(517) 334-6206

Minnesota
Department of Commerce
Commissioner of Commerce
500 Metro Square Building
Seventh and Robert Streets
St. Paul, MN 55101
(612) 296-6848

Mississippi
Office of the Secretary of State,
Securities Division
Secretary of State
401 Mississippi Street
P.O. Box 136
Jackson, MS 39205
(601) 359-1350

Missouri
Office of the Secretary of State
Secretary of State
Harry S. Truman State Office
Building
301 West High Street
Jefferson City, MO 65102
(314) 751-4136

Montana
Office of the State Auditor,
Securities Department
State Auditor and Securities
Commissioner
126 N. Sanders
Mitchell Building, Room 270
Helena, MT 59601
Mailing:
Box 4009, Helena, MT 59604
(406) 444-2040

Nebraska
Department of Banking and
Finance, Bureau of Securities
Director of Banking and Finance
301 Centennial Mall South
P.O. Box 95006
Lincoln, NE 68509-5006
(402) 471-3445

Nevada
Department of State, Securities
Division
Deputy Secretary of State
2501 E. Sahara Ave.,
Suite 201
Las Vegas, NV 89158
(702) 486-4400

New Hampshire
Office of Securities Regulation
Director
157 Manchester Street
Concord, NH 03301
(603) 271-1463

New Jersey
Department of Law & Public
Safety, Bureau of Securities
Chief of Securities Bureau
Two Gateway Center,
8th Floor
Newark, NJ 07102
(201) 648-2040

New Mexico
Regulation and Licensing
Department, Securities Division
Director
Bataan Memorial Building,
Room 165
Santa Fe, NM 87503
(505) 827-7754

New York
Department of Law, Bureau of
Investor Protection and Securities
Attorney General
120 Broadway,
23rd Floor
New York, NY 10271
(212) 341-2222

North Carolina
Department of the Secretary of
State, Securities Division
300 North Salisbury Street
Room 404
Raleigh, NC 27611
(919) 733-3924

North Dakota
Office of Securities
Commission
Commissioner
State Capital, 9th Floor
Bismarck, ND 58505
(701) 224-2910

Ohio
Department of Commerce,
Division of Securities
Commissioner
77 South High Street,
22nd Floor
Columbus, OH 43266-0548
(614) 644-7381

Oklahoma
Department of Securities
Administrator
Will Rogers Memorial Office
Building, 4th Floor
2401 Lincoln Boulevard
P.O. Box 53595
Oklahoma City, OK 73152
(405) 521-2451

Oregon
Department of Insurance and
Finance, Securities Section
Department Director
21 Labor & Industries
Building
Salem, OR 97310
(503) 378-4387

Pennsylvania
Securities Commission
Chairman
1010 N. Seventh Street,
2nd Floor
Harrisburg, PA 17102-1410
(717) 787-6828

Puerto Rico
Office of the Commissioner of
Financial Institutions
Securities Office
Commissioner of Financial
Institutions
437 Ponce de Leon Avenue
Hato Rey, PR 00918
Mailing: P.O. Box 70324,
San Juan, PR 00936
(809) 751-5606

Rhode Island
Department of Business
Regulation, Securities
Division
Chief Securities Examiner
233 Richmond Street,
Suite 232
Providence, RI 02903-4232
(401) 277-3048

South Carolina
Department of State, Securities
Division
Secretary of State & Securities
Commissioner
1205 Pendleton Street
Edgar Brown Building,
Suite 501
Columbia, SC 29201
(803) 734-1087

South Dakota
Division of Securities
Director
910 East Sioux Avenue
Pierre, SD 57501
(605) 773-4823

Tennessee
Department of Commerce and
Insurance, Securities
Division
Commissioner of Commerce and
Insurance
500 James Robertson Parkway,
6th Floor
Volunteer Plaza
Nashville, TN 37219
(615) 741-2947

Texas
State Securities Board
Securities Commissioner
P.O. Box 13167
Capitol Station
Austin, TX 78711-3167
(512) 474-2233

Utah
Department of Commerce, Utah
Division of Securities
Director
P.O. Box 45802
Salt Lake City, UT 84145
(801) 530-6600

Vermont
Department of Banking &
Insurance, Securities Division
Commissioner of Banking and
Insurance
120 State Street
Montpelier, VT 05602
(802) 828-3420

Virginia
Division of Securities and Retail
Franchising
State Corporation Commission
Director
P.O. Box 1197
Richmond, VA 23209
(804) 786-7751

Washington
Department of Licensing
Business & Professions
Administration
Securities Division
Administrator
P.O. Box 648
Olympia, WA 98504
(206) 753-6928

West Virginia
State Auditor's Office, Securities
Division
State Auditor & Commissioner of
Securities
State Capitol Building
Charleston, WV 25305

Wisconsin
Office of Commissioner of
  Securities
Commissioner
P.O. Box 1768
111 West Wilson Street
Madison, WI 53701
(608) 266-3433

Wyoming
Secretary of State, Securities
  Division
Secretary of State & Securities
  Commissioner
State Capitol Building
Cheyenne, WY 82002-0020
(307) 777-7370

Chapter 14

INDUSTRY FORECASTS

INDEX OF INDUSTRY FORECASTS

Each industry's Standard Industrial Classification (SIC) Code, where applicable, is noted in parentheses.

Source: U.S. Industrial Outlook, U.S. Department of Commerce, Washington, D.C.

14.2 INDUSTRIAL FORECASTS: LONG-TERM PROSPECTS OF SELECTED INDUSTRIES

Advanced Ceramics

During the next 10 to 15 years, major growth in market share is expected for advanced ceramics products in end-use applications such as cutting tools, bearings, and bioceramics. Beyond that period, advanced ceramics are likely to be used for automotive turbine engines and diesel and military components.

Aerospace

Increasing shipments of large commercial aircraft, spurred in part by the gradual retirement of older planes, should bring a gradual increase in profit margins for the aerospace sector. Cuts in defense spending, however, will have a dampening effect on aerospace companies that rely heavily on military contracts. Assuming continuing improvements in U.S. aerospace technology and open markets overseas, the aerospace industry should remain strong, with an average annual real growth rate of 3 percent through 1995.

Agricultural Chemicals

Nitrogenous fertilizer product shipments are expected to grow about 1 percent per year. While the United States will continue to lead in world phosphate supply and consumption, the U.S. market share will drop as Morocco continues to exploit its own rich phosphate resources. The biggest immediate challenges facing the pesticides industry, the other main agricultural chemical sector, are questions of food safety, which have become a growing political issue, and a negative environmental image.

The world market for pesticides should grow about 2.5 to 3 percent per year, while the U.S. pesticide market is expected to grow 1 percent over the next five years.

Air-Conditioning, Refrigeration, and Heating Equipment

In terms of real growth, the industry is expected to attain positive average annual growth of 2.6 percent into the mid-1990s. Developmental research and application testing for substitute refrigerants, stepped-up equipment maintenance, and recovery and reclamation of refrigerants will be of the highest priority as use of chlorofluorocarbon refrigerants is phased out due to environmental concerns. Meanwhile, ongoing advances in electric motors, compressors, and heat-exchanger technology will enable the industry to meet federally mandated conservation requirements. Foreign control of U.S. manufactured products will increase as foreign companies increase their investments in U.S. manufacturing facilities. U.S. companies, however, will continue to expand their overseas production in the European Community and the Pacific Rim.

Airline Industry

The airline industry's profits and losses track periods of growth and recession in the nation's economy. The industry has now entered a new phase of the deregulation process—globalization. This, combined with other free market movements around the world, could lead to creation of multinational megacarriers. The race is now on among the world's carriers to see which of them can put together the most effective global system.

Commercial carriers will likely continue to expand their present hub systems and to develop new secondary hubs and medium and small airports.

Despite a projected period of slow growth in the early part of the decade, the airline industry will resume its growth into the next century.

Alcoholic Beverages

The adverse consequences of the 1991 tax increases and slowing domestic economy are likely to have far-reaching consequences on the U.S. alcoholic beverage industry. Furthermore, health and social concerns, which have somewhat depressed demand, are not likely to abate in the next few years. The industry is thus predicted to decline between 0.03 and 0.06 percent annually during the first half of the decade.

Aluminum

The domestic aluminum industry will continue to modernize and to emphasize value-added mill products. Despite many plans for new capacity construction abroad, supply and demand should remain in relative equilibrium into the early 1990s. U.S. aluminum shipments are expected, therefore, to increase at a compound annual rate of about 3 percent throughout this period. Aluminum's recyclability will continue to ensure its demand in the canning industry, and advances in engine science and product packaging suggest that aluminum composite materials and new types of aluminum packaging will become commercially successful.

Apparel

The industry will face both challenges and opportunities in the years ahead. The overriding challenge stems from the intensely competitive environment within the U.S. apparel industry and the need to anticipate how best to attract the interest of today's sophisticated consumers. Opportunities will include anticipated demographic changes. The fastest popoulation growth is expected in the over 45 age group, which typically has rising income and high consumption rates and is therefore a key element in the growth of demand for apparel. Manufacturers whose strategies best integrate the elements of manufacturing costs, technology, marketing, and flexibility will meet with the greatest success.

Artificial Intelligence

Entering the 1990s, artificial intelligence (AI) is expected to become commonly used in desktop computing to solve major strategic problems in various businesses. The AI hardware and software environment of the future will feature expert systems tools on a broad spectrum of equipment, integrated and networked throughout organizations with existing computers and databases. AI users will find AI hardware and software more compact, powerful, economical, portable, and easier to use. The cumulative results of the increased use of AI technologies promise to affect profoundly the competitiveness of the U.S. industry in the future. Neural networks, emerging from the research stage, will combine with such radical developments as fuzzy logic, creating powerful new tools to help U.S. businesses compete more effectively in the marketplace.

Automotive Parts and Accessories

The continuing internationalization of this industry has important long-term consequences for all U.S. auto parts firms. Pressures from foreign competition will keep domestic parts firms striving to maximize efficiency, hold down prices, and improve product quality. Not only will the competition continue to be unyielding, but industry customers will expect more from their suppliers than in the past. Quality is an industry priority, and more attention to design, research, and development is expected from parts firms. The firms that survive this major industry restructuring will be those that recognize and act on these challenges.

Biotechnology

By the early 1990s, the market value of new biotechnology-derived products should reach $4 to $5 billion, and by the early twenty-first century, the market could be worth $15 to $40 billion. During this time, some of the 80-odd biotechnology-derived drugs and vaccines now in research and testing may be approved. Improved livestock could appear on the market by the late 1990s, biosensors by the year 2000, genetically engineered plants and microorganisms by the mid-1990s, and genetically engineered bacteria by the early 1990s. The potential sales of these products will vary widely, depending on their effectiveness, quality, safety, and uses, as well as on competitive factors.

Book Publishing

A positive set of demographic, economic, and technological trends should help the U.S. book publishing industry achieve annual shipments growth averaging 3.5 percent—adjusted for price increases—through 1995. Publishers' output should be aided by changes in technology, improved distribution patterns, and new product developments. More widespread use of low-cost desktop publishing and electronic editing systems should increase U.S. title output, and improvements in computer ordering systems, linking publishers, wholesalers, and retailers, will make possible more efficient distribution of these titles to bookstores. Publishers will make increased use of tapes, computer discs, and other media as alternatives to printing on paper.

Bottled and Canned Soft Drinks

Between 1991 and 1995, the inflation-adjusted value of bottled and canned soft drink industry shipments is expected to increase 1.5 to 2.0 percent a year. A slowly growing population will provide fewer new consumers, and demographic shifts—especially a rising elderly population—will also affect consumption, as people over 45 consume fewer bottled and canned soft drinks. Franchise companies are likely to increase their company-owned and -operated bottling networks, which will increase profits and result in added competitive pressure on other brands.

Cement

Expectations are for record levels of cement requirements in the next decade, driven by the need for renovation and repair work and, to a lesser extent, new construction. The U.S. infrastructure issue is tied to national domestic and international competitiveness. Without considerable capacity additions, and none are currently under way, the domestic market will likely rely more on foreign cement. If that happens, prices will be determined increasingly by foreign suppliers.

Coal

U.S. coal production is expected to increase by 1.5 percent a year through 1995, with the most rapid growth concentrated in low-sulfur Western coal and the slowest growth in high-sulfur Midwest output. The growth in utility demand for coal is expected to be slower in the next five years than it has been in the last five years. In absolute terms, however, coal consumption will continue to rise as new coal-fired plants are used more intensively. Coal exports, however, are expected to increase only marginally in the next few years because of oversupply in the world market. Increased output of Australian coal, for instance, will probably reduce U.S. exports to the Far East.

Coatings and Adhesives

Advanced and specialty coatings will continue to be in demand for the forseeable future and account for a higher percentage of industry sales than in the past. Demand for all major types of coatings required by the reindustrialization of Eastern Europe will provide U.S. firms with numerous direct investment and joint venture opportunities. Foreign investment in the U.S. industry does not show any signs of slowing down and will probably continue.

Commercial Banking

The evolution of electronic technology in the form of electronic funds transfer (EFT) will continue to affect every aspect of the financial services industry. Bank customer use of EFT is mainly concentrated on automated teller machines (ATMs), but point-of-sale (POS) technology is the natural outgrowth of these systems. Such technology permits retail customers to pay for goods and services by using a computerized method to debit their bank accounts. Closer cooperation among commercial banks, other depository institutions, and retail merchants will be required in order to achieve uniform standards, lower costs to customers, and improved security in these potentially popular systems. Home banking might also grow, especially if tied in to other services such as bill paying, financial planning services, home shopping, airline reservations, electronic mail, and educational and entertainment programs.

Commercial banks are also trying to expand into the securities industry. The Federal Reserve has allowed some institutions to participate in this area via holding companies on a restricted basis. The next few years will probably see increased lobbying by the banking industry to loosen further regulations barring banks from acting as brokers and underwriting corporate debt.

Meanwhile bank failures will continue to be a source of major concern as overextended institutions file for bankruptcy. Even the healthiest banks will likely face some financial difficulties in the coming decade.

Commercial Printing

The continued attractiveness of the U.S. printed product as an advertising and informational vehicle should permit the printing industry to sustain average annual shipments growth of 3.5 percent—adjusted for price increases—through 1995. Changing patterns of U.S. advertising—with less emphasis on building a product's brand awareness and stronger emphasis on supporting sales promotion—may lead to reduced revenue opportunities for magazine printers. These trends will, however, increase shipments by printers of catalogs, direct mail materials and advertising inserts.

Computer Professional Services

This industry sector should achieve average annual growth rates in current dollar revenues approaching $85 billion. Computer training and consulting will continue to gain market shares. Acquisition and use of computers by those who are marginally computer literate will increase and will continue to reconfigure the professional services market. Computer and telecommunications services represent the infrastructure of the information age. The growing importance of service industries will increase dependence on this infrastructure. Providers of computer professional services have a very bright future.

Construction Machinery

U.S. construction machinery industry shipments are expected to grow at about 2.3 percent during the 1991–1995 period. Along with new construction, a growing market for remodeling existing homes and office buildings is anticipated. Furthermore, public works construction is likely to be a large market segment assuring growth for the U.S. construction machinery industry. Highway and bridge repair will continue to provide a major source of market demand, as will the construction of new power plants and water supply facilities.

Because the industry tends to market its products globally, many large manufacturers have subsidiaries in primary foreign markets. Through effective worldwide distribution and service, product improvements, and a reputation for quality products, the United States will remain a leader in sales of construction machinery.

Consumer Electronics
Shipments of consumer electronics are expected to increase moderately at an estimated annual rate of 3 percent into the mid-1990s. For U.S. companies in this field, the outlook is not promising, except in niche areas such as large-screen television sets and high-quality loudspeakers. Import, export, and domestic production decisions in the consumer electronics field will be made more and more by foreign-owned companies during this period, unless new forces enter the market in such areas of advanced technology as high-definition television and recordable compact discs. Yet prospects are dim that any such advances will be transformed into domestically designed and produced goods, since the United States is no longer a supplier of many components vital to the production of electronics items. Research and development may also be constrained now that the largest forces in the market are controlled by interests outside the United States.

Copper
In the coming decade, U.S. consumption of copper is expected to grow at an annual rate of 2 percent, while worldwide, it will increase at an annual rate of 2.7 percent. The advent of fiber optic telecommunication cable originally appeared to threaten copper's long term prospects. In fact, however, the use of fiber optics has actually created additional demand for copper wire, which carries the electrical charge that generates the light carrying the fiber optic signal.

Corrugated and Solid Fiber Boxes
The outlook for the corrugating industry in the early 1990s is for a 2.2 percent annual rate of growth. Exports of corrugated products are forecast to increase at a fairly steady rate of growth in both tonnage and value. While Mexico and Canada will continue as the principal foreign markets, sales of U.S. corrugated products to the Caribbean Basin are also expected to show significant growth over the forecast period. Corrugated products will continue to be under market pressure from flexible plastics, but corrugated producers will easily continue to hold their dominant packaging market share. Principal growth areas are expected

to be shipping containers used as retail point-of-purchase displays for paper and allied products, sporting goods and novelty items, and food products.

Cosmetics

The value of cosmetics industry shipments is predicted to increase an average of 4 percent a year through the early 1990s. The cosmetics and fragrance industry is becoming increasingly multinational and international in scope, and competition will intensify as the number of companies shrinks. On the positive side, however, the expansion of two wage earner households will tend to increase personal spending for health and beauty aids. The growing importance of skin care products for the prevention of aging will enhance the sales of skin care products.

Crude Petroleum and Natural Gas

In the aftermath of the Persian Gulf War, the outlook for the U.S. crude petroleum and natural gas industries remains uncertain, although prices seem to have stabilized for the short term. Reserves of natural gas are large, however, and gas is projected to be the fastest-growing source of energy in the next decade. Gas contains less carbon and suphur than oil, which makes it a cleaner burning fuel. Eventually, the transportation sector may be using natural gas to meet more stringent emissions restraints and mileage requirements. Electric utilities will contribute substantially to the projected increase in demand for gas. Total U.S. energy production is expected to be somewhat greater in 1995 than it was in 1990.

Dairy Products

Into the mid-1990s, total constant dollar shipments will grow 1 percent a year. Led by demand for Italian types of cheese, the cheese sector should experience a 1.5 percent annual rise, assisted by changing demographic and taste trends. Meanwhile, popular demand for premium ice cream should continue to decline over the next five years. This trend should lead manufacturers of ice cream and frozen desserts to introduce a variety of low-calorie products—adhering to FDA standards of identity—which will generate a 1.3 percent annual growth. For the fluid milk sector, sales of yoghurt, reduced-fat milk, and cottage cheese should assure continuation of the sector's 1 percent annual growth.

Data Processing Services

The U.S. data processing industry is expected to maintain an average annual growth rate of about 16 percent into the mid-1990s, and the facilities management market should reach $45 billion. Consolidation within the industry will continue as firms attempt to maintain or increase their market shares. Electronic data interchange is expected to show phenomenal growth, and more data processintg firms will include the service in their offerings. The revenues of companies that provide electronic data interchange services in the United States are projected to grow by over $1 billion by the mid-1990s.

Electronic Components Other Than Semiconductors
Growth in domestic shipments is anticipated to increase by an average of 5 percent annually in the 1990–1995 period. A continued consolidation of the producer base within each component segment is expected.

In the short term, electron tubes and assorted components like microwave components, switches, and printed circuit assemblies will experience the strongest growth rates. In the ceramics sector, chip capacitators for surface-mount applications should account for 80 percent of shipments by 1995.

Electronic Information Services
Demand for electronic database services is expected to increase at a high rate into the mid-1990s. If no serious downturns affect the economies of industrial countries and telecommunications costs are maintained, the industry will have an average annual growth rate of 20 percent. The audiotex market is expected to grow to $3 billion by 1993. The market for CD-ROM products is projected to reach $1.2 billion. During the 1990s, businesses will consider many electronic information services strategic rather than luxury services. U.S. firms will face increased competition from European and Japanese firms in the delivery of electronic database services. The European Community, for instance, has developed an ambitious plan to establish a European information services industry to compete with the United States. To counter this development, U.S. companies are forming strategic alliances in Europe and in Japan to protect their positions and to take advantage of increased business opportunities.

Equipment Leasing
The next three to five years will see a modest growth in equipment leasing. Historically, growth in leasing has depended on overall equipment investment. Leasing will continue to be most attractive in the high-tech areas, though there will be opportunities in other sectors as well.

Growth will be fragmented, depending on the specific market, lease product, and transaction size. Providing superior or different services and taking more risk will be a strategic option for the more entrepreneurial lessors. Because leasing has become a truly global industry, U.S. companies in this sector will face competition from foreign concerns. The global market, however, offers much opportunity for U.S. firms to expand their activities.

Fabricated Structural Metal
Production of fabricated structural metal will decline for the foreseeable future, reflecting the chronic low level of new construction of office

buildings, multifamily housing, and highway bridges. Not before these markets improve, probably in the mid-1990s, will shipments start to grow.

Farm Machinery

The need for farm machinery will increase as the world progresses toward production of sufficient sustenance for its nations. The traditional U.S. share of the global market will fall, however, as both developed and developing countries expand local production of farm machinery. The fact that some foreign products are technologically more advanced than their U.S. counterparts will accelerate loss of U.S. producers' shares of the market. Large, well-managed, and innovative U.S. companies will survive, while others may drop by the wayside. In the next 5 to 25 years, government policies, good domestic growing weather, and poor weather in competing countries could coincide to produce 2 to 5 years of rapid growth. Reversal could follow just as easily.

Foundry Industry

Long-term prospects for the foundry industry will depend on a number of factors. From a technological standpoint, new casting technology will stimulate sales of more intricate castings. Lighter weight castings reduce shipping costs and have superior weight-to-strength ratios. Offering stronger, lighterweight, higher-value products may also enhance the industry's future exports.

When machining is required, CAD/CAM (computer-aided design/computer-aided manufacturing) systems, already in use in many foundries, will find increased application. Precise machining adds further value to the castings, resulting in a significant increase in the value per ton of castings shipped. While gross tons shipped may decline, value per ton will increase over the long term. Automation in foundry process technology, especially coremaking and general materials handling, will continue to reduce foundry labor intensity and therefore costs. Finally, more cooperative research and development, joint venture projects, and further industry restructuring in the form of mergers and acquisitions are likely to occur.

Glass Containers

The glass container industry is expected to grow at an average constant dollar rate of 1 percent annually during the early 1990s. The end-use markets for glass will become more concentrated because of declines in the general packaging category: most glass containers will be used for food, beverages, and products that require containers with characteristics inherent in glass or a "premium" image. If state legislation stipulating mandatory recycling rates becomes more widespread, glass will benefit from a decrease in plastic's market share. Food and beverage products that are packaged in multilayer plastics would be the most likely candidates to convert back to glass.

Health and Medical Services

Health care expenditures will rise at an average annual rate of 12 to 15 percent into the mid-1990s. Hospitals will undoubtedly increase their fees to make up for past losses. Managed health care organizations will also increase premiums to continue to provide quality care. The health care situation, meanwhile, will continue to change as more managed care organizations enter the market, hospitals and nursing homes affiliate with one another, and other companies enter the home care business. Hospitals will have to develop more aggressive marketing strategies to compete with the growing number of managed care organizations. A number of nonprofit health care organizations needing corporate reorganization may end up becoming for-profit subsidiaries. The proliferation of for-profit enterprises in the health care industry may weaken the professional bond between patient and physician.

Home Entertainment

Home video rentals and purchases should expand by approximately 6 percent through 1993, while VCR sales can be expected to level off at 9.5 million to 10 million annually. Although the industry will continue to benefit from the popularity of U.S. feature films, any major increases in viewership are likely to occur only with the advent of new, cinema-quality video equipment that takes advantage of digital technology and fiber optic cable. A growing population of U.S. viewers who prefer home entertainment should be a natural stimulus for such innovations. U.S. home video sales abroad will be heavily influenced by the ability of the U.S. Government to obtain the cooperation of foreign governments in combating video piracy.

The cable industry's profit margins will likely continue to narrow through the early 1990s, particularly in view of the threat of rate caps and a market that is becoming saturated. Overall revenue growth should equal 5 to 8 percent, while an estimated 60 percent of U.S. television households will be wired for cable by 1993.

Household Appliances

Product shipments are expected to increase at a real compound annual rate of 1 percent during the next 5 years. The appliance industry is a mature industry with replacements accounting for most shipments. New housing, which historically has accounted for approximately 20 to 25 percent of shipments, is expected to account for a smaller share in the 1990s due to fewer housing starts. In addition, refrigerator sales will suffer to the extent that chlorofluorocarbon replacement results in higher costs to consumers. Furthermore, appliance products are mature, showing little difference from one manufacturer to another. Nor are there any radically new products to stimulate sales. The latest innovative product to become widely accepted was the microwave oven.

Household Furniture
Household furniture will have a compound annual growth rate of 2.7 to 3 percent from 1992 to 1995. The demographic outlook is favorable for the furniture industry: By 1995, over 31 million consumers, more than 12 percent of the population, will be between 45 to 54 years old and in their peak earning years. Persons in their peak earning years often purchase higher quality furniture, frequently replacing items bought earlier in life.

U.S. exports of household furniture will continue to grow over the next five years as well, particularly to Canada, where the Free Trade Agreement will have eliminated all bilateral tariffs by the end of 1992.

International Engineering and Construction
Industry success early in the decade does not ensure U.S. designers and constructors will maintain their edge in the international marketplace indefinitely. Opportunities clearly exist in the international marketplace for firms possessing the ability to promote and market their services effectively. Success for U.S. international design houses and contractors will depend on superior technology and top-quality service.

The international design construction market will most likely continue to expand well into the next century. Export markets will remain important to the U.S. construction industry. Provided U.S. firms continue their strong efforts to develop these markets and build on their present successes, they may look forward to full participation in a dynamically expanding international design and construction market.

Laboratory Instruments and Apparatus
The laboratory instruments and apparatus industry should experience stable growth at about a 4 percent constant dollar rate through 1995. Moderate growth in the economy and in capital and R&D expenditures, combined with increased emphasis on environmental monitoring, energy conservation, and new materials development, should stimulate domestic markets. The need for new technological approaches to meet the requirements of the pharmaceutical and biomedical industries will also support growth. Exports will continue to provide a significant share in shipments of laboratory instruments, even though U.S. manufacturers will encounter challenges from foreign competitors.

Lead
U.S. consumption of refined lead is forecast to grow around 1.8 percent per year, from 1.18 million metric tons in 1989 to about 1,385,000 metric tons by the mid-1990s. Storage batteries will continue to be the largest end-use sector, growing in significance as other end uses contract or remain flat. Several new uses for lead show long-term potential, including use as a stabilizing agent in road asphalt and asphalt roofing shingles.

Life Insurance

Major changes in the market may drastically alter the nature of the industry. Competition for premiums will intensify. New competition will come from other financial service firms, such as banks, which will expand their sales and underwriting capabilities if legal barriers fall. Insurers will diversify and expand their product lines. Life insurance companies will have to reduce costs in order to remain competitive. The stability and solvency of the industry could be affected by the growing incidence of AIDS, further weakness in real estate markets, and an inordinate amount of high-risk junk bonds in some insurers' portfolios. The industry could be headed for a period of consolidation as noncompetitive companies are acquired.

Logging Operators

Log shipments could decline another 5 percent by the end of the period. However, much will depend on what happens in the Pacific Northwest. Harvest levels of timber from federal lands could decline significantly if logging is prohibited in old-growth forests located there. Meanwhile, domestic end-use markets should stabilize. Exports, at least over the near term, will remain at or near their present level. Indications are that the private sector could make up most of the volume that new legislation may restrict from export.

Lumber

The U.S. lumber industry is faced with some serious problems over the next few years. Tight log supplies, decreasing housing starts, and a sluggish economy will contribute to a slowing down in this industry over the next five years as will continued environmental pressures. Between 1985 and 1990 the industry grew at an average rate of about 4 percent. Over the next five years, it is expected to grow at an average annual rate of 1 percent. If concessions are gained as part of the Uruguay Round of the General Agreement on Tariffs and Trade (GATT), they could stimulate increased exports of many of this industry's products.

Machine Tools

U.S. machine tool shipments are expected to expand by 3 percent a year over the next five years. An imminent shortage of skilled labor heads the list of issues that will have a significant impact on this industry. This problem will force all the metalworking industries to invest in more productive manufacturing facilities, including automated production equipment. The globalization of markets has led to more outsourcing—the production of components in newly industrialized countries. Furthermore, the U.S. industry must tackle the issue of product liability reform: Currently, 25 percent of U.S. machine tool manufacturers have no product liability insurance. For these firms, a single product liability could bring bankruptcy.

Management, Consulting, and Public Relations Services
Management, consulting, and public relations will continue to be an expanding industry and should be able to maintain significant growth into the next decade. Increased use of high-technology equipment and systems will boost productivity. The foreign market will keep growing at a rapid pace, although U.S. firms will face increased competition from European and Asian companies.

Meat and Poultry Products
By 1995, the value of shipments by the meat and poultry products industry is expected to grow 1 to 2 percent annually, adjusted for price changes. Exports should have a greater increase, 9 percent a year, to $7 billion. The Pacific Rim will continue to be a major export market. By middecade, there will be 25 percent more meat-and-poultry processing plants than meat-only plants, and by 1995, poultry products should account for 26 percent of total industry shipments. Total U.S. per capita consumption of poultry as a percentage of total meat consumed will increase from 42 to 44 percent.

Metal Cans
The metal can industry is expected to grow at an average annual rate of 3 percent, measured in constant dollars, during the early to mid-1990s. This moderate growth will be sustained because the can is reliable, cost efficient, and profitable at the retail level. Metal cans for food and beverage will continue to enjoy modest demand because of the nature of the products packaged and the characteristics of the container. Aluminum will be the preferred package among brewers, bottlers, and distributors because of the product's compactness, adaptability to high-speed filling lines, light weight, low distribution costs, and high operating profit per packaged ounce. Food staples, excepting juice products, will continue to be packaged primarily in steel, as this is a mature and cost-efficient technology. There is the potential for stronger growth for steel in the food category during this period, as microwavable metal containers challenge plastic, paper, and composite packaging forms.

Metals and Materials Mining
The trend toward joint ventures in this industry is likely to accelerate. The number and scope of environmental studies required for new mining operations will continue to increase, further delaying the time between exploration and the commencement of mining, increasing costs in the process. Both the European economic unification and the U.S.-Canada free trade agreement offer mining companies opportunities for new markets. At the same time, however, international competition will increase to new levels as more and more companies operate worldwide and adopt global strategies.

Mining Machinery

The U.S. mining machinery industry will grow at an annual rate of about 2.3 percent into the mid-1990s. Mining equipment demand will be supported by the continued need for basic mined products such as iron ore and strategic materials, including titanium for high performance applications. Increased demand for advanced materials—such as metal composites—that are formed from mined ores and demand from less developed countries should stimulate growth in the U.S. mining industry. Recycling of metal products could slow the demand for mining equipment in some regions. The U.S. mining machinery market will also be strongly affected by federal, state, and local regulations controlling land use, pollution, and land reclamation.

Motion Pictures

Motion picture theaters are competing successfully with the home video format and should remain an important source of entertainment revenue throughout the world. With production starts continuing at adequate levels and ticket prices edging up, box office receipts are expected to recover from the current downturn and begin growing at an average of 1.5 percent through 1994.

Music

Revenues of the prerecorded music industry are expected to grow at an average annual rate of about 4 percent through the first half of the 1990s. Technological developments promise to provide better quality and contribute to industry growth in the long term. On the other hand, the future of the digital audio tape (DAT) machine remains in doubt. Even if the disagreements about DAT are resolved, the medium may never become popular. For many consumers, cassette tapes provide adequate quality at a lower price. In addition, other formats may pass DAT by, such as a recordable, erasable compact disc. This proliferation of formats may restrain sales of hardware and recordings. The influence of these new technologies on industry revenues remains difficult to predict.

Mutual Fund Industry

The phenomenal growth of mutual fund investing of the 1980s will not be sustained. The industry anticipates a slower but steady expansion. The graying of the baby boom generation bodes well for financial service firms that can assist people to save and accumulate capital for their retirement years.

Although there probably will be fewer new products, many mutual funds will repackage their products to appeal to specific markets. Furthermore, the distinction between load and no-load funds is becoming increasingly blurred. Some load funds are reducing sales charges in response to the demands of a better informed and more cost-conscious investing public, while some no-load funds are actually including charges. Distribution methods will also be changed in order to make investment easier. Finally, by the mid-1990s, if regulatory issues can be settled, fund sales may become truly international, with domestic investment companies marketing funds abroad and foreign concerns selling to U.S. investors.

Newspaper Publishing

During the next five years, newspaper industry receipts are expected to grow at a yearly rate of 1 to 1.5 percent in constant dollars. The growth rate for newspapers will likely trail the rate for the total printing and publishing industry sector. Faced with aggressive competition from other media, telecommunication, and entertainment sources, newspapers will need to mount stronger customer service and marketing programs to retain or increase their advertising and circulation bases. Industry analysts predict that, during the 1990s, competition for advertising revenue will be even tougher than it was in the previous decade. Although newspapers' major competitors will still be television, cable, radio, direct mail, Yellow Pages, and magazines, these will be joined by other media and new types of selling.

In addition to meeting these domestic challenges, the larger U.S. newspaper companies may give more consideration to investing in foreign newspapers and other media as the media and telecommunications industries increasingly become global markets. Many of these companies already own broadcast media properties outside the United States.

Nickel

U.S. primary nickel consumption will increase at a rate of 0.6 percent annually to about 110,000 metric tons in 1995. Promising new markets continue to cluster in commercial building construction; environmental control and waste treatment equipment; aerospace components; machinery and equipment for urban and regional transportation systems; processing equipment for petroleum, plastics, and higher-quality steel; and machinery for electrical power generation. Other than Glenbrook Nickel's possible reopening of the Nickel Mountain mine, no domestic nickel mine production is expected over the next five years.

Numerical Controls

During the next five years, numerical control (NC) production will grow by an average rate of 5 percent a year in real terms. Quality and productivity are the key to continued competitiveness of U.S. firms. NC technology has improved the accuracies of machines and permitted skilled machinists to operate multiple units or even multiple cells. Nonetheless, U.S. firms must continue to improve the ratio of automated machinery to total equipment stock if the United States is to regain market share lost to foreign industry.

NC builders have markedly improved their use of new computer technology. Furthermore, research and development continues on the "next generation controller" both here and abroad. Furthermore, NC builders have markedly improved their use of recent computer technology. These advances in control technology and NC equipment's growing share of total equipment sold ensure that NC demand will outpace general industrial equipment demand.

Oil Field Machinery

Into the mid-1990s, the U.S. oil field machinery industry will grow at an annual real rate of about 3.4 percent, assuming a long-term rise in oil prices. However, industry shipments could be uneven due to unstable petroleum prices and uncertainties regarding the world supply and demand for petroleum. U.S. regulations controlling the leasing of offshore areas and federal lands will also have a major effect on the level of U.S. oil and natural gas exploration and development. The U.S. petroleum equipment industry will face stronger competition from foreign countries, including the United Kingdom, Germany, France, and Japan. As foreign countries take on a greater role in their petroleum industries, U.S. manufacturers will be encouraged to form joint ventures and licensing agreements with local firms. This will accelerate U.S. technology transfer to foreign markets.

Organic Chemicals

Shipments of organic chemicals are expected to grow at the same rate as the gross national product through 1995. The strength of the U.S. economy, the value of the dollar, and the willingness of overseas producers to export to the United States and accept lower returns than in previous years will largely determine the level of domestic production. Over the long-term, the United States will become more dependent on imports of organic chemicals. Competition with foreign concerns will become increasingly fierce, and prices of U.S. organic chemicals will come under severe pressure. This could lead to a decline in the industry's profitability.

Paper and Paperboard Mills

Expansion in domestic and foreign demand for paper and paperboard is expected over the 1991–1995 period, but growth will be at a more moderate pace. Sales of paper and paperboard will increase roughly 2 percent per year over the forecast period, depending on several economic variables. Unless burdened by a stronger U.S. dollar, domestic manufacturers are cost competitive worldwide and are expected to maintain their share of paper and paperboard sales.

The projected slow growth for the nation's GNP over the next five years will affect the paper and paperboard sectors, which traditionally correlate closely with the performance of the domestic economy. Nonetheless, U.S. paper and board companies have increased their international competitiveness by lowering operating and input costs dramatically over the past five years, making the United States one of the lowest-cost paper producers in the world.

Passenger Cars

The industry can expect further, but slow, growth as long as the economy expands, Competitive pressure from new entrant countries and from new U.S. manufacturers will continue to grow for the foreseeable future, possibly forcing industry restructuring. The increasingly competitive environment will continue to exert pressure on firms to cut costs, improve quality, and identify and exploit market niches. The growing demand for larger and more spacious vehicles suggests that the traditional domestic manufacturers may be able to recover some of the market share lost to the subcompact and compact makers. However, U.S. dominance in the larger-vehicle segment will be threatened to a degree by the imminent introduction of large Japanese luxury cars. This challenge, perhaps the greatest U.S. automakers have ever faced, will determine the nature of the auto market in North America well into the next century.

Periodicals

If, into the mid-1990s, the economy grows an average rate of about 3 percent in constant dollars, magazine industry revenues should grow at an average yearly rate of 1.5 to 3 percent after adjustment for inflation. During this period, magazine publishers will need to focus on providing advertisers with high-quality marketing demographics to demonstrate the advantages of advertising in their magazines. While a great deal of the growth in the magazine industry will come from special interest magazines, some of them are likely to become victims of shakeouts caused by saturation of these special market niches. Cable television could become a significant threat to magazines in the next few years because it targets the same audience as they do. As the domestic market for magazine titles become more crowded, magazine publishers may look for more opportunities to sell their products or engage in joint ventures and licensing arrangements abroad.

Personal Computers

As a result of continual advances in systems and component technology and software development, significantly more powerful, functional, and easy-to-use personal computers will be introduced over the next five years. By 1992, therefore, the U.S. PC market may exhibit higher growth rates as pressure to upgrade to more powerful machines intensifies. By 1995, the performance of an average system should reach at least 50 megahertz (MHz), or 5 times what currently exists. Typical memory capacity will equal 16 megabytes (MB), and access times may fall below 60 nanoseconds with the advent of faster, 16-megabit dynamic random access memory (DRAM) chips. The brisk rate of growth in personal computers will continue as peripherals, software, and networks are developed to take advantage of the availability of faster, more powerful chips.

Petrochemicals

A projected weakening global economy may eventually cause production cutbacks in the petrochemical industry. Reduced production would occur first with privately held petrochemical companies in free market countries; producers in managed economy countries would soon follow. The depth and breadth of any slowdown in petrochemical production and trade cannot be predicted. Furthermore, worldwide concern about global warming and the need to reduce hydrocarbon emissions casts uncertainty over future fuel and feedstock prices.

Petroleum Refining

Environmental constraints pose the most serious challenge to the economic viability of the U.S. refining industry. Transportation fuels are a major focus of pending clean air regulations because they are a major source of pollution in crowded, urban areas. Growing demand for a lighter mix of environmentally suitable refined products, especially unleaded gasoline, will require more processing, thereby straining an already tight downstream capacity. Refiners may be forced to make major adjustments in a short time to meet current levels of demand with products that satisfy as yet undefined legislative criteria. Because stricter environmental controls will pose refinery configuration problems, U.S. refinery output is not likely to increase significantly.

Pharmaceutical Preparations

The value of pharmaceutical shipments is projected to increase 3 to 4 percent a year in constant dollars into the mid-1990s. More direct consumer access to a greater variety of nonprescription drugs could reduce health expenditures by more than $35 billion by the end of the decade. Additional research and development, with emphasis on causes instead of symptoms and on more effective delivery systems, is planned for the next few years. Finally, sales for generic drugs may reach $13.2 billion by 1995, up from $4 billion in 1989.

Photographic Equipment and Supplies

Technological advances and product innovations should stimulate periods of industry growth into the mid-1990s. With a pattern of industry expansions and contractions forecast for the next five years, however, shipments are projected to decline in constant dollars by 3 to 5 percent. Meanwhile, consumer interest in 35mm photography should continue, and moderate growth should be expected in the photofinishing area as well. Finally, manufacturers of digital and full-color copiers will attempt to establish a foothold in the office environment and in photographic/service areas. These machines could also be a key component in the development of multifunctional machines that combine copying, printing, and facsimile.

Plastic Bottles

Because of the solid waste crisis that the country is facing and the growing percentage of such waste that plastic represents, the future prospects of the plastic bottle industry are uncertain. The states or the Congress may press for punitive legislation to ban certain types of plastic and/or particular kinds of containers. Despite that prospect, major conversions from plastic into other materials seem unlikely because the U.S. consumer is accustomed to the safety and convenience provided by plastic. By the end of the five-year period, however, the industry will have begun to overcome many of the problems that have been limiting shipments. The advent of heat-resistant resins that can withstand high temperature processing and provide greater resistance to permeation will fuel movement into the food and "other" beverage category.

Plastics Materials

Overall demand for plastics materials should grow at an annual rate of 2 percent during the early 1990s. The trend toward substituting plastics for traditional materials such as metals, wood, and glass will support this growth. Future developments of new alloys, blends, additives, and composites will foster new applications for plastics materials. The U.S. plastics industry will have to face the challenge of European competition, however, which will increase after the 1992 economic union.

Private Nonresidential Construction

Total private nonresidential construction is likely to decline over the next five years, given high vacancy rates for commercial buildings, continued liquidation of failing thrift institutions, and the relatively modest five-year macroeconomic forecast. The decline will be entirely caused by the slump in commercial construction, however: Industrial, utility, and hospital construction will probably increase during the period. Finally, the need to modernize existing U.S. capital stock, including buildings, will boost the market for repair and renovation work.

Private Residential Construction

Declining home ownership in the 1980s probably represents affordability difficulties more than declining consumer preference for housing, pointing to strong pent-up demand for housing in the 1990s. Nonetheless, homebuilding is expected to grow more slowly than the overall economy through the mid-1990s, while expenditures for home improvement and repair are expected to remain strong throughout the 1990s as the housing stock ages.

Processed Fruits, Vegetables, and Specialties

Into the mid-1990s, the value of shipments by the processed fruit, vegetable, and specialty food industry is expected to increase at a compound annual rate of 1.2 to 2.5 percent, adjusted for price changes. The sales of salad dressings and asceptically packaged juices will start to slow, while frozen breakfast items, low-calorie and ethnic frozen dinners, and other microwavable convenience foods will show growth. But unless it can increase its exports, the canned fruit and vegetable industry will remain sluggish. U.S. processed foods companies will also increase sales through increased exports and joint ventures.

Property/Casualty Insurance

The property/casualty industry will probably face increased competition through the 1990s. Rates for commercial insurance will rise for a couple of years, but this competition will keep them from rising too fast or too far. The prospect for some form of federal regulation will increase, especially if solvency problems grow. The insurance industry will also be affected by how such major problems as escalating health care costs are resolved.

Publicly Owned Construction

Public works construction will continue to increase modestly during the early 1990s, given the macroeconomic forecast of continued economic growth and fairly stable interest rates. Although several state and local governments are undertaking dramatic new infrastructure initiatives, most state and local governments appear unlikely to embark on massive increases in construction spending, and some are scaling back public works spending because of increasing budgetary constraints. For these reasons, maintenance and repair spending will probably increase faster than will new construction spending.

Pulp Mills

Slow, continued growth is expected for the U.S. market pulp industry through 1995, with pulp shipments increasing 2 percent annually over the five-year period. A number of anticipated economic factors will have a positive effect on U.S. pulp producers' market share and profitability, including higher domestic and foreign pulp paper and board demand and a stable U.S. dollar relative to other supplier currencies. Furthermore, the U.S. pulp industry is expected to make further technical advances in its bleaching and pulpmaking capacities, which will keep costs down and profit margins acceptable.

Radio Communication and Detection Equipment

The 1990s hold great promise for improvements in search and navigation technology. Two of the latest developments—advanced phase array radar and laser radar—appear to be the most important and promising. However, the performance of much of the radio equipment and detection equipment industry is highly dependent on defense contracts, and the Defense Department plans to reduce expenditures 25 percent by 1995. New demands in the international defense market could offset a decrease in domestic demand. In the civilian sector, the evolution of the next generation of wireless communications services is likely to generate strong new demand for radio communications equipment over the next 5 to 10 years. Dozens of companies in the United States, Europe, and Japan are investing large sums to develop new types of mobile communications services. Operators, manufacturers, and users will benefit as this market expands to encompass a wider array of price versus performance options. The challenge will be integrating and merging these services into a cost-effective and seamless transmission network.

Railroads (Freight Service)

Modest freight traffic growth is projected for the railroad industry through the early 1990s. Rail tonnage is expected to rise an average of 1 to 1.5 percent a year. Coal is likely to continue to make up close to 40 percent of rail traffic during this period. Railroads' future prospects for attracting bulk commodities and other goods will be affected by their ability to meet competition from other modes of transport. Railroads should be able to hold or improve their traffic base because of (1) improvements in overall efficiency of rail service resulting from mergers, better equipment utilization, and technological innovations and (2) increasing attention to service quality, aggressive marketing, and effective use of railroad-shipper contracts.

Railroads (Passenger Service)

Amtrak passenger-miles have the potential to grow by 2 to 3 percent per year through the early 1990s. Ridership is highly sensitive to economic activity and airline fares, however, so year-to-year fluctuations are likely to occur. Travel times and reliability of service on the Northeast Corridor should continue to improve as the railroad realizes the benefits of long-term improvements in plant and equipment. Amtrak will also maintain its program of tight control over costs in response to the scarcity of federal funds and other pressures on the operating budget.

Retailing

Along with the manufacturing sector, U.S. retailers are undergoing a quiet reorganization of their physical premises and marketing objectives to use capital and manpower more efficiently and to meet consumer requirements. Retailers are trying new means of distribution, including warehouse-type stores and hypermarkets and are employing cable television and computer-assisted technology to sell merchandise. Where nonretailers perceive that different management could improve net profits, they will not hesitate to acquire retailers. Well-managed firms that offer the public a choice of upscale merchandise or good quality wares at a discount price will prosper. With an increasing amount of disposable income available to Americans, enterprising retailers should be richly rewarded at the cash register.

Robotics

The outlook for the robotics industry is promising, with shipments expected to grow 7 percent over the next five years. Despite heavy investment aimed at developing new robotics applications, however, the industry still remains too dependent on orders from the automotive industry. Promising new applications in the revitalized U.S. electronics and appliance industries will emerge after the robotics industry successfully diversifies. The emergence of a secondary market for robotics, coupled with the continuing shortage of U.S. skilled industrial labor, will support continued demand for robotics industry production. The increasing diffusion of robotics products into the U.S. industrial environment will eventualy create a wide customer base capable of supporting a viable and competitive industry.

Rubber Products

Ongoing consolidation in the tire and inner tube industry means that the smaller private label manufacturers will have to cooperate more closely with independent tire dealers and with original equipment manufacturers in order to survive. Furthermore, competition for the lucrative replacement sales market is likely to intensify. In the rubber and plastics footwear industry, shifts in favor of low-cost producers will make it more difficult for U.S. producers to compete in the recreational and athletic markets. Perceived differences in quality will enable certain brands to continue to attract image-conscious consumers regardless of price. Finally, in the rubber and plastics hose and belting industry, growth will be dependent on factors like automobile production and the health of the manufacturing sector as a whole. Competitive pressure from transplant operations and imports in the slow-growth market of the early 1990s will make it difficult for the U.S. industry to compete unless cost-cutting measures are continued.

Savings Institutions

Many observers predict the disappearance of the savings institutions industry within several years. An industry dedicated to housing finance may no longer be necessary because mortgage banking companies can originate residential mortgages, and secondary mortgage market investors will ultimately fund them. On the other hand, savings institutions that have specialized in residential mortgage lending are very profitable and highly solvent. They have a comparative advantage in the origination and holding of mortgage loans, and the secondary mortgage market may not be big enough to fill the void should they cease to exist.

Semiconductor Manufacturing Equipment

The early 1990s will be a period of intense competition in the semiconductor manufacturing equipment industry. U.S. firms must have adequate domestic capital sources such as tax credits and/or subsidies or pooled development/production funds to pursue new technologies. The future of this industry also depends on forging much closer business relations with U.S. device producers. The plethora of joint development contracts between U.S. and Japanese companies is yielding mixed re-sults. While these arrangements provide needed capital infusions, it's questionable whether they have given the U.S. partners any real Japanese market penetration.

Semiconductors and Related Devices

Demand for semiconductors will continue to be driven by the computer, telecommunications, and automotive markets. The use of chip sets and custom devices, such as analog to digital circuits in the automotive industry, is expected to soar. The EC and East Asia will be the fastest growing market for semiconductors from 1990 to 1994, outperforming the domestic U.S. market. Capital expenditure by semiconductor manufacturers is expected to increase most rapidly in the EC from 1991 to 1994, with that region's 20 percent increase outperforming the United States and Japan, both of which will each experience 15 percent growth.

Shipbuilding and Repair

Increasing orders for merchant ships worldwide may provide U.S. first-tier shipyards with some contracts. In addition, there are likely to be increasing opportunities for U.S. shipbuilders in the 1990s as a result of other developments, including the Oil Pollution Act of 1990, the elimination of subsidies for foreign shipbuilders, and a growing demand for replacement of aging ship tonnage. First-tier shipyards are primarily supported by U.S. naval contracts, however, and planned U.S. Navy budget cuts will require cutbacks in active shipbuilding base employment. In second-tier shipyards, the outlook for barge construction should gradually become more favorable during the latter part of the decade. Higher oil prices and possible shortages of petroleum would also stimulate the demand for exploratory drill rigs and support vessels for the offshore oil industry. Sustained demand for the repair and replacement of rigs and support vessels would improve second-tier shipyard employment.

Shoes and Slippers (nonrubber)

Industry production is expected to increase gradually over the next five years. Assembly of footwear from cut and sewn uppers and lowers produced offshore will increase substantially. Weaker firms will continue to close. Stronger companies will consolidate plants and invest in new technology designed to narrow the disparity between U.S. and foreign labor costs. The industry's capacity to respond quickly and effectively to changes in the market at the retail level is improving rapidly. Success in this area is essential to offset partially the lower costs of new Southeast Asian suppliers.

Soaps and Detergents

Real growth in soap and detergent industry product shipments is fore-cast to average 2 to 3 percent a year through the mid-1990s. Heavy-duty liquids will hold about 40 percent of the market, although profit margins will be higher on powdered detergents. The greatest industry opportunities will be in specialty chemicals that can replace phosphates and add water-softening and other properties to existing detergent formulas.

Software
By 1995, the world packaged software market could approach $100 billion, with the U.S. and European software markets in the forefront. The Japanese market should also show significant growth, due to the increasing competitiveness of Japanese suppliers and the continued shift of users toward packaged solutions and away from custom software.

Steel Mill Products
The demand for steel mill products is likely to be relatively stable over the next five years. The long-term decline in steel consumption appears to have lessened, and steel may be better able to maintain—or in some cases improve its market share. The problem of overcapacity that so plagued the industry during the mid-1980s does not seem likely to be a concern in the next decade. Most developed countries substantially downsized their steel industries and will likely continue reducing capacity. In developing countries, increases in capacity are more likely to keep in balance with demand. As a result, operating rates are expected to remain much higher than during the mid-1980s.

Supercomputers
Supercomputers with large numbers of processors will continue to make their way into the mainstream of the industry, dependent upon the ability of companies to develop software applications. Those systems defined as moderately parallel, having around 25 processors or less, will maintain their superior performance capability as multiuse systems and be especially successful as workhorses at the high end of the market.

Surgical and Medical Instruments
Into the mid-1990s, industry shipments of medical and surgical instruments are forecast to increase about 5 percent annually (in 1987 dollars). Domestically, medical devices used in infection control of contagious diseases are expected to plateau after the sharp growth in the late 1980s. The market may be rekindled if Congress approves a bill providing $4 billion to health care institutions for treating AIDS patients. Disposal of medical waste will remain a primary concern of medical instruments and supplies companies. While the industry prefers to resolve the problem of solid waste disposal with an integrated and comprehensive system for waste processing and disposal, states are focusing on legislation requiring manufacturers to use biodegradable plastics to reduce the large and growing volume of solid waste.

Surgical Appliances and Supplies
Industry shipments of surgical appliances and supplies are projected to

rise at an annual constant dollar rate of 8 to 20 percent into the mid-1990s. The changing health care environment will strongly affect this medical equipment industry. Alternate site facilities, spearheaded by immediate care and ambulatory care centers, will continue to grow as a source for primary care at the expense of the traditional doctor's office and hospital emergency room. Orthopedic supplies and basic patient care items will benefit most from this change.

Telephone and Telegraph Equipment

Overall, telephone and telegraph equipment industry shipments are expected to grow slowly but steadily during the early 1990s at an annual rate of 2 to 3 percent (in constant dollars). Shipments of customer premises equipment are forecast to increase at an annual rate of 2 percent. During the same period, employment in the telecommunications equipment industry is expected to decline slightly. Low-technology products and technologically outdated equipment will continue to be phased out; data communications equipment, integrated voice data workstations, and protocol converters will experience fairly strong growth rates. Local service providers will stress their abilities to meet customers' needs for low-cost, enhanced services available through simultaneous voice/data transmission capabilities. Increased competition for limited product and service markets will reduce profitability of companies and lead to acquisitions and mergers among companies specializing in similar product areas.

Titanium

The outlook for titanium mill products depends primarily upon demand from the military and to a lesser extent the commercial aircraft industries, which will accout for 70–75 percent of titanium consumption through the mid-1990s. However, other industrial uses of titanium are expected to become more important, with a growth rate of 5 to 10 percent. Prices for the metal will remain soft, which will help titanium compete with alternative materials, such as advanced composites. The major challenge for the industry during this period will be to enlarge the nonaerospace sector of the marketplace.

Travel Services

Travel and tourism should show steady growth during the 1990s. Even though U.S. population growth will be slower in the 1990s than in previous decades, qualitative changes in the U.S. population will be favorable to travel. These include the aging of the population, the increase in labor force participation among women, smaller families, delayed childbearing, and higher levels of education and income. Meanwhile, increasing competition will promote greater industry specialization.

Trucking

No dramatic change is forecast for the trucking industry. Instead, trends already under way will intensify. Competition pervades the industry's various subsectors, not only from within the industry, but from railroads in the vast truckload subsector and from small-package and package-express carriers in the smaller less than truckload market. This competition will produce an industry increasingly characterized by computer and telecommunications links, larger trucks, more sophisticated global carriers and shippers, and blurred modal distinctions.

Trucks

Overall class 1 and 2 truck sales will advance modestly for the next several years, mirroring developments in the passenger car industry. Numerous new product offerings, coupled with increased availability of established models, will generate more competition in the compact passenger van market. Meanwhile, because of their novelty, sales of all sport-utility vehicles could increase 20 percent by 1992. The market share of imported compact light trucks is expected to decline further as domestic manufacturers become more competitive in price and quality.

Sales of medium to heavy trucks, especially in classes 3 and 4, will increase rapidly as their usefulness for local delivery and service industries becomes more recognized. Class 8 manufacturers are pursuing major programs to improve truck design in order to increase profitability. Nonetheless, the long-distance trucking industry is grappling with depressed profits, increasing fuel costs, and shortages of both drivers and repair technicians.

Water Transportation (Deep-sea Foreign Transportation)

Total U.S. containerized trade is expected to grow at an annual rate of 3.7 percent through 1995. However, capacity is expected to increase more rapidly than trade because of continuing world orders for large new containerships. Excess capacity will exist on the most profitable routes and put pressures on rates as operators try to capture and maintain market share. U.S. liner imports are expected to grow about 3.8 percent annually, and exports are expected to grow about 3.7 percent. As supply and demand for world bulk carrier trades reach equilibrium, conditions will continue to improve. U.S. flag bulk vessels are not generally active in the international market, except on subsidized routes, because of their high operating costs.

Water Transporation (Domestic Shipping)

The long-term outlook for the domestic liner industry is tied closely to that of the national economy, although added capacity in the Hawaiian liner trade is likely to put downward pressure on freight rates in this service. Meanwhile, current indications are that demand for domestic tankers will begin to fall in the 1990s. Long-term prospects for Great Lakes shipping depends on the level of shipments of iron ore, coal, and limestone carried by U.S.-flag lakers and the continuing prosperity of the regional steel industry. Average traffic on the inland waterways is projected to grow 1 to 3 percent by the end of the century. The commodities with the highest expected annual growth rates are industrial and agricultural chemicals, farm products, and coal. New barge construction may be needed to satisfy expected demand, but operators must manage their programs to avoid overbuilding.

Workstations

The U.S. workstation industry can expect significant challenges to both its market and technological leadership over the next five years. At the low end of the market, it will face growing competition from personal computer suppliers and Asian clones with comparable processing power, memory, and graphics capabilities. In the more advanced workstation market, U.S. manufacturers will have to contend with large, vertically integrated Japanese companies. The ability of U.S. firms to protect intellectual property rights, provide customers with better service and support, and keep the lead in software development will determine whether they remain dominant in the workstation industry.

X-ray and Electromedical Equipment

Into the mid-1990s, industry shipments of X-ray apparatus and tubes are projected to grow at a compound annual rate of 3 to 4 percent. Hospital demand for X-ray and related products runs in a cyclical pattern, as older products become obsolete or are substantially upgraded. Sales of traditional cancer therapy products, including those for chemotherapy and radiation therapy, may decline as cheaper products with less severe side effects are developed. Industry shipments for electromedical equipment are expected to grow at a compound annual rate of 6 percent. Domestically, demographics will drive the electromedical industry, as the aging population utilizes a large share of electrodiagnostic and therapeutic devices. Internationally, competition will remain fierce. European and Japanese competitors are becoming increasingly adept at introducing new electromedical products resulting from their R&D efforts.

Zinc

The zinc industry will experience sustained growth in demand, with consumption rising about 2 percent a year to total 1,050,000 metric tons by the mid-1990s. Galvanizing will continue to be the largest end-use sector of zinc, with diecasting continuing to show signs of improvement. Zinc consumption in both of these end-use sectors will continue to be acutely sensitive to the strength of the dollar and imports of semifabricated metal products and finished consumer goods.

Chapter 15_____

THE ECONOMY

After a decade that witnessed unparalleled growth, worsening economic conditions at the beginning of the 1990s have caused many to wonder if all the prosperity will be undone. The recession of 1990 and 1991 brought to a head many negative influences on the economy. Many areas of the country have been deeply affected by the recession, and even the most optimistic forecasters see a slow recovery.

Economic uncertainty is frightening to most people, largely because they don't know what to expect. All they hear are stories of travail, and many lay awake at night wondering when economic calamity will befall their families. The only thing that can be said with certainty about economic downturns is that they are certain to occur. Financial professionals, of course, are constantly called upon to offer their own opinions about the present and future condition of the economy.

People who regularly and diligently try to enhance their personal financial circumstances are, of course, best prepared to cope with less robust economic climates. Put more succinctly, nothing can beat some money in the bank to weather economic storms. How differently someone must view the possibility of temporary unemployment if they have accumulated a nice nest egg than someone who is living hand to mouth. Conservative spending habits, adequate savings, and relatively little or no indebtedness are perhaps the best ways to handle whatever negatives a recession can inflict. Moreover, those who are on a firm financial footing may be able to take advantage of weakness in some market segments, for example, real estate when the economy is floundering.

The next decade is most probably not going to be a repeat of the prosperity of the 1980s. Pervasive uncertainty about future economic conditions often causes investors to become unreasonably conservative. Many make wholesale changes in their portfolios, often preferring cash-equivalent investments. Successful long-term investors (particularly those who have been through a few recessions) prefer to maintain a steady course through all economic conditions. Investors who make major shifts in their portfolios in response to short-term market and economic vacillations almost always do the wrong thing. They are often selling when they should be buying and vice versa. Most often the best thing to do in the face of uncertainty is nothing, because if the investor already has a well-balanced, diversified investment portfolio, and other personal financial planning matters continue to be dealt with effectively, he or she will prosper under any economic conditions.

The financial professional needs to keep abreast of current economic conditions and trends. Moreover, he or she needs to develop a sense of historical perspective in economic and market matters, because those who have a good understanding of past economic conditions are most likely to respond appropriately to current conditions.

15.1 LEADING ECONOMIC INDICATOR INTERPRETER

While the leading economic indicators receive a lot of media attention, many people don't understand what they mean to the economy. This section is a brief summary of some of the more commonly used economic indicators.

15.1.1 Three-Month Treasury-Bill Rate

This is the interest rate paid to buyers of U.S. Treasury bills (at auction) and best predicts the direction that the interest rates will take. It is published every Tuesday after the weekly auction on Monday. Because it is quoted every week, trends may be hard to spot.

15.1.2 Wage Settlements

The results of major wage contracts can indicate the magnitude of the rise in the cost of goods and services. Lower annual salary increase agreements usually mean lower inflation. These figures appear in news stories of major labor settlements.

15.1.3 Payroll Employment

This figure—the number of employees on company payrolls—is issued on the first Friday of each month in most major newspapers. It not only reflects the employment situation but it also best predicts future consumer spending patterns, which depend heavily on employment.

15.1.4 The Dollar Index

This indicates future interest rates and corporate profits and shows the value of the dollar against a group of foreign currencies compiled by Morgan Guaranty Trust. It is published Monday through Friday in some newspapers. Because it is issued so frequently, minor fluctuations should be ignored.

15.1.5 Inventory-to-Sales Ratio

This is a crude but useful measure of the extent to which the demand for goods is satisfied and thus indicates sales patterns that affect corporate profits.

It consists of the dollar value of business inventory nationwide divided by sales and is issued near the tenth working day of each month by the Census Bureau. When the economy is flagging, this ratio may be as high as 1.5:1, as inventories build up and sales slow. A 1.3:1 ratio is balanced by experts' opinion, as businesses like to keep a little extra inventory on hand. This indicator should be scrutinized, because changes of a quarter of a point are usually important.

15.1.6 The Standard & Poor's (S&P) 500 Stock Index

The stock market predicts general economic recoveries as no other indicator can, but it has also predicted nine out of the last five recessions. The S&P 500 Stock Index is quoted daily in most newspapers and best predicts the economy's future prospects, because it reflects a broader array of stocks than other stock averages.

15.2 CONSUMER PRICE INDEXES BY MAJOR GROUP

Table 15.1 shows annual changes in consumer prices by major category since 1960.

Table 15.1 Consumer Price Index by Major Groups, 1960–1990

YEAR	All items	Energy	Food	Shelter	Apparel and upkeep	Trans-portation	Med-ical care	Fuel oil	Elec-tricity	Utility (piped gas)	Tele-phone ser-vices	All com-modities
1960.	29.6	22.4	30.0	25.2	45.7	29.8	22.3	13.5	29.9	17.6	58.3	33.6
1961.	29.9	22.5	30.4	25.4	46.1	30.1	22.9	14.0	29.9	17.9	58.5	33.8
1962.	30.2	22.6	30.6	25.8	46.3	30.8	23.5	14.0	29.9	17.9	58.5	34.1
1963.	30.6	22.6	31.1	26.1	46.9	30.9	24.1	14.3	29.9	17.9	58.6	34.4
1964.	31.0	22.5	31.5	26.5	47.3	31.4	24.6	14.0	29.8	17.9	58.6	34.8
1965.	31.5	22.9	32.2	27.0	47.8	31.9	25.2	14.3	29.7	18.0	57.7	35.2
1966.	32.4	23.3	33.8	27.8	49.0	32.3	26.3	14.7	29.7	18.1	56.5	36.1
1967.	33.4	23.8	34.1	28.8	51.0	33.3	28.2	15.1	29.9	18.1	57.3	36.8
1968.	34.8	24.2	35.3	30.1	53.7	34.3	29.9	15.6	30.2	18.2	57.3	38.1
1969.	36.7	24.8	37.1	32.6	56.8	35.7	31.9	15.9	30.8	18.6	58.0	39.9
1970.	38.8	25.5	39.2	35.5	59.2	37.5	34.0	16.5	31.8	19.6	58.7	41.7
1971.	40.5	26.5	40.4	37.0	61.1	39.5	36.1	17.6	33.9	21.0	61.6	43.2
1972.	41.8	27.2	42.1	38.7	62.3	39.9	37.3	17.6	35.6	22.1	65.0	44.5
1973.	44.4	29.4	48.2	40.5	64.6	41.2	38.8	20.4	37.4	23.1	66.7	47.8
1974.	49.3	38.1	55.1	44.4	69.4	45.8	42.4	32.2	44.1	26.0	69.5	53.5
1975.	53.8	42.1	59.8	48.8	72.5	50.1	47.5	34.9	50.0	31.1	71.7	58.2
1976.	56.9	45.1	61.6	51.5	75.2	55.1	52.0	37.4	53.1	36.3	74.3	60.7
1977.	60.6	49.4	65.5	54.9	78.6	59.0	57.0	42.4	56.6	43.2	75.2	64.2
1978.	65.2	52.5	72.0	60.5	81.4	61.7	61.8	44.9	60.9	47.5	76.0	68.8
1979.	72.6	65.7	79.9	68.9	84.9	70.5	67.5	63.1	65.6	55.1	75.8	76.6
1980.	82.4	86.0	86.8	81.0	90.9	83.1	74.9	87.7	75.8	65.7	77.7	86.0
1981.	90.9	97.7	93.6	90.5	95.3	93.2	82.9	107.3	87.2	74.9	84.6	93.2
1982.	96.5	99.2	97.4	96.9	97.8	97.0	92.5	105.0	95.8	89.8	93.2	97.0
1983.	99.6	99.9	99.4	99.1	100.2	99.3	100.6	96.5	98.9	104.7	99.2	99.8
1984.	103.9	100.9	103.2	104.0	102.1	103.7	106.8	98.5	105.3	105.5	107.5	103.2
1985.	107.6	101.6	105.6	109.8	105.0	106.4	113.5	94.6	108.9	104.8	111.7	105.4
1986.	109.6	88.2	109.0	115.8	105.9	102.3	122.0	74.1	110.4	99.7	117.2	104.4
1987.	113.6	88.6	113.5	121.3	110.6	105.4	130.1	75.8	110.0	95.1	116.5	107.7
1988.	118.3	89.3	118.2	127.1	115.4	108.7	138.6	75.8	111.5	94.5	116.0	111.5
1989.	124.0	94.3	125.1	132.8	118.6	114.1	149.3	80.3	114.7	97.1	117.2	116.7
1990.	130.7	102.1	132.4	140.0	124.1	120.5	162.8	98.6	117.4	97.3	117.7	122.8

Source: U.S. Bureau of Labor Statistics, *Monthly Labor Review* and *Handbook of Labor Statistics*, periodic.

15.3 CONSUMER PRICE INDEXES FOR SELECTED ITEMS AND GROUPS

Table 15.2 shows the percentage change in the consumer price indexes for various commodities and groups, and, along with Table 15.1, can aid the financial professional in preparing financial projections.

Table 15.2 Consumer Price Index for Selected Items and Groups, 1970-1990

ITEM	1970	1975	1980	1983	1984	1985	1986	1987	1988	1989	1990
All items	**38.8**	**53.8**	**82.4**	**99.6**	**103.9**	**107.6**	**109.6**	**113.6**	**118.3**	**124.0**	**130.7**
Food and beverages	40.1	60.2	86.7	99.5	103.2	105.6	109.1	113.5	118.2	124.9	132.1
Food	39.2	59.8	86.8	99.4	103.2	105.6	109.0	113.5	118.2	125.1	132.4
Food at home	39.9	61.8	88.4	99.1	102.8	104.3	107.3	111.9	116.6	124.2	132.3
Cereals and bakery products	37.1	62.9	83.9	99.6	103.9	107.9	110.9	114.8	122.1	132.4	140.0
Cereals	(NA)	(NA)	76.3	99.9	105.3	111.3	117.3	124.1	132.9	147.9	158.6
Bakery products	(NA)	(NA)	83.8	99.6	104.2	108.2	111.1	115.0	121.8	131.5	139.2
Meats, poultry, fish and eggs	44.6	67.0	92.0	99.2	101.3	100.1	104.5	110.5	114.3	121.3	130.0
Meats	43.8	66.3	92.7	99.5	99.8	98.9	102.0	109.6	112.2	116.7	128.5
Beef and veal	43.5	61.9	98.4	99.1	100.3	98.2	98.8	106.3	112.1	119.3	128.8
Ground beef other than canned	47.0	62.3	104.6	99.4	98.4	95.9	94.9	100.2	103.4	108.6	118.1
Chuck roast	42.8	62.6	99.8	98.7	99.6	95.6	95.0	103.8	108.1	116.8	130.3
Round steak	45.8	66.5	98.9	99.3	99.2	97.0	98.4	105.3	110.6	116.6	125.1
Sirloin steak	42.4	61.7	96.2	99.0	101.7	99.7	102.3	111.2	120.0	126.0	130.6
Pork	45.4	77.1	81.9	100.1	98.8	99.1	107.2	116.0	112.5	113.2	129.8
Poultry	53.2	79.7	93.7	97.0	107.3	106.2	114.2	112.6	120.7	132.7	132.5
Fresh and frozen chicken parts	(NA)	(NA)	91.7	96.6	108.4	104.6	114.6	114.4	123.3	135.7	135.9
Fish and seafood	31.3	53.9	87.5	99.3	102.5	107.5	117.4	129.6	137.4	143.6	146.7
Canned fish and seafood	(NA)	(NA)	93.7	99.9	97.6	97.8	98.6	103.0	117.0	124.3	119.5
Eggs	65.6	82.4	88.6	97.7	109.1	91.0	97.2	91.5	93.6	118.5	124.1
Dairy products	44.7	62.6	90.9	100.0	101.3	103.2	103.3	105.9	108.4	115.6	126.5
Fruits and vegetables	37.8	56.9	82.1	97.3	105.7	108.4	109.4	119.1	128.1	138.0	149.0
Fresh fruits	35.6	51.8	84.8	95.1	105.6	116.3	118.7	132.0	143.0	152.4	170.9
Apples	37.1	56.4	92.1	94.6	106.6	113.1	130.6	131.0	134.2	140.5	147.5
Bananas	39.0	57.4	91.5	106.0	97.9	99.9	105.0	104.2	119.2	131.3	138.2
Oranges, tangerines	30.6	41.4	72.6	83.1	112.4	119.7	108.6	135.9	144.6	147.0	160.6
Fresh vegetables	39.4	55.6	79.0	97.6	108.2	103.5	107.7	121.6	129.3	143.1	151.1
Potatoes	38.0	57.7	81.0	91.3	116.0	101.6	96.1	116.0	119.1	153.5	162.6
Lettuce	35.4	49.6	77.8	103.2	96.1	106.1	112.7	136.4	148.6	151.5	150.3
Tomatoes	46.3	63.6	81.9	100.8	105.7	103.6	111.3	116.8	123.1	136.2	160.8
Processed fruits	38.4	59.7	82.1	98.1	105.2	109.5	106.3	110.6	122.0	125.9	136.9
Processed vegetables	36.6	62.2	83.1	98.6	103.3	104.4	104.2	107.1	112.2	124.2	127.5
Coffee	31.7	46.4	111.6	98.8	102.7	105.5	132.7	116.2	115.0	120.4	117.5
Alcoholic beverages	52.1	65.9	86.4	100.4	103.0	106.4	111.1	114.1	118.6	123.5	129.3
Alcoholic beverages at home	(NA)	(NA)	87.3	100.6	102.4	105.2	109.3	111.5	114.2	117.9	123.0
Beer and ale	49.2	63.4	84.8	100.7	104.2	106.7	108.7	110.9	114.4	118.2	123.6
Distilled spirits	(NA)	(NA)	89.8	100.4	101.4	105.3	113.3	114.4	116.1	119.9	125.7
Wine	49.7	65.5	89.5	100.5	99.1	100.2	102.4	105.7	107.8	110.9	114.4
Alcoholic beverages away from home	(NA)	(NA)	82.9	99.8	105.1	111.1	118.5	123.4	130.6	137.4	144.4
Lunch away from home	(NA)	(NA)	83.8	100.0	103.8	107.8	112.0	116.6	121.5	127.6	133.9
Dinner away from home	(NA)	(NA)	84.2	99.7	104.4	108.8	112.7	117.0	121.6	126.9	132.3
Housing	36.4	50.7	81.1	99.5	103.6	107.7	110.9	114.2	118.5	123.0	128.5
Shelter	35.5	48.8	81.0	99.1	104.0	109.8	115.8	121.3	127.1	132.8	140.0
Renters' cost	(NA)	(NA)	(NA)	103.0	108.6	115.4	121.9	128.1	133.6	138.9	146.7
Rent, residential	46.5	58.0	80.9	100.1	105.3	111.8	118.3	123.1	127.8	132.8	138.4
Tenants' insurance	(NA)	(NA)	78.9	100.7	104.8	109.4	115.8	120.4	124.9	128.3	130.6
Homeowners' costs	(NA)	(NA)	(NA)	102.5	107.3	113.1	119.4	124.8	131.1	137.3	144.6
Owners' equivalent rent	(NA)	(NA)	(NA)	102.5	107.3	113.2	119.4	124.8	131.1	137.4	144.8
Household insurance	(NA)	(NA)	(NA)	103.2	102.5	112.4	119.2	124.0	129.0	132.6	135.3
Maintenance and repair	35.8	54.1	82.4	99.9	103.7	106.5	107.9	111.8	114.7	118.0	122.2
Services	33.1	51.3	80.0	99.7	105.7	108.7	111.2	114.8	117.0	120.6	126.4
Commodities	43.7	61.9	88.0	100.2	101.0	103.7	103.7	107.8	110.4	114.6	116.6
Fuels and other utilities	29.1	45.4	75.4	100.2	104.8	106.5	104.1	103.0	104.4	107.8	111.6
Fuels	23.1	39.4	74.8	100.5	104.0	104.5	99.2	97.3	98.0	100.9	104.5
Fuel oil and other	17.0	36.4	86.1	97.2	99.4	95.9	77.6	77.9	78.1	81.7	99.3
Fuel oil	16.5	34.9	87.7	96.5	98.5	94.6	74.1	75.8	75.8	80.3	98.6
Gas (piped) and electricity	25.4	40.1	71.4	101.5	105.4	107.1	105.7	103.8	104.6	107.5	109.3
Electricity	31.8	50.0	75.8	98.9	105.3	108.9	110.4	110.0	111.5	114.7	117.4
Utility (piped) gas	19.6	31.1	65.7	104.7	105.5	104.8	99.7	95.1	94.5	97.1	97.3
Telephone services	58.7	71.7	77.7	99.2	107.5	111.7	117.2	116.5	116.0	117.2	117.7
Local charges	(NA)	(NA)	72.8	97.9	111.6	120.4	132.7	139.3	141.3	146.5	149.3
Interstate toll charges	(NA)	(NA)	83.3	101.5	99.2	94.9	88.4	75.3	72.3	70.0	68.2
Intrastate toll charges	(NA)	(NA)	85.2	100.4	105.9	106.8	106.8	104.7	101.5	97.0	95.1
Water and sewerage maintenance	34.3	48.4	74.0	100.4	107.0	113.4	119.4	125.8	132.7	140.8	150.2
Cable television	(NA)	(NA)	(NA)	(NA)	103.9	110.6	115.5	123.1	132.9	144.0	158.4
Refuse collection	(NA)	(NA)	(NA)	(NA)	103.2	109.9	118.7	130.3	142.5	155.6	171.2

15.4 PURCHASING POWER OF THE DOLLAR

Table 15.3 shows the erosion in the purchasing power of the dollar, based on indexes measuring the levels of consumer prices and producer prices. This information can be useful as an illustration of the impact of inflation over time. Note that while inflation today may be somewhat high by historical standards, it is much lower than it was during the mid-1970s and early 1980s.

Table 15.3 Purchasing Power of the Dollar, 1950–1990

[Indexes: PPI, 1982 = $1.00; CPI, 1982-84 = $1.00. Producer prices prior to 1961, and consumer prices prior to 1964, exclude Alaska and Hawaii. Producer prices based on finished goods index. Obtained by dividing the average price index for the 1982 = 100, PPI; 1982-84 = 100, CPI base periods (100.0) by the price index for a given period and expressing the result in dollars and cents. Annual figures are based on average of monthly data]

YEAR	ANNUAL AVERAGE AS MEASURED BY—		YEAR	ANNUAL AVERAGE AS MEASURED BY—		YEAR	ANNUAL AVERAGE AS MEASURED BY—	
	Producer prices	Consumer prices		Producer prices	Consumer prices		Producer prices	Consumer prices
1950	$3.546	$4.151	1964	2.985	3.220	1978	1.433	1.532
1951	3.247	3.846	1965	2.933	3.166	1979	1.289	1.380
1952	3.268	3.765	1966	2.841	3.080	1980	1.136	1.215
1953	3.300	3.735	1967	2.809	2.993	1981	1.041	1.098
1954	3.289	3.717	1968	2.732	2.873	1982	1.000	1.035
1955	3.279	3.732	1969	2.632	2.726	1983	0.984	1.003
1956	3.195	3.678	1970	2.545	2.574	1984	0.964	0.961
1957	3.077	3.549	1971	2.469	2.466	1985	0.955	0.928
1958	3.012	3.457	1972	2.392	2.391	1986	0.969	0.913
1959	3.021	3.427	1973	2.193	2.251	1987	0.949	0.880
1960	2.994	3.373	1974	1.901	2.029	1988	0.926	0.846
1961	2.994	3.340	1975	1.718	1.859	1989	0.880	0.807
1962	2.985	3.304	1976	1.645	1.757	1990	0.839	0.766
1963	2.994	3.265	1977	1.546	1.649			

Source: U.S. Bureau of Labor Statistics. Monthly data in U.S. Bureau of Economic Analysis, *Survey of Current Business.*

15.5 ANNUAL PERCENTAGE CHANGES IN CONSUMER PRICE INDEXES

Table 15.4 shows the annual percentage changes for major consumer price index categories since 1960. It is interesting to note the wide disparity among some of the components of these indexes. For example, energy costs dropped 13.2 percent during 1986, but food rose 3.2 percent and shelter rose 5.5 percent.

Table 15.4 Consumer Price Indexes—Percent Change in Major Groups, 1960–1990

YEAR	All items	Energy	Food	Shelter	Apparel and upkeep	Trans-portation	Medical care	Fuel oil	Elec-tricity	Utility (piped) gas	Tele-phone services	All commod-ities
1960	1.7	2.3	1.0	2.0	1.6	-	3.7	-1.5	1.4	6.7	1.6	0.9
1961	1.0	0.4	1.3	0.8	0.9	1.0	2.7	3.7	-	1.7	0.3	0.6
1962	1.0	0.4	0.7	1.6	0.4	2.3	2.6	-	-	-	-	0.9
1963	1.3	-	1.6	1.2	1.3	0.3	2.6	2.1	-	-	0.2	0.9
1964	1.3	-0.4	1.3	1.5	0.9	1.6	2.1	-2.1	-0.3	-	-	1.2
1965	1.6	1.8	2.2	1.9	1.1	1.6	2.4	2.1	-0.3	0.6	-1.5	1.1
1966	2.9	1.7	5.0	3.0	2.5	1.3	4.4	2.8	-	0.6	-2.1	2.6
1967	3.1	2.1	0.9	3.6	4.1	3.1	7.2	2.7	0.7	-	1.4	1.9
1968	4.2	1.7	3.5	4.5	5.3	3.0	6.0	3.3	1.0	0.6	-	3.5
1969	5.5	2.5	5.1	8.3	5.8	4.1	6.7	1.9	2.0	2.2	1.2	4.7
1970	5.7	2.8	5.7	8.9	4.2	5.0	6.6	3.8	3.2	5.4	1.2	4.5
1971	4.4	3.9	3.1	4.2	3.2	5.3	6.2	6.7	6.6	7.1	4.9	3.6
1972	3.2	2.6	4.2	4.6	2.0	1.0	3.3	-	5.0	5.2	5.5	3.0
1973	6.2	8.1	14.5	4.7	3.7	3.3	4.0	15.9	5.1	4.5	2.6	7.4
1974	11.0	29.6	14.3	9.6	7.4	11.2	9.3	57.8	17.9	12.6	4.2	11.9
1975	9.1	10.5	8.5	9.9	4.5	9.4	12.0	8.4	13.4	19.6	3.2	8.8
1976	5.8	7.1	3.0	5.5	3.7	10.0	9.5	7.2	6.2	16.7	3.6	4.3
1977	6.5	9.5	6.3	6.6	4.5	7.1	9.6	13.4	6.6	19.0	1.2	5.8
1978	7.6	6.3	9.9	10.2	3.6	4.6	8.4	5.9	7.6	10.0	1.1	7.2
1979	11.3	25.1	11.0	13.9	4.3	14.3	9.2	40.5	7.7	16.0	-0.3	11.3
1980	13.5	30.9	8.6	17.6	7.1	17.9	11.0	39.0	15.5	19.2	2.5	12.3
1981	10.3	13.6	7.8	11.7	4.8	12.2	10.7	22.3	15.0	14.0	8.9	8.4
1982	6.2	1.5	4.1	7.1	2.6	4.1	11.6	-2.1	9.9	19.9	10.2	4.1
1983	3.2	0.7	2.1	2.3	2.5	2.4	8.8	-8.1	3.2	16.6	6.4	2.9
1984	4.3	1.0	3.8	4.9	1.9	4.4	6.2	2.1	6.5	0.8	8.4	3.4
1985	3.6	0.7	2.3	5.6	2.8	2.6	6.3	-4.0	3.4	-0.7	3.9	2.1
1986	1.9	-13.2	3.2	5.5	0.9	-3.9	7.5	-21.7	1.4	-4.9	4.9	-0.9
1987	3.6	0.5	4.1	4.7	4.4	3.0	6.6	2.3	-0.4	-4.6	-0.6	3.2
1988	4.1	0.8	4.1	4.8	4.3	3.1	6.5	-	1.4	-0.6	-0.4	3.5
1989	4.8	5.6	5.8	4.5	2.8	5.0	7.7	5.9	2.9	2.8	1.0	4.7
1990	5.4	8.3	5.8	5.4	4.6	5.6	9.0	22.8	2.4	0.2	0.4	5.2

- Represents zero.

Source: U.S. Bureau of Labor Statistics, *Monthly Labor Review*.

15.6 MONTHS OF DURATION OF BUSINESS CYCLE EXPANSIONS AND CONTRACTIONS

Table 15.5 shows the months of duration of peak-to-trough business cycles from 1919 to 1989.

**Table 15.5 Business Cycle Expansions and Contractions—
Months of Duration, 1919–1990**

[The lower turning point of a cycle is considered a trough, the upper turning point a peak. Business cycle reference dates are
determined by the National Bureau of Economic Research, Inc.]

BUSINESS CYCLE REFERENCE DATE		Contraction (trough from previous peak)	Expansion (trough to peak)	LENGTH OF CYCLE	
Trough	Peak			Trough from previous trough	Peak from previous peak
March 1919.	January 1920 .	[1]7	10	[2]51	[1]17
July 1921 .	May 1923 .	18	22	28	40
July 1924 .	October 1926 .	14	27	36	41
November 1927.	August 1929.	13	21	40	34
March 1933.	May 1937 .	43	50	64	93
June 1938.	February 1945 .	13	80	63	93
October 1945 .	November 1948 .	8	37	88	45
October 1949 .	July 1953.	11	45	48	56
May 1954 .	August 1957.	10	39	55	49
April 1958.	April 1960 .	8	24	47	32
February 1961.	December 1969 .	10	106	34	116
November 1970.	November 1973 .	11	36	117	47
March 1975.	January 1980 .	16	58	52	74
July 1980 .	July 1981.	6	12	64	18
November 1982.	July 1990.	16	92	28	108
Average, all cycles:					
1919-1945 (6 cycles) .		18	35	53	53
1945-1990 (8 cycles) .		11	[3]50	56	[3]61

[1] Previous peak: August 1918.   [2] Previous trough: December 1914.   [3] For 9 cycles.

Source: U.S. Bureau of Economic Analysis, *Survey of Current Business*, April 1991.

15.7 MONEY INCOME OF HOUSEHOLDS—PERCENTAGE DISTRIBUTION BY INCOME LEVEL

Table 15.6 shows the percentage distribution of income and median income of households according to a variety of characteristics.

15.8 SELECTED WORKLIFE INDEXES BY SEX, RACE, AND EDUCATIONAL ATTAINMENT

Table 15.7 shows average duration of work life at various ages, along with other data pertaining to work life.

15.9 MEDIAN MONEY INCOME OF YEAR-ROUND FULL-TIME WORKERS WITH INCOME

Table 15.8 shows trends in the median level of income for full-time workers in various age groups by gender and by race.

Table 15.6 Money Income of Households—Percent Distribution by Income Level, March 1988

CHARACTERISTIC	Number of house-holds (1,000)	PERCENT DISTRIBUTION OF HOUSEHOLDS BY INCOME LEVEL								Median income (dol-lars)
		Under $5,000	$5,000-$9,999	$10,000-$14,999	$15,000-$24,999	$25,000-$34,999	$35,000-$49,999	$50,000-$74,999	$75,000 and over	
1988										
Total [1]	92,830	6.2	10.8	10.3	18.6	16.0	17.3	13.4	7.4	27,225
White	79,734	5.0	9.8	9.8	18.6	16.5	18.1	14.2	7.9	28,781
Black	10,561	15.4	18.4	13.1	19.4	12.5	11.4	7.3	2.6	16,407
Hispanic [2]	5,910	9.9	13.6	13.7	22.1	15.5	14.3	7.3	3.5	20,359
Family households	65,837	3.8	6.6	8.7	17.7	16.9	20.2	16.7	9.3	32,491
Married-couple families	52,100	1.5	4.2	7.4	16.8	17.5	22.2	19.4	11.1	36,436
Male householder [3]	2,847	4.6	6.4	10.4	21.4	17.7	22.0	12.0	5.4	28,642
Female householder [3]	10,890	14.7	18.2	14.4	21.2	14.0	10.3	5.3	2.0	16,051
Nonfamily households	26,994	11.9	21.0	14.0	20.9	13.8	10.2	5.4	2.7	16,148
Male householder	11,874	9.0	14.6	12.4	21.6	16.4	13.9	7.7	4.4	20,999
Female householder	15,120	14.3	26.1	15.3	20.4	11.7	7.2	3.5	1.5	12,877
1989										
Total [1]	93,347	5.3	10.3	9.7	17.9	15.9	17.3	14.5	9.0	28,906
Age of householder:										
15-24 years	5,121	12.1	13.7	13.5	26.5	17.6	11.2	4.3	1.0	18,663
25-34 years	20,472	4.5	6.7	8.3	20.5	19.9	21.0	13.9	5.2	29,823
35-44 years	20,554	3.4	5.1	5.9	14.1	16.7	22.3	20.8	11.8	37,635
45-54 years	14,514	4.0	4.6	5.8	12.2	14.0	19.9	21.7	17.9	41,523
55-64 years	12,529	5.7	8.6	9.4	16.7	15.5	16.9	15.4	11.8	30,819
65 years and over	20,156	7.1	23.6	17.1	22.0	12.2	8.6	5.6	3.9	15,771
White	80,163	4.2	9.4	9.4	17.8	16.2	18.1	15.2	9.7	30,406
Black	10,486	14.1	17.2	11.9	19.6	13.8	12.0	8.5	2.9	18,083
Hispanic [2]	5,933	8.1	13.4	12.2	21.9	15.8	14.7	9.7	4.2	21,921
Northeast	19,127	4.3	9.9	8.4	15.9	14.4	17.6	17.2	12.4	32,643
Midwest	22,760	5.2	10.3	9.4	18.1	16.6	18.5	14.5	7.4	28,750
South	32,262	7.0	11.4	11.1	18.9	16.1	15.9	12.3	7.3	25,870
West	19,197	3.7	8.9	9.0	18.3	16.2	18.1	15.5	10.4	31,086
Size of household:										
One person	22,999	11.4	23.6	15.4	21.8	13.3	8.9	3.7	1.9	14,829
Two persons	30,114	3.6	7.2	10.1	20.0	17.6	18.3	14.4	8.9	29,862
Three persons	16,128	3.7	5.7	6.6	15.2	16.6	21.1	19.2	11.9	36,277
Four persons	14,456	2.7	4.1	5.3	12.3	16.0	22.7	22.8	14.0	40,744
Five persons	6,213	2.4	4.7	5.9	14.5	15.8	22.0	21.1	13.6	39,281
Six persons	2,143	3.6	6.1	7.3	17.5	15.0	17.4	18.7	14.3	35,304
Seven persons or more	1,295	3.8	6.3	8.4	18.3	15.4	15.6	18.7	13.3	32,644
Family households	66,090	3.4	6.1	7.9	16.6	16.5	20.0	18.0	11.5	34,633
Married-couple families	52,317	1.4	3.8	6.6	15.4	16.8	21.8	20.6	13.6	38,664
Male householder [3]	2,884	3.5	7.1	8.1	20.7	18.7	19.2	14.7	8.0	30,336
Female householder [3]	10,890	13.1	16.8	14.3	21.2	14.6	11.2	6.4	2.5	17,383
Nonfamily households	27,257	10.0	20.5	14.0	21.2	14.4	11.0	6.0	2.9	17,115
Male householder	11,606	7.3	13.5	12.0	21.8	16.9	15.1	8.7	4.7	22,423
Female householder	15,651	12.0	25.8	15.4	20.8	12.5	7.9	4.0	1.5	13,755
Education attainment of householder: [4]										
Elementary school, 8 years or less	10,695	13.4	26.9	16.2	20.8	10.5	7.3	3.6	1.3	12,696
High school	41,318	5.4	11.4	11.7	20.3	17.7	17.4	11.9	4.3	25,608
1-3 years	10,091	9.7	17.9	15.0	21.9	14.7	11.7	6.9	2.2	17,767
4 years	31,227	4.0	9.3	10.6	19.8	18.6	19.2	13.5	5.0	28,060
College	36,214	1.9	3.7	5.0	13.2	15.2	21.1	22.1	17.7	42,153
1-3 years	15,842	2.6	5.8	6.9	16.8	17.7	22.3	18.9	8.9	35,083
4 years or more	20,372	1.4	2.1	3.5	10.4	13.3	20.3	24.5	24.5	49,180
Tenure:										
Owner occupied	59,846	2.9	7.3	8.0	15.5	15.5	19.9	18.4	12.5	35,481
Renter occupied	31,895	9.4	15.4	12.7	22.3	16.7	13.0	7.7	2.8	20,302
Occupier paid no cash rent	1,606	14.3	21.8	12.1	22.0	14.8	8.2	5.2	1.7	15,829

[1] Includes other races not shown separately.   [2] Hispanic persons may be of any race.   [3] No spouse present.   [4] 25 years old and over.

Source: U.S. Bureau of the Census, *Current Population Reports*, series P-60, Nos. 166 and 168, and unpublished data.

Table 15.7 Selected Worklife Indexes by Sex, Race, and Educational Attainment

[In years, except percent. For the civilian noninstitutional population. For methodological details, see source]

INDEX AND AGE	MALE						FEMALE					
		Race		Educational attainment				Race		Educational attainment		
	Total	White	Black and other	Less than high school	High school to 14 years	15 years or more	Total	White	Black and other	Less than high school	High school to 14 years	15 years or more
Life expectancy:												
At birth...................	70.0	70.7	65.3	70.0	70.0	70.0	77.6	78.3	73.9	77.6	77.6	77.6
At age 25	47.3	47.9	43.3	47.3	47.3	47.3	54.2	54.7	51.0	54.2	54.2	54.2
At age 60	17.5	17.6	16.5	17.5	17.5	17.5	22.4	22.6	21.0	22.4	22.4	22.4
At age 65	14.2	14.3	13.8	14.2	14.2	14.2	18.5	18.7	17.7	18.5	18.5	18.5
Worklife expectancy:												
At birth..................	38.8	39.8	32.9	34.6	39.9	41.1	29.4	29.7	27.4	22.3	30.1	34.9
At age 25	33.1	33.8	28.6	29.2	33.8	36.1	24.0	24.1	23.5	17.9	24.4	27.9
At age 60	4.4	4.5	3.3	3.3	4.7	6.3	3.0	3.0	3.0	2.3	3.3	3.5
At age 65	2.3	2.3	1.8	1.8	2.4	3.6	1.5	1.5	1.5	1.2	1.8	1.8
Percent of life economically active: [1]												
From birth...............	55.4	56.3	50.4	49.4	57.0	58.7	37.9	37.9	37.1	28.7	38.8	45.0
From age 25	70.0	70.6	66.1	61.7	71.5	76.3	44.3	44.1	46.1	33.0	45.0	51.5
From age 60	25.1	25.6	20.0	18.9	26.9	36.0	13.4	13.3	14.3	10.3	14.7	15.6
From age 65	16.2	16.1	13.0	12.7	16.9	25.4	8.1	8.0	8.5	6.5	9.7	9.7
Number of times person enters labor force per:												
Person born	3.9	3.9	4.3	4.3	3.7	4.6	5.5	5.6	5.4	5.8	5.6	5.6
Person age 25	1.5	1.5	1.8	2.0	1.5	1.4	3.0	3.0	3.1	3.3	3.2	2.7
Expected duration per entry remaining: [2]												
From birth................	9.9	10.2	7.7	8.0	10.8	8.9	5.3	5.3	5.1	3.8	5.4	6.2
From age 25	22.1	22.5	15.9	14.6	22.5	25.8	8.0	8.0	7.6	5.4	7.6	10.3
Number of times person voluntarily leaves labor force:												
From birth................	3.6	3.6	3.9	4.0	3.6	4.5	5.4	5.5	5.4	5.7	5.7	4.7
From age 25	2.3	2.3	2.4	2.7	2.3	2.2	3.8	3.8	3.7	3.8	4.0	3.6

[1] Ratio of worklife expectancy to life expectancy.   [2] Worklife expectancy divided by number of times person enters labor force.

Source: U.S. Bureau of Labor Statistics, *Monthly Labor Review*, August 1985.

Table 15.8 Money Income of Year-Round Full-Time Workers with Income, 1980–1989

ITEM	FEMALE					MALE				
	1980	1985	1987 [1]	1988	1989	1980	1985	1987 [1]	1988	1989
Total with income	$11,591	$16,252	$17,564	$18,545	$19,643	$19,173	$24,999	$26,681	$27,342	$28,605
15-19 years old.	6,779	8,372	} 12,329	13,183	13,653	7,753	9,050	} 14,170	14,863	15,501
20-24 years old.	9,407	11,757				12,109	13,827			
25-34 years old.	12,190	16,740	17,552	18,486	19,706	17,724	22,321	23,554	24,284	24,991
35-44 years old.	12,239	18,032	19,934	20,635	21,498	21,777	28,966	30,802	31,847	32,370
45-54 years old.	12,116	17,009	19,299	20,174	20,905	22,323	29,880	32,237	32,701	35,356
55-64 years old.	11,931	16,761	18,047	18,347	19,895	21,053	28,387	30,869	31,645	34,505
65 years old and over	12,342	18,336	19,502	19,493	21,505	17,307	26,146	28,593	29,070	34,110
White	11,703	16,482	17,889	18,823	19,873	19,720	25,693	27,303	28,262	29,846
Black . . .₂.	10,915	14,590	15,978	16,867	17,908	13,875	17,971	19,522	20,716	20,706
Hispanic [2]	9,887	13,522	14,802	15,201	16,006	13,790	17,344	17,680	18,190	18,570

[1] Beginning 1987, based on revised processing procedures; data not directly comparable with prior years. See text, section 14, and source.   [2] Persons of Hispanic origin may be of any race.

Source of tables 735 and 736: U.S. Bureau of the Census, *Current Population Reports*, series P-60, No. 168, and earlier issues.

15.10   EASY MONEY AND TIGHT MONEY

Figure 15.1 shows the implications of easy money and tight money policies. An easy money policy is one in which the Federal Reserve seeks to increase aggregate demand. It is usually followed when the Fed is attempting to increase employment and output. Tight money policies are implemented when the Fed wants to fight inflation.

FIGURE 15.1   *FEDERAL RESERVE ACTION:* EASY MONEY AND TIGHT MONEY

Easy Money
Lowers reserve requirement *or* lowers discount rate *or* buys government securities

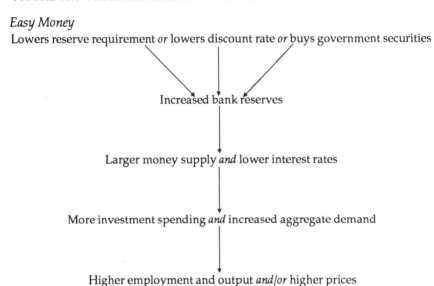

Increased bank reserves

Larger money supply *and* lower interest rates

More investment spending *and* increased aggregate demand

Higher employment and output *and/or* higher prices

Tight Money
Raises reserve requirement *or* raises discount rate *or* sells government securities

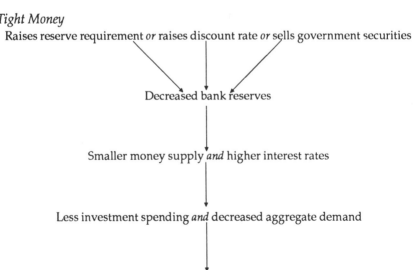

Decreased bank reserves

Smaller money supply *and* higher interest rates

Less investment spending *and* decreased aggregate demand

Lower employment and output *and/or* lower prices

15.11 EARNINGS BY EDUCATIONAL ATTAINMENT, SEX, AND AGE

Table 15.9 shows earnings categorized by age, sex, and education. Not surprisingly, those with higher education levels achieve higher income levels as well.

Table 15.9 Mean Money Earnings by Educational Attainment, Sex, and Age, March 1988

AGE AND SEX	Total	Ele-men-tary, 8 years or less	SECONDARY			COLLEGE			
			Total	1-3 years	4 years	Total	1-3 years	4 years	5 or more years
Male, total	32,558	18,903	26,292	22,430	27,139	39,671	31,543	40,415	50,262
25-34 years old	26,520	14,923	22,698	18,915	23,434	31,035	26,486	32,956	37,354
35-44 years old	36,044	20,455	27,922	22,737	28,777	42,343	32,698	43,087	53,692
45-54 years old	37,039	20,348	29,487	24,935	30,660	47,248	38,158	47,432	57,164
55-64 years old	33,975	20,713	27,930	25,231	28,852	45,073	34,500	49,272	51,860
65 years old and over	28,659	13,941	26,517	21,630	27,961	38,176	32,990	34,124	45,742
Female, total	20,531	11,710	16,856	13,834	17,336	24,933	21,310	25,674	31,189
25-34 years old	19,593	11,009	15,728	11,724	16,166	22,970	19,526	24,688	27,740
35-44 years old	21,740	12,201	17,108	13,967	17,551	26,432	22,334	27,220	32,957
45-54 years old	21,563	12,273	18,288	14,738	18,953	27,242	23,680	26,812	33,667
55-64 years old	19,047	11,445	16,865	15,134	17,321	24,769	21,215	25,465	31,080
65 years old and over	15,570	9,430	14,257	11,963	14,891	18,674	18,414	13,054	25,858

Source: U.S. Bureau of the Census, *Current Population Reports*, series P-60, unpublished data.

15.12 AVERAGE DRIVING COSTS

Table 15.10 shows trends in the average costs of owning and operating an automobile. For most families, it is second only to housing as the largest expense category, and for some it is the largest.

Table 15.10 Cost of Owning and Operating an Automobile, 1975–1989

ITEM	Unit	1975	1980	1984	1985	1986	1987	1988	1989
Cost per mile [1]	Cents	18.31	27.95	31.32	27.20	29.59	32.64	33.40	38.20
Cost per 10,000 miles [1]	Dollars	1,831	2,795	3,132	2,720	2,959	3,264	3,341	3,820
Variable cost	Cents/mile	6.45	7.62	7.86	8.04	6.52	7.20	7.60	7.90
Gas and oil	Cents/mile	4.82	5.86	6.19	6.16	4.48	4.80	5.20	5.20
Maintenance	Cents/mile	0.97	1.12	1.04	1.23	1.37	1.60	1.60	1.90
Tires	Cents/mile	0.66	0.64	0.63	0.65	0.67	0.80	0.80	0.80
Fixed cost	Dollars	1,186	2,033	2,346	2,441	2,596	2,782	3,061	3,534
Insurance	Dollars	383	490	505	503	509	535	573	663
License and registration	Dollars	30	82	106	115	130	140	139	151
Depreciation	Dollars	773	1,038	1,207	1,253	1,320	1,506	1,784	2,094
Finance charge	Dollars	(NA)	423	528	570	637	601	565	626

NA Not available. [1] Beginning 1985, not comparable to previous data.

Source: Motor Vehicle Manufacturers Association of the United States, Inc. *Motor Vehicle Facts and Figures* (Detroit, MI: Motor Vehicle Manufacturer's Association of the United States, annual).

15.13 FEDERAL RESERVE BANKS

A list of the locations, addresses, and telephone numbers of the Federal Reserve Bank branches and the Board of Governors appears in Table 15.11.

**Table 15.11 Federal Reserve Bank Branches and
The Board of Governors**

Atlanta
104 Marietta St. N.W.
Atlanta, GA 30303
(404) 586-8500

Boston
600 Atlantic Ave.
Boston, MA 02106
(617) 973-3000

Chicago
230 S. LaSalle St.
P.O. Box 834
Chicago, IL 60690
(312) 322-5322

Cleveland
1455 E. Sixth St.
P.O. Box 6387
Cleveland, OH 44101
(216) 241-2800

Dallas
400 S. Akard St.
Station K
Dallas, TX 75222
(214) 651-6111

Kansas City, Mo.
925 Grand Ave.
Federal Reserve Station
Kansas City, MO 64198
(816) 881-2000

Minneapolis
250 Marquette Ave.
Minneapolis, MN 55480
(612) 340-2345

New York
33 Liberty St.
New York, NY 10045
(212) 791-5000

Philadelphia
100 N. Sixth St.
P.O. Box 66
Philadelphia, PA 19105
(215) 574-6000

Richmond
701 E. Byrd St.
P.O. Box 27622
Richmond, VA 23261
(804) 643-1250

St. Louis
411 Locust St.
P.O. Box 442
St. Louis, MO 63166
(314) 444-8444

San Francisco
400 Sansome St.
P.O. Box 7702
San Francisco, CA 94120
(415) 544-2000

Board of Governors
Board of Governors of the Federal
Reserve System
20th and Constitution Ave.
N.W.
Washington, D.C. 20551
(202) 452-3000

15.14   FEDERAL INFORMATION CENTERS

Federal Information Centers can eliminate the maze of referrals that people often experience in contacting the federal government. They are clearinghouses for information about the federal government. Persons with questions about a government program or agency and who are unsure of which office can help may call or write to their nearest center. Table 15.12 provides Federal Information Center locations and telephone numbers.

Table 15.12   Federal Information Centers

State/City	Address	Telephone
Alabama	75 Spring St. SW, Atlanta, GA 30303	
Birmingham		205/322-8591
Mobile		205/438-1421
Alaska		
Anchorage	Box 33, 701 C St., 99513	907/271-3650
Arizona		
Phoenix	880 Front St., San Diego, CA 92188	602/261-3313
Arkansas		
Little Rock	819 Taylor St., Forth Worth, TX 76102	501/378-6177
California		
Los Angeles	300 N. Los Angeles St., 90012	213/894-3800
Sacramento	1825 Bell, 95825	916/978-4010
San Diego	880 Front St., 92188	619/557-6030
San Francisco	Box 36082, 450 Golden Gate Ave., 94102	415/556-6600
Santa Ana	880 Front St., San Diego 92188	714/836-2386
Colorado		
Colorado Springs		719/471-9491
Denver	1961 Stout St., P.O. Drawer 3526, Denver 80294	719/544-9523
Pueblo		719/544-9523
Connecticut		
Hartford	Rm. 2-110, 26 Federal Plaza, New York, NY 10278	203/527-2617
New Haven		203/624-4720

Table 15.12 Federal Information Centers

State/City	Address	Telephone
Florida		
Ft. Lauderdale	Rm. 105, 144 1st Ave. S., St. Petersburg 37701	305/522-8531
Jacksonville		904/354-4756
Miami		305/536-4155
Orlando		407/422-1800
St. Petersburg		813/893-3495
Tampa		813/229-7911
West Palm Beach		813/229-7911
Georgia		
Atlanta	75 Spring St. SW., 30303	404/331-6891
Hawaii		
Honolulu	Box 50091, 300 Ala Moana Blvd., 96850	808/541-1365
Illinois		
Chicago	33d Floor, 230 S. Dearborn St., 60604	312/353-4242
Indiana	Rm. 7411, 550 Main St., Cincinnati, OH 45202	
Gary		219/883-4110
Indianapolis		317/269-7373
Iowa	215 N. 17th St., Omaha, NE 68102	800/532-1556
Kansas	Rm. 529, 210 N. Tucker Blvd., St. Louis, MO 63101	800/432-2934
Kentucky		
Louisville	Rm. 7411, 550 Main St., Cincinnati, OH 45202	502/582-6261
Louisiana		
New Orleans	515 Rusk Ave., Houston, TX 77002	504/589-6696

Table 15.12 (continued)

State/City	Address	Telephone
Maryland		
Baltimore	Rm. 1337, 9th and Market Sts., Philadelphia, PA 19107	301/962-4980
Massachusetts		
Boston	Rm. 216, 10 Causeway St., 02222	617/565-8121
Michigan		
Detroit	Rm. M-25, 477 Michigan Ave., Detroit, 48226	313/226-7016
Grand Rapids		616/451-2628
Minnesota		
Minneapolis	33d Fl., 230 S. Dearborn St., Chicago, IL 60604	612/349-3333
Missouri	Rm. 529, 210 N. Tucker Blvd., St. Louis 63101	
St. Louis		314/425-4106
From elsewhere in Missouri		800/392-7711
Nebraska		
Omaha	215 N. 17th St., Omaha 68102	402/221-3353
From elsewhere in Nebraska		800/642-8383
New Jersey		
Northern NJ	Rm. 2-110, 26 Federal Plaza, New York, NY 10278	
Southern NJ	Rm. 1337, 9th and Market Sts., Philadelphia, PA 19107	
Newark		201/645-3600
Trenton		609/396-4400
New Mexico		
Albuquerque	819 Taylor St., Fort Worth, TX 67102	505/766-3091

Table 15.12 (continued)

State/City	Address	Telephone
New York		
Albany	111 W. Huron, 14202	518/463-4421
Buffalo		716/846-4010
New York	Rm. 2-110, 26 Federal Plaza, 10278	212/264-4464
Rochester		716/546-5075
Syracuse		315/476-8545
North Carolina		
Charlotte	75 Spring St. SW., Atlanta, GA 30303	704/376-3600
Ohio	Rm. 7411, 550 Main St., Cincinnati 45202	
Akron		216/375-5638
Cincinnati		513/684-2801
Cleveland		216/522-4040
Columbus		614/221-1014
Dayton		513/223-7377
Toledo		419/241-3223
Oklahoma		
Oklahoma City	819 Taylor St., Forth Worth, TX 76102	405/231-4868
Tulsa		918/584-4193
Oregon		
Portland	Box 18, 1220 SW. 3d Ave. 97204	918/584-4193
Pennsylvania	Rm. 1337, 9th and Market Sts., Philadelphia 19107	
Philadelphia		215/597-7042
Pittsburgh		412/644-3456

Table 15.12 (continued)

State/City	Address	Telephone
Rhode Island		
Providence	Rm. 216, 10 Causeway St., Boston, MA 02222	401/331-5565
Tennessee	75 Spring St. SW., Atlanta, GA 30303	
Chattanooga		615/265-8231
Memphis		901/521-3265
Nashville		615/242-5064
Texas		
Austin	515 Rusk Ave., Houston 77002	512/472-5494
Dallas	819 Taylor St., Forth Worth 76102	214/767-8585
Forth Worth	819 Taylor St. 76102	817/334-3624
Houston	515 Rusk Ave 77002	713/229-2552
San Antonio	515 Rusk Ave., Houston 77002	512/224-4471
Utah		
Salt Lake City	1961 Stout St., P.O. Drawer 3526, Denver, CO 80294	801/524-5353
Virginia	Rm. 1337, 9th and Market Sts., Philadelphia, PA 19107	
Norfolk		804/441-3101
Richmond		804/643-4926
Roanoke		703/982-8591
Washington	Box 18, 1220 SW. 3d Ave., Portland, OR 97204	
Seattle		206/442-0570
Tacoma		206/383-7970
Wisconsin		
Milwaukee	33d Fl., 230 S. Dearborn St., Chicago, IL 60604	414/271-2273

Chapter 16

FINANCIAL TABLES

Tables 16.1 through 16.8 can be used in conjunction with the financial analysis and the preparation of financial projections. The tables presented are

- Present value
- Future value
- Mortgage amortization
- Sinking fund payment
- Growth of a $100 monthly deposit
- Number of years money will last at a given withdrawal rate
- Compound interest rates
- Dollar/decimal equivalence of fractions

16.1 PRESENT VALUE TABLES

Financial analysis frequently involves the process of estimating cash flows. Present value tables (or a financial calculator) are essential for making accurate and appropriate estimates.

Table 16.1 is the present value of a single sum, which represents the value today of a single amount that is to be received in the future, based on a level compound interest rate.

> *EXAMPLE. A 45-year-old client plans to invest in 20-year, zero-coupon, tax-exempt bonds that yield 8 percent. Upon retirement at age 65, he wants to have accumulated $100,000. The present value of $100,000 to be received 20 years hence at 8 percent compound annually is expressed as:*
>
> *$100,000 × Present value of 1 for 20 periods at 8% = Present value*
>
> *Reference to the "present value of 1" table provides the following equation:*
>
> *$100,000 × 0.2145 = $21,450*

Table 16.2 is the present value of an annuity, which represents the value today of a level stream of income to be received each period for a finite number of periods.

> **EXAMPLE.** *A recent retiree wants to invest part of his lump-sum retirement benefits to assure himself an annual income of $12,500 for 25 years. He invests the amount at an annual interest rate of 9 percent. The calculation for the present value of this annuity ($12,500 for 25 years) is:*
>
> *$12,500 × Present value of an annuity factor for 25 years at 9% = Present value*
>
> *Reference to the "present value of annuity of one" table provides the following equation:*
>
> *$12,500 × 9.8226 = $122,783*

16.2 FUTURE VALUE TABLES

Financial analysis frequently involves the process of estimating cash flows. Future value tables (or a financial calculator) are essential for making accurate and appropriate estimates.

Table 16.3 is the future value of a single sum, which represents the value at a special date in the future of a single amount invested today:

> **EXAMPLE.** *A client purchased a $200,000 home that he plans to sell in 11 years. He expects the value of the home to appreciate at about 7 percent per year and wants to know what it will be worth at that rate in 11 years. The future value of $200,000 in 11 years at 7 percent is expressed as*
>
> *$200,000 × Future value of 1 for 11 periods at 7% = Future value*
>
> *Reference to the "future value of 1" table provides the following equation:*
>
> *$200,000 × 2.1049 = $420,980*

Table 16.4 is for the future value of an annuity which represents the value at a specified date in the future of a level stream of investments made each period at a level compound interest rate.

> **EXAMPLE.** *A 30-year-old client begins annual individual retirement account (IRA) payments of $2,250 for himself and his spouse. He wants to know how much he will have accumulated if he earns 10 percent on his money and does not begin withdrawing it until age 70. The computation is made as follows:*
>
> *$2,250 × Future value of an annuity for 40 periods at 10% = Future value*
>
> *Referenced to the "future value of an annuity of 1" table provides the following equation:*
>
> *$2,250 × 442.59 = $995,828*

Table 16.1 The Present Value of a Future Amount of 1 (P/F)

n	1%	2%	3%	4%	5%	6%	7%	8%	9%	10%	11%	12%	13%	14%	15%
1	9901	9804	9709	9615	9524	9434	9346	9259	9174	9091	9009	8929	8850	8772	8696
2	9803	9612	9426	9246	9070	8900	8734	8573	8417	8264	8116	7972	7831	7695	7561
3	9706	9423	9151	8890	8638	8396	8163	7938	7722	7513	7312	7118	6931	6750	6575
4	9610	9239	8885	8548	8227	7921	7629	7350	7084	6830	6587	6355	6133	5921	5718
5	9515	9057	8626	8219	7835	7473	7130	6806	6499	6209	5934	5674	5428	5194	4972
6	9420	8880	8375	7903	7462	7050	6663	6302	5963	5645	5346	5066	4803	4556	4323
7	9327	8706	8131	7599	7107	6651	6228	5835	5470	5132	4817	4524	4251	3996	3759
8	9235	8535	7894	7307	6768	6274	5820	5403	5019	4665	4339	4039	3762	3506	3269
9	9143	8368	7664	7026	6446	5919	5439	5002	4604	4241	3909	3606	3329	3075	2843
10	9053	8204	7441	6756	6139	5584	5084	4632	4224	3855	3522	3220	2946	2697	2472
11	8963	8043	7224	6496	5847	5268	4751	4289	3875	3505	3173	2875	2607	2366	2149
12	8874	7885	7014	6246	5568	4970	4440	3971	3555	3186	2858	2567	2307	2076	1869
13	8787	7730	6810	6006	5303	4688	4150	3677	3262	2897	2575	2292	2042	1821	1625
14	8700	7579	6611	5775	5051	4423	3878	3405	2993	2633	2320	2046	1807	1597	1413
15	8614	7430	6419	5553	4810	4173	3625	3152	2745	2394	2090	1827	1599	1401	1229
16	8528	7284	6232	5339	4581	3936	3387	2919	2519	2176	1883	1631	1415	1229	1069
17	8444	7142	6050	5134	4363	3714	3166	2703	2311	1978	1696	1456	1252	1078	0929
18	8360	7002	5874	4936	4155	3503	2959	2502	2120	1799	1528	1300	1108	0946	0808
19	8277	6864	5703	4746	3957	3305	2765	2317	1945	1635	1377	1161	0981	0829	0703
20	8195	6730	5537	4564	3769	3118	2584	2145	1784	1486	1240	1037	0868	0728	0611
21	8114	6598	5375	4388	3589	2942	2415	1987	1637	1351	1117	0926	0768	0638	0531
22	8034	6468	5219	4220	3418	2775	2257	1839	1502	1229	1007	0826	0680	0560	0462
23	7954	6342	5067	4057	3256	2618	2109	1703	1378	1117	0907	0738	0601	0491	0402
24	7876	6217	4919	3901	3101	2470	1971	1577	1264	1015	0817	0659	0532	0431	0349
25	7798	6095	4776	3751	2953	2330	1842	1460	1160	0923	0736	0588	0471	0378	0304
26	7721	5976	4637	3607	2812	2198	1722	1352	1064	0839	0663	0525	0417	0332	0264
27	7644	5859	4502	3468	2678	2074	1609	1252	0976	0763	0597	0469	0369	0291	0230
28	7568	5744	4371	3335	2551	1956	1504	1159	0896	0693	0538	0419	0326	0255	0200
29	7493	5631	4244	3206	2429	1846	1406	1073	0822	0630	0485	0374	0289	0224	0174
30	7419	5521	4120	3083	2314	1741	1314	0994	0754	0573	0437	0334	0256	0196	0151
31	7346	5412	4000	2965	2204	1643	1228	0920	0692	0521	0394	0298	0226	0172	0131
32	7273	5306	3883	2851	2099	1550	1147	0852	0634	0474	0354	0266	0200	0151	0114
33	7201	5202	3770	2741	1999	1462	1072	0789	0582	0431	0319	0238	0177	0133	0099
34	7130	5100	3660	2636	1904	1379	1002	0731	0534	0391	0288	0212	0157	0116	0086
35	7059	5000	3554	2534	1813	1301	0937	0676	0490	0356	0259	0189	0139	0102	0075
36	6989	4902	3450	2437	1727	1227	0875	0626	0449	0324	0234	0169	0123	0089	0065
37	6920	4806	3350	2343	1644	1158	0818	0580	0412	0294	0210	0151	0109	0078	0057
38	6852	4712	3252	2253	1566	1092	0765	0537	0378	0267	0190	0135	0096	0069	0049
39	6784	4620	3158	2166	1492	1031	0715	0497	0347	0243	0171	0120	0085	0060	0043
40	6717	4529	3066	2083	1420	0972	0668	0460	0318	0221	0154	0107	0075	0053	0037
41	6650	4440	2976	2003	1353	0917	0624	0426	0292	0201	0139	0096	0067	0046	0033
42	6584	4353	2890	1926	1288	0865	0583	0395	0268	0183	0125	0086	0059	0041	0028
43	6519	4268	2805	1852	1227	0816	0545	0365	0246	0166	0113	0077	0052	0036	0025
44	6454	4184	2724	1781	1169	0770	0509	0338	0226	0151	0101	0068	0046	0031	0021
45	6391	4102	2644	1712	1113	0727	0476	0313	0207	0137	0091	0061	0041	0027	0019
46	6327	4021	2567	1646	1060	0685	0445	0290	0190	0125	0082	0054	0036	0024	0016
47	6265	3943	2493	1583	1010	0647	0416	0269	0174	0113	0074	0049	0032	0021	0014
48	6203	3865	2420	1522	0961	0610	0389	0249	0160	0103	0067	0043	0028	0019	0012
49	6141	3790	2350	1463	0916	0575	0363	0230	0147	0094	0060	0039	0025	0016	0011
50	6080	3715	2281	1407	0872	0543	0340	0213	0135	0085	0054	0035	-0022	0014	0009

Table 16.1 (continued)

n	16%	17%	18%	19%	20%	21%	22%	23%	24%	25%	30%	35%	40%	45%	50%
1	8621	8547	8475	8403	8333	8264	8197	8130	8065	8000	7692	7407	7143	6897	6667
2	7432	7305	7182	7062	6944	6830	6719	6610	6504	6400	5917	5487	5102	4756	4444
3	6407	6244	6086	5934	5787	5645	5507	5374	5245	5120	4552	4064	3644	3280	2963
4	5523	5337	5158	4987	4822	4665	4514	4369	4230	4096	3501	3011	2603	2262	1975
5	4761	4561	4371	4190	4019	3855	3700	3552	3411	3277	2693	2230	1859	1560	1317
6	4104	3898	3704	3521	3349	3186	3033	2888	2751	2621	2072	1652	1328	1076	0878
7	3538	3332	3139	2959	2791	2633	2486	2348	2218	2097	1594	1224	0949	0742	0585
8	3050	2848	2660	2487	2326	2176	2038	1909	1789	1678	1226	0906	0678	0512	0390
9	2630	2434	2255	2090	1938	1799	1670	1552	1443	1342	0943	0671	0484	0353	0260
10	2267	2080	1911	1756	1615	1486	1369	1262	1163	1074	0725	0497	0346	0243	0173
11	1954	1778	1619	1476	1346	1229	1122	1026	0938	0859	0558	0368	0247	0168	0116
12	1685	1520	1372	1240	1122	1015	0920	0834	0757	0687	0429	0273	0176	0116	0077
13	1452	1299	1163	1042	0935	0839	0754	0678	0610	0550	0330	0202	0126	0080	0051
14	1252	1110	0986	0876	0779	0693	0618	0551	0492	0440	0254	0150	0090	0055	0034
15	1079	0949	0835	0736	0649	0573	0507	0448	0397	0352	0195	0111	0064	0038	0023
16	0930	0811	0708	0618	0541	0474	0415	0364	0320	0281	0150	0082	0046	0026	0015
17	0802	0693	0600	0520	0451	0391	0340	0296	0258	0225	0116	0061	0033	0018	0010
18	0691	0592	0508	0437	0376	0324	0279	0241	0208	0180	0089	0045	0023	0012	0007
19	0596	0506	0431	0367	0313	0267	0229	0196	0168	0144	0068	0033	0017	0009	0004
20	0514	0433	0365	0308	0261	0221	0187	0159	0135	0115	0053	0025	0012	0006	0003
21	0443	0370	0309	0259	0217	0183	0154	0129	0109	0092	0040	0018	0008	0004	0002
22	0382	0316	0262	0218	0181	0151	0126	0105	0088	0074	0031	0014	0006	0003	0001
23	0329	0270	0222	0183	0151	0125	0103	0085	0071	0059	0024	0010	0004	0002	0001
24	0284	0231	0188	0154	0126	0103	0085	0070	0057	0047	0018	0007	0003	0001	0001
25	0245	0197	0160	0129	0105	0085	0069	0056	0046	0038	0014	0005	0002	0001	0000
26	0211	0169	0135	0109	0087	0070	0057	0046	0037	0030	0011	0004	0002	0001	0000
27	0182	0144	0115	0091	0073	0058	0047	0037	0030	0024	0008	0003	0001	0000	0000
28	0157	0123	0097	0077	0061	0048	0038	0030	0024	0019	0006	0002	0001	0000	0000
29	0135	0105	0082	0064	0051	0040	0031	0025	0019	0015	0005	0002	0001	0000	0000
30	0116	0090	0070	0054	0042	0033	0026	0020	0016	0012	0004	0001	0000	0000	0000
31	0100	0077	0059	0045	0035	0027	0021	0016	0013	0010	0003	0001	0000	0000	0000
32	0087	0066	0050	0038	0029	0022	0017	0013	0010	0008	0002	0001	0000	0000	0000
33	0075	0056	0043	0032	0024	0018	0014	0011	0008	0006	0002	0001	0000	0000	0000
34	0064	0048	0036	0027	0020	0015	0012	0009	0007	0005	0001	0000	0000	0000	0000
35	0055	0041	0030	0023	0017	0013	0010	0007	0005	0004	0001	0000	0000	0000	0000
36	0048	0035	0026	0019	0014	0011	0008	0006	0004	0003	0001	0000	0000	0000	0000
37	0041	0030	0022	0016	0012	0009	0006	0005	0003	0003	0001	0000	0000	0000	0000
38	0036	0026	0019	0014	0010	0007	0005	0004	0003	0002	0000	0000	0000	0000	0000
39	0031	0022	0016	0011	0008	0006	0004	0003	0002	0002	0000	0000	0000	0000	0000
40	0026	0019	0013	0010	0007	0005	0003	0002	0002	0001	0000	0000	0000	0000	0000
41	0023	0016	0011	0008	0006	0004	0003	0002	0002	0001	0000	0000	0000	0000	0000
42	0020	0014	0010	0007	0005	0003	0002	0002	0001	0001	0000	0000	0000	0000	0000
43	0017	0012	0008	0006	0004	0003	0002	0001	0001	0001	0000	0000	0000	0000	0000
44	0015	0010	0007	0005	0003	0002	0002	0001	0001	0001	0000	0000	0000	0000	0000
45	0013	0008	0006	0004	0003	0002	0001	0001	0001	0000	0000	0000	0000	0000	0000
46	0011	0007	0005	0003	0002	0002	0001	0001	0001	0000	0000	0000	0000	0000	0000
47	0009	0006	0004	0003	0002	0001	0001	0001	0001	0000	0000	0000	0000	0000	0000
48	0008	0005	0003	0002	0002	0001	0001	0001	0000	0000	0000	0000	0000	0000	0000
49	0007	0005	0003	0002	0001	0001	0001	0000	0000	0000	0000	0000	0000	0000	0000
50	0006	0004	0002	0002	0001	0001	0001	0000	0000	0000	0000	0000	0000	0000	0000

Table 16.2 The Present Value of an Ordinary Annuity of 1 (P/A)

n	1%	2%	3%	4%	5%	6%	7%	8%	9%	10%	11%	12%	13%	14%	15%
1	.9901	.9804	.9709	.9615	.9524	.9434	.9346	.9259	.9174	.9091	.9009	.8929	.8850	.8772	.8696
2	1.9704	1.9416	1.9135	1.8861	1.8594	1.8334	1.8080	1.7833	1.7591	1.7355	1.7125	1.6901	1.6681	1.6467	1.6257
3	2.9410	2.8839	2.8286	2.7751	2.7232	2.6730	2.6243	2.5771	2.5313	2.4869	2.4437	2.4018	2.3612	2.3216	2.2832
4	3.9020	3.8077	3.7171	3.6299	3.5459	3.4651	3.3872	3.3121	3.2397	3.1699	3.1024	3.0374	2.9745	2.9137	2.8550
5	4.8534	4.7135	4.5797	4.4518	4.3295	4.2124	4.1002	3.9927	3.8897	3.7908	3.6959	3.6048	3.5172	3.4331	3.3522
6	5.7955	5.6014	5.4172	5.2421	5.0757	4.9173	4.7666	4.6229	4.4859	4.3553	4.2305	4.1114	3.9976	3.8887	3.7845
7	6.7282	6.4720	6.2303	6.0021	5.7864	5.5824	5.3893	5.2064	5.0330	4.8684	4.7122	4.5638	4.4226	4.2883	4.1604
8	7.6517	7.3255	7.0197	6.7328	6.4632	6.2098	5.9713	5.7466	5.5348	5.3349	5.1461	4.9676	4.7988	4.6389	4.4873
9	8.5660	8.1622	7.7861	7.4353	7.1078	6.8017	6.5152	6.2469	5.9953	5.7590	5.5371	5.3282	5.1317	4.9464	4.7716
10	9.4713	8.9826	8.5302	8.1109	7.7217	7.3601	7.0236	6.7101	6.4177	6.1446	5.8892	5.6502	5.4262	5.2161	5.0188
11	10.3676	9.7868	9.2526	8.7605	8.3064	7.8869	7.4987	7.1390	6.8052	6.4951	6.2065	5.9377	5.6869	5.4527	5.2337
12	11.2551	10.5753	9.9540	9.3851	8.8633	8.3839	7.9427	7.5361	7.1607	6.8137	6.4924	6.1944	5.9177	5.6603	5.4206
13	12.1338	11.3484	10.6349	9.9857	9.3936	8.8527	8.3577	7.9038	7.4869	7.1034	6.7499	6.4235	6.1218	5.8424	5.5832
14	13.0037	12.1062	11.2961	10.5631	9.8986	9.2950	8.7455	8.2442	7.7862	7.3667	6.9819	6.6282	6.3025	6.0021	5.7245
15	13.8651	12.8492	11.9379	11.1184	10.3797	9.7123	9.1079	8.5595	8.0607	7.6061	7.1909	6.8109	6.4624	6.1422	5.8474
16	14.7179	13.5777	12.5611	11.6523	10.8378	10.1059	9.4467	8.8514	8.3126	7.8237	7.3792	6.9740	6.6039	6.2651	5.9542
17	15.5623	14.2919	13.1661	12.1657	11.2741	10.4773	9.7632	9.1216	8.5436	8.0216	7.5488	7.1196	6.7291	6.3729	6.0472
18	16.3983	14.9920	13.7535	12.6593	11.6896	10.8276	10.0591	9.3719	8.7556	8.2014	7.7016	7.2497	6.8399	6.4674	6.1280
19	17.2260	15.6785	14.3238	13.1339	12.0853	11.1581	10.3356	9.6036	8.9501	8.3649	7.8393	7.3658	6.9380	6.5504	6.1982
20	18.0456	16.3514	14.8775	13.5903	12.4622	11.4699	10.5940	9.8181	9.1285	8.5136	7.9633	7.4694	7.0248	6.6231	6.2593
21	18.8570	17.0112	15.4150	14.0292	12.8212	11.7641	10.8355	10.0168	9.2922	8.6487	8.0751	7.5620	7.1016	6.6870	6.3125
22	19.6604	17.6580	15.9369	14.4511	13.1630	12.0416	11.0612	10.2007	9.4424	8.7715	8.1757	7.6446	7.1695	6.7430	6.3587
23	20.4558	18.2922	16.4436	14.8569	13.4886	12.3034	11.2722	10.3711	9.5802	8.8832	8.2664	7.7184	7.2297	6.7921	6.3988
24	21.2434	18.9139	16.9355	15.2470	13.7987	12.5504	11.4693	10.5288	9.7066	8.9847	8.3481	7.7843	7.2829	6.8352	6.4338
25	22.0232	19.5234	17.4132	15.6221	14.0940	12.7834	11.6536	10.6748	9.8226	9.0770	8.4217	7.8431	7.3300	6.8729	6.4641
26	22.7952	20.1210	17.8768	15.9828	14.3752	13.0032	11.8258	10.8100	9.9290	9.1610	8.4880	7.8956	7.3717	6.9061	6.4906
27	23.5596	20.7069	18.3270	16.3296	14.6430	13.2106	11.9867	10.9352	10.0266	9.2372	8.5478	7.9425	7.4086	6.9352	6.5135
28	24.3165	21.2813	18.7641	16.6631	14.8981	13.4062	12.1371	11.0511	10.1161	9.3066	8.6016	7.9844	7.4412	6.9607	6.5335
29	25.0658	21.8444	19.1885	16.9837	15.1411	13.5907	12.2777	11.1584	10.1983	9.3696	8.6501	8.0218	7.4701	6.9831	6.5509
30	25.8077	22.3964	19.6005	17.2920	15.3725	13.7649	12.4091	11.2578	10.2737	9.4269	8.6938	8.0552	7.4957	7.0027	6.5660
31	26.5423	22.9377	20.0005	17.5885	15.5928	13.9291	12.5318	11.3498	10.3428	9.4790	8.7331	8.0850	7.5183	7.0199	6.5791
32	27.2696	23.4683	20.3888	17.8736	15.8027	14.0841	12.6466	11.4350	10.4062	9.5264	8.7686	8.1116	7.5383	7.0350	6.5905
33	27.9897	23.9885	20.7658	18.1477	16.0026	14.2303	12.7538	11.5139	10.4644	9.5694	8.8005	8.1353	7.5560	7.0482	6.6003
34	28.7027	24.4986	21.1319	18.4112	16.1929	14.3682	12.8540	11.5870	10.5178	9.6086	8.8293	8.1565	7.5717	7.0599	6.6091
35	29.4086	24.9986	21.4872	18.6646	16.3742	14.4983	12.9477	11.6546	10.5668	9.6442	8.8552	8.1755	7.5856	7.0701	6.6166
36	30.1075	25.4888	21.8323	18.9083	16.5469	14.6211	13.0352	11.7172	10.6118	9.6765	8.8786	8.1924	7.5979	7.0790	6.6231
37	30.7995	25.9694	22.1673	19.1426	16.7113	14.7368	13.1170	11.7752	10.6530	9.7059	8.8996	8.2075	7.6087	7.0868	6.6288
38	31.4847	26.4406	22.4925	19.3679	16.8679	14.8460	13.1935	11.8289	10.6908	9.7327	8.9186	8.2210	7.6183	7.0937	6.6338
39	32.1631	26.9026	22.8082	19.5845	17.0171	14.9491	13.2650	11.8786	10.7255	9.7570	8.9356	8.2330	7.6269	7.0998	6.6380
40	32.8347	27.3555	23.1148	19.7928	17.1591	15.0464	13.3317	11.9246	10.7574	9.7791	8.9510	8.2438	7.6344	7.1051	6.6418
41	33.4997	27.7995	23.4124	19.9931	17.2944	15.1381	13.3941	11.9672	10.7866	9.7991	8.9649	8.2534	7.6410	7.1097	6.6450
42	34.1581	28.2348	23.7014	20.1857	17.4232	15.2246	13.4525	12.0067	10.8134	9.8174	8.9774	8.2619	7.6469	7.1138	6.6478
43	34.8100	28.6615	23.9819	20.3708	17.5459	15.3062	13.5070	12.0432	10.8380	9.8340	8.9885	8.2696	7.6522	7.1173	6.6503
44	35.4555	29.0799	24.2543	20.5489	17.6628	15.3833	13.5579	12.0771	10.8605	9.8491	8.9988	8.2764	7.6568	7.1205	6.6524
45	36.0945	29.4901	24.5187	20.7201	17.7741	15.4559	13.6055	12.1084	10.8812	9.8628	9.0079	8.2825	7.6609	7.1232	6.6543
46	36.7273	29.8923	24.7755	20.8847	17.8801	15.5244	13.6500	12.1374	10.9002	9.8753	9.0161	8.2880	7.6645	7.1256	6.6559
47	37.3537	30.2866	25.0247	21.0430	17.9810	15.5891	13.6916	12.1643	10.9176	9.8866	9.0235	8.2928	7.6677	7.1277	6.6573
48	37.9740	30.6731	25.2667	21.1952	18.0772	15.6501	13.7305	12.1891	10.9336	9.8969	9.0302	8.2972	7.6705	7.1296	6.6585
49	38.5881	31.0521	25.5017	21.3415	18.1687	15.7077	13.7668	12.2122	10.9482	9.9063	9.0362	8.3010	7.6730	7.1312	6.6596
50	39.1961	31.4236	25.7298	21.4822	18.2559	15.7619	13.8008	12.2335	10.9617	9.9148	9.0416	8.3045	7.6753	7.1327	6.6605

Table 16.2 (continued)

n	16%	17%	18%	19%	20%	21%	22%	23%	24%	25%	30%	35%	40%	45%	50%
1	.8621	.8547	.8475	.8403	.8333	.8264	.8197	.8130	.8065	.8000	.7692	.7407	.7143	.6897	.6667
2	1.6052	1.5852	1.5656	1.5465	1.5278	1.5095	1.4915	1.4740	1.4568	1.4400	1.3609	1.2894	1.2245	1.1653	1.1111
3	2.2459	2.2096	2.1743	2.1399	2.1065	2.0739	2.0422	2.0114	1.9813	1.9520	1.8161	1.6959	1.5889	1.4933	1.4074
4	2.7982	2.7432	2.6901	2.6386	2.5887	2.5404	2.4936	2.4483	2.4043	2.3616	2.1662	1.9969	1.8492	1.7195	1.6049
5	3.2743	3.1993	3.1272	3.0576	2.9906	2.9260	2.8636	2.8035	2.7454	2.6893	2.4356	2.2200	2.0352	1.8755	1.7366
6	3.6847	3.5892	3.4976	3.4098	3.3255	3.2446	3.1669	3.0923	3.0205	2.9514	2.6428	2.3852	2.1680	1.9831	1.8244
7	4.0386	3.9224	3.8115	3.7057	3.6046	3.5079	3.4155	3.3270	3.2423	3.1611	2.8021	2.5075	2.2628	2.0573	1.8830
8	4.3436	4.2072	4.0776	3.9544	3.8372	3.7256	3.6193	3.5179	3.4212	3.3289	2.9247	2.5982	2.3306	2.1085	1.9220
9	4.6065	4.4506	4.3030	4.1633	4.0310	3.9054	3.7863	3.6731	3.5655	3.4631	3.0190	2.6653	2.3790	2.1438	1.9480
10	4.8332	4.6586	4.4941	4.3389	4.1925	4.0541	3.9232	3.7993	3.6819	3.5705	3.0916	2.7150	2.4136	2.1681	1.9653
11	5.0286	4.8364	4.6560	4.4865	4.3271	4.1769	4.0354	3.9019	3.7757	3.6564	3.1474	2.7519	2.4383	2.1849	1.9769
12	5.1971	4.9884	4.7932	4.6105	4.4392	4.2785	4.1274	3.9852	3.8514	3.7251	3.1903	2.7792	2.4559	2.1965	1.9846
13	5.3423	5.1183	4.9095	4.7147	4.5327	4.3624	4.2028	4.0530	3.9124	3.7801	3.2233	2.7994	2.4685	2.2045	1.9897
14	5.4675	5.2293	5.0081	4.8023	4.6106	4.4317	4.2646	4.1082	3.9616	3.8241	3.2487	2.8143	2.4775	2.2100	1.9932
15	5.5755	5.3242	5.0916	4.8759	4.6755	4.4890	4.3152	4.1530	4.0013	3.8593	3.2682	2.8254	2.4839	2.2138	1.9954
16	5.6685	5.4053	5.1624	4.9377	4.7296	4.5364	4.3567	4.1894	4.0333	3.8874	3.2833	2.8337	2.4885	2.2164	1.9970
17	5.7487	5.4746	5.2223	4.9897	4.7746	4.5755	4.3908	4.2190	4.0591	3.9099	3.2948	2.8397	2.4918	2.2182	1.9980
18	5.8179	5.5338	5.2732	5.0333	4.8122	4.6079	4.4187	4.2431	4.0799	3.9279	3.3037	2.8443	2.4941	2.2195	1.9986
19	5.8775	5.5845	5.3163	5.0700	4.8435	4.6346	4.4415	4.2627	4.0967	3.9424	3.3106	2.8476	2.4958	2.2203	1.9991
20	5.9288	5.6278	5.3528	5.1009	4.8696	4.6567	4.4603	4.2786	4.1103	3.9539	3.3158	2.8501	2.4970	2.2209	1.9994
21	5.9732	5.6648	5.3837	5.1268	4.8913	4.6749	4.4756	4.2915	4.1212	3.9631	3.3199	2.8519	2.4979	2.2213	1.9996
22	6.0113	5.6964	5.4099	5.1486	4.9094	4.6900	4.4882	4.3021	4.1300	3.9705	3.3230	2.8533	2.4985	2.2216	1.9997
23	6.0443	5.7234	5.4321	5.1669	4.9245	4.7025	4.4985	4.3106	4.1371	3.9764	3.3254	2.8543	2.4989	2.2218	1.9998
24	6.0726	5.7465	5.4510	5.1823	4.9371	4.7128	4.5070	4.3176	4.1428	3.9811	3.3272	2.8550	2.4992	2.2219	1.9999
25	6.0971	5.7662	5.4669	5.1952	4.9476	4.7213	4.5139	4.3232	4.1474	3.9849	3.3286	2.8556	2.4994	2.2220	1.9999
26	6.1182	5.7831	5.4805	5.2060	4.9563	4.7284	4.5196	4.3278	4.1511	3.9879	3.3297	2.8560	2.4996	2.2221	1.9999
27	6.1364	5.7975	5.4919	5.2151	4.9636	4.7342	4.5243	4.3316	4.1541	3.9903	3.3306	2.8563	2.4997	2.2221	2.0000
28	6.1521	5.8099	5.5016	5.2228	4.9697	4.7390	4.5281	4.3346	4.1566	3.9923	3.3312	2.8565	2.4998	2.2221	2.0000
29	6.1656	5.8204	5.5099	5.2293	4.9747	4.7430	4.5312	4.3371	4.1585	3.9938	3.3317	2.8567	2.4998	2.2222	2.0000
30	6.1772	5.8294	5.5168	5.2347	4.9789	4.7463	4.5338	4.3391	4.1601	3.9950	3.3321	2.8568	2.4999	2.2222	2.0000
31	6.1873	5.8371	5.5227	5.2392	4.9825	4.7490	4.5359	4.3407	4.1614	3.9960	3.3324	2.8569	2.4999	2.2222	2.0000
32	6.1959	5.8437	5.5277	5.2431	4.9854	4.7512	4.5376	4.3420	4.1624	3.9968	3.3326	2.8569	2.4999	2.2222	2.0000
33	6.2034	5.8493	5.5320	5.2463	4.9878	4.7531	4.5390	4.3431	4.1632	3.9975	3.3328	2.8570	2.5000	2.2222	2.0000
34	6.2098	5.8541	5.5356	5.2490	4.9899	4.7546	4.5402	4.3440	4.1639	3.9980	3.3329	2.8570	2.5000	2.2222	2.0000
35	6.2153	5.8582	5.5386	5.2512	4.9915	4.7559	4.5411	4.3447	4.1644	3.9984	3.3330	2.8571	2.5000	2.2222	2.0000
36	6.2201	5.8617	5.5412	5.2531	4.9930	4.7569	4.5419	4.3453	4.1649	3.9987	3.3331	2.8571	2.5000	2.2222	2.0000
37	6.2243	5.8647	5.5434	5.2547	4.9941	4.7578	4.5425	4.3458	4.1652	3.9990	3.3332	2.8571	2.5000	2.2222	2.0000
38	6.2278	5.8673	5.5453	5.2561	4.9951	4.7585	4.5431	4.3461	4.1655	3.9992	3.3332	2.8571	2.5000	2.2222	2.0000
39	6.2309	5.8695	5.5468	5.2572	4.9959	4.7591	4.5435	4.3464	4.1657	3.9993	3.3332	2.8571	2.5000	2.2222	2.0000
40	6.2335	5.8713	5.5482	5.2582	4.9966	4.7596	4.5439	4.3467	4.1659	3.9995	3.3333	2.8571	2.5000	2.2222	2.0000
41	6.2358	5.8729	5.5493	5.2590	4.9972	4.7600	4.5441	4.3469	4.1660	3.9996	3.3333	2.8571	2.5000	2.2222	2.0000
42	6.2377	5.8743	5.5503	5.2596	4.9977	4.7603	4.5444	4.3471	4.1662	3.9997	3.3333	2.8571	2.5000	2.2222	2.0000
43	6.2394	5.8755	5.5511	5.2602	4.9980	4.7606	4.5446	4.3472	4.1663	3.9997	3.3333	2.8571	2.5000	2.2222	2.0000
44	6.2409	5.8765	5.5518	5.2607	4.9984	4.7608	4.5447	4.3473	4.1663	3.9998	3.3333	2.8571	2.5000	2.2222	2.0000
45	6.2422	5.8773	5.5523	5.2611	4.9986	4.7610	4.5448	4.3474	4.1664	3.9998	3.3333	2.8571	2.5000	2.2222	2.0000
46	6.2432	5.8781	5.5528	5.2614	4.9989	4.7611	4.5450	4.3475	4.1665	3.9999	3.3334	2.8571	2.5000	2.2222	2.0000
47	6.2442	5.8787	5.5533	5.2617	4.9991	4.7613	4.5450	4.3475	4.1665	3.9999	3.3334	2.8571	2.5000	2.2222	2.0000
48	6.2450	5.8792	5.5536	5.2619	4.9992	4.7614	4.5451	4.3476	4.1665	3.9999	3.3334	2.8571	2.5000	2.2222	2.0000
49	6.2457	5.8797	5.5539	5.2621	4.9994	4.7615	4.5452	4.3476	4.1666	3.9999	3.3334	2.8571	2.5000	2.2222	2.0000
50	6.2463	5.8801	5.5542	5.2623	4.9995	4.7615	4.5452	4.3477	4.1666	3.9999	3.3334	2.8571	2.5000	2.2222	2.0000

Table 16.3 The Future Value of a Present Amount of 1 (F/P)

n	1%	2%	3%	4%	5%	6%	7%	8%	9%	10%	11%	12%	13%	14%
1	1.0100	1.0200	1.0300	1.0400	1.0500	1.0600	1.0700	1.0800	1.0900	1.1000	1.1100	1.1200	1.1300	1.1400
2	1.0201	1.0404	1.0609	1.0816	1.1025	1.1236	1.1449	1.1664	1.1881	1.2100	1.2321	1.2544	1.2769	1.2996
3	1.0303	1.0612	1.0927	1.1249	1.1576	1.1910	1.2250	1.2597	1.2950	1.3310	1.3676	1.4049	1.4429	1.4815
4	1.0406	1.0824	1.1255	1.1699	1.2155	1.2625	1.3108	1.3605	1.4116	1.4641	1.5181	1.5735	1.6305	1.6890
5	1.0510	1.1041	1.1593	1.2167	1.2763	1.3382	1.4026	1.4693	1.5386	1.6105	1.6851	1.7623	1.8424	1.9254
6	1.0615	1.1262	1.1941	1.2653	1.3401	1.4185	1.5007	1.5869	1.6771	1.7716	1.8704	1.9738	2.0820	2.1950
7	1.0721	1.1487	1.2299	1.3159	1.4071	1.5036	1.6058	1.7138	1.8280	1.9487	2.0762	2.2107	2.3526	2.5023
8	1.0829	1.1717	1.2668	1.3686	1.4775	1.5938	1.7182	1.8509	1.9926	2.1436	2.3045	2.4760	2.6584	2.8526
9	1.0937	1.1951	1.3048	1.4233	1.5513	1.6895	1.8385	1.9990	2.1719	2.3579	2.5580	2.7731	3.0040	3.2520
10	1.1046	1.2190	1.3439	1.4802	1.6289	1.7908	1.9671	2.1589	2.3674	2.5937	2.8394	3.1059	3.3946	3.7072
11	1.1157	1.2434	1.3842	1.5395	1.7103	1.8983	2.1049	2.3316	2.5804	2.8531	3.1518	3.4786	3.8359	4.2262
12	1.1266	1.2682	1.4258	1.6010	1.7959	2.0122	2.2522	2.5182	2.8127	3.1384	3.4984	3.8960	4.3345	4.8179
13	1.1381	1.2936	1.4685	1.6651	1.8856	2.1329	2.4098	2.7196	3.0658	3.4523	3.8833	4.3635	4.8980	5.4924
14	1.1495	1.3195	1.5126	1.7317	1.9799	2.2609	2.5785	2.9372	3.3417	3.7975	4.3104	4.8871	5.5348	6.2614
15	1.1610	1.3459	1.5580	1.8009	2.0789	2.3966	2.7590	3.1722	3.6425	4.1772	4.7846	5.4736	6.2543	7.1379
16	1.1726	1.3728	1.6047	1.8730	2.1829	2.5403	2.9522	3.4259	3.9703	4.5950	5.3109	6.1304	7.0673	8.1373
17	1.1843	1.4002	1.6528	1.9479	2.2920	2.6928	3.1588	3.7000	4.3276	5.0545	5.8951	6.8661	7.9861	9.2765
18	1.1961	1.4282	1.7024	2.0258	2.4066	2.8543	3.3799	3.9960	4.7171	5.5599	6.5435	7.6900	9.0243	10.5752
19	1.2081	1.4568	1.7535	2.1068	2.5269	3.0256	3.6165	4.3157	5.1417	6.1159	7.2633	8.6128	10.1974	12.0557
20	1.2202	1.4859	1.8061	2.1911	2.6533	3.2071	3.8697	4.6609	5.6044	6.7275	8.0623	9.6463	11.5231	13.7435
21	1.2324	1.5157	1.8603	2.2788	2.7860	3.3996	4.1406	5.0338	6.1088	7.4002	8.9491	10.8039	13.0211	15.6676
22	1.2447	1.5460	1.9161	2.3699	2.9253	3.6035	4.4304	5.4365	6.6586	8.1403	9.9336	12.1003	14.7139	17.8611
23	1.2572	1.5769	1.9736	2.4647	3.0715	3.8197	4.7405	5.8714	7.2579	8.9543	11.0262	13.5524	16.6267	20.3616
24	1.2697	1.6084	2.0328	2.5633	3.2251	4.0489	5.0724	6.3412	7.9111	9.8497	12.2391	15.1787	18.7881	23.2122
25	1.2824	1.6406	2.0938	2.6658	3.3864	4.2919	5.4274	6.8485	8.6231	10.8347	13.5854	17.0001	21.2306	26.4620
26	1.2953	1.6734	2.1566	2.7725	3.5557	4.5494	5.8073	7.3963	9.3991	11.9181	15.0798	19.0401	23.9906	30.1666
27	1.3082	1.7069	2.2213	2.8834	3.7335	4.8223	6.2139	7.9880	10.2451	13.1100	16.7386	21.3249	27.1094	34.3900
28	1.3213	1.7410	2.2879	2.9987	3.9201	5.1117	6.6488	8.6271	11.1671	14.4210	18.5798	23.8839	30.6336	39.2046
29	1.3345	1.7758	2.3566	3.1186	4.1161	5.4184	7.1142	9.3172	12.1722	15.8631	20.6236	26.7500	34.6159	44.6932
30	1.3478	1.8114	2.4273	3.2434	4.3219	5.7435	7.6122	10.0626	13.2677	17.4494	22.8922	29.9600	39.1160	50.9503
31	1.3613	1.8476	2.5001	3.3731	4.5380	6.0881	8.1451	10.8676	14.4617	19.1943	25.4104	33.5552	44.2011	58.0833
32	1.3749	1.8845	2.5751	3.5081	4.7649	6.4534	8.7152	11.7370	15.7633	21.1137	28.2055	37.5818	49.9473	66.2150
33	1.3887	1.9222	2.6523	3.6484	5.0032	6.8406	9.3253	12.6760	17.1820	23.2251	31.3081	42.0917	56.4851	75.4851
34	1.4026	1.9607	2.7319	3.7943	5.2533	7.2510	9.9781	13.6901	18.7284	25.5476	34.7520	47.1427	63.7777	86.0530
35	1.4166	1.9999	2.8139	3.9461	5.5160	7.6861	10.6765	14.7853	20.4139	28.1023	38.5747	52.7998	72.0688	98.1004
36	1.4308	2.0399	2.8983	4.1039	5.7918	8.1472	11.4239	15.9681	22.2512	30.9126	42.8179	59.1358	81.4377	111.8350
37	1.4451	2.0807	2.9852	4.2681	6.0814	8.6361	12.2236	17.2456	24.2538	34.0038	47.5279	66.2321	92.0246	127.4910
38	1.4595	2.1223	3.0748	4.4388	6.3855	9.1542	13.0792	18.6252	26.4366	37.4042	52.7560	74.1799	103.9880	145.3400
39	1.4741	2.1647	3.1670	4.6164	6.7047	9.7035	13.9948	20.1152	28.8159	41.1446	58.5591	83.0815	117.5060	165.6880
40	1.4889	2.2080	3.2620	4.8010	7.0400	10.2857	14.9744	21.7244	31.4094	45.2591	65.0006	93.0513	132.7820	188.8840
41	1.5038	2.2522	3.3599	4.9931	7.3920	10.9028	16.0226	23.4624	34.2362	49.7850	72.1507	104.2170	150.0440	215.3280
42	1.5188	2.2972	3.4607	5.1928	7.7616	11.5570	17.1442	25.3394	37.3175	54.7635	80.0872	116.7240	169.5490	245.4740
43	1.5340	2.3432	3.5645	5.4005	8.1497	12.2504	18.3443	27.3665	40.6760	60.2398	88.8968	130.7300	191.5910	279.8400
44	1.5493	2.3901	3.6715	5.6165	8.5571	12.9854	19.6284	29.5558	44.3369	66.2638	98.6754	146.4180	216.4980	319.0180
45	1.5648	2.4379	3.7816	5.8412	8.9850	13.7646	21.0024	31.9203	48.3272	72.8902	109.5300	163.9880	244.6420	363.6800
46	1.5805	2.4866	3.8950	6.0748	9.4342	14.5904	22.4725	34.4739	52.6766	80.1792	121.5780	183.6670	276.4460	414.5950
47	1.5963	2.5363	4.0119	6.3178	9.9006	15.4658	24.0456	37.2318	57.4175	88.1971	134.9520	205.7070	312.3840	472.6390
48	1.6122	2.5871	4.1323	6.5705	10.4013	16.3938	25.7288	40.2104	62.5851	97.0168	149.7960	230.3920	352.9940	538.8080
49	1.6283	2.6388	4.2562	6.8333	10.9213	17.3774	27.5298	43.4272	68.2177	106.7190	166.2740	258.0390	398.8830	614.2410
50	1.6446	2.6916	4.3839	7.1067	11.4674	18.4201	29.4569	46.9014	74.3573	117.3900	184.5640	289.0030	450.7380	700.2350

Table 16.3 (continued)

n	15%	16%	17%	18%	19%	20%	21%	22%	23%	24%	25%
1	1.1500	1.1600	1.1700	1.1800	1.1900	1.2000	1.2100	1.2200	1.2300	1.2400	1.2500
2	1.3225	1.3456	1.3689	1.3924	1.4161	1.4400	1.4641	1.4884	1.5129	1.5376	1.5625
3	1.5209	1.5609	1.6016	1.6430	1.6852	1.7280	1.7716	1.8158	1.8609	1.9066	1.9531
4	1.7490	1.8106	1.8739	1.9388	2.0053	2.0736	2.1436	2.2153	2.2889	2.3642	2.4414
5	2.0114	2.1003	2.1924	2.2878	2.3864	2.4883	2.5937	2.7027	2.8153	2.9316	3.0518
6	2.3131	2.4364	2.5652	2.6996	2.8398	2.9860	3.1384	3.2973	3.4628	3.6352	3.8147
7	2.6600	2.8262	3.0012	3.1855	3.3793	3.5832	3.7975	4.0227	4.2593	4.5077	4.7684
8	3.0590	3.2784	3.5115	3.7589	4.0214	4.2998	4.5950	4.9077	5.2389	5.5895	5.9605
9	3.5179	3.8030	4.1084	4.4355	4.7854	5.1598	5.5599	5.9874	6.4439	6.9310	7.4506
10	4.0456	4.4114	4.8068	5.2338	5.6947	6.1917	6.7275	7.3046	7.9259	8.5944	9.3132
11	4.6524	5.1173	5.6240	6.1759	6.7767	7.4301	8.1403	8.9117	9.7489	10.6571	11.6415
12	5.3503	5.9360	6.5801	7.2876	8.0642	8.9161	9.8497	10.8722	11.9912	13.2148	14.5519
13	6.1528	6.8858	7.6987	8.5994	9.5964	10.6993	11.9182	13.2641	14.7491	16.3863	18.1899
14	7.0757	7.9875	9.0075	10.1473	11.4198	12.8392	14.4210	16.1822	18.1414	20.3191	22.7374
15	8.1371	9.2655	10.5387	11.9738	13.5895	15.4070	17.4494	19.7423	22.3140	25.1956	28.4217
16	9.3576	10.7480	12.3303	14.1290	16.1715	18.4884	21.1138	24.0856	27.4462	31.2426	35.5271
17	10.7613	12.4677	14.4265	16.6723	19.2441	22.1861	25.5477	29.3844	33.7588	38.7408	44.4089
18	12.3755	14.4625	16.8790	19.6733	22.9005	26.6233	30.9127	35.8490	41.5233	48.0386	55.5112
19	14.2318	16.7765	19.7484	23.2145	27.2516	31.9480	37.4044	43.7358	51.0737	59.5679	69.3890
20	16.3666	19.4608	23.1056	27.3931	32.4294	38.3376	45.2593	53.3576	62.8206	73.8642	86.7362
21	18.8216	22.5745	27.0336	32.3238	38.5910	46.0052	54.7637	65.0963	77.2694	91.5916	108.4200
22	21.6448	26.1864	31.6293	38.1421	45.9233	55.2062	66.2641	79.4175	95.0413	113.5740	135.5250
23	24.8915	30.3762	37.0062	45.0077	54.6487	66.2474	80.1796	96.8893	116.9010	140.8310	169.4070
24	28.6252	35.2364	43.2973	53.1091	65.0320	79.4969	97.0173	118.2050	143.7880	174.6310	211.7580
25	32.9190	40.8743	50.6579	62.6688	77.3881	95.3963	117.3910	144.2100	176.8590	216.5420	264.6980
26	37.8569	47.4142	59.2697	73.9491	92.0918	114.4760	142.0430	175.9360	217.5370	268.5120	330.8720
27	43.5354	55.0004	69.3455	87.2600	109.5890	137.3710	171.8720	214.6420	267.5700	332.9550	413.5900
28	50.0657	63.8005	81.1343	102.9670	130.4110	164.8450	207.9650	261.8640	329.1120	412.8640	516.9880
29	57.5756	74.0086	94.9271	121.5010	155.1890	197.8140	251.6380	319.4740	404.8070	511.9520	646.2350
30	66.2119	85.8500	111.0650	143.3710	184.6750	237.3760	304.4820	389.7580	497.9130	634.8200	807.7940
31	76.1437	99.5860	129.9460	169.1780	219.7640	284.8520	368.4230	475.5040	612.4330	787.1770	1009.7400
32	87.5653	115.5200	152.0360	199.6300	261.5190	341.8220	445.7920	580.1150	753.2930	976.0990	1262.1800
33	100.7000	134.0030	177.8830	235.5630	311.2073	410.1870	539.4080	707.7410	926.5500	1210.3600	1577.7200
34	115.8050	155.4430	208.1230	277.9650	370.3370	492.2240	652.6840	863.4430	1139.6600	1500.8500	1972.1500
35	133.1760	180.3140	243.5040	327.9980	440.7010	590.6690	789.7470	1053.4000	1401.7800	1861.0500	2465.1900
36	153.1520	209.1640	284.8990	387.0380	524.4340	708.8030	955.5940	1285.1500	1724.1900	2307.7100	3081.4900
37	176.1250	242.6310	333.3320	456.7050	624.0760	850.5630	1156.2700	1567.8800	2120.7500	2861.5600	3851.8600
38	202.5440	281.4520	389.9990	538.9120	742.6510	1020.6800	1399.0900	1912.8200	2608.5200	3548.3300	4814.8300
39	232.9260	326.4840	456.2980	635.9160	883.7540	1224.8100	1692.8900	2333.6400	3208.4800	4399.9300	6018.5300
40	267.8650	378.7220	533.8690	750.3810	1051.6700	1469.7700	2048.4000	2847.0300	3946.4300	5455.9100	7523.1700
41	308.0440	439.3170	624.6270	885.4490	1251.4800	1763.7300	2478.5700	3473.3800	4854.1100	6765.3300	9403.9600
42	354.2510	509.6080	730.8130	1044.8300	1489.2700	2116.4700	2999.0600	4237.5300	5970.5600	8389.0200	11754.9000
43	407.3880	591.1450	855.0520	1232.9000	1772.2300	2539.7700	3628.8700	5169.7800	7343.7800	10402.4000	14693.7000
44	468.4970	685.7280	1000.4100	1454.8200	2108.9500	3047.7200	4390.9300	6307.1300	9032.8600	12898.9000	18367.1000
45	538.7710	795.4450	1170.4800	1760.6900	2509.6500	3657.2700	5313.0300	7694.7000	11110.4000	15994.7000	22958.9000
46	619.5870	922.7160	1369.4600	2025.6900	2986.4800	4388.7200	6428.7600	9387.5400	13665.8000	19833.4000	28698.6000
47	712.5250	1070.3500	1602.2700	2390.3200	3553.9200	5266.4600	7778.8000	11452.8000	16808.9000	24593.4000	35873.2000
48	819.4040	1241.6100	1874.6600	2820.5800	4229.1600	6319.7600	9412.3500	13972.4000	20675.0000	30495.9000	44841.6000
49	942.3150	1440.2600	2193.3500	3328.2800	5032.7000	7583.7100	11388.9000	17046.3000	25430.2000	37814.9000	56051.9000
50	1083.6600	1670.7100	2566.2200	3927.3700	5988.9100	9100.4500	13780.6000	20796.5000	31279.2000	46890.5000	70064.9000

Table 16.4 The Future Value of an Ordinary Annuity of 1 (F/A)

n	1%	2%	3%	4%	5%	6%	7%	8%	9%	10%	11%	12%	13%	14%
1	1.0000	1.0000	1.0000	1.0000	1.0000	1.0000	1.0000	1.0000	1.0000	1.0000	1.0000	1.0000	1.0000	1.0000
2	2.0100	2.0200	2.0300	2.0400	2.0500	2.0600	2.0700	2.0800	2.0900	2.1000	2.1100	2.1200	2.1300	2.1400
3	3.0301	3.0604	3.0909	3.1216	3.1525	3.1836	3.2149	3.2464	3.2781	3.3100	3.3421	3.3744	3.4069	3.4396
4	4.0604	4.1216	4.1836	4.2465	4.3101	4.3746	4.4399	4.5061	4.5731	4.6410	4.7097	4.7793	4.8498	4.9211
5	5.1010	5.2040	5.3091	5.4163	5.5256	5.6371	5.7507	5.8666	5.9847	6.1051	6.2278	6.3528	6.4803	6.6101
6	6.1520	6.3081	6.4684	6.6330	6.8019	6.9753	7.1533	7.3359	7.5233	7.7156	7.9129	8.1152	8.3227	8.5355
7	7.2135	7.4343	7.6625	7.8983	8.1420	8.3938	8.6540	8.9228	9.2004	9.4872	9.7833	10.0890	10.4047	10.7305
8	8.2857	8.5830	8.8923	9.2142	9.5491	9.8975	10.2598	10.6366	11.0285	11.4359	11.8594	12.2997	12.7573	13.2328
9	9.3685	9.7546	10.1591	10.5828	11.0266	11.4913	11.9780	12.4876	13.0210	13.5795	14.1640	14.7757	15.4157	16.0853
10	10.4622	10.9497	11.4639	12.0061	12.5779	13.1808	13.8164	14.4866	15.1929	15.9374	16.7220	17.5487	18.4197	19.3373
11	11.5668	12.1687	12.8078	13.4864	14.2068	14.9716	15.7836	16.6455	17.5603	18.5312	19.5614	20.6546	21.8143	23.0445
12	12.6825	13.4121	14.1920	15.0258	15.9171	16.8699	17.8885	18.9771	20.1407	21.3843	22.7132	24.1331	25.6502	27.2707
13	13.8093	14.6803	15.6178	16.6268	17.7130	18.8821	20.1406	21.4953	22.9534	24.5227	26.2116	28.0291	29.9847	32.0887
14	14.9474	15.9739	17.0863	18.2919	19.5986	21.0151	22.5505	24.2149	26.0192	27.9750	30.0949	32.3926	34.8827	37.5811
15	16.0969	17.2934	18.5989	20.0236	21.5786	23.2760	25.1290	27.1521	29.3609	31.7725	34.4054	37.2797	40.4175	43.8424
16	17.2579	18.6393	20.1569	21.8245	23.6575	25.6725	27.8881	30.3243	33.0034	35.9497	39.1899	42.7533	46.6717	50.9804
17	18.4304	20.0121	21.7616	23.6975	25.8404	28.2129	30.8402	33.7502	36.9737	40.5447	44.5008	48.8837	53.7391	59.1176
18	19.6147	21.4123	23.4144	25.6454	28.1324	30.9057	33.9990	37.4502	41.3013	45.5992	50.3959	55.7497	61.7251	68.3941
19	20.8109	22.8406	25.1169	27.6712	30.5390	33.7600	37.3790	41.4463	46.0185	51.1591	56.9395	63.4397	70.7494	78.9692
20	22.0190	24.2974	26.8704	29.7781	33.0660	36.7856	40.9955	45.7620	51.1601	57.2750	64.2028	72.0524	80.9468	91.0249
21	23.2392	25.7833	28.6765	31.9692	35.7193	39.9927	44.8652	50.4229	56.7645	64.0025	72.2651	81.6987	92.4599	104.7684
22	24.4716	27.2990	30.5368	34.2480	38.5052	43.3923	49.0057	55.4568	62.8733	71.4027	81.2143	92.5026	105.4910	120.4360
23	25.7163	28.8450	32.4529	36.6179	41.4305	46.9958	53.4361	60.8933	69.5319	79.5430	91.1479	104.6029	120.2048	138.2970
24	26.9735	30.4219	34.4265	39.0826	44.5020	50.8156	58.1767	66.7648	76.7898	88.4973	102.1742	118.1552	136.8315	158.6586
25	28.2432	32.0303	36.4593	41.6459	47.7271	54.8645	63.2490	73.1059	84.7009	98.3471	114.4133	133.3339	155.6196	181.8708
26	29.5256	33.6709	38.5530	44.3117	51.1135	59.1564	68.6765	79.9544	93.3240	109.1818	127.9988	150.3339	176.8501	208.3327
27	30.8209	35.3443	40.7096	47.0842	54.6691	63.7058	74.4838	87.3508	102.7231	121.0999	143.0786	169.3740	200.8406	238.4993
28	32.1291	37.0512	42.9309	49.9676	58.4026	68.5281	80.6977	95.3388	112.9682	134.2099	159.8173	190.6989	227.9499	272.8892
29	33.4504	38.7922	45.2189	52.9663	62.3227	73.6398	87.3465	103.9659	124.1354	148.6309	178.3972	214.5828	258.5834	312.0937
30	34.7849	40.5681	47.5754	56.0849	66.4388	79.0582	94.4608	113.2832	136.3075	164.4940	199.0209	241.3327	293.1992	356.7868
31	36.1327	42.3794	50.0027	59.3283	70.7608	84.8017	102.0730	123.3459	149.5752	181.9434	221.9132	271.2926	332.3151	407.7370
32	37.4941	44.2270	52.5028	62.7015	75.2988	90.8898	110.2182	134.2135	164.0370	201.1378	247.3236	304.8477	376.5161	465.8202
33	38.8690	46.1116	55.0778	66.2095	80.0638	97.3432	118.9334	145.9506	179.8003	222.2515	275.5292	342.4294	426.4632	532.0350
34	40.2577	48.0338	57.7302	69.8579	85.0670	104.1838	128.2588	158.6267	196.9823	245.4767	306.8374	384.5210	482.9034	607.5199
35	41.6603	49.9945	60.4621	73.6522	90.3203	111.4348	138.2369	172.3168	215.7108	271.0244	341.5896	431.6635	546.6808	693.5727
36	43.0769	51.9944	63.2759	77.5983	95.8362	119.1209	148.9135	187.1021	236.1247	299.1268	380.1644	484.4631	618.7493	791.6729
37	44.5076	54.0343	66.1742	81.7022	101.6281	127.2681	160.3374	203.0703	258.3759	330.0395	422.9825	543.5987	700.1868	903.5071
38	45.9527	56.1149	69.1594	85.9703	107.7095	135.9042	172.5610	220.3159	282.6298	364.0434	470.5106	609.8305	792.2110	1030.9981
39	47.4123	58.2372	72.2342	90.4092	114.0950	145.0585	185.6403	238.9412	309.0665	401.4478	523.2667	684.0102	895.1985	1176.3378
40	48.8864	60.4020	75.4013	95.0255	120.7998	154.7620	199.6351	259.0565	337.8824	442.5926	581.8261	767.0914	1013.7043	1342.0251
41	50.3752	62.6100	78.6633	99.8265	127.8398	165.0477	214.6096	280.7810	369.2919	487.8518	646.8269	860.1424	1146.4858	1530.9086
42	51.8790	64.8622	82.0232	104.8196	135.2318	175.9505	230.6322	304.2435	403.5281	537.6370	718.9779	964.3595	1296.5290	1746.2359
43	53.3978	67.1595	85.4839	110.0124	142.9933	187.5076	247.7765	329.5830	440.8457	592.4007	799.0655	1081.0826	1466.0777	1991.7089
44	54.9318	69.5027	89.0484	115.4129	151.1430	199.7580	266.1209	356.9496	481.5218	652.6408	887.9627	1211.8125	1657.6679	2271.5481
45	56.4811	71.8927	92.7199	121.0294	159.7002	212.7435	285.7493	386.5056	525.8587	718.9048	986.6386	1358.2300	1874.1647	2590.5648
46	58.0459	74.3306	96.5015	126.8706	168.6852	226.5081	306.7518	418.4261	574.1860	791.7953	1096.1688	1522.2176	2118.8061	2954.2439
47	59.6263	76.8172	100.3965	132.9454	178.1194	241.0986	329.2244	452.9002	626.8628	871.9748	1217.7474	1705.8838	2395.2509	3368.8381
48	61.2226	79.3535	104.4084	139.2632	188.0254	256.5645	353.2701	490.1322	684.2804	960.1723	1352.6996	1911.5898	2707.6335	3841.4754
49	62.8348	81.9406	108.5406	145.8337	198.4267	272.9584	378.9990	530.3427	746.8656	1057.1896	1502.4966	2141.9806	3062.6259	4380.2820
50	64.4632	84.5794	112.7969	152.6671	209.3480	290.3359	406.5289	573.7702	815.0835	1163.9085	1668.7712	2400.0182	3459.5072	4994.5215

Table 16.4 (continued)

n	15%	16%	17%	18%	19%	20%	21%	22%	23%	24%	25%
1	1.0000	1.0000	1.0000	1.0000	1.0000	1.0000	1.0000	1.0000	1.0000	1.0000	1.0000
2	2.1500	2.1600	2.1700	2.1800	2.1900	2.2000	2.2100	2.2200	2.2300	2.2400	2.2500
3	3.4725	3.5056	3.5389	3.5724	3.6061	3.6400	3.6741	3.7084	3.7429	3.7776	3.8125
4	4.9934	5.0665	5.1405	5.2154	5.2913	5.3680	5.4457	5.5242	5.6038	5.6842	5.7656
5	6.7424	6.8771	7.0144	7.1542	7.2966	7.4416	7.5892	7.7396	7.8926	8.0484	8.2070
6	8.7537	8.9775	9.2068	9.4420	9.6830	9.9299	10.1830	10.4423	10.7079	10.9801	11.2588
7	11.0668	11.4139	11.7720	12.1415	12.5227	12.9159	13.3214	13.7396	14.1708	14.6153	15.0735
8	13.7268	14.2401	14.7733	15.3270	15.9020	16.4991	17.1189	17.7623	18.4300	19.1229	19.8419
9	16.7858	17.5185	18.2847	19.0859	19.9234	20.7989	21.7139	22.6700	23.6690	24.7125	25.8023
10	20.3037	21.3215	22.3931	23.5213	24.7089	25.9587	27.2738	28.6574	30.1128	31.6434	33.2529
11	24.3493	25.7329	27.1999	28.7551	30.4035	32.1504	34.0013	35.9620	38.0388	40.2379	42.5661
12	29.0017	30.8502	32.8239	34.9311	37.1802	39.5805	42.1416	44.8737	47.7877	50.8950	54.2077
13	34.3519	36.7862	39.4040	42.2187	45.2445	48.4966	51.9913	55.7459	59.7788	64.1097	68.7596
14	40.5047	43.6720	47.1027	50.8180	54.8409	59.1959	63.9095	69.0100	74.5280	80.4961	86.9495
15	47.5804	51.6595	56.1101	60.9653	66.2607	72.0351	78.3305	85.1922	92.6694	100.8151	109.6868
16	55.7175	60.9250	66.6488	72.9390	79.8502	87.4421	95.7799	104.9345	114.9834	126.0108	138.1085
17	65.0751	71.6730	78.9792	87.0680	96.0218	105.9306	116.8937	129.0201	142.4295	157.2534	173.6357
18	75.8364	84.1407	93.4056	103.7403	115.2659	128.1167	142.4413	158.4045	176.1883	195.9942	218.0446
19	88.2118	98.6032	110.2846	123.4135	138.1664	154.7400	173.3540	194.2535	217.7116	244.0328	273.5558
20	102.4436	115.3797	130.0329	146.6280	165.4180	186.6880	210.7584	237.9893	268.7853	303.6006	342.9447
21	118.8101	134.8405	153.1385	174.0210	197.8474	225.0256	256.0176	291.3469	331.6059	377.4648	429.6809
22	137.6316	157.4150	180.1721	206.3448	236.4385	271.0307	310.7813	356.4432	408.8753	469.0563	538.1011
23	159.2764	183.6014	211.8013	244.4868	282.3618	326.2369	377.0454	435.8607	503.9166	582.6298	673.6264
24	184.1678	213.9776	248.8076	289.4945	337.0105	392.4842	457.2249	532.7501	620.8174	723.4610	843.0329
25	212.7930	249.2140	292.1049	342.6035	402.0425	471.9811	554.2422	650.9551	764.6055	898.0916	1054.7912
26	245.7120	290.0883	342.7627	405.2721	479.4306	567.3773	671.6330	795.1653	941.4647	1114.6336	1319.4890
27	283.5688	337.5024	402.0323	479.2211	571.5224	681.8528	813.6760	971.1016	1159.0016	1383.1457	1650.3612
28	327.1041	392.5028	471.3778	566.4809	681.1116	819.2233	985.5479	1185.7440	1426.5720	1716.1007	2063.9515
29	377.1697	456.3032	552.5121	669.4474	811.5228	984.0680	1193.5130	1447.6077	1755.6835	2126.9648	2580.9394
30	434.7451	530.3117	647.4391	790.9480	966.7122	1181.8815	1445.1507	1767.0814	2160.4907	2640.9164	3227.1743
31	500.9569	616.1616	758.5038	934.3186	1151.3875	1419.2579	1749.6323	2156.8393	2658.4036	3275.7363	4034.9678
32	577.1005	715.7475	888.4494	1103.4960	1371.1511	1704.1094	2118.0551	2632.3439	3270.8364	4062.9131	5044.7098
33	664.6655	831.2671	1040.4858	1303.1252	1632.6698	2045.9313	2563.8467	3212.4596	4024.1288	5039.0122	6306.8873
34	765.3654	965.2698	1218.3684	1538.6878	1943.8771	2456.1176	3103.2545	3920.2007	4950.6784	6249.3751	7884.6091
35	881.1702	1120.7130	1426.4910	1816.6516	2314.2137	2948.3411	3755.9380	4783.6448	6090.3344	7750.2252	9856.7614
36	1014.3457	1301.0270	1669.9945	2144.6489	2754.9143	3539.0093	4545.6849	5837.0467	7492.1113	9611.2792	12321.9517
37	1167.4975	1510.1914	1954.8936	2531.6857	3279.3480	4247.8112	5501.2788	7122.1970	9216.2970	11918.9862	15403.4396
38	1343.6222	1752.8220	2288.2255	2988.3891	3903.4241	5098.3734	6657.5474	8690.0803	11337.0453	14780.5428	19255.2996
39	1546.1655	2034.2735	2678.2238	3527.2991	4646.0747	6119.0481	8056.6323	10602.8979	13945.5657	18328.8733	24070.1243
40	1779.0903	2360.7573	3134.5218	4163.2130	5529.8289	7343.8577	9749.5250	12936.5355	17154.0459	22728.8027	30088.6553
41	2046.9539	2739.4784	3668.3905	4913.5913	6581.4964	8813.6293	11797.9253	15783.5734	21100.4763	28184.7153	37611.8193
42	2354.9969	3178.7950	4293.0169	5799.0378	7832.9807	10577.3551	14276.4897	19256.9595	25954.5859	34950.0469	47015.7739
43	2709.2465	3688.4022	5023.8298	6843.8646	9322.2471	12693.8260	17275.5525	23494.4905	31925.1406	43339.0586	58770.7178
44	3116.6335	4279.5465	5878.8009	8076.7602	11094.4740	15233.5913	20904.4187	28664.2786	39268.9229	53741.4326	73464.3965
45	3585.1285	4965.2739	6879.2906	9531.5770	13203.4240	18281.3096	25295.3464	34971.4199	48301.7754	66640.3760	91831.4961
46	4123.8978	5760.7178	8049.7700	11248.2609	15713.0746	21938.5713	30608.3694	42666.1323	59412.1836	82635.0664	114790.3701
47	4743.4824	6683.4326	9419.2310	13273.9479	18699.5586	26327.2856	37037.1270	52053.6812	73077.9863	102468.4824	143488.9629
48	5456.0048	7753.7818	11021.5002	15664.2584	22253.4749	31593.7427	44815.9233	63506.4912	89886.9229	127061.9180	179362.2031
49	6275.4055	8995.3870	12896.1553	18484.8250	26482.6350	37913.4912	54228.2676	77478.9189	110561.9150	157557.7793	224203.7539
50	7217.7164	10435.6488	15089.5016	21813.0935	31515.3357	45497.1895	65617.2041	94525.2812	135992.1562	195372.6465	280255.6914

16.3 MORTGAGE AMORTIZATION TABLE

Table 16.5 shows the percentage of the principal amount of a loan needed each year to pay off the loan when the actual payments are monthly and are paid in arrears. Divide the percentage or the result by 12 to get the level monthly payment that includes both interest and principal. If payments are made in advance, rather than in arrears, the payment amount will be slightly smaller than the amounts derived from this table.

> EXAMPLE: *The annual amount needed to pay off a $75,000, 10 percent, 30 year mortgage if payments are made monthly and in arrears is $7,905 (factor of 10.54% × $75,000). The monthly payment, therefore, is $658.75 ($7,905 ÷ 12 months). If the loan is to be paid off over 15 years, rather than 30 years, the annual payment is $9,675 (factor of 12.90% × $75,000) and the monthly payment is $806.25 ($9,675 ÷ 12 months). In other words, by paying $147.50 more per month ($806.25 − $658.75), the mortgage will be paid off in 15 years rather than 30 years.*

16.4 SINKING FUND PAYMENT TABLE

Table 16.6 shows the amount which, when deposited at the end of each period shown, grows to $1 in the future.

> EXAMPLE: *The amount of $15,000 will be needed in 10 years. At 7 percent interest, an annual deposit of $1,086 deposited at the end of each year will grow to $15,000 in 10 years. The 10-year factor at 7 percent is .072378. $15,000 × .072378 = $1,086.*

16.5 GROWTH OF A $100 MONTHLY DEPOSIT

Table 16.7 shows what a monthly deposit of $100 grows to over a period of years. Compounding is monthly, and deposits are assumed to have been made at the beginning of the month.

> EXAMPLE: *A newlywed couple wants to save some money on a monthly basis, and they are interested in what they can accumulate over 30 years, assuming they can earn 9½ percent on their savings. As the table shows, if they save $100 per month, they will have $204,913 in savings after 30 years, based on a 9½ percent annual return. If they can manage to save $150 per month over the same period, they will have accumulated $307,369 ($204,913 × 1.5).*

Table 16.5 Mortgage Amortization

Interest Rate	10 yr	15 yr	20 yr	25 yr	30 yr
8.00	14.56	11.47	10.04	9.27	8.81
8.25	14.72	11.65	10.23	9.47	9.02
8.50	14.88	11.82	10.42	9.67	9.23
8.75	15.04	12.00	10.61	9.87	9.45
9.00	15.21	12.18	10.80	10.08	9.66
9.25	15.37	12.36	11.00	10.28	9.88
9.50	15.53	12.54	11.19	10.49	10.10
9.75	15.70	12.72	11.39	10.70	10.31
10.00	15.86	12.90	11.59	10.91	10.54
10.25	16.03	13.08	11.78	11.12	10.76
10.50	16.20	13.27	11.99	11.34	10.98
10.75	16.37	13.46	12.19	11.55	11.21
11.00	16.54	13.64	12.39	11.77	11.43
11.25	16.71	13.83	12.60	11.98	11.66
11.50	16.88	14.02	12.80	12.20	11.89
11.75	17.05	14.21	13.01	12.42	12.12
12.00	17.22	14.41	13.22	12.64	12.35
12.25	17.40	14.60	13.43	12.87	12.58
12.50	17.57	14.80	13.64	13.09	12.81
12.75	17.75	14.99	13.85	13.31	13.05
13.00	17.92	15.19	14.06	13.54	13.28
13.25	18.10	15.39	14.28	13.77	13.51
13.50	18.28	15.58	14.49	13.99	13.75
13.75	18.46	15.78	14.71	14.22	13.99
14.00	18.64	15.99	14.93	14.45	14.22
14.25	18.82	16.19	15.15	14.68	14.46
14.50	19.00	16.39	15.36	14.91	14.70
14.75	19.18	16.60	15.59	15.14	14.94
15.00	19.37	16.80	15.81	15.37	15.18

Table 16.6 Sinking Fund Payment

Years	4%	5%	6%	7%	8%	9%	10%	11%	12%	13%	14%
1	1.000000	1.000000	1.000000	1.000000	1.000000	1.000000	1.000000	1.000000	1.000000	1.000000	1.000000
2	.490196	.487805	.485437	.483092	.480769	.478469	.476190	.473934	.471698	.469484	.467290
3	.320349	.317209	.314110	.311052	.308034	.305055	.302115	.299213	.296349	.293522	.290731
4	.235490	.232012	.228591	.225228	.221921	.218669	.215471	.212326	.209234	.206194	.203205
5	.184627	.180975	.177396	.173891	.170456	.167092	.163797	.160570	.157410	.154315	.151284
6	.150762	.147017	.143363	.139796	.136315	.132920	.129607	.126377	.123226	.120153	.117157
7	.126610	.122820	.119135	.115553	.112072	.108691	.105405	.102215	.099118	.096111	.093192
8	.108528	.104722	.101036	.097468	.094015	.090674	.087444	.084321	.081303	.078387	.075570
9	.094493	.090690	.087022	.083486	.080080	.076799	.073641	.070602	.067679	.064869	.062168
10	.083291	.079505	.075868	.072378	.069029	.065820	.062745	.059801	.056984	.054290	.051714
11	.074149	.070389	.066793	.063357	.060076	.056947	.053963	.051121	.048415	.045841	.043394
12	.066552	.062825	.059277	.055902	.052695	.049651	.046763	.044027	.041437	.038986	.036669
13	.060144	.056456	.052960	.049651	.046522	.043567	.040779	.038151	.035677	.033350	.031164
14	.054669	.051024	.047585	.044345	.041297	.038433	.035746	.033228	.030871	.028667	.026609
15	.049941	.046342	.042963	.039795	.036830	.034059	.031474	.029065	.026824	.024742	.022809
16	.045820	.042270	.038952	.035858	.032977	.030300	.027817	.025517	.023390	.021426	.019615
17	.042199	.038699	.035445	.032425	.029629	.027046	.024664	.022471	.020457	.018608	.016915
18	.038993	.035546	.032357	.029413	.026702	.024212	.021930	.019843	.017937	.016201	.014621
19	.036139	.032745	.029621	.026753	.024128	.021730	.019547	.017563	.015763	.014134	.012663
20	.033582	.030243	.027185	.024393	.021852	.019546	.017460	.015576	.013879	.012354	.010986
21	.031280	.027996	.025005	.022289	.019832	.017617	.015624	.013838	.012240	.010814	.009545
22	.029199	.025971	.023046	.020406	.018032	.015905	.014005	.012313	.010811	.009479	.008303
23	.027309	.024137	.021278	.018714	.016422	.014382	.012572	.010971	.009560	.008319	.007231
24	.025587	.022471	.019679	.017189	.014978	.013023	.011300	.009787	.008463	.007308	.006303
25	.024012	.020952	.018227	.015811	.013679	.011806	.010168	.008740	.007500	.006426	.005498
26	.022567	.019564	.016904	.014561	.012507	.010715	.009159	.007813	.006652	.005655	.004800
27	.021239	.018292	.015697	.013426	.011448	.009735	.008258	.006989	.005904	.004979	.004193
28	.020013	.017123	.014593	.012392	.010489	.008852	.007451	.006257	.005244	.004387	.003664
29	.018880	.016046	.013580	.011449	.009619	.008056	.006728	.005605	.004660	.003867	.003204
30	.017830	.015051	.012649	.010586	.008827	.007336	.006079	.005025	.004144	.003411	.002803

Table 16.6 (continued)

Years	15%	16%	17%	18%	19%	20%	21%	22%	23%	24%	25%
1	1.000000	1.000000	1.000000	1.000000	1.000000	1.000000	1.000000	1.000000	1.000000	1.000000	1.000000
2	.465116	.462963	.460829	.458716	.456621	.454545	.452489	.450450	.448430	.446429	.444444
3	.287977	.285258	.282574	.279924	.277308	.274725	.272175	.269658	.267173	.264718	.262295
4	.200265	.197375	.194533	.191739	.188991	.186289	.183632	.181020	.178451	.175926	.173442
5	.148316	.145409	.142564	.139778	.137050	.134380	.131765	.129206	.126700	.124248	.121847
6	.114237	.111390	.108615	.105910	.103274	.100706	.098203	.095764	.093389	.091074	.088819
7	.090360	.087613	.084947	.082362	.079855	.077424	.075067	.072782	.070568	.068422	.066342
8	.072850	.070224	.067690	.065244	.062885	.060609	.058415	.056299	.054259	.052293	.050399
9	.059574	.057082	.054691	.052395	.050192	.048079	.046053	.044111	.042249	.040465	.038756
10	.049252	.046901	.044657	.042515	.040471	.038523	.036665	.034895	.033208	.031602	.030073
11	.041069	.038861	.036765	.034776	.032891	.031104	.029411	.027807	.026289	.024852	.023493
12	.034481	.032415	.030466	.028628	.026896	.025265	.023730	.022285	.020926	.019648	.018448
13	.029110	.027184	.025378	.023686	.022102	.020620	.019234	.017939	.016728	.015598	.014543
14	.024688	.022898	.021230	.019678	.018235	.016893	.015647	.014491	.013418	.012423	.011501
15	.021017	.019358	.017822	.016403	.015092	.013882	.012766	.011738	.010791	.009919	.009117
16	.017948	.016414	.015004	.013710	.012523	.011436	.010441	.009530	.008697	.007936	.007241
17	.015367	.013952	.012662	.011485	.010414	.009440	.008555	.007751	.007021	.006539	.005759
18	.013186	.011885	.010706	.009639	.008676	.007805	.007020	.006313	.005676	.005102	.004586
19	.011336	.010142	.009067	.008103	.007238	.006642	.005769	.005148	.004593	.004098	.003656
20	.009761	.008667	.007690	.006820	.006045	.005357	.004745	.004202	.003720	.003294	.002916
21	.008417	.007416	.006530	.005746	.005054	.004444	.003906	.003432	.003016	.002649	.002327
22	.007266	.006353	.005550	.004846	.004229	.003690	.003218	.002805	.002446	.002132	.001858
23	.006278	.005447	.004721	.004090	.003542	.003065	.002652	.002294	.001984	.001716	.001485
24	.005430	.004673	.004019	.003454	.002967	.002548	.002187	.001877	.001611	.001382	.001186
25	.004699	.004013	.003423	.002919	.002487	.002119	.001804	.001536	.001308	.001113	.000948
26	.004070	.003447	.002917	.002467	.002086	.001762	.001489	.001258	.001062	.000897	.000758
27	.003526	.002963	.002487	.002087	.001750	.001467	.001229	.001030	.000863	.000723	.000606
28	.003057	.002548	.002121	.001765	.001468	.001221	.001015	.000843	.000701	.000583	.000485
29	.002651	.002192	.001810	.001494	.001232	.001016	.000838	.000691	.000570	.000470	.000387
30	.002300	.001886	.001545	.001264	.001034	.000846	.000692	.000566	.000463	.000379	.000310

Table 16.7 Growth of a $100 Monthly Deposit

Interest Rate	5 Years	10 Years	15 Years	20 Years	25 Years	30 Years	35 Years	40 Years
5%	$6,829	$15,593	$26,840	$41,275	$ 59,799	$ 83,573	$114,083	$153,238
5½	6,920	16,024	28,002	43,762	64,498	91,780	127,675	174,902
6	7,012	16,470	29,227	46,435	69,646	100,954	143,183	200,145
6½	7,106	16,932	30,519	49,308	75,289	111,217	160,898	229,599
7	7,201	17,409	31,881	52,397	81,480	122,709	181,156	264,012
7½	7,298	17,904	33,318	55,719	88,274	135,587	204,345	304,272
8	7,397	18,417	34,835	59,295	95,737	150,030	230,918	351,428
8½	7,497	18,947	36,435	63,144	103,937	166,240	261,395	406,726
9	7,599	19,497	38,124	67,290	112,953	184,447	296,385	471,643
9½	7,703	20,066	39,908	71,756	122,872	204,913	336,590	547,933
10	7,808	20,655	41,792	76,570	133,789	227,933	382,828	637,678

16.6 NUMBER OF YEARS MONEY WILL LAST AT A GIVEN WITHDRAWAL RATE

Figure 16.1 shows the number of years that a nest egg will last at a given annual rate of withdrawal. Retirees are often concerned about how long their money will last. Someone who withdraws money at an annual rate that is less than its rate of return will never run out of money. For example, someone who takes 5 percent of invested funds that are earning 8 percent per year will never invade principal. On the other hand, taking 10 percent out each year from a nest egg that is earning 8 percent, as Figure 16.1 shows, will exhaust the money in 20 years. This can be determined by looking at the box where the 10 percent rate of withdrawal column intersects with the 8 percent rate of return column.

16.7 COMPOUND INTEREST RATE TABLE

The frequency with which a time deposit is compounded can have a significant difference in total yield. Table 16.8 summarizes the true annual rate of return based upon commonly offered rates of compounding.

FIGURE 16.1 NUMBER OF YEARS A NEST EGG WILL LAST AT A GIVEN ANNUAL RATE

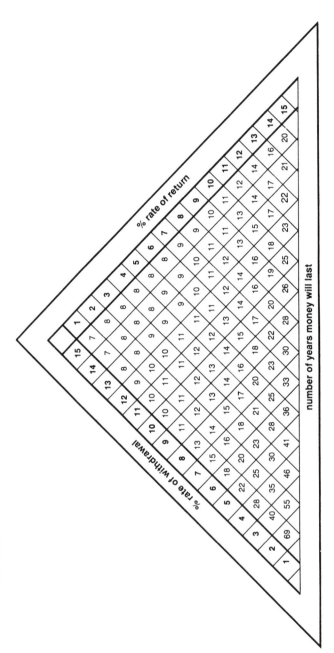

Table 16.8   Compound Interest Rate Table

Nominal Annual Rate	Semi-Annually	The True Annual Rate If Compounded . . .			
		Quarterly	Monthly	Weekly	Daily
3.00	3.0225	3.0339	3.0415	3.0445	3.0453
3.25	3.2764	3.2898	3.2988	3.3023	3.3032
3.50	3.5306	3.5462	3.5566	3.5607	3.5617
3.75	3.7851	3.8030	3.8151	3.8197	3.8209
4.00	4.0400	4.0604	4.0741	4.0794	4.0808
4.25	4.2951	4.3182	4.3337	4.3397	4.3413
4.50	4.5506	4.5765	4.5939	4.6007	4.6024
4.75	4.8064	4.8352	4.8547	4.8623	4.8642
5.00	5.0625	5.0945	5.1161	5.1245	5.1267
5.25	5.3189	5.3542	5.3781	5.3874	5.3898
5.50	5.5756	5.6144	5.6407	5.6509	5.6536
5.75	5.8326	5.8751	5.9039	5.9151	5.9180
6.00	6.0900	6.1363	6.1677	6.1799	6.1831
6.25	6.3476	6.3980	6.4321	6.4454	6.4488
6.50	6.6056	6.6601	6.6971	6.7115	6.7152
6.75	6.8639	6.9227	6.9627	6.9783	6.9823
7.00	7.1225	7.1859	7.2290	7.2457	7.2500
7.25	7.3814	7.4495	7.4958	7.5138	7.5185
7.50	7.6406	7.7135	7.7632	7.7825	7.7875
7.75	7.9001	7.9781	8.0312	8.0519	8.0573
8.00	8.1600	8.2432	8.2999	8.3220	8.3277
8.25	8.4201	8.5087	8.5692	8.5927	8.5988
8.50	8.6806	8.7747	8.8390	8.8641	8.8706
8.75	8.9414	9.0413	9.1095	9.1362	9.1430
9.00	9.2025	9.3083	9.3806	9.4089	9.4162
9.25	9.4639	9.5758	9.6524	9.6823	9.6900
9.50	9.7256	9.8438	9.9247	9.9563	9.9645
9.75	9.9876	10.1123	10.1977	10.2310	10.2397
10.00	10.2500	10.3812	10.4713	10.5064	10.5155
11.00	11.3025	11.4621	11.5718	11.6148	11.6259
12.00	12.3600	12.5508	12.6825	12.7340	12.7474
13.00	13.4225	13.6475	13.8032	13.8643	13.8802
14.00	14.4900	14.7523	14.9342	15.0057	15.0242
15.00	15.5625	15.8650	16.0754	16.1583	16.1798

16.8   DOLLAR/DECIMAL EQUIVALENCE OF FRACTIONS

Dollar/decimal equivalences of fractions are often needed for the price and premium calculations of a variety of financial instruments. Table 16.9 shows the decimal equivalents of fractions.

Table 16.9   Decimal Equivalents of Fractions

Fractions				Decimals
1/32				.03125
2/32	1/16			.0625
3/32				.09375
4/32	2/16	1/8		.125
5/32				.15625
6/32	3/16			.1875
7/32				.21875
8/32	4/16	2/8	1/4	.25
9/32				.28125
10/32	5/16			.3125
11/32				.34375
12/32	6/16	3/8		.375
13/32				.40625
14/32	7/16			.4375
15/32				.46875
16/32	8/16	4/8	1/2	.5
17/32				.53125
18/32	9/16			.5625
19/32				.59375
20/32	10/16	5/8		.625
21/32				.65625
22/32	11/16			.6875
23/32				.71875
24/32	12/16	6/8	3/4	.75
25/32				.78125
26/32	13/16			.8125
27/32				.84375
28/32	14/16	7/8		.875
29/32				.90625
30/32	15/16			.9375
31/32				.96875

GLOSSARY

Abatement - A diminution in testamentary gifts as a result of an insufficient amount of assets in a testator's estate.

Accrued benefit - A benefit that an employee has earned (or accrued) through participation in an employee benefit plan. In a defined contribution plan, the accrued benefit of a participant is the balance in his or her individual account at a given time. In a defined benefit plan, the accrued benefit is determined by reference to the benefit that will be provided to a participant when he or she reaches normal retirement age as specified by the plan.

Actual cash value - In many insurance policies, the amount awarded for physical damage losses; commonly defined as replacement cost less depreciation.

Adjustable life insurance - A type of insurance that allows the policyholder to change the plan of insurance, raise or lower the face amount of the policy,increase or decrease the premium, and lengthen or shorten the protection period.

Administrator - For estate purposes, a person designated to manage the administration of a decedent's estate. If a person is named in the will, then he is an executor (if a woman, an executrix). If a person is appointed by a court, then he is an administrator (for a woman, an administratrix).

Advance-decline ratio - A barometer of the market's condition. Following an upward sweep, speculative interest is concentrated on the small number of stocks that struggle forward, while, masked by the performance of those few, the rest of the market fades.

Aggressive growth fund - A mutual fund whose investment objective is capital appreciation. Most investments are in common stocks of higher-growth potential and risk.

Alpha - The excess return over a risk-free rate of a given stock when the excess return of the stock market as a whole (or a selected segment of the market) is zero. A positive alpha indicates that the investment has earned on the average a premium above that expected for the level of

503

market variability. A negative alpha indicates that the investment received on the average a premium lower than that expected for the level of market variability.

Alternate valuation date - Property passing from a decedent's estate can be valued for estate tax purposes either on the date of death or the alternate valuation date, whichever is chosen by the administrator or executor. The alternate valuation date is either six months from the date of death or the date the property is disposed of (if less than six months from the date of death). It can be elected only if the total value of an estate can be reduced.

American depository receipt (ADR) - A form similar to a stock certificate which is registered in the holder's name. The certificate represents a certain number of shares in an alien corporation. Such shares are held by an alien bank that serves as the agent for a domestic commercial bank which has released the depository receipt.

Annual exclusion - An amount ($10,000 per donee) a donor can gift during a period of one year which is excluded from gift tax computation. The donee must have an immediate right to ownership.

Annuity - A series of periodic payments, usually level in amount or adjusted according to some index (e.g., cost of living) that typically continue for the lifetime of the recipient.

Annuity trust - A trust arrangement typically providing periodic fixed payments, regardless of the trust's income, to one or more beneficiaries.

Arbitrage - Simultaneous purchasing and selling of the identical item in different markets in order to yield profits. The result is that the price of an item becomes equal in all markets. The purchase of foreign exchange, stocks, bonds, silver, gold, or other commodities in one market at a profit. The simultaneous purchase and sale of mortgages, future contracts, or mortgage-based securities in different markets to profit from price differences.

Asset play - A security that is appealing because its current price fails to reflect truly the value of the firm's assets.

Balanced fund - A mutual fund which has an investment policy of balancing its portfolio, generally by including bonds, preferred stocks, and common stocks.

Basis - In calculating capital gains or losses, the value employed as the original property cost, which may or may not be the true cost.

Bear spread - An option technique where the investor purchases one type of option (either a put or a call) and sells the other on the same underlying security simultaneously. The option that is bought has a higher striking price than the one sold. The investor profits by a decrease in the market price of the underlying stock.

Beneficiary - A person designated by a participant or one who, by the terms of the plan, is or may be eligible for benefits under the plan if the participant dies.

Bequest - The transfer of personal property, as opposed to real property, pursuant to a will; a legacy. Such inheritance is not included in a beneficiary's gross income for income tax purposes. The basis of such property is the fair market value on either the date of the testator's death, date of receipt, or alternate valuation date, whichever is chosen by the estate's administrator.

Beta - A measure of a stock's sensitivity to the movement of the general market, in either direction. A beta of greater than one indicates that the stock's excess return varies more than proportionately with the excess return of the market, and thus presents greater opportunity for gain and greater risk for loss than the market as a whole.

Bid price - In the case of open-end shares, the price at which the holder may redeem their shares; in most cases, it is the current net asset value per share. In the case of closed-end shares, the highest price then offered for stock in the public market.

Blind pool partnership (or program) - A limited real estate partnership investment where assets to be bought are unknown to investors at the time of investment.

Blue sky law - The name given to certain laws enacted by the various states to regulate the sale and issuance of securities, specifically, attempting to prevent fraud in their sale and disposition.

Bond, original issue discount (OID) - A bond offered below face value at time of the initial offering, the difference between redemption price and original issue price is treated as income, rather than capital gains, over the life of the bond.

Bond, strip - Where traders clip the coupons off a fixed-interest bond or note and then sell the principal and interest parts separately to two groups of investors. Those seeking current income buy the strip of coupons, and those wanting a lump sum at maturity and a capital gain buy the principal or "corpus" portion. Because each portion is worth less than its whole before taxes, both are sold at a deep discount from their face values.

Bond, zero-coupon - A security sold at a deep discount from its face value and redeemed at the full amount at maturity. The difference between the cost of the bond and its value when redeemed is the investor's return. These notes provide no interest payment to holders.

Bond swap - The simultaneous sale of one bond issue and the purchase of another.

Bottom fisher - An investor searching for a stock or commodity that has dropped to a bottom level before turning around. In some situations, people who purchase stocks and bonds of bankrupt or near-bankrupt organizations.

Bull spread - A spread option technique where an investor purchases one type of option, either a call or put, and sells the other on the same underlying stock simultaneously. The option sold has a higher striking price than the one purchased. The investor profits by an increase in the market price of the underlying stock.

Buy and write strategy - A conservative options technique involving purchasing securities and then writing covered call options on them. An investor receives both dividends from the stock and the premium income from the call options. A disadvantage is that the investor may be required to sell the security below the current market price if the call is exercised.

Callable - A bond issue or preferred stock, all or part of which may be redeemed by the issuing corporation under definite conditions, before maturity.

Call option - Giving the option buyer the right to buy 100 shares of stock at a stated price at any time before a deadline, at which point the option expires.

Capital gains distribution - A distribution to investment company (mutual fund) shareholders from net long-term capital gains realized by a regulated investment company on the sale of portfolio securities.

Capitalization rate (cap rate) - Net operating income divided by the cost. On a cash asset, the capitalization rate is the yield that the owner receives.

Cash equivalent - An item readily converted to cash with little or no change in current market value (e.g., money market funds, Treasury bills).

Cash-on-cash return - The yield on investor's contributed capital (e.g., the cash distributed divided by the cash invested).

Cash or deferred plan - A qualified profit-sharing or stock bonus plan that gives a participant an option to take cash or to have the employer contribute the money to a qualified profit sharing plan as an "employer" contribution to the plan (i.e., an "elective deferral"). These arrangements are often called "401(k) plans."

Charitable lead trust - Generally, a trust to which a grantor transfers income-producing property, from which contributions are made to various qualified charitable organizations, with a remainder interest vested in a chosen individual (e.g., a family member). In effect, this gives the grantor an income tax deduction each year for income that would have been earned by him or her, a gift and estate tax deduction for qualifying trusts, as well as the advantage of retaining the property in the family.

Charitable lead (or upfront) trust - A trust for a fixed term of years wherein a charity is the income beneficiary and the remainder goes to a noncharitable beneficiary.

Charitable remainder annuity trust - A trust that provides a certain sum, not less than 5 percent of initial fair market value of all property placed in trust, to be distributed at least annually to a noncharitable beneficiary, with remainder to a qualified charity.

Charitable remainder trust - A trust formed to pay income to a noncharitable beneficiary and to pay the entire remainder interest to a qualified charitable organization or purpose. Charitable deductions are allowed for qualified contributions of a remainder interest in trust for income, gift, and estate taxes. Such trusts must either be a charitable remainder annuity trust or a charitable remainder unitrust.

Charitable remainder unitrust - A trust that provides a fixed percentage, not less than 5 percent of net fair market value of property, valued annually, to be distributed at least annually to a noncharitable beneficiary, with remainder to a qualified charity.

Charitable trust - Any trust created to support religion, education, relief of poverty, health, a governmental or municipal purpose, or other cause that is qualified by the Internal Revenue Service.

Closed-end funds (CEF) - Investment companies with a fixed capitalization. Their shares, like those of public corporations, are priced by the forces of supply and demand. These funds are traded on a securities exchange or over the counter, so buyers and sellers deal with one another (not with the fund itself), in acquiring or disposing of shares. These funds often trade at a discount below the net asset value, and at other times trade at a premium above the net asset value.

Codicil - An explanation, addition, or alteration to an existing will. If a testator dies leaving a will and one or more codicils, then the last will constitutes all such documents take together. Thus, codicils are merely used to change a will rather than to implement an entirely new one or to revoke an old one completely.

Coinsurance - A provision in an insurance policy under which the insured agrees to carry a certain amount of insurance expressed as a percentage of the value of the property. It provides for the full payment, up to the amount of the policy, of all losses if the insurance carried is at least equal to the specified percentage. If the insured fails to carry the necessary amount of insurance, he or she assumes a proportionate share of the loss.

Collateralized mortgage obligation (CMO) - A security that allows investors to choose whether they want a piece of the early, middle, or late maturities in a single pool of mortgages. The cash flow is managed so that investors get their share of interest payments, but principal payments initially go to investors having the shortest-maturity bonds.

College Work-Study Program (CWSP) - A federally sponsored program that provides jobs for students with demonstrated financial need. Students typically work 10 to 15 hours a week during the academic year (and more during vacation periods) and are paid at least the federal minimum wage. Students employed through CWSP may work for colleges as well as public and private nonprofit organizations.

Complex trust - Used for tax purposes, any trust not classified as a simple trust. Generally, a trust allowing the trustee control over distribution of trust income or at least one of whose beneficiaries is a qualifying charitable organization.

Conservator - A court-appointed official responsible for the protection of the interests of an estate.

Contractual plan - A mutual fund accumulation plan with a stated paying-in period and provision for regular investments at monthly or quarterly dates. Substantially synonymous with period charge plan.

Contributory plan - A pension plan under which employee contributions are required as a condition of participation.

Conversion premium - The percentage that the price of the convertible trades above its conversion value. One of the axioms of convertible bond trading is that the lower the premium, the more closely it will trade in step with the common. The higher the premium, the more likely the issue will trade on its merits as a bond.

Convertible term insurance - Term insurance which can be exchanged, at the option of the policyholder and without evidence of insurability, for another plan of insurance; credit life insurance; term life insurance issued through a lender or lending agency to cover payment of a loan, installment purchase, or other obligation, in case of death.

Convertibles - Interest-paying debentures and dividend-paying preferred shares that can be exchanged for the common stock of the issuing company on a preset basis. The conversion privilege becomes valuable only if the market value of the debenture or preferred stock is below that of the total value of the common shares into which it can be converted.

Corpus - A term used in trust companies and trust accounting to describe all the property in a trust; also referred to as the "body" of the trust. A corpus may consist of real estate, stocks, bonds, and other personal property; cash in the form of bank accounts; and any other items that the donor may wish to have included.

Cost basis - The original price or cost of an asset usually based on the purchase price or, in the case of assets received from an estate, on the appraised value of the assets at the death of the donor or some anniversary or other fixed date.

Covered call - A call whose seller (writer) owns the underlying security (or a call thereon with an exercise price equal to or less than the exercise price of the call sold) or a security convertible into the underlying security; a call whose holder has sold the underlying security short.

Covered put - A put whose seller (writer) owns a put on the same underlying security with an exercise price equal to or greater than the exercise price of the put written, or who has sold the underlying security short; a put whose holder owns the underlying security or a security convertible into the underlying security.

Covered writing - Most commonly, writing calls against a long position in the underlying stock. By receiving a premium, the writer intends to realize additional return on the underlying common stock in his or her portfolio or gain some element of protection (limited to the amount of the premium less transaction costs) from a decline in the value of that underlying stock. The covered writer is long the underlying stock or a convertible security such as warrants, convertible bonds, convertible preferreds, or a listed option of the same class. He or she is willing to forsake possible appreciation in his underlying issues in return for payment of the premium.

Crummey trust - A trust having special powers, one of which permits the beneficiary to withdraw limited amounts of trust income or corpus or both, generally, up to the amount excludible from gift tax ($10,000).

CUSIP number - A number assigned to every common stock, preferred stock, and corporate and municipal bond for security identification needs. CUSIP is the American Bankers Association's Committee on Uniform Securities Identification Procedures.

Cyclical stocks - Securities that go up and down in value with the trend of business, rising faster in periods of rapidly improving business conditions and declining noticeably when business conditions deteriorate.

Declaration date (DD) - The date on which payment of a dividend is authorized by a corporation's board of directors.

Deep discount bond - A bond selling substantially below face value; a general measure is below $800 on a bond with a face value of $1,000.

Defensive stocks - Stocks that frequently withstand selling pressure in falling markets. Favored by long-term investors seeking price stability.

Deferred annuity - An annuity contract that provides for the postponement or start of an annuity until after a specified period or until the annuitant attains a specified age.

Defined benefit plan - A plan that is designed to provide participants with a definite benefit at retirement. Contributions under the plan are determined by reference to the benefits provided, not on the basis of a percentage of compensation.

Defined contribution plan - A plan that provides an individual account for each participant and in which benefits are based solely upon the amount contributed to the account (plus or minus any income, expenses, gain, and losses allocated to the account).

Development drilling program - Searching for oil and gas in an area with proven reserves to a depth known to have been productive in the past.

Devise - The transfer of real estate by a will.

Directed trust - A trust in which the trustee has less than full managerial authority. This will be the case whenever somebody else, who is not a trustee, has the power to control particular actions of the trustees.

Discretionary formula plan - A profit-sharing plan that provides that the amount of each year's contribution will be determined by the board of directors (or responsible official(s)) of the sponsoring employer, in its discretion. Contributions must be "recurring and substantial" to keep the plan in a qualified status.

Discretionary trust - Any trust where the trustee has the right to accumulate income for future distribution or trust income is to be paid at the discretion of the trustee.

Distribution date - The date when a dividend or other payment or distribution is made to holders of an instrument.

Dollar cost averaging - A system of buying securities at regular intervals with a fixed dollar amount. The investor buys by the dollars' worth rather than by the number of shares. If each investment is of the same number of dollars, payments buy more shares when the price is low and fewer when it rises.

Donative trust - A trust created for the benefit of another by the acquisition of property on behalf of a beneficiary and without any payment required by the beneficiary.

Dry trust - A trust where the trustee's only duty is to distribute trust assets to the beneficiaries.

Dual-purpose fund - A closed-end investment firm issuing two types of capital stock. The first (income shares) receives dividends from investments; the second (capital shares) receives dividends from the appreciation of investments.

Employee stock ownership plan (ESOP) - A profit-sharing, stock bonus, or money purchase pension plan, the funds of which must be invested primarily in employer company stock. Unlike other plans, an ESOP may borrow from the employer or use the employer's credit to acquire company stock.

Employer-sponsored IRA - An IRA that is sponsored by the employer for purposes of helping its employees make a tax-deductible contribution to an IRA and to invest the funds in a particular type of investment.

Endowment - Life insurance payable to the policyholder if living on the maturity date stated in the policy, or to a beneficiary if the insured dies prior to that date.

Endowment insurance - Life insurance on which premiums are paid for a given period, during which the insured is covered. If the person survives beyond the end of the premium period, he or she collects the face value.

Eurobond - A bond released by a U.S. or other non-European company for sale in Europe. In this market, corporations and governments issue medium-term securities, typically 10 to 15 years in length.

Eurodollar - U.S. dollars retained on deposit and circulated among bank and financial firms around the world that are used for short-term trade financing.

Excess insurance - A policy or bond covering the insured against certain hazards, applying only to loss or damage in excess of a stated amount. The risk of initial loss or damage (excluded from the excess policy or bond) may be carried by the insured himself or herself or may be insured by another policy or bond, providing what is known as primary insurance.

Ex-dividend (ex div, XD) - Indentifying the period during which the quoted price of a security excludes the payment of any declared dividend to the buyer and the dividend reverts to the seller.

Executor - A person designated by an individual in a will to carry out the administration of the latter's estate upon his or her death.

Executory trust - A trust that requires further settlement or conveyance to be made by either the trust's creator or the trustee.

Exercise price - The fixed price for which a stock can be purchased in a call contract or sold in a put contract.

Expense ratio - A ratio, expressed in cents per $100 of investment, that compares mutual fund expenses for management and other overhead costs to the average net asset value of outstanding shares. This ratio is reported in a mutual fund's annual report.

Exploratory drilling program - A program that searches for an undiscovered reservoir of gas or oil. Such programs are often syndicated, and units are sold to limited partners.

Extended coverage insurance - Protection for the insured against property damage caused by windstorm, hail, smoke, explosion, riot, riot attending a strike, civil commotion, vehicle, and aircraft. This is provided in conjunction with the fire insurance policy and the various "package" policies.

Extended term insurance - A form of insurance available as a nonforfeiture option. It provides the original amount of insurance for a limited period of time.

Family Financial Statement (FFS) - A financial information collection document of the American College Testing Program's Financial Aid Services, used by parents of dependent students or by independent students to supply information about their income, assets, expenses, and liabilities. The ACT Program uses this information in estimating how much money a family is able to contribute toward a student's college expenses, but aid sponsors make the final determination.

Fed funds rate - The rate of interest payable on federal funds; considered the key short-term interest rate because it indicates the intentions of the government.

Financial Aid Form (FAF) - A financial information collection document of the College Scholarship Service (CSS), used by parents of dependent students or by independent students to supply information about their income, expenses, assets, and liabilities. The CSS uses this information in estimating how much money a family is able to contribute toward a student's college expenses, but aid sponsors make the final decision.

Fixed annuity - An annuity contract providing payments that remain constant throughout the annuity period. These payments do not vary with investment experience.

Flexible premium policy or annuity - A life insurance policy or annuity under which the policyholder or contractholder may vary the amounts or timing of premium payments.

Flexible premium variable life insurance - A life insurance policy that combines the premium flexibility feature of universal life insurance with the equity-based benefit feature of variable life insurance.

Forfeitures - The benefits that a participant loses if he or she terminates employment before becoming eligible for full retirement benefits under a pension plan.

Forward contract - A cash market transaction in which two parties agree to the purchase and sale of a commodity at some future time under such conditions as the two agree. The terms of forward contracts are not standardized; a contract is not transferable and usually can be canceled only with the consent of the other party, which often must be obtained for consideration and under penalty.

403(b) plan - Section 403(b) of the Internal Revenue Code permits employees of certain charitable organizations and public school systems to establish tax-sheltered retirement programs which may be funded with annuities and mutual fund shares.

Future interest - The delayed privilege of possession or enjoyment in land or other property. Such privilege of possession or enjoyment will arise upon the occurrence of a future event. Examples include a remainder interest, reversionary interest, or contingent interest.

General obligations (GO) - Long-term municipal borrowings that are backed by the full faith, credit, and taxing powers of the issuing locality rather than income generated by a specific project.

Generation-skipping tax - Generally, a tax imposed on a generation-skipping transfer of property, right, or virtually any ability to receive property as a result of such transfer. A generation-skipping transfer is a transfer which splits a beneficial interest between two generations, where one generation is at least two generations younger than that of the transferor.

Generation-skipping trust - A trust which transfers a beneficial interest between two generations, where one generation is two or more generations subsequent to that of the creator. A generation-skipping trust may or may not be subject to the generation-skipping tax, depending upon the amount and other circumstances involved.

Global funds - Mutual funds that invest in both U.S. and foreign securities.

GNMA mortgage-backed securities - Securities guaranteed by the Government National Mortgage Association ("Ginnie Mae") and issued primarily by mortgage bankers (but also by others approved by GNMA). The GNMA security is pass-through in nature, and the holder is protected by the "full faith and credit of the U.S. government." It is collateralized by FHA or VA mortgages.

Good-'til-canceled order (GTC) - An order to buy or sell that remains in effect until it is either executed or canceled.

Grantor trust - A type of trust in which the grantor retains control over the trust's assets or income (or both) and is taxed on income generated by the trust.

Greenmail - What can occur when a hostile investor buys a sizable portion of a company's stock. Desperate to rid itself of the raider, the company buys back the investor's shares for more than the going rate.

Gross lease - A lease whereby the landlord is responsible for all taxes, insurance, and repairs and maintenance.

Growth fund - A mutual fund whose holdings are made up primarily of growth stocks.

Growth stock - Stock of a corporation whose existing and projected earnings are sufficiently positive to indicate an appreciable and constant increase in the stock's market value over an extended time period, the rate of increase being larger than those of most corporate stocks.

Guaranteed Student Loan Program (GSL) - A federal program that lets students borrow money for education expenses directly from banks and other lending institutions (sometimes the colleges themselves). Dependent students may borrow up to specified amounts per academic year up to a specified maximum for the total undergraduate program. Students must demonstrate need in order to qualify. The federal government pays the interest while the student is in college. Repayment terms are favorable, and repayment need not begin until the student graduates or leaves school. Deferments for limited periods are available under certain conditions.

Guaranteed insurability - An option that permits the policyholder to buy additional amounts of life insurance at stated times with evidence of insurability.

Hedge fund - A mutual fund that uses hedging practices by purchasing stocks on margin, selling short, or trading in options in an effort to maximize its profits at risk; any limited partnership of investors that invests in speculative stocks.

Horizontal spread - A spread option technique involving the purchase and sale of option contracts within the same class and on the same underlying stock and having the same striking price but different expiration dates.

Immediate payment annuity - An annuity contract purchased with one payment and with a stated payout plan.

Incentive stock options (ISO) - A form of stock option provided under the tax laws and subject to tax preference over unqualified stock options.

Income approach - A method of appraising property by basing the value upon the net operating income produced by the property. It is calculated by subtracting from the total revenue of the property the operating expenses (excluding depreciation and interest) to determine the operating income. The value of the property is then determined by taking the net operating income of a property and dividing it by the yield required by an all-cash purchaser.

Indenture - A formal agreement between an issuer of bonds and the bondholder covering such concerns as form of the bond, amount of the issue, property pledged, protective covenants, working capital, current ratio, and redemption rights or call privileges. Provides for appointment of a trustee to act on behalf of the bondholders.

Index fund - A mutual fund whose investment objective is to match the composite investment performance of a large group of publicly traded common stocks, for example, the Standard & Poor's 500 Composite Stock Index.

Index futures - Contracts that promise to buy or sell a standardized amount of a stock index by a specified date. Futures are regulated by the Commodity Futures Trading Commission.

Index options - Option contracts issued by the Options Clearing Corporation, based on a stock index instead of an underlying security. When exercised, settlement is made by a cash payment, not delivery of shares.

Insurance trust - A trust that receives the insurance proceeds upon the death of an insured. A trustee then invests and distributes the proceeds in a manner described in the trust agreement. Although there are many possible alternatives, some agreements give the trustee absolute discretion to allocate income or principal among beneficiaries as they require money under specified circumstances. Whatever the arrangement, lump-sum proceeds and installments under a "settlement option" are avoided, which allows the principal to remain intact until the occurrence of specified events.

Internal rate of return (IRR) - A return on an investment calculation that uses the time value of money. The present value of the partnership investment is compared to the present value of future benefits. The internal rate of return is an attempt to compare dissimilar investments with dissimilar returns.

International funds - Funds that buy securities traded in securities markets outside the United States.

Inter vivos trust - A trust created and executed during the grantor's life, as opposed to a testamentary trust which takes effect upon the death of the grantor.

Intestate - Without a will. When a person dies without making a will, he or she is said to have died "intestate." It is commonly used to signify the property of a person dying without a will: the intestate's property.

Inverted yield curve - A condition where short-term interest rates are higher than long-term rates.

Investment Advisors Act - Federal legislation of 1940 to regulate investment advisors, in order to protect the public from misrepresentation and dishonest investment tactics, by identifying specific unlawful activities. All investment advisors are required to register with the Securities and Exchange Commission, the administrator of the Investment Advisors Act.

Investment company - A company or trust that uses its capital to invest in other companies. There are two principal types: the closed-end type and the open-end, or mutual fund. (1) Shares in closed-end investment companies are readily transferable in the open market and are bought and sold like other shares. Capitalization of these companies remains the same unless action is taken to change, which is seldom. (2) Open-end funds sells their own new shares to investors and are not listed. Open-end funds are so called because their capitalization is not fixed; more shares are issued as people want them.

Investment grade - An investment situation where the firm shows a very strong balance sheet, is well capitalized, has a record of continuous dividends, and is recognized as a leader in the industry; a bond rating of Baa/BBB or higher. Bonds recognized as investment grade quality are suitable for purchases by fiduciaries.

Irrevocable living trust - A trust created by a living grantor who cannot cancel or repeal the trust. Transferred property may be taxable to the grantor, trust income is generally taxable to beneficiaries, and transfer of assets may avoid estate taxes.

Irrevocable trust - Any trust that cannot be revoked by its creator.

Joint and survivor annuity - An annuity paid for the life of the participant with a survivor annuity for his or her spouse. The survivor annuity must be at least 50 percent, but not more than 100 percent, of the annuity received by the participant during his or her lifetime. Also, the joint and survivor annuity must be the actuarial equivalent of a single life annuity that would have been paid to the participant.

Joint life insurance - Insurance on two or more persons, the benefits of which are payable on the first death to occur.

Joint tenancy - Two or more people holding equal ownership of property. Upon the death of one of the parties, the decedent's interest automatically passes on to the surviving owner(s).

Joint tenants by the entireties - An account held in two or more names from which either owner may withdraw but for which each owner is considered to own all the funds.

Joint tenants with right of survivorship - Property (bank account, safe deposit box) held in two or more names, to which any single owner has access without notifying the other(s). Right of survivorship indicates that in the event of the death of one owner, the remaining tenant(s) immediately become(s) owner(s) of the property.

Keogh plan - A qualified retirement plan, either a defined contribution plan or a defined benefit plan that covers a self-employed person. (Other employees might also be covered.)

Leading indicators - Twelve indicators, issued by the Bureau of Economic Analysis, chosen for their record in predicting turns in the business cycle, released late in the month for the previous month.

LIBOR - See **London Inter-Bank Offered Rate.**

Life estate - An estate in property which only lasts during an individual's lifetime. That is, an estate which is not inheritable as directed by the owner.

Life insurance trust - A trust created by an individual for the benefit of his or her heirs, the major portion of which is in the form of life insurance.

Load - The portion of the offering price of shares of open-end investment companies that cover sales commissions and all other costs of distribution. The load is usually incurred only on purchase.

London Inter-Bank Offered Rate - A measure of what major international banks charge each other for large-volume loans of Eurodollars or dollars on deposit outside the United States.

Lump-sum distribution - The one time payment to a beneficiary covering the entire amount of an agreement. Used extensively with IRAs, pension plans, and executive stock option plans.

Maintenance - The sum of cash or securities deposited in a brokerage account to fulfill the brokerage firm's margin requirements.

Margin - The amount paid by the customer when he or she used a broker's credit to buy a security. Under Federal Reserve regulations, the initial margin required in past decades has ranged from 50 to 100 percent of the purchase price.

Marital deduction - An unlimited deduction for the entire amount of inter vivos and testamentary gifts made between a husband and wife.

Marital deduction trust - Generally, any trust designed to take advantage of the unlimited marital deduction.

Master limited partnership (MLP) - An investment vehicle that combines the tax shelter attractions of conventional limited partnerships with the marketability of publicly traded issues like stocks. There are two types of MLPs: (1) the rollout, in which a company spins off assets to stockholders, and (2) the rollup, in which dozens of private partnerships are combined and exchanged for publicly traded units.

Maximum capital gains fund - A mutual fund whose goal is to produce significant capital gains for its stockholders.

Money market deposit account (MMDA) - A market-sensitive bank deposit account. Interest rates are generally, but not always, lower than rates on money market funds. On the other hand, most MMDAs are federally insured, subject to dollar limitations.

Money market fund (MMF) - An investment vehicle whose primary objective is to make higher-interest securities available to the average investor who wants immediate income and high investment safety. This is accomplished through the purchase of large denomination money market instruments, such as U.S. government securities, repurchase agreements, and commercial paper.

Money purchase pension plan - A defined contribution plan under which the employer's contributions are mandatory and are usually based on each participant's compensation. Retirement benefits under the plan are based on the amount in the participant's individual account at retirement.

Naked calls - The selling of options on stock that is not owned.

Negative yield curve - The condition where yields on short-term debt securities are higher than those on long-term debt securities of the same quality.

Net operating income - In real estate, the gross potential income minus vacancies and all operating expenses. The balance is what is available to an all-cash owner or to pay debt service.

Nominal interest rate - The contractual interest rate shown on the face and in the body of a bond and representing the amount of interest to be paid, in contrast to the effective interest rate.

Noncontributory plan - A pension plan under which employees are eligible to participate and receive accrued benefits without contributing to the plan.

Nonforfeiture options - Privileges allowed under terms of a life insurance contract after cash values have been created. Four privileges exist: (1) surrender for full cash value; (2) loans up to the full amount of the cash value; (3) paid-up policy for the amount of insurance that cash value, as a single premium, will buy at net rates; and (4) term insurance for full face amount of the original policy for as long as the cash value will last to pay necessary premiums.

Offshore funds - As they affect U.S. citizens, mutual funds that have their headquarters outside the United States. Usually, such funds are not available to Americans but are sold to investors in other parts of the world.

Open-end fund - A mutual fund where new shares of the fund are sold whenever there is a request.

Option income fund - The investment objective of these funds is to seek a high current return by investing primarily in dividend-paying common stocks on which call options are traded on national securities exchanges. Current return generally consists of dividends, premiums from expired call options, net short-term gains from sales of portfolio securities on exercises of options or otherwise, and any profits from closing purchase transactions.

Option premium - The dollar amount paid to the writer for the option. This amount is generally determined by supply and demand, duration of the contract difference between the fluctuations, among other considerations.

Option writer - A seller of a stock option contract with an obligation to purchase or sell shares of the underlying stock at a preset price within a given period of time.

Parent Loans for Undergraduate Students (PLUS) - A federal program that lets parents of undergraduate dependent students borrow for their children's education expenses directly from banks and other lending institutions. Parents may borrow up to $4,000 per academic year and up to $20,000 for the total undergraduate program of each child. The federal government guarantees the loan against loss due to death, disability, or default and subsidizes the interest rate. Repayment begins within 60 days after disbursement and may extend up to 10 years. The interest rate is set annually, to a maximum of 12 percent.

Parking - Putting assets in a safe investment while other investment alternatives are being considered, for example, parking the proceeds of a stock or bond sale in an interest-bearing money market fund while evaluating what other stocks or bonds to buy.

Pell Grant Program (formerly Basic Education Opportunity Grant Program or BEOG) - A federally sponsored and administered program that provides grants based on need to undergraduate students. Congress annually sets the dollar range of Pell Grants. Students apply using a need analysis form or a form submitted directly to the federal government.

Perkins Loan (formerly the National Direct Student Loan or NDSL Program) - A federally funded program that provides loans for undergraduates up to a specified maximum. Repayment need not begin until the student graduates or leaves school; service in the military, Peace Corps, VISTA, or comparable organizations may carry other special provisions for deferment or cancellation. Repayment terms are favorable, and repayment may be partially or wholly waived for certain kinds of employment.

Per stirpes - In the distribution of estate assets, a method of dividing such assets so that the children of a deceased beneficiary will receive a share of an ancestor's estate, just as their parent would have received if still living.

Pooled income fund - A fund to which several donors transfer property, retaining an income interest and giving the remainder to a single charity.

Positive yield curve - A condition where interest rates are higher on long-term debt securities than on short-term debt securities of the same quality.

Pour-over - A provision in a trust or will that directs property into another trust or will upon the happening of a specified event.

Power of appointment - Generally, an authority given to a donee to dispose of property in a manner that the donor has described.

Preliminary prospectus - An advance report giving the details of a planned offering of corporate stock. The issue is still in the process of being registered by the SEC and cannot be sold until clearance is received.

Present interest - The immediate use, possession, or enjoyment of property rather than at a future time.

Price/earnings (P/E) ratio - The price of a share of stock divided by earnings per share for a 12-month period. For example, a stock selling for $60 a share and earning $4 a share is said to be selling at a price/earnings ratio of 15:1.

Private annuity - As used in estate planning, an annuity generally provided to an individual who exchanges income-producing property to another person (typically a family member) in return for an annuity. The primary purpose of using a private annuity is to pass income property to beneficiaries while simultaneously reducing the annuitant's gross estate.

Profit-sharing plan - A defined contribution plan under which the employer agrees to make discretionary contributions (usually out of profits). A participant's retirement benefits are based on the amount in his or her individual account at retirement.

Purchase-money mortgage - Used by real estate sellers when they act as the lender themselves. The mortgage is actually a short-term instrument that runs no more than five years. In most cases, a purchase-money mortgage is a second mortgage, supplementing the buyer's bank financing.

Purchasing power risk - In investments, used to refer to the risk that the price level may move, thus affecting the relative valuations of various categories of securities, for example, stocks versus bonds.

Put option - A bondholder's right to redeem a bond prior to its maturity; a contract granting the right to sell at a specified price a given number of shares by a stated date. A put option purchaser gains this right in return for payment of an option premium. The put option seller assumes this obligation in return for receiving the option premium.

Qualified pension plan (qualified plan) - A plan that meets the requirements of the Internal Revenue Code (generally Section 401(a)). The advantage of qualification is that the plan is eligible for special tax considerations. For example, employers are permitted to deduct contributions to the plan even though the benefits provided under the plan are deferred to a later date.

Qualified terminable interest property (QTIP) - Qualifying property that is eligible for the marital deduction, even though it is terminable interest property, because the surviving spouse receives the entire income from such property and during the surviving spouse's life the property cannot be appointed to anyone except the surviving spouse.

Qualified terminable interest property trust - Permits assets to be transferred between spouses. A QTIP grantor directs income from the assets to his or her spouse for life having the power of distributing the assets upon the spouse's death. Qualifies the grantor for the unlimited marital deduction.

Qualified total distribution - One or more distributions from a plan (1) within one taxable year of the employee made on account of the termination of the plan or a complete discontinuance of contributions to the plan or (2) that constitute a lump-sum distribution. A distribution of accumulated deductible employee contributions is also a qualified total distribution. A qualified total distribution may be rolled over to an IRA.

Rated plicy - Sometimes called an "extra-risk" policy, an insurance policy issued at a higher than standard premium rate to cover the extra risk where, for example, an insured has impaired health or a hazardous occupation.

Record date - The date on which a person must be registered as a shareholder on the stock book of a company in order to receive a declared dividend, or among other things, to vote on company affairs.

Red herring - An advance report giving the details of a planned offering of corporate stock. The issue is still in the process of being registered by the SEC and cannot be sold until clearance is received.

Reinvestment rate - The rate of return resulting from reinvestment of the interest from a fixed-income security or a bond. Other than zero-coupon bonds, the reinvestment rate on coupon bonds has little predictability because it rises and falls with market interest rates.

Remainder interest - A future interest which will become an interest in possession after the termination of a prior interest created at the same time and by the same instrument as the future interest.

Remaindermen - Those persons who receive the proceeds from the final distribution of a trust or estate.

Renewable term insurance - Insurance that offers a guaranteed option to renew without a health examination up to retirement age and sometimes beyond.

Repurchase agreement (Repo) - An arrangement allowing the owner of debt securities (usually Treasury bills) to borrow money by selling the securities to a buyer while promising to repurchase them at a fixed price on a specified date.

Residuary estate - What remains in an estate after all claims to the estate have been properly disposed of.

Revenue anticipation notes (RANs) - Short-term municipal borrowings that fund current operations and are to be funded by revenues other than taxes, especially federal aid.

Reverse-annuity mortgage - Designed for retirees and other fixed-income homeowners who owe little or nothing on their houses. Typically, it permits them to use some or all of the equity already in the home as supplemental income, while retaining ownership. In effect, they are borrowing against the value of the house on a monthly basis. The longer they borrow, of course, the less equity they retain in the house. The loan becomes due either on a specific date or when a specified event occurs such as the sale of the property or death of the borrower.

Revocable trust - A trust that reserves the right of the grantor to reacquire the trust's property. A revocable trust is not exempt from gift taxes or estate taxes upon the grantor's death, but may reduce administrative costs and burdens of ownership that will affect the beneficiary.

Rider - A special policy provision or group of provisions that may be added to a policy to expand or limit the benefits otherwise payable.

Rollover IRA account - An individual retirement account that is established for the sole purpose of receiving a distribution from a qualified plan so that the assets can subsequently be rolled over into another qualified plan.

Rule against perpetuities - Principle that a property interest is invalid unless it is created to vest (if at all) within a period prescribed by state statute, which is generally a life in being plus 21 years. The rule against perpetuities is especially influential in drafting instruments relating to trusts and estates.

Running in the shorts - Purchasing securities where there is a substantial short position for the purpose of advancing the price so that those who are short the stock will purchase their securities back, or cover their short selling contracts, and hence lead to an additional climb in price.

Salary-reduction plan - Under this type of cash or deferred arrangement, each eligible employee may elect to reduce his or her current compensation or to forgo a salary increase and have these amounts instead contributed to the plan on his or her behalf on a pretax basis.

Savings and loan association - A mutual, cooperative quasi-public financial institution, owned by its members (depositors), and chartered by a state or by the federal government. The association receives the savings of its members and uses these funds to finance long-term amortized mortgage loans to its members and to the general public. Such an association may also be organized as a corporation owned by stockholders.

Savings bank - A banking association whose purpose is to promote thrift and savings habits in a community. It may be either a stock organization (a bank with a capital stock structure) or a "mutual savings bank."

Sector funds - Mutual funds that concentrate on trading a range of securities within a broad industry group, such as technology, energy, or financial services.

Secular trend - A long-term trend either up or down in the price or level of a commodity, price structure, inflation rate, and so on, that is not influenced by seasonal variations or distortions.

Settlement options - Provisions in a life insurance policy or annuity contract for alternative methods of settlement in place of lump-sum payments.

Settlor - A person who creates a trust.

Short sale - A transaction made by a person who believes a stock will decline and places a sell order, though he or she does not own any of these shares. Stock exchange and federal regulations govern and limit the conditions under which a short sale may be made. Sometimes a person will sell short a stock already owned to protect a paper profit.

Simple trust - A trust which distributes all income and does not have the authority to make charitable distributions.

Simplified employee pension (SEP) - A company retirement program that places retirement contributions into eligible employees' individual retirement accounts (subject to special rules on contributions and eligibility).

Single-premium deferred annuity (SPDA) - A tax-deferred investment similar to an individual retirement account, but free of the IRA restrictions. An investor makes a lump-sum payment to an insurance company selling the annuity. Proceeds are taxed only when distributions are taken. Unlike IRAs, there is no maximum to the amount that can be invested in a SPDA, nor must the holder wait until age 59½ to begin drawing the benefits.

Single-state municipal bond fund - A mutual fund that invests entirely in tax-exempt obligations of governments and government agencies within one state. Dividends paid on fund shares that apply to interest are exempt from state taxes for residents of that particular state and are also exempt from federal taxes. Capital gains, if any, are taxable.

Speculative stocks - Securities issued by relatively new firms of unproved financial status, and so on, and by firms with below average financial strength.

Spendthrift trust - A trust created to provide income to a beneficiary, while protecting the trust's assets from the beneficiary and his or her creditors. The primary effect is to keep a beneficiary from spending all the money placed in trust for his or her benefit.

Split dollar life insurance - A life insurance plan in which the employer and employee join in purchasing a cash value policy on the employee's life. The employer pays that part of the annual premium that represents the increase in cash value, and the employee pays the balance of the annual premium. The employer is entitled to receive, out of the proceeds of the policy, an amount equal to the cash surrender value, and the employee's beneficiary is entitled to the remainder.

Sprinkling trust - A trust providing the trustee a discretionary power to distribute any amount of income to various beneficiaries and to accumulate any undistributed income.

Stock index future - A security that combines features of traditional commodity futures trading with securities trading employing composite stock indexes. Investors can speculate on general market performance or purchase an index future contract to hedge a long position or short position against a drop in value.

Stock index options - Similar to traditional options to buy or sell individual stocks with one exception. It is impractical for an option holder to exercise his or her right to sell or buy a whole basket of securities. Therefore, any profit or loss is settled in cash.

Stop limit order - A stop order to a broker that becomes a limit order after the specified stop price has been reached.

Stop-loss order - An order to a broker that sets the sell price of a stock below the current market price; used to protect profits that have already been made or to prevent further losses should the security decline.

Stop order - An order to buy at a price above or sell at a price below the current market. Stop buy orders are generally used to limit loss or to protect unrealized profits on a short sale. Stop sell orders are generally used to protect unrealized profits or to limit loss on a holding or to protect unrealized profits on a short sale. A stop order becomes a market order when the stock sells at or beyond the specified price and thus may not necessarily be executed at that price.

Straddle - The purchase or sale of an equivalent number of puts and calls on a given underlying stock with the same exercise price and expiration date.

Supplemental Educational Opportunity Grant Program (SEOG) - A federal program administered by colleges to provide need-based aid to undergraduate students.

Systematic risk - The tendency of the asset price to move along with the market index. The measure of systematic risk is widely known as "beta." If beta is one (1.0), the asset price tends to fall in the same proportion that the market falls, other things being equal, and to rise by the same proportion that the market rises.

Taxable estate - The gross estate of a citizen or resident less allowable administrative and funeral expenses; indebtedness; taxes; losses; transfer for public, charitable, and religious uses; transfer to a surviving spouse; and a specific exemption.

Tax anticipation note (TAN) - Short-term notes issued by municipalities to fulfill short-term requirements, in anticipation of tax receipts.

Tax-deferred - Any item, such as money contributed to an IRA, which is not taxed until it is withdrawn or distributed at an authorized time.

Tax-free rollover - A provision whereby an individual receiving a lump-sum distribution from a qualified pension or profit-sharing plan can preserve the tax-deferred status of these funds by a "rollover" into an IRA or another qualified plan if rolled over within 60 days of receipt.

Technical analysis - The study and use of market prices and indexes related to the supply and demand for stocks. Used to forecast future price movements.

Tenancy by the entirety - Tenancy by a husband and wife in such a manner that, except in concert with the other, neither husband nor wife has a disposable interest in the property during the lifetime of the other. Upon the death of either, the property goes to the survivor.

Tenancy in common - Ownership of property by two or more persons, each holding a separate interest. No right of survivorship exists.

Terminable interest - An interest in property that will terminate upon the occurrence of a specified event, such as a leasehold.

Testamentary disposition - The disposition of property by deed, will or otherwise in such a manner that it shall not take effect unless or until the grantor dies.

Testamentary trust - A trust created by a testator's will and effective upon his or her death.

Thrift plan - A defined contribution plan that is contributory in the sense that employer contributions are geared to mandatory contributions by the employee. Employer contributions are made on a matching basis— for example, 50 percent of the total contribution made by the employee.

Totten trust - A revocable trust subject to state laws that is created by an individual with separate funds deposited in a savings account in his or her own name as trustee for another (usually a dependent). After the depositor's death, the money ordinarily becomes the beneficiary's property.

Umbrella liability insurance - Insurance that covers losses in excess of amounts covered by other liability insurance policies; also protects the insured in many situations not covered by the usual liability policies. Also called extended personal liability insurance.

Uncovered writer - A writer of a stock option contract who does not own shares of the underlying stock.

Uniform Gift to Minors Act (UGMA) - A law adopted by most states establishing regulations for the distribution and administration of assets in the name of a child. The Act provides for a custodian of the assets, often the parents, but sometimes an independent trustee.

Uniform Transfer to Minors Act (UTMA) - Similar to Uniform Gifts to Minors Act, but more flexible as to property allowed to be placed in the minor's account. UTMA also permits transfers by will.

Unit investment trust (UIT) - An investment vehicle that buys a fixed portfolio of income-producing securities, such as corporate, municipal, or government bonds; mortgage-backed securities; or preferred stock. Unit holders receive an undivided interest in both the principal and the income portion of the portfolio in proportion to the amount of capital they have invested.

Universal life insurance - A flexible premium life insurance policy under which the policyholder may change the death benefit from time to time (with satisfactory evidence of insurability for increases) and vary the amount or timing of premium payments. Premiums (less expense charges) are credited to a policy account from which mortality charges are deducted and to which interest is credited at rates which may change from time to time.

Up tick - A transaction made at a price higher than the preceding transaction. A stock may be sold short only on an up tick (i.e., a transaction at the same price as the preceding trade but higher than the preceding different price).

Variable annuity - An annuity contract in which the amount of each periodic income payment may fluctuate. The fluctuation may be related to securities market values, a cost-of-living index, or some other variable factor. A variable deferred annuity is one that allows the investor to invest his or her funds in any of a variety of stock and interest-earning mutual funds.

Variable life insurance - Life insurance under which the benefits relate to the value of assets behind the contract at the time the benefit is paid. The amount of death benefit payable would, under variable life policies that have been proposed, never be less than the initial death benefit payable under the policy.

Vested benefits - Accrued benefits of a participant that have become non-forfeitable under the vesting schedule adopted by the plan.

Voluntary contributions - Amounts that a participant voluntarily contributes to a plan in addition to the contributions made by the employer. IRS permits "reasonable" amounts of employee contributions. Up to 10 percent of the employee's compensation is generally considered reasonable. Voluntary contributions are not deductible on the employee's tax return.

Vulture funds - Dollars pooled by investors in search of troubled office buildings, apartment complexes, and tracts of land that can be picked up at bargain basement prices.

Waiver of premium - Nearly all life insurance companies will add to their contracts, upon payment of a small additional premium, a clause providing that if the insured becomes totally and permanently disabled, his or her insurance policy will be continued in full force and the company will exempt the insured from paying further premiums during disability.

Whole life insurance - A type of insurance policy continuing in force throughout the policyholder's lifetime and payable on his or her death or when he or she attains a specified age. Whole life insurance builds up cash surrender values over the life of the insured.

Wraparound mortgage - A mortgage in which the lender pays all underlying mortgages. One payment is made to the wraparound mortgage holder who is responsible for paying all of the other subordinate or junior mortgages.

Writer - A seller of a stock option contract with an obligation to purchase or sell shares of the underlying stock at a preset price within a given period of time.

Year of service - A 12-month period during which an employee is credited with at least 1,000 hours of service.

Yield curve - A graph indicating the term structure of interest rates by plotting the yields of all bonds of the same quality with maturities ranging from the shortest to the longest available.

Yield to call - Measures the return on a bond investment an individual would receive stated as an average yearly return from purchase date to call date.

Yield to maturity (YTM) - The percentage rate of return on an investment if it is held until maturity.

Zero-coupon security - A security making no periodic interest payment but instead is sold at a deep discount from its face value. The purchaser of this bond receives the rate of return by the gradual appreciation of the security, which is redeemed at face value on a given maturity date.

INDEX

tax basis of securities, determining, 10.8
tax deductions, 10.9
year-end tax planning, 10.1
Time-sharing, 6.1.1.2
Treasury bills, 2.1.4
Treasury securities, 4.2
  issue date calendar, 4.3
Trusts, 12.1.7

U

U.S. savings bonds, 4.4, 4.5, 4.6

V

Vacation homes, 6.1.1.2
Value-Line Rankings, 3.3.2

W

Wilshire 5000 Index, 3.7.8
Wiesenberger Mutual Fund Portfo-
lios Index, 5.7
Wills, 12.2
Work life indexes, 15.8
Work-study programs,
9.3.3

Y

Yields,
  bond and stock, 1.7
  double tax-exempt and equivalent taxable, 4.11
  federal tax-exempt and equivalent taxable, 4.10